Adobe

CERTIFIED ASSOCIATE
Approved Courseware

FlashCS6

Revealed

Adobe

CERTIFIED ASSOCIATE
Approved Courseware

Flash CS6

Revealed

Jim Shuman

DELMAR
CENGAGE Learning

Australia • Brazil • Japan • Korea • Mexico • Singapore • Spain • United Kingdom • United States

DELMAR
CENGAGE Learning®

Adobe Flash CS6 Revealed

Jim Shuman

Vice President, Career and Professional Editorial:
 Dave Garza

Director of Learning Solutions: Sandy Clark

Senior Acquisitions Editor: Jim Gish

Managing Editor: Larry Main

Product Managers: Jane Hosie-Bounar, Nicole Calisi

Editorial Assistant: Sarah Timm

Vice President Marketing, Career and Professional:
 Jennifer Baker

Executive Marketing Manager: Deborah S. Yarnell

Marketing Coordinator: Erin DeAngelo

Production Director: Wendy Troeger

Senior Content Project Manager: Kathryn B. Kucharek

Developmental Editor: Pam Conrad

Technical Editor: Sarah Mosser

Director of Design: Bruce Bond

Cover Design: Riezebox Holzbaur/Tim Heraldo

Cover Photo: Riezebox Holzbaur/Andrei Pasternak

Text Designer: Liz Kingslein

Production House: Integra Software Services Pvt. Ltd.

Proofreader: Harold Johnson

Indexer: Alexandra Nickerson

Technology Project Manager: Jim Gilbert

Adobe® Premiere Pro®, Adobe After Effects®, Adobe® Bridge®, Adobe Audition®, Adobe® Encore®, Adobe® Photoshop®, Adobe® Illustrator®, Adobe® InDesign®, Adobe® Flash®, Adobe® Dreamweaver®, Adobe® Fireworks®, and Adobe® Creative Suite® are trademarks or registered trademarks of Adobe Systems, Inc. in the United States and/or other countries. Third party products, services, company names, logos, design, titles, words, or phrases within these materials may be trademarks of their respective owners.

Adobe product screenshot(s) reprinted with permission from Adobe Systems Incorporated.

The Adobe Approved Certification Courseware logo is a proprietary trademark of Adobe. All rights reserved. Cengage Learning and Adobe Flash CS6–Revealed are independent from ProCert Labs, LLC and Adobe Systems Incorporated, and are not affiliated with ProCert Labs and Adobe in any manner. This publication may asssist students to prepare for an Adobe Certified Expert exam, however, neither ProCert Labs nor Adobe warrant that use of this material will ensure success in connection with any exam.

Adobe Certified Associate Approved Courseware logo is a proprietary trademark of Adobe. All rights reserved. Cengage Learning and the Revealed Series are independent from ProCert Labs, LLC and Adobe Systems Incorporated, and are not affiliated with ProCert Labs and Adobe in any manner. This publication may assist students to prepare for an Adobe Certified Associate exam, however, neither ProCert Labs nor Adobe warrant that use of this material will ensure success in connection with any exam.

Library of Congress Control Number: 2011945472

ISBN-13: 978-1-133-69321-5
ISBN-10: 1-133-69321-0

Delmar
5 Maxwell Drive
Clifton Park, NY 12065-2919
USA

Cengage Learning is a leading provider of customized learning solutions with office locations around the globe, including Singapore, the United Kingdom, Australia, Mexico, Brazil, and Japan. Locate your local office at: **international.cengage.com/region**

Cengage Learning products are represented in Canada by Nelson Education, Ltd.

To learn more about Delmar, visit **www.cengage.com/delmar**

Purchase any of our products at your local college store or at our preferred online store **www.cengagebrain.com**

Notice to the Reader
Publisher does not warrant or guarantee any of the products described herein or perform any independent analysis in connection with any of the product information contained herein. Publisher does not assume, and expressly disclaims, any obligation to obtain and include information other than that provided to it by the manufacturer. The reader is expressly warned to consider and adopt all safety precautions that might be indicated by the activities described herein and to avoid all potential hazards. By following the instructions contained herein, the reader willingly assumes all risks in connection with such instructions. The publisher makes no representations or warranties of any kind, including but not limited to, the warranties of fitness for particular purpose or merchantability, nor are any such representations implied with respect to the material set forth herein, and the publisher takes no responsibility with respect to such material. The publisher shall not be liable for any special, consequential, or exemplary damages resulting, in whole or in part, from the readers' use of, or reliance upon, this material.

Printed in the United States of America
1 2 3 4 5 6 7 16 15 14 13 12

Revealed Series Vision

The Revealed Series is your guide to today's hottest multimedia applications. For years, the Revealed Series has kept pace with the dynamic demands of the multimedia community, and continues to do so with the publication of 13 new titles covering the latest Adobe Creative Suite products. Each comprehensive book teaches not only the technical skills required for success in today's competitive multimedia market, but the design skills as well. From animation, to web design, to mobile app development, to digital image editing and interactive media skills, the Revealed Series has you covered. We recognize the unique learning environment of the multimedia classroom, and we deliver text books that include:

- Comprehensive step-by-step instructions
- In-depth explanantions of the "why" behind a skill
- Creative projects for additional practice
- Full-color visuals for a clear explanation of concepts
- Comprehensive online material offering additional instruction and skills practice
- Video tutorials for skills reinforcement as well as the presentation of additional features

- NEW icons to highlight features that are new since the previous release of the software With the Revealed Series, we've created books that speak directly to the multimedia and design community–one of the most rapidly growing computer fields today.

—The Revealed Series

New to This Edition!

The latest edition of Adobe Flash CS6 Revealed includes many new and exciting features, some of which are listed below:

- A new chapter on using Flash to develop mobile applications, including design considerations, scaling content, and using code snippets to add Touch and Gesture events such as pinch to zoom, drag, and swipe.
- Coverage of how to publish AIR for Android and AIR for iOS (Apple) applications for smartphones.
- Coverage of how to test mobile applications on a smartphone via a USB port.
- Coverage of how to test mobile applications, including the use of the Accelerometer, using the Mobile Content Simulator.

CourseMate

A CourseMate is available to accompany *Adobe Flash CS6 Revealed*, which helps you make the grade! This CourseMate includes:

- An interactive eBook, with highlighting, note-taking, and search capabilities
- Interactive learning tools, including:
  - Chapter quizzes
  - Flash cards
  - Instructional video lessons from Total Training, the leading provider of video instruction for Adobe software; these video lessons are tightly integrated with the book, chapter by chapter, and include assessment
  - And more!

Go to login.cengagebrain.com to access these resources you have purchased.

AUTHOR'S VISION

Writing a textbook on an application development and animation program is quite challenging. How do you take such a feature-rich program like Adobe Flash Professional CS6 and put it in a context that helps users learn? My goal is to provide a comprehensive, yet manageable, introduction to Adobe Flash Professional CS6—just enough conceptual information to provide the needed context—and then move right into working with the application. My thought is that you'll get so caught up in the hands-on activities and compelling projects that you'll be pleasantly surprised at the level of Flash skills and knowledge you've acquired at the end of each chapter.

What a joy it has been to be a part of such a creative and energetic publishing team. The Revealed Series is a great format for teaching and learning Flash, and the Revealed Series team took the ball and ran with it. I would like to thank Jim Gish, who provided the vision for the project, and Jane Hosie-Bounar for her management expertise, and everyone at Delmar and Cengage Learning for their professional guidance. A special thanks to my Developmental Editor Pam Conrad for her hard work, editorial expertise, and constant encouragement. Jane and Pam made this book possible for me. I also want to give a heartfelt thanks to my wife, Barbara, for her patience, support, and use of her remarkable artwork. This book is dedicated to my two precious granddaughters, Daniela and Mariana, who bring such joy to my life.

—Jim Shuman

Introduction to Adobe Flash CS6

Welcome to *Adobe Flash CS6—Revealed*. This book offers creative projects, concise instructions, and complete coverage of basic to advanced Adobe Flash CS6 skills, helping you to create and publish Flash animations, mobile applications, and websites. Use this book both while you learn and as your own reference guide.

This text is organized into 12 chapters with a bonus Chapter 13 posted online! In these chapters, you will learn many skills to create interesting graphics-rich applications that include animation, sound, video, and interactivity. In addition, you will learn how to publish your own Flash applications.

What You'll Do

A What You'll Do figure begins every lesson. This figure gives you an at-a-glance look at what you'll do in the chapter, either by showing you a page or pages from the current project or a tool you'll be using.

Comprehensive Conceptual Lessons

Before jumping into instructions, in-depth conceptual information tells you "why" skills are applied. This book provides the "how" and "why" through the use of professional examples. Also included in the text are tips and sidebars to help you work more efficiently and creatively, or to teach you a bit about the history or design philosophy behind the skill you are using.

Step-by-Step Instructions

This book combines in-depth conceptual information with concise steps to help you learn Flash CS6. Each set of steps guides you through a lesson where you will create, modify, or enhance a Flash CS6 file. Step references to large colorful images and quick step summaries round out the lessons. The Data Files for the steps are provided on Cengage Brain. For information on how to access Cengage Brain, see "Read This Before You Begin."

PROJECT BUILDER 2

You have been asked to develop a prototype application that demonstrates the use of the swipe event on a phone application. You will start with a template and repurpose it.

Use a template to create a swipe application.

1. Open a new AIR for Android Swipe Gallery template application, then save it as **swipePrototype.fla**.
2. Change the view to 50%.
3. Open the imageHolder movie clip in the edit window.
4. Click on a numbered screen and note the size of the graphic, which is smaller than the size of the Stage.
5. Return to the main Timeline.
6. Obtain three graphics, such as JPG photos, and resize them to fit the dimension of the swipe template screen (that is, the colored area with the number).

7. Import the three graphics to the Library.
8. Drag each file to the stage, change it to a movie clip, and delete it from the Stage.
9. Open the imageHolder movie clip in the edit window and change the view to 50%.
10. Delete the number 1 on the first screen, then add a title, change it to a movie clip, and give it an instance name.
11. Delete the other numbers, swap symbols with the three new movie clips, and remove the tint from each image.
12. Return to the main Timeline.
13. Display the Mobile Content Simulator.
14. Use the Touch and Gesture Swipe gesture to display the screens.
15. Close the AIR preview window.

Add a zoom gesture.

1. Open the imageHolder in the edit window.
2. Select the movie clip on the second screen on the Stage and give it an instance name.
3. Insert a Pinch to Zoom Event for the movie clip from the Mobile Gestures Events options.
4. Return to the main Timeline.
5. Display the Mobile Content Simulator.
6. Use the Touch and Gesture Swipe gesture to swipe and display the second screen.
7. Change to the Zoom gesture and zoom in and out on the screen.
8. Close the AIR preview window.
9. Save and close the application.

Figure 39 *Sample completed Project Builder 2*
Photos courtesy of J. Shuman.

FLASH 12-40

Developing Mobile Applications

Create a button

1. Insert a **new layer** above the top layer on the Timeline, then name the layer **signal**.
2. Select the **Rectangle Primitive tool** [ ], then set the **Stroke Color** to **No Stroke**.

TIP The No Stroke icon [ ] is in the upper-right corner of the color palette.

3. Set the **Fill Color** to the **red gradient color swatch** in the bottom row of the color palette.
4. Display the Properties panel, click the **Reset button** in the RECTANGLE OPTIONS area, then set the corner radius to **5**.
5. Draw the **rectangle** shown in Figure 20.
6. Click the **Zoom tool** [ ] on the Tools panel, then click the **rectangle** to enlarge it.
7. Select the **Gradient Transform tool** [ ] on the Tools panel.

TIP You may need to click and hold the Free Transform tool first.

8. Click the **rectangle**, then drag the **diagonal arrow** toward the center of the rectangle as shown in Figure 21 to make the red area more round.
9. Click the **Selection tool** [ ] on the Tools panel, then drag a **marquee** around the rectangle to select it.
10. Click **Modify** on the menu bar, then click **Convert to Symbol**.
11. Type **b_signal** in the Name text box, click the **Type list arrow**, click **Button**, then click **OK**.
12. Display the Library panel, then drag the **b_signal symbol** to the Buttons folder.

You created a button symbol on the Stage and dragged it to the Buttons folder in the Library panel.

FLASH 3-18

Working with Symbols and Interactivity

Figure 20 *The rectangle object*

The Car Race — Rectangle object

Finish Line

Figure 21 *Adjusting the gradient*

Finish Line — Center circle indicates round red area

Drag the diagonal arrow from the outside ring toward the center of the rectangle

Projects

This book contains a variety of end-of-chapter materials for additional practice and reinforcement. The Skills Review contains hands-on practice exercises that mirror the progressive nature of the lesson material. The chapter concludes with four projects: two Project Builders, one Design Project, and one Portfolio Project. The Project Builders and the Design Project require you to apply the skills you've learned in the chapter. The Portfolio Project encourages you to solve challenges based on the content explored in the chapter and then add the completed projects to your portfolio.

What Instructor Resources Are Available with This Book?

The Instructor Resources are Delmar's way of putting the resources and information needed to teach and learn effectively into your hands. All the resources are available for both Macintosh and Windows operating systems. These resources can be found online at **http://login.cengage.com**. Once you log in or create an account, search for the title under 'My Dashboard' using the ISBN. Then select the instructor companion site resources and click 'Add to my Bookshelf.'

Instructor's Manual

Available as an electronic file, the Instructor's Manual includes chapter overviews and detailed lecture topics for each chapter, with teaching tips.

Sample Syllabus

The Sample Syllabus includes a suggested syllabus for any course that uses this book.

PowerPoint Presentations

Each chapter has a corresponding PowerPoint presentation that you can use in lectures, distribute to your students, or customize to suit your course.

Data Files for Students

To complete most of the chapters in this book, your students will need Data Files, which are available online. Instruct students to use the Data Files List at the end of this book. This list gives instructions on organizing files.

To access the Data Files for this book, take the following steps:

1. Open your browser and go to http://www.cengagebrain.com
2. Type the author, title, or ISBN of this book in the Search window. (The ISBN is listed on the back cover.)
3. Click the book title in the list of search results.
4. When the book's main page is displayed, click the Access button under Free Study Tools.
5. To download Data Files, select a chapter number and then click on the Data Files tab on the left navigation bar to download the files.

Solutions to Exercises

Solution Files are Data Files completed with comprehensive sample answers. Use these files to evaluate your students' work. Or distribute them electronically so students can verify their work. Sample solutions to all lessons and end-of-chapter material are provided with the exception of some of the Portfolio Projects.

ACA Certification

This book covers the objectives necessary for Adobe Flash ACA certification. Use the Certification Grid at the back of the book to find out where an objective is covered.

Additional Resources and Certification

To access additional resources for this book, including information about ACE certification, follow Steps 1 through 4 under Data Files for Students, above, and then:

1. Click ACE information or, to access additional materials, click the Additional Materials tab under Book Resources to download the files.

Test Bank and Test Engine

ExamView is a powerful testing software package that allows instructors to create and administer printed and computer (LAN-based) exams. ExamView includes hundreds of questions that correspond to the topics covered in this text, enabling students to generate detailed study guides that include page references for further review. The computer-based and LAN-based/online testing component allows students to take exams using the EV Player, and also saves the instructor time by grading each exam automatically.

BRIEF CONTENTS

CONTENTS

 CHAPTER 1: GETTING STARTED WITH FLASH

CHAPTER 4: CREATING ANIMATIONS

CHAPTER 6:   PREPARING AND PUBLISHING APPLICATIONS

CHAPTER 7:   IMPORTING AND MODIFYING GRAPHICS

CHAPTER 8: BUILDING COMPLEX ANIMATIONS

CHAPTER 11: ADDING SOUND AND VIDEO

CHAPTER 12: DEVELOPING MOBILE APPLICATIONS

Intended Audience

This book is designed for the beginner or intermediate user who wants to learn how to use Adobe Flash CS6. The book is designed to provide basic and in-depth material that not only educates, but encourages you to explore the nuances of this exciting program.

Approach

The book allows you to work at your own pace through step-by-step tutorials. A concept is presented and the process is explained, followed by the actual steps. To learn the most from the use of the text, you should adopt the following habits:

- Proceed slowly: Accuracy and comprehension are more important than speed.
- Understand what is happening with each step before you continue to the next step.
- After finishing a process, ask yourself: Can I do the process on my own? If the answer is no, review the steps.

Icons, Buttons, and Pointers

Symbols for icons, buttons, and pointers are shown each time they are used.

Fonts

Data Files contain a variety of commonly used fonts, but there is no guarantee that these fonts will be available on your computer. Each font is identified in cases where fonts other than Arial or Times New Roman are used. If any of the fonts in use are not available on your computer, you can make a substitution, realizing that the results may vary from those in the book.

Windows and Macintosh

Adobe Flash CS6 works virtually the same on Windows and Macintosh operating systems. In those cases where there is a difference, the abbreviations (Win) and (Mac) are used.

Windows System Requirements

Adobe Flash CS6 requires the following:
- Intel® Pentium® 4 or AMD Athlon® 64 processor
- Microsoft® Windows® XP with Service Pack 3 or Windows 7
- 2GB of RAM (3GB recommended)

- 3.5GB of available hard-disk space for installation; additional free space required during installation (cannot install on removable flash storage devices)
- 1024x768 display (1280x800 recommended)
- DVD-ROM drive
- QuickTime 7.6.6 software required for multimedia features

Macintosh System Requirements

Adobe Flash CS6 requires the following:
- Multicore Intel processor
- Mac OS X v10.6 or v10.7
- 2GB of RAM (3GB recommended)
- 4GB of available hard-disk space for installation; additional free space required during installation (cannot install on a volume that uses a case-sensitive file system or on removable flash storage devices)
- 1024x768 display (1280x800 recommended)
- DVD-ROM drive
- QuickTime 7.6.6 software required for multimedia features
- Java Runtime Environment 1.6

Data Files

To complete the lessons in this book, you need the Data Files. To access the Data Files for this book, take the following steps:

1. Open your browser and go to http://www.cengagebrain.com
2. Type the author, title, or ISBN of this book in the Search window. (The ISBN is listed on the back cover.)
3. Click the book title in the list of search results.
4. When the book's main page is displayed, click the Access button under Free Study Tools.
5. To download Data Files, select a chapter number and then click on the Data Files tab on the left navigation bar to download the files.
6. To access additional materials, including information about ACE certification, click the Additional Materials tab under Book Resources to download the files.

Your instructor will tell you where to store the files as you work, such as the hard drive, a network server, or a USB drive. The instructions in the lessons will refer to "the drive and folder where you store your Data Files" when referring to the Data Files for the book.

Projects

Several projects are presented at the end of each chapter that allow students to apply the skills they have learned in the unit. Two projects, Ultimate Tours and the Portfolio, build from chapter to chapter. You will need to contact your instructor if you plan to work on these without having completed the previous chapter's project.

Creating a Portfolio

The Portfolio Project and Project Builders allow students to use their creativity to come up with original Flash animations, screen designs and applications. Creating a portfolio is an excellent way to store and display original work.

Certification

This book covers the objectives necessary for Adobe Flash ACA certification. This book, along with material posted on Cengage Brain, also covers the objectives necessary for Adobe Flash ACE certification. Use the ACA Certification Grid at the back of the book to find out where an ACA objective is covered, and the ACE Certification grid posted on Cengage Brain to find out where each ACE objective is covered. To access Cengage Brain, take the following steps:

1. Open your browser and go to http://www.cengagebrain.com
2. Type the author, title, or ISBN of this book in the Search window. (The ISBN is listed on the back cover.)
3. Click the book title in the list of search results.
4. When the book's main page is displayed, click the Access button under Free Study Tools.

CHAPTER 1

GETTING STARTED WITH
FLASH

1. Understand the Flash workspace
2. Open a document and play a Flash movie
3. Create and save a Flash movie
4. Work with the Timeline
5. Distribute a Flash movie/application
6. Plan an application

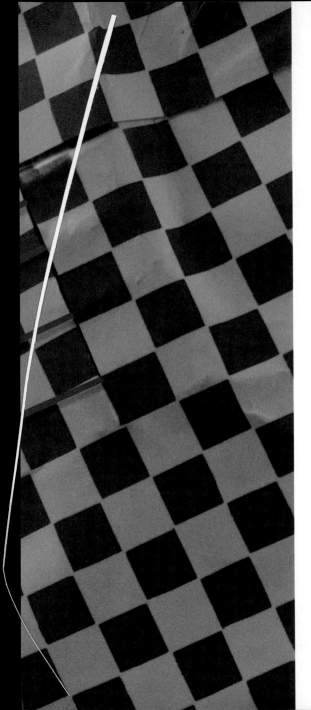

CHAPTER 1

GETTING STARTED WITH FLASH

Introduction

Adobe has created the Adobe® Flash® Platform, which is an integrated set of tools and technologies used to develop and deliver compelling applications running on computers, websites, and mobile devices. The Adobe Flash Platform includes Adobe Catalyst used to create interactive designs, Flash Builder and Flex both used for programming, Flash Player used to display Flash content on the Web, and Adobe AIR used to deploy Flash applications on desktops, mobile devices, and televisions. At the heart of the Adobe Flash Platform is Adobe Flash Professional.

Adobe Flash Professional CS6 is a development tool that allows you to create compelling interactive applications, which often include animation. Flash is an excellent program for creating applications that are used for the following: **entertainment** (such as, multiplayer social games running on Facebook); **business** (such as, stock market analytic tools); **education** (such as, interactive museum exhibits); **government** (such as, interactive national park tours); and **personal use** (such as, GPS-based interactive street maps).

Flash is popular with developers because they can create these applications and deliver them in multiple ways: on desktop computers, smartphones, tablets, and even TVs. An example is Sesame Street. Using Flash technologies Sesame Street developers were able to repurpose their television content to create games and other applications that run on computers, smartphones (iPhone, Windows, and Android models), and tablets such as the iPad. Flash is helping them leverage resources, both personnel and content, because the ability to create one application and use it on several devices saves development time and money.

Flash has become the standard for both professional and casual application developers, as well as for web developers. It is the leading program for creating animations, such as product demonstrations and banner ads, used in websites. It has exceptional drawing tools and tools for creating interactive controls, such as navigation buttons and menus. Furthermore, it provides the ability to incorporate sounds and video easily into an application. This chapter provides an overview of Flash and presents concepts that are covered in more detail in later chapters.

Understand the
FLASH WORKSPACE

What You'll Do

 In this lesson, you will learn about the development workspace in Adobe Flash and how to change Flash settings to customize your workspace.

Organizing the Flash Workspace

As a designer, one of the most important things for you to do is to organize your workspace—that is, to decide what to have displayed on the screen and how to arrange the various tools and panels. Because **Flash** is a powerful program with many tools, your workspace may become cluttered. Fortunately, it is easy to customize the workspace to display only the tools needed at any particular time.

The development process in Flash operates according to a movie metaphor: objects placed on the Stage also are incorporated in frames on a Timeline. As you work in Flash, you create a movie by arranging objects (such as graphics and text) on the Stage, and then animating the objects using the Timeline. You can play the movie on the Stage as you are working on it by using the movie controls (start, stop, rewind, and so on). Once completed, the movie can become part of an application, such as a game, or used in a website. Unless otherwise noted, the term *movie* refers to Flash-created movies.

When you start Flash, three basic parts of the workspace are displayed: a menu bar that organizes commands within menus, a Stage

where objects are placed, and a Timeline used to organize and control the objects on the Stage. In addition, one or more panels may be displayed. Panels, such as the Tools panel, are used when working with objects and features of the movie. Figure 1 shows a typical Flash workspace.

Stage

The **Stage** contains all of the objects (such as drawings, photos, animations, text, and videos) that are part of the movie that will be seen by your viewers. It shows how the objects behave within the movie and how they interact with each other. You can resize the Stage and change the background color applied to it. You can draw objects directly on the Stage or drag them from the Library panel to the Stage. You can also import objects developed in another program directly to the Stage. You can specify the size of the Stage (in pixels), which will be the size of the display area for the application on your smartphone or within your browser window. The gray area surrounding the Stage is the Pasteboard. You can place objects on the Pasteboard as you are creating a movie. However, neither the Pasteboard nor the objects on it will appear when the movie is played.

Timeline (Frames and Layers)

The **Timeline** is used to organize and control the movie's contents by specifying when each object appears on the Stage. The Timeline is critical to the creation of movies because a movie is merely a series of still images that appear over time. The images are contained within **frames**, which are segments of the Timeline. Frames in a Flash movie are similar to frames in a motion picture. When a Flash movie is played, a playhead moves from frame to frame on the Timeline, causing the content of each frame to appear on the Stage in a linear sequence.

The Timeline indicates where you are at any time within the movie and allows you to insert, delete, select, copy, and move frames. The Timeline contains **layers** that help to organize the objects on the Stage. You can draw and edit objects on one layer without affecting objects on other layers. Layers are a way to stack objects so they can overlap and give a 3D appearance on the Stage.

Panels

Panels are used to view, organize, and modify objects and features in a movie. The most commonly used panels are the Tools panel, the Properties panel (also called the Property inspector), and the Library panel. The **Tools panel** contains a set of tools, such as the rectangle, oval and text tools, used to draw and edit graphics and text. The **Properties panel** is used to display and change the properties of an object, such as the size and transparency of a circle. The **Library panel** is used to store and organize the various assets in your movie such as graphics, buttons, sounds, and video.

You can control which panels are displayed individually or you can choose to display

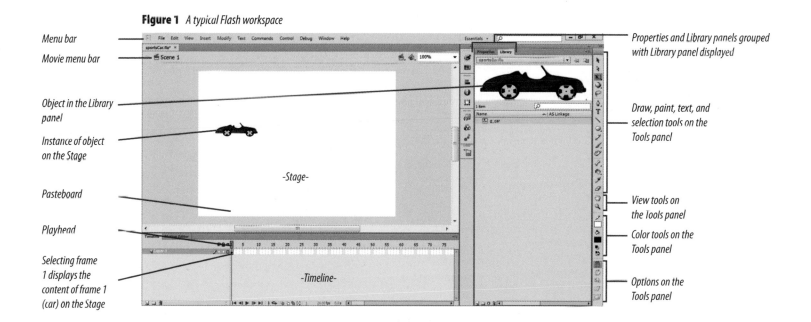

Figure 1 *A typical Flash workspace*

Menu bar

Movie menu bar

Object in the Library panel

Instance of object on the Stage

Pasteboard

Playhead

Selecting frame 1 displays the content of frame 1 (car) on the Stage

-Stage-

-Timeline-

Properties and Library panels grouped with Library panel displayed

Draw, paint, text, and selection tools on the Tools panel

View tools on the Tools panel

Color tools on the Tools panel

Options on the Tools panel

panel sets. **Panel sets** are groups of the most commonly used panels. For example, the Properties and the Library panels are often grouped together to make a panel set.

Although several panels open automatically when you start Flash, you may choose to close them and then display them only when they are needed. This keeps your workspace from becoming too cluttered. Panels are floating windows, meaning that you can move them around the workspace. This allows you to group (dock) panels together as a way to organize them in the workspace. In addition, you can control how a panel is displayed. That is, you can expand a panel to show all of its features or collapse it to show only the title bar. Collapsing panels reduces the clutter on your workspace, provides a larger area for the Stage, and still provides easy access to often used panels.

If you choose to rearrange panels, first decide if you want a panel to be grouped (docked) with another panel, stacked above or below another panel, placed as a floating panel, or simply positioned as a stand-alone panel. An example of each of these is shown in Figure 2. When panels are grouped and expanded, clicking on a panel's tab makes it the active panel so that the panel features are displayed.

The key to rearranging panels is the blue drop zone that appears when a panel is being moved. The drop zone is the area to which the panel can move and is indicated by either a blue line or a rectangle with a blue border. A single blue line indicates the position for stacking a panel above or below another panel. A rectangle with a blue border indicates the position for grouping panels. If you move a panel without using a drop zone, the panel becomes a floating panel and is neither grouped nor stacked with other panels. To move a panel, you drag the panel by its tab until the desired blue drop zone appears, then you release the mouse button. Figure 3 shows the Library panel being grouped with the Properties panel. The process is to drag the Library

Figure 2 *Arranging panels*

Collapsed panel sets showing the icon for each panel in a panel set

Grouped panels: Properties/Library

Stand-alone panel (Tools)

Floating panel

panel tab adjacent to the Properties panel tab. Notice the rectangle with the blue border that surrounds the Properties panel. This indicates the drop zone for the Library panel. (*Note:* Dragging a panel by its tab moves only that panel. To move a panel set you must drag the group by its title bar.)

Floating panels can be resized by dragging the left side, right side, or bottom of the panel. Also, you can resize a panel by dragging one of the bottom corners. In addition to resizing panels, you can collapse a panel so that only its title bar appears, and then you can expand it to display the entire panel. The Collapse to Icons button is located in the upper-right corner of each panel's title bar, as shown in Figure 3. The

Collapse to Icons button is a toggle button, which means it changes or toggles between two states. When clicked, the Collapse to Icons button changes to the Expand Panels button.

If you want to close a panel, you can click the Panel options button (shown in Figure 3) to display a drop down menu and then click the Close option. Alternately, you can right-click (Win) or [control]-click (Mac) the panel tab and choose close. If the panel is a floating panel you can click the Close button on the title bar. Finally, if the panel is expanded, you can display the Windows menu and deselect the panel (or panel group).

Arranging panels can be a bit tricky. It's easy to start moving panels around and find

that the workspace is cluttered with panels arranged in unintended ways. To clean up your workspace, you can close a panel(s) or simply display the default Essentials workspace described below.

Flash provides several preset workspace configurations that provide panels and panel sets most often used by designers, developers, and animators. The default workspace, shown in Figure 4, is named Essentials and can be displayed by clicking the Essentials button on the menu bar and choosing Reset 'Essentials'. (*Note:* Your Essentials button may be below your menu bar.) Alternately, you can choose Reset 'Essentials' from the Workspace command on the Window menu. This workspace includes

Figure 3 *Grouping the Library panel with the Properties panel*

Click ▶▶ or ◀◀ to toggle between the Collapse to Icons button and the Expand Panels button

Panel options button ▼≡

Library panel being dragged

Rectangle with blue border indicates drop zone

the Timeline panel (grouped with the Motion Editor, which is used to edit animations); the Tools panel which is expanded; the Properties and Library panels grouped and expanded; and several other panel sets that are stacked and collapsed. Your Essentials workspace may open with additional panel sets that are grouped depending on user settings and previous use. You can expand and collapse these grouped panels sets by clicking the Expand Panels button or the Collapse to Icons button. To open a single panel set, you click an icon in the set. The Essentials workspace is a good development environment when learning Flash.

Regardless of how you decide to customize your development workspace, the Stage and the menu bar are always displayed. Usually, you display the Timeline, Tools panel, Library panel, Properties panel, and one or more other panels.

Other changes that you can make to the workspace are to change the size of the Stage, move the Stage around the Pasteboard, and change the size of the Timeline panel. To increase the size of the Stage so that the objects on the Stage can be edited more easily, you can change the magnification setting using commands on the View menu or by using the Zoom tool on the Tools panel. The Hand tool on the Tools panel and the scroll bars at

the bottom and right of the Stage can be used to reposition the Stage. The Timeline can be resized by dragging the top border. As your Flash movie gets more complex, you will use more layers on the Timeline. Increasing the size of the Timeline allows you to view more layers at one time.

Figure 4 *The Essentials workspace*

Your panel sets may vary; mouse over an icon to see the name of a collapsed panel

Figure 5 *The Flash Welcome screen*

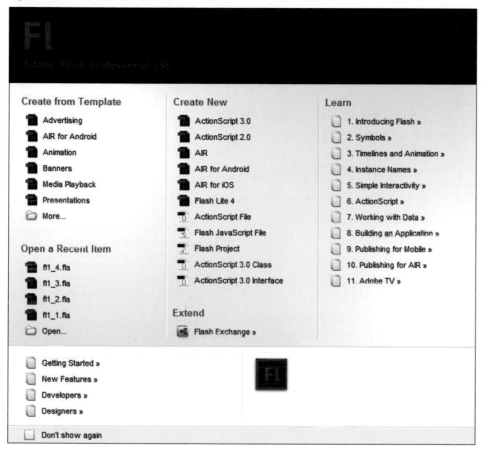

Create from Template

- Advertising
- AIR for Android
- Animation
- Banners
- Media Playback
- Presentations
- More...

Open a Recent Item

- fl1_4.fla
- fl1_3.fla
- fl1_2.fla
- fl1_1.fla
- Open...

Create New

- ActionScript 3.0
- ActionScript 2.0
- AIR
- AIR for Android
- AIR for iOS
- Flash Lite 4
- ActionScript File
- Flash JavaScript File
- Flash Project
- ActionScript 3.0 Class
- ActionScript 3.0 Interface

Extend

- Flash Exchange »

Learn

- 1. Introducing Flash »
- 2. Symbols »
- 3. Timelines and Animation »
- 4. Instance Names »
- 5. Simple Interactivity »
- 6. ActionScript »
- 7. Working with Data »
- 8. Building an Application »
- 9. Publishing for Mobile »
- 10. Publishing for AIR »
- 11. Adobe TV »

- Getting Started »
- New Features »
- Developers »
- Designers »

FI

- Don't show again

Start Adobe Flash and work with panels

1. Start the Adobe Flash Professional CS6 program ▣.

   The Adobe Flash CS6 Welcome screen appears, as shown in Figure 5. This screen allows you to open a recent document or create a new Flash file.

2. Click **ActionScript 3.0** under Create New.

3. Click the **Essentials button** on the menu bar, then click **Reset 'Essentials'**.

   Note: The Essentials button may be under the menu bar.

   TIP When you open a new file or as you are rearranging your workspace, use the Reset 'Essentials' option to display the default workspace.

4. Click **Window** on the menu bar, then note the panels with check marks.

   The check marks identify which panels and panel sets are open.

   TIP The Properties, Library, Colors, Swatches, Align, Info, Transform, Code Snippets, Components, Motion Presets, and Projects panels may be grouped, stacked, and/or collapsed, depending upon the configuration of your Essentials workspace. If so, only the panel that is active will have a check mark.

5. With the Windows menu still open, click **Hide Panels**.

6. Click **Window** on the menu bar, then click **Timeline**.

7. Click **Window** on the menu bar, then click **Tools**.

8. Click **Window** on the menu bar, then click **Library**.

   The Library and Properties panels are grouped, and the Library panel is the active panel.

   (continued)

9. Click the **Properties panel tab**.

   The Properties panel is the active tab and the panel's features are displayed.

10. Click the **Library panel tab**, then drag the **Library panel** to the left side of the Stage as a floating panel.

11. Click the **Collapse to Icons button** on the Library panel title bar.

12. Click the **Expand Panels button** on the Library panel title bar.

13. Click the **Library panel tab**, drag the **Library panel tab** to the right of the Properties panel tab, then when a rectangle with a blue border appears, as shown in Figure 6, release the mouse button to group the panels.

    Note: If the panels do not appear grouped, repeat the step making sure there is a rectangle with a blue border before releasing the mouse button.

14. Click the **Collapse to Icons button** in the upper-right corner of the grouped panels, as shown in Figure 6.

15. Click the **Expand Panels button** to display the grouped panels.

16. Click **Essentials** on the menu bar, then click **Reset 'Essentials'**.

17. Click the **Color panel button** 🎨.

    The Color panel is expanded and shown grouped with the Swatches panel.

18. Click the **Collapse to Icons button** ▶▶ for the Color panel set.

19. Click **Essentials** on the menu bar, then click **Reset 'Essentials'**.

You started Flash and configured the workspace by hiding, moving, and displaying panels.

Figure 6 *Library panel grouped with the Properties panel*

Click to toggle between Collapse to Icons button and Expand Panels button

Grouped panels share one title bar

Library tab placed next to Properties tab

Blue rectangle shows drop zone

Understanding Your Workspace

Organizing the Flash workspace is like organizing your desktop. You may work more efficiently if you have many of the most commonly used items in view and ready to use. Alternately, you may work better if your workspace is relatively uncluttered, giving you more free "desk space." Fortunately, Flash makes it easy for you to decide which items to display and how they are arranged while you work. You should become familiar with quickly opening, collapsing, expanding, and closing the various windows, toolbars, and panels in Flash, and experimenting with different layouts and screen resolutions to find the workspace that works best for you. Be sure to use screentips, such as those associated with the Collapse to Icons button, the Expand Panels buttons, and panel sets, to help you identify components of your workspace.

Figure 7 *Changing the size of the Timeline panel*

View list arrow

Double-headed pointer

Alternate Ways to Complete a Task

Flash often provides alternative ways to complete the same task. For instance, if you want to change the view (zoom in and out) of the Stage you could use the following methods:

- the magnification command on the View menu
- the View list options on the movie menu
- the Zoom tool on the Tools panel
- the Zoom in and Zoom out commands on the View menu
- the various combinations of shortcut keys displayed on the View menu

Change the Stage view and display of the Timeline

1. Click the **Hand tool** 🖐 on the Tools panel, click the middle of the Stage, then drag the **Stage** around the Pasteboard.
2. Click **View** on the menu bar, point to **Magnification**, then click **50%**.
3. Move the pointer to the top of the Timeline title bar then, when the pointer changes to a double-headed pointer ↕, click and drag the **title bar** up to increase the height of the Timeline, as shown in Figure 7.
   Increasing the height of the Timeline panel allows you to view more layers as you add them to the Timeline.
4. Move the pointer to the top of the Timeline title bar then, when the pointer changes to a double-headed pointer ↕, click and drag the **title bar** down to decrease the height of the Timeline.
5. Double-click the word **Timeline** to collapse the Timeline.
6. Click the word **Timeline** again to expand the Timeline.
7. Click the **View list arrow** on the movie menu bar as shown in Figure 7, then click **100%**.
8. Click **Essentials** on the menu bar, then click **Reset 'Essentials'**.
9. Click **File** on the menu bar, then click **Save**.
10. Navigate to the drive and folder where your Data Files are stored, type **workspace** for the filename, then click **Save**.
11. Click **File** on the menu bar, then click **Close**.

You used a View command to change the magnification of the Stage; you used the Hand tool to move the Stage around the workspace; you resized, collapsed, and expanded the Timeline panel; then you saved the document.

Open a Document and
PLAY A FLASH MOVIE

What You'll Do

In this lesson, you will open a Flash document (movie); preview, test, and save the movie; then change the movie's Stage settings.

Opening a Movie in Flash

Flash files are called documents (or movies, interchangeably) and have an .fla file extension. If you have created a movie in Flash and saved it with the name myMovie, the filename will be myMovie.fla. Files with the .fla file extension can only be opened and edited using Flash. After they are opened, you can edit and resave them.

In order for Flash movies to be viewed on computers that do not have the Flash program installed, the movies must be saved in a different file format. The two most common file formats for distributing Flash movies are Flash Player (.swf) and Adobe AIR (.air). Flash Player files are used on websites for everything from interactive product demonstrations to banner ads. Adobe AIR files are used for a much broader range of applications such as interactive games, tutorials, product demonstrations, and productivity software. An important feature of AIR applications, also called apps, is that they can be played on any device (computer, mobile, TV) without the Flash Player and without a browser. The Publish command is used to convert a Flash FLA movie to a SWF or an AIR format. Depending on the target

you specify, Flash Player or Air, the filename extension will be changed to match the target you specifiy, either Flash Player (.fla) or Air (.air). For example, when a Flash file named myMovie.fla is published using the Publish command and the target is Flash Player (the default target), a new file named myMovie.swf is created. Flash SWF movies can be played in a browser without the Flash program, but the Flash Player must be installed on the computer. Flash Players are pre-installed on almost all computers. For those that do not have the player, it can be downloaded free from the Adobe website, *www.adobe.com*. Because .swf files cannot be edited in the Flash program, you should preview the Flash .fla files on the Stage and test them before you publish them. Be sure to keep the original .fla file so that you can make changes, if needed, at a later date.

Previewing a Movie

After creating a new Flash movie or opening a previously saved movie, you can preview it within the workspace in several ways. When you preview a movie, you play the frames by directing the playhead to move through the Timeline as you watch the movement on the Stage.

Control Menu Commands (and Keyboard Shortcuts)

Figure 8 shows the Control menu commands, which resemble common DVD-type options:

- Play ([Enter] (Win) or [return] (Mac)) begins playing the movie frame by frame, from the location of the playhead to the end of the movie. For example, if the playhead is on frame 5 and the last frame is frame 40, choosing the Play command will play frames 5–40 of the movie.

QUICK TIP

When a movie starts, the Play command changes to a Stop command. You can also stop the movie by pressing [Enter] (Win) or [return] (Mac).

- Rewind ([Shift][,]) (Win) or ([option] ⌘ [R]) (Mac) moves the playhead to frame 1.
- Go To End ([Shift][.]) moves the playhead to the last frame of the movie.

- Step Forward One Frame (.) moves the playhead forward one frame at a time.
- Step Backward One Frame (,) moves the playhead backward one frame at a time.

You can turn on the Loop Playback setting to allow the movie to continue playing repeatedly. A check mark next to the Loop Playback command on the Control menu indicates that the feature is active. To turn off this feature, click the Loop Playback command.

Control Buttons

You can also preview a movie using the Control buttons located on the status bar at the bottom of the Timeline. Figure 8 shows these buttons.

QUICK TIP

The decision of which controls to use (the Control menu, keyboard shortcuts, or the Control buttons on the Timeline status bar) is a matter of personal preference.

Testing a Movie

When you play a movie within the Flash workspace, some interactive functions (such as navigation buttons that are used to jump from one part of the movie to another) do not work. To preview the full functionality of a movie, you can use the Test Movie command on the Control menu to play the movie in a Flash Player window or in a browser on a computer using the SWF format. In addition, the Test Movie command can be used to play

Figure 8 *Methods to control a movie*

DVD-type commands

Control buttons on the Timeline status bar

Control menu

a movie on a mobile device that is attached to your computer using a USB cable.

Documents, Movies, and Applications

As you work in Flash, you are creating a document. When you save your work as an .fla file, you are saving the document. This is consistent with other Adobe products, such as Photoshop, that use the word *document* to refer to work created in that program. In addition, because Flash uses a movie metaphor with a Stage, Timeline, frames, animations, and so on, the work done in Flash is often referred to as a movie. So, the phrase *Flash document* and the phrase *Flash movie* are synonymous. Movies can be as small and simple as a ball bouncing across the screen or as complex as a full-length interactive adventure game. Products such as games and educational software, as well as online advertisements and product demonstrations, are referred to as applications (see Figure 9). Applications usually contain multiple Flash documents or movies that are linked.

Using the Flash Player

To view a Flash movie on the web, your computer needs to have the Flash Player installed. An important feature of multimedia players, such as the Flash Player, is the ability to decompress a file that has been compressed. Compressing a file gives it a small file size, which means it can be delivered more quickly over the Internet than its uncompressed counterpart. In addition to Adobe, companies such as Apple (QuickTime) and Microsoft (Windows Media Player) create players that allow applications to be viewed on the web. These applications can be created by Apple, Microsoft, or other companies. The multimedia players are distributed free and can be downloaded from the company's website. The Flash Player is created by Adobe and the latest version is available at *www.adobe.com*.

Figure 9 *Example of an application*
Courtesy of New York Philharmonic Kidzone. http://www.nyphilkids.org/games/main.phtml?

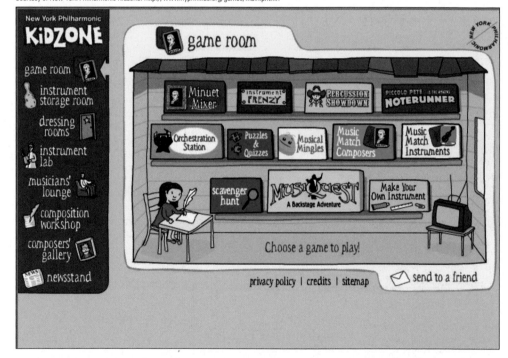

Figure 10 *Playhead moving across Timeline*

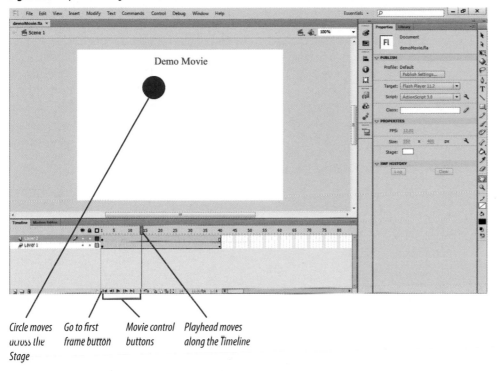

Circle moves across the Stage   *Go to first frame button*   *Movie control buttons*   *Playhead moves along the Timeline*

Using Options and Shortcuts

As you know, there is often more than one way to complete a particular command when using Flash. For example, if you want to rewind a movie you can use the control on the Control menu, use the control on the Timeline status bar, press [Shift] + [,], or drag the playhead to frame 1. In addition, Flash provides context menus that are relevant to the current selection. For example, if you point to a graphic and right-click (Win) or [control]-click (Mac), a menu opens with graphic-related commands, such as cut and copy. Shortcut keys are also available for many of the most common commands, such as [Ctrl][Z] (Win) or [command][Z] (Mac) for Undo.

Open and play a movie using the Control menu and movie control buttons

1. Open fl1_1.fla from the drive and folder where your Data Files are stored, then save it as **demoMovie.fla**.

2. Verify the view is set to 100%.

   The view setting is displayed on the movie menu bar, which is above and to the right of the Stage.

3. Click **Control** on the menu bar, then click **Play**.

   Notice how the playhead moves across the Timeline as the blue circle moves from the left of the Stage to the right, as shown in Figure 10.

4. Click **Control** on the menu bar, then click **Rewind**.

5. Press [**Enter**] (Win) or [**return**] (Mac) to play the movie, then press [**Enter**] (Win) or [**return**] (Mac) again to stop the movie before it ends.

6. Click the **Go to first frame button** at the bottom of the Timeline status bar, as shown in Figure 10.

7. Use all the movie control buttons on the Timeline status bar to preview the movie.

8. Click and drag the **playhead** back and forth to view the contents of the movie frame by frame.

9. Click number **1** on the Timeline to select the frame.

10. Press the **period key** several times, then press the **comma key** several times to move the playhead one frame at a time forward and backward.

You opened a Flash movie and previewed it, using various controls.

Test a movie

1. Click **Control** on the menu bar, point to **Test Movie**, then click **in Flash Professional**.

   The Flash Player window opens, as shown in Figure 11, and the movie starts playing automatically.

2. Click **Control** on the menu bar of the Flash Player window (Win) or application menu bar (Mac), then review the available commands.

3. Click **File** on the menu bar of the Flash Player window (Win) or application menu bar (Mac), then click **Close** to close the Flash Player window.

4. Use your file management program to navigate to the drive and folder where you saved the demoMovie.fla file and notice the demoMovie.swf file.

TIP   When you test a movie, Flash automatically creates a file that has an .swf extension in the folder where your movie is stored and then plays the movie in the Flash Player.

5. Return to the Flash program.

6. Click **View** on the menu bar, point to **Magnification**, then click **100%** if it is not already selected.

7. Click **1** on the Timeline.

You tested a movie in the Flash Player window and viewed the .swf file created as a result of testing the movie, set the magnification, and then displayed the contents of frame 1.

Figure 11 *Flash Player window*

Auto Save and Data Recovery

Flash provides an Auto Save feature that periodically saves each document. In addition, the Auto Recover feature enables Flash to periodically take a snapshot of all open documents so that the user can recover from any sudden data loss event. If a dialog box titled Document save and auto-recovery opens, you can choose to save the document, disable the auto-recovery feature, and/or prevent the dialog box from reappearing. The Auto-Save feature is turned on and off in the Document Properties dialog box.

Figure 12 *Document Settings dialog box*

Background color swatch

Figure 13 *Completed changes to the document properties*

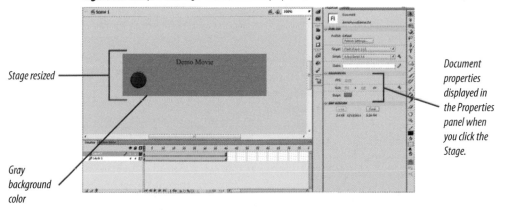

Stage resized

Gray
background
color

Document
properties
displayed in
the Properties
panel when
you click the
Stage.

Change the document properties

1. Click **Modify** on the menu bar, then click **Document**.

    The Document Settings dialog box opens.

2. Double-click in the **height text box** to select the number, then type **160**.

3. Click the **Background color swatch**, then click the **gray (#999999) color swatch** in the far-left column of the Color Swatch palette.

    Note: The color code for a color appears next to the sample color swatch above the palette as you point to a color. The Color Swatch palette allows you to click a color to choose it or to enter a number that represents the color.

4. Review the remaining default values shown in Figure 12, then click **OK**.

    The dialog box closes.

5. Click the **Stage**.

    TIP You can use the Properties Panel to change the Document properties as shown in Figure 13. You must click the Stage to display the settings.

6. Press **[Enter]** (Win) or **[return]** (Mac) to play the movie.

7. Click **File** on the menu bar, then click **Save As**.

8. Navigate to the drive and folder where your Data Files are stored, type **demoMovieBanner** for the filename, then click **Save**.

9. Click **File** on the menu bar, then click **Close**.

You set the document properties including the size of the Stage and the background color, then you saved the document.

Create and
SAVE A FLASH MOVIE

What You'll Do

In this lesson, you will create a Flash movie that will include a simple animation, add animation effects, and then save the movie.

Creating a Flash Movie

Flash movies are created by placing objects (graphics, text, sounds, photos, and so on) on the Stage, editing these objects (for example, changing their brightness), animating the objects, and adding interactivity with buttons and menus. You can create graphic objects in Flash using the drawing tools, or you can create them in another program, such as Adobe Illustrator, Photoshop, or Fireworks, and then import them into a Flash movie. In addition, you can acquire clip art and stock photographs and import them into a movie. When objects are placed on the Stage, they are automatically placed on a layer and in the selected frame on the Timeline.

Figure 14 shows a movie that has a circle object created in Flash. Notice that the playhead is on frame 1 of the movie. The object placed on the Stage appears in frame 1 and appears on the Stage when the playhead is on frame 1. The dot in frame 1 on the Timeline indicates that this frame is a keyframe. The concept of keyframes is critical to understanding how Flash works. A **keyframe** indicates that there is a change in the movie, such as the start of an animation,

or the resizing of an object on the Stage. A keyframe is automatically designated in frame 1 of every layer. In addition, you can designate any frame to be a keyframe.

The circle object in Figure 14 was created using the Oval tool. To create an oval or a rectangle, you select the desired tool and then drag the pointer over an area on the Stage. *Note:* Flash uses one button on the Tools panel to group the Oval and Rectangle tools, along with three other drawing tools. To display a menu of these tools, click and hold the rectangle (or oval) button on the Tools panel to display the menu and then click the tool you want to use. If you want to draw a perfect circle or square, press and hold [Shift] after the tool is selected, and then drag the pointer. If you make a mistake, you can click Edit on the menu bar, and then click Undo. To make changes to an object, such as resizing or changing its color, or to animate an object, you must first select it. You can use the Selection tool to select an entire object or group of objects. You drag the Selection tool pointer around the entire object to make a **marquee**. An object that has been selected displays a dot pattern or a blue border.

Creating an Animation

Figure 15 shows a movie that has 24 frames, as specified by the blue shading on the Timeline. The blue background color on the Timeline indicates a motion animation that starts in frame 1 and ends in frame 24. The dotted line on the Stage indicates the path the object will follow during the animation. In this case, the object will move from left to right across the Stage. The movement of the object is caused by having the object in different places on the Stage in different frames of the movie. In this case, frame 12 displays the object midway through the animation and frame 24 displays the object at the end of the animation. A basic motion animation requires two keyframes. The first keyframe sets the starting position of the object, and the second keyframe sets the ending position of the object. The number of frames from keyframe to keyframe determines the length of the animation. If the starting keyframe is frame 1 and the ending keyframe is frame 24, the object will be animated for 24 frames. As an object is being animated, Flash automatically fills in the frames between these keyframes, with a process called **motion tweening**.

The Motion Tween Animation Process

Having an object move around the screen is one of the most common types of animations. Flash provides a process called motion tweening that makes it relatively simple to move objects. The process is to select an object on the Stage, then select the Motion Tween command from the Insert menu. If the object is not a symbol, a dialog box opens asking if you want to convert the object to a symbol. Creating a symbol allows you to reuse the object for this and other movies, as well as to apply a motion tween. Only symbols and text blocks can be motion tweened. The final

Figure 14 *Circle object in frame 1*

Object on the Stage is in frame 1 on the Timeline

Figure 15 *Motion animation*

Dotted line indicates the path the object will follow during animation

Blue shading indicates a motion tween animation

step in the animation process is to select the ending frame for the animation and drag the object to another location on the Stage.

Two important things happen during the animation process. First, the Timeline shows the **tween span** (also called **motion span**), which is the number of frames in the motion tween. The tween span can be identified on the Timeline by a blue color, which, in this example, extends for 24 frames. The default tween span when starting from frame 1 of a new movie is determined by the number of frames per second setting. In this example, we used the default setting of 24 frames per second, so the initial number of frames in a tween for this movie is 24 frames.

The length of the motion tween is determined by the last frame in the movie automatically or by you manually if you designate a frame other than the last frame of the movie as the end of the animation. If a movie has an ending frame beyond frame 1, the tween span will extend to the end of the movie. For example, if a movie has 50 frames and you insert a motion tween starting at frame 1, the tween span will extend from frames 1 through 50. Likewise, if a movie has an ending frame in frame 10 and you insert a motion tween in frame 1, the motion tween will extend from frame 1 to frame 10. Finally, a motion tween does not have to start in frame 1. You can start a motion tween in a frame other than frame 1 by clicking the frame on the layer you want to contain the motion tween, inserting a keyframe in that frame, and then continuing with the steps to insert a motion tween (selecting or creating

the object to be tweened, inserting the tween and moving the object).

You can increase or decrease the length of the animation by pointing to either end of the **tween** span and dragging it to a new frame. The tween span will have more or fewer frames based on this action. The duration of the tween will still be based on the number of frames per second setting. For example, if we drag the tween span from frame 24 to frame 48, there are now 48 frames in the tween span. The tween span will still play at 24 frames

per second because we did not change that setting. It will take two seconds to play the new tween span.

Second, a dotted line, called the **motion path**, represents the path the object takes from the beginning frame to the ending frame. This path can be reshaped to cause the object to travel in a non-linear way, as shown in Figure 16. Reshaping a path can be done by using the Selection tool on the Tools panel. You see the tween span on the Timeline and the motion path on the Stage.

Figure 16 *A reshaped motion path*

Motion path line

Motion Presets

Flash provides several preconfigured motion tweens that you can apply to an object on the Stage. These allow you to bounce an object across the Stage, fly-in an object from off the Stage, cause an object to pulsate and to spiral in place, as well as many other types of object animations. Figure 17 shows the Motion Presets panel where you choose a preset and apply it to an object. You can preview each preset before applying it and you can easily change to a different preset, if desired.

Adding Effects to an Object

In addition to animating the location of an object (or objects), you can also animate an object's appearance. Objects have properties such as color, brightness, and size. You can alter an object's properties as it is being animated using the motion tween process. For example, you could give the appearance of the object fading in by changing its transparency (alpha setting) or having it grow larger by altering its size over the course of the animation. Another useful effect is applying filters, such as drop shadows or bevels. All of these changes can be made by selecting the object, and then using commands in the Properties panel.

Figure 17 *Panel set with Motion Presets panel active*

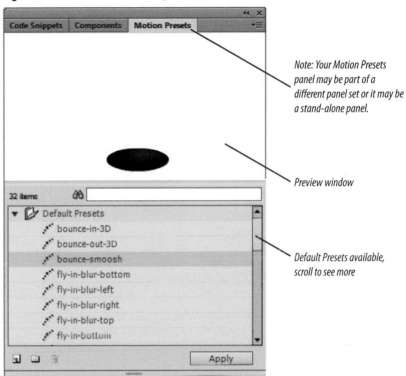

Note: Your Motion Presets panel may be part of a different panel set or it may be a stand-alone panel.

Preview window

Default Presets available, scroll to see more

Create objects using drawing tools

1. Click **ActionScript 3**.0 to open a new Flash document.

2. Save the movie as **tween.fla**.

3. Verify the view is set to 100%.

4. Click and hold the **Rectangle tool** ⬜ (or the Oval tool ⬭ if it is displayed) on the Tools panel to display the list of tools, as shown in Figure 18, then click the **Oval tool** ⬭.

5. Verify that the Object Drawing option ⬜ in the Options area of the Tools panel is not active, as shown in Figure 18.

6. Click the **Fill Color tool color swatch** ⬚ on the Tools panel, then, if necessary, click the **red color swatch** in the left column of the color palette.

7. Verify the Stroke Color tool color swatch on the Tools panel is black, as seen in Figure 20.

8. Press and hold **[Shift]**, drag the **pointer** on the left side of the Stage to draw the circle, as shown in Figure 19, then release the mouse button.

   Pressing and holding [Shift] creates a circle.

TIP Use the Undo command on the Edit menu to undo an action.

9. Click the **Selection tool** ▸ on the Tools panel, drag a **marquee** around the object to select it, as shown in Figure 20, then release the mouse button.

   The object appears covered with a dot pattern.

You created an object using the Oval tool, and then selected the object using the Selection tool.

Figure 18 *Drawing tools menu*

Rectangle tool

Oval tool

Stroke color tool color swatch

Fill color tool color swatch

Object Drawing option is not active

Figure 19 *Drawing a circle*

Figure 20 *Creating a marquee selection*

Use the Selection tool to draw a marquee, which selects the entire object

Getting Started with Flash

Figure 21 *The circle on the right side of the Stage*

Indicates the active frame, which is frame 24

Create a motion tween animation

1. Click **Insert** on the menu bar, then click **Motion Tween**.

   The Convert selection to symbol for tween dialog box opens.

2. Click **OK**.

   A blue border surrounds the object indicating that the object is a symbol. Notice that, in this example, the playhead automatically moved to frame 24, the last frame in the tween span. When you move the object to a new location on the Stage, the object's new location will be reflected in frame 24.

3. Click and then drag the **circle** to the right side of the Stage, as shown in Figure 21, then release the mouse button.

4. Press **[Enter]**(Win) or **[return]**(Mac) to play the movie.

   The playhead moves through frames 1–24 on the Timeline, and the circle moves across the Stage.

5. Click **frame 12** on Layer 1 on the Timeline.

   Verify the frame number on the status bar of the Timeline is 12, and notice that the object is halfway across the screen. This is the result of the tweening process in which the frames between 1 and 24 are filled in with the object in the correct location for each frame.

   (continued)

6. Verify the Selection tool ![selection tool icon] is active, then point to the end of the tween span until the pointer changes to a double-headed arrow ↔, as shown in Figure 22.

7. Click and drag the **tween span** to frame 48, then verify the frame number on the status bar is 48, or adjust as needed.

8. Press **[Enter]**(Win) or **[return]**(Mac) to play the movie.

   Notice it now takes longer (2 seconds, not 1 second) to play the movie. Also notice that a diamond symbol appears in frame 48 indicating that it is now a Property keyframe. A Property keyframe indicates a change in the property of an object. In this case, it indicates the location of the object on the Stage has changed from frame 24 to frame 48.

9. Click **frame 24** and notice that the object is now halfway across the screen.

10. Click **File** on the menu bar, then click **Save**.

You created a motion tween animation and changed the length of the tween span.

Figure 22 *Pointing to the end of the tween span*

Double-headed arrow over end of tween span

Figure 23 *Using the Selection tool to reshape a motion path*

Reshape the motion path

1. Click **File** on the menu bar, click **Save As**, then save the document with the filename **tweenEffects.fla**.

2. Verify the Selection tool ▶ is active.

3. Click **frame 1** to select it.

   Note: When you see the direction to click a frame, click the frame on the layer not the number on the Timeline.

4. Point to just below the middle of the path until the pointer changes to a pointer with an arc ▶⌣, as shown in Figure 23.

   (continued)

5. Click and drag the **path** to reshape the path, as shown in Figure 24.

6. Play the movie.

   Note: When you see the direction to play the movie, press [Enter] (Win) or [return] (Mac).

7. Test the movie.

   Note: When you see the direction to test the movie, click Control on the menu bar, point to Test Movie, then click in Flash Professional. Alternately, you can press [Ctrl]+[Enter] (Win) or [command]+[return](Mac).

8. View the movie, then close the Flash Player window.

9. Click **Edit** on the menu bar, then click **Undo Reshape**.

   Note: The Undo command starts with the most recent action and moves back through the actions. As a result, you may have to click Undo more than one time before you are able to click Undo Reshape.

You used the Selection tool to reshape a motion path and the Undo command to undo the reshape.

Figure 24 *Reshaping the motion path*

Figure 25 *The Properties panel displayed*

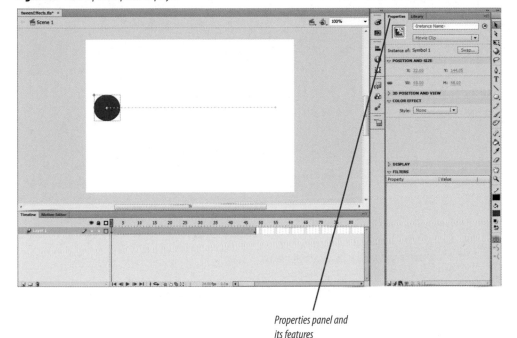

Properties panel and its features

Change the transparency of an object

1. Click **frame 1** to select it, then click the **circle object** on the Stage to select it.

2. Click the **Properties panel tab** to display the Properties panel, as shown in Figure 25.

   Note: If the Properties panel is not open, click Window on the menu bar, then click Properties.

   Note: To verify the object is active, review the available settings in the Properties panel. Make sure POSITION AND SIZE is one of the options.

3. Click **COLOR EFFECT** on the Properties panel to display the Color Effect area if it is not already displayed, click the **Style list arrow**, then click **Alpha**.

4. Drag the **Alpha slider** △ to **0**.

   The object becomes transparent. The bounding box indicates the location of the object and displays the Stage color, white.

5. Click **frame 48** on the layer to select it.

6. Click the bounding box on the Stage to select the object and check that the object's properties are displayed in the Properties panel.

   Note: To verify the object is active, review the available settings in the Properties panel. Make sure POSITION AND SIZE is one of the options.

7. Drag the **Alpha slider** △ to **100**.

8. Play the movie.

9. Test the movie, then close the Flash Player window.

You used the Color Effect option on the Properties panel to change the transparency of an object.

Resize an object

1. Click **frame 1** to select it.
2. Click inside the bounding box on the Stage to select the **circle object**.
3. Click **POSITION AND SIZE** on the Properties panel if this area is not already open.
4. Review the W (width) and H (height) settings of the object.

   The width and height are the dimensions of the bounding box around the circle.

5. Click **frame 48** to select it, then click the **circle object** to select it.
6. Verify the Lock icon ⊜ in the Properties panel is not broken.

   Note: If the lock is broken, click the broken lock to lock it, as shown in Figure 26, to ensure the width and height change proportionally.

7. Point to the number next to W: and when the pointer changes to a double-headed arrow ↔, drag the ↔ **pointer** left to decrease the width so that the circle shrinks to about half its size, as shown in Figure 26.

   Hint: You can also double-click a value in the Properties panel and type a value.
   Note: Resizing the object will reposition it.

8. Click the **circle object** on the Stage.
9. Play the movie.
10. Test the movie, then close the Flash Player window.
11. Click **frame 1**, click the **circle object** to select it, then drag the **Alpha slider** △ to **100**.

You used the Position and Size option on the Properties panel to change the size of an object.

Figure 26 *Resizing the circle*

Make sure the Lock icon is not broken

Your values may differ

Drag the number for width left to decrease the size

Figure 27 *The Add filter icon*

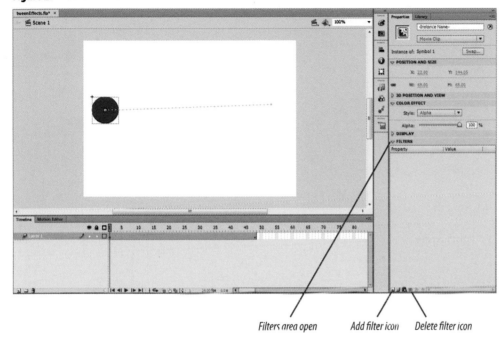

Filters area open   Add filter icon   Delete filter icon

Add a filter to an object

1. Verify the object is selected by viewing the Properties panel and verifying the object's properties are displayed.

2. Click **FILTERS** on the Properties panel to display the Filters area if it is not already displayed.

3. Click the **Add filter icon** ⬧ at the bottom of the Filters area, as shown in Figure 27.

4. Click **Drop Shadow**, point to the number for the angle, then when the pointer changes to a double-headed arrow ⬧, drag the ⬧ **pointer** right to change the number of degrees to **100**.

5. Click **frame 1** to select it, then play the movie.

6. Click **frame 1** to select it, then click the **circle object** to select it.

7. Click **Drop Shadow** in the Filters area, then click the **Delete Filter icon** ⬧ at the bottom of the Filters area.

   The drop shadow filter is removed from the circle object.

8. Click the **Add filter icon** ⬧ at the bottom of the Filters area.

9. Click **Bevel**, test the movie, then close the Flash Player window.

You used the Filters option in the Properties panel to add and delete filters.

Add a motion preset

1. Verify the playhead is on frame 1, then click the object to select it.

2. Click **Window** on the menu bar, then click **Motion Presets**.

   The Motion Presets panel opens. It may open as a stand-alone panel or it may be grouped with other panels.

3. Drag the **Motion Presets panel or the panel set** by its title bar (not one of the tabs) to the right so that it does not obscure the Stage.

4. Click the **expand icon** ▶ for the Default Presets, then click **bounce-smoosh** and watch the animation in the preview widow, as shown in Figure 28.

5. Click **Apply**.

   A dialog box opens asking if you want to replace the current motion object with the new selection. You can only apply one motion tween or motion preset to an object at any one time.

6. Click **Yes**.

   The bevel filter is deleted and a new path is displayed.

7. Play the movie, then test the movie.

   Notice the circle object disappears from the Stage.

   (continued)

Figure 28 *The Motion Presets panel*

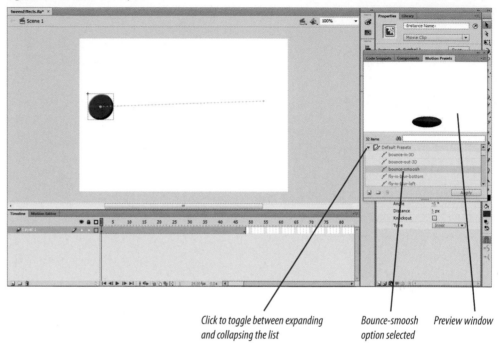

Click to toggle between expanding and collapsing the list

Bounce-smoosh option selected

Preview window

Getting Started with Flash

Figure 29 *Diamond symbols indicating Property keyframes*

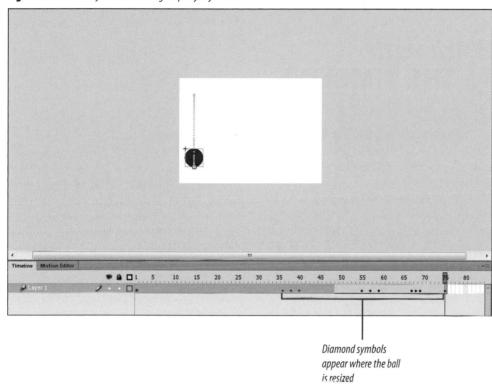

Diamond symbols
appear where the ball
is resized

8. Close the Flash Player window.

9. Click **View** on the menu bar, point to **Magnification**, then click **50%**.

10. Click **frame 1**, click the **Selection tool** ▶ , draw a **marquee** around the circle object and the path to select both of them.

11. Press the **up arrow key [↑]** on the keyboard to move the circle object and the path toward the top of the Stage.

12. Play the movie.

    Notice the Timeline has several diamond symbols, as shown in Figure 29. Each one is a Property keyframe and indicates that there is a change in the object during the motion tween, such as when the ball is resized.

13. Click **frame 1** to select it, then drag the **playhead** from frame 1 to the last frame and notice the change that occurs at each keyframe.

14. Scroll the list of motion presets, click **pulse**, click **Apply**, then click **Yes**.

15. Play the movie.

16. Close the Motion Presets panel or panel set if the Motion Presets panel is part of a panel set.

17. Save and close the movie.

You applied motion presets to an object and viewed how keyframes identify changes in the motion tween.

Work with
THE TIMELINE

What You'll Do

 In this lesson, you will add another layer, allowing you to create an additional animation, and you will use the Timeline to help organize the contents of your movie.

Understanding the Timeline

The Timeline organizes and controls a movie's contents over time. By learning how to read the information provided on the Timeline, you can identify what will be happening in a movie, frame by frame. You can identify which objects are animated, what types of animations are being used, when the various objects will appear in a movie, when changes are made to the properties of an object, which objects will appear on top of others, and how fast the movie will play. Features of the Timeline are shown in Figure 30 and explained in this lesson.

Using Layers

Each new Flash movie contains one layer, named Layer 1. **Layers** are like transparent sheets of plastic that are stacked on top of each other, as shown in Figure 31, which also shows how the stacked objects appear on the Stage. Each layer can contain one or more objects. In Figure 31, the tree is on one layer, the heading Solitude is on another layer, and the colored backdrop is on a third layer. You can add layers using the Timeline command on the Insert menu or by clicking the New Layer icon on the Timeline status bar. Placing objects on different layers and locking the layers helps avoid accidentally making changes to one object while editing another.

Figure 30 *Elements of the Timeline*

New Layer button   Layers   Playhead   Movie control buttons   Current frame   Frame rate   Elapsed time   Status bar   Scroll bar   Frames   Frame View icon

When you add a new layer, Flash stacks it on top of the other layer(s) on the Timeline. The stacking order of the layers on the Timeline is important because objects on the Stage appear in the same stacking order. For example, if you have two overlapping objects, and the top layer has a drawing of a tree and the bottom layer has a drawing of a house, the tree appears as though it is in front of the house. You can change the stacking order of layers simply by dragging them up or down in the list of layers. You can name layers, hide them so their contents do not appear on the Stage, and lock them so that they cannot be edited.

Using Frames and Keyframes

The Timeline is made up of individual segments called **frames**. The contents of each layer appear as the playhead moves over the frames, so any object in frame 1, no matter which layer it is on, appears on the Stage whenever frame 1 is played. Frames are numbered in increments of five for easy reference. The upper-right corner of the Timeline contains a Frame View icon. Clicking this icon displays a menu that provides different views of the Timeline, for example, showing more frames or showing a preview (thumbnails) of the objects on a layer. The status bar at the bottom of the Timeline indicates the current frame (the frame that the playhead is currently on), the frame rate (frames per second, also called fps), and the elapsed time from frame 1 to the current frame. Frames per second is the unit of measure for movies. If the frame rate is set to 24 frames per second and the movie has 48 frames, the movie will take 2 seconds to play.

Keyframes are locations on the Timeline where a new occurrence of an object appears

or a change is made in the object. So, if you draw an object on the Stage, the current frame will need to be changed to a keyframe. In addition, if you create a motion tween, the first frame of the tween span will be a keyframe. One type of keyframe is a Property keyframe, which is used to specify locations on the Timeline where you want an animation or object to change. For example, you may have an animation of an object that moves across the Stage in frames 1 through 20. If you decide to resize the object in frame 5, a Property keyframe will appear on the Timeline in frame 5 when you make the change to that object. Another type of keyframe is a Blank keyframe, which is used to indicate that no content (objects) appears in that frame.

Interpreting the Timeline

The Timeline provides many clues to what is happening on the Stage. Interpreting these clues is essential to learning Flash. These clues are in the form of symbols and colors that appear on the Timeline. Figure 32 shows the most common symbols and colors. These are explained next. Others will be discussed in subsequent chapters. The top layer on the Timeline in Figure 32 shows that frame 1 is a blank keyframe as indicated by the unfilled circle. No content will appear in frame 1 of this layer. In addition, the white background which extends to frame 24 indicates a span of blank frames. An unfilled rectangle appears at the end of the span and indicates the end of the blank frames. The next layer shows a keyframe with content as indicated by the filled circle. The content

Figure 31 *The concept of layers*

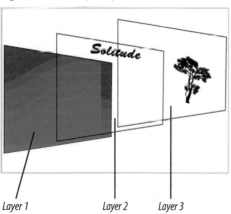

Layer 1   Layer 2   Layer 3

The Stage

in this frame also appears in frames 2-24 as indicated by the gray background. Again, an unfilled rectangle appears at the end of the span and indicates the end of the frames with the same content. The next layer shows a keyframe in frame 1 and a motion tween using the contents of frame 1 as indicated by the blue background in frames 2-24. A property keyframe (indicated by a diamond) appears at the end of this span because a change has been made to the object being animated, such as moving it to a different location on the Stage. The bottom layer shows a keyframe in frame 1 and property keyframes (indicated by diamonds) in frames 5, 10, 15, 20 and 24.

Figure 33 shows the Timeline of a movie created in Lesson 3 but now a second object, a square at the top of the Stage, has been added to the movie. By studying the Timeline, you can learn several things about the square object and this movie. First, the darker blue color highlighting Layer 2 indicates that this layer is active. Second, the square object is placed on its own layer, Layer 2 (indicated by the darker blue color that highlights the layer name and the motion animation). Third, the layer has a motion animation (indicated by the blue background in the frames and the motion path on the Stage). Fourth, the animation runs from frame 1 to frame 48. Fifth, if the objects intersect during the animation, the square will be on top of the circle, because the layer it is placed on (Layer 2) is above the layer that the circle

is placed on (Layer 1). Sixth, the frame rate is set to 24, which means that the movie will play 24 frames per second. Seventh,

the playhead is at frame 1, which causes the contents of frame 1 for both layers to appear on the Stage.

Figure 32 *Common symbols and colors on the Timeline*

Figure 33 *The Timeline of a movie with a second object*

Getting Started with Flash

Figure 34 *Drawing a square*

Figure 35 *Positioning the square at the bottom of the Stage*

Add a layer

1. Open tween.fla, then save it as **layers.fla**.
2. Click **frame 1** on Layer 1.
3. Click **Insert** on the menu bar, point to **Timeline**, then click **Layer**.

   A new layer—Layer 2—appears at the top of the Timeline.

You added a layer to the Timeline.

Create a second animation

1. Click **frame 1** on Layer 2.
2. Click and hold the **Oval tool** on the Tools panel, then click the **Rectangle tool** on the menu that opens.
3. Click the **Fill Color tool color swatch** on the Tools panel, then click the **blue color swatch** in the left column of the color palette.
4. Press and hold [**Shift**], then draw a **square** resembling the dimensions and position of the square shown in Figure 34.
5. Click the **Selection tool** on the Tools panel, then drag a **marquee** around the square to select the object.
6. Click **Insert** on the menu bar, click **Motion Tween**, then click **OK** in the Convert selection to symbol for tween dialog box.
7. Click **frame 48** on Layer 2, then drag the **square** to the bottom of the Stage, as shown in Figure 35.

   When you click frame 48, the circle object moves to the right side of the Stage. Remember, when a frame is selected, all objects in that frame on every layer appear on the Stage.

(continued)

8. Play the movie.

The square appears on top if the two objects intersect.

You drew an object and used it to create a second animation.

Work with layers and view Timeline features

1. Click **Layer 2** on the Timeline, then drag **Layer 2** below Layer 1.

Layer 2 is now the bottom layer, as shown in Figure 36.

2. Play the movie and notice how the square appears beneath the circle if the objects intersect.

3. Click **Layer 2** on the Timeline, then drag **Layer 2** above Layer 1.

4. Play the movie and notice how the square now appears on top of the circle if they intersect.

5. Click the **Frame View icon** ▾≣ on the right corner of the Timeline title bar, as shown in Figure 37, to display the menu.

6. Click **Tiny** to display more frames.

Notice how more frames appear on the Timeline, but each frame is smaller.

7. Click the **Frame View icon** ▾≣ , then click **Short**.

8. Click the **Frame View icon** ▾≣ , then click **Preview**.

The object thumbnails appear in frame 1 on the Timeline.

9. Click the **Frame View icon** ▾≣ , then click **Normal**.

You changed the order of the layers, the display of frames, and the way the Timeline is viewed.

Figure 36 *Changing the stacking order of layers*

Figure 37 *Changing the view of the Timeline*

Frame View icon   Frame View options

Getting Started with Flash

Figure 38 *Changing the frame rate*

Pointer changes to
double-headed arrow

Figure 39 *Displaying the Properties option*

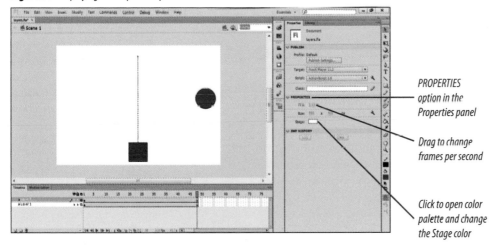

PROPERTIES
option in the
Properties panel

Drag to change
frames per second

Click to open color
palette and change
the Stage color

Modify the frame rate and change the layer names

1. Point to the **Frame Rate (fps)** on the Timeline status bar so the pointer changes to the double-headed arrow 🖐, as shown in Figure 38.

2. Drag the 🖐 **pointer** left to change the frame rate to **3**.

TIP Alternately, you can click the frame rate number, then type a new number.

3. Play the movie and notice that the speed of the movie changed.

4. Click a blank area of the Stage, then verify the Properties panel is the active panel. If not, click **Window**, then click **Properties**.

5. If the PROPERTIES options are not displayed, as shown in Figure 39, click **PROPERTIES** on the Properties panel.

   When the Stage is clicked, the Properties panel provides information about the Stage, including size and background color.

6. Use the Properties panel to change the frame rate (fps) to **18** and the Stage color to **black**.

7. Click the **tick mark** for **24** on the Timeline and notice the position of the objects on the Stage.

8. Drag the **playhead** left and right to display frames one by one.

9. Double-click **Layer 1** on the Timeline, type **circle**, then press **[Enter]**(Win) or **[return]**(Mac).

10. Change the name of Layer 2 to **square**.

11. Play the movie, then save your work.

You changed the frame rate of the movie and named layers.

Distribute a
FLASH MOVIE/APPLICATION

What You'll Do

 In this lesson, you will prepare a movie for distribution on the web.

Distributing Movies for Viewing on a Website

Flash is an excellent program for creating animations, such as banner ads, that are part of a website. When you develop Flash movies, the program saves them in a file format (.fla) that only users who have the Flash program installed on their computers can view. Web browsers, such as Internet Explorer, Safari, Chrome, and Firefox, cannot play Flash FLA files. Flash FLA files must be converted into a Flash Player file (.swf) so that the web browser knows the type of file to play (.swf) and the program needed to play the file (Flash Player). In addition, the HTML code needs to be created that instructs the web browser to play the SWF file. Fortunately, Flash generates both the SWF and HTML files when you use the Flash Publish command.

The process for publishing a Flash movie is to create and save a movie and then select the Publish command on the File menu. You can specify various settings, such as dimensions for the window in which the movie plays in the browser, before publishing the movie. Targeting the Flash Player when publishing a

movie creates two files: an HTML file and a Flash Player (SWF) file. Both the HTML and SWF files retain the same name as the Flash movie file, but with different file extensions:

- .html—the HTML document
- .swf—the Flash Player file

So, publishing a movie named layers.fla generates two files–layers.html and layers.swf. The HTML document contains the code that the browser interprets to display the movie on the web. The code also specifies which Flash Player movie the browser should play. Sample HTML code referencing a Flash Player movie is shown in Figure 40: the movie source is set to layers.swf; the display dimensions (determined by the size of the Stage) are set to 550 × 400; and the background color is set to black (#000000 is the code for black).

Specifying a Stage color for a Flash document will cause the HTML document that is created when using the Publish command to fill the browser window with the color. If you want to display a background color only for the dimensions of the Stage, you can add a layer to the Flash document and draw a rectangle the same dimensions of the Stage and with the desired fill color. Be sure this backdrop layer is the bottom layer. Then, when you publish the Flash document and view it in a browser, the movie will be displayed in a browser window using the dimensions of the Stage and the color you identified for the backdrop rectangle. The rest of the browser window will be the Stage color. A shortcut to previewing a Flash document within an HTML document is to use the Default – (HTML) option from the Publish Preview command in the File menu or simply pressing [F12].

Distributing Movies for Viewing on a Computer or Mobile Device

Flash is also an excellent program for developing applications, such as games, that are displayed on computers (without using a browser) and mobile devices (smartphones and tablets). These applications are created as AIR (Adobe Integrated Runtime) files and do not use a web browser. An AIR application has an .air file extension and can be run by simply clicking on an icon displayed on the computer or mobile device. An example would be the MazeBall game that is downloaded from the Android Market for mobile phones and the Apple store for the iPad. The process for creating an AIR application is to choose one of the AIR settings: AIR for Android, AIR for iOS or AIR (for desktop and laptop computers) before you start developing the application or to create an application and use the Publish setting to select the desired target device(s). Developing applications can be quite a bit more involved, both in scope and technically, than creating animations for a website.

Other Distribution Options

Flash provides another way to distribute your movies that may or may not involve delivery on the web. You can create an executable file called a **projector**. When you create a projector file, you specify the type of file you want to create, such as Windows .exe files and Macintosh .app files. Projector files maintain the movie's interactivity. So, if a movie has buttons that the user clicks to play an animation, the buttons will work in a projector file.

Projector files do not need the Flash Player to play them. You can play projector files directly from a computer, or you can incorporate them into an application, such as a game, that is downloaded or delivered on a CD or DVD. In addition, Flash provides options for creating movies specifically for mobile devices, such as cell phones. This lesson will focus on creating a Flash Player SWF file. Later you will learn how to create AIR and projector files.

Figure 40 *Sample HTML code*

```
<!DOCTYPE html PUBLIC "-//W3C//DTD XHTML 1.0 Strict//EN" "http://www.w3.org/TR/xhtml1/DTD/xhtml1-strict.dtd">
<html xmlns="http://www.w3.org/1999/xhtml" lang="en" xml:lang="en">
    <head>
        <title>layers</title>
        <meta http-equiv="Content-Type" content="text/html; charset=utf-8" />
        <style type="text/css" media="screen">
        html, body { height:100%; background-color: #000000;}
        body { margin:0; padding:0; overflow:hidden; }
        #flashContent { width:100%; height:100%; }
        </style>
    </head>
    <body>
        <div id="flashContent">
            <object classid="clsid:d27cdb6e-ae6d-11cf-96b8-444553540000" width="550" height="400" id="layers" align="middle">
                <param name="movie" value="layers.swf" />
                <param name="quality" value="high" />
                <param name="bgcolor" value="#000000" />
```

Movie source   Stage background color   Dimensions

Publish a movie for distribution on the web

1. Verify layers.fla is open, then save it as **layersWeb.fla**.

2. Click **File** on the menu bar, then click **Publish**.

   The files layersWeb.html and layersWeb.swf are automatically generated and saved in the same folder as the Flash document.

3. Use your file management program to navigate to the drive and folder where you save your work.

4. Notice the three files that begin with "layersWeb," as shown in Figure 41.

   The three files are layersWeb.fla, the Flash movie; layersWeb.html, the HTML document; and layersWeb.swf, the Flash Player file.

5. Double-click **layersWeb.html** to play the movie in the browser.

   Note: Depending on your browser, browser settings and version, you may need to complete additional steps (such as accepting blocked content) to view the layers.html document.

TIP   Click the browser button on the taskbar if the movie does not open automatically in your browser.

   Notice the animation takes up only a portion of the browser window, as shown in Figure 42. This is because the Stage size is set to 550 x 440, which is smaller than the browser window. Notice also that the entire browser window has been filled with the black background. This is because a background color was used rather than creating a backdrop layer.

6. Close the browser, and return to Flash.

You used the Publish command to create an HTML document (.html) and a Flash Player file (.swf), then you displayed the HTML document in a web browser.

Figure 41   *The three layers files after publishing the movie*

Your files may be listed in a different order

Your file sizes may vary slightly

Figure 42   *The animation played in a browser window*

Figure 43 *Drawing a rectangle the size of the Stage*

Create a backdrop color layer for the Stage

1. Click the **Stage** to select it.
2. Use the document properties in the Properties panel to change the Stage color to **white**.
3. Click **square** on the Timeline to select the square layer.
4. Click **Insert** on the menu bar, point to **Timeline**, then click **Layer**.
5. Double-click **Layer 3** on the Timeline to select the name of the new layer, type **backdrop**, then press **[Enter]** (Win) or **[return]** (Mac).
6. Click **frame 1** on the backdrop layer.
7. Click the **Rectangle tool** □ on the Tools menu.
8. Use the Tools panel to set the Fill Color to **black** and the Stroke Color to **black**.
9. Draw a **rectangle** that covers the Stage, as shown in Figure 43.
10. Click **backdrop** on the Timeline, then drag the **backdrop** layer below the circle layer.
11. Click **File** on the menu bar, point to **Publish Preview**, then click **Default – (HTML)**.

    Notice how the HTML document has a white background and the Flash movie plays in an area the size of the Stage.

    Note: If a warning message opens, follow the directions to allow blocked content.
12. Close the browser and return to Flash.
13. Save and close the layersWeb.fla document.

You changed the Stage color of a Flash document and added a backdrop color layer.

Plan an
APPLICATION

What You'll Do

Purpose	"What do we want to accomplish?"
Audience	"Who will use our application or website?"
Treatment	"What is the look and feel?"
Specifications	"What does the application include and how does it work?"

In this lesson, you will learn how to plan a Flash application. You will also learn about the guidelines for screen design and the interactive design of applications.

Planning an Application

Flash can be used to develop entire products, such as games that run on smartphones, or animations that are part of a product, such as an educational tutorial, and delivered via the Internet, a CD, or a DVD. You can use Flash to create enhancements to web pages, such as animated logos, interactive navigation buttons, and banner ads. No matter what the application, the first step is planning. Often, the temptation is to jump right into the program and start developing movies. The problem is that this invariably results in a more time-consuming process at best; and wasted effort, resources, and money at worst. The larger and more complex the project is, the more critical the planning process becomes. Planning an application should involve the following steps:

Step 1: Stating the Purpose (Goals). "What, specifically, do we want to accomplish?"

Determining the goals is a critical step in planning because goals guide the development process, keep the team members on track, and provide a way to evaluate the application, both during and after its development.

Step 2: Identifying the Target Audience. "Who will use our application?"

Understanding the potential viewers helps in developing an application that can address their needs. For example, children respond to exploration and surprise, so having a dog wag its tail when the mouse pointer rolls over it might appeal to this audience.

Step 3: Determining the Treatment. "What is the look and feel?"

The treatment is how the application will be presented to the user, including the tone, approach, and emphasis.

Tone. Will the application be humorous, serious, light, heavy, formal, or informal? The tone of an application can often be used to make a statement, for instance, projecting a progressive, high-tech, well-funded corporate image.

Approach. How much direction will be provided to the user? An interactive game might focus on exploration such as when the user points to an object on the screen and the object becomes animated; while an informational application might provide lots of direction and include lists of options in the form of drop-down menus.

Emphasis. How much emphasis will be placed on the various multimedia elements? For example, a company may want to develop a business application that shows the features of its new product line, including video demonstrations and sound narrations of how each product works. The budget might not allow for the expense of creating the videos, so the emphasis would shift to still pictures with text descriptions.

Step 4: Developing the Specifications and Storyboard. "What precisely does the application include and how does it work?"

The **specifications** state what will be included in each screen, including the arrangement of each element and the functionality of each object (for example, what happens when you click the button labeled Skip Intro). Specifications should include the following:

Playback System. The choice of what configuration to target for playback is critical, especially Internet connection speed, browser versions, screen resolution, screen size (especially when targeting mobile devices), and plug-ins.

Elements to Include. The specifications should include details about the various elements that are to be included in the application. What are the dimensions for the animations, and what is the frame rate? What are the sizes of the various objects such as photos, buttons, and so on? What fonts, font sizes, and font formatting will be used? Should video or sound be included?

Functionality. The specifications should include the way the program reacts to an action by the user, such as a mouse click. For example, clicking a door (object) might cause a doorbell to ring (sound), the door to open (an animation), an "exit the program" message to appear (text), or an entirely new screen to be displayed.

Using Screen Design Guidelines

The following screen design guidelines are used by application developers. The implementation of these guidelines is affected by the goals of the application, the intended audience, and the content.

Balance in screen design refers to the distribution of optical weight in the layout. Optical weight is the ability of an object to attract the viewer's eye, as determined by the object's size, shape, color, and so on. The screen in Figure 44 shows a somewhat balanced design with the bright buttons at the bottom balanced against the heading near the top; and the icons on the left balanced against the satellite image on the right. However, the overall feel is less formal than a precisely balanced layout would project. In general, a balanced design is more appealing to a viewer. However, for a game application a balanced layout may not be desired.

Figure 44 *Sample screen design*
nasa.gov http://spaceplace.nasa.gov/satellite-insight/en/#/review/satelliteinsight/SatelliteInsight.swf

Unity helps the screen objects reinforce each other. **Intra-screen unity** has to do with how the various screen objects relate and how they all fit in. For example, a children's game might only use cartoon characterizations of animals for all the objects—including navigation buttons and sound control buttons, as well as the on-screen characters. **Inter-screen unity** refers to the design that viewers encounter as they navigate from one screen to another, and it provides consistency throughout the application. For example, all navigation buttons are located in the same place on each screen.

Movement refers to the way the viewer's eyes move through the objects on the screen. Different types of objects and various animation techniques can be used to draw the viewer to a location on the screen.

For example, a photo of a waterfall may cause the viewer's eyes to follow the flow of the water down, especially if the waterfall is animated. The designer could then place an object, such as a logo or a sales message, below the waterfall.

Using Interactive Design Guidelines

In addition to screen design guidelines, interactive guidelines determine the interactivity of the application. The following guidelines are not absolute rules since they are affected by the goals of the application, the intended audience, and the content:

- Make it simple, easy to understand, and easy to use so that viewers do not have to spend time learning what the application is about and what they need to do.
- Build in consistency in the navigation scheme. Help the users know where they are in the application and help them avoid getting lost.
- Provide feedback. Users need to know when an action, such as clicking a button, has been completed. Changing its color or shape, or adding a sound can indicate this.
- Give the user control. Allow the user to skip long introductions; provide controls for starting, stopping, and rewinding animations, video, and audio; and provide controls for adjusting audio.

Using Storyboards

Simple applications such as a banner ad on a website may consist of a single Flash animation, but complex applications, such as games, often include several animations within one or more Flash movies. No matter how extensive the application, storyboards can be invaluable in the development process. A storyboard is a series of pictures that illustrate the sequence of events in an animation. See Figure 45. A storyboard can be extremely elaborate and include color images, scripts,

Figure 45 *Sample storyboard*

and notations for dialog, sound effects, transitions, and movement. Or, it can be as simple as black and white stick figures. Storyboards can be created using templates and even computer programs or simply sketched out. As part of the pre-production process, storyboards are an easy way to test out an idea by helping you visualize the progression of events. This allows you to make adjustments before development begins. Then the storyboard becomes a basic blueprint for the creation of the animation and a guide for those involved in the development process such as Flash designers, developers, and artists.

Rich Media Content and Accessibility

Flash provides the tools that allow you to create compelling applications and websites by incorporating rich media content, such as animations, sound, and video. Generally, incorporating rich media enhances the user's experience. However, accessibility becomes an issue for those persons who have visual, hearing, or mobility impairments, or have a cognitive disability. Designers need to utilize techniques that help ensure accessibility, such as providing consistency in navigation and layout, labeling graphics, captioning audio content throughout the applications and website, and providing keyboard access.

The Flash Workflow Process

After the planning process, you are ready to start work on the Flash documents. The following steps can be used as guidelines in a general workflow process suggested by Adobe.

Step 1: Create and/or acquire the elements to be used in the application. The elements include text, photos, drawings, video, and audio. The elements become the raw material for the graphics, animations, menus, buttons, and content that populate the application and provide the interactivity. You can use the various Flash drawing and text tools to create your own images and text content; or, you can use another program, such as Adobe Photoshop, to develop the elements, and then import them into Flash. Alternately, you can acquire stock clip art and photographs. You can produce video and audio content in-house and import it into Flash or you can acquire these elements from a third party.

Step 2: Arrange the elements and create the animations. Arrange the elements (objects) on the Stage and on the Timeline to define when and how they appear in your application. Once the elements are available, you can create the various animations called for in the specifications.

Step 3: Apply special effects. Flash provides innumerable special effects that can be applied to the various media elements and animations. These include graphic and text filters, such as drop shadows, blurs, glows, and bevels. In addition, there are effects for sounds and animations such as fade-ins and fade-outs, acceleration and deceleration, morphing, and even 3D effects.

Step 4: Create the interactivity. Flash provides a scripting feature, ActionScript, which allows you to develop programming code to control how the media elements behave, including how various objects respond to user interactions, such as clicking buttons and rolling over images.

Step 5: Test and publish the application. Testing can begin before the actual development process with usability testing, which involves potential users being observed as they navigate through thumbnail sketches of the storyboard. Testing should continue throughout the development process, including using the Test Movie feature in the Control menu to test the movie using the Flash Player and to publish the movie in order to test it in a browser.

Project Management

Developing any extensive application, such as a game, involves project management. A project plan needs to be developed that provides the project scope and identifies the milestones, including analyzing, designing, building, testing, and launching. Personnel and resource needs are identified, budgets built, tasks assigned, and schedules developed. Successful projects are a team effort relying on the close collaboration of designers, developers, project managers, graphic artists, programmers, testers, and others. Adobe provides various product suites, such as the Creative Suite 6 (CS6) Web Collection, that include programs such as Flash, Dreamweaver, Photoshop, Illustrator, and Fireworks. These are the primary tools needed to develop interactive applications. These programs are designed for easy integration. So, a graphic artist can use Photoshop to develop an image that can easily be imported into Flash and used by an animator. In addition, other tools in the suites, such as Adobe Bridge, help ensure efficient workflow when working in a team environment. Adobe Flash Builder and Flex are tools that are used by Flash developers who focus on creating sophisticated Flash applications by writing ActionScript code.

Using the Flash Help Feature

As you are planning the application and while you are developing it, you may have specific questions about how to incorporate what you are planning using Flash. Fortunately, Flash provides a comprehensive Help feature that can be very useful when first learning the program. You access the Help feature from the Help menu. The Help feature is organized by categories, including Using Flash Professional CS6, which have several topics such as Workspace and Managing documents. In addition, the Help feature has a Help Search feature. You use the Help Search feature to search for topics using keywords, such as Timeline. Searching by keywords accesses the Flash Community Help feature, which displays links to content relevant to the search terms. Another option in the Help menu is Adobe Online Forums. This is a link to Flash Professional forums sponsored by Adobe. You can ask questions and join groups discussing various Flash-related topics. Other resources not affiliated with Adobe are available through the web. You may find some by searching the web for Flash resources.

Figure 46 *The Flash Help categories*

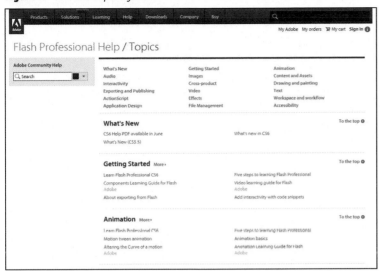

Figure 47 *The Flash Community Help site*

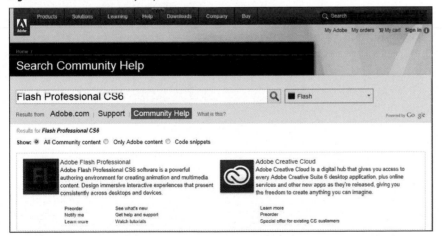

Use Flash Help

1. Start a new Flash document.

2. Click **Help** on the menu bar, then click **Flash Help**.

   Note: If you see a page not found message, be sure you are connected to the Internet.

3. Maximize the Help window to view the Help screen, as shown in Figure 46.

4. Scroll down, display the **Workspace and workflow** section, click **The Timeline**, then read through the text in About the Timeline.

5. Scroll down the page and review the information that is provided.

6. Scroll to display the top of the Help window.

7. Click in the **Search text box**, type **Flash Professional CS6**, then verify the Flash icon is displayed to the right of the Search text box.

   Your search is refined to the Flash product when the Flash icon is displayed.

8. Press **[Enter]** (Win) or **[return]** (Mac) to access the Community Help site, as seen in Figure 47.

9. Scroll down the page and study the various links provided on the site.

10. Close the Flash Help site, then exit the Flash program.

You used the Flash Help feature to access information on the Timeline and the community help feature.

Open a document and understand the Flash workspace.

1. Start Flash, open fl1_2.fla, then save it as **skillsDemo1.fla**. This movie has two layers. Layer 1 contains the heading and the rectangle at the top of the Stage. Layer 2 contains an animation that runs for 75 frames.
2. Change the magnification to 50% using the View menu. (*Hint*: Click View, point to Magnification, then click 50%.)
3. Change the magnification to Fit in Window.
4. Change the Timeline view to Small, then change it back to Normal. (*Hint*: Click the Frame View icon in the upper-right corner of the Timeline title bar.)
5. Hide all panels.
6. Display the Tools panel, Timeline panel, Properties panel, and the Library panel if it did not open with the Properties panel.
7. Group the Library and Properties panels if they are not already grouped.
8. Drag the Library panel from the Properties panel, then position it on the Stage.
9. Collapse the Library panel.
10. Close the Library panel to remove it from the screen.
11. Reset the Essentials workspace.

Play and test a Flash movie.

1. Drag the playhead to view the contents of each frame. Use the commands on the Timeline status bar to play and rewind the movie.
2. Press [Enter] (Win) or [return] (Mac) to play and stop the movie.

3. Test the movie in the Flash Player window, then close the Flash Player window.

Change the document size and Stage color.

1. Use the document properties settings in the Properties panel to change the document height to 380. (*Hint:* Click a blank area of the Stage to select it.)
2. Change the Stage color to a medium gray color (#999999).
3. Change the magnification to 100%.
4. Play the movie.

Create and save a Flash movie.

1. Insert a new layer above Layer 2, then select frame 1 on the new layer, Layer 3.
2. Draw a green ball in the middle of the left side of the Stage, approximately the same size as the red ball. (*Hint*: The green gradient color can be used to draw the ball. Several gradient colors are found in the bottom row of the color palette when you click the Fill Color tool in the Tools panel.)
3. Use the Selection tool to draw a marquee around the green ball to select it, then create a motion tween to animate the green ball so that it moves across the screen from left to right. (*Hint*: After inserting the motion tween, select frame 75 on Layer 3 before repositioning the green ball.)
4. Use the Selection tool to reshape the motion path to an arc by dragging the middle of the path downward.
5. Play the movie.

6. Use the Undo command to undo the reshape. (*Note*: You may need to use the Undo feature twice.)
7. Use the Selection tool to select frame 75 of the Layer 3, click the green ball if it is not already selected to select it, then use the Properties panel to change the transparency (alpha) from 100% to 20%. (*Hint*: If the Properties panel COLOR EFFECT option is not displayed, make sure the Properties panel is open and click the green ball to make sure it is selected.)
8. Play the movie.
9. Click frame 75 on Layer 3 and click the green ball to select it.
10. Use the Properties panel to decrease the width of the ball to approximately half its size. (*Hint*: Make sure the lock width and height value icon in the Properties panel is unbroken. You may need to click the Stage to have the new value take effect.)
11. Play the movie.
12. Select frame 1 on Layer 3, then click the green ball to select it.
13. Use the Filters option in the Properties panel to add a drop shadow.
14. Play the movie.
15. Select frame 1 on Layer 2, then click the red ball to select it.
16. Open the Motion Presets panel, then add a bounce-smoosh preset.
17. Move Layer 3 below Layer 2.
18. Play the movie.
19. Save the movie.

Work with the Timeline.

1. Change the frame rate to 8 frames per second, play the movie, change the frame rate to 24, then play the movie again.
2. Change the view of the Timeline to display more frames.
3. Change the view of the Timeline to display a preview of the object thumbnails.
4. Change the view of the Timeline to display the Normal view.
5. Click frame 1 on Layer 1, use the playhead to display each frame, then compare your screens to Figure 48.
6. Save the movie.

Distribute a Flash movie.

1. Click File on the menu bar, then click Publish.
2. Open your browser, then open skillsDemo1.html.
3. View the movie, close your browser, then return to Flash.

Work with the Flash workspace.

1. Use the Document Settings dialog box to change the document Stage color to white.
2. Insert a new layer, then rename the layer **gray backdrop**.
3. Select frame 1 of the gray backdrop layer.
4. Select the rectangle tool, then set the Fill Color and the Stroke Color to the same shade of gray.
5. Draw a rectangle that covers the Stage.
6. Drag the gray backdrop layer to the bottom of the list of layers on the Timeline.

7. Rename the layers using these names: **heading**, **green ball**, and **red ball**. Use clues on the Timeline to help you know what to name each layer.

8. Play the movie in the browser, then close the browser window.
9. Save and close the Flash document.

Figure 48 *Completed Skills Review*

A friend cannot decide whether to sign up for a class in Flash or Dreamweaver. You help her decide by showing her what you already know about Flash. You want to show her how easy it is to create a simple animation because you think she'd enjoy a class in Flash. You decide to animate three objects. The first object is placed on the center of the Stage and pulsates throughout the movie. The second object enters the Stage from the left side and moves across the middle of the Stage and off the right side of the Stage. The third object enters the Stage from the right side and moves across the middle of the Stage and off the left side of the Stage. The motion paths for the two objects that move across the Stage are reshaped so they go above and below the pulsating object in the middle of the Stage.

1. Open a Flash document, then save it as **demonstration.fla**.
2. Verify the view is set to 100%.
3. Use the tools on the Tools panel to create a circle (or object of your choice) and color of your choice on the middle of the Stage.
4. Draw a marquee around the object to select it and apply a pulse motion preset.
5. Insert a new layer, then select frame 1 on the layer.
6. Create a simple shape or design using a color of your choice, and place it off the left side of the Stage and halfway down the Stage.

7. Select the object and insert a motion tween that moves the object directly across the screen and off the right side of the Stage. (*Hint*: After inserting the motion tween, select the last frame in the motion span and drag the object off the right side of the Stage.)
8. Reshape the motion path so that the object goes in an arc below the center pulsating object.
9. Insert a new layer, then select frame 1 on the new layer.
10. Create an object using the color of your choice and place it off the right side of the Stage and halfway down the Stage.

11. Draw a marquee to select the object and insert a motion tween that moves the object directly across the screen and off the left side of the Stage.
12. Reshape the motion path so that the object goes in an arc above the center pulsating object.
13. Play the movie.
14. Add a Stage color.
15. Rename the layers with descriptive names.
16. Play the movie, test it , then close the Flash Player window.
17. Save the movie, then compare your movie to the sample provided in Figure 49.

Figure 49 *Sample completed Project Builder 1*

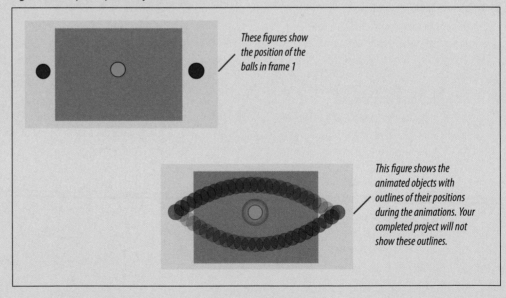

These figures show the position of the balls in frame 1

This figure shows the animated objects with outlines of their positions during the animations. Your completed project will not show these outlines.

You've been asked to develop a simple movie about recycling for a day care center. For this project, you will add two animations to an existing movie. You will show three objects that appear on the screen at different times, and then move each object to a recycle bin at different times. You can create the objects using any of the Tools on the Tools panel.

1. Open fl1_3.fla, then save it as **recycle.fla**.
2. Play the movie and study the Timeline to familiarize yourself with the movie's current settings. Currently, there are no animations.
3. Insert a new layer above Layer 2, click frame 1 on the new layer, then draw a small object in the upper-left corner of the Stage.
4. Create a motion tween that moves the object to the recycle bin. (*Hint*: After inserting the motion tween, be sure to select frame 40 on the new layer before moving the object to the recycle bin. *Note*: At this time, the object will appear on top of the recycle bin when it is placed in the bin.)
5. Reshape the path so that the object moves in an arc to the recycle bin.
6. Insert a new layer above the top layer, click frame 1 on the new layer, draw a small object in the upper-center of the Stage, then create a motion tween that moves the object to the recycle bin.
7. Insert a new layer above the top layer, click frame 1 on the new layer, draw a small object in the

upper-right corner of the Stage, then create a motion tween that moves the object to the recycle bin.
8. Reshape the path so that the object moves in an arc to the recycle bin.
9. Move Layer 1 to the top of all the layers. (*Note:* Layer 1 contains the front of the box. Moving Layer 1 above the other layers causes the objects on those layers to be hidden behind the front of the box.)
10. Play the movie and compare your movie to the sample provided in Figure 50.
11. Save the movie.

Figure 50 *Sample completed Project Builder 2*

This figure shows the animated objects with outlines of their positions during the animations. Your completed project will not show these outlines.

DESIGN PROJECT

Figure 51 shows screens from a mobile app that is described on the NASA website. Study the figure and answer the following questions. For each question, indicate how you determined your answer.

1. Connect to the Internet, then go to *www.nps.gov/nama/photosmultimedia/app-page.htm* (*Note:* The screens displayed on the website may be different than those in Figure 51.)

2. Open a document in a word processor or open a new Flash document, save the file as **dpc1**, then answer the following questions. (*Hint:* Use the Flash Text tool if you open a Flash document.)
   - Whose app is this?
   - What is the goal(s) of the app?
   - Who is the target audience?
   - What treatment (look and feel) is used?

   - What are the design layout guidelines being used (balance, movement, etc.)?
   - How can animation enhance this page?
   - Do you think this is an effective design for the organization, its products, and its target audience? Why, or why not?
   - What suggestions would you make to improve the design, and why?

Figure 51 *Design Project*
Courtesy of National Park Service website – www.nps.gov; © Google 2012. www.nps.gov/nama/photosmultimedia/app-page.htm

There are numerous companies in the business of developing websites and applications for others. Many of these companies use Flash as one of their primary development tools. These companies promote themselves through their own websites and usually provide online portfolios with samples of their work. Log onto the Internet, then use your favorite search engine and keywords such as Flash developers and Flash animators to locate three of these companies, and generate the following information for each one. A sample website is shown in Figure 52.

1. Company name:
2. Contact information (address, phone, and so on):
3. Website URL:
4. Company mission:
5. Services provided:
6. Sample list of clients:
7. Describe three ways the company seems to have used Flash in its website. Were these effective? Why, or why not?
8. Describe three applications of Flash that the company includes in its portfolio (or showcases or samples). Were these effective? Why, or why not?
9. Would you want to work for this company? Why, or why not?
10. Would you recommend this company to another company that was looking to create an application or enhance its website? Why, or why not?

Figure 52 *Sample website for Portfolio Project*
Copyright © 2012 2Advanced Studios, LLC. http://www.2advanced.com/#/work

CHAPTER **2** DRAWING OBJECTS IN
ADOBE FLASH

1. Use the Flash drawing and alignment tools
2. Select objects and apply colors
3. Work with drawn objects
4. Work with text and text objects
5. Work with layers and objects

2 DRAWING OBJECTS IN ADOBE FLASH

Introduction

Computers can display graphics in either a bitmap or a vector format. The difference between these formats is in how they describe an image. A bitmap graphic represents an image as an array of dots, called **pixels**, which are arranged within a grid. Each pixel in an image has an exact position on the screen and a precise color. To make a change in a bitmap graphic, you modify the pixels. When you enlarge a bitmap graphic, the number of pixels remains the same, resulting in jagged edges that decrease the quality of the image. A vector graphic represents an image using lines and curves, which you can resize without losing image quality. Also, the file size of a vector image is generally smaller than the file size of a bitmap image, which makes vector images particularly useful for an application. However, vector graphics are not as effective as bitmap graphics for representing photo-realistic images. Even so, one of the most compelling features of Flash is the ability to create and manipulate vector graphics.

Images (objects) created using Flash drawing tools are vector graphics, and have a stroke (border line), a fill, or both. In addition, the stroke of an object can be segmented into smaller lines. You can modify the size, shape, rotation, and color of each stroke, fill, and segment.

Flash provides two drawing modes, called models. In the Merge Drawing Model, when you draw two shapes and one overlaps the other, a change in the top object may affect the object it overlaps. For example, if you draw a circle on top of a rectangle and then move the circle off the rectangle, the portion of the rectangle covered by the circle is removed. The Object Drawing Model allows you to overlap shapes which are then kept separate, so that changes in one object do not affect another object. Another way to avoid having changes in one object affect another is to place the objects on separate layers on the Timeline as you did in Chapter 1.

Use the Flash Drawing
AND ALIGNMENT TOOLS

What You'll Do

In this lesson, you will use several drawing tools to create various vector graphics.

Using Flash Drawing and Editing Tools

When you point to a tool on the Tools panel, its name appears next to the tool. Figure 1 identifies the tools described in the following paragraphs. Several of the tools have options that modify their use. For example, the Brush tool has options for changing the size and shape of the brush head. These options are available in the Options area of the Tools panel when the tool is selected.

Selection—Used to select an object or parts of an object, such as the stroke or fill, and to reshape and reposition objects. The options for the Selection tool are Snap to Objects (aligns objects), Smooth (smooths lines), and Straighten (straightens lines).

Subselection—Used to select, drag, and reshape an object. Vector graphics are composed of lines and curves (each of which is a segment) connected by **anchor points**. Selecting an object with this tool displays the anchor points and allows you to use them to edit the object.

Free Transform—Used to rotate, scale, skew, and distort objects.

Gradient Transform—Used to transform a gradient fill by adjusting the size, direction, or center of the fill.

The Free and Gradient Transform tools are grouped within one icon on the Tools panel. To see the menu containing grouped tools, click and hold the tool icon until the menu opens.

3D Rotation—Used to create 3D effects by rotating movie clips in 3D space on the Stage.

3D Translation—Used to create 3D effects by moving movie clips in 3D space on the Stage.

The 3D Rotation and the 3D Translation tools are grouped within one icon on the Tools panel.

Lasso—Used to select objects or parts of objects. The Polygon Mode option allows you to draw straight lines when selecting an object.

Pen—Used to draw lines and curves by creating a series of dots, known as anchor points, that are automatically connected. Other tools used to add, delete, and convert the anchor points created by the Pen tool are grouped with the Pen tool.

Text—Used to create and edit text.

Line—Used to draw straight lines. You can draw vertical, horizontal, and 45° diagonal lines by pressing and holding [Shift] while drawing the line.

Rectangle—Used to draw rectangular shapes. Press and hold [Shift] to draw a perfect square.

Oval—Used to draw oval shapes. Press and hold [Shift] to draw a perfect circle.

Primitive Rectangle and Oval—Used to draw objects with properties, such as corner radius or inner radius, that can be changed using the Properties panel.

PolyStar—Used to draw polygons and stars.

The Rectangle, Oval, Primitive, and PolyStar tools are grouped within one tool on the Tools panel.

Pencil—Used to draw freehand lines and shapes. The Pencil Mode option displays a menu with the following commands: Straighten (draws straight lines), Smooth (draws smooth curved lines), and Ink (draws freehand with no modification).

Brush—Used to draw (paint) with brush-like strokes. Options allow you to set the size and shape of the brush, and to determine the area to be painted, such as inside or behind an object.

Spray Brush—Used to spray colors and patterns onto objects. Dots are the default pattern for the spray. However, you can use a graphic symbol, such as a flag, to create a pattern.

The Brush and Spray Brush tools are grouped together.

Deco—Used to turn graphic shapes into geometric patterns or to create kaleidoscopic-like effects.

Bone—Used to animate objects that have joints. For example you could use a series of linked objects, such as arms and legs to create character animations.

Bind—Used to adjust the relationships among individual bones. The Bone and Bind tools are grouped together.

Paint Bucket—Used to fill enclosed areas of a drawing with color. Options allow you to fill areas that have gaps and to make adjustments in a gradient fill.

Ink Bottle—Used to apply line colors and thickness to the stroke of an object.

The Paint Bucket and Ink Bottle are grouped together.

Eyedropper—Used to select stroke, fill, and text attributes so they can be copied from one object to another.

Eraser—Used to erase lines and fills. Options allow you to choose what part of the object to erase, as well as the size and shape of the eraser.

Hand—Used to move the Stage around the Pasteboard by dragging the Stage.

Zoom—Used to change the magnification of an area of the Stage. Clicking an area of the Stage zooms in and holding down [Alt] (Win) or [option] (Mac) and clicking zooms out.

Stroke Color—Used to set the stroke color of drawn objects.

Figure 1 *Flash tools*

Selection
Subselection
Free Transform (Gradient)
3D Rotation (3D Translation)
Lasso
Pen (Add Anchor Point, etc.)
Text
Line
Rectangle (Oval, etc.)
Pencil
Brush (Spray)
Deco
Bone (Bind)
Paint Bucket (Ink Bottle)
Eyedropper
Eraser
Hand
Zoom

Stroke Color

Fill Color

Black and White
Swap Color

Options area (options change depending on which tool is selected)

Fill Color—Used to set the fill color of drawn objects.

Black and White—Used to set the stroke color to black and the fill color to white.

Swap Color—Used to swap the stroke and fill colors.

Options—Used to select an option for a tool, such as the type of rectangle (object drawing mode) or size of the brush when using the Brush tool.

Working with Grouped Tools

To display a list of grouped tools, you click the tool and hold the mouse button until the menu opens. For example, if you want to select the Oval tool and the Rectangle tool is displayed, you click and hold the Rectangle tool. Then, when the menu opens, you click the Oval tool option. You know a tool is a grouped tool if you see an arrow in the lower-right corner of the tool icon.

Working with Tool Options

Some tools have additional options that allow you to modify their use. For example, the brush tool has options to set the brush size and to set where the brush fill will be applied. If additional options for a tool are available, they appear at the bottom of the Tools panel in the Options area when the tool is selected. If the option has a menu associated with it, such as a list of brush sizes for the brush tool, then the option icon will have an arrow in the lower-right corner. Click and hold the option until the menu opens.

Tools for Creating Vector Graphics

The Oval, Rectangle, Pencil, Brush, Line, and Pen tools are used to create vector objects.

Positioning Objects on the Stage

The Stage dimensions are made up of pixels (dots) matching the Stage size. So, a Stage size of 550 × 400 would be 550 pixels wide and 400 pixels high. Each pixel has a location on the Stage designated as the X (across) and Y (down) coordinates. The location of any object on the Stage is determined by its position from the upper-left corner of the Stage, which is 0,0 and the object's registration point. The registration point of an object is used to align it with the coordinates. The registration point, which is shown as a crosshair, is initially set at the upper-left corner of an object, as shown in Figure 2. So, an object having coordinates of 100,100 would be positioned at 100 pixels across and 100 pixels down the Stage, as shown in Figure 2. The Properties panel displays the X,Y values of any selected object. The most precise way to position an object on the Stage is to use the Properties panel to enter X and Y values for the object. Other ways to position objects on the Stage include using rulers, gridlines, and guides, as well as the align options. The Rulers, Grid, and Guides commands, which are found on the View menu, are used to turn on and off these features. Figure 2 shows the rulers and the ruler lines, which are used to indicate the position of an object. (*Note:* Normally

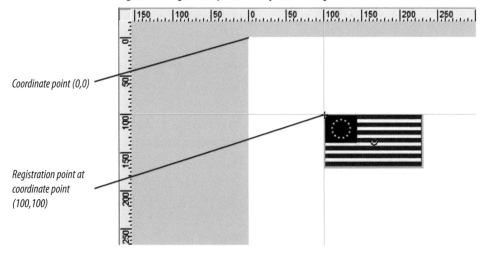

Figure 2 *Using rulers to position an object on the Stage*

Coordinate point (0,0)

Registration point at coordinate point (100,100)

Drawing Objects in Adobe Flash

ruler lines display on top of objects on the Stage. In Figure 2, the registration point is displayed above the ruler lines to show its exact placement.)

After displaying the rulers, you can drag the lines from the top ruler or the left side ruler to the Stage. To remove a ruler line, you drag the ruler line up to the top ruler or across to the left ruler.

Figure 3 shows the Stage with gridlines displayed. The gridlines can be used to position an object. You can modify the grid size and color. In addition to using rulers and guides to help place objects, you can create a new layer as a Guide layer that you use to position objects on the Stage. When you turn gridlines and guides on, they appear on the Stage. However, they do not appear in the Flash movie when you test or publish it.

Using the Align Panel

Figure 4 shows the Align panel, which allows you to position objects on the Stage either relative to the Stage or to other objects. The Align panel has four areas (Align, Distribute, Match size, Space) each with options. The Align options are used to align the edge or center of an object with the edge or center of the Stage—or, if multiple objects are selected, to align their edges and centers. The Distribute options are used to position objects across or down the Stage. The Match size options are used to resize selected objects to match the height and/or width of the largest object or to match the Stage if the Align to stage option is selected. The Space options are used to space out objects evenly across and down the Stage.

Figure 3 *Using gridlines to position an object on the Stage*

Figure 4 *The Align panel*

Show gridlines and check settings

1. Open fl2_1.fla from the drive and folder where your Data Files are stored, then save it as **tools.fla**.

2. Click **Essentials** on the menu bar, then click **Reset 'Essentials'**.

3. Click **View** on the menu bar, point to **Magnification**, then click **Fit in Window**.

4. Click the **Stroke Color tool color swatch** ✎ on the Tools panel, then click the **red color swatch** in the left column of the Color palette.

   Note: The color swatches shown in the Tools panel reflect the last selection and may not be the colors shown for the icons in Steps 4 and 5.

5. Click the **Fill Color tool color swatch** ▨ on the Tools panel, then click the **blue color swatch** in the left column of the Color palette.

6. Click **View** on the menu bar, point to **Grid**, then click **Show Grid** to display the gridlines.

7. Point to each tool on the Tools panel, then read its name.

8. Click the **Text tool** T , click **CHARACTER** on the Properties panel to open the area if it is not open already.

   Notice the options in the Properties panel including the CHARACTER and PARAGRAPH areas, as shown in Figure 5. The Properties panel options change depending on the tool selected. For the Text tool the properties include the character family and the paragraph family.

   You opened a document, saved it, set up the workspace, changed the stroke and fill colors, displayed the grid, viewed tool names on the Tools panel, then viewed the Text tool options in the Properties panel.

Figure 5 *Tool name on the Tools panel*

A percent may appear here when you choose Fit in Window

Your settings may vary

Point to a tool to display its name

Stroke Color tool (red selected)

Fill Color tool (blue selected)

Figure 6 *Objects created with drawing tools*

Use the Rectangle, Oval, and Line tools

1. Click the **Rectangle tool** 🔲 on the Tools panel.

   Note: If the Rectangle tool is not displayed, click and hold the Oval tool to display the group of tools.

2. Verify that the Object Drawing option 🔘 in the Options area of the Tools panel is not active.

   TIP When the Object Drawing option is not active, the object is drawn so that its stroke and fill can be selected separately.

3. Draw **three rectangle shapes** using Figure 6 as a guide.

   TIP Use the grid to approximate shape sizes, and press and hold [Shift] to draw a square. To undo an action, click the Undo command on the Edit menu.

   Notice the blue color for the fill and the red color for the strokes (border lines).

4. Click and hold the **Rectangle tool** 🔲 on the Tools panel, then click the **Oval tool** 🔘.

5. Draw **three oval shapes** using Figure 6 as a guide.

   TIP Press and hold [Shift] to draw a perfect circle.

6. Click the **Line tool** ╲ , then draw **three lines** using Figure 6 as a guide.

   TIP To snap the line to the nearest 45-degree increment, such as 45, 90, 180 and so on, press and hold [Shift], draw the line, use the line tool pointer to rotate the line, then release [Shift].

You used the Rectangle, Oval, and Line tools to draw objects on the Stage.

Use the Pen, Pencil, and Brush tools

1. Click **Insert** on the menu bar, point to **Timeline**, then click **Layer**.

   A new layer—Layer 2—appears above Layer 1.

2. Click **frame 5** on Layer 2.

3. Click **Insert** on the menu bar, point to **Timeline**, then click **Keyframe**.

   Since the objects were drawn in frame 1 on Layer 1, they are no longer visible when you insert a keyframe in frame 5 on Layer 2. A keyframe allows you to draw in any location on the Stage on the specified frame.

4. Click the **Zoom tool** 🔍 on the Tools panel, click near the upper-left quadrant of the Stage to zoom in, then scroll as needed to see more of the grid.

5. Click the **Pen tool** ✒ on the Tools panel, position it in the upper-left quadrant of the Stage, as shown in Figure 7, then click to set an anchor point.

   (continued)

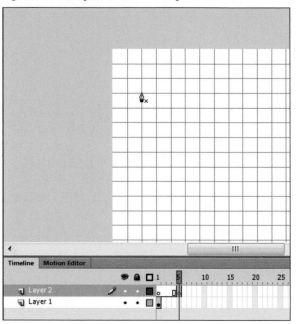

Figure 7 *Positioning the Pen Tool on the Stage*

Drawing Objects in Adobe Flash

Figure 8 *Setting anchor points to draw an arrow*

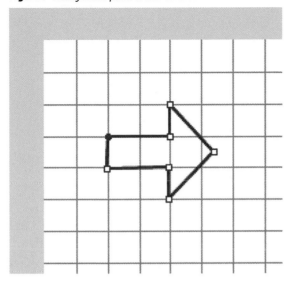

6. Using Figure 8 as a guide, click the remaining anchor points to finish drawing an arrow.

TIP To close an object, be sure to re-click the first anchor point as your last action.

7. Click the **Paint Bucket tool** 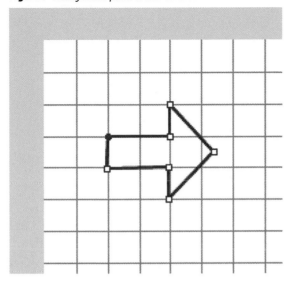, then click inside the arrow.

8. Click **View** on the menu bar, point to **Magnification**, then click **Fit in Window**.

9. Click **View** on the menu bar, point to **Grid**, then click **Show Grid** to turn off the gridlines.

10. Click **Insert** on the menu bar, point to **Timeline**, click **layer**, then insert a **keyframe** in frame 10.

(continued)

11. Click the **Pencil tool** ✐ on the Tools panel.

12. Click **Pencil Mode** S or ⌐ in the Options area of the Tools panel, then click the **Smooth** option, as shown in Figure 9.

13. Draw the **left image** shown in Figure 10.

14. Click the **Brush tool** ✐ on the Tools panel.

15. Click the **Brush Size Icon** ▪ in the Options area at the bottom of the Tools panel, then click the fifth option from the top.

16. Draw the **right image** shown in Figure 10.

   Notice the Pencil tool displays the stroke color and the Brush tool displays the fill color.

You added a layer, inserted a keyframe, then used the Pen tool to draw an arrow; you selected the Smooth option for the Pencil tool and drew an object; you selected a brush size for the Brush tool and drew an object.

Figure 9 *Pencil Tool options*

Click the Pencil Mode Smooth icon to display the 3 options (Note: The Straighten icon might be displayed instead of the Smooth icon)

Click the Smooth option

Figure 10 *Images drawn using drawing tools*

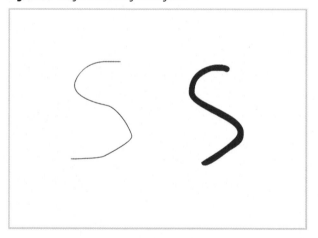

Figure 11 *The dot pattern indicating the object is selected*

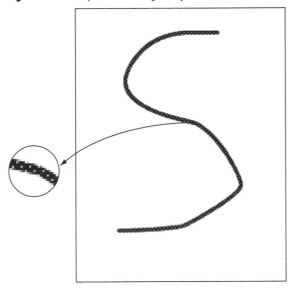

Modify an object using tool options

1. Click the **Selection tool** ↖ on the Tools panel, then drag a **marquee** around the left object to select it.

   The line displays a dot pattern, as shown in Figure 11, indicating that it is selected.

2. Click the **Pencil Mode Smooth icon** ⟋ in the Options area of the Tools panel **three times**. The line becomes smoother as the curves tend to flatten.

3. Click and hold the **Stroke slider** 🔺 in the FILL AND STROKE area of the Properties panel, then drag the **Stroke slider** 🔺 to change the stroke size to **20.**

TIP You can also type a Stroke value in the Stroke text box.

4. Click the **Style list arrow** in the FILL AND STROKE area, then click **Dotted**.

5. Repeat Step 4 and change the line style to **Hatched**.

6. Repeat Step 4 and change the line style to **Solid**.

7. Set the Stroke to **1**.

8. Save your work.

You smoothed objects using the tool options.

Use the Spray tool with a symbol

1. Click **Insert** on the menu bar, point to **Timeline**, then click **Layer**.

2. Click **frame 15** on Layer 4.

3. Click **Insert** on the menu bar, point to **Timeline**, then click **Keyframe**.

4. Click and hold the **Brush tool** 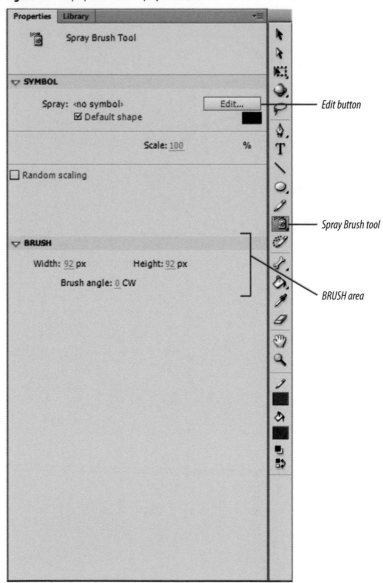 on the Tools panel, then click the **Spray Brush tool** .

5. Display the Properties panel if it is not already displayed, then click the **Edit button** in the SYMBOL area of the Properties panel, as shown in Figure 12.

   Note: If the Properties panel does not display the options for the Spray Brush tool, click the Selection tool, then click the Spray Brush tool.

6. Click **flag** in the Select Symbol dialog box.

   The flag symbol is a graphic that was imported into this Flash document.

   (continued)

Figure 12 *The properties for the Spray Brush tool*

Edit button

Spray Brush tool

BRUSH area

Drawing Objects in Adobe Flash

Figure 13 *A design created using the Spray Brush tool*

7. Click OK.

8. Click the **Random rotation check box** to select it, then click to deselect the **Rotate symbol check box** and the **Random scaling check box** if they are checked.

9. Display the **Brush area** on the Properties panel if it is not already open, then set the width and height to **8 px**.

TIP You can drag the number to the left or you can click the number next to Width or Height, and then type the number in the text box that appears to set the value.

10. Point to the upper left of the stage, then slowly draw the **U** in USA, as shown in Figure 13.

11. Continue to use the **Spray brush tool** to draw the **S** and **A**.

    Hint: If you need to redo the drawing, use the Undo command on the Edit menu or use the Selection tool to draw a marquee around the drawing, then delete the selection.

12. Save your work, then close the document.

You specified a symbol as a pattern and used the Spray Brush tool to complete a drawing.

Use XY coordinates to position objects on the Stage

1. Open fl2_2.fla, then save it as **alignObjects.fla**.

2. Click the **Selection tool** ▶ on the Tools panel, click the **flag** on the Stage, then display the Properties panel, if it is not displayed.

   Notice the X and Y coordinates are set to 100.

3. Click **View** on the menu bar, then click **Rulers**.

4. Click and hold the **horizontal ruler** at the top of the Stage, then drag a **ruler line** down to 100 on the vertical ruler, as shown in Figure 14.

5. Click and hold the **vertical ruler** at the left of the Stage, then drag a **ruler line** across to 100 on the horizontal ruler.

   The point where the two ruler lines cross identifies the X,Y coordinates 100,100. The ruler lines meet at the registration point of the object.

6. Click the **flag**, click **100** next to X: on the Properties panel, type **0**, then press **[Enter]** (Win) or **[Return]** (Mac).

   This aligns the registration point of the object to the left edge of the Stage.

7. Repeat Step 6 to change the Y value to **0**.

8. Type **550** for the X value and **400** for the Y value.

   Notice the flag is positioned off the Stage because the registration point is in the upper-left corner of the object.

9. Change the view to **50%**.

(continued)

Figure 14 *Positioning an object on the Stage using XY coordinates*

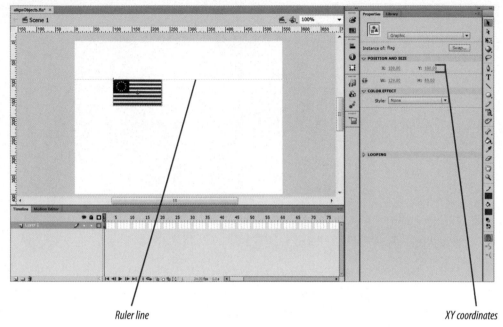

Ruler line

XY coordinates

Drawing Objects in Adobe Flash

Figure 15 *Setting the registration point*

Registration point options

Note: Your Type may be different

10. Point to the **flag**, then click and drag the **flag** around the Stage noticing how the values for X and Y in the Properties panel change.

11. Drag the **flag** to approximately the middle of the Stage.

12. Change the view to **100%**.

13. Use the **arrow keys** on the keyboard to move the flag one pixel at a time in all four directions, then observe the changes to the X and Y values in the Properties panel as you move the object.

14. Click the **flag** to select it, click **Modify** on the menu bar, then click **Convert to Symbol**.

    The Convert to Symbol dialog box opens allowing you to change the registration point.

15. Click the **lower-right icon** as shown in Figure 15, then click **OK**.

    Notice the registration point is now located on the lower-right corner of the flag.

16. Change the **X** and **Y** values in the Properties panel to **100** and **100**.

    Notice the flag is now positioned using the new location of the registration point.

17. Drag each **ruler line** to its respective ruler to remove it from the Stage.

18. Click **View** on the menu bar, then click **Rulers** to remove them from view.

19. Save, then close the Flash document.

You used the X and Y values of an object to position it on the Stage. You used the Convert to Symbol dialog box to change the registration point of an object.

Use the Align options

1. Open fl2_3.fla, then save it as **alignOptions.fla**.

   This document has three objects (flags) of different sizes randomly placed on the Stage.

2. Click **Essentials** on the menu bar, then click **'Reset Essentials'**.

3. Click **Window** on the menu bar, then click **Align** to open the Align panel set.

TIP Alternately, you can click the Align icon that is part of a collapsed panel set on your workspace.

4. Drag the **Align panel set** by its title bar, not its tab, and position it adjacent to the right side of the Stage, as shown in Figure 16.

5. Verify the Align to stage check box in the Align panel is active (checked).

6. Click the **largest flag** to select it, then click the **Align left edge icon** ⊨ .

7. Point to the next **Align icon** ⧰ , read the name that appears, then click the **Align horizontal center icon** ⧰ and notice the new position of the object on the Stage.

8. Click the other **Align options** on the top row of the Align panel.

9. Click the **Align horizontal center icon** ⧰ , then click the **Align vertical center icon** ▤ .

   When you use these two align options together, they position the center of the object with the center of the Stage.

10. Click the **Match width icon** ▣ , then click the **Match height icon** ▤ .

(continued)

Figure 16 *Positioning the Align panel*

Be sure Align to stage is active (checked)

Drawing Objects in Adobe Flash

Figure 17 *All three objects selected*

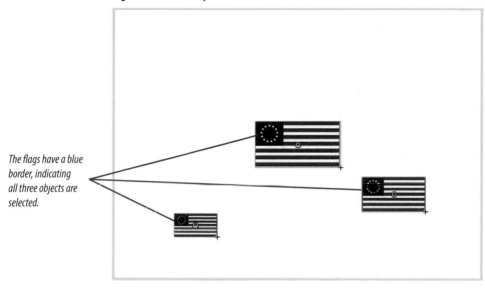

The flags have a blue border, indicating all three objects are selected.

11. Click **Edit** on the menu bar, then click **Undo Match Size**.

12. Click **Edit** on the menu bar, then click **Undo Match Size**.

13. Use the **Selection tool** ▶ to draw a marquee around all three flags to select them, as shown in Figure 17.

14. Click the **Align left edge icon** 🖫 , then click the **Align horizontal center icon** 🖴 .

15. Click the **Space evenly vertically icon** ⬛ , then click the **Align vertical center icon** ⬛ .

16. Click the **Align to stage check box** to make this feature not active.

17. With all three objects selected, click each of the **Align options** on the top row of the Align panel.

    Notice that the objects align to each other instead of the Stage.

18. Click the **Match width and height icon** 🖴 .

    This changes the dimension of each object to match the size of the largest object.

19. Close the Align panel set, then save and close the Flash document.

You used the Align panel to position objects on the Stage relative to the Stage and to each other.

Select Objects
AND APPLY COLORS

What You'll Do

In this lesson, you will use several techniques to select objects, change the color of strokes and fills, and create a gradient fill.

Selecting Objects

Before you can edit a drawing, you must first select the object, or the part of the object, on which you want to work. Drawn objects are made up of a stroke and a fill. A stroke can have several segments. For example, a rectangle has four stroke segments, one for each side of the object. These can be selected separately or as a whole. Flash highlights objects that have been selected, as shown in Figure 18. When the stroke of an object is selected, a dotted colored line appears. When the fill of an object is selected, a dot pattern appears. When the stroke and fill of an object are selected, both the stroke and the fill appear dotted. When a group of objects is selected, a bounding box appears.

Using the Selection Tool

You can use the Selection tool to select part or all of an object, and to select multiple objects. To select only the fill, click just the fill; to select only the stroke, click just the stroke. To select both the fill and the stroke of one object, double-click the object, hold [Shift] and click the fill and stroke or draw a marquee around it. To select part of an object, drag a marquee that defines the area you want to select, as

shown in Figure 18. To select multiple objects or combinations of strokes and fills, press and hold [Shift], then click each stroke or fill you want to select. To deselect an object(s), click a blank area of the Stage.

Using the Lasso Tool

The Lasso tool provides more flexibility than the Selection tool when selecting an object(s) or parts of an object on the Stage. You can use the tool in a freehand manner to draw any shape that then selects the object(s) within the shape. Alternately, you can use the Polygon Mode option to draw straight lines and connect them to form a shape that will select any object(s) within the shape.

Drawing Model Modes

Flash provides two drawing modes, called models. In the Merge Drawing Model mode, the stroke and fill of an object are separate. Thus, as you draw an object such as a circle, the stroke and fill can be selected individually as described earlier. When using the Object Drawing Model mode, the stroke and fill are combined and cannot be selected individually. However, you can use the Break Apart option from the Modify menu to separate the

Drawing Objects in Adobe Flash

stroke and fill so that they can be selected individually. You can toggle between the two modes by clicking the Object Drawing option in the Options area of the Tools panel.

Working with Colors

Flash allows you to change the color of the stroke and fill of an object. Figure 19 shows the Colors area of the Tools panel. To change a color, you click the color swatch of the Stroke Color tool or the color swatch of the Fill Color tool, and then select a color swatch on the Color palette. The Color palette, as shown in Figure 20, allows you to select a color from the palette or type in a six-character code that represents the values of three colors (red, green, blue), referred to as RGB. When these characters are combined in various ways, they can represent virtually any color. The values are in a hexadecimal format (base 16), so they include letters and digits (A–F + 0–9 = 16 options), and they are preceded by a pound sign (#). The first two characters represent the value for red, the next two for green, and the last two for blue. For example, #000000 represents black (lack of color); #FFFFFF represents white; and #FFCC33 represents a shade of gold. You do not have to memorize the codes. There are reference manuals with the codes, and many programs allow you to set the values visually by selecting a color from a palette. You can also use the Properties panel to change the stroke and fill colors.

You can set the desired colors before drawing an object, or you can change a color of a previously drawn object. You can use the Ink Bottle tool to change the stroke color, and you can use the Paint Bucket tool to change the fill color. You can turn off either the stroke or the fill by selecting the No Stroke icon or the No Fill icon in the color palette.

Working with Gradients

A gradient is a color fill that makes a gradual transition from one color to another. Gradients can be very useful for creating a 3D effect, drawing attention to an object, and generally enhancing the appearance of an object. You can apply a gradient fill by using the Paint Bucket tool. The position of the Paint Bucket tool over the object is important because it determines the direction of the gradient fill. The Color palette can be used to create and alter custom gradients.

Figure 18 *Objects or parts of objects are highlighted when selected*

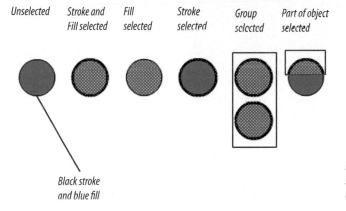

Unselected | Stroke and Fill selected | Fill selected | Stroke selected | Group selected | Part of object selected

Black stroke and blue fill

Figure 19 *The Colors area of the Tools panel*

Stroke Color tool

Fill Color tool

Black and white tool changes stroke to black and fill to white

Swap colors tool swaps the stroke and fill colors

Figure 20 *Color palette showing the hexadecimal number*

Hexadecimal number for shade of gold color

Preset gradient fills

No Stroke icon or No Fill icon (depending on which Color palette is open)

Select a drawing using the Selection tool

1. Open tools.fla, then click **1** on the Timeline.

TIP The options available to you in the Properties panel differ depending on whether you click a number on the Timeline or a frame on a layer.

2. Click the **Selection tool** ▶ on the Tools panel if it is not already selected, then drag a **marquee** around the circle to select the entire object (both the stroke and the fill).

3. Click anywhere on the Stage to deselect the object.

4. Click **inside the circle** to select the fill only, then click outside the circle to deselect it.

5. Click the **stroke** of the circle to select it, as shown in Figure 21, then deselect it.

6. Double-click the **circle** to select it, press and hold **[Shift]**, double-click the **square** to select both objects, then click the **Stage** to deselect both objects.

7. Click the **right border** of the square to select it, as shown in Figure 22, then deselect it.

   Objects, such as rectangles, have border segments that can be selected individually.

(continued)

Figure 21 *Using the Selection tool to select the stroke of the circle*

Figure 22 *Using the Selection tool to select a segment of the stroke of the square*

Figure 23 *Separating the stroke and fill of an object*

8. Drag a **marquee** around the square, circle, and diagonal line to select all three objects.

9. Click a blank area of the Stage to deselect the objects.

10. Click **inside the oval** in row 2 to select the fill, then drag the **fill** outside the stroke, as shown in Figure 23.

11. Look at the Properties panel.

   Notice the stroke color is none and the fill color is blue. This is because only the object's fill is selected. You can use the Properties panel to verify what you have selected when working with the Selection tool.

12. Click **Edit** on the menu bar, then click **Undo Move**.

You used the Selection tool to select the stroke and fill of an object, and to select multiple objects.

Change fill and stroke colors

1. Click **Layer 4,** click **Insert** on the menu bar, point to **Timeline,** then click **Layer.**

2. Click **frame 20** of the new layer, click **Insert** on the menu bar, point to **Timeline,** then click **Keyframe.**

3. Select the **Oval tool** on the Tools panel, then draw **two circles** similar to those shown in Figure 24.

4. Click the **Fill Color tool color swatch** on the Tools panel, then click the **green color swatch** in the left column of the Color palette.

5. Click the **Paint Bucket tool** on the Tools panel, then click the **fill** of the right circle.

6. Click the **Stroke Color tool color swatch** on the Tools panel, then click the **green color swatch** in the left column of the color palette.

7. Click and hold the **Paint Bucket tool** on the Tools panel, click the **Ink Bottle tool** , point to the **red stroke line** of the left circle as shown in Figure 25, then click to change the stroke color to green.

8. Click **Edit** on the menu bar, then click **Undo Stroke.**

You used the Paint Bucket and Ink Bottle tools to change the fill and stroke colors of an object.

Figure 24 *Circles drawn with the Oval tool*

Figure 25 *Changing the stroke color*

Figure 26 *Selecting the red gradient*

Click red gradient color
swatch to select it. If solid
color appears, repeat
the selection.

Hex Edit text box

Figure 27 *Clicking the right side of the circle*

Apply a gradient and make changes to the gradient

1. Click the **Fill Color tool color swatch** 🏠 on the Tools panel, then click the **red gradient color swatch** in the bottom row of the Color palette, as shown in Figure 26.

2. Click and hold the **Ink Bottle tool** 🖋 on the Tools panel, click the **Paint Bucket tool** 🪣, then click the **green circle**.

3. Click different parts of the right circle to view how the gradient changes, then click the **right side** of the circle, as shown in Figure 27.

4. Click and hold the **Free Transform tool** 🔲 on the Tools panel, then click the **Gradient Transform tool** 🏠.

5. Click the **gradient-filled circle**.

(continued)

6. Drag each handle shown in Figure 28 to see its effect on the gradient, then click the **Stage** to deselect the circle.

7. Click the **Selection tool** ⬉ on the Tools panel, then click inside the left circle.

8. Click the **Fill Color tool color swatch** ⬧ ▪ in the FILL AND STROKE area of the Properties panel, click the **Hex Edit text box**, type **#006637** (two zeros).

   The Fill color swatch in the Properties panel changes to a shade of green.

9. Press **[Enter]** (Win) or **[return]** (Mac), then save your work.

   The fill of the circle changes to a shade of green.

You applied a gradient fill, you used the Gradient Transform tool to alter the gradient, and you applied a new color using its Hexadecimal number.

Figure 28 *Gradient Transform handles*

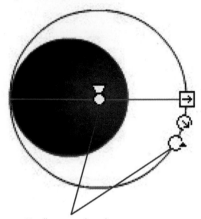

Handles are used to adjust the gradient effect

Figure 29 *Circle drawn using the Object Drawing Model mode*

Blue bounding box indicates
the object is selected

Object Drawing option
active; active mode is Object
Drawing Model

Work with Object Drawing Model mode

1. Insert a **new layer**, then insert a **keyframe** on frame 25.
2. Select the **Oval tool** ⬭ , click the **Stroke Color tool color swatch** , then click the **red swatch**.
3. Click the **Fill Color tool color swatch** , then click the **black swatch**.
4. Click the **Object Drawing option** ⬭ in the Options area of the Tools panel to make the icon active.

   The icon is active and the mode changes to Object Drawing Model.
5. Draw a **circle** as shown in Figure 29.

   Notice that when you use Object Drawing Model mode, the object is selected automatically, which means both the stroke and fill areas of the circle are selected.
6. Click the **Selection tool** �\ on the Tools panel, then click a blank area of the Stage to deselect the object.
7. Click the **circle** once, then drag the **circle** around the Stage.

   The entire object is selected, including the stroke and fill areas.
8. Click **Modify** on the menu bar, then click **Break Apart**.

   Breaking apart an object drawn in Object Drawing Model mode allows you to select the strokes and fills individually.
9. Click a blank area of the Stage, click the **fill** area of the circle, drag to the right, then save your work.

   Notice the fill moves but the stroke stays.

You used the Object Drawing Model mode to draw an object, deselect it, then break it apart to display and then separate the stroke and fill.

Work with Drawn OBJECTS

What You'll Do

In this lesson, you will copy, move, and transform (resize, rotate, and reshape) objects.

Copying and Moving Objects

To copy an object, select it, and then click the Copy command on the Edit menu. To paste the object, click one of the Paste commands on the Edit menu. You can copy an object to another layer by selecting the frame on the layer you want to copy the object to, and then pasting the object. You can copy and paste more than one object by selecting all the objects before using the Copy or Paste commands.

You move an object by selecting it and dragging it to a new location. You can position an object more precisely by selecting it and then pressing the arrow keys, which move the selection up, down, left, and right in small increments. In addition, you can change the X and Y coordinates in the Properties panel to position an object exactly on the Stage.

Transforming Objects

You use the Free Transform tool and the Transform panel to resize, rotate, skew, and reshape objects. After selecting an object, you click the Free Transform tool to display eight square-shaped handles used to transform the object, and a circle-shaped transformation point located at the center of the object.

The transformation point is the point around which the object can be rotated. You can also change its location.

Resizing an Object

You enlarge or reduce the size of an object using the Scale option, which is available when the Free Transform tool is active. The process is to select the object and click the Free Transform tool, and then click the Scale option in the Options area of the Tools panel. Eight handles appear around the selected object. You drag the corner handles to resize the object without changing its proportions. That is, if the object starts out as a square, dragging a corner handle will change the size of the object, but it will still be a square. On the other hand, if you drag one of the middle handles, the object will be reshaped as taller, shorter, wider, or narrower. In addition, you can change the Width and Height settings in the Properties panel to resize an object in increments of one-tenth of one pixel.

Rotating and Skewing an Object

You use the Rotate and Skew option of the Free Transform tool to rotate an object and

Drawing Objects in Adobe Flash

to skew it. The process is to select the object, click the Free Transform tool, and then click the Rotate and Skew option in the Options area of the Tools panel. Eight handles appear around the object. You drag the corner handles to rotate the object, or you drag the middle handles to skew the object, as shown in Figure 30. The Transform panel can be used to rotate and skew an object in a more precise way; select the object, display the Transform panel (available via the Window menu), enter the desired rotation or skew in degrees, and then press [Enter] (Win) or [return] (Mac).

Distorting an Object

You can use the Distort and Envelope options to reshape an object by dragging its handles. The Distort option allows you to reshape an object by dragging one corner without affecting the other corners of the object. The Envelope option provides more than eight handles to allow more precise distortions. These options are accessed through the Transform command on the Modify menu.

Flipping an Object

You use a Flip option on the Transform menu to flip an object either horizontally or vertically. You select the object, click the Transform command on the Modify menu, and then choose Flip Vertical or Flip Horizontal. Other Transform options allow you to rotate and scale the selected object.

The Remove Transform command allows you to restore an object to its original state.

Reshaping a Segment of an Object

You use the Subselection tool to reshape a segment of an object. You click an edge of the object to display handles that can be dragged to reshape the object.

You use the Selection tool to reshape objects. When you point to the edge of an object, the pointer displays an arc symbol. Using the Arc pointer, you drag the edge of the object you want to reshape, as shown in Figure 31. If the Selection tool points to a corner of an object, the pointer changes to an L-shape. You drag the pointer to reshape the corner of the object.

Figure 30 *Using handles to manipulate an object*

Drag corner handle to rotate an object

Drag middle handle to skew an object

Transformation point

Figure 31 *Using the Selection tool to distort an object*

Copy and move an object

1. Click **5** on the Timeline.

2. Click the **Selection tool** ⬉ on the Tools panel, then draw a **marquee** around the arrow object to select it.

3. Click **Edit** on the menu bar, click **Copy**, click **Edit** on the menu bar, then click **Paste in Center**.

4. Drag the newly copied **arrow** to the upper-right corner of the Stage, as shown in Figure 32.

5. Verify the right arrow object is selected on the Stage, press the **down arrow key [↓]** on the keyboard.

   The object moves down in approximately one-pixel increments and the Y coordinate in the Properties panel changes each time the arrow key is pressed.

6. Press the **right arrow key [→]** on the keyboard.

   The object moves right in one-pixel increments and the X coordinate in the Properties panel changes each time the arrow key is pressed.

7. Select the number in the X coordinate box in the Properties panel, type **450** as shown in Figure 33, then press **[Enter]** (Win) or **[return]** (Mac).

8. Select the **number** in the Y coordinate box in the Properties panel, type **30**, then press **[Enter]** (Win) or **[return]** (Mac).

9. Drag a **marquee** around the left arrow object, then set the X and Y coordinates to **36** and **30**, respectively.

10. Click a blank area of the Stage to deselect the object.

You used the Selection tool to select an object, then you copied and moved the object.

Figure 32 *Moving the copied object*

Figure 33 *Changing the X coordinate in the Properties panel*

This value 450 indicates the X coordinate position of the selected object

Figure 34 *Resizing an object using the corner handles*

Pointer used to drag
corner handle

Figure 35 *Reshaping an object using the middle handles*

Pointer used to reshape
the object

Resize and reshape an object

1. Click the **Free Transform tool** ▓ on the Tools panel.

   Note: You may need to click and hold the Gradient tool to display the Free Transform tool.

2. Draw a **marquee** around the arrow object on the right side of the Stage to select the object.

3. Click the **Scale option** ▣ in the Options area on the Tools panel to make it active.

4. Drag each **corner handle** toward and then away from the center of the object, as shown in Figure 34.

   As you drag a corner handle, the object's size is changed, but its proportions remain the same.

5. Click **Edit** on the menu bar, then click **Undo Scale**.

6. Repeat Step 5 until the arrow returns to its original size.

TIP The object is its original size when the option Undo Scale is no longer available on the Edit menu.

7. Verify the arrow is still selected and the handles are displayed, then select the **Scale option** ▣ in the Options area on the Tools panel to make it active.

8. Drag each **middle handle** toward and then away from the center of the object, as shown in Figure 35.

   As you drag the middle handles, the object's size and proportions change.

9. Click **Edit** on the menu bar, then click **Undo Scale** as needed to return the arrow to its original size.

You used the Free Transform tool and the Scale option to display an object's handles, and you used the handles to resize and reshape the object.

Skew, rotate, and flip an object

1. Verify that the Free Transform tool and the right arrow are selected (handles displayed), then click the **Rotate and Skew option** in the Options area of the Tools panel.

2. Click and drag the **upper-middle handle** to the right.

3. Click and rotate the **upper-right corner handle** of the object clockwise.

   The arrow slants down and to the right.

4. Click **Edit** on the menu bar, click the **Undo Rotate** command, then repeat, selecting the Undo Rotate and Undo Skew commands until the arrow is in its original shape and orientation.

5. Click the **Selection tool** on the Tools panel, verify that the right arrow is selected, click **Window** on the menu bar, then click **Transform**.

6. Click the **Rotate text box**, then type **45**, as shown in Figure 36.

7. Press **[Enter]** (Win) or **[return]** (Mac).

8. Click **Edit** on the menu bar, click **Undo Transform**, then close the Transform panel set if it is still open.

9. Draw a **marquee** around the arrow in the upper-left corner of the Stage to select the object.

10. Click **Modify** on the menu bar, point to **Transform**, then click **Flip Horizontal**.

11. Save your work.

You used options on the Tools panel and the Transform panel, as well as commands on the Modify menu to skew, rotate, and flip an object.

Figure 36 *Using the Transform panel to rotate an object*

Rotate text box

Transform Options

Different transform options, such as rotate, skew, and scale, can be accessed through the Options area on the Tools panel when the Free Transform tool is active, the Transform command on the Modify menu, and the Transform panel via the Transform command on the Window menu.

Drawing Objects in Adobe Flash

Figure 37 *Using the Subselection tool to select an object*

Click the tip of the
object to display the
handles

Figure 38 *Using the Subselection tool to drag a handle to reshape the object*

Figure 39 *Using the Selection tool to drag an edge to reshape the object*

Click here, then drag

Use the Zoom, Subselection, and Selection tools

1. Drag a **marquee** around the arrow in the upper-right corner of the Stage, click **Edit** on the menu bar, click **Copy**, click **Edit** on the menu bar, then click **Paste in Center**.

2. Click the **Zoom tool** 🔍 on the Tools panel, then click the **middle of the arrow** in the center of the Stage to enlarge the view.

3. Click the **Subselection tool** ▷ on the Tools panel, then click the **tip of the arrow** to display the handles, as shown in Figure 37.

TIP The handles allow you to change any segment of the object.

4. Click the **handle** at the tip of the arrow, then drag it, as shown in Figure 38.

5. Select the **Oval tool** ⬭ on the Tools panel, then click the **Object Drawing option** 🔲 in the Options area of the Tools panel so the option is not active.

6. Verify the Fill color is set to blue, then draw a **circle** to the left of the arrow you just modified.

7. Click the **Selection tool** ▶ on the Tools panel, then point to the **left edge of the circle** until the Arc pointer ⬎ is displayed.

8. Drag the ⬎ **pointer** to the position shown in Figure 39.

9. Change the **View** of the Stage to **100%**.

10. Save your work.

You used the Zoom tool to change the view, and you used the Subselection and Selection tools to reshape objects.

Use the Rectangle Primitive and Oval tools

1. Insert a **new layer** above Layer 6, click **frame 30** on Layer 7, then insert a **keyframe**.

2. Click and hold the **Oval tool** ⊙ to display the menu.

3. Click the **Rectangle Primitive tool** ▭ , then click the **Reset button** in the Properties panel RECTANGLE OPTIONS area to clear all of the settings.

4. Press and hold **[Shift]**, point to the **middle of the Stage**, then draw the **square** shown in Figure 40.

5. Click the **Selection tool** ➤ in the Tools panel, then drag the **upper-right corner handle** toward the center of the object.

   As you drag the corner, the radius of each of the four corners is changed.

6. Click the **Reset button** in the Properties panel to clear the setting.

7. Slowly drag the **slider** ◠ in the RECTANGLE OPTIONS area to the right until the radius changes to 100, then slowly drag the **slider** ◠ to the left until the radius changes to -100.

8. Click the **Reset Button** on the Properties panel to clear the radius settings.

9. Click the **Lock corner radius icon** ⟲ in the Properties panel RECTANGLE OPTIONS area to unlock the individual controls.

10. Type **-60** in the upper-left corner radius text box, type **-60** in the upper-right corner text box as shown in Figure 41, then press **[Enter]** (Win) or **[return]** (Mac).

(continued)

Figure 40 *Drawing an object with the Rectangle Primitive tool*

The corner handles can be dragged to change the radius of the corners; in addition, the Properties panel can be used to make changes to the object

Figure 41 *Setting the corner radius of two corners*

Your values will differ

Type the values

Broken lock allows you to change individual settings

Use the slider to quickly change the radius of the corners

Drawing Objects in Adobe Flash

Figure 42 *Drawing an object with the Oval Primitive tool*

Figure 43 *Setting the stroke value to 12*

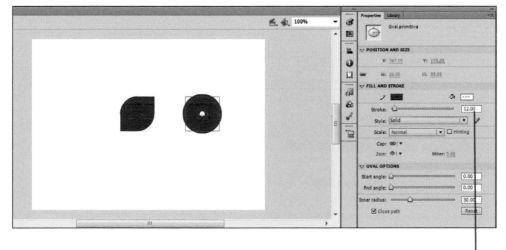

Set the Stroke
value to 12

11. Click the **Reset button** in the Properties panel to clear the radius settings.

12. Click the **Lock corner radius icon** 🔗 to unlock the individual controls.

13. Set the upper-left corner radius to **60** and the lower-right corner to **60**.

14. Click a blank area of the Stage to deselect the object.

15. Click and hold the **Rectangle Primitive tool** 🔲, click the **Oval Primitive tool** 🔵 on the Tools panel, then press and hold **[Shift]** and draw the **circle** shown in Figure 42.

TIP Remember some tools are grouped. Click and hold a grouped tool, such as the Oval tool, to see the menu of tools in the group.

16. Click the **Reset button** in the Properties panel OVAL OPTIONS area to clear any settings.

17. Drag the **Start angle slider** ⌂ and the **End angle slider** ⌂ to view their effect on the circle, then drag each **slider** back to 0.

18. Click the **Reset button** to clear the settings.

19. Drag the **Inner radius slider** ⌂ to see the effect on the circle, then set the inner radius to **30**.

20. Display the FILL AND STROKE area of the Properties panel, then set the Stroke value to **12**, as shown in Figure 43.

21. Save your work.

You used the Primitive tools to create objects and the Properties panel to alter them.

Work with Text
AND TEXT OBJECTS

What You'll Do

 In this lesson, you will enter text using text blocks. You will also resize text blocks, change text attributes, and transform text.

Learning About Text

Flash provides a great deal of flexibility when using text. Among other settings for text, you can specify the typeface (font), size, style (bold, italic), and color (including gradients). You can transform the text by rotating, scaling, skewing, and flipping it. You can even break apart a letter and reshape its segments. There are two different text engines for working with text: Classic Text and Text Layout Framework (TLF). Classic Text mode is appropriate for many text applications and is easy to work with. Text Layout Framework mode provides advanced features and is appropriate for more text intensive applications.

Entering Text and Changing the Text Block for Classic Text

It is important to understand that text is entered into a text block, as shown in Figure 44. You use the Text tool to place a text block on the Stage and to enter and edit text. A text block expands as more text is entered and may even extend beyond the edge of the Stage. You can adjust the size of the text block so that it is a fixed width by dragging the handle in the upper-right corner of the block.

Figure 45 shows the process of using the Text tool to enter text and resize the text block. Once you select the Text tool, you click the Stage where you want the text to appear. An insertion point indicates where the next character will appear in the text block when it is typed. You can resize the text block to a fixed width by dragging the circle handle. After resizing the text block, the circle handle changes to a square, indicating that the text block now has a fixed width. Then, when you enter more text, it automatically wraps within the text block. You can resize the width of a text block at any time by selecting it with the Selection tool (either clicking on the text or drawing a marquee around it) and dragging any handle.

Changing Text Attributes

You can use the Properties panel to change the font, size, and style of a single character or an entire text block. Figure 46 shows the Properties panel when a text object is selected. You select text, display the Properties panel, and make the changes. You use the Selection tool to select the entire text block by drawing a marquee around it. You use the Text tool to select a single character or string of characters by dragging the I-beam pointer over the text you want to select, as shown in Figure 47.

Working with Paragraphs

When working with large bodies of text, such as paragraphs, Flash provides many of the features found in a word processor. You can align paragraphs (left, right, center, justified) within a text block, set margins (space between the border of a text block and the paragraph text), set indents for the first line of a paragraph, and set line spacing (distance between paragraphs) using the Properties panel.

Transforming Text

It is important to understand that a text block is an object. Therefore, you can apply filters, such as drop shadows, and you can transform (reshape, rotate, skew, and so on) a text block in the same way you transform other objects. If you want to transform individual characters within a text block, you must first break apart the text block. To do this, you use the Selection tool to select the text block, then you click the Break Apart command on the Modify menu. Each character (or a group of characters) in the text block can now be selected and transformed.

The Text Layout Framework (TLF)

Text Layout Framework (TLF) provides several advanced text features such as character color highlighting, underlining, strikethrough, and rotation. Text in the TLF format is displayed in a container, similar to a text block. Containers can be resized and linked using a Container icon. This allows you to flow text between them. The containers can have a border and background color, and the text in containers can be formatted into columns. Containers can also have tab stops. Using TFL text reduces the size of SWF files while increasing their performance.

Figure 44 *A text block*

This is a text block used to enter text.

Figure 45 *Using the Text tool*

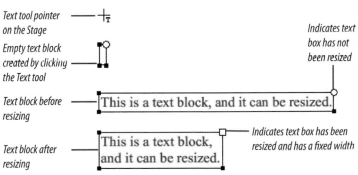

Text tool pointer on the Stage

Empty text block created by clicking the Text tool

Indicates text box has not been resized

Text block before resizing

This is a text block, and it can be resized.

Text block after resizing

This is a text block, and it can be resized.

Indicates text box has been resized and has a fixed width

Figure 46 *The Properties panel when a text object is selected*

Click to expand and see available options

Figure 47 *Dragging the I-beam pointer to select text*

This is a text block, and it can be resized.

I-beam pointer

Enter text and change text attributes

1. Click **Layer 7**, insert a **new layer**, then insert a **keyframe** in frame 35 of the new layer.

2. Click the **Text tool** T , then verify the Text engine is set to Classic Text mode and the Text type is set to Static Text in the T area on the Properties panel.

3. Click the left-center of the Stage, then type **We have great events each year including a Rally**!

4. Click the **I-Beam pointer** ⌐ before the word "Rally" as shown in Figure 48, then type **Car** followed by a space.

5. Drag the **I-Beam pointer** ⌐ across the text to select all the text.

6. Make the following changes in the CHARACTER area of the Properties panel: Family: **Arial**; Style: **Bold**; Size: **16**; Color: **#990000**, then click the **text box**.

   Your Properties panel should resemble Figure 49.

7. Verify the text block is selected, position the **text pointer** ⊣⌐ over the circle handle until the pointer changes to a double arrow ⟷, then drag the **handle** to just before the word each, as shown in Figure 50.

8. Select the text using the I-Beam pointer ⌐ , then click the **Align center icon** 📃 in the PARAGRAPH area of the Properties panel.

9. Click the **Selection tool** ▸ on the Tools panel, click the **text object**, then drag the **object** to the lower-middle of the Stage.

TIP The Selection tool is used to select the text block, and the Text tool is used to select and edit the text within the text block.

You entered text and changed the font, type size, and text color; you also resized the text block and changed the text alignment.

Figure 48 *Using the Text tool to enter text*

We have great events each year including a Rally!

Figure 49 *Changes to the CHARACTER area of the Properties panel*

Text engine list arrow displays the text modes

Text type list arrow

Figure 50 *Resizing the text block*

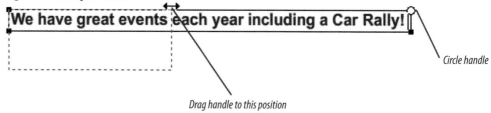

Circle handle

Drag handle to this position

Figure 51 *The Filters options in the Properties panel*

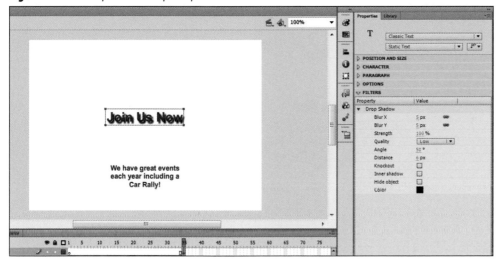

Using Filters

You can apply special effects, such as drop shadows, to text using options in the FILTERS area of the Properties panel. The process is to select the desired text, display the FILTERS area of the Properties panel, choose the desired effect, and make any adjustments, such as changing the angle of a drop shadow. You can copy and paste a filter from one object to another using the clipboard icon in the FILTERS area of the Properties panel.

Add a Filter effect to text

1. Click the **Text tool** T on the Tools panel, click the center of the Stage, then type **Join Us Now**. *Hint*: If the text box does not appear, double-click the Stage.

2. Drag the **I-Beam pointer** I across the text to select it, then use the Properties panel to change the Font size to **30** and the Text (fill) color to **#003399**.

3. Click **CHARACTER** on the Properties panel to close the CHARACTER area, then close all areas in the Properties panel except for the FILTERS area.

4. Click the **Selection tool** ▶ on the Tools panel, then verify the text block is selected.

5. Click the **Add filter icon** at the bottom of the FILTERS area, then click **Drop Shadow**.

6. Point to the **Angle value** in the FILTERS area of the Properties panel, then, when the pointer changes to a double-headed arrow, drag the pointer to the right to view the effect on the shadow, then set the Angle to **50**.

7. Point to the **Distance value**, when the pointer changes to a double-headed arrow, drag the pointer to the right and notice the changes in the drop shadow.

8. Set the Distance to **6**.

9. Click the **Selection tool** ▶, click the text box to select it, drag the **text box** as needed to match the placement shown in Figure 51, then save your work.

You used the Filter panel to create a drop shadow, then made changes to it.

Skew text and align objects

1. Click the **Text tool** T to select it, click the ┼ᴛ **pointer** near the top left of the Stage, then type **Classic Car Club**.

2. Click **CHARACTER** in the Properties panel to display the CHARACTER area.

   The attributes of the new text reflect the most recent settings entered in the Properties panel.

3. Drag the **I-Beam pointer** Ⅰ to select the text, then use the CHARACTER area of the Properties panel to change the font size to **40** and the fill color to **#990000**.

4. Click the **Selection tool** ▸ on the Tools panel, click the **text box** to select it, then click the **Free Transform tool** on the Tools panel.

5. Click the **Rotate and Skew option** ⟳ in the Options area of the Tools panel.

6. Drag the **top middle handle** to the right, as shown in Figure 52, to skew the text.

7. Click the **Selection tool** ▸ on the Tools panel.

8. Drag a **marquee** around all of the objects on the Stage to select them.

9. Click **Modify** on the menu bar, point to **Align**, click **Align to stage** to make it active.

10. Click **Modify** on the menu bar, point to **Align**, then click **Horizontal Center**.

11. Click a blank area of the Stage to deselect the objects.

You entered a heading, changed the font size and color, and skewed text using the Free Transform tool, then you aligned the objects on the Stage.

Figure 52 *Skewing the text*

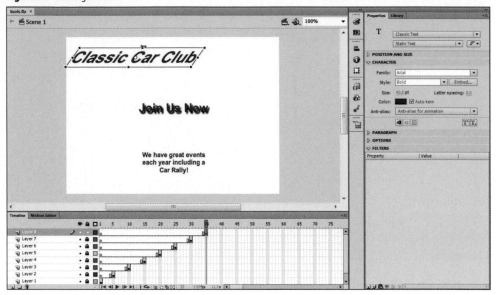

Figure 53 *Reshaping a letter*

Drag this anchor point; notice the lines are drawn from the anchor points on either side of the anchor point being dragged

Figure 54 *Applying a gradient fill to each letter*

Reshape and apply a gradient to text

1. Click the **Selection tool** , click the **Classic Car Club text block** to select it, click **Modify** on the menu bar, then click **Break Apart**.

   The letters are now individual text blocks.

2. Click **Modify** on the menu bar, then click **Break Apart**.

   The letters are filled with a dot pattern, indicating that they can now be edited.

3. Click the **Zoom tool** on the Tools panel, then click the first **"C"** in Classic.

4. Click the **Subselection tool** on the Tools panel, then click the **edge** of the letter **"C"** to display the object's segment handles.

5. Drag a **lower anchor point** on the "C" in Classic, as shown in Figure 53.

6. Click the **Selection tool** , then click a blank area of the Stage to deselect the objects.

7. Click the **View list arrow** on the movie menu bar, then click **Fit in Window**.

8. Click the **Fill Color tool color swatch** on the Tools panel, then click the **red gradient color swatch** in the bottom row of the Color palette.

9. Click the **Paint Bucket tool** on the Tools panel, then click the **top** of each letter to change the fill to a red gradient, as shown in Figure 54.

   Note: Click the Ink Bottle tool if you do not see the Paint Bucket tool.

10. Use the status bar to change the movie frame rate to **3**, test the movie, watch the movie, then close the Flash Player window.

11. Save your work, then close the document.

You broke apart a text block, reshaped text, and added a gradient to the text.

Use the Text Layout Framework

1. Open fl2_4.fla, then save it as **TLF.fla**.

2. Click the **Text tool** T on the Tools panel, then click the **text block** on the Stage.

3. Click the **Text engine list arrow** in the T area on the Properties panel, then click **TLF Text**.

   The text block on the Stage changes to a container and displays two container icons.

4. Scroll the Properties panel as needed, then click **CONTAINER AND FLOW** to display the CONTAINER AND FLOW options.

5. Click the **Behavior list arrow**, then click **Multiline**.

6. Change the Column value to **2**, change it to **3**, then change it to **1**.

7. Point to the **middle handle** on the right side of the container, when the pointer changes to a double-headed arrow ↔, click and drag the **middle handle** left to the position shown in Figure 55, then release the mouse pointer.

8. Click the **Flow icon** on the right side of the container, position the **Flow pointer** ⊞ as shown in Figure 56, then click the mouse button.

   Another container appears that is linked to the first container and with the text flowing from the first container.

9. Click before **From** in the first container, then type **By the 1970s, the car had become a collector's item**.

   Notice as you type in the first container that the text flows to the second container.

(continued)

Figure 55 *Reshaping the text container*

Container icon

Indicates where container will be resized

Figure 56 *Positioning the Flow icon pointer*

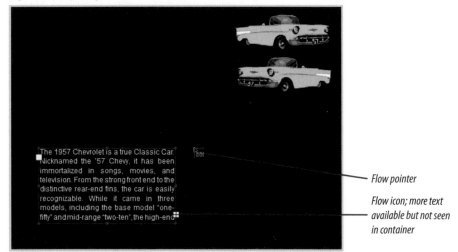

Flow pointer

Flow icon; more text available but not seen in container

Figure 57 *Repostioning the text container*

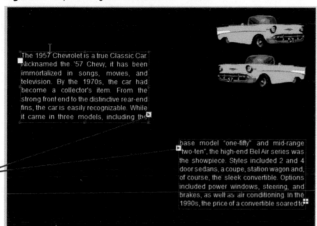

Indicates these
containers are linked

Figure 58 *Repositioning the second text container*

Containers are still linked   Drag to enlarge container

10. Click the **Selection tool** , then click and
    drag the **first container** to the position shown
    in Figure 57.

11. Drag the **second container** to the position
    shown in Figure 58.

12. Click and drag the **bottom middle handle**
    of the second container down to display all
    the text if some of the text is not visible.

NEW

13. **Double-click** the first container to display
    the ruler.

    The ruler allows you to set tab stops and adjust
    the left and right margins of the container text.

14. Point to just above the **1** in 1957 on the ruler,
    then **click** to set a tab stop.

TIP Be sure you click the ruler, and not above or below
    the ruler.

(continued)

15. Point to the beginning of the paragraph, then **click** to set an insertion point, as shown in Figure 59.

16. Press the **Tab key**.

    The first line of the paragraph is indented.

17. Click a blank area of the Stage to remove the ruler.

18. Use the Properties panel to complete the following settings: Text type: **TFL Text**; Font Family: **Times New Roman**; Style: **Regular**; Size: **16 pt**; Color: **White**.

19. Insert **a new layer** above the text layer, then name it **heading**.

20. Click **frame 1** on the heading layer.

21. Click above the first container, then type the heading shown in Figure 60.

22. Click the **Selection tool** on the Tools panel, then verify the text box is selected.

23. Click the **Rotation list arrow** in the CHARACTER area on the Properties Panel, then click **270⁰**.

    The text rotates within the container.

24. Click **Modify** on the menu bar, point to **Transform**, then click **Rotate 90⁰ CW**.

25. Click the **heading**, then use the **arrow keys** to position the container between the two text containers.

(continued)

Figure 59 *Setting an insertion line*

Tab set

Insertion line inserted at beginning of the paragraph

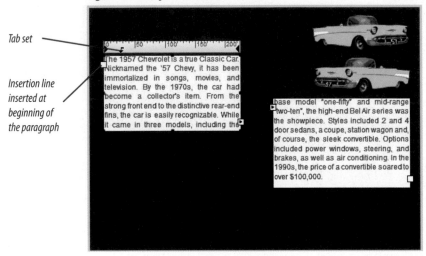

Figure 60 *Typing a heading*

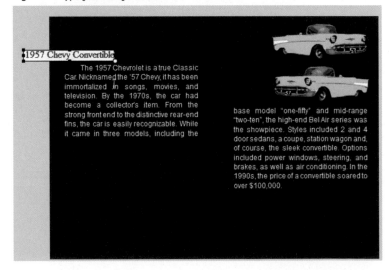

Figure 61 *Adding a container border*

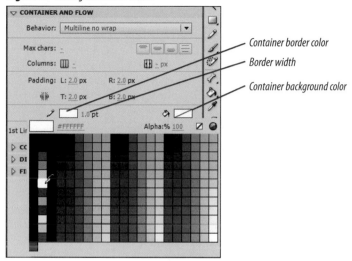

Container border color

Border width

Container background color

26. Click the **Container border color icon** in the CONTAINER AND FLOW area, then click **white**.

    The border color swatch changes to white, as shown in Figure 61.

27. Change the border width to **2**.

28. Click the **Container background color icon** , then set the color to **#333333**.

29. Click the **Text tool** T , then click and drag the pointer to select the words '57 Chevy.

30. In the CHARACTER area of the Properties panel, change the Style to **bold** and the Color to **black**.

31. Click the **Highlight color icon** in the CHARACTER area on the Properties panel, then click the **car** with the **Eyedropper** tool to select the color.

32. Repeat steps 29–31 for the **$100,000** text.

33. Use the **Selection tool** to position the cars, as shown in Figure 62.

34. Test the movie, then save and close it.

You used the Text Layout Framework feature to display columns, create containers, add highlight color to text, add background and stroke color to a container, and rotate text.

Figure 62 *The completed document*

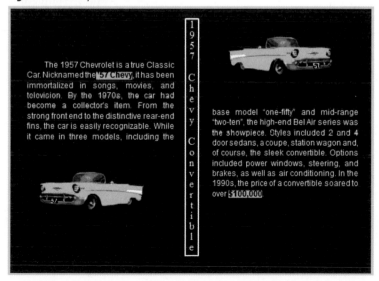

Work with Layers
AND OBJECTS

What You'll Do

 In this lesson, you will create, rename, reorder, delete, hide, and lock layers. You will also add text on top of an object.

Learning About Layers

Flash uses two types of spatial organization. First, there is the position of objects on the Stage, and then there is the stacking order of objects that overlap. An example of overlapping objects is text placed on a banner. In this case, the banner background might be placed on one layer and the banner text might be placed on a different layer. Layers are used on the Timeline as a way of organizing objects. Placing objects on their own layer makes them easier to work with, especially when reshaping them, repositioning them on the Stage, or rearranging their order in relation to other objects. In addition, layers are useful for organizing other elements such as sounds, animations, and ActionScript.

There are five types of layers, as shown in the Layer Properties dialog box displayed in Figure 63 and discussed next.

Normal—The default layer type. All objects on these layers appear in the movie.

Mask—A layer that hides and reveals portions of another layer.

Masked—A layer that contains the objects that are hidden and revealed by a Mask layer.

Folder—A layer that can contain other layers.

Guide (Standard and Motion)—You use a Standard Guide layer to set a reference point (such as a guide line) for positioning objects on the Stage. You use a Motion Guide layer to create a path for animated objects to follow.

Motion Guide, Mask, and Masked layer types are covered in a later chapter.

Working with Layers

The Layer Properties dialog box, accessed through the Timeline command on the Modify menu, allows you to specify the type of layer. It also allows you to name, show (and hide), and lock layers. Naming a layer provides a clue to the objects on that layer. For example, naming a layer Logo might indicate that the object on the layer is the company's logo. Hiding a layer(s) may reduce the clutter on the Stage and make it easier to work with selected objects on the layer(s) that are not hidden. Locking a layer(s) prevents the objects from being accidentally edited. Other options in the Layer Properties dialog box allow you to view layers as outlines, change the outline color, and change layer height. Outlines can be used to help you determine which objects are on a layer. When you turn on this feature, each layer has a colored box that corresponds with the color of the objects on its layer. Icons on the Layers area of the Timeline, as shown in Figure 64, correspond to features in the Layer Properties dialog box.

Figure 63 *The Layer Properties dialog box*

Figure 64 *The Layers area of the Timeline*

Create and reorder layers

1. Open fl2_5.fla from the drive and folder where your Data Files are stored, then save it as **layers2.fla**.

2. Click the **Selection tool** ![arrow] , click the **View list arrow** on the movie menu bar, then click **Fit in Window**.

3. Click the **New Layer icon** ![icon] on the bottom of the Timeline (below the layer names) to insert a new layer, Layer 2.

4. Click **frame 1** on Layer 2.

5. Select the **Rectangle tool** ![icon] on the Tools panel, then set each corner radius to **10** in the RECTANGLE OPTIONS area of the Properties panel, and set the Stroke to **2** in the FILL AND STROKE area.

6. Click the **Fill Color tool color swatch** ![icon] on the Tools panel, click the **Hex Edit text box**, type **#999999**, then press **[Enter]** (Win) or **[return]** (Mac).

7. Click the **Stroke Color tool color swatch** ![icon] on the Tools panel, click the **Hex Edit text box**, type **#000000**, then press **[Enter]** (Win) or **[return]** (Mac).

8. Draw the **rectangle** shown in Figure 65 so it covers the text heading.

9. Drag **Layer 1** above Layer 2 on the Timeline, as shown in Figure 66.

10. Click the **Selection tool** ![arrow] on the Tools panel.

11. Click a blank area of the Stage to deselect the objects.

You added a layer, drew an object on the layer, and reordered layers.

Figure 65 *Drawing a rectangle with a rounded corner*

New Layer icon

Figure 66 *Dragging Layer 1 above Layer 2*

Drag Layer 1 above Layer 2

Drawing Objects in Adobe Flash

Figure 67 *Renaming layers*

Your outline colors may vary

The amount of text you see may vary

Timeline icon

Figure 68 *Hiding all the layers*

No objects are visible on the Stage

Red X indicates layer is hidden

Icon to lock individual layer

Rename and delete layers, expand the Timeline, and hide and lock layers

1. Double-click **Layer 1** on the Timeline, type **heading** in the Layer Name text box, then press **[Enter]** (Win) or **[return]** (Mac).

2. Rename Layer 2 as **heading background**.

3. Point to the **Timeline icon** ▥, which is on the Timeline status bar and shown in Figure 67.

4. When the pointer changes to a double arrow ◀▮▶, drag the **pointer** ◀▮▶ to the right to display all the layer names.

5. Click the **heading layer**, then click the **Delete icon** 🗑 on the Timeline status bar.

6. Click **Edit** on the menu bar, then click **Undo Delete Layer**.

7. Click the **Show or Hide All Layers icon** 👁 to hide all layers, then compare your image to Figure 68.

8. Click the **Show or Hide All Layers icon** 👁 to show all the layers.

9. Click the **Show or Hide This Layer icon** ⬜ next to the **heading background layer** name twice to hide and then show the layer.

10. Click the **Lock or Unlock All Layers icon** 🔒 to lock all layers, then try to select and edit an object.

11. Click the **Lock or Unlock All Layers icon** 🔒 again to unlock the layers.

12. Click the **Lock or Unlock This Layer icon** ⬜ next to the **heading background layer** to lock the layer.

13. Save the document, then exit Flash

You renamed layers to associate them with objects on the layers, deleted and restored a layer, hid layers, and locked layers to prevent accidently editing their contents.

Use the Flash drawing and alignment tools.

1. Start Flash, open fl2_6.fla, then save it as **skillsDemo2.fla**. Refer to Figure 69 as you complete these steps. (*Note*: Figure 69 shows the objects after changes have been made to them. For example, in Step 5 you draw a rectangle in the middle of the Stage. Then, in a later step you rotate the rectangle 45 degrees.)
2. Set the view to Fit in Window, then display the Grid.
3. Select the Oval tool, then set the stroke size to 1, the stroke color to black (Hex: **#000000**) and the fill color to blue (Hex: **#0000FF**).
4. Use the Oval tool to draw an oval on the left side of the Stage, then draw a circle beneath the oval. (*Hint*: Use the Undo command as needed.)
5. Use the Rectangle tool to draw a rectangle in the middle of the Stage, then draw a square beneath the rectangle. (*Hint*: Reset the RECTANGLE OPTIONS as needed.)
6. Use the Line tool to draw a horizontal line on the right side of the Stage, then draw a vertical line beneath the horizontal line and a diagonal line beneath the vertical line.
7. Use the Pen tool to draw an arrow-shaped object above the rectangle. (*Hint*: Use the Zoom tool to enlarge the area of the Stage.)
8. Use the Paint Bucket tool to fill the arrow with the blue color. (*Hint*: If the arrow does not fill, be sure you closed the arrow shape by clicking the first anchor point as your last action.)
9. Use the Pencil tool to draw a freehand curved line above the oval, then select the line and use the Smooth option to smooth out the line.

10. Use the Rectangle Primitive tool to draw a rectangle below the square. (*Hint*: Reset the RECTANGLE OPTIONS as needed after drawing the rectangle.)
11. Use the Selection tool to drag a corner to round all the corners.
12. Save your work.

Select objects and apply colors.

1. Use the Selection tool to select the stroke of the circle, then deselect the stroke.
2. Use the Selection tool to select the fill of the circle, then deselect the fill.
3. Use the Paint Bucket tool to change the fill color of the square to a red gradient.
4. Use the Ink Bottle tool to change the stroke color of the circle to red (Hex: **#FF0000**).
5. Change the fill color of the oval to a blue gradient.
6. Save your work.

Work with drawn objects.

1. Copy and paste in center the arrow object.
2. Move the copied arrow to another location on the Stage.
3. Use the Properties panel to set the height of each arrow to 30.
4. Flip the copied arrow horizontally.
5. Rotate the rectangle to a 45° angle.
6. Skew the square to the right.
7. Copy one of the arrows and use the Subselection tool to reshape it, then delete it.
8. Use the Selection tool to reshape the circle to a crescent shape.
9. Save your work.

Work with text and text objects.

1. Select the Text tool, set the text mode to Classic Text and the type to Static Text, then enter the following text in a text block at the top of the Stage: **Gateway to the Pacific.**
2. Select the text, then change the text to font: Tahoma, size: 24, color: red.
3. Use the Align option on the Modify menu to horizontally center the text block.
4. Use the Selection tool and the up and down arrow keys on the keyboard to align the text block with a gridline.
5. Skew the text block to the right.
6. Save your work.

Work with layers.

1. Insert a layer into the document.
2. Change the name on the new layer to **heading bkgnd**, then click frame 1 on the layer.
3. Use the Rectangle Primitive tool to draw a rounded corner rectangle with a blue fill and a black stroke that covers the words Gateway to the Pacific.
4. Switch the order of the layers.
5. Lock all layers.
6. Unlock all layers.
7. Hide the heading bkgnd layer.
8. Show the heading bkgnd layer.
9. Add a layer, name it **subheading**, and use the Text tool to type **Seattle** below the heading, using Tahoma, Regular, 24 pt, and the color blue.
10. Align Seattle so it is centered horizontally across the Stage, then save your work.

Drawing Objects in Adobe Flash

Use the Merge Drawing Model mode.

1. Insert a new layer and name it **MergeDraw**.
2. Select the Rectangle tool and verify that the Object Drawing option is not active.
3. Draw a square in the upper-right of the Stage, then use the Oval tool to draw a circle with a different color that covers approximately half of the square.
4. Select the stroke and fill of the circle, then using the Selection tool drag the circle off the square. (*Note*: Depending on the size of the circle and where you drew it to overlap the square, your results may vary from what is shown in Figure 69.)

Use the Object Drawing Model mode.

1. Insert a new layer and name it **ObjectDraw**.
2. Select the Rectangle tool and select the Object Drawing option to make it active.
3. Draw a square with a blue fill color, then use the Oval tool to draw a circle with a different color that covers approximately half of the square.
4. Use the Selection tool to drag the circle off the square.
5. Change the name of Layer 1 to **objects**.
6. Save your work, then compare your image to the example shown in Figure 69.

Use the Spray tool with a symbol.

1. Turn off the gridlines.
2. Add a new layer to the Timeline, then name the layer **aces wild**.
3. Add a keyframe to frame 5 of the new layer.
4. Select the Text tool and change the Text option to TLF Text, then verify rotation is set to auto and the

Align option in the PARAGRAPH area of the properties panel is set to Justify with last line aligned to start.
5. Drag the pointer to create a text box that covers the lower one-fourth of the Stage, then set the Behavior option in the CONTAINER AND FLOW area of the Properties panel to Multiline.
6. Type the following using Arial, 14 pt text, black:

Ace's Wild has been providing novelty items, gifts, and toys to Seattleites since 1975. Located in Seattle's Greenlake district, we provide one stop shopping for the most unusual and unique costumes, party supplies, crafts, and the strangest collection of toys ever assembled. Visit Ace's Wild to have a fun time choosing that perfect present for the hard to buy for person in your life.

7. Divide the text block into two text Containers, then use the Selection tool to position them as shown in Figure 69. (*Note:* You can drag any middle handle to resize the container.)
8. Use the Text tool to select the top Container, set a first line paragraph indent, then create a **2** pt blue border (#0000FF) and a gray (#CCCCCC) background.
9. Select the bottom Container and create the same border and background.
10. Use the Text tool to select Ace's Wild in the top Container, then create a white highlight.
11. Select the Spray Brush tool.
12. Click the Edit button in the Symbol area of the Properties panel, then select the Ace symbol.
13. Set the Scale width and height to **50**, turn on Rotate symbol (*Hint*: Be sure the check box has a check mark) and turn off the other options (*Hint*: Be sure all other check boxes do not have check marks), set the Brush width and height to 3 px, then draw the letters for Ace's as shown in Figure 69.
14. Change the Stage color to a shade of blue (#3399FF).
15. Test the movie, then save and close the document. (*Note*: If the movie displays too quickly, adjust the frame rate.)
16. Exit Flash.

Figure 69 *Completed Skills Review*

A local travel company, Ultimate Tours, has asked you to design a sample opening screen for its new application. The goal of the application is to inform potential customers of its services. The company specializes in exotic treks, tours, and cruises. Thus, while its target audience spans a wide age range, they are all looking for something out of the ordinary. This screen may become part of a website, a mobile app, and/or a link on a Facebook site.

1. Open a new Flash document using ActionScript 2.0 and save it as **ultimateTours2.fla**. Create the Flash movie shown in Figure 70. (*Note*: ActionScript 2.0 is used because in subsequent chapters the ultimateTours project will require this version of ActionScript.)

2. Set the document properties, including the Stage size and Stage color. (*Note*: You can use your choice of colors.)

3. Create the following on separate layers and name the layers:
   - A text heading; select a font size and font color. Skew the heading, break it apart, then reshape one or more of the characters.
   - A subheading with a different font size and color.
   - At least three objects that will be the background for button symbols.
   - Text that will appear on the top of the button background.

Note: You can use different colors, shapes, and placement but your project should have all the elements shown in Figure 70.

4. Use one or more of the align features (gridlines, rulers, Align command on the Modify menu, arrow keys) to align the objects on the Stage.

5. Lock all layers.

6. Compare your image to the example shown in Figure 70.

7. Save your work.

8. Test the movie, close the Flash Player window, then close the movie.

Drawing Objects in Adobe Flash

Figure 70 *Sample completed Project Builder 1*

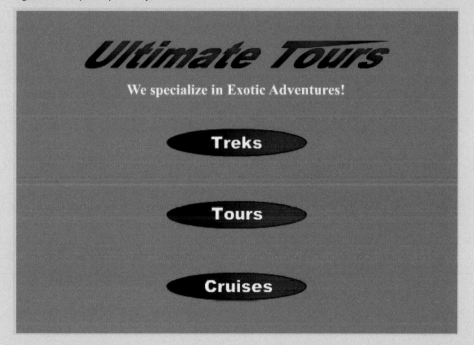

You have been asked to create several sample designs for the opening screen of an application of a new organization called The Jazz Club. The club is being organized to bring together music enthusiasts for social events and charitable fundraising activities. The club members plan to sponsor weekly jam sessions and a show once a month. Because the club is just getting started, the organizers are looking to you for help in developing an application. This screen may become part of a website, a mobile app, and/or a link on a Facebook site.

1. Plan the application by specifying the goal, target audience, treatment ("look and feel"), and elements you want to include (text, graphics, sound, and so on).

2. Sketch out a screen design that shows the layout of the objects. Be creative in your design.

3. Open a new Flash document and save it as **theJazzClub2.fla**.

4. Set the document properties, including the Stage size and Stage color, if desired.

5. Display the gridlines and rulers and use them to help align objects on the Stage.

6. Create a heading, text objects, and drawings (such as the lines) to be used as links to the categories of information provided on the application. (*Note*: Some of the characters are individual text blocks [e.g. the S in Sessions] allowing you to move the text block without moving the other characters. *Hint*: Use the Oval, Line, and Brush tools to create the notes. After selecting the Brush tool, experiment with the different Brush tool shapes found in the Options area at the bottom of the Tools panel.)

7. Hide the gridlines and rulers.

8. Save your work, then compare your image to the example shown in Figure 71.

Figure 71 *Sample completed Project Builder 2*

Figure 72 shows the home page of a website. Study the figure and complete the following. For each question indicate how you determined your answer.

1. Connect to the Internet, go to *www.nps.gov*, then select Explore Nature.
2. Open a document in a word processor or open a new Flash document, save the file as **dpc2**, then answer the following questions. (*Hint*: Use the Text tool in Flash.)
   - Whose website is this?
   - What is the goal(s) of the site?
   - Who is the target audience?
   - What treatment ("look and feel") is used?
   - What are the design layout guidelines being used (balance, movement, and so on)?
   - If you wanted to add animation to this screen, what element might you animate?
   - Do you think this is an effective design for the organization, its goals, and its target audience? Why or why not?
   - How might TLF text be used in this layout?
   - What suggestions would you make to improve the design and why?

Figure 72 *Design Project*
Courtesy of National Park Service website. www.nps.gov

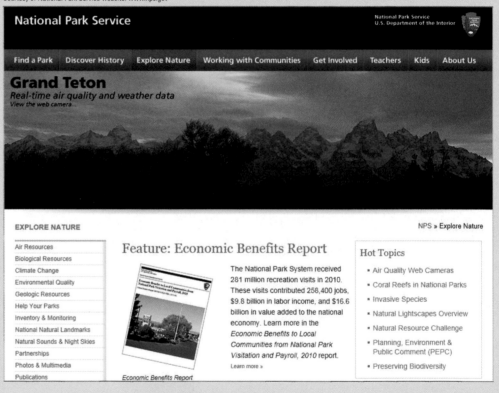

You have decided to create a personal portfolio of your work that you can use when you begin your job search. The portfolio will be part of a website with a link on your Facebook page.

1. Research what should be included in a portfolio.
2. Plan the site by specifying the goal, target audience, treatment ("look and feel"), and elements you want to include (text, graphics, sound, and so on).
3. Sketch an opening screen that shows the layout of the objects. Be creative in your design.
4. Design the opening screen to include personal data (such as a Biography object that will link to your personal data, work history, and education), contact information (such as a Contact me object that will link to your contact information), and samples of your work (such as Animations, Graphics, and Screen Designs objects that will link to samples of your work) The categories and titles are up to you.
5. Open a new Flash document using ActionScript 2.0 and save it as **portfolio2.fla**. (*Note*: ActionScript 2.0 is used because, in subsequent chapters, the portfolio project will require this version of ActionScript.)
6. Set the document properties, including the Stage size and Stage color, if desired.
7. Display the gridlines and rulers and use them to help align objects on the Stage. (*Note:* The sample completed Portfolio Project shown in Figure 73 uses

four layers. As you complete the following steps include layers for:
- the border
- the placeholder for the image
- the background ovals for the heading and the categories
- the text for the heading and the categories)
8. Add a border the size of the Stage. (*Hint*: Use the Rectangle tool, then set the Stroke color to a color of your choice and the Fill color to no color ☑ .
9. Create a heading with its own background.
10. Create the background ovals for the categories.
11. Create the text objects that will be used as links to the categories of information provided on the website. (*Hint*: In the example shown here, the Brush Script Std font is used. You can replace this font with Impact or any other appropriate font on your computer.)
12. Hide the gridlines and rulers.
13. Lock all the layers.
14. Save your work, then compare your image to the example shown in Figure 73.

Figure 73 *Sample completed Portfolio Project*

CHAPTER 3 WORKING WITH SYMBOLS AND INTERACTIVITY

1. Create symbols and instances
2. Work with libraries
3. Create buttons
4. Assign actions to frames and buttons
5. Import graphics

3 WORKING WITH SYMBOLS AND INTERACTIVITY

Introduction

An important benefit of Flash is its ability to create movies with small file sizes. This allows the movies to be delivered from the web or displayed on a mobile device more quickly. One way to keep the file size small is to create reusable graphics, buttons, and movie clips. Flash allows you to create a graphic (drawing) and then make unlimited copies, which you can use throughout the current movie and in other movies. Flash calls the original drawing a **symbol** and the copied drawings **instances**. Flash stores symbols in the Library panel—each time you need a copy of the symbol, you can open the Library panel and drag the symbol to the Stage, which creates an instance (copy) of the symbol. Using instances reduces the movie file size because Flash stores only the information about the symbol's properties (size, shape, color), and a link is established between the symbol and an instance so that the instance has the same properties (such as color and shape) as the symbol. There are two especially valuable editing features of this process. First, if you have created several instances of a symbol and decide to change the same property for every instance, all that is needed is to edit the symbol. For example, if a logo appears in several places in an application and you need to change the color of each instance of the logo, you simply change the color of the symbol. Because the instances are linked to the symbol they are automatically updated. Second, you can change the properties of an individual instance of a symbol in one of two ways. You can change properties associated with the whole instance, such as size or transparency, and you can skew or rotate the instance. So if you have a symbol that is a tree, you can make the tree bigger or smaller, or you can make the tree lean to the left as if it is blowing in the wind. However, if you want to change individual parts of the instance, then you must break the link between the instance and the symbol. When you break the link between an instance and a symbol, the instance becomes an object that can be edited. For example, thinking about our tree now as an object, you can make the leaves on the tree different colors. You can only do this if you break the link between the instance and the symbol. When you break the link, changes you make to the object are not reflected in the symbol or any instances of the symbol. Likewise, if subsequently you make changes to the symbol, the changes will not be reflected in the unlinked object. The process for unlinking an instance is to select the instance on the Stage and choose the Break Apart command from the Modify menu.

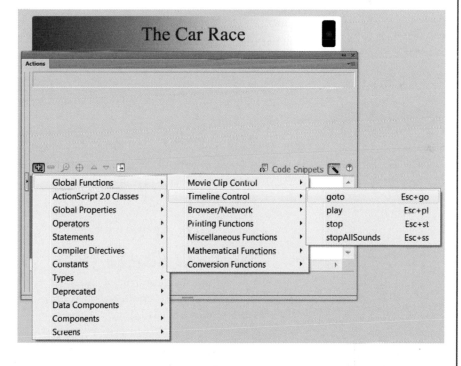

Create Symbols
AND INSTANCES

What You'll Do

In this lesson, you will create graphic symbols, turn them into instances, and then edit the instances.

Understanding Symbol Types

There are three categories of symbols: graphic, button, and movie clip. A graphic symbol is useful because you can reuse a single image and make changes in each instance of the image. A button symbol is useful because you can create buttons for interactivity, such as starting or stopping a movie. A movie clip symbol is useful for creating complex animations because you can create a movie within a movie. For example, you could have a movie with a car moving across the screen and its wheels rotating. The wheel animation would be created as one movie clip symbol and attached to each wheel of the animated car. Symbols can be created from objects you draw using the Flash drawing tools. In addition, you can import graphics into a Flash document that can then be converted to symbols.

Creating a Graphic Symbol

You can use the New Symbol command on the Insert menu to create and then draw a symbol. You can also draw an object and then use the Convert to Symbol command on the Modify menu to convert the object to a symbol. The Convert to Symbol dialog box, shown in Figure 1, allows you to name

the symbol and specify the type of symbol you want to create (Movie Clip, Button, or Graphic). When naming a symbol, it's a good idea to use a naming convention that allows you to quickly identify the type of symbol and to group like symbols together. For example, you could identify all graphic symbols by naming them g_*name* and all buttons as b_*name*. In Figure 1, the drawing on the Stage is being converted to a graphic symbol.

After you complete the Convert to Symbol dialog box, Flash places the symbol in the Library panel, as shown in Figure 2. In Figure 2, an icon identifying the symbol as a graphic symbol and the symbol name are listed in the Library panel, along with a preview of the selected symbol. To create an instance of the symbol, you simply drag a symbol from the Library panel to the Stage. To edit a symbol, you can double-click it in the Library panel or you can use the Edit Symbols command on the Edit menu. Either way displays the symbol in an edit window, where changes can be made to it. When you edit a symbol, the changes are reflected in all instances of that symbol in your movie. For example, you can draw a car, convert the car to a symbol, and then create several instances of the car.

You can uniformly change the size of all the cars by double-clicking the car symbol in the Library panel to open the edit window, and then rescaling it to the desired size.

Working with Instances

You can have as many instances as needed in your movie, and you can edit each one to make it somewhat different from the others. You can rotate, skew (slant), and resize graphic and button instances. In addition, you can change the color, brightness, and transparency. However, there are some limitations. An instance is a single object with no segments or parts, such as a stroke and a fill. You cannot select a part of an instance. Therefore, any changes to the color of the instance are made to the entire object. Of course, you can use layers to stack other objects on top of an instance to change its appearance. In addition, you can use the Break Apart command on the Modify menu to break the link between

an instance and a symbol. Once the link is broken, you can make any changes to the object, such as changing its stroke and fill color. However, because the link is broken, the object is no longer an instance of the original symbol. So, if you make any changes to the original symbol, then the unlinked object is not affected.

The process for creating an instance is to open the Library panel and drag the desired symbol to the Stage. Once the symbol is on the Stage, you select the instance by using the Selection tool to drag a marquee around it. A blue bounding

box indicates that the object is selected. Then, you can use the Free Transform tool options (such as Rotate and Skew, or Scale) to modify the entire image, or you can use the Break Apart command to break apart the instance and edit individual strokes and fills.

Figure 2 *A graphic symbol in the Library panel*

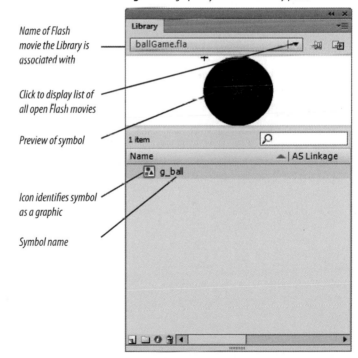

Name of Flash movie the Library is associated with

Click to display list of all open Flash movies

Preview of symbol

Icon identifies symbol as a graphic

Symbol name

Figure 1 *Using the Convert to Symbol dialog box to convert an object to a symbol*

Create a symbol

1. Open fl3_1.fla from the drive and folder where your Data Files are stored, then save it as **coolCar.fla**.

   This document has one object, a car, that was created using the Flash drawing tools.

2. Verify the Properties panel, the Library panel, and the Tools panel are displayed.

3. Set the magnification to **Fit in Window**.

4. Click the **Selection tool** on the Tools panel, then drag a **marquee** around the car to select it.

5. Click **Modify** on the menu bar, then click **Convert to Symbol**.

6. Type **g_car** in the Name text box.

7. Click the **Type list arrow** to display the symbol types, then click **Graphic**, as shown in Figure 3.

8. Set the **registration** to the upper-left corner as shown in Figure 3 if necessary, then click **OK**.

9. Click the **Library panel tab**, study the Library panel as shown in Figure 4, then save your work.

   The Library panel displays the symbol (red car) in the Item Preview window, an icon ![icon] indicating that this is a graphic symbol, and the name of the symbol (g_car). The symbol is contained in the library, and the car on the Stage is now an instance of the symbol.

You opened a file with an object, converted the object to a symbol, and displayed the symbol in the Library panel.

Figure 3 *Options in the Convert to Symbol dialog box*

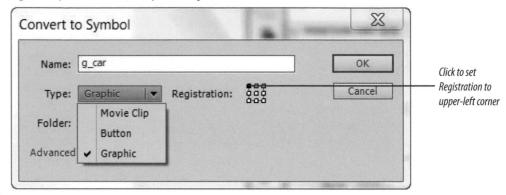

Click to set Registration to upper-left corner

Figure 4 *Newly created symbol in the Library panel*

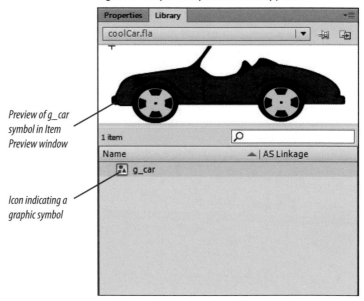

Preview of g_car symbol in Item Preview window

Icon indicating a graphic symbol

Working with Symbols and Interactivity

Figure 5 *Creating an instance*

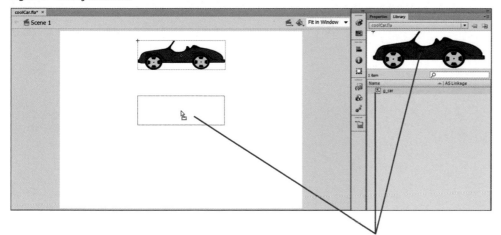

Drag the car image, the name of the symbol,
or its icon from the Library panel to below
the original instance to create a second
instance of the symbol

Figure 6 *The alpha set to 50%*

This area may not be open   Transparency set to 50%

Create and edit an instance

1. Point to the **car image** in the Item Preview window of the Library panel, then drag the **image** to the Stage beneath the first car, as shown in Figure 5.

   Both cars on the Stage are instances of the graphic symbol in the Library panel.

   TIP You can also drag the name of the symbol or its icon from the Library panel to the Stage.

2. Verify the bottom car is selected, click **Modify** on the menu bar, point to **Transform**, then click **Flip Horizontal**.

3. Display the Properties panel, then display the COLOR EFFECT area if it is not already showing.

4. Click the **Style list arrow**, then click **Alpha**.

5. Drag the **Alpha slider** left then right, then set the transparency to **50%**.

   Notice how the transparency changes. Figure 6 shows the transparency set to 50%.

6. Click a blank area of the Stage to deselect the object, then save your work.

   Changing the alpha setting gives the car a more transparent look.

You created an instance of a symbol and edited the instance on the Stage.

Lesson 1   Create Symbols and Instances

Edit a symbol in the edit window

1. Display the Library panel, double-click the **g_car symbol icon** in the Library panel to display the edit window, then compare your screen to Figure 7.

    The g_car symbol appears in the edit window, indicating that you are editing the g_car symbol.

TIP You can also edit a symbol by selecting it, clicking Edit on the menu bar, then clicking Edit Symbols.

2. Click a blank area of the window to deselect the car.

3. Verify the Selection tool is selected, then click the **light gray hubcap** inside the front wheel to select it.

4. Press and hold **[Shift]**, then click the **hubcap** inside the back wheel so both hubcap fills are selected.

5. Set the **Fill Color** to the **blue gradient color swatch** in the bottom row of the color palette, compare your image to Figure 8, then deselect the image.

6. Click **Scene 1** at the top left of the edit window to exit the edit window and return to the main Timeline and main Stage, then save your work.

    Changes you make to the symbol affect every instance of the symbol on the Stage. The hubcap fill becomes a blue gradient in the Library panel and on the Stage.

You edited a symbol in the edit window that affected all instances of the symbol.

Figure 7 *Edit window*

Graphic symbol indicates you are in the edit window

Name of symbol

Figure 8 *Edited symbol*

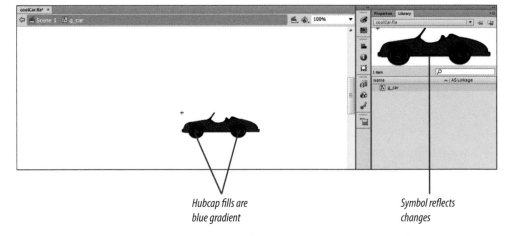

Hubcap fills are blue gradient

Symbol reflects changes

Figure 9 *The car with the maroon body selected*

Figure 10 *Changing the symbol affects only the one instance of the symbol*

Instance of the symbol ——

Object that is no
longer an instance
of the symbol ——

Break apart an instance

1. Drag a **marquee** around the bottom car to
    select it if it is not selected.
2. Click **Modify** on the menu bar, then click
    Break Apart.

    The object is no longer linked to the symbol, and
    its parts (strokes and fills) can now be edited.
3. Click a blank area of the Stage to deselect
    the object.
4. Click the blue **front hubcap**, press and hold
    [Shift], then click the **blue back hubcap** so
    both hubcaps are selected.
5. Set the **Fill Color** to the **light gray color
    swatch (#999999)** in the left column of the
    color palette.
6. Double-click the **g_car symbol icon**
    in the Library panel to display the edit window.
7. Click the **maroon front body** of the car to select
    it, press and hold **[Shift]**, then click the **maroon
    back body** of the car, as shown in Figure 9.
8. Set the **Fill Color** to the **red gradient color
    swatch** in the bottom row of the color palette.
9. Click **Scene 1** at the top left of the edit window,
    then compare your images to Figure 10.

    The body color of the car in the original instance
    is a different color, but the body color of the car
    to which you applied the Break Apart command
    remains unchanged.
10. Save your work.

*You used the Break Apart command to break the link between
one instance and its symbol, you edited the object created using
the Break Apart command, and then you edited the symbol,
which only affected the instance still linked to the symbol.*

Work with LIBRARIES

What You'll Do

 In this lesson, you will use the Library panel to organize the symbols in a movie.

Understanding the Library

The library in a Flash document contains the symbols and other items such as imported graphics, movie clips, and sounds. The Library panel provides a way to view and organize the items, and allows you to change the item name, display item properties, and add and delete items. Figure 11 shows the Library panel for a document. Refer to this figure as you read the following descriptions of the parts of the library.

Tab title—Identifies the panel title, in this case, the Library panel.

Panel options menu— Labeled in Figure 11 and shown in Figure 12, the Panel options menu provides access to several features used to edit symbols (such as renaming symbols) and organize symbols (such as creating a new folder).

Display movies list arrow—Opens a menu showing all open movies. You use this menu to select an open document (movie) and display the Library panel associated with that open document. This allows you to use the items from one movie in another movie. For example, you may have developed a drawing in one Flash movie that you converted to a symbol and now you want to use that symbol in the movie you are working on. With both documents open, you simply use the Display movies list arrow to display the library with the desired symbol, and then drag the symbol to the Stage of the current movie. This will automatically place the symbol in the library for the current movie. In addition to the movie libraries, you can create permanent libraries that are available whenever you start Flash. Flash also has sample libraries that contain buttons and other objects. The permanent and sample libraries are accessed through the Common Libraries command on the Window menu. All assets in all of these libraries are available for use in any movie.

Item Preview window—Displays the selected item. If the item is animated or a sound file, a control button appears, allowing you to preview the animation or play the sound.

Name list box—Lists the folder and item names. Each item type has a different icon associated with it. Clicking an item name or icon displays the item in the Item Preview window.

Working with Symbols and Interactivity

Toggle Sorting Order icon—Allows you to reorder the list of folders and items within folders.

New Symbol icon—Displays the Create New Symbol dialog box, allowing you to create a new symbol.

New Folder icon—Allows you to create a new folder.

Properties icon—Displays the Properties dialog box for the selected item.

Delete icon—Deletes the selected item or folder.

To make changes to an item, you can double-click either the item icon in the Library panel, the item in the Item Preview window, or the item on the Stage to display the edit window.

Figure 11 *The Library panel*

Tab title

Item Preview window

Name list box

Panel options list arrow

Display movies list arrow; click to display list of all open Flash movies; click a movie to open Library panel for that movie

Toggle Sorting Order Icon (position may vary)

New Symbol icon

New Folder icon

Properties icon

Delete icon

Figure 12 *The Panel options menu*

New Symbol...
New Folder
New Font...
New Video...
Rename
Delete
Duplicate...
Move to...
Edit
Edit with...
Edit with Audition
Edit Class
Play
Update...
Properties...
Component Definition...
Runtime Shared Library URL...
Select Unused Items
Expand Folder
Collapse Folder
Expand All Folders
Collapse All Folders
Help
Close
Close Group

Create folders in the Library panel

1. Open fl3_2.fla, then save it as **carRace.fla**.

2. Verify the Properties panel, the Library panel, and the Tools panel are displayed.

3. Set the magnification to **Fit in Window**.

   This movie has eight layers containing various objects such as text blocks, lines, and a backdrop. Two layers contain animations of cars.

4. Test the movie, then close the Flash Player window.

5. Click the **Show or Hide All Layers icon** 👁 on the Timeline to hide all of the layers.

6. Click each **red X** in the Show or Hide All Layers column to show the contents of each layer, click the **Show or Hide This Layer icon** ⬚ to hide the contents of that layer, then after viewing the contents of each layer, click the **Show or Hide All Layers icon** 👁 on the Timeline to show all of the layers.

   Note: The resetBTN layer shows an empty Stage. This is because the word Reset is located in frame 65 at the end of the movie and does not appear in frame 1.

7. Click each item in the Library panel to display it in the Item Preview window.

   Notice that there is one button symbol (b_reset) and five graphic symbols.

8. Click **Name** on the Name list box title bar, as shown in Figure 13, and notice how the items are sorted.

9. Repeat Step 8 and notice how the items are sorted.

You opened a Flash movie and sorted items in the Library panel.

Figure 13 *The open Library panel*

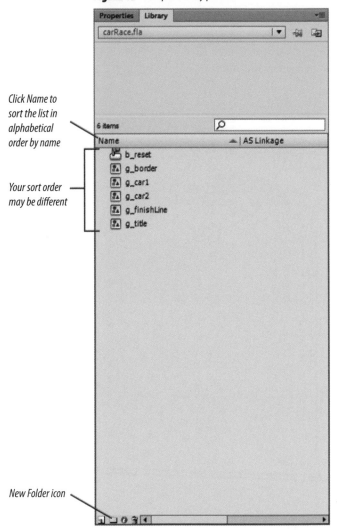

Click Name to sort the list in alphabetical order by name

Your sort order may be different

New Folder icon

Figure 14 *The Library panel with the folders added*

Buttons folder

Graphics folder

Figure 15 *The Library panel after moving the symbols to the folders*

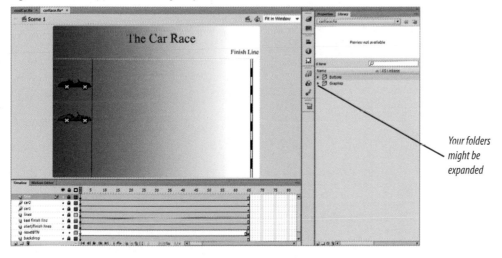

Your folders
might be
expanded

Organize items within Library panel folders

1. Click the **New Folder icon** in the Library panel, as shown in Figure 13.
2. Type **Graphics** in the Name text box for the new folder, then press [**Enter**] (Win) or [**return**] (Mac).
3. Click the **New Folder icon** on the Library panel.
4. Type **Buttons** in the Name text box for the new folder, then press [**Enter**] (Win) or [**return**] (Mac).

   Your Library panel should resemble Figure 14.
5. Drag the **g_title symbol** in the Library panel to the Graphics folder.
6. Drag the other graphic symbols to the Graphics folder.
7. Drag the **b_reset symbol** to the Buttons folder, then compare your Library panel to Figure 15.
8. Click the **Graphics folder expand icon** to open it and display the graphic symbols.
9. Click the **Buttons folder expand icon** to open it and display the button symbol.
10. Click the **Graphics folder collapse icon** to close the folder.
11. Click the **Buttons folder collapse icon** to close the folder.

   Note: To remove an item from a folder, drag the item down to a blank area of the Library panel.

You created new folders, organized the symbols within the folders, and then opened and closed the folders.

Rename symbols and delete a symbol

1. Click the **expand icon** ▶ for the Graphics folder to display the symbols.

2. Right-click (Win) or [control]-click (Mac) the **g_car1 symbol**, then click **Rename**.

3. Type **g_redCar** in the Name text box, then press **[Enter]** (Win) or **[return]** (Mac).

4. Repeat Steps 2 and 3 to rename the g_car2 symbol as **g_blueCar**.

5. Study the Stage and notice there are two yellow lines, one near the top and the other at the bottom of the Stage.

6. Click **g_border** in the Library panel to select it.

7. Click the **Delete icon** 🗑 at the bottom of the Library panel.

8. Study the Stage and notice the yellow border lines are deleted.

   Your Library panel should resemble Figure 16.

TIP You can also select an item and press [Delete], or you can use the Panel options menu in the Library panel to remove an item from the library. The Undo command in the Edit menu can be used to undelete an item.

You used the Library panel to rename symbols and delete a symbol.

Figure 16 *Updated Library panel*

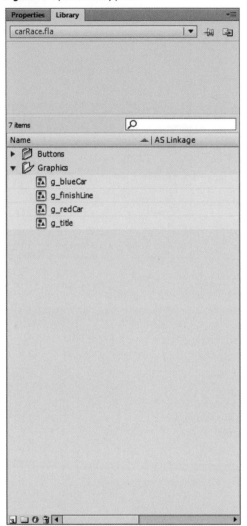

Working with Symbols and Interactivity

Figure 17 *The carRace.fla document and the coolCar.fla Library panel*

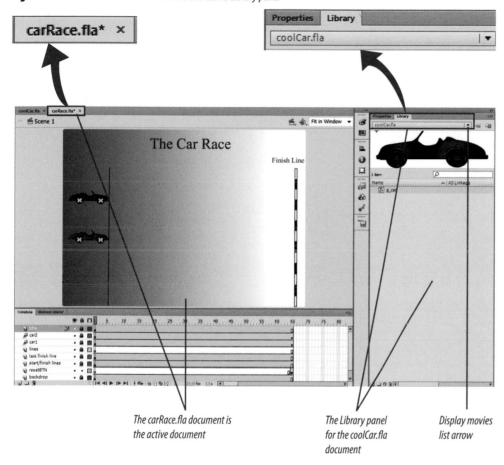

The carRace.fla document is
the active document

The Library panel
for the coolCar.fla
document

Display movies
list arrow

Use multiple Library panels

1. Click the **Display movies list arrow** near the top of the Library panel to display a list of open documents.

2. Click **coolCar.fla**, then click **g_car**.

   The Library panel for the coolCar document is displayed. However, the carRace document remains open, as shown in Figure 17.

3. Click **frame 1** on the resetBTN layer, then drag the [📷] **g_car symbol** from the Library panel to the center of the Stage.

   The reset BTN layer is the only unlocked layer. Objects cannot be placed on locked layers.

4. Click the **Display movies list arrow** to display the open documents.

5. Click **carRace.fla** to view the carRace document's Library panel.

   Notice the g_car symbol is added automatically to the Library panel of the carRace document.

6. Click the **g_car symbol** in the Library panel.

7. Click the **Delete icon** 🗑 at the bottom of the Library panel.

   You deleted the g_car symbol from the carRace library but it still exists in the coolCar library. The car was also deleted from the Stage.

8. Save your work.

9. Click the **coolCar.fla tab** at the top of the workspace to display the document.

10. Close the coolCar document and save the document if asked.

You used the Library panel to display the contents of another library and added an object from that library to the current document.

Create BUTTONS

What You'll Do

In this lesson, you will create a button, edit the four button states, and test a button.

Understanding Buttons

Button symbols are used to provide interactivity. When you click a button, an action occurs, such as starting an animation or jumping to another frame on the Timeline. Any object, including Flash drawings, text blocks, and imported graphic images, can be made into buttons. Unlike graphic symbols, buttons have four states: Up, Over, Down, and Hit. These states correspond to the use of the mouse and recognize that the user requires feedback when the mouse is pointing to a button and when the button has been clicked. This is often shown by a change in the button (such as a different color or different shape). An example of a button with different colors for the four different states is shown in Figure 18. These four states are explained in the following paragraphs.

Up—Represents how the button appears when the mouse pointer is not over it.

Over—Represents how the button appears when the mouse pointer is over it.

Down—Represents how the button appears after the user clicks the mouse.

Hit—Defines the area of the screen that will respond to the pointer. In most cases, you will want the Hit state to be the same or similar to the Up state in location and size.

When you create a button symbol, Flash automatically creates a new Timeline. The Timeline has only four frames, one for each button state. The Timeline does not play; it merely reacts to the mouse pointer by displaying the appropriate button state.

The process for creating and previewing buttons is as follows:

Create a button symbol—Draw an object or select an object that has already been created and placed on the Stage. Use the Convert to

Figure 18 *The four button states*

Up   Over   Down   Hit

Symbol command on the Modify menu to convert the object to a button symbol and to enter a name for the button.

Edit the button symbol—Select the button and choose the Edit Symbols command on the Edit menu or double-click the button symbol in the Library panel. This displays the edit window, which includes the button Timeline, shown in Figure 19. You use the button Timeline to work with the four button states. The Up state is the original button symbol. Flash automatically places it in frame 1. You need to determine how the original object will change for the other states. To change the button for the Over state, click frame 2 and insert a keyframe. This automatically places a copy of the button that is in frame 1 into frame 2. Then, alter the button's appearance for the Over state, for instance, by changing the fill color. Use the same process for the Down state. For the Hit state, you insert a keyframe in frame 4 and then specify the area on the screen that will respond to the pointer. If you do not specify a hit area, the image for the Down state is used for the hit area. You add a keyframe to the Hit frame only if you are going to specify the hit area.

Return to the main Timeline—Once you've finished editing a button, you choose the Edit Document command on the Edit menu or click Scene 1 above the edit window to return to the main Timeline.

Preview the button—By default, Flash disables buttons so that you can manipulate them on the Stage. You can preview a button by choosing the Enable Simple Buttons command on the Control menu. You can also choose the Test Movie command on the Control menu to play the movie and test the buttons.

Figure 19 *The edit window showing the button symbol and the button Timeline*

The Up state of the button symbol

Create a button

1. Insert a **new layer** above the top layer on the Timeline, then name the layer **signal**.
2. Select the **Rectangle Primitive tool** ▭, then set the **Stroke Color** to **No Stroke**.

TIP The No Stroke icon ⊘ is in the upper-right corner of the color palette.

3. Set the **Fill Color** to the **red gradient color swatch** in the bottom row of the color palette.
4. Display the Properties panel, click the **Reset button** in the RECTANGLE OPTIONS area, then set the corner radius to **5**.
5. Draw the **rectangle** shown in Figure 20.
6. Click the **Zoom tool** ⌕ on the Tools panel, then click the **rectangle** to enlarge it.
7. Select the **Gradient Transform tool** ▦ on the Tools panel.

TIP You may need to click and hold the Free Transform tool first.

8. Click the **rectangle**, then drag the **diagonal arrow** toward the center of the rectangle as shown in Figure 21 to make the red area more round.
9. Click the **Selection tool** ▶ on the Tools panel, then drag a **marquee** around the rectangle to select it.
10. Click **Modify** on the menu bar, then click **Convert to Symbol**.
11. Type **b_signal** in the Name text box, click the **Type list arrow**, click **Button**, then click **OK**.
12. Display the Library panel, then drag the **b_signal symbol** to the Buttons folder.

You created a button symbol on the Stage and dragged it to the Buttons folder in the Library panel.

Figure 20 *The rectangle object*

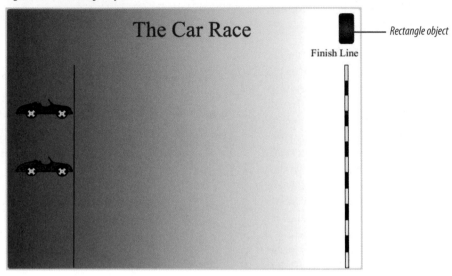

The Car Race

Rectangle object

Finish Line

Figure 21 *Adjusting the gradient*

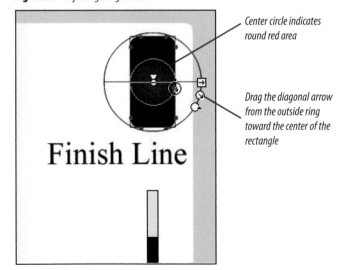

Center circle indicates round red area

Drag the diagonal arrow from the outside ring toward the center of the rectangle

Finish Line

Figure 22 *Specifying the hit area*

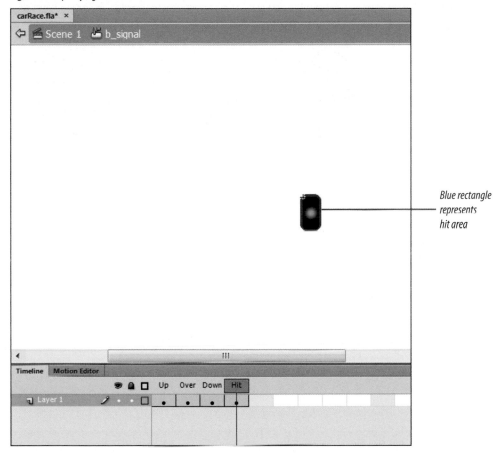

Blue rectangle
represents
hit area

Edit a button and specify a hit area

1. Open the Buttons folder, right-click (Win) or control-click (Mac) **b_signal** in the Library panel, then click **Edit**.

   Flash displays the edit window showing the Timeline with four button states.

2. Click the blank **Over frame** on Layer 1, then insert a **keyframe**.

TIP The [F6] key inserts a keyframe in the selected frame. The [fn] key may need to be used with some Mac keyboards.

3. Set the **Fill Color** to the **gray gradient color swatch** on the bottom of the color palette.

TIP If the gradient is not selected, try clicking the edge of the gradient swatch rather than the middle.

4. Insert a **keyframe** in the Down frame on Layer 1.

5. Set the **Fill Color** to the **green gradient color swatch** on the bottom of the color palette.

6. Insert a **keyframe** in the Hit frame on Layer 1.

7. Select the **Rectangle tool** on the Tools panel then set the **Fill Color** to the **blue color swatch** in the left column of the color palette.

8. Draw a **rectangle** slightly larger than the button as shown in Figure 22, then release the mouse button.

TIP The Hit area will not be visible on the Stage when you return to the main Timeline.

9. Click **Scene 1** above the edit window to return to the main Timeline.

You edited a button by changing the color of its Over and Down states, and you specified the Hit area.

Test a button

1. Click the **Selection tool** ➤ , then click a blank area of the Stage.
2. Click **Control** on the menu bar to display the Control menu, then click **Enable Simple Buttons** if it is not already checked.

   This command allows you to test buttons on the Stage without viewing the movie in the Flash Player window.

3. Point to the **signal button** on the Stage, then compare your image to Figure 23.

   The pointer changes to a hand 🖑, indicating that the object is clickable, and the button changes to a gray gradient, the color you selected for the Over state.

4. Press and hold the **mouse button**, then notice that the button changes to a green gradient, the color you selected for the Down state, as shown in Figure 24.

5. Release the mouse and notice that the button changes to a gray gradient, the color you selected for the Over state.

   (continued)

Figure 23 *The button's Over state*

Figure 24 *The button's Down state*

The Button Hit Area

All buttons have an area that responds to the mouse pointer, including rolling over the button and clicking it. This hit area is usually the same size and shape as the button itself. However, you can specify any area of the button to be the hit area. For example, you could have a button symbol that looks like a target with just the bulls-eye center being the hit area.

Figure 25 *The button's Up state*

Finish Line

6. Move the mouse away from the signal button, and notice that the button returns to a red gradient, the Up state color, as shown in Figure 25.

7. Click **Control** on the menu bar, then click **Enable Simple Buttons** to turn off the command.

8. Click the **View list arrow** above the Stage, then click **Fit in Window**, as shown in Figure 26.

   This shortcut allows you to change the magnification view without using the Magnification command on the View menu or the Zoom tool in the Tools panel.

9. Save your work.

You used the mouse to test a button and view the button states.

Figure 26 *View options from the View list*

— *View options for the Stage*

Within the figure: carRace.fla* — Scene 1 — Fit in Window / Show Frame / Show All / 25% / 50% / 100% / 200% / 400% / 800% — ace — Finish Line

Lesson 3 Create Buttons

Assign Actions
TO FRAMES AND BUTTONS

What You'll Do

In this lesson, you will use ActionScript to assign actions to frames and buttons.

Understanding Actions

In a basic movie, Flash plays the frames sequentially without stopping for user input. However, you often want to provide users with the ability to interact with the movie by allowing them to perform actions, such as starting and stopping the movie or jumping to a specific frame in the movie. One way to provide user interaction is to assign an action to the Down state of a button. Then, whenever the user clicks the button, the action occurs. Flash provides a scripting language, called ActionScript, that allows you to add actions to buttons and frames within a movie. For example, you can place a stop action in a frame that pauses the movie, and then you can assign a play action to a button that starts the movie when the user clicks the button.

Analyzing ActionScript

ActionScript, which is a powerful scripting language, allows those with even limited programming experience to create complex actions. For example, you can create order forms that capture user input or volume controls that display when sounds are played. A basic ActionScript involves an event (such as a mouse click) that causes some action to occur by triggering the script. The following is an example of a basic ActionScript:

```
on (release) {

gotoAndPlay(10);

}
```

In this example, the event is a mouse click (indicated by the word release) that causes the movie's playhead to go to frame 10 and play the frame. This is a simple example of ActionScript code and it is easy to follow. Other ActionScript code can be quite complex and may require programming expertise to understand.

ActionScript 2.0 and 3.0

Adobe has identified two types of Flash CS6 users, designers and developers. Designers focus more on the visual features of a Flash movie, including the user interface design, drawing objects, and acquiring and editing additional assets (such as graphic images). Whereas, developers focus more on the programming aspects of a Flash movie, including creation of complex animations and writing the code that specifies how the movie responds

Working with Symbols and Interactivity

to user interactions. In many cases, designers and developers work together to create sophisticated Flash applications. In other cases, designers work without the benefit of a developer's programming expertise. In order to accommodate the varying needs of these two types of users, Flash CS6 provides two versions of ActionScript, 2.0 and 3.0, called AS2 and AS3. ActionScript 3.0 is used by developers because it provides a programming environment that is more familiar to them and can be used to create movies that download more quickly. However, the differences between AS2 and AS3 are transparent to designers who do not have programming expertise. AS2 allows new Flash users to create compelling applications even if they do not have a background in programming. At the same time, AS2 provides an introduction to ActionScript that can be the basis for learning ActionScript 3.0. ActionScript 2.0 will be used in this chapter. You can specify ActionScript 2.0 when creating a new document or you can use the Flash tab in the Publish Settings dialog box, which can be opened using the Publish Settings command found on the File menu, to specify AS2.

An advantage of using AS2 is a feature called Script Assist, which provides an easy way to use ActionScript without having to learn the scripting language. The Script Assist feature within the Actions panel allows you to assign basic actions to frames and objects, such as buttons. Figure 27 shows the Actions panel displaying an ActionScript indicating that when the user clicks the selected object (a button, in this example, b_signal), the movie goes to and plays frame 2.

Figure 27 *The Actions panel displaying an ActionScript*

Event
on (release)

Action
gotoAndPlay(2)

Action assigned
to this button
symbol

Script Assist
active

The process for assigning actions to buttons, shown in Figure 28, is as follows:

1. Select the button on the Stage that you want to assign an action to.
2. Display the Actions panel, using the Window menu.
3. Click the Script Assist button to display the Script Assist panel within the ActionScript panel, and verify the button symbol and name appear in the lower-left corner of the Actions panel.
4. Click the Add a new item to the script button to display a list of Script categories and associated menus.
5. Click the appropriate category from a menu. Flash provides several categories, such as the Timeline Control category accessed via the Global Functions menu. You can use the actions available via the Timeline Control menu to start and stop movies, as well as jump to (goto) specific frames. These can be in response to user mouse movements and keystrokes.

■ Select the desired action, such as goto.
■ Specify the event that triggers the action, such as on (release). This step in the process is not shown in Figure 28.

Button actions respond to one or more mouse events, including:

Release—With the pointer inside the button Hit area, the user presses and releases (clicks) the mouse button. This is the default event.

Key Press—With the button displayed, the user presses a predetermined key on the keyboard.

Roll Over—The user moves the pointer into the button Hit area.

Drag Over—The user holds down the mouse button, moves the pointer out of the button Hit area, and then back into the Hit area.

Using Frame Actions

In addition to assigning actions to buttons, you can assign actions to frames. Actions assigned to frames are executed when the playhead reaches the frame. A common frame action is stop, which is often assigned to the first and last frame of a layer on the Timeline.

Figure 28 *The process for assigning actions to buttons*

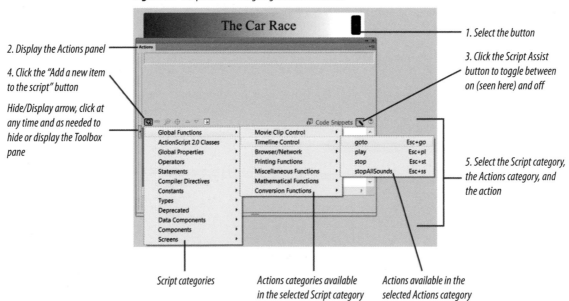

Working with Symbols and Interactivity

Understanding the Actions Panel

The Actions panel has two panes. The left pane (also called the Toolbox pane) uses folders to display the Script categories. The right pane, called the Script pane, is used with the Script Assist feature and it displays the ActionScript code as the code is being generated. When using the Script Assist feature, it is best to close the left pane. This is done by clicking the Hide/Display arrow, which is shown in Figure 28 and Figure 29. In Figure 28, the Toolbox pane is collapsed, and in Figure 29, the Toolbox pane is expanded.

The lower-left corner of the Script pane displays the symbol name or the frame to which the action(s) will apply. Always verify that the desired symbol or frame is displayed. When the Script Assist feature is turned off (not active), you can type ActionScript code directly into the Script pane.

Using Frame Labels

Buttons are often used to move the playhead to a specific location on the Timeline. For example, clicking a Start button might cause the playhead to jump from frame 1 to frame 10 to start an animation. In addition to referencing frame numbers, like 10, you can reference frame labels in the ActionScript code. Frame labels have an advantage over frame numbers, especially in large and complex applications, because adding or deleting frames will not disrupt the navigation to a frame reference you already have in actions because the label remains attached to the frame even if the frame moves. The process is to select a frame and use the Properties panel to specify a name. Then use the frame name in the ActionScript code instead of the frame number. Figure 30 shows the Timeline with a frame label and the Actions panel with the code that references the label.

Figure 29 *The Actions panel*

Toolbox pane

Hide/Display arrow for the Toolbox pane

Button that the code will be applied to

Script Assist off

Figure 30 *The Timeline with a frame label*

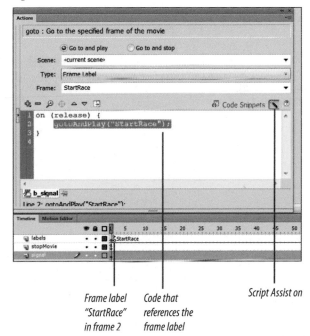

Frame label "StartRace" in frame 2

Code that references the frame label

Script Assist on

Assign a stop action to frames

1. Click **Control** on the menu bar, point to **Test Movie**, then click **in Flash Professional**.

   The movie plays and continues to loop.

2. Close the Flash Player window.

3. Insert a **new layer**, name it **stopMovie**, then click **frame 1** on the layer to select the frame.

4. Click **Window** on the menu bar, then click **Actions** to display the Actions panel.

5. Study the Actions panel. If the Toolbox pane is displayed as shown in Figure 31, then click the **Hide/Display arrow** to hide the pane.

6. Click the **Script Assist button** 🖉 to turn on the Script Assist feature if Script Assist is not active.

7. Verify stopMovie:1 (indicating the layer and frame to which the action will be applied) is displayed in the lower-left corner of the Script pane.

8. Click the **Add a new item to the script button** 🔖 to display the Script categories, point to **Global Functions**, point to **Timeline Control**, then click **stop**, as shown in Figure 32.

9. Insert a **keyframe** in frame 65 on the stopMovie layer, then open the Actions panel if it is no longer open.

TIP You can collapse the Actions panel to view more of the Stage, then expand the Actions panel when needed. Alternately, you can drag the bottom or sides of the Actions panel up to make the panel smaller.

(continued)

Figure 31 *The Actions panel Toolbox pane*

Hide/Display arrow for the Toolbox pane

Figure 32 *Assigning an action to frame 1 on the stopMovie layer*

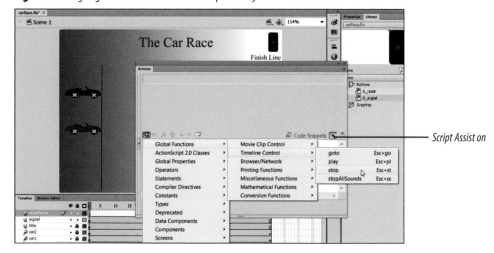

Script Assist on

Working with Symbols and Interactivity

Figure 33 *Script for the stopMovie layer*

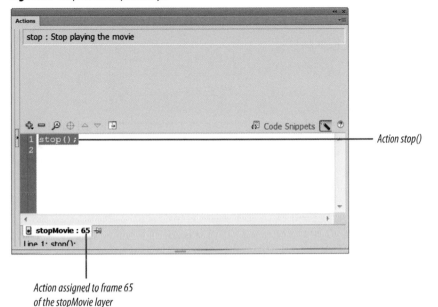

Action stop()

Action assigned to frame 65
of the stopMovie layer

Figure 34 *Assigning an event and an action to a button*

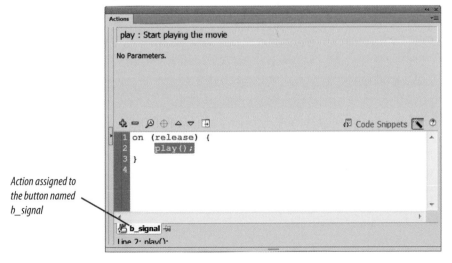

Action assigned to
the button named
b_signal

10. Verify stopMovie: 65 is displayed in the lower-left corner of the Script pane, then repeat Step 8. Compare your screen to Figure 33.

11. Test the movie.

The movie does not play because there is a stop action assigned to frame 1.

12. Close the Flash Player window.

You inserted a layer and assigned a stop action to the first and last frames on the layer.

Assign a play action to a button

1. Click **frame 1** on the signal layer.

2. Move the **Actions panel** to view the signal button on the Stage, if necessary.

3. Click the **Selection tool** ▶ on the Tools panel, then click the **button** on the Stage.

4. Verify b_signal is displayed in the lower left of the Actions panel.

This ensures that the actions specified in the Actions panel will apply to the b_signal button.

5. Click ⊕ to display the Script categories, point to **Global Functions**, point to **Timeline Control,** then click **play.**

Release is the default event for a button, as shown in Figure 34. The "play" action causes the playhead to move to the next frame. To jump to a specific frame, the "goto" action and frame number would be used.

6. Click **Control** on the menu bar, point to **Test Movie,** then click **in Flash Professional.**

7. Click the **signal button** to play the animation.

8. Close the Flash Player window.

You used the Actions panel to assign a play action to a button.

Assign a goto frame action to a button

1. Click **Control** on the menu bar, point to **Test Movie**, then click **in Flash Professional**.

2. Click the **signal button**.

   The movie plays and stops, and the word Reset, which is actually a button, appears.

3. Click the **Reset button** and notice nothing happens because it does not have an action assigned to it.

4. Close the Flash Player window.

5. Click **frame 65** on the resetBTN layer to display the Reset button on the Stage.

   Note: You many need to close and/or move the Actions panel to view the Reset button on the Stage.

6. Click the **Reset button** on the Stage to select it.

7. Verify b_reset is displayed in the lower left of the Actions panel.

8. Verify Script Assist in the Actions panel is active ![icon], click ![icon], point to **Global Functions**, point to **Timeline Control**, click **goto**, then verify Frame 1 is specified, as shown in Figure 35.

9. Click **Control** on the menu bar, point to **Test Movie**, then click **in Flash Professional**.

10. Click the **signal button** to start the movie, then when the movie stops, click the **Reset button**.

    The goto action you assigned to the Reset button causes the playhead to jump to frame 1, the beginning of the movie.

11. Close the Flash Player window.

You used the Actions panel to assign an action to a button.

Figure 35 *Assigning a goto action to a button*

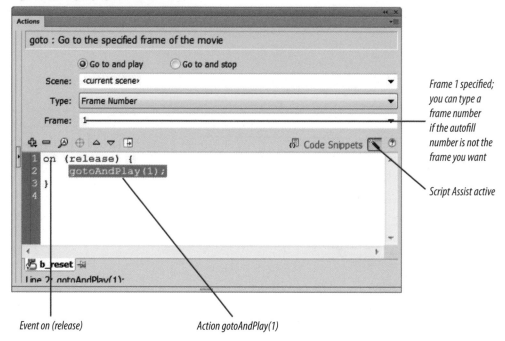

Frame 1 specified; you can type a frame number if the autofill number is not the frame you want

Script Assist active

Event on (release)

Action gotoAndPlay(1)

Global Functions: Timeline Control and Movie Clip Control

The most common actions for including interactivity in a movie when using ActionScript 2.0 are added using the Global Functions categories Timeline Control and Movie Clip Control. Timeline Control actions focus on controlling the playhead (play, stop), jumping to a specific frame (goto), and stopping sounds (stopAllSounds). These actions are generally assigned to buttons. Movie Clip Control actions focus on manipulating movie clips (startDrag, stopDrag, removeMovieClip, and so on). They also provide mouse (on Release) and keyboard (Key Press) actions that can be assigned to buttons.

Figure 36 *Assigning a keyPress action to a button*

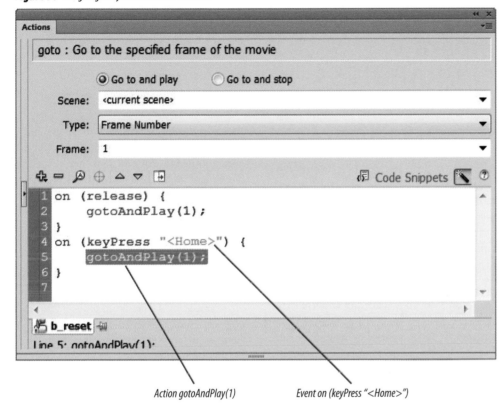

Action gotoAndPlay(1)   Event on (keyPress "<Home>")

keyPress Events

Not all keys on a keyboard can be used for keyPress events. In addition, some keys such as [Home] will only work when the movie is played in a browser and not when the movie is played in the Flash Player window. You may need to use another key such as *r* or *h* which will work in a browser or the Flash Player window. Test your movie to make sure the keyPress events work for the intended playback system.

Assign a second event to a button

1. Click the **right curly brace** (}) in the Actions panel to highlight the brace in line 3 of the ActionScript.

2. Click ⊕, point to **Global Functions**, point to **Movie Clip Control**, then click **on**.

   The Script Assist window displays several event options. Release is selected.

3. Click the **Release check box** to deselect the option.

4. Click the **Key Press check box** to select it, then press the **[Home] key** on the keyboard.

   TIP If your keyboard does not have a [Home] key, use [fn]+[←] (Mac) or a letter, such as *r*, to complete the steps.

5. Click ⊕, point to **Global Functions**, point to **Timeline Control**, then click **goto**.

   The ActionScript now indicates that pressing the [Home] key will cause the playhead to go to frame 1, as shown in Figure 36.

   The Reset button can now be activated by clicking it or by pressing the [Home] key.

6. Click **File** on the menu bar, point to **Publish Preview**, then click **Default – (HTML)**.

   The movie opens in your default browser.

   Note: If a warning message opens, follow the messages to allow blocked content.

7. Click the **signal button** to start the movie, then when the movie stops, press the **[Home] key**.

   TIP Use the key(s) you assigned to the keypress event if it is different from the Home key.

8. Close the browser window, close the Actions panel, then save and close the movie.

You added a keypress event that triggers a goto frame action.

Import GRAPHICS

What You'll Do

Photo courtesy of J. Shuman

In this lesson, you will import and work with bitmap and vector graphics.

Understanding Graphic Types

Flash provides excellent drawing tools, which allow you to create various objects that can be changed into symbols. In addition, you can import graphics and other assets, such as photographs and sounds. There are two types of graphic files, bitmap graphics and vector graphics. They are distinguished by the way in which the image is represented.

Bitmap images are made up of a group of tiny dots of color called **pixels** (picture elements). Bitmap graphics are often used with photographic images because they can represent subtle gradients in color. However, one disadvantage of bitmap graphics is the inability to enlarge the graphic without distorting the image. This is because both the computer screen's resolution (pixels per inch) and the number of pixels making up the image are a fixed number. So, when you enlarge an image each pixel must increase in size to fill the larger image dimensions. This causes the pixels to display jagged edges, as shown in Figure 37.

Vector graphics represent an image as a geometric shape made up of lines and arcs that are combined to create various shapes, such as circles and rectangles. This is similar to Flash drawings that include strokes and fills. Flash drawing tools create vector graphics. One advantage of vector graphics is that they can be resized without distorting the image. The reason is that the geometric shapes are based on mathematical models that are recalculated when the image is resized. Figure 38 shows an example of a vector graphic before and after resizing. Vector graphics are best used for drawings rather than for images requiring photographic quality.

There are several programs that allow you to create and edit graphics including Adobe Illustrator, Fireworks, and Photoshop. There are also clip art and stock photograph collections that are available online. Filename extensions identify the file type. For example, .jpg, .tif, .png, and .gif are file formats for bitmap graphics; while .ai is a vector file format.

Importing and Editing Graphics

Once you have identified the graphic you would like to include in a Flash document, you can use the Import feature to bring the graphic into Flash. The process for importing is to select the Import command from the File menu and specify where to import (Stage or Library). Then you navigate to the location where the file is stored and select it. After importing a vector graphic you can work with it as you would any graphic. Because bitmap graphics are not easy to edit in Flash, you may want to use another program, such as Photoshop, to obtain the desired size, color, and other enhancements before importing the graphic.

Figure 37 *Bitmap graphic enlarged*

Photo courtesy of J. Shuman

Figure 38 *Vector graphic enlarged*

Import graphics

1. Start a new Flash document, then save it as **sailing.fla**.

2. Click **File** on the menu bar, point to **Import**, then click **Import to Library**.

   The Preparing to import process make take a few moments.

3. Navigate to the folder where your Data Files are stored, click **islandview.jpg**, then click **Open**.

   Islandview.jpg is a digital photo that was edited in Photoshop and saved as a .jpg file.

4. Display the Library panel and notice the icon used for bitmap graphics.

5. Drag the **islandview icon** to the Stage, then lock the layer.

6. Click **File** on the menu bar, point to **Import**, then click **Import to Library**.

7. Navigate to the folder where your Data Files are stored, then click **sailboat.ai**.

   This graphic was created using Adobe Illustrator and is made up of several layers.

8. Click **Open**.

   A dialog box appears asking you to choose the layers to import. All layers are selected by default.

9. Click **OK**.

   The graphic is added to the Library panel as a symbol.

10. Add a new layer to the Timeline, click **frame 1** on the layer, then drag the **sailboat icon** to the Stage, as shown in Figure 39.

    (continued)

Figure 39 *Positioning the sailboat image on the Stage*

Photo courtesy of J. Shuman

Vector graphic of a sailboat

Bitmap graphic of a sailboat

Symbol identifies this object as a bitmap graphic

Working with Symbols and Interactivity

Figure 40 *Changing the color of the sail*
Photo courtesy of J. Shuman

Figure 41 *Rotating and skewing the sailboat image*
Photo courtesy of J. Shuman

11. Click **Modify** on the menu bar, click **Break apart**, then repeat this step until the dotted pattern that indicates the image is no longer a symbol appears.

12. Click the **Selection tool** , then click a blank area of the Pasteboard.

13. Click the **left sail**, set the **Fill color icon** to the **rainbow pattern** to change the sail color, as shown in Figure 40.

    Hint: The rainbow color is found at the bottom of the palette for the Fill Color tool.

14. Use the **Selection tool** to drag a **marquee** around the entire sailboat to select it, then convert the image to a graphic symbol named **g_rainbowSail**.

15. Display the Properties panel, verify the Lock icon is not broken, then change the width of the boat to **60**.

16. Click the **Zoom tool** on the Tools panel, click the **sailboat** twice, then scroll as needed to view each sailboat.

    Notice how the bitmap photograph becomes distorted, while the vector sailboat does not.

17. Change the view to **Fit in Window**, click the **Selection tool** , then click the **sailboat** with the rainbow sail.

18. Click the **Free Transform tool** , click the **Rotate and Skew option** , skew the sailboat to the left, verify the Lock icon is not broken, change the width to **50**, then position the sailboat as shown in Figure 41.

19. Test the movie, close the Flash Player window, then save your work and exit Flash.

You imported a bitmap and a vector graphic, and edited the vector graphic.

Create a symbol.

1. Start Flash, open fl3_3.fla, then save it as **skillsDemo3.fla**. This document consists of a single object that was created using the Flash drawing tools.
2. Use the Selection tool to drag a marquee around the ball to select it.
3. Convert the ball to a graphic symbol with the name **g_beachBall**.
4. Double-click the g_beachBall symbol on the Library panel to open the edit window, change the fill color to a rainbow gradient, add a text block that sits on top of the ball with the words **BEACH BALL** (see Figure 42), formated with white, Times New Roman, 12-pt, bold, then click Scene 1 to return to the main Timeline.
5. With the ball selected, create a motion tween animation that moves the ball from the left edge of the Stage to the right edge of the Stage.
6. Use the Selection tool to drag the middle of the motion path up to near the middle of the Stage to create an arc.
7. Select the last frame of the animation on the Timeline and set Rotate to 1 time in the Rotation area of the Properties panel.
8. Play the movie.
   The ball should move across the Stage in an arc and spin at the same time.
9. Lock the beachBall spin layer.

Create and edit an instance.

1. Insert a new layer and name it **blueBall**.
2. Click frame 1 on the blueBall layer, then drag the g_beachBall symbol from the Library panel so it is on top of the ball on the Stage.

3. Use the arrow keys as needed to align the ball so that it covers the ball on the Stage.
4. Click the Selection tool, click the ball to select it, and break apart the object.
5. Change the fill color of the ball to a blue gradient and change the text to **BLUE BALL**.
6. Insert a new layer and name it **greenBall**.
7. Click frame 12 on the greenBall layer, then insert a keyframe.
8. Drag the g_beachBall symbol from the Library panel so it is on top of the ball that is near the middle of the Stage. (*Note*: Align only the balls, not the text.)
9. With the ball selected, break apart the object and change the fill color of the ball to a green gradient and the text to **GREEN BALL**.
10. Move the beachBall spin layer to above the other layers.
11. Insert a new layer and name it **title.**
12. Click frame 1 on the title layer, create a text block at the top middle of the Stage with the words **BeachBall Spin** using Arial as the font, blue as the color, and 20-pt as the font size, then center the text block horizontally on the Stage.
13. Insert a new layer above the title layer and name it **titleBkgnd**.
14. Draw a primitive rectangle with a corner radius of 10, a medium gray fill (#999999) and no stroke that covers the BeachBall Spin title text.
15. Verify the rectangle is selected, convert it to a graphic symbol, then name it **g_Bkgnd**.
16. Move the title layer so it is above the titleBkgnd layer.
17. Play the movie, then save your work.

Work with libraries.

1. Click the New Folder button at the bottom of the Library panel to create a new folder.
2. Name the folder **Graphics**, then move the two graphic symbols to the Graphics folder.
3. Expand the Graphics folder.
4. Rename the g_Bkgnd symbol to **g_titleBkgnd** in the Library panel.
5. Save your work.

Create a button.

1. Insert a new layer above the title layer and name it **startButton**.
2. Click frame 1 of the new layer.
3. Create a text block with the word **Start** formatted with white, bold, 20-pt Arial, then center the text block horizontally near the bottom of the Stage.
4. Select the text. (*Hint*: Drag a marquee around the object.)
5. Convert the selected object to a button symbol and name it **b_start.**
6. Create a new folder named **Buttons** in the Library panel and move the b_start button symbol to the folder.
7. Open the Buttons folder, then display the edit window for the b_start button.
8. Insert a keyframe in the Over frame.
9. Select the text and change the color to a lighter shade of gray than the background rectangle.
10. Insert a keyframe in the Down frame.
11. Select the text and change the color to blue.
12. Insert a keyframe in the Hit frame.

13. Draw a rectangular object that covers the button area for the Hit state.
14. Click Scene 1 to exit the edit window and return to the main Timeline.
15. Save your work.

Test a button.

1. Click Control on the menu bar, then click Enable Simple Buttons to turn on Enable Simple Buttons.
2. Point to the button and notice the color change.
3. Click the button and notice the other color change.
4. Turn off Enable Simple Buttons.

Stop a movie by assigning an action to a frame.

1. Insert a new layer and name it **stopMovie**.
2. Insert a keyframe in frame 24 on the new layer.
3. With frame 24 selected, display the Actions panel.
4. Assign a stop action to the frame.
5. Click frame 1 on the stopMovie layer.
6. Assign a stop action to frame 1.
7. Save your work.

Assign a goto action to a button.

1. Use the Selection tool to select the Start button on the Stage.
2. Use Script Assist in the Actions panel to assign an event and a goto action to the button. (*Hint*: Refer to the section on assigning a goto action as needed.)
3. Test the movie.

Import a graphic.

1. Import BeachScene.jpg from the drive and folder where your Data Files are stored to the Library panel.
2. Insert a new layer and name the layer **backDrop**.
3. Select frame 1 on the backDrop layer, then drag the BeachScene image to the Stage.
4. Convert the BeachScene image to a graphic symbol with the name **g_beachScene**.

5. Move the backDrop layer to the bottom of the Timeline.
6. Move the graphic symbols to the Graphics folder in the Library panel.
7. Test the movie, then compare your image to Figure 42.
8. Close the Flash Player window, then save your work.
9. Exit Flash.

Figure 42 *Completed Skills Review*

The Ultimate Tours travel company has asked you to design a sample navigation scheme for its application. The company wants to see how its opening screen will link with one of its main categories (Treks). Figure 43 shows a sample opening screen and Treks screen. Using the figures or the opening screen you created in Chapter 2 as a guide, you will add a Treks screen and link it to the opening screen (*Hint*: Assume that all of the drawings on the opening screen are on frame 1, unless noted.)

1. Open ultimateTours2.fla (the file you created in Chapter 2 Project Builder 1), then save it as **ultimateTours3.fla**. (*Note*: If you create a new file, you must create an ActionScript 2.0 file. You can check the ActionScript version by selecting Publish Settings from the File menu and clicking the Flash tab.)
2. Insert a layer above the subheading layer and name it **logo**.
3. Import the UTLogo.png file from the drive and folder where your Data Files are stored to the Library panel.
4. Select frame 1 on the logo layer, then drag the logo image to the lower-right corner of the Stage.
5. Select the logo and convert it to a graphic symbol with the name **g_UTLogo**.
6. Set the last frame of the movie by inserting a keyframe on a frame on the Logo layer at least five frames farther along the Timeline, then lock the logo layer. (*Note*: You see the logo because the keyframe you inserted on the last frame of the movie ensures everything on this layer appears on this last frame.)
7. Select the layer that the Ultimate Tours text block is on, then insert a keyframe on the last frame of the movie. (*Hint*: This should be the same frame number as the frame you set as the last frame of the movie in Step 6. *Note*: You see the logo and the heading Ultimate Tours because the keyframe you inserted on the last frame of the movie ensures everything on this layer appears on this last frame.)
8. Insert a new layer, name it **treks headings**, insert a keyframe on the last frame of the movie, then create the Treks screen shown in Figure 43, except for the home button.
9. Convert the Treks graphic on the opening screen to a button symbol named **b_treks**, then edit the symbol so that different colors appear for the different states and be sure to set a hit area.
10. Assign a goto action to the Treks button that jumps the playhead to the Treks screen when the Treks button is clicked. (*Hint*: You can jump to the Treks screen by typing the frame number for the screen in the Actions panel. See Figure 35.)
11. Insert a new layer and name it **stopMovie**. Add stop actions that cause the movie to stop after displaying the opening screen and after displaying the Treks screen. Make sure there is a keyframe in the last frame of the stopMovie layer.
12. Insert a new layer and name it **homeButton**, insert a keyframe on the last frame of the movie, then draw the home button image with the Home text.
13. Convert the image to a button symbol named **b_home**, then edit the symbol so that different colors appear for the different states. Assign a goto action for the Home button that jumps the movie to frame 1.
14. Test the movie.
15. Save your work, then compare your screens to the samples shown in Figure 43.

Figure 43 *Sample completed Project Builder 1*

Opening screen

Convert to a button symbol

Treks screen

Convert to a button symbol

You have been asked to assist the International Student Association (ISA). The association sponsors a series of monthly events, each focusing on a different culture from around the world. The events are led by a guest speaker who makes a presentation, followed by a discussion. The events are free and they are open to everyone. ISA would like you to design a Flash movie that will be used with its website and on its mobile app. The movie starts by providing information about the series, and then provides links to the upcoming event and to a schedule. Refer to Figure 44 as you create the Flash movie. Depending on the font you choose, your screen may not appear exactly the same as Figure 44. (*Hint*: Keep the following in mind as you complete this project:

- Insert a blank keyframe in a frame on a layer when you do not want the text or objects from the previous frame to appear in the frame where you are inserting a blank keyframe.
- Use the align panel and the rulers to help place objects, such as the buttons on the page, in the same location from screen to screen. If copying an object you can use the Paste in Place command to have the object copied to the exact location it was selected from.
- Remember to break apart a button to change its name, then select the object and convert the updated object to a new button with a new name.)

1. Open a new Flash ActionScript 2.0 document and save it as **isa3.fla**.
2. Change the Stage size to width: 320 and height: 480. (*Note*: There will be three screens with each screen being on a separate frame. Frame 1 will display the opening screen; frame 2 will display the Next Event screen; and frame 3 will display the Schedule screen.)
3. Draw a border that surrounds the stage. (*Hint*: Use the rectangle tool, select the "no color" ☑ color swatch in the color palette, then use the stroke color of your choice. Set the border stroke to at least 2.)
4. On another layer create the heading and subheading (top two lines) that will appear on all three screens. Be sure to add a keyframe in the last frame on this layer of the movie so that the heading and subheading appear on every frame of the movie. (*Note*: The last frame will be frame 3.)
5. On another layer add the text to the opening screen in frame 1. (*Hint:* After adding the text in frame 1, be sure to insert a blank keyframe in frame 2 of the new layer. To add a blank keyframe, select the desired frame, click Insert on the menu, point to Timeline, and then click Blank Keyframe. You add a blank keyframe in frame 2 so that the text you added in frame 1 will not appear in frame 2.)
6. Create the Next Event screen in frame 2 by adding a layer and entering the title (Next Event) and the text for the screen. (*Hint*: Be sure to insert a keyframe in frame 2 of the new layer and a blank keyframe in frame 3 of that same layer.)
7. Create the Schedule screen in frame 3 by adding a layer and entering the title (Schedule) and the text

for the screen. (*Hint*: Be sure to insert a keyframe in frame 3 of the new layer.)
8. Insert a layer and create a Next Event button with the name **b_nextEvent** on the opening screen that jumps the movie to the Next Event screen. Create a Schedule button with the name **b_schedule** on another layer that jumps the movie to the Schedule screen. For each button you create, specify different colors for each state of the button.
9. Insert another layer and on the Next Event screen, create a Home button with the name **b_home**, that jumps the movie back to the opening screen. Be sure to specify different colors for each state when you create the Home button.
10. Copy an instance of the Home button you created in Step 6 to the Schedule screen. (*Hint*: You can select the button with the Selection tool, select Copy from the Edit menu, display the Schedule screen and select Copy in Place from the Edit menu.)
11. On the Next Event screen, copy an instance of the Schedule button you created in Step 5 that jumps the movie to the Schedule screen.
12. On the Schedule screen, copy an instance of the Next Event button you created in Step 5 that jumps the movie to the Next Event screen.
13. Insert a layer and add an action to each frame on that layer that stops the movie on that frame.
14. Rename all of the layers using appropriate names.
15. Test the movie.
16. Save your work, then compare your movie to the sample shown in Figure 44.

Figure 44 *Sample completed Project Builder 2*

Sample general
information screen

Sample next
event screen

Sample series screen

Figure 45 shows the home page of a website. Study the figure and complete the following questions. For each question, indicate how you determined your answer.

1. Connect to the Internet and go to *www.zoo.org*. Notice that this website has images that change as you visit the website.
2. Open a document in a word processor or open a new Flash document, save the file as **dpc3**, then answer the following questions. (*Hint*: Use the Text tool in Flash.)
   - Whose website is this?
   - What is the goal(s) of the site?
   - Who is the target audience?
   - What treatment ("look and feel") is used?
   - What are the design layout guidelines being used (balance, movement, and so on)?
   - What may be animated on this home page?
   - Do you think this is an effective design for the company, its products, and its target audience? Why or why not?
   - What suggestions would you make to improve the design, and why?

Figure 45 *Design Project*
Courtesy of zoo.org. www.zoo.org

This is a continuation of the Chapter 2 Portfolio Project, which is the development of a personal portfolio. In this project, you will create a button that will be used to link the opening screen of your portfolio to the animations page. Next, you will create another button to start the animation.

1. Open portfolio2.fla (the file you created in Portfolio Project, Chapter 2), then save it as **portfolio3.fla**.
2. Unlock the layers as needed.
3. Insert a new layer, name it **sampleAnimations**, then insert a keyframe in frame 2.
4. On this new layer, create a Sample Animations screen that has a text block with an oval background and the words **Sample Animations** at the top of the Stage, then add another text block and oval background with the word **Tweened**. *(Note:* This screen will have several animation samples added to it later.)
5. Insert a new layer, name it **home button**, then insert a keyframe in frame 2.
6. Add a text block that says **Home** and has an oval background at the bottom of the Stage.
7. Insert a new layer, name it **tweenedAnimation**, then insert a keyframe in frame 3.
8. Create an animation(s) of your choice using objects you draw or import, or objects from the Library panel of another document. *(Note:* To create a motion tween animation when starting in a frame other than frame 1, you need to specify the beginning frame of the animation by inserting a keyframe in

the starting frame, placing or drawing the object on the Stage, selecting the object and converting it into a graphic symbol, inserting a motion tween, inserting a keyframe in the ending frame of the animation, and repositioning the object. *(Hint:* To create more than one animation that plays at the same time, put each animation on its own layer, such as tweenedAnimationRedCar and tweenedAnimationBlueCar.)

9. Insert a new layer, name it **animationHeading**, insert a keyframe in frame 3, then add a heading, such as Passing Cars in the sample in Figure 46, that describes the animation(s).
10. On the Sample Animations screen, convert the Tweened and Home text blocks into button symbols, then edit each symbol so that different colors appear for the different states. For the Tweened button, assign an action that jumps to the frame that plays an animation. For the Home button, assign an

action to the Home button that jumps to the frame that displays My Portfolio. *(Hint:* You need to use ActionScript 2.0.)
11. Change the Animations graphic on the home page to a button, then edit the symbol so that different colors appear for the different states. Assign an action to the Animations button that jumps to the Sample Animations screen.
12. Insert a new layer, then name it **stopMovie**. Insert keyframes and assign stop actions to the appropriate frames.
13. Insert a new layer at the bottom of the layers pane and name it **backdrop**. Insert a keyframe in frame 3 on the backdrop layer. This is the same frame where the tween animation begins. Add a color background to the animation screen.
14. Test the movie.
15. Save your work, then compare your movie to the sample shown in Figure 46.

Figure 46 *Sample completed Portfolio Project*

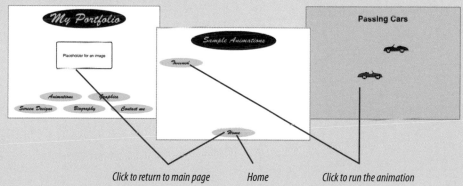

Click to return to main page   Home   Click to run the animation

CHAPTER 4 CREATING
ANIMATIONS

1. Create motion tween animations

2. Create classic tween animations

3. Create frame-by frame animations

4. Create shape tween animations

5. Create movie clips

6. Animate text

CHAPTER 4

CREATING ANIMATIONS

Introduction

Animation can be an important part of your application or website, whether the focus is on entertainment (provides interactive games), e-commerce (attracts attention and provides product demonstrations), or education (simulates complex processes such as DNA replication).

How Does Animation Work?

The perception of motion in an animation is actually an illusion. Animation is like a motion picture in that it is made up of a series of still images. Research has found that our eye captures and holds an image for one-tenth of a second before processing another image. By retaining each impression for one-tenth of a second, we perceive a series of rapidly displayed still images as a single, moving image. This phenomenon is known as **persistence of vision** and it provides the basis for the frame rate in animations. Frame rates of 10–12 frames-per-second (fps) generally provide an acceptably smooth computer-based animation. Lower frame rates result in a jerky image, while frame rates

over 30 fps may result in a blurred image. In addition, higher frame rates may increase file size because more frames are needed for a 5 second animation running at 30 fps than at 10 fps. After creating an animation you can experiment with various frame rates to obtain the desired effect. Flash uses a default frame rate of 24 fps.

Flash Animation

Creating animation is one of the most powerful features of Flash, yet developing basic animations is a simple process. Flash allows you to create animations that can move and rotate an object around the Stage, as well as change its size, shape, or color. You can also use the animation features in Flash to create special effects, such as an object zooming or fading in and out. You can combine animation effects so that an object changes shape and color as it moves across the Stage. Animations are created by changing the content of successive frames. Flash provides two animation methods: frame-by-frame animation and tweened animation. Tweened animations can be motion, classic, or shape tweens.

TOOLS YOU'LL USE

Create Motion Tween
ANIMATIONS

What You'll Do

 In this lesson, you will create and edit motion tween animations.

Understanding Motion Tween Animations

An animation implies some sort of movement in an object. However, the concept of animation is much broader. Objects have specific properties such as position, size, color, and shape. Any change in a property of an object over time (i.e., across frames on the Timeline) can be considered an animation. So, having an object start at the left of the screen in frame 1 and then having it move across the screen and end up at the right side in frame 10 would be a change in the position property of the object. Each of the in-between frames (2-9) would show the position of the object as it moves across the screen. In a motion tween animation, you specify the position of the object in the beginning and ending frames and Flash fills in the in-between frames, a process known as **tweening**. Fortunately, you can change several properties with one motion tween. For example, you could have

a car move across the screen and, at the same time, you could have the size of the car change to give the impression of the car moving away from the viewer.

The process for creating a motion tween animation is to select the frame and layer where the animation will start. If necessary, insert a keyframe (by default, frame 1 of each layer has a keyframe). Select the object on the Stage, then select the Motion Tween command from the Insert menu. If the object is not already a symbol, you will be asked if you want to convert it to a symbol. You must convert the object to a symbol if prompted because only symbols and text fields can have a motion tween applied. Then you select the ending frame and make any changes to the object, such as moving it to another location or resizing it. After you make the change, a keyframe automatically appears in the ending frame you selected. When you create a motion tween, a tween span appears on the Timeline.

Tween Spans

Figure 1 shows a motion tween animation of a car that starts in frame 1 and ends in frame 24. The Onion Skin feature is enabled so that outlines of the car are displayed for each frame of the animation in the figure. The Onion Skin feature is useful when developing an animation, but it is not how the completed animation will appear. Figure 1 shows the button that turns the Onion Skin feature on and off.

After turning the feature on, the numbers of the frames that will be affected are highlighted on the Timeline. You can change which frames display as outlines by dragging either end of the highlight. Notice a blue highlight appears on the Timeline for the frames of the animation. The blue highlighted area is called the tween or motion span. The length of the motion tween is determined by the last frame in the movie or by other keyframes on the layer. (*Note:*

The default tween span when starting from frame 1 of a new movie is determined by the number of frames in one second of the movie. So, if the frame rate is 24 frames per second, then the span is 24 frames.) You can increase or decrease the number of frames in the span by dragging the end of the span. In addition, you can move the span to a different location on the Timeline, and you can copy the span to have it apply to another object.

Figure 1 *Sample motion tween animation*

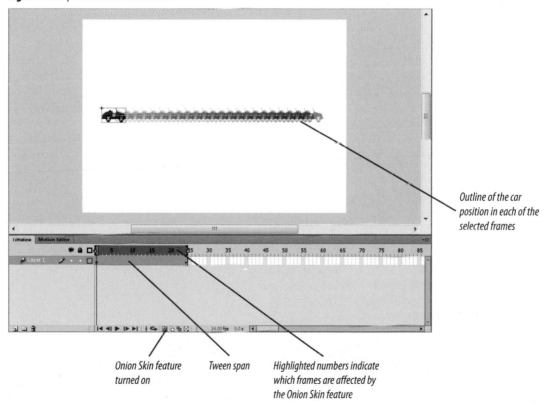

Outline of the car position in each of the selected frames

Onion Skin feature turned on

Tween span

Highlighted numbers indicate which frames are affected by the Onion Skin feature

Motion Path

The animation shown in Figure 2 includes a position change (from frame 1 to frame 24); a motion path showing the position change is displayed on the Stage. Each dot on the path corresponds to a frame on the Timeline and indicates the location of the object (in this example, the car) when the frame is played. A motion path can be altered by dragging a point on the path using the Selection tool or by using the Subselection tool to manipulate Bezier handles as shown in Figure 3. Bezier curves employ a mathematical method for drawing curves. The shape of a Bezier curve can be altered by moving the handles attached to the end points of the curve.

In addition, an entire path can be moved around the Stage and reshaped using the Free Transform tool.

Property Keyframes

A keyframe indicates a change in a Flash movie, such as the start or ending of an animation. Motion tween animations use property keyframes that are specific to each property such as a position keyframe, color keyframe, or rotation keyframe. In most cases these are automatically placed on the Timeline as the motion tween animation is created.

Keep in mind:

- Only one object on the Stage can be animated in each tween span.

- You can have multiple motion tween animations playing at the same time if they are on different layers.
- A motion tween is, in essence, an object animation because, while several changes can be made to an object's properties, only one object is animated for each motion tween.
- The types of objects that can be tweened include graphic, button, and movie clip symbols, as well as text fields.
- You can remove a motion tween animation by clicking the tween span on the Timeline and choosing Remove Tween from the Insert menu.

Figure 3 *Bezier handles used to alter the path*

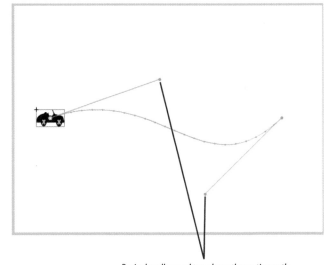

Bezier handles used to reshape the motion path

Figure 2 *The motion path*

The transformation point determines an object's placement along the path

Motion path with dots; each dot corresponds to a frame on the Timeline and shows the location of the car when the frame is played

Creating Animations

Figure 4 *Positioning the car object*

Figure 5 *Changing the end of the tween span*

Drag pointer to here

Create a motion tween animation

1. Open fl4_1.fla from the drive and folder where your Data Files are stored, then save it as **motionTw.fla**.

    This document has one drawn object—a car that has been converted to a symbol.

2. Click the **Selection tool** on the Tools panel, then click the **car** to select it.

3. Click **Insert** on the menu bar, then click **Motion Tween**.

    Notice the tween span appears on the Timeline. Because you started in frame 1, the number of frames in the span equals the frames per second for the movie.

4. Verify the playhead is on the last frame of the tween span, then drag the **car** to the right side of the Stage, as shown in Figure 4.

    A motion path appears on the Stage with dots indicating the position of the object for each frame. A diamond symbol appears in frame 24, which is the end of the tween span. The diamond symbol is a position keyframe and it is automatically inserted at the end of the tween path.

    Note: The end of this tween span is determined by the document frame rate, which is 24 fps. To see the diamond symbol more clearly, move the playhead.

5. Point to the end of the tween span, when the pointer changes to a double arrow ←→, drag the **tween span** to frame 40, as shown in Figure 5.

    (continued)

6. Click on the Timeline, then press the **period key** to move the playhead one frame at a time and notice the position of the car for each frame.

7. Play the movie.

8. Test the movie, then close the Flash Player window.

9. Save your work.

You created a motion tween animation, extended the length of the animation, and viewed the position of the animated object in each frame of the animation.

Edit a motion path

1. Click the **Selection tool** ▶ on the Tools panel, then click a blank area of the Stage.

2. Click **frame 1** on Layer 1.

3. Point to the middle of the motion path, as shown in Figure 6.

4. When the pointer changes to a pointer with an arc ▶⌣, drag the ▶⌣ **pointer** down, as shown in Figure 7.

(continued)

Figure 6 *Pointing to the middle of the path*

Figure 7 *Dragging the motion path down*

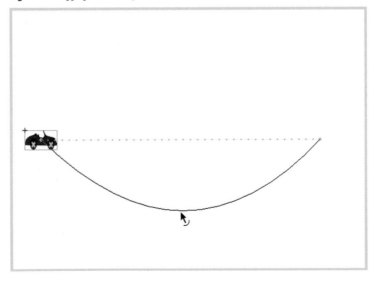

z

Figure 8 *Displaying the Bezier handles*

Point here

Figure 9 *Using the Bezier handles to alter the shape of the path*

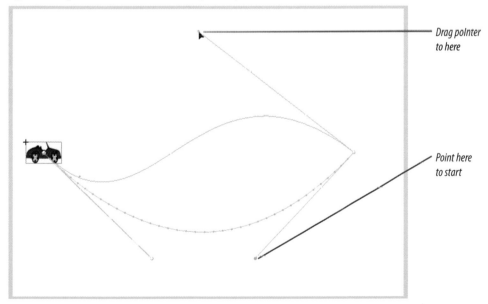

Drag pointer
to here

Point here
to start

5. Play the movie.

   Notice the car is not oriented to the path. That is, the front of the car does not align with the path. Later in this lesson you will learn to orient an object to a curved path.

6. Click **frame 1** on Layer 1.

7. Click the **Subselection tool** ⌕ on the Tools panel, point to the end of the motion path, then, when the pointer changes into an arrow with a small square ⌕ ₒ, click the end of path to display Bezier handles, as shown in Figure 8.

8. Point to the **lower-right handle**, then when the pointer changes to a delta symbol ►, drag the **handle** up and toward the center of the Stage to form a horizontal S shape, as shown in Figure 9.

9. Click the **Selection tool** ► on the Tools panel, then click a blank area of the Stage.

10. Play the movie, then save your work.

You edited a motion path by using the Selection tool to drag the path and by using the Subselection tool to display and reposition Bezier handles.

Change the ease value of an animation

1. Play the movie and notice that the car moves at a constant speed.

2. Click **frame 1** on Layer 1, then display the Properties panel.

3. Point to the **Ease value**, when the pointer changes to a hand with a double arrow 👆⇄, drag the 👆⇄ **pointer** to the right to set the value at **100**, as shown in Figure 10.

4. Play the movie.

    The car starts out moving fast and slows down near the end of the animation. Notice the word "out" is displayed next to the ease value on the Properties panel indicating that the object will ease out, that is slow down, at the end of the animation.

5. Click **frame 1** on Layer 1.

6. Point to the Ease value on the Properties panel, then drag the 👆⇄ **pointer** to the left to set the value to **−100**.

7. Play the movie.

    The car starts out moving slowly and speeds up near the end of the animation. Notice the word "in" is displayed next to the ease value on the Properties panel. Also, notice the dots are grouped closer together at the beginning of the motion path indicating that the object does not move very far in that section of the path.

8. Click **frame 1** on Layer 1, then set the ease value to **0**.

9. Save your work.

You changed the ease out and ease in values of the animation.

Figure 10 *Changing the ease value*

Drag the pointer to the right

Figure 11 *Changing the width of the object*

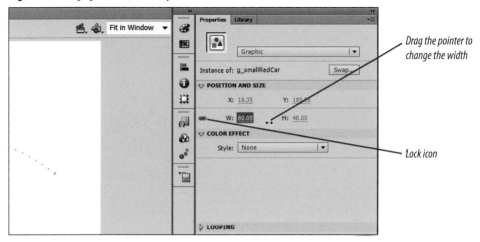

Drag the pointer to change the width

Lock icon

Figure 12 *Using the Free Transform tool to skew the object*

Point to the middle handle and drag the pointer to the right

Resize and reshape an object

1. Verify frame 1 is selected, click the **Selection tool** , then click the **car**.

2. Display the Properties panel, verify the lock icon is not broken, point to the **W: value**, then, when the pointer changes to a hand with a double arrow , drag the **pointer** to the right to set the value to **80**, as shown in Figure 11.

   The car in frame 1 is now wider and taller.

3. Play the movie.

4. Click **frame 40** on Layer 1, then click the **car**.

5. Point to the **W: value** on the Properties panel, then drag the **pointer** to the left to set the value to **30**.

   The car in frame 40 is now less wide and tall.

6. Play the movie.

   The car starts out large and ends up small.

7. Click **frame 20** on Layer 1.

8. Click the **Free Transform tool** on the Tools panel, then click the **Rotate and Skew option** if it is not active.

9. Point to the **top middle handle**, then, when the pointer changes to a double line , drag the **pointer** to the right to skew the object, as shown in Figure 12.

   A keyframe indicating a change in the property (skew) of the object appears in frame 20.

10. Play the movie, use the Undo command on the Edit menu to undo the skew, then save the movie.

    Note: You may have to click the Undo command more than one time to undo the skew.

    The skew keyframe is removed from frame 20.

You resized and skewed a motion tween object.

Create a color effect

1. Click the **Selection tool** ↖ on the Tools panel.

2. Click **frame 40** on Layer 1.

3. Click the **car** to select it.

4. Click **COLOR EFFECT** to display that area if it is not open, then click the **Style list arrow** in the COLOR EFFECT area of the Properties panel.

5. Click **Alpha**, then drag the **slider**△ to set the value to **0%**, as shown in Figure 13.

6. Play the movie.

   Notice the car slowly becomes transparent.

7. Click frame 40 on Layer 1, click the object to select it, then reset the Alpha to **100%**.

TIP Click just inside the bounding box if you have trouble selecting the object.

8. Click **frame 40** on Layer 1.

9. Click the **car** to select it.

10. Click the **Style list arrow** in the COLOR EFFECT area of the Properties panel.

11. Click **Advanced**, then set the x R + value for Red to **100**, as shown in Figure 14.

12. Play the movie.

    Notice the car slowly changes to a new shade of red. Because the car is a symbol, it is one part (not a composite of pieces). As a result, changes made to the color value affect the entire car.

13. Set the x R + value back to **0**, then save your work.

You changed the alpha and advanced color option for an object.

Figure 13 *Setting the Alpha (transparency) value*

Click to collapse or expand the COLOR EFFECT area   Drag the slider to the left   Alpha set to 0

Figure 14 *Changing a color value for the object*

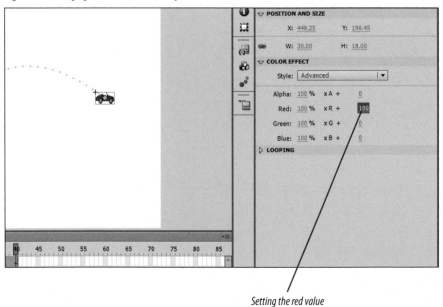

Setting the red value

Figure 15 *Aligning the car to the path*

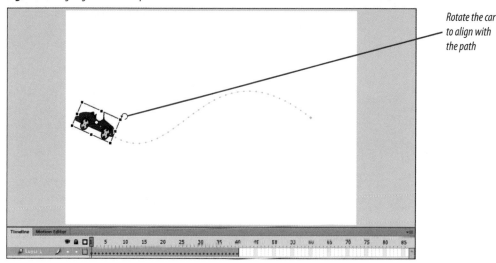

Rotate the car to align with the path

Figure 16 *Aligning the car to the end of the motion path*

Orient an object to a path

1. Play the movie.

   Notice the car follows the path but it is not oriented to the path.

2. Click **frame 1** on Layer 1.

3. Click the **Orient to path check box** in the ROTATION area of the Properties panel.

4. Click the **Free Transform tool** on the Tools panel, then click the **Rotate and Skew option** in the Options area of the Tools panel if it is not active.

5. Point to the upper-right corner of the car, then, when the pointer changes into a circular arrow, rotate the front of the car so that it aligns with the path, as shown in Figure 15.

6. Click **frame 40** on Layer 1, then rotate the back end of the car so that its back end aligns with the path, as shown in Figure 16.

7. Play the movie.

   The car is oriented to the path.

   Notice the diamond symbols in the frames on Layer 1. These are rotation keyframes that indicate the object will change in each frame as it rotates to stay oriented to the path.

8. Test the movie, then close the Flash Player window.

9. Save your work, then close the document.

You oriented an object to a motion path and aligned the object with the path in the first and last frames of the motion tween.

Copy a motion path

1. Open fl4_2.fla, save it at **tweenEdits.fla**, then play the movie.

   This movie has a motion tween that animates from frame 1 to frame 40. Notice the rotation keyframes on the biker layer.

2. Insert a **new layer** at the top of the Timeline, then name it **biker2**.

   Notice the last frame of the new layer is the same (50) as the last frame of the movie.

3. Click **frame 1** on the biker2 layer.

4. Click the **Selection tool** on the Tools panel, then display the Library panel.

5. Click the **g_biker symbol** in the Library panel to display the image in the Preview window.

6. Drag the **g_biker symbol** from the Library panel to the Stage, as shown in Figure 17.

   This creates a new instance of the g_biker symbol.

7. Click any frame on the tween span on the biker layer, then click the **original biker** on the Stage.

   The motion tween is selected as indicated by the blue highlight on the biker layer.

8. Click **Edit** on the menu bar, point to **Timeline**, then click **Copy Motion**.

9. Click the **new instance** of the biker, click **Edit** on the menu bar, point to **Timeline**, then click **Paste Motion**.

10. Play the movie.

11. Hide the biker layer.

12. Click **frame 1** on the biker2 layer, click the **Free Transform tool** on the Tools panel, then click the path to select it, as shown in Figure 18.

(continued)

Figure 17 *Dragging the biker symbol to the Stage*

Preview window

Drag g_biker symbol from the Library panel and position it on the Stage

Figure 18 *Selecting the path to display the handles*

Click the path to select it

Eight handles used to alter the path appear when the path is selected

Figure 19 *Positioning the path*

Figure 20 *Aligning the biker to the path*

13. Click **Modify** on the menu bar, point to **Transform**, then click **Flip Horizontal**.

14. Play the movie.

    The direction of the biker on the path is reversed, but the direction the biker faces is not reversed.

15. Click **frame 1** on the biker2 layer.

16. Click the **path** to select it.

17. Use the arrow keys on the keyboard to position the path, as shown on Figure 19.

18. Click the **biker object** to select it.

19. Click **Modify** on the menu bar, point to **Transform**, then click **Flip Horizontal**.

20. Use the Free Transform tool ⬚ and the arrow keys to align the biker, as shown in Figure 20.

21. Play the movie.

22. Save your work.

You copied a motion path to another object, adjusted the position of the path and oriented the object to the path.

Rotate an object

1. Click **frame 1** on the biker2 layer, then display the Properties panel.

2. Point to the **Rotate times value** in the ROTATION area of the Properties panel, then, when the pointer changes to a hand with a double arrow ⊕, drag the ⊕ **pointer** to the right to set the count to **1**, as shown in Figure 21.

3. Click the **Direction list arrow**, click **CW** (Clockwise), click **frame 1** on the biker2 layer, then play the movie.

   The biker object rotates one time in a clockwise direction. Look at the Timeline. Notice the rotation keyframes have been removed from the motion tween span. This is because, as the biker rotates, he is no longer oriented to the path. Motion tweens do not allow an object to be rotated and oriented to a path simultaneously because orienting an object to a path rotates the object in each frame along the path. You can use a classic tween to rotate and orient an object to a path at the same time. The remaining keyframes at the beginning and ending of the tween span are used to align the biker to the ramp.

4. Click **frame 1** on the biker2 layer, set the rotation count to **2**, set the Direction to **CCW** (Counter Clockwise), then play the movie.

5. Click **Orient to path** to select it.

   The rotate value is automatically set to no times (indicated by a 0), as shown in Figure 22.

6. Play the movie, then save your work.

You caused an object to rotate by setting the rotate value and specifying a rotation direction.

Figure 21 *Changing the rotate value*

Drag the pointer to change the rotate value

Direction list arrow

Figure 22 *The Properties panel showing that the rotate value is set to 0 times*

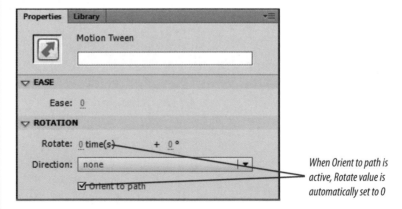

When Orient to path is active, Rotate value is automatically set to 0

Figure 23 *Timeline showing the motion tween removed*

Removal of motion tween in the biker2 layer removes the blue highlight on the Timeline

Remove a motion tween

1. Unhide the **biker layer**, then play the movie.
2. Double-click **frame 1** on the biker2 layer to select the tween span on the Timeline.

   Note: You can double-click any frame on the tween span to select it.
3. Click **Insert** on the menu bar, then click **Remove Tween**.
4. Click **frame 1** on the ramps and buses layer, then notice that the blue highlight on the biker2 layer is gone, as shown in Figure 23.
5. Play the movie and notice that the biker on the biker2 layer is visible but it does not move.
6. Use the Undo command in the Edit menu to undo the Remove Tween process.

   Note: You may need to select the Undo command more than one time.
7. Click **biker2** on the Timeline to select the layer.
8. Click the **Delete icon** 🗑 on the Timeline status bar to delete the biker2 layer that includes the motion tween.
9. Test the movie, then close the Flash Player window.
10. Save your work.

You removed an object's motion tween, undid the action, then deleted a layer containing a motion tween.

Work with multiple motion tweens

1. Click frame **40** on the biker layer, then click the **biker** on the Stage.

2. Lock the **biker layer**, then insert a **new layer** above the biker layer and name it **bikeOffStage**.

3. Click frame **40** on the bikeOffStage layer.

4. Click **Insert** on the menu bar, point to **Timeline**, then click **Keyframe**.

5. Display the Library panel.

6. Drag an instance of the **g_biker symbol** from the Library panel so it is on top of the biker on the Stage, as shown in Figure 24.

7. Verify the **Free Transform tool** is selected, then click the **Rotate and Skew option** in the Options area of the Tools panel.

8. Rotate the object to orient it to the other biker, then use the arrow keys on the keyboard to align the two biker objects.

9. Click frame **41** on the **bikeOffStage** layer, then insert a **keyframe**.

10. Use the **arrow keys** on the keyboard and the **Free Transform tool** to align the biker with the bottom of the ramp, as shown in Figure 25.

(continued)

Figure 24 *Placing an instance of the g_biker symbol on top of the object on the Stage*

Figure 25 *Aligning the biker with the ramp*

Creating Animations

Figure 26 *Dragging the biker object off the Stage*

Drag the object off the Stage

11. Click the **Selection tool** ▶, then click the **biker**.

12. Use the Magnification options on the View menu to display the entire Stage and part of the Pasteboard.

13. Click **Insert** on the menu bar, then click **Motion Tween**.

14. Click **frame 45** on the bikeOffStage layer, then drag the **biker** off the Stage, as shown in Figure 26.

15. Test the movie, close the Flash Player window, save your work, then close the document.

You created a second motion tween for the movie.

Create Classic Tween
ANIMATIONS

What You'll Do

In this lesson, you will create a motion guide and attach an animation to it.

Understanding Classic Tweens

Classic tweens are similar to motion tweens in that you can create animations that change the properties of an object over time. Motion tweens are easier to use and allow the greatest degree of control over tweened animations. Classic tweens are a bit more complex to create, however, they provide certain capabilities that some developers desire. For example, with a motion tween (which consists of one object over the tween span), you can alter the ease value so that an object starts out fast and ends slow. But, with a classic tween, you can alter the ease value so that an object starts out fast, slows down, and then speeds up again. The process for creating a classic tween animation that moves an object is to select the starting frame and, if necessary, insert a keyframe. Next, insert a keyframe at the ending frame. The two keyframes and all the frames between them will be used for the animation. Next, click any frame on the layer between the keyframes. Then select classic tween from the Insert menu, select the ending frame, and move the object to the position you want it to be in the ending frame.

Understanding Motion Guides

When you use motion tweening to generate an animation that moves an object, a motion path that shows the movement is automatically created on the Stage. When you use classic tweening, the object moves in a straight line from the beginning location to the ending location on the Stage. There is no path displayed. You can draw a path, called a **motion guide**, that can be used to alter the path of a classic tween animation, as shown in Figure 27. A motion guide is drawn on the motion guide layer with the classic tween animation placed on its own layer beneath a motion guide layer, as shown in Figure 28. The process for creating a motion guide and attaching a classic tween animation to it is:

■ Create a classic tween animation.
■ Insert a new layer above the classic tween animation layer and change the layer properties to a Guide layer. Drag the classic tween animation layer to the guide layer so that it indents, as shown in Figure 28. This indicates that the classic tween animation layer is associated with the motion guide layer.

- Click the Guide layer and draw a path using the Pen, Pencil, Line, Circle, Rectangle, or Brush tools.
- Attach the object to the path by clicking the first keyframe of the layer that contains the animation, and then dragging the object by its transformation point to the beginning of the path. Click the end keyframe and then repeat the steps to attach the object to the end of the path.

Depending on the type of object you are animating and the path, you may need to orient the object to the path.

The advantages of using a motion guide are that you can have an object move along any path, including a path that intersects itself, and you can easily change the shape of the path, allowing you to experiment with different motions. A consideration when using a motion guide is that, in some instances, orienting the object along the path may result in an unnatural-looking animation. You can fix this by stepping through the animation one frame at a time until you reach the frame where the object is positioned poorly. You can then insert a keyframe and adjust the object as desired.

Transformation Point and Registration Point

Each symbol has a transformation point in the form of a circle (O) that is used to orient the object when it is being animated.

For example, when you rotate a symbol, the transformation point is the pivot point around which the object rotates. The transformation point is also the point that snaps to a motion guide, as shown in Figure 27. When attaching an object to a path, you can drag the transformation point to the path. The default position for a transformation point is the center of the object. You can reposition the transformation point while in the symbol edit mode by dragging the transformation point to a different location on the object. Objects also have a registration point (+) that determines the X and Y coordinates of an object on the Stage. The transformation and registration points can overlap—this is displayed as a plus sign within a circle ⊕.

Figure 27 *A motion guide with an object (motorbike) attached*

Transformation point with registration point ⊕; use the Zoom tool as needed to see the transformation point

Figure 28 *A motion guide layer with a classic tween on the layer beneath it*

Motion guide layer containing the path

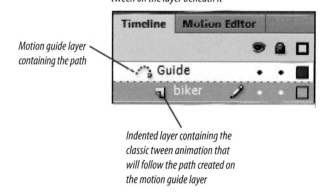

Indented layer containing the classic tween animation that will follow the path created on the motion guide layer

Create a classic tween animation

1. Open fl4_3.fla, then save it as **cTween.fla**.
2. Insert a **new layer**, then name it **biker**.
3. Click **frame 1** on the biker layer, then drag the **biker symbol** from the Library panel to the Stage, as shown in Figure 29.
4. Click **frame 30** on the biker layer, click **Insert** on the menu bar, point to **Timeline**, then click **Keyframe**.
5. Drag the **biker** to the position shown in Figure 30.
6. Click **frame 2** on the biker layer, click **Insert** on the menu bar, then click **Classic Tween**.

   An arrow appears on the Timeline indicating that this is a classic tween.
7. Play the movie.

You created an animation using a classic tween.

Add a motion guide and orient the object to the guide

1. Insert a **new layer**, then name it **Guide**.
2. Click **Modify** on the menu bar, point to **Timeline**, then click **Layer Properties**.
3. Click the **Guide option button**, click **OK**, then drag the **biker layer** up to the Guide layer, as shown in Figure 31.

   The biker layer indents below the Guide layer.
4. Click **frame 1** on the Guide layer, click the **Pencil tool** on the Tools panel, select **Smooth** in the Options area at the bottom of the Tools panel, then set the stroke color to **black**.
5. Point to the middle of the biker, then draw a **line** with a loop similar to the one shown in Figure 32.

(continued)

Figure 29 *Positioning the biker symbol on the Stage*

Drag g_biker symbol from the Library panel and position it on the Stage

Figure 30 *Repositioning the biker*

Figure 31 *Dragging the biker layer up to the Guide layer*

Drag biker layer up to but not above the Guide layer

Figure 32 *Drawing a guide path on a Guide layer*

Point to the middle of the biker object

Figure 33 *Aligning the object with the guide path*

Align this handle to the path

Figure 34 *Aligning the object with the end of the guide path*

Align this handle to the path

6. Click **frame 30** on the biker layer, click the **Selection tool** , then drag the **biker** so that the **transformation point** touches the end of the path.

   Hint: Use the Zoom tool to zoom in on the biker to make it easier to see you have placed the transformation point on the path.

7. Play the movie.

   The biker should follow the path. If not, make sure the biker is attached to the beginning and end of the path.

8. Click **frame 1** on the biker layer, then click the **biker** to select the object.

9. Click the **Free Transform tool** on the Tools panel, then rotate the **biker,** as shown in Figure 33.

10. Click **frame 30** on the biker layer, then rotate the **biker**, as shown in Figure 34.

11. Click the **Selection tool** , then click **frame 1** on the biker layer.

12. Display the Properties panel, then click the **Orient to path check box.**

13. Play the movie.

14. Click **frame 1** on the biker layer, set the Ease value on the Properties panel to **100**, then click **frame 1** on the biker layer to accept the value.

15. Click each frame on the **biker layer** until you locate the highest point on the motion path, insert a **keyframe** on that frame, set the ease value to **100**, then click **frame 1** on the biker layer to accept the value. Setting the ease values in steps 14 and 15 will cause the biker to start out fast, slow down at the top of the loop and speed up again.

16. Test the movie, save your work, then close the document.

You added a motion guide, oriented the animated object to the guide, and set ease values.

Lesson 2   Create Classic Tween Animations

Create Frame-by-Frame
ANIMATIONS

What You'll Do

 In this lesson, you will create frame-by-frame animations.

Understanding Frame-by-Frame Animations

A frame-by-frame animation (also called a frame animation) is created by specifying the object that is to appear in each frame of a sequence of frames. Figure 35 shows three images that are variations of a cartoon character. In this example, the head and body remain the same, but the arms and legs change to represent a walking motion. If these individual images are placed into succeeding frames (with keyframes), an animation is created.

Frame-by-frame animations are useful when you want to change individual parts of an image. The images in Figure 35 are simple—only three images are needed for the animation. However, depending on the complexity of the image and the desired movements, the time needed to display each change can be substantial. When creating a frame-by-frame animation, you need to consider the following points:

- *The number of different images.* The more images there are, the more effort is needed to create them. However, the greater the number of images, the less change you need to make in each image and the more

realistic the movement in the animation may seem.

- *The number of frames in which each image will appear.* Changing the number of frames in which the object appears may change the effect of the animation. If each image appears in only one frame, the animation may appear rather jerky, since the frames change very rapidly. However, in some cases, you may want to give the impression of a rapid change in an object, such as rapidly blinking colors. If so, you could make changes in the color of an object from one frame to another.

- *The movie frame rate.* Frame rates below 10 may appear jerky, while those above 30 may appear blurred. The frame rate is easy to change, and you should experiment with different rates until you get the desired effect.

Keyframes are critical to the development of frame animations because they signify a change in the object. Because frame animations are created by changing the object, each frame in a frame animation may need to be a keyframe. The exception is when you want an object displayed in several frames before it changes.

Creating a Frame-by-Frame Animation

To create a frame animation, select the frame on the layer where you want the animation to begin, insert a keyframe, and then place the object on the Stage. Next, select the frame where you want the change to occur, insert a keyframe, and then change the object. You can also add a new object in place of the original one. Figure 36 shows the first three frames of an animation in which three different objects are placed one on top of the other in succeeding frames. In the figure, the movement is shown as shadows. These shadows are visible because the Onion Skin feature is turned on. In this movie, the objects stay in place during the animation. However, a frame animation can also involve movement of the object around the Stage.

Using the Onion Skin Feature

Normally, Flash displays one frame of an animation sequence at a time on the Stage. Turning on the Onion Skin feature allows you to view an outline of the object(s) in any number of frames. This can help in positioning animated objects on the Stage.

Figure 35 *Three images used in an animation*

Figure 36 *A frame-by-frame animation of three figures appearing to walk in place*

Onion Skin feature is turned on so that all of the objects in frames 1-3 are viewable even though the playhead is on frame 1

The 3 objects placed on top of each other on the Stage, each in its own frame on the same layer on the Timeline

Create an in-place frame-by-frame animation

1. Open fl4_4.fla, then save it as **frameAn.fla**.

2. Set the view to **Fit in Window**.

3. Insert a **new layer**, name it **stickfigs**, click **frame 1** of the stickfigs layer, then drag **stickfig1** from the Library panel to the center of the Stage so it touches the white walkway.

   Note: You can use the Align panel to center the object horizontally across the Stage.

4. Click **frame 2** of the stickfigs layer to select it, click **Insert** on the menu bar, point to **Timeline**, then click **Keyframe**.

5. Drag **stickfig2** so it is on top of stickfig1, as shown in Figure 37, use the arrow keys on the keyboard to align the heads, then click a blank area of the Stage to deselect stickfig2.

6. Select **stickfig1** by clicking the foot that points up as shown in Figure 38, then press **[Delete]**.

7. Click **frame 3** on the stickfigs layer to select it, insert a **keyframe,** drag **stickfig3** so it is on top of stickfig2, then use the **arrow keys** on the keyboard to align the heads.

8. Click a blank area of the Stage to deselect stickfig3.

9. Select stickfig2 by clicking the foot that points down as shown in Figure 39, then press **[Delete]**.

10. Change the frame rate to **12**.

11. Play the movie.

You created a frame-by-frame animation.

Figure 37 *Dragging stickfig2 on top of stickfig1*

Figure 38 *Selecting stickfig1*

Click foot that points up

Figure 39 *Selecting stickfig2*

Click foot that points down

Creating Animations

Figure 40 *Moving the houses layer below the stickfigs layer*

Timeline	Motion Editor												

(Timeline graphic showing layers: stickfigs, houses, backdrop, frames 1–50)

Figure 41 *Positioning the houses symbol on the Stage*

Figure 42 *Repositioning the houses object*

Copy frames and add a moving background

1. Click **frame 1** of the stickfigs layer, press and hold **[Shift]**, then click **frame 3**.

2. Click **Edit** on the menu bar, point to **Timeline**, click **Copy Frames**, then click **frame 4** of the stickfigs layer.

3. Click **Edit** on the menu bar, point to **Timeline**, then click **Paste Frames**.

4. Click **frame 7**, then repeat step 3.

5. Click **frame 10** of the stickfigs layer, press and hold **[Shift]**, then click **frame 13**.

6. Click **Edit** on the menu bar, point to **Timeline**, then click **Remove Frames**.

7. Play the movie.

8. Insert a **new layer**, name the layer **houses**, then drag the **houses layer** below the stickfigs layer, as shown in Figure 40.

9. Click **frame 1** of the houses layer, drag the **houses symbol** from the Library panel to the Stage, position the houses as shown in Figure 41, then play the movie.

10. Click **frame 1** of the houses layer, click **Insert** on the menu bar, then click **Motion Tween**.

11. Click **frame 9** on the houses layer, then drag the **houses object** to the left, as shown in Figure 42.

12. Test the movie, close the Flash Player window.

    To slow down the animation you can reduce the frame rate and/or extend the length of the movie.

13. Save your work, then close the document.

You copied frames and added a motion tween to a movie with an in-place frame-by-frame animation.

Create a frame-by-frame animation of a moving object

1. Open fl4_5.fla, then save it as **frameM.fla**.

   This document has a backdrop layer that contains a row of houses and clouds.

2. Insert a **new layer**, then name it **stickFigs**.

3. Use the Magnification options on the View menu to display the entire Stage and part of the Pasteboard.

4. Click **frame 5** on the stickFigs layer, then insert a **keyframe**.

5. Drag **stickfig1** from the Library panel to the left edge of the Stage, as shown in Figure 43.

6. Click **frame 6** on the stickFigs layer, click **Insert** on the menu bar, point to **Timeline**, then click **Blank Keyframe**.

   A blank keyframe keeps the object in the previous frame from appearing in the current frame.

7. Click the **Edit Multiple Frames button** 🖿 on the Timeline status bar to turn it on.

   This allows you to view the contents of more than one frame at a time.

8. Drag **stickfig2** from the Library panel to the right of stickfig1, as shown in Figure 44.

9. Click **frame 7** on the stickFigs layer, then insert a **Blank Keyframe**.

10. Drag **stickfig3** to the right of stickfig2, as shown in Figure 45.

(continued)

Figure 43 *Positioning stickfig1 on the Stage*

Figure 44 *Positioning stickfig2 on the Stage*

Figure 45 *Positioning stickfig3 on the Stage*

Creating Animations

Figure 46 *Adding stickfig3 as the final object*

Working with Frames

Selecting frames

To select one frame: click the frame.

To select a range of contiguous frames: Shift-click additional frames.

To select non-contiguous frames: Control-click (Win) or ⌘-click (Mac).

To select a span of frames: double-click between keyframes.

To select all frames on the Timeline: choose Select All Frames from the Timeline option on the Edit menu.

Removing frames

Select the frame(s), then choose Remove Frames from the Timeline option on the Edit menu.

This removes frames from the timeline and moves the contents of succeeding frames left based on the number of frames removed.

Copy and paste

Select the frame(s), choose Copy Frames from the Timeline option on the Edit menu, select the frame to copy to, then choose Paste Frames from the Timeline option on the Edit menu.

Clear contents

Select the frame(s), then choose Clear Frames from the Timeline option on the Edit menu.

This leaves the frame(s) on the Timeline but the content is cleared and not available for pasting. (*Note*: If you select a frame within a motion tween and choose the Clear Frames option, all of the frames of the motion tween will cleared.)

11. Click **frame 8** on the stickFigs layer, insert a **Blank Keyframe**, then drag **stickfig1** from the Library panel to the right of stickfig3.

    Note: In this frame-by-frame animation each object must be placed individually rather than using a copy and paste process.

12. Click **frame 9** on the stickFigs layer, insert a **Blank Keyframe**, then drag **stickfig2** to the right of stickfig1.

13. Click **frame 10** on the stickFigs layer, insert a **Blank Keyframe**, then drag **stickfig3** to the right of stickfig2.

14. Click **frame 11** on the stickFigs layer, insert a **Blank Keyframe**, then drag **stickFig1** to the right of stickFig2 and partially off the Stage.

    Your screen should resemble Figure 46.

15. Test the movie.

    Notice how the figure seems to hesitate at the end of the movie before looping to the start of the movie. This is because there are still frames in the movie that have no content.

16. Close the Flash Player window, click **frame 12** on the stickFigs layer, then insert a **Blank Keyframe**.

17. Click the **Edit Multiple Frames button** on the Timeline status bar to turn it off.

18. Test the movie, then close the Flash Player window.

19. Change the frame rate to **6 fps**.

20. Test the movie, then close the Flash Player window.

21. Save the movie, then close the document.

You created a frame-by-frame animation that causes objects to appear to move across the screen.

Create Shape Tween
ANIMATIONS

What You'll Do

 In this lesson, you will create a shape tween animation and specify shape hints.

Understanding Shape Tweening

In previous lessons, you learned that you can use motion tweening to change the shape of an object. You accomplish this by selecting the Free Transform tool and then dragging the handles to resize and skew the object. While this is easy and allows you to include motion along with the change in shape, there are two drawbacks. First, you are limited in the type of changes (resizing and skewing) that can be made to the shape of an object. Second, you must work with the same object throughout the animation. When you use **shape tweening**, however, you can have an animation change the shape of an object to any form you desire, and you can include two objects in the animation with two different shapes. As with motion tweening, you can use shape tweening to change other properties of an object, such as its color, location, and size.

Using Shape Tweening to Create a Morphing Effect

Morphing involves changing one object into another, sometimes unrelated, object. For example, you could turn a robot into a human, or turn a football into a basketball. The viewer sees the transformation as a series of incremental changes. In Flash, the first object appears on the Stage and changes into the second object as the movie plays. The number of frames included from the beginning to the end of this shape tween animation determines how quickly the morphing effect takes place. The first frame in the animation displays the first object and the last frame displays the second object. The in-between frames display the different shapes that are created as the first object changes into the second object.

When working with shape tweening, you need to keep the following points in mind:

- Shape tweening can be applied only to editable graphics. To apply shape tweening to instances, groups, symbols, text blocks, or bitmaps, you must break apart the object to make it editable. To do this, you use the Break Apart command on the Modify menu. When you break apart an instance of a symbol, it is no longer linked to the original symbol.
- You can shape tween more than one object at a time as long as all the objects are on

Creating Animations

the same layer. However, if the shapes are complex and/or if they involve movement in which the objects cross paths, the results may be unpredictable.

- You can use shape tweening to move an object in a straight line, but other options, such as rotating an object, are not available.
- You can use the settings in the Properties panel to set options (such as the ease value, which causes acceleration or deceleration) for a shape tween.
- Shape hints can be used to control more complex shape changes.

Properties Panel Options

Figure 47 shows the Properties panel options for a shape tween. The options allow you to adjust several aspects of the animation, as described in the following:

- Adjust the rate of change between frames to create a more natural appearance during the transition by setting an ease value. Setting the value between −1 and −100 will begin the shape tween gradually and accelerate it toward the end of the animation. Setting the value between 1 and 100 will begin the shape tween rapidly and decelerate it toward the end of the animation. By default, the rate of change is set to 0, which causes a constant rate of change between frames.
- Choose a blend option. The Distributive option creates an animation in which the in-between shapes are smoother and more irregular. The Angular option preserves the corners and straight lines and works only with objects that have these features. If the objects do not have corners, Flash defaults to the Distributive option.

Shape Hints

You can use shape hints to control the shape's transition appearance during animation. Shape hints allow you to specify a location on the beginning object that corresponds to a location on the ending object. Figure 48 shows two shape animations of the same objects, one using shape hints and the other not using shape hints. The figure also shows how the object being reshaped appears in one of the in-between frames. Notice that with the shape hints, the object in the in-between frame is more recognizable.

Figure 47 *The Properties panel options for a shape tween*

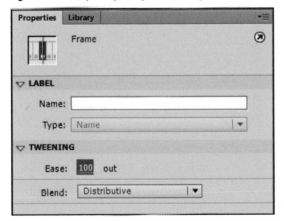

Figure 48 *Two shape animations (A morphing into B) with and without shape hints*

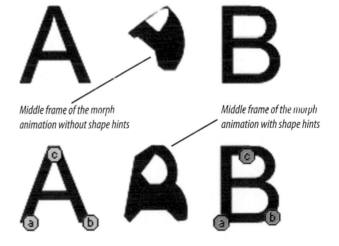

Middle frame of the morph animation without shape hints

Middle frame of the morph animation with shape hints

Create a shape tween animation

1. Open fl4_6.fla, then save it as **antiqueCar.fla**.

2. Set the view to **Fit in Window**.

3. Click **frame 30** on the shape layer, then insert a **keyframe**.

4. Click the **Selection tool** 🔧 on the Tools panel. Notice the graphic is editable as indicated by the dot pattern.

5. Click a blank area of the pasteboard to deselect the car.

6. Move the pointer towards the top of the car near the right side until it changes to an arc pointer ↖, then use the arc pointer ↖ to drag the **car top** to above the steering wheel, as shown in Figure 49.

   Note: Be sure you are using the arc pointer and not the corner pointer.

7. Click anywhere on the shape layer between frames 1 and 30.

8. Click **Insert** on the menu bar, then click **Shape Tween**.

9. Click **frame 1** on the shape layer, then play the movie.

10. Click **frame 30** on the shape layer.

11. Click the **Selection tool** 🔧 on the Tools panel, then drag a **marquee** around the car to select it if it is not already selected.

12. Drag the **car** to the right side of the Stage, then change the fps to **12**.

13. Test the movie, then close the Flash Player window.

14. Change the fps to **24**, save the movie and close it.

You created a shape tween animation, causing an object to change shape as it moves over several frames.

Figure 49 *Reshaping the object*

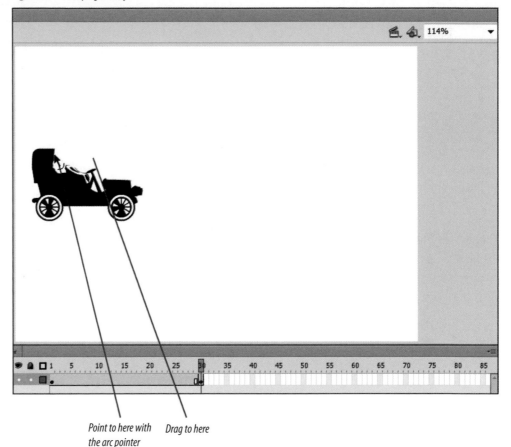

Point to here with the arc pointer   Drag to here

Figure 50 *Positioning the car instance on the Stage*

Transformation point appears when the mouse is released

Line up both cars so it appears that there is only one car; use the spokes on the wheels to help you know when the two objects are aligned

Create a morphing effect

1. Open fl4_7.fla, then save it as **morphCar.fla**.
2. Click **frame 40** on the morph layer.
3. Click **Insert** on the menu bar, point to **Timeline**, then click **Blank Keyframe**.

   TIP Inserting a blank keyframe prevents the object in the preceding keyframe from automatically being inserted into the frame with the blank keyframe. This is necessary when morphing two objects.

4. Click the **Edit Multiple Frames button** on the Timeline status bar.

   Turning on the Edit Multiple Frames feature allows you to align the two objects to be morphed.

5. Drag the **g_antiqueCarTopDown graphic** symbol from the Library panel directly on top of the car on the Stage, as shown in Figure 50.

   TIP Use the arrow keys to move the object as needed.

6. Make sure the g_antiqueCarTopDown object is selected, click **Modify** on the menu bar, then click **Break Apart**.

   This allows the object to be reshaped.

7. Click the **Edit Multiple Frames button** to turn off the feature.

8. Click anywhere between frames 1 and 40 on the morph layer, click **Insert** on the menu bar, then click **Shape Tween**.

9. Click **frame 1** on the Timeline, then play the movie.

   The first car morphs into the second car.

10. Save the movie.

You created a morphing effect, causing one object to change into another.

Adjust the rate of change in a shape tween animation

1. Click **frame 40** on the morph layer.

2. Click the **Selection tool** ![cursor] on the Tools panel, then drag a **marquee** around the car to select it, if it is not already selected.

3. Drag the **car** to the right side of the Stage.

4. Click **frame 1** on the morph layer.

5. Set the ease value on the Properties panel to **–100**, as shown in Figure 51.

6. Click the **Stage** to deselect the car.

7. Play the movie.

   The car starts out slow and speeds up as the morphing process is completed.

8. Repeat Steps 4 and 5, but change the ease value to **100**.

9. Click **frame 1** on the Timeline, then play the movie.

   The car starts out fast and slows down as the morphing process is completed.

10. Test the movie, then close the Flash Player window.

11. Save your work, then close the movie.

You added motion to a shape tween animation and changed the ease value.

Figure 51 *Setting the ease value of the morph*

Creating Animations

Figure 52 *Positioning a shape hint*

Figure 53 *Adding shape hints*

Figure 54 *Matching shape hints*

Use shape hints

1. Open fl4_8.fla, then save it as **shapeHints.fla**.
2. Play the movie and notice how the L morphs into a Z.
3. Change the view to 200%, then click **frame 15** on the Timeline, the midpoint of the animation.

   Notice the shape is unrecognizable.
4. Click **frame 1** on the hints layer to display the first object.
5. Make sure the object is selected, click **Modify** on the menu bar, point to **Shape**, then click **Add Shape Hint**.
6. Drag the **Shape Hint icon** 🔴 to the location shown in Figure 52.
7. Repeat Steps 5 and 6 to set a second and third Shape Hint icon, as shown in Figure 53.

   Notice the shape hints are placed at the major points of the image. For more complex objects you can use more shape hints and experiment with their placement.
8. Click **frame 30** on the hints layer.

   The shape hints are stacked on top of each other.
9. Drag the **Shape Hint icons** to match Figure 54.
10. Click **frame 15** on the hints layer, then notice how the object is more recognizable now that the shape hints have been added.
11. Click **frame 1** on the Timeline, then play the movie.
12. Save your work, then close the movie.

You added shape hints to a morph animation.

Create Movie
CLIPS

What You'll Do

In this lesson, you will create, edit, and animate a movie clip.

Understanding Movie Clip Symbols

Until now you have been working with two kinds of symbols, graphic and button. A third type is a **movie clip symbol**, which provides a way to create more complex types of animations. A movie clip is essentially a movie within a movie. Each movie clip has its own Timeline, which is independent of the main Timeline. This allows you to nest a movie clip that is running one animation within another animation or in a scene on the main Timeline. Because a movie clip retains its own Timeline, when you insert an instance of the movie clip symbol into a Flash document, the movie clip continues in an endless loop even if the main Timeline stops.

The wheels on a car rotating while the car is moving across the screen is an example of a movie (the moving car) with a nested animation (the rotating wheels). The nested animation is a movie clip. To create the animated movie clip, a drawing of a wheel separate from the car is converted into a movie clip symbol. Then the movie clip symbol is opened in the edit window, which includes a Timeline that is unique to the movie clip. In the edit window, an animation is created that causes the wheel to rotate. After exiting the edit window and returning to the main Timeline, an instance of the movie clip symbol is placed on each wheel of the car. Finally, the car, including the wheels, is animated on the main Timeline. As the car is moving across the screen, each wheel is rotating according to the movie clip Timeline. This process is shown in Figure 55.

In addition to allowing you to create more complex animations, movie clips help to organize the different reusable pieces of a movie and provide for smaller movie file sizes. This is because only one movie clip symbol needs to be stored in the Library panel while an unlimited number of instances of the symbol can be used in the Flash document.

An animated movie clip can be viewed in the edit window that is displayed when you double-click the movie clip symbol in the Library panel; and it can be viewed when you test or publish the movie that contains the movie clip. It is important to note that an animated movie clip cannot be viewed simply by playing the movie on the main Timeline.

In this lesson, you will learn how to create a movie clip symbol from a drawn object, edit the movie clip to create an animation, and nest the movie clip in another animation.

Figure 55 *The process of nesting a movie clip within an animation*

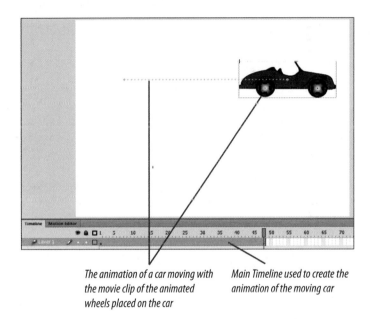

The movie clip of a wheel that has been animated to rotate shown in the edit window

Timeline in the edit window used to create the animation of the rotating wheel

The animation of a car moving with the movie clip of the animated wheels placed on the car

Main Timeline used to create the animation of the moving car

Break apart a graphic symbol and select parts of the object to separate from the graphic

1. Open fl4_9.fla, then save it as **mClip.fla**.

   This document has one graphic symbol—a car that has been placed on the Stage.

2. Click the **Selection tool** ➤ on the Tools panel, then click the **car** to select it.

3. Click **Modify** on the menu bar, then click **Break Apart**.

4. Click a blank area of the Stage to deselect the object.

5. Click the **Zoom tool** 🔍 on the Tools panel, then click the **front wheel** two times to zoom in on the wheel.

6. Click the **Selection tool** ➤ on the Tools panel.

7. Click the **gray hubcap**, press and hold **[Shift]**, then click the rest of the wheel, as shown in Figure 56.

   Hint: There are several small parts to the wheel, so click until a dot pattern covers the entire wheel, but do not select the tire. Use the Undo command if you select the tire.

8. Drag the **selected area** down below the car, as shown in Figure 57.

9. Compare your selected wheel to Figure 57, if your wheel does not match the figure, use the Undo command to move the wheel back to its original position, and repeat step 7.

You broke apart a graphic symbol and selected parts of the object to separate from the graphic.

Figure 56 *Selecting the wheel*

Figure 57 *Separating the wheel from the car*

Figure 58 *Selecting the gray area of the wheel*

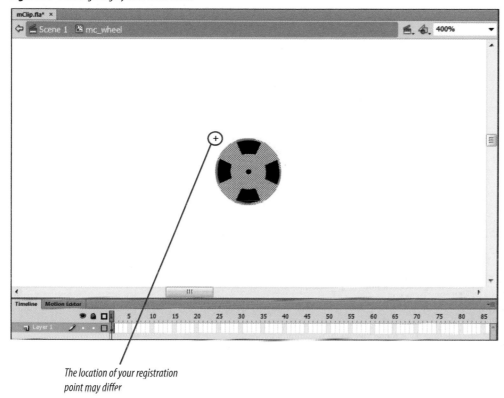

The location of your registration
point may differ

Create and edit a movie clip

1. Verify the wheel is selected, click **Modify** on the menu bar, then click **Convert to Symbol**.

2. Type **mc_wheel** for the name, select **Movie Clip** for the Type, then click **OK**.

3. Display the Library panel.

   Notice the mc_wheel movie clip and the movie clip icon appear in the Library panel.

4. Double-click the **mc_wheel icon** on the Library panel to display the edit window.

5. Click the **Zoom tool** on the Tools panel, then click the **wheel** twice to zoom in on the wheel.

   The movie clip has been broken apart as indicated by the dot pattern.

6. Click the **Selection tool** , click a blank area of the Stage to deselect the object, then click the **gray area** of the wheel to select it, as shown in Figure 58.

7. Click the **Fill color tool color swatch** on the Tools panel, then click the **gray gradient color swatch** in the bottom row of the palette.

You created a movie clip symbol and edited it to change the color of the object.

Animate a movie clip

1. Click the **Selection tool** ↖ , then drag a **marquee** around the entire wheel to select it.

2. Click **Insert** on the menu bar, click **Motion Tween**, then click **OK** for the Convert selection to symbol for tween dialog box.

3. Point to the end of the tween span on Layer 1 of the Timeline, then, when the pointer changes to a double-headed arrow ↔, drag the **span** to frame 48, as shown in Figure 59.

4. Click **frame 1** on Layer 1.

5. Display the Properties panel.

6. Change the rotate value to **4** times and verify the Direction is CW (Clockwise), as shown in Figure 60.

   Hint: If you don't see the Rotate option, click the Selection tool, then drag a marquee around the object.

7. Set the frame rate on the Timeline status bar to **12**.

8. Press **[Enter]** (Win) or **[Return]** (Mac) to play the Timeline for the mc_wheel movie clip symbol.

9. Click **Scene 1** near the top left side of the edit widow to exit the edit window.

10. Drag the **wheel** on the Stage up and position it so it is back inside the front tire of the car.

(continued)

Figure 59 *Increasing the motion span on the Timeline*

Movie clip symbol Timeline   Movie clip symbol in edit window   Drag the motion span to frame 48

Figure 60 *Changing the rotate value*

Creating Animations

Figure 61 *Repositioning the car*

11. Display the Library panel, then drag the **mc_wheel movie clip** from the Library panel and position it using the arrow keys as needed so it is on the back wheel.

12. Click **View** on the menu bar, point to **Magnification**, then click **Fit in Window**.

13. Test the movie and notice how the wheels turn, then close the Flash Player window.

14. Click the **Selection tool** , then drag a **marquee** around the car to select it and the wheels.

15. Click **Insert** on the menu bar, click **Motion Tween**.

16. Click **OK** to convert the selection to a symbol for tweening.

17. Drag the **tween span** on Layer 1 to frame 48.

    This will match the number of frames in the mc_wheel movie clip.

18. Click **frame 48** on Layer 1, then drag the **car** to the right side of the Stage, as shown in Figure 61.

19. Test the movie, then close the Flash Player window.

20. Save your work, then close the document.

You edited a movie clip to create an animation, then nested the movie clip in an animation on the main Timeline.

Animate TEXT

What You'll Do

▶ In this lesson, you will animate text by scrolling, rotating, zooming, and resizing it.

Animating Text

You can motion tween text block objects just as you do graphic objects. You can resize, rotate, reposition, and change the colors of text blocks. Figure 62 shows three examples of animated text with the Onion Skin feature turned on. When the movie starts, each of the following occurs one after the other:

- The Classic Car Club text block scrolls in from the left side to the top center of the Stage. This is done by creating the text block, positioning it off the Stage, and creating a motion-tweened animation that moves it to the Stage.
- The Annual text block appears and rotates five times. This occurs after you create the Annual text block, position it in the middle of the Stage under the heading, and use the Properties panel to specify a clockwise rotation that repeats five times.
- The ROAD RALLY text block slowly zooms out and appears in the middle of the Stage. This occurs after you create the text block and use the Free Transform tool handles to resize it to a small block at the beginning of the animation. Then, you resize the text block to a larger size at the end of the animation.

Once you create a motion animation using a text block, the text block becomes a symbol and you are unable to edit individual characters within the text block unless you use the Break Apart command. You can, however, edit the symbol as a whole.

Figure 62 *Three examples of animated text*

Text scrolls from off the Stage to the center of the Stage

THE CLASSIC CAR CLUB

Text rotates

Annual

Text zooms

Select, copy, and paste frames

1. Open fl4_10.fla, then save the movie as **textAn.fla**.

   This document has a heading and a frame-by-frame animation of a car where the front end rotates up and down, and then the car moves off the Stage.

2. Play the movie, then click **1** on the Timeline.

3. Press the **period key** to move through the animation one frame at a time and notice the changes to the car object in each frame.

4. Change the view to **Fit in Window**.

5. Click **frame 1** on the carGo layer, press and hold **[Shift]**, then click **frame 9** to select all the frames, as shown in Figure 63.

6. Click **Edit** on the menu bar, point to **Timeline**, then click **Cut Frames**.

7. Click **frame 72** on the carGo layer.

8. Click **Edit** on the menu bar, point to **Timeline**, then click **Paste Frames**.

   The frames are pasted in the new location, as shown in Figure 64.

9. Click **frame 1** on the carGo layer.

10. Play the movie, then save your work.

You selected frames and moved them from one location on the Timeline to another location on the Timeline.

Figure 63 *Selecting a range of frames*

Click frame 1 first

Hold [Shift] and click frame 9 to select the range of frames

Figure 64 *The Pasted Frame*

Frames copied to new location on the Timeline

Figure 65 *Positioning the text block outside the Stage*

Figure 66 *Centering the text block*

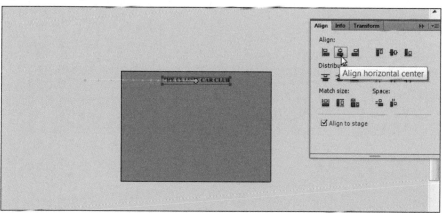

Animate text using a motion preset

1. Use the Magnification options on the View menu to display the entire Stage and part of the Pasteboard.

2. Click **frame 1** on the flyInText layer.

3. Open the Motion Presets panel, display the Default Presets, then click **fly-in-left**.

4. Click **Apply**, read the information box, then click **OK**.

   A motion tween is applied to the text block and a motion path appears.

5. Click the **Selection tool** , then draw a **marquee** around the text and the path.

6. Use the **left arrow key** to position the object and path, as shown in Figure 65.

   Alternately, you can drag the object and path to reposition it. Using the arrow key prevents any vertical movement when repositioning the object and path.

7. Click **frame 24** on the flyInText layer.

8. Click a blank area of the Stage to deselect the object and the path.

9. Click the **text object** to select it, then use the align panel to **center** the text horizontally across the Stage, as shown in Figure 66.

10. Click **frame 80** on the flyInText layer, then insert a **keyframe**.

11. Change the view to **Fit in Window**.

12. Test the movie, then close the Flash Player window.

You used a motion preset to animate an object by having it fly in from the left side of the Stage.

Create rotating text

1. Insert a **new layer**, then name it **rotateText**.

2. Insert a **keyframe** in frame 24 on the rotateText layer.

3. Click the **Text tool** T on the Tools panel, position the pointer under the "A" in "CLASSIC," then click.

4. Change the Character properties in the Properties panel to **Times New Roman**, size **24**, style **bold** and color **blue** (#0000FF).

5. Type **Annual**, then compare your image to Figure 67.

6. Click the **Selection tool** on the Tools panel, then use the Align panel to center the text block horizontally across the Stage.

7. Verify Annual is selected, click **Insert** on the menu bar, then click **Motion Tween**.

8. Click **frame 24** on the rotateText layer, then set the Rotate value on the Properties panel to **2** times with a **CW** (clockwise) direction.

9. Point to the end of the tween span (frame 80), then drag the ↔ **pointer** to frame 34, as shown in Figure 68.

10. Click **frame 80** on the rotateText layer, then insert a **keyframe**.

    The keyframe is needed to display the word Annual in frames 34 to 80.

11. Click **1** on the Timeline, then play the movie.

    The Annual text rotates clockwise two times.

You inserted a new layer, created a rotating text block, applied a motion tween to text, and used the Properties panel to rotate the text block.

Figure 67 *Adding the Annual text block*

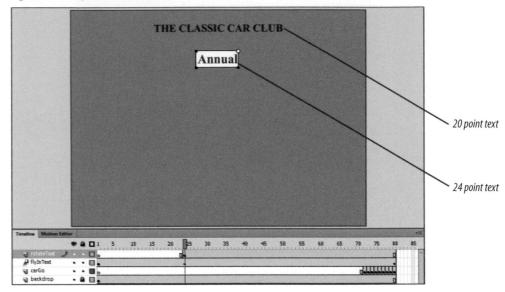

20 point text

24 point text

Figure 68 *Resizing the motion span from frame 80 to frame 34*

Drag to here

Start here

Creating Animations

Figure 69 *Using the Text tool to type ROAD RALLY*

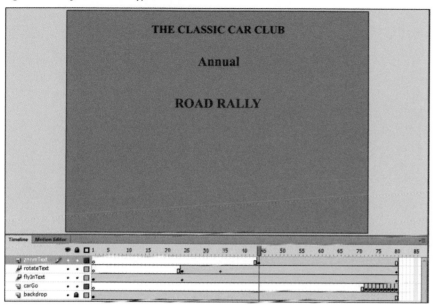

THE CLASSIC CAR CLUB

Annual

ROAD RALLY

Figure 70 *Resizing the Text block*

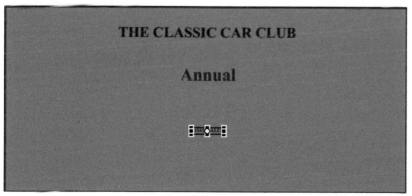

THE CLASSIC CAR CLUB

Annual

Resize and fade in text

1. Insert a **new layer**, name it **zoomText**, then insert a **keyframe** in frame 44 on the layer.

2. Click the **Text tool** T , position the pointer beneath the Annual text block, then type **ROAD RALLY**, as shown in Figure 69.

3. Click the **Selection tool** , then use the Align panel to center the text block horizontally across the Stage.

4. Click **frame 44** on the zoomText layer, click **Insert** on the menu bar, then click **Motion Tween**.

5. Click **frame 44** on the zoomText layer, click the **Free Transform tool** , then click the **Scale option** in the Options area of the Tools panel.

6. Drag the **upper-left corner handle** inward to resize the text block, as shown in Figure 70.

7. Click **frame 80** on the zoomText layer, verify the Scale option in the Options area of the Tools panel is selected, then drag the **upper-left corner handle** outward to resize the text block to approximately its original size.

TIP If the text appears upside down or backwards, you can use the Undo feature several times to return the text to its original size before you resized the text in step 6. Then repeat step 6, being careful not to resize the text too small.

8. Test the movie, then close the Flash Player window.

You created a motion animation that caused a text block to zoom out.

Make a text block into a button

1. Insert a **new layer**, then name it **continueBTN**.

2. Insert a **keyframe** in frame 72 on the continueBTN layer.

3. Click the **Text** tool ⊤ on the Tools panel, position the **Text tool pointer** ⊥⊤ beneath the car, then type **Click to continue**.

4. Drag the **pointer** over the text to select it, then change the character size to **12** using the Properties panel.

5. Click the **Selection tool** ▶ on the Tools panel, center the text block horizontally across the Stage, then compare your image to Figure 71.

6. Verify that the text block is selected, click **Modify** on the menu bar, click **Convert to Symbol**, type **b_continue** in the Name text block, set the Type to **Button**, then click **OK**.

7. Double-click the **text block** to edit the button.

8. Insert a **keyframe** in the Over frame, then set the fill color to the **black color swatch** in the left column of the color palette.

9. Insert a **keyframe** in the Down frame, set the fill color to the **bright green color swatch** in the left column of the color palette.

10. Insert a **keyframe** in the Hit frame, click the **Rectangle tool** ▭ on the Tools panel, then draw a **rectangle** that covers the text block, as shown in Figure 72.

11. Click **Scene 1** at the top left of the edit window to return to the main Timeline.

You made the text block into a button.

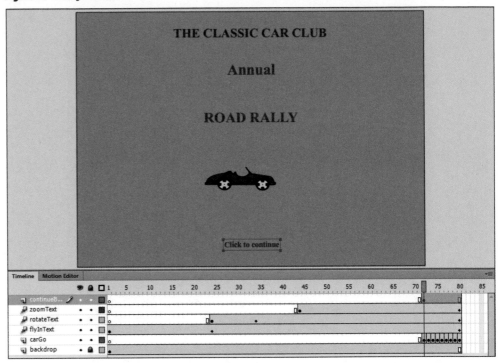

Figure 71 *Adding a button*

Figure 72 *The rectangle that defines the hit area*

Creating Animations

Figure 73 *Adding a play action*

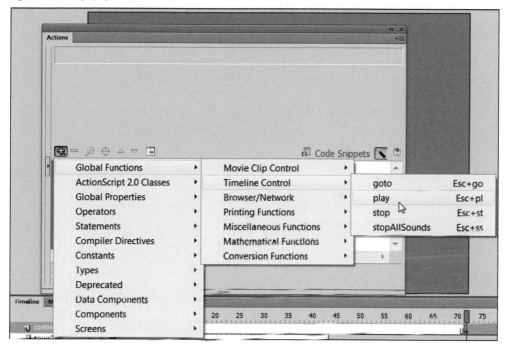

Add an action to the button

1. Display the Actions panel.

2. Click the **Selection tool** on the Tools panel, then click the **Click to continue button** on the Stage.

3. Verify the Script Assist button is turned on, then verify the button symbol and b_continue are displayed in the lower-left corner of the Actions panel.

   Note: You need to have ActionScript 2.0 active. You can check your ActionScript version by choosing Publish Settings on the File menu, then selecting the Flash tab.

4. Click the **Add a new item to the script button** in the Script Assist window, point to **Global Functions**, point to **Timeline Control**, then click **play**, as shown in Figure 73.

5. Insert a **new layer**, name it **stopMovie**, then insert a **keyframe** in frame 72 on that layer.

6. Verify that stopmovie:72 is displayed in the lower-left corner of the Actions panel.

7. Click the **Add a new item to the script button** in the Script Assist window, point to **Global Functions**, point to **Timeline Control**, then click **stop**.

8. Click **Control** on the menu bar, point to **Test Movie**, click **in Flash Professional**, then click the **Click to continue button** when it appears.

   The movie begins by playing the animated text blocks. When you click the Click to continue button the movie plays the animated car and then the movie loops back to frame 1.

9. Close the Flash Player movie window, save and close the movie, then exit Flash.

You inserted a play button and added a play action to it, then inserted a stop action on another layer.

Create a motion tween animation.

1. Start Flash, open fl4_11.fla, then save it as **skillsDemo4.fla**.
2. Insert a keyframe in frame 20 on the ballAn layer.
3. Display the Library panel, then drag the g_vball graphic symbol to the lower-left corner of the Stage.
4. Click frame 20 on the ballAn layer, then insert a motion tween.
5. Point to the end of frame 20, when the pointer changes to a double-headed arrow, drag the pointer to frame 40 to set the tween span from frames 20 to 40.
6. With frame 40 selected, drag the object to the lower-right corner of the Stage.
7. Insert a blank keyframe in frame 41.
8. Play the movie, then save your work.

Edit a motion tween.

1. Click frame 20 on the ballAn layer, then use the Selection tool to alter the motion path to form an arc.
2. Use the Subsection tool to display the Bezier handles, use them to form a curved path, then play the movie.
3. Select frame 20, use the Properties panel to change the ease value to **100**, then play the movie.
4. Select frame 20, change the ease value to **−100**, then play the movie.
5. Select frame 40, select the object, use the Properties panel to change the width of the object to **30**, then play the movie. (*Hint*: Click the object on the Stage, then verify the Lock width and height values together chain is not broken. This will ensure that when one value is changed, the other value changes proportionally.)

6. Select frame 35, select the object, use the Free transform tool to skew the object, then play the movie.
7. Select frame 40, select the object, use the Properties panel to change the alpha setting to **0**, then play the movie.
8. Select frame 40, select the object and change the alpha setting back to **100**. (*Hint:* Click the area of the Stage where the ball should be.)
9. Select frame 40, select the object, then use the Advanced Style option in the COLOR EFFECT area of the Properties panel to create a red color.
10. Lock the ballAn layer.
11. Play the movie, then save your work.

Create a classic tween.

1. Insert a new layer and name it **v-ball**.
2. Insert a keyframe in frame 76 on the v-ball layer.
3. Insert a keyframe in frame 41 on the v-ball layer.
4. Drag an instance of the g_vball symbol from the Library panel to the lower-left corner of the Stage.
5. Insert a keyframe in frame 50 on the v-ball layer and drag the ball to the lower-right corner of the Stage.
6. Click any frame between 41 and 50 on the v-ball layer and insert a Classic tween.
7. Insert a blank keyframe at frame 51 on the v-ball layer.
8. Play the movie, then save your work.

Create a motion guide.

1. Insert a new layer above the v-ball layer and name it **path**.
2. Insert a keyframe in frame 76 on the path layer.
3. Change the path layer to a Guide layer.
4. Insert a keyframe in frame 41 on the path layer.

5. Select the pencil tool, point to the middle of the ball and draw a path with a loop.
6. Insert a keyframe in frame 50 on the path layer.
7. Drag the v-ball layer up to the path layer so that it indents below the path layer.
8. Click frame 41 on the v-ball layer and use the Selection tool to attach the ball to the path.
9. Click frame 50 on the v-ball layer and attach the ball to the path.
10. Click frame 41 on the v-ball layer and use the Properties panel to orient the ball to the path.
11. Lock the v-ball and path layers.
12. Hide the path layer.
13. Play the movie, then save the movie.

Create a frame-by-frame animation.

1. Insert a new layer above the path layer and name it **corner-ball**.
2. Insert a keyframe in frame 76 on the corner-ball layer.
3. Insert a keyframe in frame 51 on the corner-ball layer, then drag the g_vball graphic from the Library panel to the lower-left corner of the Stage.
4. Insert a blank keyframe in frame 55 on the corner-ball layer, then drag g_vball graphic from the Library panel to the upper-left corner of the Stage.
5. Insert a blank keyframe in frame 59 on the corner-ball layer, then drag the g_vball graphic from the Library panel to the upper-right corner of the Stage.
6. Insert a blank keyframe in the frame 63 on the corner-ball layer, then drag the g_vball graphic from the Library panel to the lower-right corner of the Stage.

Creating Animations

7. Insert a blank keyframe in frame 67 on the corner-ball layer.
8. Lock the corner-ball layer.
9. Change the movie frame rate to 3 frames per second, then play the movie.
10. Change the movie frame rate to 12 frames per second, play the movie, then save your work.

Create a movie clip.

1. Insert a new layer and name it **spin-ball**.
2. Insert a keyframe at frame 76 on the spin-ball layer.
3. Insert a keyframe at frame 51 on the spin-ball layer.
4. Drag an instance of the g_vball symbol from the Library panel to the center of the Stage.
5. Use the align panel to center, both horizontally and vertically, the instance of the g_vball on the Stage.
6. Select the ball and convert it to a movie clip with the name **mc_ball**.
7. Display the edit window for the mc_ball movie clip.
8. Create a motion tween that rotates the ball 6 times counterclockwise in 12 frames.
9. Exit the edit window.
10. Insert a blank keyframe in frame 67 of the spin-ball layer.
11. Lock the spin-ball layer.
12. Test the movie, close the Flash Player window, then save your work.

Animate text.

1. Insert a new layer above the spin-ball layer and name it **heading**.
2. Click frame 1 on the heading layer.
3. Use the Text tool to click at the top-center of the Stage, then type **Having fun with a**.
4. Change the text to Arial, 20 point, light gray (#CCCCCC), and bold.
5. Use the Selection tool to select the heading and center the heading across the Stage.
6. Select frame 1 on the heading layer and create a pulse motion using the Motion Presets panel.
7. Drag the motion span to frame 76.
8. Play the movie and save your work.
9. Lock the heading layer.
10. Insert a new layer and name it **zoom**.
11. Insert a keyframe in frame 76 on the zoom layer.
12. Insert a keyframe in frame 11 on the zoom layer.
13. Use the Text tool to type **Volleyball** below the heading, then center it as needed.
14. Select frame 11 on the zoom layer and create a motion tween.
15. Insert a keyframe in frame 20 on the zoom layer.
16. Click frame 11 on the zoom layer and select the text block.
17. Use the Free Transform tool to resize the text block to approximately one-fourth its original size.

18. Select frame 20 on the zoom layer, and resize the text block to approximately the size shown in Figure 74.
19. Lock the zoom layer.
20. Test the movie, close the Flash Player window, save your work.

Create a Shape Tween Animation.

1. Insert a new layer above the zoom layer and name it **morph**.
2. Insert a keyframe in frame 66 on the morph layer.
3. Drag the g_vball symbol to the center of the Stage so it covers the other ball (mc_ball movie clip) in the center of the Stage. Because the mc_ball movie clip (spinning ball) ends in frame 66 and the morph begins in frame 66, this will give the impression of the spinning ball morphing.
4. Use the Properties panel to resize the width to **60 px**. (*Hint*: Verify the Lock width and height values together chain is not broken. This will ensure that when one value is changed, the other value changes proportionally.)
5. Reposition the smaller ball so it is over the center of the larger ball, then break apart the object.
6. Insert a blank keyframe in frame 76 on the morph layer.
7. Turn on the Edit Multiple Frames feature.

8. Drag the g_fball symbol to the Stage and use the Properties panel to resize the width to **60 px**. (*Hint*: Verify the Lock width and height values together chain is not broken. This will ensure that when one value is changed, the other value changes proportionally.)
9. Center the football on top of the volleyball.
10. Break apart the football object.
11. Turn off the Edit Multiple Frames feature.
12. Click frame 66 on the morph layer and insert a shape tween.
13. Test the movie, then close the Flash Player window.
14. Add shape hints to the volleyball and the football.
15. Lock the morph layer.
16. Test the movie, close the Flash Player window, then save your work.
17. Exit Flash.

Figure 74 *Completed Skills Review*

Creating Animations

The Ultimate Tours travel company has asked you to design several sample animations for its application. Figure 75 shows a sample opening screen and the Cruises screen. Using these as a guide, complete the following:

1. Open fl4_12.fla and save it as **ultimateTours4.fla**. (*Note:* This Flash document does not have any objects on the Stage. However, it does have all of the objects you will need to complete the project located in the Library panel. If you completed Project Builder 1 in chapter 3 you will notice that all of the objects have been converted to either graphic symbols (so they can be animated) or button symbols.)
2. Display the Library panel, click each item and view it in the Preview window.
3. Change the name of Layer 1 to **heading**.
4. Select frame 1 of the heading layer, drag the Ultimate Tours heading to the top of the Stage and center it. (*Hint:* Be sure the Align to stage check box is checked.)
5. Animate the heading Ultimate Tours using the Free Transform tool and the scale option so that it zooms out from a transparent (alpha = 0) state in frame 1 to an alpha setting of 100 at the end of the tween.
6. Insert a keyframe in frame 80 of the headings layer. (*Note:* In the following steps when you add a layer give the layer an appropriate name.)
7. Add a layer and have the logo appear on the screen next.
8. After the heading and logo appear, make the subheading We Specialize in Exotic Adventures! appear on its own layer.

9. Using separate layers, create motion tweens that cause each of the button shapes (Treks, Tours, Cruises) to scroll from the bottom of the Stage to its position on the Stage. Stagger the buttons on the Timeline so they scroll onto the Stage one after the other. (*Hint:* When adjusting the position of on object that has a motion tween be sure to select the desired frame (starting or ending) of the tween before repositioning the object.)
10. Add a layer and assign a stop action after the opening screen appears, that is after the buttons scroll onto the screen.
11. Remove the frames from the cruises, tours, treks and subheading layers that come after the stop action frame to prevent these objects from appearing on the next screen. (*Note:* To remove a group of frames you can drag the mouse to highlight the frames or click a frame, hold [Shift] and click another frame in a series. After highlighting the desired frames you can select Remove Frames from the Timeline option of the Edit menu.)
12. Add a new layer, add a keyframe one frame after the stop action and create the text blocks shown in Figure 75 (Featured Cruises, Panama Canal, Caribbean, Galapagos).
13. Import the graphic file ship.gif from the drive and folder where your Data Files are stored to the Library panel. (*Hint:* To import a graphic to the Library panel, click File on the menu bar, point to Import, then click Import to Library. Navigate to the drive and folder where your Data Files are stored, then select the desired file and click Open.)

14. Add a new layer, add a keyframe in the same frame as the one in the cruise headings layer and drag the ship.gif from the Library panel to the Stage.
15. Convert the ship graphic to a graphic symbol named **g_ship**, create a motion tween animation that moves the ship across the screen, then alter the motion path to cause a dip in it, similar to the path shown in Figure 75. (*Hint:* Use the Selection tool to create an arc in the path. Then use the Subselection tool to display the Bezier handles and further alter the path.)
16. Use the Free Transform tool and the Rotate and Skew option to attach the ship to the beginning and then to the end of the path, then orient the boat to the motion path.
17. Assign a goto action to the Cruises button on the opening screen so it jumps to the frame that has the Cruises screen.
18. Assign a stop action to a frame on the stop action layer so that the movie stops at the Featured Cruises screen after the ship animation is complete.
19. Add a layer, position the Home button on the cruises screen, and add an action to the button that jumps to the opening screen.
20. Check the ActionScript for all of your buttons and make sure the button name appears in the Actions panel along with the desired frame to jump to.
21. Lock all layers.
22. Test the movie, then compare your movie to the example shown in Figure 75.

Figure 75 *Sample completed Project Builder 1*

Opening screen

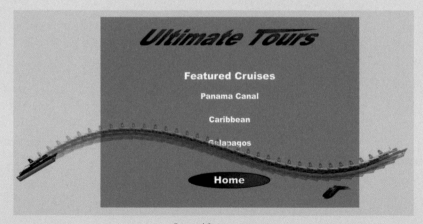

Featured Cruises screen

You have been asked to demonstrate some of the animation features of Flash. You have decided to create a movie clip that includes a frame-by-frame animation and then use the movie clip in a motion tween animation. Figure 76 shows the stick figure that will walk across the screen and jump up as it moves along. The movement across the screen is created using a motion tween. The jumping up is created using a movie clip, as shown in Figure 76.

To complete this project, do the following:

1. Open fl4_13.fla, then save the movie as **jumper4.fla**.
2. Display the Library panel, then click on each of the graphic symbols and view them in the Preview window.

3. Add a color for the Stage, then add the sidewalk, the lines for the sidewalk, and the houses, adding layers as needed and naming them appropriately.
4. Create a new movie clip. (*Note*: You can create a new movie clip by selecting New Symbol from the Insert menu, then you can drag objects from the Library panel to the movie clip edit window.)
5. In the edit window, edit the clip to create a frame-by-frame animation of the stick figures walking in place. In the edit window, place a keyframe in the first six frames of the movie clip Timeline. Click frame 1, then drag stickFig1 to the Stage. Use the transformation point to place the figure. Click frame 2, then drag stickFig2 to the Stage. Continue until each of the six frames has one stick figure.

6. Click frame 1, then use the period to click through the movie. Click one frame and move the stick figure in that frame so it is above its original location. This placement creates the jumping effect.
7. Exit the edit window and place the movie clip on the Stage on its own layer, then create a motion tween that moves the movie clip from the left side to the right side of the Stage.
8. Add keyframes to the other layers to be sure objects on those layers appear on the Stage for the full length of the movie.
9. Test the movie. Change the fps setting as needed to create a more realistic effect, then retest the movie. (*Note*: Movie clips do not play from the Stage, you must use the Test Movie command.)
10. Close the Flash Player movie, then save the movie.

Figure 76 *Sample completed Project Builder 2*

Jumper4 movie

mc_stickfigs symbol in edit window

Figure 77 shows a website for kids. Study the figure and complete the following. For each question, indicate how you determined your answer.

1. Connect to the Internet, then go to *www.smokeybear.com/kids*.
2. Open a document in a word processor or open a new Flash document, save the file as **dpc4**, then answer the following questions. (*Hint*: Use the Text tool in Flash.)
   - What seems to be the purpose of this site?
   - Who is the target audience?
   - How would you use a frame animation in this site?
   - How would you use a motion tween animation?
   - How would you use a motion guide?
   - How would you use motion animation effects?
   - How would you animate the text?

Figure 77 *Design Project*
Smokey Bear image used with the permission of the USDA Forest Service. www.smokeybear.com/kids

Creating Animations

This is a continuation of the Portfolio Project in Chapter 3, which is the development of a personal portfolio. In this project, you will create several buttons for the sample animations screen and link them to the animations.

1. Open portfolio3.fla (the file you created in Portfolio Project, Chapter 3) and save it as **portfolio4.fla**.
2. Create button symbols using the ovals with text at the bottom of your opening screen (for example, Graphics, Screen Designs, Biography, and Contact me buttons).
3. Delete the layers that contain the text and background for these buttons, create a new layer, and place all of these buttons on the layer, including the Animations button you created in Chapter 3, on frame 1 of the layer.
4. Add layers and create buttons with labels, as shown in Figure 78, for the tweened animation, frame-by-frame animation, motion path animation, and animated text.
5. Create a tween animation or use the passing cars animation from Chapter 3, and link it to the appropriate button on the Sample Animations screen by assigning a goto action to the button.
6. Create a frame-by-frame animation, and link it to the appropriate button on the Sample Animations screen.
7. Create a motion path animation, and link it to the appropriate button on the Sample Animations screen.
8. Create several text animations, using scrolling, rotating, and zooming; then link them to the appropriate button on the Sample Animations screen.
9. Create a shape tween animation, and link it to the appropriate button on the Sample Animations screen.
10. Create a shape tween animation that produces a morphing effect, and link it to the appropriate button on the Sample Animations screen.
11. Create a shape tween animation that produces a morphing effect using shape hints, and link it to the appropriate button on the Sample Animations screen.
12. Add a layer and create a Home button that links the Sample Animations screen to the Home screen.
13. Create frame actions that cause the movie to return to the Sample Animations screen after each animation has been played.
14. Test the movie.
15. Save your work, then compare sample pages from your movie to the example shown for two of the screens in Figure 78.

Figure 78 *Sample completed Portfolio Project*

Sample Animations page

A sample animation

CHAPTER 5 CREATING SPECIAL EFFECTS

1. Create a mask effect
2. Add sound
3. Add video
4. Create an animated navigation bar
5. Create character animations using inverse kinematics
6. Create 3D effects
7. Use the Deco tool

CHAPTER 5 CREATING SPECIAL EFFECTS

Introduction

Now that you are familiar with the basics of Flash, you can begin to apply some of the special features, such as special effects and sound effects, that can enhance a movie. Special effects can provide variety and add interest to a movie, as well as draw the viewer's attention to a location or event in the movie. One type of special effect is a spotlight that highlights an area(s) of the movie or reveals selected content on the Stage as it passes over the content. You can use sound effects to enhance a movie by creating moods and dramatizing events. In addition, you can add sound to a button to provide feedback to the viewer when the button is clicked. Video can be incorporated into a Flash movie and effects, such as fading in and out, can be applied to the display of the video.

Another type of special effect is an animated navigation bar, for example, one that causes a drop-down menu to open when the user rolls over a button. This effect can be created using masks and invisible buttons.

Additional features of Adobe Flash CS6 are Inverse Kinematics, 3D Effects, and the Deco tool. Inverse kinematics allows you to easily create character animations and even allows users to interact with the character when viewing the Flash movie. The 3D tools allow you to create 3D effects such as objects moving and rotating through 3D space. The Deco tool provides a variety of drawing effects that can be used to create environments and decorative patterns.

Create A
MASK EFFECT

What You'll Do

Clas

ssic (

Car (

Club

 In this lesson, you will apply a mask effect.

Understanding Mask Layers

A **mask layer** allows you to cover up the objects on one or more layers and, at the same time, create a window through which you can view objects on those layer(s). You can determine the size and shape of the window and specify whether it moves around the Stage. Moving the window around the Stage can create effects such as a spotlight that highlights certain content on the Stage, drawing the viewer's attention to a specific location. Because the window can move around the Stage, you can use a mask layer to reveal only the area of the Stage and the objects you want the viewer to see.

You need at least two layers on the Timeline when you are working with a mask layer. One layer, called the mask layer, contains the window object through which you view the objects, which are on a second layer below the mask layer. The second layer, called the masked layer, contains the object(s) that are viewed through the window. Figure 1 shows how a mask layer works: The top part of the figure shows the mask layer with the window in the shape of a circle. The next part of the figure shows the

layer to be masked. The last part of the figure shows the result of applying the mask. Figure 1 illustrates the simplest use of a mask layer. In most cases, you want to have other objects appear on the Stage and have the mask layer affect only a certain portion of the Stage.

The process for using a mask layer follows:

- Insert a new layer that will become the masked layer—add the objects that you want to display through the mask layer window. Alternately, you can use an existing layer that already contains the objects you want to mask.
- Insert a new layer above the masked layer that will become the mask layer. A mask layer always masks the layer(s) immediately below it.
- Draw a filled shape, such as a circle, or create an instance of a symbol that will become the window on the mask layer. Flash ignores bitmaps, gradients, transparency colors, and line styles on a mask layer. On a mask layer, filled areas become transparent and non-filled areas become opaque when viewed over a masked layer.

- Select the layer you want to be the mask layer and open the Layer Properties dialog box. To open the Layer Properties dialog box, click Modify on the menu bar, point to the Timeline, then click Layer Properties. In the Layer Properties dialog box, select Mask as the layer type. Flash converts the layer to the mask layer.
- Select the layer you want to apply the mask to and open the Layer Properties dialog box, then select Masked as the layer type. Flash converts the layer to the masked layer.
- Lock both the mask and masked layers.
- To mask additional layers: Drag an existing layer beneath the mask layer, or create a new layer beneath the mask layer and use the Layer Properties dialog box to convert it to a masked layer. Adding additional masked layers allows you to reveal more than one object with the same mask layer. For example, you could have a mask layer that reveals constellations on one masked layer and animated shooting stars on another masked layer.
- To unlink a masked layer: Drag it above the mask layer, or select it and select Normal from the Layer Properties dialog box.

Figure 1 *A mask layer with a window*

Mask layer with window (the filled circle, which becomes transparent when viewed over a masked layer)

Classic Car Club

Masked layer before applying mask

'las

Masked layer after applying mask; you only see what appears through the window as the window moves across the Stage

Create a mask layer

1. Open fl5_1.fla, then save it as **classicCC.fla**.

2. Insert a **new layer**, name it **mask**, then click **frame 1** on the mask layer.

3. Select the **Oval tool** ⬭ on the Tools panel, set the Stroke Color to **No Stroke** 🗹 on the top row of the color palette.

4. Set the Fill Color to the **black color swatch** in the left column of the color palette.

5. Draw the circle shown in Figure 2, click the **Selection tool** ▸ on the Tools panel, then drag a **marquee** around the circle to select it.

6. Click **Insert** on the menu bar, click **Motion Tween**, then click **OK** to convert the drawing into a symbol so that it can be tweened.

   Note: Flash converts the object to a movie symbol as the default symbol type. To convert the object to a different symbol type, you must convert the symbol manually.

7. Click **frame 40** on the mask layer, then drag the **circle** to the position shown in Figure 3.

8. Click **mask** on the Timeline to select the mask layer, click **Modify** on the menu bar, point to **Timeline**, then click **Layer Properties**.

9. Verify that the Show check box is selected in the Name area, click the **Lock check box** to select it, click the **Mask option button** in the Type area, then click **OK**.

   The mask layer has a shaded mask icon next to it on the Timeline.

   Hint: Alternately, you can lock the layer using the Lock This Layer icon on the Timeline.

   (continued)

Figure 2 *Object to be used as the window on a mask layer*

Figure 3 *Repositioning the circle*

Creating Special Effects

Figure 4 *The completed Layer Properties dialog box*

Show selected

Masked selected

Your color may vary

Lock selected

10. Play the movie from frame 1 and notice how the circle object covers the text on the heading layer as it moves across the Stage.

    Note: The circle object will not become transparent until a masked layer is created beneath it.

You created a mask layer containing a circle object that moves across the Stage.

Create a masked layer

1. Click **heading** on the Timeline to select the heading layer, click **Modify** on the menu bar, point to **Timeline,** then click **Layer Properties** to open the Layer Properties dialog box.

2. Verify that the Show check box Is selected in the Name area, click the **Lock check box** to select it, click the **Masked option button** in the Type area, compare your dialog box to Figure 4, then click **OK.**

    The text on the Stage seems to disappear. The heading layer is indented and has a shaded masked icon next to it on the Timeline.

3. Play the movie and notice how the circle object acts as a window to display the text on the heading layer.

4. Click **Control** on the menu bar, point to **Test Movie,** then click **in Flash Professional.**

5. View the movie, then close the Flash Player window.

6. Save your work, then close the movie.

You used the Layer Properties dialog box to create a masked layer.

LESSON 2

Add
SOUND

What You'll Do

 In this lesson, you will add sound to an animation and to a button click event.

Incorporating Animation and Sound

Sound can be extremely useful in a Flash movie. Sounds are often the only effective way to convey an idea, elicit an emotion, dramatize a point, and provide feedback to a user's action, such as clicking a button. How would you describe in words or show in an animation the sound a whale makes? Think about how chilling it is to hear the footsteps on the stairway of a haunted house. Consider how useful it is to hear the pronunciation of "buenos dias" as you are studying Spanish. All types of sounds can be incorporated into a Flash movie: for example, CD-quality music that might be used as background for a movie; narrations that help explain what the user is seeing; various sound effects, such as a car horn beeping; and recordings of special events, such as a presidential speech or a rock concert.

The process for adding a sound to a movie follows:

- Import a sound file into a Flash movie; Flash places the sound file in the movie's library.

- Create a new layer.
- Select the desired frame on the new layer where you want the sound to play and drag the sound symbol to the Stage.

Instead of dragging the sound symbol to the Stage, you can use the Properties panel, as shown in Figure 5, to select the desired sound file. You can also use options in the Properties panel to specify special effects (such as Fade in and Fade out).

In addition to adding a sound to a layer, you can sync a sound with a button. For example, you might want to have a sound play when a button is clicked. The process for synchronizing a sound to a button follows:

- Display the Edit window for the button.
- Add a layer. The sound should be on its own layer.
- Select the frame for the desired button event (such as down).
- Use the Properties panel to select the sound file.
- Select Event as the Sync option.
- Exit the Edit window and return to the Stage.

You can place more than one sound file on a layer, and you can place sounds on layers that have other objects. However, it is recommended that you place each sound on a separate layer so that it is easier to identify and edit. In Figure 6, the sound layer shows a wave pattern that extends from frame 1 to frame 24. The wave pattern gives some indication of the volume of the sound at any particular frame. The higher spikes in the pattern indicate a louder sound. The wave pattern also gives some indication of the pitch.

The denser the wave pattern, the lower the pitch. You can alter the sound by adding or removing frames. However, removing frames may create undesired effects. It is best to make changes to a sound file using a sound-editing program.

You can import the following sound file formats into Flash:

- ASND (Windows or Macintosh)
- WAV (Windows only)
- AIFF (Macintosh only)

- MP3 (Windows or Macintosh)

If you have QuickTime 4 or later installed on your computer, you can import these additional sound file formats:

- AIFF (Windows or Macintosh)
- SD 2 (Sound Designer II; Macintosh only)
- MOV or QT (Sound Only QuickTime Movies; Windows or Macintosh)
- AU (Sun AU; Windows or Macintosh)
- SND (System 7 Sounds; Macintosh only)
- WAV (Windows or Macintosh)

Figure 5 *Properties panel Sound options*

Name list arrow; click to see list of available sounds

Click Sync button to see menu

Effect menu

Figure 6 *A wave pattern displayed on a sound layer*

Add sound to a movie

1. Open fl5_2.fla, then save it as **rallySnd.fla**.

2. Play the movie and notice that there is no sound.

3. Click the **stopMovie layer**, insert a **new layer**, then name it **carSnd**.

4. Insert a **keyframe** in frame 72 on the carSnd layer.

5. Click **File** on the menu bar, point to **Import**, then click **Import to Library**.

6. Use the Import to Library dialog box to navigate to the drive and folder where your Data Files are stored, click the **CarSnd.wav file**, then click **Open**.

7. Display the Library panel, click **CarSnd.wav**, then click the **Play button** ▶ in the Preview window.

8. Click **frame 72** on the carSnd layer.

9. Drag the **CarSnd sound symbol** ◀ to the Stage, as shown in Figure 7.

   After releasing the mouse button, notice the wave pattern that has been placed on the carSnd layer starting in frame 72.

TIP The wave pattern may not appear on the layer until the movie is played one time.

10. Change the frame rate to **12 fps**.

11. Click **Control** on the menu bar, point to **Test Movie**, then click **in Flash Professional**.

12. Click the **Click to continue button** to move the playhead to the frame that starts the sound.

13. Close the Flash Player window.

You imported a sound and added it to a movie.

Figure 7 *Dragging the CarSnd symbol to the Stage*

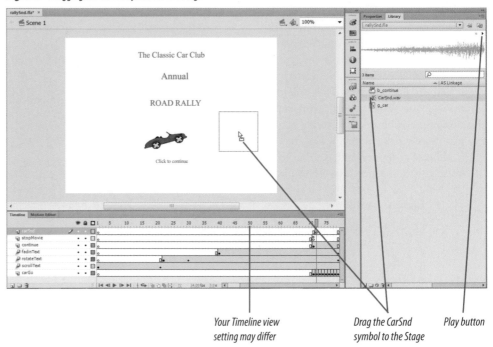

Your Timeline view setting may differ

Drag the CarSnd symbol to the Stage

Play button

Figure 8 *The Timeline for the button with the sound layer*

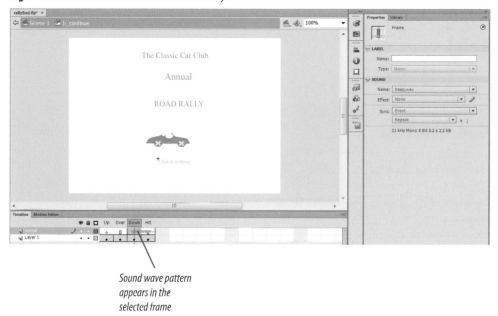

Sound wave pattern
appears in the
selected frame

Adding Sounds to a Movie's Timeline and to a Button's Timeline

When adding a sound to a movie's Timeline, the sound will play when the playhead reaches the frame containing the sound wave. In some instances, the user may need to click a button to cause the playhead to move to the frame containing the sound wave. However, in these instances, the sound is not associated with the button because the sound is part of the movie's Timeline and not part of the button's Timeline. To associate a sound with a button, you place the sound wave on the Timeline for the button. Then, whenever the button is pressed, the sound plays.

Add sound to a button

1. Click **frame 71** on the carSnd layer.
2. Click the **Selection tool** ![pointer icon] on the Tools panel, drag a **marquee** around "Click to continue" to select the button, then double-click the **button** to display the button's Timeline.
3. Insert a **new layer** above Layer 1, then name it **sound**.
4. Click the **Down frame** on the sound layer, click **Insert** on the menu bar, point to **Timeline**, then click **Blank Keyframe**.
5. Click **File** on the menu bar, point to **Import**, then click **Import to Library**.
6. Use the Import to Library dialog box to navigate to the drive and folder where your Data Files are stored, click the **beep.wav file**, then click **Open**.
7. Display the Properties panel, click the **Name list arrow** in the SOUND area, then click **beep.wav**.
8. Click the **Sync list arrow** in the Properties panel, click **Event**, then compare your screen to Figure 8.
9. Click **Scene 1** on the upper left of the edit window title bar to display the main Timeline.
10. Test the movie.
11. Click the **Click to continue button** and listen to the sounds, then close the Flash Player window.
12. Save your work, then close the movie.

You added a sound layer to a button, imported a sound, then attached the sound to the button.

Add
VIDEO

What You'll Do

In this lesson, you will import a video, add actions to video control buttons, and then synchronize sound to a video clip.

Incorporating Video

Adobe Flash allows you to import FLV (Flash video) files that then can be used in a Flash document. Flash provides several ways to add video to a movie, depending on the application and, especially, the file size. Video content can be embedded directly into a Flash document, progressively downloaded, or streamed.

Embedded video becomes part of the SWF file similar to other objects, such as sound and graphics. A placeholder appears on the Stage and is used to display the video during playback. If the video is imported as a movie clip symbol, then the placeholder can be edited, including rotating, resizing, and even animating it. Because embedded video becomes part of the SWF file, the technique of embedding video is best used for small video clips in order to keep the document file size small. The process for embedding video is to import a video file using the Import Video Wizard. Then, you place the video on the Stage and add controls as desired. Figure 9 shows a

video placeholder for an embedded video. The video file (fireworks.flv) is in the Library panel and the video layer on the Timeline contains the video object. The embedded video plays when the Play button is clicked.

Progressive downloading allows you to use ActionScript to load an external FLV file into a SWF file; the video then plays when the SWF file is played. With progressive downloading, the FLV file resides outside the SWF file. As a result, the SWF file size can be kept smaller than when the video is embedded in the Flash document. The video begins playing soon after the first part of the file has been downloaded.

Streaming video provides a constant connection between the user and the video delivery. Streaming has several advantages over the other methods of delivering video, including starting the video more quickly and allowing for live video delivery. However, streaming video requires the Flash Media Server, an Adobe software product designed specifically for streaming video content.

Creating Special Effects

Using the Import Video Wizard

The Import Video Wizard is used to import FLV files into Flash documents. The wizard, in a step-by-step process, leads you through a series of windows that allow you to select the file to be imported and the deployment method (embedded, progressive, streaming). In addition, you can specify whether or not to have the video converted to a movie clip symbol which allows you to animate the placeholder. The wizard appears when you choose the Import Video command from the Import option on the File menu.

Using the Adobe Media Encoder

The Adobe Media Encoder is an application used by Flash to convert various video file formats, such as .mov, .avi, and .mpeg, to the FLV (Flash Video) format so the videos can be used with Flash. The Encoder allows you to, among other things, choose the size of the placeholder the video will play in, edit the video, and insert cue points that can be used to synchronize the video with animations and sound. Figure 10 shows the Encoder, which is open and ready to convert the fireworks.mov video (Source Name) to fireworks.flv (Output File). The Start Queue button is used to start the process. When the conversion is complete, a green check mark is displayed in the Status column. The Adobe Media Encoder can be accessed through the Import Video Wizard.

Figure 9 *An embedded video*

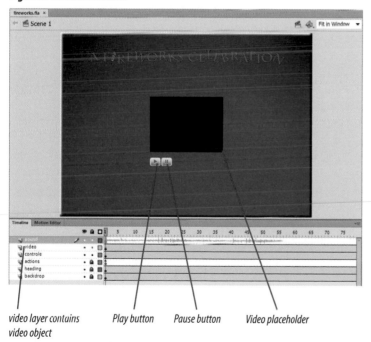

video layer contains
video object   Play button   Pause button   Video placeholder

Figure 10 *The Adobe Media Encoder*

Import a video

1. Open fl5_3.fla, then save it as **fireworks.fla**.

   The movie has four layers and 85 frames. The backdrop layer contains a blue gradient backdrop object. The heading layer contains the text object. The actions layer has a stop action in frame 1. The controls layer contains Play and Pause buttons that will be used to control the video. The Library panel contains the two button symbols and a sound file as well as graphics and movie clip files.

2. Set the view to **Fit in Window**.

3. Insert a **new layer** above the controls layer, name it **video**, then click **frame 1** on the video layer.

4. Click **File** on the menu bar, point to **Import**, then click **Import Video**.

   The Import Video Wizard begins by asking for the path to the video file and the desired method for importing the file, as shown in Figure 11.

5. Click the **Embed FLV in SWF and play in timeline option button**.

6. Click **Browse**, navigate to the drive and folder where your Data Files are stored, click **fireworks.mov**, then click **Open**.

   A message appears indicating that the video format is not valid for embedding video. You must convert the file to the FLV format.

7. Click **OK**, then click the **Launch Adobe Media Encoder button**.

   Note: If a message about browsing to the file after it is converted opens, click OK.

   (continued)

Figure 11 *The Import Video Wizard*

Creating Special Effects

Figure 12 *The completed Select Video window*

Start Queue button

Your path may vary

After several moments the encoder opens.

Note: Click the Adobe Media Encoder button on the taskbar if the encoder does not open automatically in its own window.

8. Click the **Start Queue button**, as shown in Figure 12.

   When the process is done, the green Start Queue arrow will dim and a green check mark will appear next to the word Done.

9. Close the encoder window.

10. Click **OK** to close the message window if one opens, then click the **Browse button**.

11. Click **fireworks.flv**, then click **Open**.

    Note: If you do not see fireworks.flv, navigate to the drive and folder where you saved your solution file.

    The Select Video screen displays the path to the fireworks.flv file below the Browse button.

12. Click **Next**.

    The Embedding screen opens, which allows you to specify how you would like to embed the video.

13. Read the screen and verify all the options have a check mark.

14. Click **Next**.

15. Read the Finish Video Import screen, then click **Finish**.

    The video is encoded and placed on the Stage and in the Library panel.

You imported a video then specified the encoding and embed type.

Attach actions to video control buttons

1. Click **Control** on the menu bar, point to **Test Movie**, then click in **Flash Professional**.

2. Click the **control buttons**.

   Nothing happens because there is a stop action in frame 1 and no actions have been assigned to the buttons.

3. Close the Flash Player window.

4. Open the Actions panel.

5. Click the **Play button** on the Stage, then verify the btn_play button symbol appears in the lower-left corner of the Script pane.

6. Turn on Script Assist if it is off.

7. Click the **Add a new item to the script button** 🔧, point to **Global Functions**, point to **Timeline Control**, then click **play** as shown in Figure 13.

8. Click the **Pause button** on the Stage, then verify the btn_pause button symbol appears in the lower-left corner of the Script pane.

9. Click the **Add a new item to the script button** 🔧, point to **Global Functions**, point to **Timeline Control**, then click **stop**.

10. Close the Actions panel.

11. Test the movie, click the **Play button**, then click the **Pause button**.

    The video plays, however there is no sound.

12. Close the Flash Player window.

You assigned play and stop actions to video control buttons.

Figure 13 *Using Script Assist to assign a play action to a button*

Play button selected

Click "play" to assign this action to the Play button

Creating Special Effects

Figure 14 *The completed Properties panel*

Synchronize sound to a video clip

1. Insert a **new layer** above the video layer, then name it **sound**.
2. Click **frame 1** on the sound layer.
3. Display the Library panel.
4. Click **fireworks.wav** to display the sound wave pattern in the Preview window.
5. Click the **Play button** ▶ in the Preview window, then click the **Stop button** ■ .
6. Display the Properties panel, then display the SOUND area options.
7. Click the **Name list arrow** in the SOUND area, then click **fireworks.wav**.
8. Click the **Sync sound list arrow** in the SOUND area, then click **Stream**.
9. Click the **Repeat list arrow**, click **Loop**, then compare your Properties panel to Figure 14.
10. Test the movie, click the **Play button**, then click the **Pause button**.
11. Close the Flash Player window.
12. Lock all layers.
13. Save your work, then close the file.

You inserted a layer, then you synchronized a sound to the video clip.

Create an Animated NAVIGATION BAR

What You'll Do

In this lesson, you will work through the process to create one drop-down menu.

Understanding Animated Navigation Bars

A common navigation scheme for a website is a navigation bar with drop-down menus, such as the one shown in Figure 15. Using a navigation bar has several advantages. First, it allows the developer to provide several menu options to the user without cluttering the screen, thereby providing more screen space for the website content. Second, it allows the user to go quickly to a location on the site without having to navigate several screens to find the desired content. Third, it provides consistency in function and appearance, making it easy for users to learn and work with the navigation scheme.

There are various ways to create drop-down menus using the animation capabilities of Flash and ActionScript. One common technique allows you to give the illusion of a drop-down menu by using masks that reveal

Figure 15 *Navigation bar with drop-down menus*

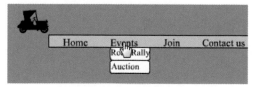

the menu. When the user points to (rolls over) a menu item on the navigation bar, a list or "menu" of buttons is displayed ("drops down"). Then the user can click a button, which might go to another location in the website or trigger some other action, depending on the action assigned to the button. The dropping down of the list is actually an illusion created by using a mask to "uncover" the menu options.

The process for creating a drop-down menu follows:

- **Create a navigation bar.** This could be as basic as a background graphic in the shape of a rectangle with buttons that represent the navigation bar menu items.
- **Position the drop-down buttons.** Add a drop-down buttons layer beneath the navigation bar layer. Next, select an empty frame adjacent to the first frame containing the navigation bar. Place the buttons that will be used to create the drop down list on the Stage below their respective menu items on the navigation bar. For example, if the navigation bar has an Events button with two choices, Road Rally and Auction, that you want to appear as buttons on

Creating Special Effects

a drop-down menu, position these two buttons below the Events button on the drop-down buttons layer.

- **Create an animated mask.** Add a mask layer above the drop-down buttons layer and create an animation of an object that starts above the drop-down buttons and moves down to reveal them. Then change the layer to a mask layer and the drop-down buttons layer to a masked layer.
- **Assign actions to the drop-down buttons.** Select each drop-down button and assign an action, such as "on (release) gotoAndPlay."
- **Assign a roll over action to the navigation bar menu item button.** The desired effect is to have the drop-down buttons appear when the user points to a navigation bar button. Therefore, you need to assign an "on rollOver" action to the navigation bar button that causes the playhead to go to the frame that plays the animation on the mask layer. This can be done using the Script Assist feature.
- **Create an invisible button.** When the user points to a navigation bar button, the drop-down menu appears showing the drop-down buttons. There needs to be a way to have the menu disappear when the user points away from the navigation bar button. This can be done by creating a button on a layer below the masked layer. This button is slightly larger than the drop-down buttons and their navigation bar button, as shown in Figure 16.

A rollOver action is assigned to this button so that when the user rolls off the drop-down or navigation bar buttons, he or she rolls onto this button and the action is carried out. This button should be made transparent so the user does not see it.

Using Frame Labels

Until now, you have worked with frame numbers in ActionScript code when creating a goto action. Frame labels can also be used in the code. You can assign a label to a frame as an identifier. For example, you could assign the label home to frame 10 and then create a goto home action that will cause the playhead to jump to frame 10. One advantage of using frame labels is that if you insert frames on the Timeline, the label adjusts for the added frames. So, you do not have to change the ActionScript that uses the frame label. Another advantage is that the descriptive labels help you identify parts of the movie

as you work with the Timeline. You assign a frame label by selecting the desired frame and typing a label in the Frame text box in the Properties panel.

Understanding Scenes

When you create a movie, the phrase Scene 1 appears above the Stage. You can add scenes to a movie at any time. Scenes are one way to organize long movies. For example, a movie created for a website could be divided into several scenes: an introduction, a home page, and content pages. Each scene has its own Timeline. You can insert a new scene by opening the Insert menu and selecting Scene. You can view a scene by opening the Other Panels option on the Windows menu and then selecting a scene to view. Scenes can be given descriptive names and referenced in ActionScript code, which allows users to jump from scene to scene. One drawback to using scenes is potentially larger file sizes.

Figure 16 *A button that will be assigned a rollOver action*

When the user rolls over any part of the blue button with the pointer, a script is executed that causes the drop-down menu to disappear

Position the drop-down buttons

1. Open fl5_4.fla, then save it as **navBar.fla**.

   This file contains a navigation bar, scenes, and many objects in the library.

2. Click **Window** on the menu bar, click **Other Panels**, click **Scene**, then click **Scene 2** to view Scene 2 and its associated Timeline.

   This scene was created as part of the entire movie by selecting Scene from the Insert menu to display a blank Timeline.

3. Press **[Enter]** (Win) or **[return]** (Mac) to play the scene, click **Scene 1**, then close the Scene panel.

   This returns you to the main scene.

4. Click the **homeBkgrnd layer**, insert a **new layer**, then name it **roadRally**.

5. Click **frame 2** on the roadRally layer, then insert a **keyframe**.

6. Display the Library panel, open the Buttons folder, then drag the **b_roadRally button** to the position just below the Events button on the Navigation bar, as shown in Figure 17.

   (continued)

Figure 17 *Positioning the b_roadRally button*

The expand icon indicates that this is a folder layer. In this case, all of the navigation bar buttons are within this folder. Clicking the arrow reveals the contents of the folder.

Drag from the library to here

Creating Special Effects

Figure 18 *Positioning the buttons*

The bottom border of the navigation bar must overlap the top border of the Road Rally button.

The bottom border of the Road Rally button must overlap the top border of the Auction button.

7. Insert a **new layer** above the homeBkgrnd layer, then name it **auction**.

8. Click **frame 2** on the auction layer, then insert a **keyframe**.

9. Drag the **b_auction button** from the Library panel and position it below the b_roadRally button.

10. Click the **Zoom tool** 🔍 on the Tools panel, then click the **Events button** on the navigation bar to enlarge the view.

11. Click the **Selection tool** 🔏 on the Tools panel, then click each button and use the arrow keys to position each button, as shown in Figure 18, making sure the bottom border overlaps with the border of the object beneath it.

You placed the drop-down buttons on the Stage and repositioned them.

Add a mask layer

1. Click the **roadRally layer**, insert a **new layer** above the roadRally layer, then name it **mask**.

2. Click **frame 2** on the mask layer, then insert a **keyframe**.

3. Select the **Rectangle tool** on the Tools panel, set the Stroke Color to **No Stroke**, then set the Fill Color to **black**.

4. Draw a **rectangle** that covers the buttons, as shown in Figure 19.

5. Click the **Selection tool** on the Tools panel, then drag the **rectangle** to above the buttons, as shown in Figure 20.

6. Verify the rectangle is selected, click **Insert** on the menu bar, click **Motion Tween**, then click **OK**.

   Note: Flash automatically converts the object to a movie symbol, which can have a motion tween applied to it. If you want the object to be a different type of symbol, you need to convert the object to the symbol type of your choice before inserting the motion tween.

   (continued)

Figure 19 *The drawn rectangle that covers the buttons*

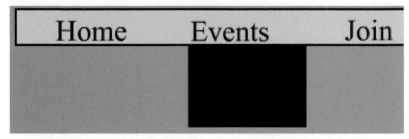

Figure 20 *Dragging the rectangle above the buttons*

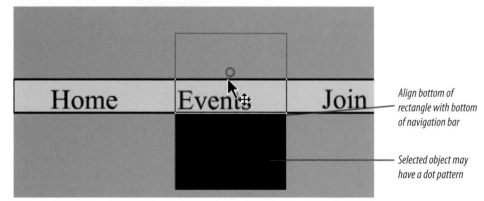

Align bottom of rectangle with bottom of navigation bar

Selected object may have a dot pattern

Creating Special Effects

Figure 21 *Positioning the rectangle over the buttons*

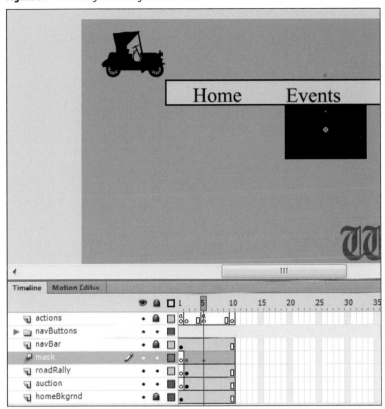

7. Click **frame 5** on the mask layer, then insert a **keyframe**.

8. Use the **Selection tool** ↖ to move the **rectangle**, as shown in Figure 21.

9. Click **mask** on the Timeline, click **Modify** on the menu bar, point to **Timeline**, click **Layer Properties**, click the **Mask option button**, then click **OK**.

10. Click **roadRally** on the Timeline.

11. Click **Modify** on the menu bar, point to **Timeline**, click **Layer Properties**, click the **Masked option button**, then click **OK**.

12. Click **auction** on the Timeline, then repeat step 11.

13. Drag the **playhead** along the Timeline, noticing how the mask hides and reveals the buttons.

You added a mask that animates to hide and reveal the menu buttons.

Assign an action to a drop-down button

1. Change the view to **Fit in Window.**

2. Click **frame 2** on the roadRally layer, then click the **Road Rally button** to select it.

3. Open the Actions panel, then verify the Script Assist button is active and b_roadRally is displayed in the lower-left corner of the Script pane, as shown in Figure 22.

   b_roadRally in the lower-left corner of the Script pane tells you that the b_roadRally button symbol is selected on the Stage and that the ActionScript you create will apply to this object.

4. Click the **Add a new item to the script icon**, point to **Global Functions,** point to **Timeline Control,** then click **goto.**

5. Click the **Scene list arrow,** point to **Scene 2** as shown in Figure 23, then click.

6. Verify the Type is set to Frame Number and the Frame is set to 1.

7. Collapse the Actions panel.

You used the Script Assist window to assign a goto action to a menu button.

Figure 22 *The Actions panel with the b_roadRally button selected*

b_roadRally button indicating the action to be created will be assigned to this button

Script Assist is active

Figure 23 *Selecting the scene to go to*

Scenes, which have their own Timeline, are a way to organize large movies. In this case, Scene 2 contains the Road Rally screen for the website.

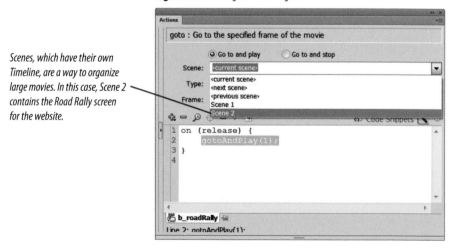

Creating Special Effects

Figure 24 *Specifying a frame label*

Figure 25 *The completed Actions panel*

Frame label

b_events button symbol indicating the action will be assigned to this button

Frame label used in the gotoAndPlay command

Add a frame label and assign a rollOver action

1. Insert a **new layer** at the top of the Timeline, name it **labels**, then insert a **keyframe** in frame 2 on the labels layer.

2. Display the Properties panel, click inside the **Name text box** in the LABEL area, then type **eventsMenu**, as shown in Figure 24.

3. Click the **Events button** on the Stage to select it.

4. Expand the Actions panel, then verify b_events is displayed in the lower-left corner of the Script pane.

5. Click the **Add a new item to the script icon** 🔧, point to **Global Functions**, point to **Movie Clip Control**, then click **on**.

6. Click the **Release check box** to deselect it, then click the **Roll Over check box** to select it.

7. Click the **Add a new item to the script icon** 🔧, point to **Global Functions**, point to **Timeline Control**, then click **goto**.

8. Click the **Type list arrow**, then click **Frame Label**.

9. Click the **Frame list arrow**, then click **eventsMenu**.

   Your screen should resemble Figure 25.

10. Click **Control** on the menu bar, point to **Test Movie**, then click **in Flash Professional**.

11. Point to **Events**, then click **Road Rally**.

12. Close the Flash Player window, collapse the Actions panel, then save your work.

You added a frame label and assigned a rollOver action using the frame label.

Add an invisible button

1. Click **Control** on the menu bar, point to **Test Movie**, then click **in Flash Professional**.

2. Move the pointer over Events on the navigation bar, then move the pointer away from Events.

   Notice that when you point to Events, the drop-down menu appears. However, when you move the pointer away from the menu, it does not disappear.

3. Close the Flash Player window.

4. Insert a **new layer** above the homeBkgrnd layer, then name it **rollOver**.

5. Insert a **keyframe** in frame 2 on the rollOver layer.

6. Click the **Zoom tool** 🔍 on the Tools panel, then click the **Events button** on the navigation bar to enlarge the view.

7. Select the **Rectangle tool** ☐ on the Tools panel, verify that the Stroke Color is set to No Stroke ☑ , then set the Fill Color to **blue**.

8. Draw a **rectangle**, as shown in Figure 26.

9. Click the **Selection tool** ▸ on the Tools panel, then click the **blue rectangle** to select it.

10. Click **Modify** on the menu bar, then click **Convert to Symbol**.

11. Type **b_rollOver** for the name, click the **Type list arrow**, click **Button**, then click **OK**.

12. Expand the Actions panel.

(continued)

Figure 26 *Drawing the rectangle*

Creating Special Effects

Figure 27 *The Actions panel displaying ActionScript assigned to the b_rollOver button symbol*

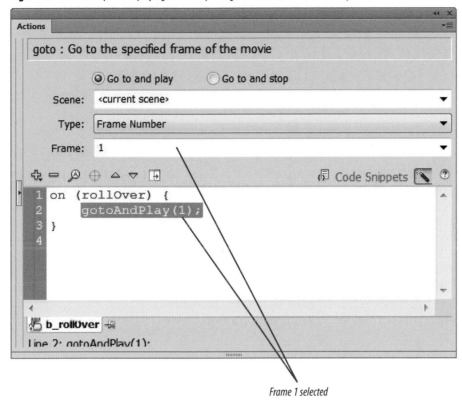

Frame 1 selected

13. Verify the rollOver button is selected and b_rollOver is displayed in the lower-left corner of the Script pane.
14. Click the **Add a new item to the script icon**, point to **Global Functions**, point to **Movie Clip Control**, then click **on**.
15. Click the **Release check box** to deselect it, then click the **Roll Over check box** to select it.
16. Click the **Add a new item to the script icon**, point to **Global Functions**, point to **Timeline Control**, then click **goto**.
17. Verify Frame 1 is specified, as shown in Figure 27.
18. Close the Actions panel.
19. Click the **Style list arrow** in the COLOR EFFECT area of the Properties panel, click **Alpha**, then set the percentage to **0**.
20. Click **Control** on the menu bar, point to **Test Movie**, then click **in Flash Professional**.
21. Point to **Events** to display the drop-down menu, then slowly move the pointer away from Events.

    The drop-down menu disappears.
22. Close the Flash Player window, then save and close the movie.

You added a button and assigned a rollOver action to it, then made the button transparent.

Create Character Animations
USING INVERSE KINEMATICS

What You'll Do

In this lesson, you will use the bone tool to create a character animation and create a movie clip that can be manipulated by the viewer.

Understanding Inverse Kinematics

One way to create character animations is to use the frame-by-frame process in which you place individually drawn objects into a series of successive frames. You did this with the stick figure graphics in an earlier chapter. Those graphics were simple to draw. However, if you have more complex drawings, such as fill shapes that are more realistic, and if you want to create animations that show an unlimited number of poses, the time required to develop all of the necessary drawings would be considerable.

Flash provides a process that allows you to create a single image and add a structure to the image that can be used to animate the various parts of the image. The process is called **inverse kinematics (IK)** and involves creating an articulated structure of bones that allow you to link the parts of an image. Once the bone structure is created, you can animate the image by changing the position of any of its parts. The bone structure causes the related parts to animate in a natural way. For example, if you draw an image of a person, create the bone structure, and then move the person's right foot, then all parts of the leg (lower leg, knee, upper leg) respond. This makes it easy to animate various movements.

Figure 28 shows a drawing of a character before and after the bone structure is added. Figure 29 shows how moving the right foot moves the entire leg. The image is made up of several small drawings, each one converted to a graphic symbol. These include a head, torso, upper and lower arms, upper and lower legs, hips, and feet. Together these form the IK object.

Creating the Bone Structure

The bone structure can be applied to a single drawn shape, such as an oval created with the Flash drawing tools. More often it is applied to an image, such as a character, made up of several drawings. When this is the case, each drawing is converted to a graphic symbol or a movie clip symbol and then assembled to form the desired image. If you import a graphic, it needs to be broken apart using the Modify menu and the individual parts of the imported graphic converted to graphic symbols or movie clip symbols. However, if the imported graphic has only one part (such as a bitmap), it needs to be broken apart and treated as a single drawn shape.

Once the image is ready, you use the Bone tool to create the bone structure, called the armature, by clicking and dragging the Bone tool pointer to link one part of the image to another. You continue adding bones to the structure until all parts of the image are linked. For a human form you would link the head to the torso and the torso to the upper left arm and the upper left arm to the lower left arm, and so on. The bones in an armature are connected to each other in a parent-child hierarchy, so that adjusting the child adjusts the parent.

Animating the IK Object

As you are creating the bone structure, a layer named Armature is added to the Timeline, and the image with the bone structure is placed in frame 1 on that layer. This new layer is called a **pose layer**. Each pose layer can contain only one armature and its associated image. Animating the image is done on this layer by inserting a keyframe in any frame after frame 1 on the Armature layer and then changing the position of one or more of the bones. This

is referred to as creating a pose. Once you specify the start and end positions of the image, Flash interpolates the position of the parts of the image for the in-between frames. So, when one bone moves, the other connected bones move in relation to it. Additional poses can be set along the Timeline by inserting keyframes and adjusting the bone structure. Animations of IK objects, other than those within movie clips, only allow you to change the shape, position, and ease in the animation.

Figure 28 *Drawings showing before and after the bone structure is added*

Figure 29 *Moving the foot moves the other parts of the leg*

Creating a Movie Clip with an IK Object

Movie clips provide a great deal of flexibility when animating IK objects. You can change properties such as the color effect and you can nest one movie clip within another. So, you could have a movie clip of a character walking and nest another movie clip within it to have its mouth move. In addition, you can apply a motion tween to a movie clip. So, you could have a movie clip of a character walking and have it play within a motion tween, which causes the character (movie clip) to jump over an obstacle.

Runtime Feature

Flash provides a runtime feature for manipulation of an IK object. That is, you can allow the user to click the object and adjust the image. This is useful if you are creating a game or just wanting to provide some interaction in an application. The process is to click a frame on the Armature layer, then use the Properties panel to set the Type to Runtime. The runtime feature only works with IK structures connected to drawn shapes or movie clip symbols, not graphic or button symbols. In addition, only one pose can used.

IK Objects

As you are working with IK objects, keep in mind the following:

- The Undo feature can be used to undo a series of actions such as undoing a mistake made when creating the bone structure.
- The bone structure may disappear as you are working on it. This could be caused by going outside the image as you are connecting the parts of the image. If the bone structure disappears, use the Undo feature to Undo your last action.
- To delete an individual bone and all of its children, click the bone and press [Delete]. You can select multiple bones to delete by holding down [Shift] and clicking each bone.
- To delete all bones, select the image and choose the Break Apart command from the Modify menu.
- To create IK animations, ActionScript 3.0 and Flash Player 10 need to be specified in the Publish Settings dialog box, which is displayed by choosing Publish Settings from the File menu.

Figure 30 *Connecting the head and torso*

Figure 31 *Connecting the torso and the upper arm*

The color of the bones may vary

Figure 32 *Connecting the upper and lower arms*

Figure 33 *The completed bone structure*

Create the bone structure

1. Open fl5_5.fla, then save it as **kicker.fla**.

    This document has a graphic symbol made up of 13 individual drawings to form a character shape.

2. Click the **Selection tool** ➤ , then drag a **marquee** around the image to select it.

    Notice the separate objects.

3. Click a blank area of the Stage to deselect the image.

4. Click the **Zoom tool** 🔍 , then click the **image** to zoom in on it.

5. Scroll the Stage to view the head, then click the **Bone tool** 🦴 on the Tools panel.

6. Point to the middle of the head, when the pointer changes to a bone with a cross ⚑ , drag the ⚑ **pointer** down to the torso as shown in Figure 30, then release the mouse button.

7. Point to the bottom of the bone, then drag the ⚑ **pointer** to the left as shown in Figure 31.

8. Point to the left end of the bone, then drag the ⚑ **pointer** down as shown in Figure 32.

    Notice that a bone connects two overlapping objects, such as the bone used to connect the upper arm and lower arm.

9. Using Figure 33 as a guide, complete the drawing of the other bones.

    Hint: Use the Undo command as needed if your connections do not match Figure 33.

10. Save your work.

You created a bone structure by connecting objects on the Stage with the Bone tool.

Animate the character

1. Change the view to **Fit in Window**.
2. Click **frame 10** on the Armature layer, then insert a **keyframe**.

   Note: The name of your Armature layer will include a number.
3. Click the **Selection tool** , then click a blank area of the Stage to deselect the object if it is selected.
4. Point to the **right foot**, then, when the pointer changes to a bone with a delta symbol , drag the **pointer** to position the foot as shown in Figure 34.
5. Point to the **right arm**, then use the pointer to position it as shown in Figure 35.
6. Use the pointer to position the left arm and left foot as shown in Figure 36.

   Hint: To position the left foot, move the left knee first, then move the left foot.
7. Click **frame 20** on the Armature layer, then insert a **keyframe**.
8. Adjust the arms and legs as shown in Figure 37.

   Hint: Move the right leg to the position shown to create a kicking motion.
9. Click the **Free Transform tool** on the Tools panel, then drag a **marquee** around the image to select it if it is not already selected.
10. Point to the **upper-right handle**, then, when the pointer changes to an arc , drag the **pointer** to the left as shown in Figure 38.
11. Test the movie, close the Flash Player window, then save the movie.

You animated the character by adjusting the armatures of the various bones.

Figure 34 *Positioning the right foot*

Figure 35 *Positioning the right arm*

Figure 36 *Positioning the left arm and left foot*

right leg

Figure 37 *Positioning the arms and legs*

right leg

Figure 38 *Rotating the object*

Figure 39 *Increasing the length of the motion span*

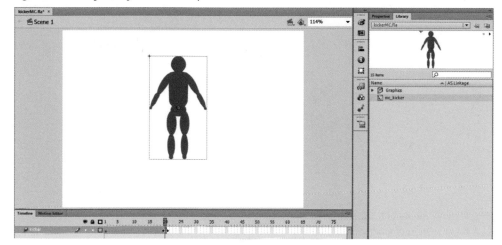

Create a movie clip of the IK object and animate the movie clip

1. Click **File** on the menu bar, click **Save as**, type **kickerMC**, then click **Save**.

2. Click **frame 1** on the Armature layer.

3. Click the **Selection tool** , then drag a **marquee** around the entire image to select it.

4. Click **Modify** on the menu bar, then click **Convert to Symbol**.

5. Type **mc_kicker** for the name, select **Movie Clip** for the Type, then click **OK**.

6. Click **Armature** on the Timeline, then click the **Delete icon** on the Timeline status bar to delete the layer.

7. Click **frame 1** on the kicker layer, display the Library panel, then drag the **mc_kicker symbol** to the Stage.

8. Insert a **motion tween**.

9. Drag the **tween span** on the Timeline to **frame 20**, as shown in Figure 39.

10. Click **frame 10** on the kicker layer.

11. Verify the object is selected, then press the **up arrow** [↑] on the keyboard 10 times.

12. Click **frame 20**, then press the **down arrow** [↓] on the keyboard 10 times.

    Steps 11 and 12 will give the impression of the character jumping up then coming down during the kicking motion.

13. Test the movie, close the Flash Player window, then save your work.

You created a movie clip and applied a motion tween to it.

Apply an ease value

1. Double-click the **mc_kicker symbol** in the Library panel to display the edit window, then scroll as needed to see the entire object.

2. Display the Properties panel.

3. Click **frame 10** on the Armature layer.

4. Set the Ease Strength to **-100**.

5. Click the **Type list arrow** in the EASE area, then click **Simple (Fastest)**

   The EASE type is set to Simple (Fastest), as shown in Figure 40. Frame 10 is the start of the motion tween where the right leg begins to kick downward. Setting the ease value to -100 will cause the leg motion to start out slow and accelerate as the leg follows through to the end of the kicking motion. This is a more natural way to represent the kick than to have the leg speed constant throughout the downward motion and follow through.

6. Click **Scene 1** on the edit window title bar to return to the main Timeline.

7. Test the movie, close the Flash Player window, save your work, then close the file.

You added an ease value to the movie clip.

Figure 40 *Setting the ease value*

Creating Special Effects

Figure 41 *The completed armature structure*

Set the play to runtime

1. Open fl5_6.fla, then save it as **kickerRT.fla**.

   This character is similar to the one used in the kicker movie, however it has been created using movie clips instead of graphic symbols. Also, only one pose is used.

2. Use the **Bone tool** , to create the armature structure as shown in Figure 41.

   Hint: Each bone should connect two body parts.

3. Click **frame 1** on the Armature layer.

   Hint: If you have trouble clicking a frame, select a larger frame view setting and try again.

4. Display the Properties panel, click the **Type list arrow** in the OPTIONS area of the Properties panel, then click **Runtime**.

5. Click **File**, point to **Publish Preview**, then click **Default - (HTML)** to display the movie in a browser.

   Hint: Press [F12] (Win) or [command][F12] (Mac) to display the movie in a browser.

6. Drag each part of the character, such as an arm or a leg.

7. Close your browser.

8. Save your work, then close the document.

You created an animated character, set the play to runtime, and manipulated the character in a browser.

Create 3D EFFECTS

What You'll Do

Photo courtesy of J. Shuman.

 In this lesson, you will create a movie with 3D effects.

Understanding 3D Effects

Flash allows you to create 3D effects by manipulating objects in 3D space on the Stage. Until now you have been working in two dimensions, width and height. The default settings for the Stage are 550 pixels wide and 400 pixels high. These are represented by an X axis (across) and a Y axis (down). Any position on the Stage can be specified by X and Y coordinates. The upper-left corner of the Stage has an X value of 0 and a Y value of 0, and the lower-right corner has an X value of 550 and a Y value of 400, as shown in Figure 42.

In 3D space there is also a Z axis that represents depth. Flash provides two tools, 3D Translation and 3D Rotation that can be used to move and rotate objects using all three axes. In addition, Flash provides two other properties that can be adjusted to control the view of an object. The Perspective Angle property controls the angle of the object and can be used to create a zooming in and out effect. The Vanishing Point property more precisely controls the direction of an object as it moves away from the viewer. The Perspective Angle and the Vanishing Point settings are found in the Properties panel.

Figure 42 *The X and Y coordinates on the Stage*

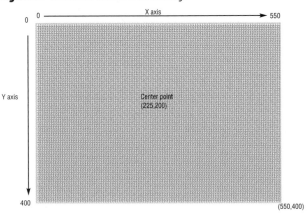

Creating Special Effects

The 3D Tools

The 3D tools are available on the Tools panel. By default the 3D Rotation tool is displayed on the Tools panel. To access the 3D Translation tool, click and hold the 3D Rotation tool to open the menu. Toggle between these two 3D tools as needed.

The process for creating 3D effects is to create a movie clip (only movie clips can have 3D effects applied to them), place the movie clip on the Stage, create a motion tween and then click the object with either of the 3D tools. When you click an object with the 3D Translation tool, the three axes X, Y, and Z appear on top of the object, as shown in

Figure 43. Each has its own color: red (X), green (Y), and blue (Z), which you see only when the 3D Rotation tool is active. The X and Y axes have arrows and the Z axis is represented by a black dot when the 3D Translation tool is active. You point to an arrow or the black dot and drag it to reposition the object. Dragging the X axis arrow moves the object horizontally. Dragging the Y axis arrow moves the object vertically. Dragging the Z axis dot zooms the object in and out.

When you click the object with the 3D Rotation tool, the three axes X, Y, and Z appear on top of the object, as shown in Figure 44. Dragging the X axis (red) will flip the object

horizontally. Dragging the Y axis (green) will flip the object vertically. Dragging the Z axis (blue) will spin the object. A fourth option, the orange circle, rotates the object around the X and Y axes at the same time.

Using a Motion Tween with a 3D Effect

Creating 3D effects requires a change in the position of an object. A motion tween is used to specify where on the Timeline the effect will take place. This allows you to create more than one effect by selecting various frames in the tween span and making adjustments as desired. If you are animating more than one object, each object should be on its own layer.

Figure 43 *The 3D Translation tool*

Photos courtesy of J. Shuman.

Figure 44 *The 3D Rotation tool*

Create a 3D animation

1. Open fl5_7.fla, then save it as **puzzle.fla**.

   Note: The document opens with the ruler feature turned on and showing the vertical and horizontal lines that intersect at the center of the Stage.

2. Change the view to **Fit in Window**.

3. Click **frame 1** on the Image 1 layer, insert a **motion tween**, then drag the **tween span** to frame 40.

4. Click **frame 20** on the Image 1 layer, then select the **3D Translation tool** ⚓ from the Tools panel.

   Note: You may need to click the 3D Rotation tool on the Tools panel to display the 3D Translation tool.

5. Click the **image** in the upper-right corner of the Stage, point to the **green arrow tip**, then use the ▶Y pointer to drag the image down to the horizontal ruler line, as shown in Figure 45.

6. Click the **red arrow tip**, then use the ▶X pointer to drag the image to the left, as shown in Figure 46.

7. Select the **3D Rotation tool** ⚪ from the Tools panel, point to the **green line Y axis** on the right side of the object, then, when the pointer changes to a delta symbol with a Y, drag the ▶Y **pointer** down and to the left, as shown in Figure 47, to flip the image horizontally.

8. Click **frame 40** on the Image 1 layer, then select the **3D Translation tool** ⚓ from the Tools panel.

(continued)

Figure 45 *Using the 3D Translation tool to position the image vertically*

Point here

Drag pointer down

Figure 46 *Using the 3D Translation tool to position the image horizontally*

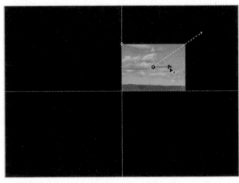

Figure 47 *Using the 3D Rotation tool to flip the image horizontally*

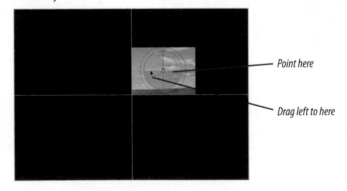

Point here

Drag left to here

Photos courtesy of J. Shuman.

Figure 48 *Using the 3D Translation tool to position the image again*

Figure 49 *Using the 3D Translation tool to position a second image*

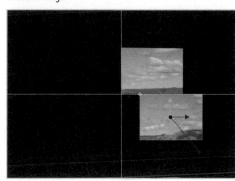

Figure 50 *Using the 3D Rotation tool to flip the image vertically*

Drag pointer left and up   Point here

Figure 51 *Using the 3D Translation tool to reposition the second image*

Photos courtesy of J. Shuman.

Lesson 6   Create 3D Effects

9. Click the **red arrow tip**, then use the ▶x pointer to move the image to the position shown in Figure 48.

10. Select the **3D Rotation tool** ⬤, point to the **green line Y axis** on the left side of the object, then drag the ▶Y **pointer** down and to the right to flip the image horizontally again.

11. Click **frame 1** on the Image 2 layer, insert a **motion tween**, then drag the **tween span** to frame 40.

12. Click **frame 20** on the Image 2 layer, then select the **3D Translation tool** ⬩.

13. Point to the **red and green arrow tips** and use the ▶x pointer and the ▶Y pointer respectively to drag the image to the position shown in Figure 49.

14. Select the **3D Rotation tool** ⬤, then point to the **bottom red line X axis** so the pointer changes to a delta symbol with an X.

15. Use the ▶x pointer to drag the **bottom red line X axis** to the left and up to flip the image vertically, as shown in Figure 50.

16. Click **frame 40** on the Image 2 layer, then select the **3D Translation tool** ⬩.

17. Point to the **red and green arrow tips** and use the ▶x pointer and the ▶Y pointer respectively to position the image as shown in Figure 51.

18. Select the **3D Rotation tool** ⬤, then point to the **bottom red line X axis** so the pointer changes to a ▶x.

19. Drag the **bottom red line X axis** to the left and up to flip the image vertically again.

(continued)

20. Click **frame 1** on the Image 3 layer, insert a **motion tween**, then drag the **tween span** to frame 40.

21. Click **frame 20** on the Image 3 layer, then select the **3D Translation tool** 🔨.

22. Point to the **red and green arrow tips** and use the ►ₓ pointer and the ►ᵧ pointer respectively to drag the image to the position shown in Figure 52.

23. Select the **3D Rotation tool** 🔵, then point to the **blue circle Z axis**, as shown in Figure 53.

    The pointer changes to ►₂.

24. Drag the **circle** to rotate the image clockwise 180 degrees, as shown in Figure 54.

25. Click **frame 40** on the Image 3 layer, then select the **3D Translation tool** 🔨.

26. Point to the **red and green arrow tips** and use the ►ₓ pointer and the ►ᵧ pointer respectively to position the image as shown in Figure 55.

27. Select the **3D Rotation tool** 🔵, point to the **blue circle Z axis**, then use the ►₂ pointer to drag the circle and to rotate the image clockwise 180 degrees again.

28. Click **frame 1** on the Image 4 layer, insert a motion tween, then drag the **tween span** to frame 40.

29. Click **frame 20** on the Image 4 layer, then select the **3D Translation tool** 🔨.

(continued)

Figure 52 *Using the 3D Translation tool to position the third image*

Figure 53 *Pointing to the blue circle Z axis on the 3D Rotation tool*

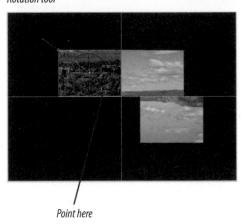

Point here

Figure 54 *Using the 3D Rotation tool to rotate the image*

Rotate the pointer clockwise to here

Figure 55 *Using the 3D Translation tool to reposition the third image*

Creating Special Effects

Figure 56 *Using the 3D Translation tool to position the fourth image*

Figure 57 *Using the 3D Rotation tool to rotate the image*

Drag pointer left to here   Point here

Figure 58 *Using the 3D Translation tool to reposition the fourth image*

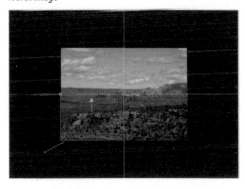

Figure 59 *The completed 3D effects movie*

30. Point to the **red and green arrow tips** and use the ▶$_x$ pointer and the ▶$_Y$ pointer respectively to position the image as shown in Figure 56.

31. Select the **3D Rotation tool** 🔵, then point to the right side of the **orange circle**.

    The pointer changes to a Delta symbol.

32. Drag the ▶ **pointer** to the middle of the image as shown in Figure 57.

33. Click **frame 40** on the Image 4 layer, point to the left side of the orange circle, then drag the ▶ **pointer** to the center of the image.

34. Use the **3D Translation tool** 🔺 to position the image as shown in Figure 58.

35. Click the **Selection tool** ▶, drag the **ruler lines** to remove them, then use the 3D tools and the red and green arrow tips to make adjustments as needed so your screen resembles Figure 59.

    Hint: Use the arrow keys on the keyboard to make minor adjustments to the position of an object.

36. Test the movie, then close the Flash Player window.

37. Save your work, then close the document.

You created a movie with 3D effects.

Use the
DECO TOOL

What You'll Do

In this lesson, you will use the Deco tool to create and animate a cityscape.

Understanding the Deco Tool

The Deco tool provides a variety of drawing effects that can be used to quickly create environments, such as city landscapes, and to create various animations. In addition, the Deco tool can be used to create decorative patterns that incorporate imported graphics and those drawn in Flash. These patterns can be animated and added to a movie to create special effects. Flash has a number of Deco tool brushes and effects. In addition, Adobe has designed the Deco tool so that other brushes and effects can be added by developers. This allows users to develop tools for their specific needs. Because the Deco tool is easy to use and can be used to quickly create a design and add animation, it is a valuable tool for creating prototypes in the early stages of developing an application. One drawback of using the Deco tool is that animations created with the Deco tool often result in movie file sizes that are large. This is because the images created with the brush tools are made up of small segments and the animations are frame-by-frame animations.

Basic Types of Deco Effects

There are 13 drawing effects available with the Deco tool, as shown in Figure 60.

Figure 60 The Deco drawing tools

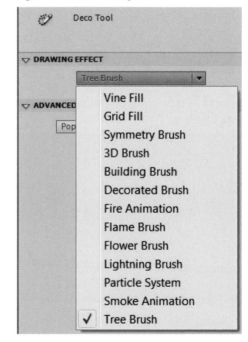

Creating Special Effects

These drawing effects are available in the Properties panel when the Deco tool is selected from the Tools panel. They are grouped into three basic types, although there is some overlap in the groups.

■ Fills—the Vine Fill, Grid Fill, and Symmetry Brush create patterns that can be used as fill for graphics or a backdrop for a movie. Figure 61 shows a vine and a grid fill. Flash allows you to create your own fill using an image of your choice, such as a logo. In addition, you can set various properties such as the pattern scale.

■ Brushes—several brushes including the building, lightning, tree, and flower brushes can be used to create drawings that can be combined to construct environments, like the one shown in Figure 62. The Decorated Brush has 20 variations, including those shown in Figure 63.

■ Animations—a few brushes, such as the Lightning Brush, Fire Animation, Smoke Animation, and Particle System, create animations as they are used. However, any effect created using the Deco tool can be selected, converted to a graphic or movie clip symbol, and animated by inserting a motion tween or using another animation process in Flash.

Hint: Select a keyframe before selecting the Deco tool and use different layers for each Deco tool effect.

Figure 61 *A vine fill and a grid fill*

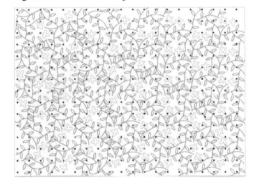

Figure 62 *Cityscape created using Deco tools*

Figure 63 *Patterns created using selected Decorative Brushes*

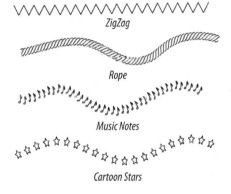

ZigZag

Rope

Music Notes

Cartoon Stars

Create screen design and animations with the Deco tool

1. Open fl5_8 .fla, then save it as **decoLand.fla**.

   This movie has six layers, dimensions of 400 x 400 pxs, a length of 65 frames, and a dark blue backdrop.

2. Change the view for the Timeline to **Small** if necessary to see all 65 frames, then set the view to **Fit in Window**.

3. Click **frame 1** on the buildings layer, click the **Deco tool** on the Tools panel, then display the Properties panel.

4. Click the **DRAWING EFFECT list arrow**, then click **Building Brush**.

5. Verify your Properties panel displays DRAWING EFFECT: Building Brush; ADVANCED OPTIONS: Random building and Building Size 1.

6. Point to the Stage, then click and drag the pointer to the position shown in Figure 64.

   Note: The Random building option may cause your building to display differently.

   Hint: You can use the undo command in the Edit menu to undo an action(s).

7. Continue to create four more buildings similar to Figure 65.

8. Click **frame 1** on the trees layer.

9. Click the **Deco tool** on the Tools panel, then use the Properties panel to change the DRAWING EFFECT to **Tree Brush** and the type to **Poplar Tree**.

10. Use the pointer to draw trees similar to the ones shown in Figure 66.

(continued)

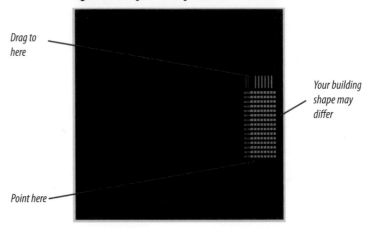

Figure 64 *Using the Building Brush tool*

Drag to here

Your building shape may differ

Point here

Figure 65 *The completed buildings*

Figure 66 *The completed trees*

Drag the Deco tool up to create the tree shape, pause and hold the mouse button down to create the leaves.

Creating Special Effects

Figure 67 *Using the Lightning Brush*

Point here →

Figure 68 *Inserting a blank keyframe*

Figure 69 *Positioning the pointer*

Point here →

Blank keyframe inserted after the
keyframes of the animation.
*Note: There may be a different number
of keyframes in your animation.*

11. Insert a **keyframe** in frame 10 on the lightning layer.
12. Click the **Deco tool** on the Tools panel, change the DRAWING EFFECT to **Lightning Brush** and the color to **white**, then verify animation is checked.
13. Point off the Stage as shown in Figure 67, then drag the **pointer** toward the trees and release the mouse button.
14. Insert a **blank keyframe** in the frame following the last keyframe in the lightning animation, as shown in Figure 68.
15. Click **frame 20** on the fire layer, then insert a **keyframe**.
16. Click the **Deco tool** on the Tools panel, then change the DRAWING EFFECT to **Fire Animation** and the Fire duration to **30 frames**.
17. Click the **tree top** on the far left of the Stage, click **frame 50** on the fire layer, then insert a **blank keyframe**.
18. Click **frame 35** on the snow layer, then insert a **keyframe**.
19. Click the **Deco tool** on the Tools panel, change the DRAWING EFFECT to **Particle System**, verify Particle 1 and Particle 2 have a check mark, and set the particle color to **white** for each particle.
20. Point to the sky, as shown in Figure 69, then click the **pointer**.
21. Click **frame 35**, repeat Steps 19 and 20 **three times** placing the **pointer** in different areas across the sky.
22. Test the movie, close the Flash Player window, save your work, then close the document.

You created a cityscape environment, including animations, with the Deco tool.

Create a mask effect.

1. Start Flash, open fl5_9.fla, then save it as **skillsDemo5.fla**. (*Hint*: When you open the file, you may receive a missing font message, meaning a font used in this document is not available on your computer. You can choose a substitute font or use a default font.)
2. Verify the frame rate is set to 12 and the Flash Publish Settings (accessed from the File menu) are set to Flash Player 10 or above and ActionScript 3.0.
3. Insert a new layer above the table layer, then name it **heading**.
4. Select frame 1 on the heading layer, then use the Text tool to create the Aces Wild heading with the following characteristics: size 48, color #006633 (a dark green), and Byington (or similar) font. (*Hint*: Look at Figure 70 and find a font that matches the heading text. Use the samples provided to find a similar font, such as Constania.)
5. Use the Selection tool to select the heading, then use the Align command in the Modify menu to center the heading across the Stage.
6. With the heading still selected, convert it to a graphic symbol with the name **g_heading**.
7. Insert a keyframe in frame 40 on the heading layer.
8. Insert a new layer above the heading layer, then name it **ending-heading**.
9. Insert a keyframe in frame 40 on the ending-heading layer.
10. Drag the g_heading symbol from the Library panel and position it on top of the heading on the Stage, then use the keyboard arrow keys as needed to position the g_heading symbol.

11. Lock the ending-heading layer.
12. Insert a new layer above the heading layer, then name it **circle**.
13. Select frame 1 on the circle layer, then use the Oval tool to create a black-filled circle with no stroke that is slightly larger in height than the heading text.
14. Place the circle to the left of the heading.
15. Convert the circle to a graphic symbol with the name **g_mask**.
16. With the circle selected, insert a motion tween.
17. Select frame 40 on the circle layer and drag the circle across and to the right side of the heading.
18. Change the circle layer to a mask layer and lock the layer.
19. Change the heading layer to a masked layer and lock the layer.
20. Insert keyframes in frame 40 on the table layer and the head and body layer but not on the card layer.
21. Insert a new layer above the table layer, name it **stopMovie**, move the stopmovie layer below the table layer, then insert a keyframe in frame 40.
22. Open the Actions panel, verify Script Assist is turned off and stopMovie: 40 is displayed in the lower-left corner of the Script pane, then type **stop( );** for the code. (*Note*: Because ActionScript 3.0 is needed when working with inverse kinematics and with the 3D feature, both of which you will do shortly, you cannot use the Script Assist feature of Flash, which is why you typed the code directly into the Actions pane.)
23. Close the Actions panel.
24. Test the movie, then save your work.

Create a character animation using inverse kinematics.

1. Select 1 on the Timeline, then use the Zoom tool to enlarge the view of the character.
2. Use the Bone tool to join the head to the body, then to join the body with the upper and lower left arm, and with the upper and lower right arm. (*Note*: The bone structure stops at the elbow on each arm.)
3. Click the Selection tool on the Tools panel, click frame 40 on the Armature layer, then insert a keyframe.
4. Select frame 6 on the Armature layer.
5. Use the Selection tool to move the ends of the arms so that the lower left and lower right arms are horizontal and touch at the chest. This will cause the elbows to point out away from the body.
6. Select frame 12 on the Armature layer.
7. Use the Selection tool to move the end of the right arm so that it is straight and pointing to the upper-left corner of the Stage.
8. Change the view to Fit in Window.
9. Test the movie, then save your work. (*Note*: If a warning dialog box opens, click OK.)

Create a frame-by-frame animation.

1. Select frame 4 on the card layer, then insert a keyframe.
2. Use the Zoom tool and the keyboard arrow keys as needed to reposition the card so that it is at the end of the right arm.
3. Select frame 5 on the card layer, then insert a keyframe.
4. Use the arrow keys on the keyboard to reposition the card so that it is at the end of the right arm.

5. Repeat steps 3 and 4 in frame 6 through frame 12 on the card layer. (*Note*: The hand moves a small increment in each frame, which is why you must reposition the card so it stays connected to the hand.)
6. Select frame 13 on the card layer, then insert a blank keyframe.
7. Test the movie, close the Flash Player window, then save your work.

Create a 3D effect.

1. Change the view to Fit in Window, insert a new layer above the card layer, then name it **ace3D**.
2. Select frame 12 on the ace3D layer, then insert a keyframe.
3. Drag the mc_aceD movie clip from the Library panel to the Stage, display the Properties panel, verify the Lock width and height values together icon is not a broken link, then resize the width to 10.6.
4. Reposition the ace so it is on top of the card held by the character.
5. Verify frame 12 on the ace3D layer is selected, then create a motion tween.
6. Verify the tween span on the Timeline extends from frame 12 through frame 40.
7. Select frame 40 on the ace3D layer.
8. Use the 3D Translation tool to reposition the card to the upper-left corner of the Stage in a diagonal line that extends from the character's right shoulder. (*Hint*: Use both the red and green arrow tips to move the card to create a diagonal line.)

9. Use the Free Transform tool and the Scale option at the bottom of the Tools panel to resize the card to a width of between 80 and 90.
10. Select frame 26 on the ace3D layer.
11. Use the 3D Rotation tool to add a 3D effect.
12. Select frame 40 on the ace3D layer.
13. Use the 3D Rotation tool to add a 3D effect that causes the card to display right side up, as seen in Figure 70.
14. Test the movie, close the Flash Player window, then save your work.

Add sound to a movie.

1. Insert a new layer at the top of the Timeline, then name it **sound**.
2. Insert a keyframe in frame 15 on the sound layer.
3. Drag introSound.wav from the Library panel to the Stage.
4. Insert a keyframe in frame 40 on the sound layer.
5. Test the movie, if a warning box opens, read the message then click OK, compare your movie to the images in Figure 70, close the Flash Player window, save your work, then close the file.

Figure 70 *Completed Skills Review-IK 3D Animation*

Add video.

1. Open fl5_10.fla, then save it as **skillsDemo5-video.fla**.
2. Add a new layer above the headings layer, then name it **video**.
3. Import the file tour-video.mov as an embedded video from the drive and folder where you store your Data Files to the Library using the Import Video command. (*Note*: You will need to use the Adobe Media Encoder to convert the file to the flv format, then you will need to browse to the drive and folder where you save your Solution Files to open the converted file.)
4. Verify that the video is in the Library panel and on the center of the Stage, notice the number of frames needed to display the entire video as indicated by the blue shading on the video layer. (*Note*: You may need to drag the video from the Library panel to the Stage. If a message appears asking if you want frames inserted into the Timeline, click Yes. *Hint*. Be sure to position the video placeholder, If necessary, to prevent overlapping the text subheading.)
5. Add a new layer, name it **controls**, then select frame 1 on the layer.

6. Use the Text tool to create a text box with the word **Play** beneath and to the left of center of the video, as shown in Figure 71. Set the text characteristics to the following: family Arial, style Narrow (Win) or Regular (Mac), size 20 pt, and color White.

7. Convert the text to a button symbol with the name **b_play**.

8. Edit the over and down states of the button symbol, for example, make the color of the letters change when the mouse pointer is over the word Play and when the user clicks the button. Be sure to add a hit area that surrounds the text.

9. Use the Actions panel and Script Assist to assign a play action to the button that plays the movie when the mouse is released.

10. Use the Text tool to create a text box with the word **Pause** beneath and to the right of center of the video, as shown in Figure 71. Use the same text characteristics used for the Play button.

11. Convert the text to a button symbol with the name **b_pause**.

12. Edit the button symbol to match what you did in step 8.

13. Use the Actions panel to assign a stop action to the button when it is released.

14. Add a new layer, then name it **stopMovie**.

15. Add a stop action to frame 1 on the stopMovie layer.

16. Add a keyframe at the end of the movie on the headings layer. (*Note*: If a message appears asking if you want frames inserted into the Timeline, click No because the frames are already inserted.)

17. Test the movie, compare your screen to Figure 71, close the Flash Player window, then save your work.

18. Close the Flash document.

Work with TLF text.

1. Open fl5_11.fla, then save it as **skillsDemo5-TLF.fla**.

2. Add a new layer and name it **photo**.

3. Select frame 1 of the photo layer and drag the g_birchBay graphic symbol from the Library panel to the center of the Stage.

4. Use the Align panel to center the graphic on the Stage.

5. Lock the heading and photo layers.

6. Add a new layer at the top of the Timeline and name it **text**.

7. Select frame 1 of the text layer and drag the g_text graphic from the Library panel to the middle of the Stage.

8. Verify the text image is selected, then click Modify on the menu bar and select Break Apart. (*Note*: The original text block was changed to a graphic symbol and placed in the Library panel. In order to edit the text, the symbol must be broken apart.)

9. Display the Properties panel and change the text from Classic Text to TLF Text.

10. Change the Size in the CHARACTER area to 13 pt.

11. Change the Behavior in the CONTAINER AND FLOW area of the Properties panel to Multiline.

12. Using Figure 72 as a guide complete the following:
   - Use the Selection tool to resize the Container and create a second linked Container.
   - Use the Text tool to type in the words "in the majestic Pacific Northwest" at the end of the first sentence.
   - Use the Selection tool to select the containers.
   - Justify the text using the "Justify with last line aligned to start" button in the PARAGRAPH area of the Properties panel, and adjust the text box widths as needed to closely match the line wrap shown in Figure 72.

13. Lock the text layer.

14. Test the movie, then close the Flash Player window.

15. Save your work.

Figure 71 *Completed Skills Review - video*

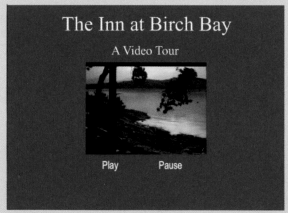

Photo courtesy of Jim Shuman.

Create the drop-down buttons.

1. Save the Flash document as **skillsDemo5-navBar.fla**.
2. Insert a new layer, name it **navBar Background**, create the white horizontal bar shown in Figure 72, then lock the layer.
3. Insert a new layer, name it **navBar Buttons**, then create the three text headings using Classic text and a black color.
4. Convert the Take a Tour heading to a button, then edit the button symbol to add a hit area around it. (*Note*: Be sure to make the hit area long enough so that it will fall below the navBar Background rectangle.)
5. Reposition the Take a Tour button so that its hit area falls below the navBar Background rectangle. (*Note*: You can test the hit area by turning on Enable Simple Buttons in the Control menu and pointing to the button.)
6. Reposition the Home and Map text to match the Take a Tour text as needed.
7. Insert keyframes in frame 10 of all the layers.
8. Insert a layer above the navBar Buttons layer, name it **videoBtn**, then insert a keyframe in frame 2 of the layer.
9. Refer again to Figure 72 and create the video button, edit the button symbol to add a hit area to the button, then position it below Take a Tour.
10. Insert a layer, name it **photosBtn**, then insert a keyframe in frame 2 of the layer.
11. Create the photos button, then position it below the video button.

Add a mask layer.

1. Insert a layer, name it **cover**, then insert a keyframe in frame 2 of the layer.

Photo courtesy of Jim Shuman.

Creating Special Effects

2. Draw a rectangle that covers the video and slide buttons and move it above Take a Tour.
3. Verify the rectangle is selected and Insert a motion tween.
4. Insert a keyframe in frame 5 of the cover layer, then move the rectangle down to cover the buttons.
5. Change the layer properties for the cover layer to mask.
6. Select the photosBtn layer and change it to a masked layer, if it has not changed to a masked layer.
7. Select the videoBtn layer and change it to a masked layer.

Assign actions to buttons and frames.

1. Click File on the menu bar, click Publish Settings, click the Script list arrow, then change the Script to ActionScript 2.0. (*Note*: ActionScript 2.0 is needed when assigning actions to buttons.)
2. When the warning message appears, click OK, then click OK to close the Publish Settings dialog box.

3. Select frame 2 on the videoBtn layer, click to select the Video button, then use ScriptAssist to add the on(release) code that causes the playhead to go to the next scene. (*Note*: The next scene will contain the video; although the scene has not been created yet, you can still assign "next scene();" to the on(release) action.)
4. Insert a layer above the cover layer, name it **labels**, then insert a keyframe in frame 2 of the layer.
5. Add a frame label named **tourMenu**.
6. Select 1 on the Timeline, select the Take a Tour button, then use ScriptAssist to add the code so the playhead goes to and plays the frame labeled tourMenu when the mouse pointer rolls over the button.
7. Insert a layer above the labels layer, name it **actions**, then, in frames 1 and 5 (be sure to add a keyframe) on the actions layer, use the Script pane (ScriptAssist turned off) to type **stop();**.
8. Insert a layer above the heading layer, name it **rollOver**, then insert a keyframe in frame 2 of the layer.

Figure 72 *Completed Skills Review - TLF and Animated Navigation Bar*

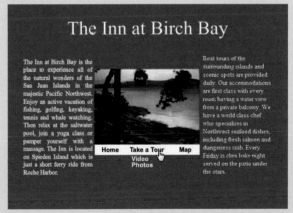

Add an invisible button.

1. Draw a rectangle that covers the Take a Tour, Video, and Photos buttons, then convert the rectangle to a button with the name **rollOverBtn**.
2. Use ScriptAssist to add ActionScript code that causes the playhead to go to frame 1 when the mouse pointer rolls over the button.
3. Select the rollOverBtn button and use the Properties panel to change the alpha setting to 0.
4. Test the movie, then save and close it.
   Note: If your text columns do not display as justified, unlock the text layer if it is locked, select a text block and set the Anti-alias option in the CHARACTER area of the Properties panel to Anti-alias for readability.

Work with the Deco tool.

This is a continuation of the Deco tool exercise you completed in this chapter. Figure 73 shows the changes you will make to the decoLand.fla document as you complete the following steps.

(*Hint*: Use the Undo command in the Edit menu to undo drawings as necessary.)

1. Open decoLand.fla and save it as **skillsDemo5-deco.fla**.
2. Change the view to Fit in Window.
3. Lock all the layers.
4. Insert a new layer above the backdrop layer, name it **road**, then select frame 1 on the road layer.
5. Select the Deco tool and display the Properties panel.
6. Change the DRAWING EFFECT to Decorated Brush, the ADVANCED OPTIONS to 18: Bumps, and the color to white.

7. Use the Deco pointer to draw the road below the buildings. (*Hint*: If no room, draw the road below the trees.)
8. Lock the road layer.
9. Insert a new layer above the snow layer and name it **stars**.
10. Select frame 1 of the stars layer.
11. Select the Deco tool and display the Properties panel.
12. Change the ADVANCED OPTIONS to 16: Shiny Stars, then set the color to white, the pattern size to 30, and the pattern width to 20.
13. Use the Deco pointer to create the stars at the top of the Stage. (*Hint*: You can click and drag the pointer, and you can move the pointer to a new location then click and drag again to create a more scattered effect.)

14. Lock the stars layer.
15. Insert a new layer above the stars layer and name it **flowers**.
16. Select frame 1 of the flowers layer.
17. Select the Deco tool and display the Properties panel.
18. Change the DRAWING EFFECT to Flower Brush, then change the ADVANCED OPTIONS to Rose, and the flower and leaf size to 50%.
19. Click and drag to create the row of flowers at the bottom of the Stage.
20. Lock the flowers layer.
21. Save the movie.
22. Test the movie, then close the Flash Player window.
23. Exit Flash.

Figure 73 *Completed Skills Review - deco*

The Ultimate Tours travel company has asked you to design several sample animations for its application. Figure 74 shows a sample Mystery Ships screen with a mask effect, as the spotlight rotates across the screen and highlights different ships. Complete the following for the Mystery Ships screen of the Ultimate Tours application.

1. Open fl5_12.fla, then save it as **assets.fla**.
2. Open ultimateTours4.fla (the file you created in Chapter 4 Project Builder 1), and save it as **ultimateTours5.fla**.
3. Insert a new layer at the top of the Timeline and select frame 1 on the layer.
4. Display the Library panel, then click the Display movies list arrow below the Library tab to display the list of open documents.
5. Select assets.fla and drag each of the symbols in the Library panel (all sound and graphic files) to the

Stage, delete the layer from the Timeline, click the assets.fla tab above the Stage, then close the assets file. (*Note*: You added the objects from the assets file to the ultimateTours5 Library panel, and then closed the assets.fla file.)
6. Display the Library panel for ultimateTours5.
7. Insert a new layer at the top of the Timeline, then name it **backdrop**.
8. Insert a keyframe in a frame that is higher than the last frame in the current movie (such as frame 100) on the backdrop layer, then draw a dark gray rectangle (#333333) that covers the Stage.
9. Insert a keyframe that is at least 30 frames higher on the backdrop layer (such as frame 130), then lock the layer. (*Note*: All of the subsequent layers you add will use the same starting frame, such as 100.)
10. Insert a new layer, name it **heading**, insert a keyframe in frame 100 (or the frame specified in Step 8), and create the Mystery Ships heading.

11. Insert a new layer, name it **lighthouse**, insert a keyframe in frame 100 (or the frame specified in Step 8), and place the g_lighthouse symbol on the Stage.
12. Insert a new layer, name it **searchlight**, insert a keyframe in frame 100 (or the frame specified in Step 8), and place the g_searchlight symbol to the left of the lighthouse, then use the Selection tool to move the tip of the searchlight to the blue window in the lighthouse. (*Hint*: The searchlight will rotate (pivot) around the transformation point (small circle) of the graphic, which is located in the tip of the searchlight. You can view the transformation point by using the Selection tool to select the searchlight on the Stage.)
13. Use the Free Transform tool to create a motion tween that causes the searchlight to rotate from the left to the right of the lighthouse.

Figure 74 *Sample completed Project Builder 1*

14. Create a new layer for each of the three ships, name each layer appropriately (**ship1**, **ship2**, and **ship3**), and insert keyframes in frame 100 (or the frame specified in Step 8) of each layer.

15. Using frame 100 (or the frame specified in Step 8), place the ships on the Stage so that the searchlight highlights them as it moves from left to right across the Stage.

16. Insert a new layer above the ship layers, name it **searchlight mask**, insert a keyframe in frame 100 (or the frame specified in Step 8), add an instance of the g_searchlight symbol from the Library panel so it is on top of the searchlight on the Stage, then add a motion tween that duplicates the one created in Step 13.

17. Change the layer properties for the four layers you just created in order to create a mask effect that has a searchlight as the mask and reveals the ships when the searchlight is over them. (*Note*: The two searchlight motion tweens are needed on different

layers because one will become a mask and will not be visible in the movie.)

18. Insert a new layer, name it **sound**, insert a keyframe in frame 100 (or the appropriate frame) on the layer, then drag the foghorn.wav sound file to the Stage.

19. Insert a new layer, name it **homeBTN**, insert a keyframe in the last frame of the movie, then add the b_home button to the bottom center of the Stage. (*Note*: This button does not appear on the MYSTERY SHIPS screen in Figure 74 because the last frame of the movie has not been reached.)

20. Add an action to the home button to have the playhead go to frame 1 of the movie when the button is clicked. (*Hint*: You may need to turn on ScriptAssist.)

21. Insert a new layer, name it **stopAction**, then add a keyframe and a stop action at the end of the movie. (*Hint*: You can turn off ScriptAssist and type stop(); into the Actions panel.)

22. Add a new layer, name it **labels**, insert a keyframe in frame 100 (or the appropriate frame), then create a frame label named **mystery**.

23. Click 1 on the Timeline, drag (scrub) the playhead on the Timeline to locate the first frame that shows the layer with the Featured Cruises heading (the layer that has the Galapagos text), then unlock the layer that has the Featured Cruises heading (or layer that has the Galapagos text).

24. Change the Galapagos text to **Mystery Ships**, center align the text, then create a button that changes the text color for the different button states.

25. Add an action to the mystery ship button to have the playhead go to the frame labeled mystery.

26. Test the movie, then compare your image to the example shown in Figure 74.

27. Close the Flash Player window.

28. Lock all layers, save your work, then close the document.

You have been asked to develop a website illustrating the signs of the zodiac. The introductory screen should have a heading with a mask effect and 12 zodiac signs, each of which could become a button. Clicking a zodiac sign button displays an information screen with a different graphic to represent the sign and information about the sign, as well as special effects such as sound, mask effect, and character animation (inverse kinematics). Each information screen would be linked to its button (e.g. zodiac) and to the introductory screen with a Home button. (*Note*: Using the inverse kinematics feature requires ActionScript 3.0, therefore, you will start with a movie that has the ActionScript for the Scorpio and Home buttons and a stop action already developed.)

1. Open fl5_13.fla, save it as **zodiac5.fla**, then change the frame rate to **12 fps**.
2. Test the movie, then study the Timeline to understand how the movie works.
3. Refer to Figure 75 as you complete the introductory screen with the following:
   - A new layer above the signs layer named **heading** with the heading, **Signs of the** that appears from frame 1 through frame 31
   - A new layer named **masked** that contains the word **Zodiac** and that appears from frame 1 through frame 31
   - A mask layer that passes across the heading Zodiac (*Notes*: Use a fill color that can be seen on the black

background. After creating the motion tween, drag the end of the tween span on the Timeline to frame 31. Be sure to set the Layer Properties for the mask and masked layers.)
   - A new layer that displays the word **Zodiac** in frame 31 only (*Note*: Remove frames 32–80 from the layer by using the Remove Frames option from the Timeline command of the Edit menu.)
   - A new layer with a sound that plays from frame 1 through frame 31 as the mask is revealing the contents of the masked layer
4. Refer to Figure 75 as you complete the scorpio screen with the following: (*Notes*: The scorpio screen starts in frame 51. Remove frames in other layers containing content that you do not want displayed after frame 31, such as the Zodiac heading.)
   - A new layer with the three-line heading

Figure 75 *Sample completed Project Builder 2*

Scorpio - the Scorpion
October 23 - November 21
Intense, Emotional, Secretive
   - An inverse kinematics animation that moves the tail (*Note*: Be sure to connect the head to the tail.)
5. Test the movie.
6. Save the movie as **zodiac5-mc.fla**.
7. Select frame 51 on the Armature layer and convert the IK animation to a movie clip.
8. Open the Edit window for the movie clip and add a stop action on a separate layer at the end of the movie clip, then return to the main Timeline.
9. Delete the Armature layer, then select frame 51 on the scorpio layer and drag the movie clip to the Stage.
10. Create a motion tween to animate the movie clip so the scorpion moves across the screen.
11. Test the movie, compare your screens to Figure 75, close the Flash Player window, then save the movie.

Tail moves while scorpion moves across the screen

Figure 76 shows the home page of a website. Study the figure and complete the following questions. For each question, indicate how you determined your answer.

1. Connect to the Internet, then go to *www.adidas.com*, and display the women's running shoes. Go to the site and explore several links to get a feeling for how the site is constructed. Use Figure 76 to answer the questions.

2. Open a document in a word processor or open a new Flash document, save the file as **dpc5**, then answer the following questions. (*Hint*: Use the Text tool in Flash.)

   - Whose site is this and what seems to be the purpose of this site?
   - Who is the target audience?
   - How would you use a character animation with inverse kinematics on this site?
   - How would you use video on this site?
   - How would you use a mask effect on this site?
   - How would you use sound on this site?
   - How would you use 3D on this site?
   - What suggestions would you make to improve the design and why?

Figure 76 *Design Project*

adidas, the 3-Bars logo, the 3-Stripe trade mark, and adizero are registered trademarks of the adidas Group, used with permission. adidas AG owns the copyright to the Image used. www.adidas.com

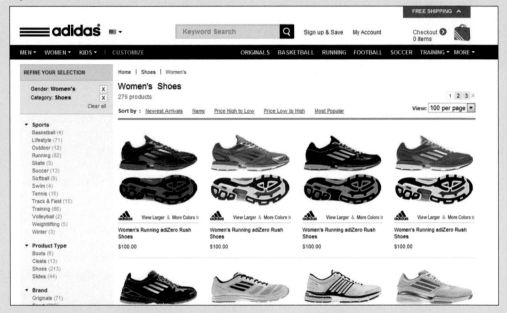

Creating Special Effects

This is a continuation of the Portfolio Project in Chapter 4, which is the development of a personal portfolio.

In this project, you will create several buttons for the Sample Animations screen and link them to their respective animations.

1. Open portfolio4.fla (the file you created in Portfolio Project, Chapter 4) and save it as **portfolio5.fla**.
2. Display the Sample Animations screen. You will be adding buttons to this screen. Each of these new buttons links to a screen that plays its corresponding animation. In each case, have the animation return to the Sample Animations screen at the end of the animation.
3. Add a button for a character animation so it appears on the Sample Animations screen, add a new layer and create a character animation (inverse kinematics) on that layer, then link the character animation button to the character animation.
4. Add a button for a mask effect so it appears on the Sample Animations screen, add new layers to create a mask effect (such as to the words My Portfolio) on that layer, add a sound that plays as the mask is revealing the contents of the masked layer, then link the mask effect button to the mask effect animation.
5. Add a button for an animated navigation bar so it appears on the Sample Animations screen, add a new layer and create an animated navigation bar on that layer, then link the navigation bar button to the animated navigation bar.
6. Test the movie, then compare your Sample Animation screen to the example shown in Figure 77.
7. Close the Flash Player window, then save your work.

Figure 77 *Sample completed Portfolio Project*

CHAPTER 6 PREPARING AND PUBLISHING APPLICATIONS

1. Publish movies using different formats

2. Reduce file size to optimize a movie

3. Create a preloader

NEW 4. Publish AIR applications

NEW 5. Create and publish applications for mobile devices

CHAPTER 6 PREPARING AND PUBLISHING APPLICATIONS

Introduction

The most common use of Flash is to develop applications for delivery on the web, on mobile devices, and on stand-alone computers. During the planning process for an Adobe Flash movie, you are concerned with, among other things, how the target audience will view the movie. Flash provides several features that help you generate the files that are necessary for delivering movies successfully to the target audience over the Internet. These features include creating HTML files that play the Flash SWF movies.

There will be times when you are not delivering Flash applications through the Internet. For example, you may have a game that resides on a desktop computer, an informational application located on a kiosk, or a mobile app that is downloaded to a smartphone. In these cases, the Flash publish settings can be used to create projector files (executable files) and AIR files. Projector files (Win and Mac) are stand-alone executable files that do not require the Flash Player.

Similarly, AIR (Adobe Integrated Runtime) files do not require the Flash Player. The AIR file format is similar to creating an executable file, however, the file size is considerably smaller than projector files. Therefore, AIR files are more suitable for mobile applications.

> **QUICK TIP**
>
> Flash provides a new feature that allows you to test a mobile application using the on-screen Simulator. The Simulator displays the application as it would appear on a mobile phone, and it allows you to use events and gestures such as touch, zoom, and swipe to see how the application reacts. Go to Cengage Brain to access a bonus lesson on the Simulator.

When you deliver content over the Internet, you want to provide compelling movies. However, it is important that you keep the file size down so that the movies play smoothly regardless of the user's connection speed. Flash allows you to test movies to determine where problems might arise during download and to make changes to optimize the movies.

Publish Movies
USING DIFFERENT FORMATS

What You'll Do

In this lesson, you will use the Flash Publish Settings feature to publish a movie, create a GIF animation, create a JPEG image from a movie, and create an executable file.

Using Publish Settings

The Flash Publish feature generates the files necessary to deliver the movies on the web. When you publish a movie using the default settings, a Flash (SWF) file is created that can be viewed using the Flash Player. In addition, an HTML file is created with the necessary code to instruct the browser to play the Flash file using the Flash Player.

Figure 1 shows the Publish Settings dialog box with a list of the available formats for publishing a Flash movie. By default, the Flash (.swf) and HTML Wrapper formats are selected. You can choose a combination of formats, and you can specify a different name (but not file extension) for each format. The GIF, JPEG, and PNG formats create still images that can be delivered on the web or within other applications. The GIF format can also be used to create GIF animations. The projector formats in the Publish Settings dialog box are executable files (which were discussed in Chapter 1). When you select a format, its settings appear. Figure 1 shows the Flash and the HTML Wrapper formats

selected in the Publish Settings dialog box, as well as the default settings associated with those formats. The options include:

- A profile, which is a set of selected settings that have been saved for later use; the Default profile is selected in Figure 1
- The target version of the Flash Player
- The version of ActionScript
- The quality for JPEG images and audio
- Other options, such as compressing the movie

> **QUICK TIP**
>
> Not all features of Flash CS6 work when using Flash Player versions earlier than version 10

Figure 2 shows the GIF format selected and its format settings. The Flash (.swf) and HTML Wrapper formats are still selected. These are optional when selecting any of the other formats. GIF files, which are compressed bitmaps, provide an easy way to create images and simple animations for delivery on the web. GIF animations are frame-by-frame animations created from Flash movie frames.

You can change several settings, including the following:

- The dimensions in pixels (or you can match the movie dimensions)
- Playback as a static image or an animated GIF
- Whether an animation plays (loops) continuously or repeats a certain number of times
- A range of appearance settings, such as optimizing colors and removing gradients

Using Publish Preview

You can use the Publish Preview command on the File menu to publish a movie and display the movie in either your default browser or the Flash Player. In addition, you can use this command to view HTML, GIF, JPEG, PNG, and Projector files.

Figure 1 *The Publish Settings dialog box*

Profile

Selected formats

Target list arrow

Script list arrow

Figure 2 *The GIF format settings*

GIF Image format selected

Publish using the default settings

1. Open fl6_1.fla from the drive and folder where your Data Files are stored, save it as **planeLoop.fla**, then play the movie.

2. Click **File** on the menu bar, then click **Publish Settings**.

3. Verify that the Flash (.swf) and HTML Wrapper check boxes are the only ones selected.

4. Verify that the version is set to Flash Player 11.2 or later and that the Compress movie check box in the ADVANCED area is selected.

TIP You may have to expand the ADVANCED area to see the options.

5. Accept the remaining default settings, click **Publish**, then click **OK**.

6. Use your file management program to navigate to the drive and folder where you save your Data Files, then notice the three files with filenames that start with "planeLoop", as shown in Figure 3.

7. Display the Flash program, click **File** on the menu bar, point to **Publish Preview**, then click **Default - (HTML)**.

   The movie plays in a browser.

   Note: If a warning message opens, follow the messages to allow blocked content.

8. Close the browser, then display the Flash program.

You published a movie using the default publish settings and viewed it in a browser.

Figure 3 *The three planeLoop files*

The Flash document file

Your browser icon may vary

The Flash Player file

Your file extensions may not appear

The HTML document file

HTML or your browser may be listed as the file type

Your file sizes may differ

Figure 4 *The completed Publish Settings dialog box for GIF settings*

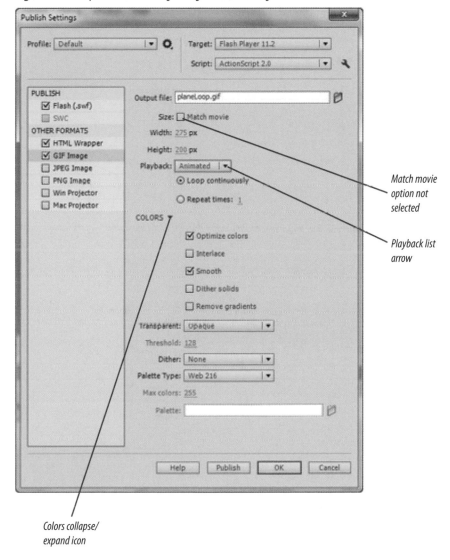

Match movie option not selected

Playback list arrow

Colors collapse/ expand icon

Create a GIF animation from a movie

1. Click **File** on the menu bar, then click **Publish Settings**.
2. Click the **GIF Image check box**.
3. Click the **Match movie check box** to the right of Size: to turn off this setting, click the **Width text box**, type **275**, click the **Height text box**, then type **200**.
4. Click the **Playback list arrow**, then click **Animated**.
5. Click the **COLORS expand icon** ▶ , then verify the remaining default settings match those shown in Figure 4.
6. Click **Publish**, then click **OK**.
7. Open your browser, then use the browser to open planeLoop.gif from the drive and folder where you save your work.

TIP Many browsers have an Open command on the File menu. Use this command to navigate to and then open files for display within the browser. If you do not see the GIF file, change the file type to All Files.

8. Notice the GIF animation plays in the browser with the modified settings.

   Because the GIF file is not an SWF file, it does not require the Flash Player to play—it can be displayed directly in a web browser.
9. Close the browser.

You changed the publish settings for a GIF image, then created a GIF animation and viewed it in your web browser.

Create a JPEG image from a frame of a movie

1. Display the Flash program, then click **10** on the Timeline.

2. Click **File** on the menu bar, then click **Publish Settings**.

3. Click the **GIF Image check box** to deselect it, then click the **JPEG Image check box** to select it.

   Deselecting the GIF format will prevent the GIF file from being created again.

4. Review the default settings, click **Publish**, then click **OK**.

5. Open your browser, then use the browser to open the planeLoop.jpg file from the drive and folder where you save your work.

TIP If you do not see the JPG file, change the file type to All Files.

6. Notice that the static JPEG image appears in the browser, as shown in Figure 5.

7. Close your browser, then display the Flash program.

You reviewed the default publish settings for a JPEG image, then created a JPEG image and viewed it in your web browser.

Figure 5 *The JPEG image displayed in a browser*

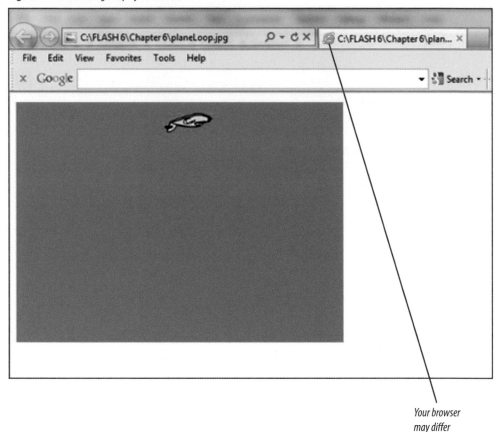

Your browser may differ

Figure 6 *The completed Win Projector format dialog box*

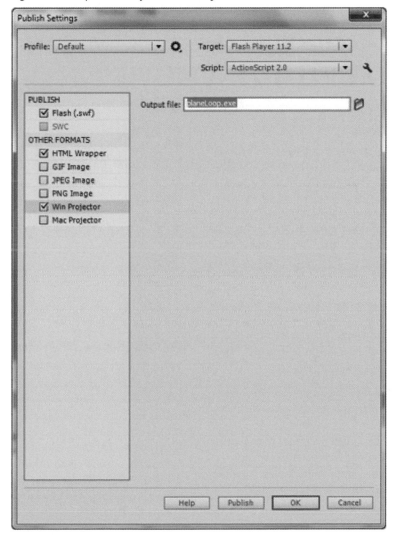

Create an executable file

1. Click **File** on the menu bar, then click **Publish Settings**.

2. Click the **JPEG Image check box** to deselect it, then click the **Win Projector** (or **Mac Projector**) **check box** to select it.

   Note: A Mac Projector file uses the extension .app.

3. Review the default settings as shown in Figure 6.

4. Click **Publish**, then click **OK**.

5. Use your file management program to navigate to the drive and folder where you save your Data Files, then notice the size of the executable file.

   Note: The file size of executable files can be very large.

6. Double-click the **filename** to run the file.

7. Close the player window.

8. Save your work, then close the movie.

You reviewed the default publish settings for an executable file, then created an executable file and viewed it.

Reduce File Size
TO OPTIMIZE A MOVIE

What You'll Do

 In this lesson, you will test a movie and reduce its file size.

Testing a Movie

The goal in publishing a movie is to provide the most effective playback for the intended audience. This requires that you pay special attention to the download time and playback speed. Users are turned off by long waits to view content, jerky animations, and audio that skips. These events can occur as the file size increases in relation to the user's Internet connection speed.

Before you publish a movie, be sure you have maximized its optimization in order to improve its delivery. As you develop Flash movies, keep in mind and practice these guidelines for optimizing movies:

- Use symbols and instances for every element that appears in a movie more than once.
- Use tween animations rather than frame-by-frame animations when possible.
- Use movie clips rather than graphic symbols for animation sequences.
- Confine the area of change to a keyframe so that the action takes place in as small an area as possible.
- Use bitmap graphics as static elements rather than in animations.

- Group elements, such as related images.
- Limit the number of fonts and font styles.
- Use gradients and alpha transparencies sparingly.

When you publish a movie, Flash optimizes it using default features, including compressing the entire movie, which is later decompressed by the Flash Player. However, Flash provides various ways to test a movie before you publish it to determine where changes/optimizations can improve its delivery. Two features for testing are discussed next.

Using the Bandwidth Profiler

When a movie is delivered over the Internet, the contents of each frame are sent to the user's computer. Depending on the amount of data in the frame and the user's connection speed, the movie may pause while the frame's contents download. The first step in optimizing a movie is to test the movie and determine which frames may create a pause during playback. The test should be done using a simulated Internet connection speed that is representative of the speed of your target audience. You can set a simulated speed using the **Bandwidth Profiler**, shown in Figure 7. The Bandwidth Profiler allows you to view a

Preparing and Publishing Applications

graphical representation of the size of each frame. Each bar represents one frame of the movie, and the height of the bar corresponds to the frame's size. If a bar extends above the red baseline, the movie may need to pause to allow the frame's contents to be downloaded. Figure 7 shows the following:

- Movie information: dimensions, frame rate, file size, duration (in frames and seconds), and preload (number of frames and amount of time it takes before the application starts playing)
- Settings: simulated bandwidth (specified in the View menu option)
- State: number of the selected frame (that is, the location of the playhead) and size of the contents in that frame

The Bandwidth Profiler shown in Figure 7 indicates that downloading frame 38 may result in a pause because of the large size of the contents in this frame in relationship to the connection speed and the frame rate. If the specified connection speed is correct for your target audience and the frame rate is needed to ensure acceptable animation quality, then the only change that can be made is in the contents of the frame.

Using the Simulate Download Feature

When testing a movie, you can simulate downloading Flash movies using different connection speeds. The most common connections are dial-up, broadband (both DSL and cable), and T1. Dial-up is a phone connection that provides a relatively slow download speed. Broadband is a type of data transmission in which a wide band of frequencies is available to transmit more

information at the same time. DSL provides a broadband Internet connection speed that is available through phone lines. DSL and cable are widely used by homes and businesses. T1 provides an extremely fast connection speed and is widely used in businesses, especially for intranet (a computer network within a company) applications. You can test the movie that you are developing at the different speeds to evaluate the download experience for potential users.

Figure 7 *The Bandwidth Profiler*

Simulated bandwidth set in the View menu

Selected frame (38)

Information about selected frame

Movie:
Dim: 550 X 400 pixels
Fr rate: 12.0 fr/sec
Size: 89 KB (91945 B)
Duration: 156 fr (13.0 s)
Preload: 15 fr (1.3 s)
Settings:
Bandwidth: 33400 B/s (2783 B/fr)
State:
Frame: 38
9 KB (9931 B)

64 KB
32 KB
16 KB
8 KB
4 KB
2.7 KB

10   20   30   40   50

Playback head at frame 38

Test the download time for a movie

1. Open fl6_2.fla, then save it as **planeFun.fla**.

2. Turn on your computer speakers or plug in headphones if you would like to hear the audio that is part of this movie.

3. Change the view to **Fit in Window**.

4. Click **Control** on the menu bar, point to **Test Movie**, then click **in Flash Professional**.

5. Maximize the Flash Player window.

6. Click **View** on the menu bar, point to **Download Settings**, then click **DSL (32.6 KB/s)**, as shown in Figure 8.

   The connection speeds (especially DSL) are affected by several factors including your Internet service provider capabilities, distance to telecom equipment, your computer and Internet connectivity equipment and the amount of Internet traffic. The Download Simulator provides relative connection speeds and is used to help determine where in a movie a download problem might exist.

7. Click **View** on the menu bar, then click **Simulate Download**.

   The movie is loaded and ready to play in the Flash Player using the simulated speed of 32.6 KB/s.

   (continued)

Figure 8 *Selecting the connection speed for a simulated download*

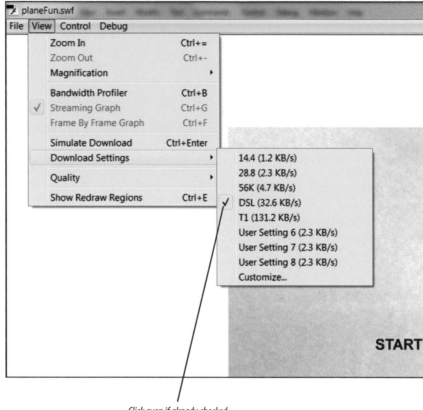

Click even if already checked

Figure 9 *A pause in the movie*

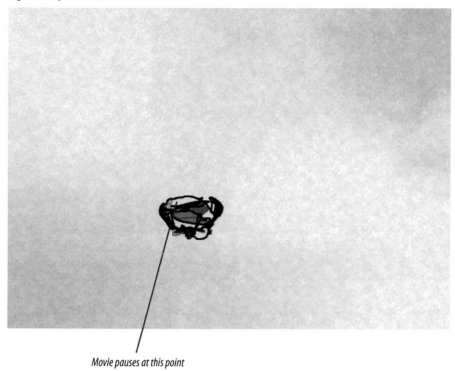

Movie pauses at this point

8. Click **Start**, then notice the pause in the movie when the plane begins to morph into the hot air balloon, as shown in Figure 9.

   You may have to wait several moments for the movie to continue. The pause is caused by the simulated browser waiting for the remaining contents of the movie to be downloaded.

9. Click **View** on the menu bar, point to **Download Settings**, then click **T1 (131.2 KB/s)**.

10. Click **View** on the menu bar, verify the Simulate Download feature is off (no check mark next to it), then click **Simulate Download** to turn on the feature.

    When you change a download setting, you need to be sure the Simulate Download feature is off, and then you must turn it on again to start the simulation with the new setting. The movie is loaded and ready to play in the Flash Player at the simulated download speed of 131.2 KB/s.

11. Click **Start**, then notice the pause in the movie is shorter with the simulated T1 line speed.

TIP If you don't notice a difference, turn the Simulate Download feature off and then on again.

Note: To see a dramatic difference, select one of the simulated dial up speeds (14.4, 28.8, or 56 K). If you do this, be prepared to wait up to several minutes for the plane to morph into a hot air balloon. If you have users that connect via a dial-up connection, be sure to simulate a dial-up connection and make adjustments as needed so the movie displays as smoothly as possible.

You used the Flash Player window to simulate the download time for a movie using different connection speeds.

Use the Bandwidth Profiler

1. Verify that the Flash Player window is still open.

2. Click **View** on the menu bar, point to **Download Settings**, then click **DSL (32.6 KB/s)** to select it.

3. Click **View** on the menu bar, then click **Bandwidth Profiler**.

4. Click **View** on the menu bar, then verify Frame By Frame Graph is selected.

5. Click **View** on the menu bar, then click **Simulate Download**.

   Notice the green bar as it scrolls at the top of the Bandwidth Profiler to indicate the frames being downloaded. The bar pauses at frame 38, as shown in Figure 10.

6. Click **frame 37** on the Timeline, then notice that the only object in the frame is the morphing balloon, and its size is less than 1 KB.

7. Click **frame 38** on the Timeline, then notice the large color photograph.

   The frame setting in the State area indicates that the file size is over 600 KB. It takes several moments to download this large image, which causes the pause in the movie. One way to optimize the movie is to replace the image with the large file size, the one that is currently in frame 38, with an image that is a smaller file size.

8. Close the Flash Player window.

You used the Bandwidth Profiler to determine which frame causes a pause in the movie.

Figure 10 *The Bandwidth Profiler indicating the pause at frame 38*

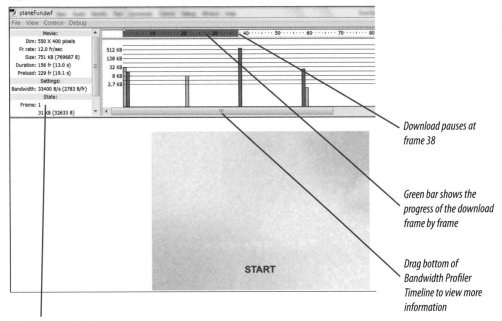

Download pauses at frame 38

Green bar shows the progress of the download frame by frame

Drag bottom of Bandwidth Profiler Timeline to view more information

There is a stop action in frame 1 causing the movie to stay at frame 1 while the rest of the movie is downloading

Figure 11 *Positioning the cloud image*

Drag the icon to adjust the   Drag the border up to   Frame 38 selected
Timeline panel width   view more layers

Optimize a movie by reducing file size

1. Point to the **top border** of the Timeline, then, when the pointer changes to a double-arrow ↕, drag the **top border** up to view the balloons-image layer.

   TIP If the layer name appears cut off, then drag the Adjust Timeline panel width icon to the right until the layer name is fully visible.

2. Click **frame 38** on the balloons-image layer to view the image on the Stage.

3. Click the **balloon photographic image** on the Stage, click **Edit** on the menu bar, then click **Cut**.

   The balloon photograph is no longer visible on the Stage.

4. Display the Library panel.

5. Verify frame 38 is selected, then drag the **cloud.png** graphic from the Library panel to the center of the Stage, as shown in Figure 11.

6. Click **Control** on the menu bar, point to **Test Movie**, click **in Flash Professional**, then maximize the Flash Player window if it is not already maximized.

7. Click **View** on the Flash Player window menu bar, click **Simulate Download**, wait for the download to finish, then click **Start**.

   Notice the movie no longer pauses.

8. Click **frame 38** on the Timeline in the Flash Player window and notice that the file size is now just above the 8 KB line.

9. Click **View**, click **Bandwidth Profiler** to close the Bandwidth Profiler, close the Flash Player window, save your work, then close the movie.

You replaced an image that had a large file size with one having a small file size to help optimize a movie.

Create a
PRELOADER

What You'll Do

Loading . . .

In this lesson, you will create a preloader for the planeFun movie.

Preloading a Movie

One way you can improve the playback performance of large or complex movies is to preload the movie frames. Preloading frames prevents the browser from playing a specified frame or series of frames until all of the frames have been downloaded. Commonly, a **preloader** frame includes a simple animation that starts in frame 1 and loops until the rest of the movie has been downloaded. The animation could consist of the words "Please wait" flashing on the screen, the word "Loading" with a series of scrolling dots, or the hand of a clock sweeping around in a circle. The purpose of the animation is to indicate to the viewer that the movie is being loaded. The animation is placed on its own layer. A second layer contains the ActionScript code that checks to see if the movie has been loaded and, if not, causes a loop that continues the preloader animation until the last frame of the movie has been loaded.

For example, assume a movie has 155 frames. An additional 10 frames could be added to the beginning of the movie for the preloader, and the preloader animation would run from frames 1 to 10. A label, such as **startofMovie**, would be added to frame 11 (the first frame of the actual movie). Another label, such as **endofMovie**, would be added to frame 165, the last frame of the entire movie. Then the following ActionScript code would be placed in frame 1 of the movie on the preLoaderScript layer:

```
ifFrameLoaded ("endofMovie") {
    gotoAndPlay ("startofMovie");
}
```

This ActionScript code is a conditional statement that checks to see if the frame labeled endofMovie is loaded. If the statement is true, then the next line of the script is executed and the playhead goes to the frame labeled startofMovie. This ActionScript code is placed in frame 1 on the preLoaderScript layer. So each time the playhead is on frame 1, there is a check to see if the entire movie has been downloaded. If the condition is false, the playhead moves on to frames 2, 3, 4, and so on. Then the following ActionScript code would be placed in frame 10.

gotoAndPlay (1);

This creates a loop. When the movie first starts, the playhead is on frame 1 and there is a check to see if the movie has been loaded. If not, the playhead continues to frame 10 (playing the preloader animation) where the script "gotoAndPlay (1)"; causes the playhead to loop back to frame 1 for another check.

The looping process continues until all movie frames have been loaded.

Figure 12 shows the Timeline that displays the two preloader layers after the preloader has been created.

Figure 12 *The completed preloader with the animation and ActionScript*

The preloader ActionScript code in frames 1 and 10

The preloader animation plays in frames 1 through 10

The startofMovie frame label in frame 11

Add layers for a preloader

1. Open fl6_3.fla, then save it as **preLoader.fla**.

   This movie is similar to the planeFun.fla movie except that the first 10 frames contain no content, and the movie again contains the larger graphic file photo of the hot air balloons.

2. Change the view to **Fit in Window**.

3. Click the **labels layer** at the top of the Timeline, then click the **New Layer icon** to insert a **new layer**.

4. Name the new layer **preLoaderScript**.

5. Insert a **new layer** above the preLoaderScript layer, then name it **preLoaderAnimation**.

6. Click **frame 10** on the preLoaderAnimation layer, then insert a **keyframe**.

7. Insert a **keyframe** in frame 10 on the preLoader-Script layer.

   Your screen should resemble Figure 13.

You added two layers that will be used to create a preloader. One layer will contain the ActionScript and the other layer will contain the animation for the preloader.

Figure 13 *The preloader layers added to the Timeline*

New layers   Keyframes

Preparing and Publishing Applications

Figure 14 *The Actions panel showing frame to which action will be applied*

The ActionScript that is to be developed will be applied to frame 1 on the preLoaderScript layer

Script Assist feature is off

Figure 15 *The ActionScript code used to check if the last frame in the movie has been downloaded*

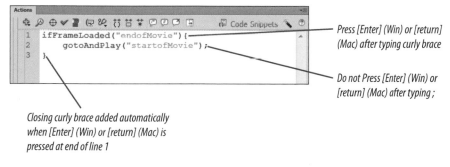

Press [Enter] (Win) or [return] (Mac) after typing curly brace

Do not Press [Enter] (Win) or [return] (Mac) after typing ;

Closing curly brace added automatically when [Enter] (Win) or [return] (Mac) is pressed at end of line 1

Add actions to the preloader

1. Open the Actions panel, then turn off the Script Assist feature if it is on.
2. Click **frame 1** on the preLoaderScript layer.
3. Verify that preLoaderScript:1 is displayed in the lower-left corner of the Actions panel Script pane, as shown in Figure 14.
4. Click the **Actions panel Script pane**, then type the following code, matching use of capital letters, spacing, and punctuation exactly.

   ifFrameLoaded ("endofMovie") {

      gotoAndPlay ("startofMovie");

   Your screen should match Figure 15.

   Note: A closing curly brace was added automatically when you pressed [Enter] (Win) or [return] (Mac) at the end of line. You do not type the closing brace. If your press [Enter] (Win) or [return] (Mac) at the end of line two, a second curly brace will be added to the code. If this happens, delete one curly brace. Be sure there is only one closing curly brace.
5. Click **frame 10** on the preLoaderScript layer, then verify preLoaderScript:10 is displayed in the lower-left corner of the Actions panel Script pane.
6. Click the **Actions panel Script pane**, then type the following code.

   gotoAndPlay (1);
7. Close the Actions panel.

You added actions to frames on the preLoaderScript layer that create a loop. The loop includes a check to see if the entire movie has been loaded and, if so, jumps to a starting place in the movie.

Create the preloader animation

1. Click **frame 1** on the preLoaderAnimation layer.

2. Click the **Text tool** T on the Tools menu, verify the text type is set to Classic Text, click the middle of the Stage, then type **Loading**.

3. Double-click to select **Loading**, then use the Properties panel to set the font to **Arial**, the style to **Bold**, the size to **20**, and the color to **blue**.

4. Insert a **keyframe** in frame 3 on the preLoader-Animation layer.

5. Using the **Text ⊤ pointer**, point to the right of the g in Loading, click, press the **spacebar**, then type a **period [.]**.

6. Insert a **keyframe** in frame 6 on the preLoaderAnimation layer.

7. Point to the right of the period, click, press the **spacebar**, then type a **period [.]**.

8. Insert a **keyframe** in frame 9 on the preLoader-Animation layer, point to the right of the period, click, press the **spacebar**, then type a **period [.]**.

   Your screen should resemble Figure 16.

9. Click **frame 10** on the preLoaderAnimation layer, click **Insert** on the menu bar, point to **Timeline**, then click **Blank Keyframe**.

   Inserting a blank keyframe prevents the contents of the previous frame from being inserted into the frame.

10. Drag the **playhead** back and forth across frames 1 through 10 and view the animation.

You created an animation that causes the word Loading to appear, followed by three dots, as the playhead loops waiting for the movie to load. You can create any animation for the preloader and use as many frames as desired.

Figure 16 *The text used in the preloader animation*

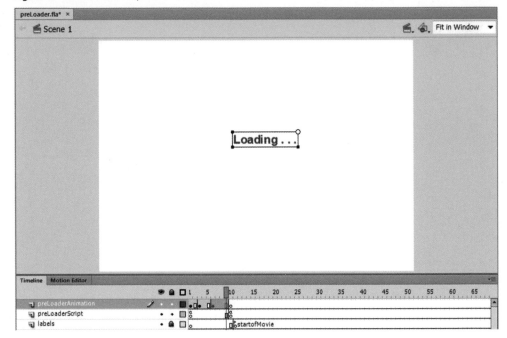

Figure 17 *The Bandwidth Profiler showing the delay in downloading frame 48*

Playhead loops while
movie is loading

Delay in downloading
frame 48

Preloader animation plays
until all frames are loaded

Testing the preloader

1. Click **Control** on the menu bar, point to **Test Movie**, then click **in Flash Professional**.

2. Maximize the Flash Player window if it is not already maximized.

3. Click **View** on the menu bar, then click **Bandwidth Profiler** to display it if it is not already displayed.

4. Click **View** on the menu bar, point to **Download Settings**, then verify that DSL (32.6 KB/s) is selected.

5. Click **View** on the menu bar, then click **Simulate Download**.

   Notice the playhead loops, causing the preloader animation "Loading . . ." to play over and over in the Flash Player window as the frames are loaded. There is a delay in downloading frame 48, as shown in Figure 17, as the large JPG file is loaded. Once all frames are loaded, the screen with the Start button appears in the Flash Player window.

6. Repeat Step 5 twice (to turn off and then turn on the Simulated Download feature) to run the simulation again, then drag the **scroll bar** on the Bandwidth Profiler to the right as needed to view the last frames of the movie (through frame 165).

7. Close the Bandwidth Profiler, then close the Flash Player window.

8. Save and close the movie.

You tested the preloader by simulating a download and you viewed the information on the Bandwidth Profiler during the simulation.

Publish AIR
APPLICATIONS

What You'll Do

In this lesson, you will publish a Flash AIR application for stand-alone delivery.

Understanding the Development Process for AIR Applications

Until now you have been creating Flash applications and publishing them as SWF files to be viewed in a web browser using the Flash Player. Flash provides another technology, AIR (Adobe Integrated Runtime), that creates applications that can be played without a browser. An AIR app can be displayed on mobile devices, on stand-alone computers, on the Internet, and even on television sets. AIR applications are cross-platform, which means they will play on different operating systems such as Windows and Apple computers. In addition, the AIR format allows a developer to create a single application and deliver it on multiple devices. This saves development time and money as the same content can be repurposed for different audiences. You can repurpose a Flash application for delivery on various devices by simply changing the publish settings. However, there are always considerations that must be taken into account as content is repurposed. For example, the screen size of mobile devices requires a different design than the screen size of typical desktop computers. In this lesson you will repurpose a Flash application so it plays as a stand-alone application on a desktop computer.

There are several files that are created when publishing an AIR app including the descriptor and installer files required to deploy it. Flash creates the application descriptor XML file, which contains the settings, the installer file that is used to install the application on a computer, and the SWF file when you publish the AIR application. You specify the settings for these files in the AIR Settings dialog box. Once you have created an AIR file, this dialog box can be opened from either the document Properties panel or the Publish Settings option on the File menu.

Figure 18 shows the Publish Settings dialog box with the default settings Flash (.swf), HTML Wrapper, and Flash Player 11.2. To create an AIR file you need to change the Publish Target setting from Flash Player to AIR 2.5, as shown in Figure 19. Then you need to open the AIR Settings dialog box and complete the settings contained within four tabs, as shown in Figure 20 and explained next.

Settings on the General Tab

The General tab of the AIR Settings dialog box contains the following options:

Output file: Name and location of the AIR file to be created when using the Publish command. The .air file extension indicates an AIR package file.

Output as: AIR package allows cross-platform delivery. Windows Installer provides a specific Windows installer (.exe) instead of a platform-independent AIR installer (.air).

App Name: Name used by the AIR application installer to generate the application

filename and the application folder. The AIR application name defaults to the name of the SWF file.

Version: Specifies a version number for the AIR application you are creating.

App ID: Identifies the AIR application with a unique ID.

Description: Used to enter a description of the AIR application, which is displayed in the installer window when the user installs the AIR application.

Copyright: Used to enter a copyright notice.

Window Style: Used to specify the window style for the user interface when the user runs the AIR application on a computer.

Render mode: Used to specify whether to use the computer's CPU or graphics card when displaying images.

Profiles: Used in the programming process when targeting various devices.

Included Files: Used to add files, such as video or sound files, to the AIR application package. By default, the AIR application descriptor XML file and the main SWF file are automatically included.

Figure 18 *The Publish Settings dialog box*

Figure 19 *Changing the Publish Target settings*

Figure 20 *Tabs on the AIR Settings dialog box*

Settings on the Signature Tab

Figure 21 shows the AIR Settings dialog box with the Signature tab active. You use the settings on this tab to create a certificate, which is a digital signature, for your application. This certificate identifies the publisher of the application and assures the user of the AIR application that the application is authentic.

Settings on the Icons Tab

Figure 22 shows the AIR Settings dialog box with the Icons tab active. An icon is the graphic that displays after you install the application and run it in the Adobe AIR runtime. It could be a logo, a drawing that represents the app,

or any graphic created by the developer. You use the settings on the Icons tab to specify icons for the application. For instance, the Icons tab in the AIR Settings dialog box allows you to specify four different square sizes for an icon (16, 32, 48 and 128 pixels) to allow for the different views in which the icon appears. For example, the icon can appear in a web browser in thumbnail, detail, and tile views. It can also appear as a desktop icon and in the title of the AIR application window, as well as in other places. The graphics need be a PNG file type. You can create PNG files using graphics programs such as Adobe Fireworks and Photoshop.

Settings on the Advanced Tab

Figure 23 shows the AIR Settings dialog box with the Advanced tab active. When you publish an AIR application for delivery as a stand-alone application, the user needs to install the application on a computer. You use settings on the Advanced tab to specify additional settings for the installation. For example, you can specify associated file types, size and placement of the initial window used to view the application, folder in which the application is installed, and Program menu folder in which to place the file.

Figure 21 *The Signature tab settings*

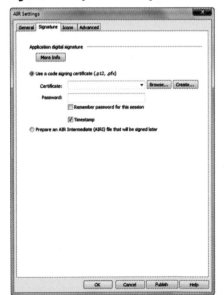

Figure 22 *Icons tab settings*

Figure 23 *Advanced tab settings*

Preparing and Publishing Applications

Figure 24 *Displaying the Publish Target list*

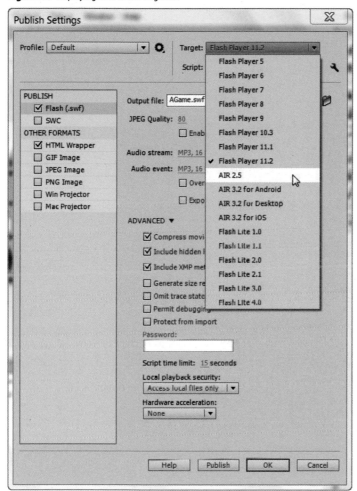

1. Open fl6_4, then save it as **AGame.fla**.

2. Click **File** on the menu bar, point to **Publish Preview**, then click **Default-(HTML)**.

   Note: If a missing font message appears in the Output area at the bottom of the screen, you can ignore the message. You will reset the workspace at the end of the lesson.

3. Play the game, then close the browser.

4. Click **File** on the menu bar, then click **Publish Settings**.

5. Click the **Target list arrow**, then click **AIR 2.5** as shown in Figure 24.

   Note: The version numbers in your list may differ from those shown in the figure.

6. Click the **Player Settings icon** 🔧 to the right of the Target list box in order to display the AIR Settings dialog box.

   The General tab settings are displayed. Study these settings and notice that the filename, AGame, is used for the Output file, App name, App ID, and the included files. You will use the General default settings.

7. Click the **Icons tab**.

8. Verify icon 16x16 is highlighted, then click the **Search icon** 🖳.

9. Navigate to the location where your data files are stored, click **Match16.png**, then click **Open**.

   Note: If a message appears indicating the icon must be copied to a folder relative to the root folder, click OK.

   (continued)

10. Click **icon 32 × 32** to highlight it, click the **Search icon** , click **Match32.png**, then click **Open**.

11. Click **icon 48 × 48** to highlight it, click the **Search icon**, click **Match48.png**, then click **Open**.

12. Click **icon 128 × 128** to highlight it, click the **Search icon**, click **Match128.png**, then click **Open**.

13. Click the **Signature tab**, then click the **Create button** (Win) or the **New button** (Mac) to begin the process for creating a Self-Signed Digital Certificate.

14. Type your name, organization unit (such as your program or department) and organization name (such as your school).

15. Type a password of your choice, making sure to remember it, then type the password again in the Confirm text box to confirm it.

    Your dialog box should resemble Figure 25.

16. Click the **Browse button** (Win) or the **Folder icon** (Mac).

    The Select File Destination dialog box appears with the folder where you store your solution files as the active folder. Notice the filename is entered and the file type is p12, designating this as a Certificate File.

    Note: The file type does not show if you do not have file extensions set to visible or if you are using a Mac.

17. Verify your solution file folder is the active destination folder, then click **Save**.

    (continued)

Figure 25 *The completed Self-Signed Digital Certificate*

Preparing and Publishing Applications

Figure 26 *The completed Signature tab settings*

18. Click **OK** in the Create Self-Signed Digital Certificate dialog box.

    After a few moments the following message appears: Self-Signed certificate has been created.

19. Click **OK** to close the message box.

20. Type your password in the Signature tab dialog box.

21. Verify Timestamp is selected, as shown in Figure 26.

22. Click the **Publish button**.

    Note: The message "AIR file has been created" appears when the process is complete.

23. Click **OK** to close the message box.

24. Click **OK** to close the AIR Settings dialog box.

25. Click **OK** to close the Publish Settings dialog box.

26. Save the application, click **Reset 'Essentials'** on the Essentials menu, then close the application.

27. Navigate to the drive and folder where you save your files, then notice the files created in this lesson that are specific to creating an AIR application.

    AGame-app.xml: a text file containing the settings that were specified in the publish process

    AGame.air: the AIR file

    AGame.p12: the Self-Signed Digital Certificate

    To launch the AIR app you need to install it. This can be done by right-clicking the AIR file and choosing Install. However, depending on the setup of your computer, you may not have permission to install applications.

28. Return to the Flash program.

You repurposed a Flash application for delivery as a stand-alone application.

Create and Publish Applications for MOBILE DEVICES

What You'll Do

In this lesson, you will publish two Flash applications for a mobile device. One has been repurposed and the other uses a pinching effect.

Understanding the Development Process for Mobile Apps

A new feature of Flash CS6 is the ability to quickly and easily develop applications for mobile devices, such as smartphones and tablets. Flash CS6 specifically targets Android and iOS (Apple) devices because of their large markets. You can start a new AIR for Android or AIR for iOS application or you can repurpose an existing Flash document. In either case, you create the application in Flash and publish it as an AIR file. The publish process requires specifying various settings by completing several dialog boxes. Figure 27 shows the Publish Settings dialog box for an AIR for Android app.

Settings on the General tab

The AIR for Android Settings dialog box has five tabs (General, Deployment, Icons, Permissions, Languages), which are explained briefly. Notice that while many of the settings available on these tabs are similar to the settings discussed in the previous lesson, there are options available specific to an application, such as AIR for Android, as discussed in this lesson.

Output file: Displays the name and location of the AIR file. The .apk file extension indicates an AIR for Android package file.

App name: Displays the name that appears on the mobile device when the app is downloaded. Also, this is the name used when searching for the app in the Android market.

App ID: Displays a string of characters that uniquely identifies the application; the characters you type are preceded by "air". when the ID is displayed.

Version: Displays a version number for the application, which can be changed as new versions of the application are published.

Version label: Used to describe the version (optional).

Aspect Ratio: Determines how the application is displayed. There are several options available: Portrait maintains the portrait orientation of the application no matter how the mobile device is turned. Landscape maintains the landscape orientation of the application no matter how the mobile device is turned. Auto, when selected along with Auto orientation, launches the application on the device in either portrait or landscape mode, depending on the current orientation of the device.

Full screen: Sets the application to run in full screen mode.

Auto orientation: Allows the application to switch from portrait to landscape mode and vice versa, depending on the current orientation of the device; must be used in conjunction with Aspect Ratio Auto mode.

Included Files: Displays the files and folders to include in your application package. Allows you to add files, such as video, audio, or SWF files. By default, the main SWF file and the application descriptor XML file are included. The descriptor XML file contains all the general settings such as the Output file, App name, Version, and so on.

While you can make changes in the General settings, the default settings are often acceptable.

Settings on the Deployment Tab

Figure 28 shows the AIR for Android Settings dialog box with the Deployment tab active. These settings allow you to create a certificate that identifies who you are to the user.

Certificate (Self-Created): The digital certificate for the application.

Password: The password for the selected digital certificate.

Android deployment type: Android applications can be deployed in three different ways: Device release allows creation of applications for the marketplace or any other distribution medium, such as a website. Emulator release is used to test the application when an emulator program is available. Device debugging allows on-device debugging.

AIR runtime: The AIR app uses an AIR runtime plug-in. There are two choices for making sure the user has the runtime plug-in: Embed AIR runtime with the application. or Get AIR runtime from: (A message will appear on a device that does not have the runtime plug-in and the user can choose to go to the specified location, Google Android Market or Amazon Appstore.)

After publishing: Two choices as listed next are available: "Install the application on an Android device connected to the computer." or "Immediately launch the application on a connected device." You can select either choice or both choices, whichever best meets your needs.

When you click the Create button, the Create Self-Signed Digital Certificate dialog box appears allowing you to identify the app developer including the Publisher name, Organization unit, and Organization name. In addition, you create a password, then specify the type of encryption and the certificate validity period (25 years minimum). The Save as option allows you to specify the filename and storage location for the certificate.

The process for creating an AIR for iOS app is similar to an AIR for Android app. However, Apple requires a mobile app developer to register with Apple and pay a fee. This lesson will focus on Android devices.

Figure 27 *The AIR for Android Settings dialog box*

Figure 28 *The Deployment tab settings*

Settings on the Icons Tab

As discussed in Lesson 3, an icon is the graphic associated with the application. For mobile devices, the icon displays on the user's mobile device when the application is downloaded. The Icon tab in the AIR for Android Settings dialog box allows you to specify three graphic files of varying sizes (36×36, 48×48, and 72×72). These sizes are in pixels and the graphics must be a PNG file type. If no icons are provided by the developer, a generic Android icon displays.

Settings on the Permissions Tab

Figure 29 shows the AIR for Android Settings dialog box with the Permissions tab active.

Figure 29 *The Permissions tab settings*

Clicking a name displays the description

You use settings on this tab to specify which services and data the application has access to on the device. Clicking on a Permission Name displays a description of the selection.

Settings on the Languages Tab

The Languages tab in the AIR for Android Settings dialog box allows you to specify the languages that will be supported by your application.

Mobile App Gestures and Events

While you can take an already developed Flash file and repurpose it for mobile devices by completing the AIR publishing process, it will not have any of the features users are accustomed to, such as pinch to zoom or swipe, unless you have specifically added these features to your Flash file. These features, called gestures and events, can easily be incorporated into a Flash file that you want to publish as a mobile app by using Code Snippets. These are small blocks of code that you apply to an object in your app or the app in general. For example, if you would like your users to be able to zoom in and out on an object, such as a map, you can select the map on the Stage and apply the Pinch to Zoom Event from the Code Snippets panel. Code Snippets are written in ActionScript 3, so the Publish Settings for your app must specify this version of ActionScript. Figure 30 shows the Code Snippets panel with the Pinch to Zoom Event highlighted under the Mobile Gesture Events category. Notice the other events including Pan, Rotate, and Swipe.

Figure 30 *Code Snippets panel with the Pinch to Zoom Event selected*

Preparing and Publishing Applications

Figure 31 *Changing the publish target to AIR for Android*

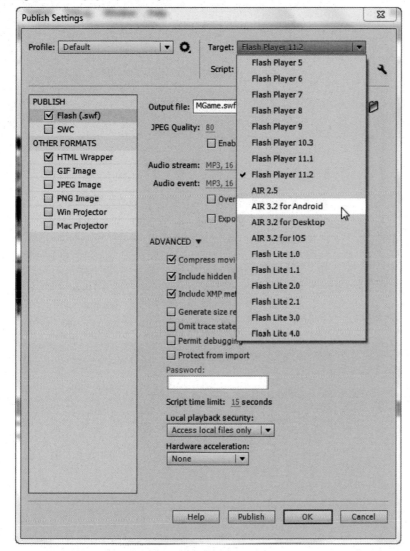

NEW Repurpose a Flash app for use on mobile devices

1. Open fl6_5, then save it as **MGame.fla**.

2. Click **File** on the menu bar, point to **Publish Preview**, then click **Default – (HTML)**.

   Note: If a missing font message appears in the Output area at the bottom of the screen, you can ignore the message. You will reset the workspace at the end of the lesson.

3. Play the game, then close the browser.

4. Click **File** on the menu bar, then click **Publish Settings**.

5. Click the **Target list arrow**, point to **AIR 3.2 for Android** as shown in Figure 31, then **click**.

6. Click the **Player Settings icon** 🔧 to the right of the Target list box in order to display the AIR for Android Settings dialog box.

   The General tab settings are displayed. Study these settings and notice that the filename, MGame, is used for the Output file, App name, App ID, and the included files. You will use the default settings.

7. Click the **Icons tab**.

8. Verify icon 36×36 is highlighted, then click the **Search icon** 📇.

9. Navigate to the location where your data files are stored, click **Game36.png**, then click **Open**.

10. Click **icon 48×48** to highlight it, click the **Search icon** 📇, click **Game48.png**, then click **Open**.

(continued)

11. Click **icon 72×72** to highlight it, click the **Search icon** , click **Game72.png**, then click **Open**.

12. Click the **Permissions tab**.

13. Click **CAMERA**, then read the description.

14. Click **INTERNET**, then read the description.

15. Click the **INTERNET check box** to select it, then click the **Languages tab**.

16. Click the **English check box** to select it, then click the **Deployment tab**.

17. Click the **Create button** to begin the process for creating a Self-Signed Certificate.

18. Type your name, organization unit (your program or department), and organization name (such as your school).

19. Type a password of your choice, making sure to remember it, then type the password again in the Confirm text box to confirm it.

    Your dialog box should resemble Figure 32.

20. Click the **Browse button**.

    The Select File Destination dialog box with the folder where your solution files are stored opens as the active folder. Notice the filename is entered and the file type is p12, designating this as a Certificate File.

21. Verify your solution file folder is the active destination folder, then click **Save**.

22. Click **OK** to close the Self-Signed Digital Certificate dialog box.

    After a few moments the following message appears: Self-signed certificate has been created.

    (continued)

Figure 32 *The completed certificate*

Testing an App on a Mobile Device

Flash CS6 allows you to test your application on a mobile device that is connected to your computer. You must configure your device to accept the app as follows.

Prepare your Android (2.2 or above) device for testing a mobile app:

1. Go to Settings for your device (such as on your smartphone).
2. Scroll to and select Applications, then verify "Unknown Sources" is checked.
3. Scroll to and select Development, then verify "USB debugging" is checked.
4. Connect your USB cable from the computer to your phone (the same cable used to charge your device).

Even if you do not have an Android device, you can still learn the mobile app publishing process by completing this lesson.

Figure 33 *The completed Deployment settings*

23. Click **OK** to close the message box.
24. Type your password.
25. Verify Device release and Embed AIR runtime with application are selected, as shown in Figure 33.

    Note: If you have an Android (2.2+) phone or tablet and you want to test this app, click the "Install application on the connected Android device checkbox" to select it. Make sure that the settings on your smartphone "Unknown Sources" and "USB debugging" have been turned on and that your Android 2.2+ mobile device is connected to the computer with a USB cable.

26. Click the **Publish button**.

    The publish process may take several moments.

27. Click **OK** to close the AIR for Android Settings dialog box when the publishing process is complete.

28. Click **OK** to close the Publish Settings dialog box

29. **Save** the application, click **Reset 'Essentials'** on the Essentials menu, then close the application.

    Note: If you connected an Android (2.2+) phone or tablet, the app icon will appear on the connected Android device as an app. You can tap the icon and play the game.

You repurposed and published a Flash application for delivery on a mobile device.

NEW Create a mobile app with events

1. Click **Air for Android** under Create New.
2. Save the file as **SantaFe.fla**.
3. Change the view to **Fit in Window**.
4. Click **File** on the menu bar, point to **Import**, then click **Import to Stage**.
5. Navigate to the drive and folder where your data files are stored, click **SFimage.jpg**, then click **Open**.
6. Click the **image** to select it.
7. Click **Modify** on the menu bar, then click **Convert to Symbol**.
8. Type **mc_sf** for the name, then select **Movie Clip** for the type.
9. Click the **center registration point** as shown in Figure 34, then click **OK**.

   The registration point determines how the graphic will zoom in and out.

10. Display the Properties panel, then type **SFimage** for the instance name, as shown in Figure 35.

    The instance name is used by the code to identify the object.

11. Click **frame 1** on the actions layer, open the Actions panel, then notice there is no code currently assigned to that frame.

    You will add code that will allow the user to zoom the application by pinching it.

    (continued)

Figure 34 *Selecting the center registration point*

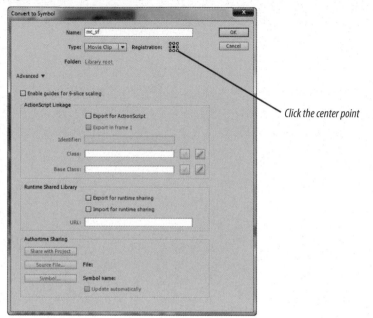

Click the center point

Figure 35 *Typing an instance name*

Type the instance name in the text box

Figure 36 *Selecting the Pinch to Zoom Event*

Figure 37 *The Code Snippet for the Pinch to Zoom Event*

12. Click **Window** on the menu bar, then click **Code Snippets**.

    Notice the folders named Mobile Touch Events, Mobile Gesture Events, and Mobile Actions.

13. Click the **Mobile Gesture Events expand icon** ▶.

14. Click **Pinch to Zoom Event**, as shown in Figure 36.

15. Click the **Show description icon** ⓘ, then read the description of the event.

16. Click the **Show code icon** { }, then scroll to the bottom of the code box, as shown in Figure 37.

    Notice the scaleX and scaleY code. This code resizes the object based on the X and Y Stage coordinates. *Note:* If "instance_name_here" appears instead of "SFimage," you do not have the image selected. Click the map and repeat steps 11-15.

17. Click the **Insert button** to insert the code into the app.

    The code is inserted in the application.

18. Click **frame 1** on the actions layer, open the actions panel, then notice the code that has been added to that frame.

You created a new AIR for Android application and used a code snippet to add a Pinch to Zoom event.

Publish a mobile app

1. Click **File** on the menu bar, then click **AIR 3.2 for Android Settings**.

   The AIR for Android Settings dialog box opens with the General tab active. No changes are needed on this tab.

2. Click the **Icons tab**, then complete the dialog box to specify sf36.png, sf48,png, and sf72.png as the graphics to use.

3. Click the **Permissions tab**, then click the **INTERNET check box** to select it.

4. Click the **Languages tab**, then click the **English check box** to select it.

5. Click the **Deployment tab**.

6. Click the **Create button** for the Certificate option.

7. Complete the Create Self-Signed Digital Certificate dialog box, except for the Save as option.

8. Click the **Browse button** for the Save as option.

9. Verify the folder where you store your solution files is the active folder in the Select File Destination dialog box, then click **Save**.

   Your screen should resemble Figure 38.

10. Click **OK** in the Create Self-Signed digital Certificate dialog box.

    After a few moments the following message appears: Self-signed certificate has been created.

11. Click **OK**.

(continued)

Figure 38 *The completed Self-Signed Digital Certificate*

Figure 39 *The completed Deployment settings*

12. Type your password in the Password text box on the Deployment tab.

13. Verify Device release and Embed AIR runtime with application are selected, as shown in Figure 39.

    Note: If you have an Android (2.2+) phone or tablet and you want to test the application once it is published, click the "Install application on the connected Android device check box" to select it. Then, connect the Android device to the computer using a USB cable.

14. Click the **Publish button**.

15. Click **OK** to close the AIR for Android Settings dialog box when the publishing process is complete.

16. Save, then close the application.

    Note: If you connected an Android (2.2+) phone or tablet to your computer, the app icon will appear on the connected Android device. You can tap the icon to display the application, then pinch the map to have it zoom in and out.

You completed the AIR for Android settings to publish an application that will display on a mobile device.

Publish using default settings.

1. Start Flash, open fl6_6.fla, then save it as **skillsDemo6.fla.** (*Notes*: When you open the file, you may receive a warning message that a font is missing. You can replace this font with the default or with any other appropriate font on your computer. If a message appears indicating that you need QuickTime, you will need to install the program to continue.)
2. Open the Publish Settings dialog box.
3. Verify that the Formats tab is selected and the Flash and HTML Wrapper options are the only Format types checked.
4. Click Publish, then click OK to close the dialog box.
5. Use your file management program to navigate to the drive and folder where you store your files to view the skillsDemo6.html and skillsDemo6.swf files.
6. Return to the Flash program.
7. Use the Publish Preview feature to display the movie in a browser.
8. Close your browser, return to the Flash program, then save your work.

Create a JPEG image.

1. Select 60 on the Timeline.
2. Open the Publish Settings dialog box.
3. Click the JPEG Image check box.
4. Click Publish, then click OK to close the dialog box.
5. Open your browser, and then open the skillsDemo6.jpg file.
6. Close the browser, return to the Flash program, then save your work.

Test a movie.

1. Test the movie in the Flash Player window, then maximize the Flash Player window if it is not already maximized.
2. Turn off the loop feature. (*Hint*: Click Control on the Flash Player menu bar, then deselect the Loop check box.)
3. Set the Download Setting to DSL (32.6 KB/s) if it is not already set to that setting.
4. Display the Bandwidth Profiler if it is not already displayed, click View on the menu bar, then click Frame By Frame Graph if it is not already selected.
5. Use controls on the Control menu to rewind, play, and then rewind the movie. (Notice the bar on the Timeline for frame 1 is just under 256 KB, which is way above the red base line. The large photo is in frame 1, which could cause the movie to have a slow start.)
6. Close the Flash Player window.

Reduce file size to optimize a movie.

1. Select frame 1 on the sedona-photo layer, verify the image is selected on the Stage, then delete the image.
2. Replace the image with the sedona-sm graphic from the Library panel.
3. Position the sedona-sm image approximately two-thirds of the way down the Stage and centered across the Stage.
4. Save the movie.
5. Test the movie within the Flash Player window by simulating a DSL download. (Notice the bar on the Timeline for frame 1 is near 32 KB. This allows the movie to start more quickly.)
6. Close the Flash Player window.

Add a background.

1. Verify skillsDemo6.fla is the active file, then insert a new layer and move it below the sedona-photo layer.
2. Name the new layer **background**.
3. Select frame 1 on the background layer.
4. Display the Library panel (if necessary).
5. Drag the g_background graphic symbol to the center of the Stage.
6. Click the last frame on the Timeline associated with content so your screen looks like Figure 40. (*Note*: Your heading font may differ.)
7. Use the Publish Preview feature to view the movie in a browser, close the browser, then save your work.

Create a preloader.

1. Click 1 on the Timeline.
2. Click Edit on the menu bar, point to Timeline, then click Select All Frames.
3. Point to any frame on the Timeline and drag the frames to the right so they start in frame 11.
4. Insert a new layer and name it **labels**.
5. Click frame 11 on the labels layer to select it, insert a keyframe, then display the Properties panel and type **startofMovie** in the Name text box in the LABEL area.
6. Insert a keyframe in frame 70 on the labels layer and type **endofMovie** in the Name text box in the LABEL area.
7. Add a new layer and name it **preLoaderScript**.
8. Insert an ifFrameLoaded action in frame 1 to check if all the frames have been loaded and, if so, go to and play the startofMovie frame. Also, insert a keyframe in frame 10 on the preLoaderScript layer, then insert a gotoAndPlay(1) action in frame 10 to cause a loop in the preloader frames.

9. Add a new layer and name it **preloader Animation**, then have the words "**Please wait**" appear in the first four frames and not appear in the last six frames of the ten frames used for the preloader. This will cause the words Please wait to flash until all the frames are loaded.
10. Test the movie, and use the Simulate Download feature to view the preloader.
11. Save your work, then close the file.

Create an AIR application.

1. Open fl6_7.fla, then save it as **skillsDemo6A.fla**. (*Note:* When you open the file, you may receive a warning message that a font is missing. You can replace this font with the default, or with any other appropriate font on your computer.)
2. Open the Publish Settings dialog box and change the Target setting to AIR 2.5.
3. Display the AIR settings dialog box and set the icons to sedona16.png, sedona32.png, sedona48.png, and sedona128.png.
4. From the Signature tab dialog box, create a Self-Signed Digital Certificate and save it with the default name.
5. Publish the AIR file.
6. Navigate to the drive and folder where your data files are located and view the files created when you published the AIR application.
7. Save your work, then close the application.

Create an AIR for Android mobile app with events.

1. Create a new AIR for Android file, then name it **skillsDemo-M.fla**.
2. Change the view to Fit in Window.

Photo courtesy of J. Shuman.

3. Import sedonaImage.png to the Stage.
4. Change the view to Fit in Window.
5. Select the image and change it to a movie clip symbol with a center registration point.
6. Select the image on the Stage and use the Properties panel to give the image an instance name.
7. Use the Code Snippets panel to assign a Pinch to Zoom Event to the image.
8. Publish the application with the following:
   - Language: English
   - Permissions: Internet
   - Icons: sedona36.png, sedona 48.png, and sedona 72.png

Figure 40 *Completed Skills Review*

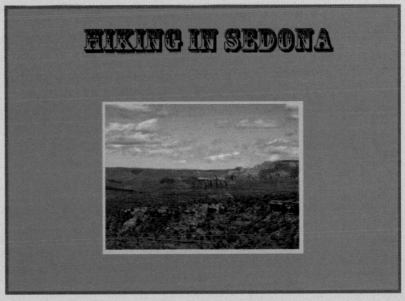

- A Self-Signed Digital Certificate you create
- The Deployment settings that include the password, Device release selected, and Embed AIR runtime with application selected.
   Note: If you have an Android mobile device, connect it to the computer and have the application display on it.
9. Save the application.
10. View the files that were created during the publish process.
11. Close the application and exit Flash.

The Ultimate Tours travel company has asked you to create a stand-alone application for the opening animation of its website.

1. Open fl6_8.fla and save it as **ultimateTours6A.fla**.
2. Use a graphics program, such as Photoshop, to create an image to be used as icons for this app. Create four sizes, in pixels, of the image for the AIR stand-alone app (16×16, 32×32, 48×48, and 128×128). These should be PNG file types. Alternately, you can use the generic icon graphics (uTours16.png, uTours32.png, uTours48.png, and uTours128.png) provided with your data files.
3. Create the AIR app as a stand-alone application by completing the Icons and Signature tab settings, including creating a Self-Signed Digital Certificate.
4. View the files created by this process.
5. Save and close the application.

Figure 41 *Icon settings for sample completed Project Builder 1*

Preparing and Publishing Applications

In this project you will choose a Flash movie you developed for this book or one you developed on your own. You will make changes to the publish settings, create an AIR stand-alone application, and create an AIR for Android application for a mobile device. Figure 42 shows a sample application.

1. Open a movie you developed from this book or one you developed on your own, then save it as **publish6.fla**.
2. Use a graphics program, such as Photoshop, to create an image to be used as icons for this app. Create four sizes, in pixels, of the image for the AIR stand-alone app (16×16, 32×32, 48×48, and 128×128). These should be PNG file types. Alternately, you can use the generic icon graphics (publish16.png, publish32.png, publish48.png, and publish128.png) provided with your data files.
3. Create the AIR app as a stand-alone application by completing the Icons and Signature tab settings including creating a Self-Signed Digital Certificate.
4. View the files created by this process.
5. Save the application.
6. Save the application as **publish6-M fla.**.
7. Use a graphics program, such as Photoshop, to create an image to be used as icons for this app. The sizes for the AIR for Android mobile app will be 36×36, 48×48 (this could be the same graphic as above), and 72×72. Alternately, you can use the generic Icon graphics (publish36.png, publish48.png, and publish72.png) provided with your data files.

8. Use the Publish Settings dialog box to change the Publish Target to AIR 3.2 for Android.
9. Create the AIR for Android mobile application by completing the Languages, Permission, Icons, and Deployment tab settings including creating a Self-Signed Digital Certificate.
10. View the files created by this process.
11. View the application on an Android mobile device, such as an Android tablet or phone, if you have one connected to the computer.
12. Save and close the application.

Figure 42 *Sample completed Project Builder 2*

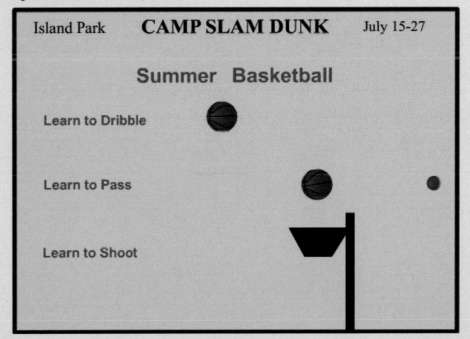

Figure 43 shows the home page of a website. Study the figure and complete the following questions. For each question, indicate how you determined your answer.

1. Connect to the Internet and go to *www.nesdis.noaa.gov/jpss/*.

2. Open a document in a word processor or open a new Flash movie, save the file as **dpc6**, then answer the following questions. (*Hint*: Use the Text tool in Flash.)

   ▪ What is the purpose of this site?
   ▪ Who is the target audience?
   ▪ How would you use the Bandwidth Profiler when developing this site?
   ▪ Assuming there is a pause in the playing of a Flash movie on the site, what suggestions would you make to eliminate the pause?
   ▪ What suggestions would you make to improve the design, and why?

Figure 43 *Design Project*

Courtesy of NOAA.gov website. www.nesdis.noaa.gov/jpss/

This is a continuation of the Portfolio Project in Chapter 5, which is the development of a personal portfolio. In this project, you will create a JPEG image of your portfolio screen. Then you will use the Bandwidth Profiler to determine where a pause may occur in a movie and make changes in the movie to eliminate the pause.

1. Open portfolio5.fla (the file you created in Portfolio Project, Chapter 5) and save it as **portfolio6.fla**.
2. Use the Publish Settings dialog box to publish the movie.
3. Use the Publish Preview feature to display the movie in the browser.
4. Create a JPEG image of the first frame of the movie.
5. Display the JPEG image in your browser.
6. Use the Bandwidth Profiler to display a frame-by-frame graph of the movie, as seen in Figure 44, and to determine which frame may cause a pause in the movie at a 28.8 (2.3 KB/s) connection speed. (*Note*: Specifying 28.8 (2.3 KB/s) as the connection speed enables you to identify any pauses and practice using the Bandwidth Profiler. This option can take a very long time to load.)
7. Make a change in the movie to help optimize it.
8. Play the movie.
9. Save and close the movie.

Figure 44 *Using the Bandwidth Profiler to improve download speeds of the sample completed Portfolio Project*

CHAPTER 7 IMPORTING AND
MODIFYING GRAPHICS

1. Understand and import graphics
2. Break apart bitmaps and use bitmap fills
3. Trace bitmap graphics

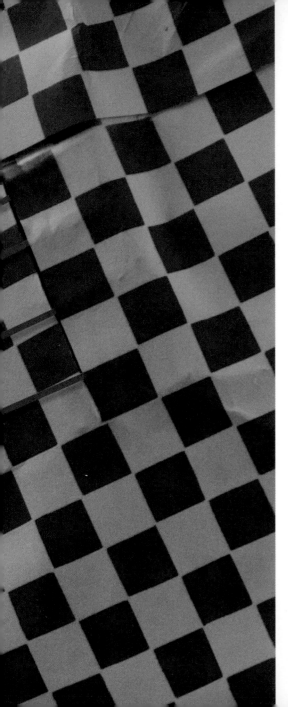

CHAPTER 7
IMPORTING AND
MODIFYING GRAPHICS

Introduction

Graphics are vital to websites and applications. A single drawing, chart, or photograph can illustrate what might take many pages of narrative text to communicate. In the end, the image may do a better job of creating a lasting impression or establishing a mood. As you create movies, you may often find yourself wanting to use a logo or image that originated in another application. In previous chapters, you learned to create graphics using the drawing tools on the Tools panel. And, as you have seen in previous chapters, you are not limited to just what you can draw within your movie. You can also import and even animate vector and bitmap graphics that have been created or modified in other applications.

Importing vector graphics from an application, such as Adobe Fireworks or Adobe Illustrator, is easy—the vector graphics are treated almost the same as if you created them in Adobe Flash. Importing bitmap graphics is easy, too, but working with them can be more difficult. Also, remember that using bitmap graphics can increase the file size of your movies dramatically, resulting in slower download times. When considering images for your movies, it is most efficient to use vector graphics or to create graphics directly within Flash.

In this chapter, you will practice importing graphics that have been created outside the Flash environment. For those who are "artistically challenged," importing graphics from other applications can often help to make up for less-than-perfect drawing skills. You can import a wide variety of vector and bitmap graphics, including drawings and photographs. Once the graphics are in your library, you can place them on the Stage, where you can trace them, break them apart, use them to fill an object, optimize them, and animate them.

Understand and
IMPORT GRAPHICS

What You'll Do

▶ *In this lesson, you will import graphics that were created using different drawing and image-editing programs.*

Understanding the Formats

Because Flash is a vector-based application, all graphics and motion within the application are calculated according to mathematical formulas. This vector-based format results in a smaller file size, as well as a robust ability to resize movies without a notable loss in quality.

When you import bitmapped graphics, you usually lose some of the vector-based benefits or these benefits change dramatically. A bitmap graphic, also called a **raster graphic**, is based on pixels, not on mathematical formulas. As discussed previously, importing multiple bitmap graphics increases the file size of your movie and decreases flexibility in terms of resizing the movie.

Flash makes it possible to import both vector and bitmap graphics from applications such as Adobe Fireworks, Illustrator, and Photoshop. In many cases, you can retain features, such as layers, transparency, and animation, when you import graphics.

Importing Different Graphic Formats: An Overview

There are several ways of bringing external graphics into your movie, including import

or cut and paste. Generally, the best way to bring a graphic into your movie is to **import** it by selecting the Import option on the File menu. Then, you can choose the Import to Stage command to have the graphic placed on the Stage and in the library, or you can choose the Import to Library command to have the graphic placed only in the library. Next, in the Import dialog box, you navigate to the graphic of your choice. Figure 1 displays the Import to Library dialog box with the All Files option selected. In most cases, you would import graphics to the Library before developing a movie. At times during the development process, you may want to add a new graphic directly to the Stage. In these cases, you could use the Import to Stage feature to save the step of dragging the graphic from the Library panel to the Stage.

If the original graphic has layers, Flash can create new layers associated with that graphic in your document, depending on the file type and the settings you specify when you import the graphic. Flash automatically places the additional layers on the Timeline or inside a movie clip symbol, when applicable.

If you are importing large numbers of graphics, you can import a group of graphics (of the same file type and from a single folder), all of which will automatically use the same settings, enabling you to choose your import preferences just once.

You can also copy and paste graphics from an application, such as a graphics-editing program, directly into a Flash movie. Some graphics applications, such as Adobe

Illustrator, create vector graphics which are maintained during the copy and paste process. However, when you copy and paste using other applications, the graphic may become a flattened bitmap, which means the advantages of using vector graphics in Flash, such as smaller file sizes, editing strokes and fills, and resizing without distortion, are lost.

Using Fireworks PNG Files

Graphics created in Fireworks are PNG files. You can import Fireworks PNG files as flattened bitmap graphics. You need QuickTime 4 or

later (a free download from Apple) to import PNG files.

Importing Adobe Illustrator Files

Adobe Illustrator is an excellent program for creating artwork that is to be imported into Flash. Graphics created in Illustrator are AI files. Illustrator AI files are vector-based. So, when imported as a movie clip, AI files preserve most of their attributes including filters (such as drop shadows) and blends (such as transparency settings). In addition, you can choose to convert Illustrator graphic

Figure 1 *Import to Library dialog box*

You can display all file types, as seen here, or you can display only files of one file type, such as AI files, by selecting that file type in the file types list

File type list (All file types listed)

List arrow for file types, name on button changes to reflect last file type selected (All Files currently selected as the file type)

layers to Flash layers, using the Import dialog box, which is shown in Figure 2. This allows quite a bit of flexibility when editing and animating an Illustrator file in Flash.

Importing Adobe Photoshop Files

Flash also allows you to import Photoshop files into a Flash document. One advantage of using Photoshop to create graphics and enhance photographs is that the drawing and selection tools, as well as the photo-retouching features, allow you to produce more creative and complex images. The Photoshop tools allow you to create high-quality artwork before you import the graphic into Flash. Graphics created in Photoshop are PSD files. In the Import

dialog box for a Photoshop file, you can choose to have the Photoshop layers imported as Flash layers. This allows you to edit individual parts of an image, such as animating text, or to use the entire graphic, such as creating a button using a photograph, once the graphic is in your Flash document.

The process for importing Photoshop files into Flash is discussed next. First, open a Flash document and select the Import option from the File menu. Next, choose to import to the Stage or to the library, and then navigate to and select the PSD file you want to import. The Import dialog box for a Photoshop file opens, as shown in Figure 3. You select options in this dialog box that

determine whether or not you want to be able to edit the contents (text, image, background, etc.) of each PSD layer. If you choose not to make a layer editable, the contents of that layer are flattened as a bitmap image. If you choose to make a layer editable, a movie clip symbol that contains the graphic information is created using the layer contents. Therefore, depending on the choices you make in the Import dialog box, you could end up with several items (graphic symbols and movie clip symbols as well as bitmaps) in the Library. All of the information (flattened bitmap images and editable images) for the PSD file is imported into one folder in your Flash movie.

When importing to the Stage, other options allow you to specify that the contents of the imported file retain the same relative position they had in Photoshop and that the Flash Stage resizes so it is the same size as the Photoshop document.

Importing Bitmaps

Flash allows you to use and modify imported bitmaps in a variety of ways. You can control the size, compression, and **anti-aliasing** of an imported bitmap. Anti-aliasing is the process of smoothing the edges of a graphic so they appear less jagged. This is done by blending colors. For example, if there is a black graphic on a white background, the pixels on the edges of the graphic would be turned to shades of gray. You can also use a bitmap as a fill, or you can convert a bitmap to a vector by tracing it or breaking it apart.

Figure 2 *The Import dialog box for an Illustrator file*

Importing and Modifying Graphics

Once you import a bitmap, it becomes a graphic object in the library. To edit the graphic from the Library panel, double-click the object to open the Bitmap Properties dialog box. Using the dialog box, you can compress the graphic and allow for smoothing (anti-aliasing) on the graphic.

When an instance of a bitmap symbol is on the Stage, you can use the Properties panel to:

- numerically change the dimensions of the graphic
- swap the bitmap for another bitmap within the Library (this is useful if you want to quickly view how another graphic will look in the same location in your movie)
- edit the bitmap in another application (for example, Photoshop if that program is available)

Copyrights

Copyright laws apply to digital images, including those obtained from companies that provide stock photographic images and clip art. These laws are intended to protect the intellectual property rights of the creator of the work, as well as to ensure compensation for the creativity and work involved by the artist. Some works, such as those created by government agencies, *may* be in the public domain, while others, such as those used for education, *may* fall under fair use and not be subject to copyright restrictions. However, unless you produce the graphics yourself, you should assume that any other graphics you want to use in your Flash movies are protected under copyright laws. Be sure to read the terms of use associated with any graphic you obtain for use in your movies and to follow the stated permissions requirements regarding that graphic.

Figure 3 *Import dialog box for Photoshop "background.psd" file*

background.psd consists of two layers: Sun and Background

Sun layer is selected; it is converted to a movie clip so its features will be editable

Once imported, each layer in background.psd will exist on its own layer in Flash

Import a layered Fireworks PNG file as a movie clip symbol

1. Start Flash, create a new **Flash (ActionScript 2.0) document**, save it as **gsamples.fla**, then verify the Stage size is 550 × 400 pixels.

2. Display the Library panel.

3. Click **File** on the menu bar, point to **Import**, click **Import to Stage**, then navigate to the drive and folder where your Data Files are stored.

TIP Alternately, you can import the image to the library, and then drag the image to the Stage.

4. Click the **list arrow** for the file types, click **All Files (*.*)**, click **dragonfly.png**, then click **Open**.

    If a message appears indicating that you need QuickTime, you will need to install the program. If this is not possible, you can import the graphic file dfly.jpg as a substitute.

TIP If you have difficulty finding the file types list arrow, refer to Figure 1.

5. Display the Library panel, then click **dragonfly.png** to display the object in the Preview window.

6. Click the **object** on the Stage to select it, then display the Properties panel.

7. Type **0** for the X and Y coordinates in the POSITION AND SIZE area, as shown in Figure 4.

8. Verify the object is selected, click **Modify** on the menu bar, then select **Convert to Symbol**.

9. Type **mc_dragonfly** for the name, select **Movie Clip** for the type, then click **OK**.

10. Name Layer 1 **dragonfly**.

You imported a Fireworks PNG file as a flattened bitmap and converted it to a movie clip symbol.

Figure 4 *Positioning the object on the Stage*

dragonfly.png moves to the 0,0 position based on the X and Y coordinate values

Setting the X and Y coordinates

Figure 5 *Tree on the Stage after importing, resizing, and repositioning*

Position coordinates
and size

Import an Adobe Illustrator file as a symbol

1. Click **File** on the menu bar, point to **Import**, then click **Import to Library**.

TIP Alternately, you can import the image to the Stage.

2. Click the **list arrow** for the file types, click **Adobe Illustrator (*.ai)**, click **tree.ai**, then click **Open**.

   The Import to Library dialog box for an Illustrator file appears. A check mark next to a layer means that layer will be imported.

3. Verify the Convert layers to option is set to Flash Layers, then verify both Import unused symbols and Import as a single bitmap image check boxes do not have check marks.

4. Click **OK**, then display the Library panel.

   A new graphic symbol, tree.ai, appears in the Library panel.

5. Insert a **new layer**, name it **tree1**, then drag the **tree1 layer** beneath the dragonfly layer.

6. Verify that frame 1 of the tree1 layer is selected, then drag the **tree.ai graphic symbol** from the Library panel to the left side of the Stage beneath the dragonfly.

7. Display the Properties panel, verify the tree is selected on the Stage, then verify the Lock width and height values together symbol 🔗 is broken.

8. Change the width to **300** and the height to **277**.

9. Set the X: coordinate to **3.0** and the Y: coordinate to **60.0**.

10. Compare your screen to Figure 5.

You imported an Illustrator file to the library, dragged the graphic symbol to the Stage, and then resized and repositioned it.

Import an Adobe Photoshop PSD file

1. Click **File** on the menu bar, point to **Import**, then click **Import to Stage**.

2. Click the **list arrow** for the file types, click **Photoshop (*.psd)**, click **background.psd**, then click **Open**.

    The Import to Stage dialog box for a Photoshop file opens. A check mark next to a layer means the layer will be imported.

3. Click the **Background layer** (not its check box), then verify the Flattened bitmap image option button is selected.

4. Click the **Sun layer** (not its check box), then click the **Editable paths and layer styles option button**.

5. Verify the Convert layers to option is set to Flash Layers, then verify the Set stage size to . . . option does not have a check mark, as shown in Figure 6.

6. Click **OK**, notice the two layers that are added to the Timeline, then press **[Esc]** to deselect the newly inserted graphics.

7. Click the **Sun layer**, then click the **Delete icon** 🗑.

8. Drag the **Background layer** below the tree1 layer.

9. Click the **background graphic** to select it, then use the Properties panel to change the width to **550** and the height to **400**.

10. Verify the X: coordinate is set to 0.00 and the Y: coordinate is set to 0.00.

    Your screen should resemble Figure 7.

11. Lock the Background layer.

You imported a PSD file to the library, resized it, set its position on the Stage, and then locked its layer.

Figure 6 *Completed Import dialog box for Photoshop "background.psd" file*

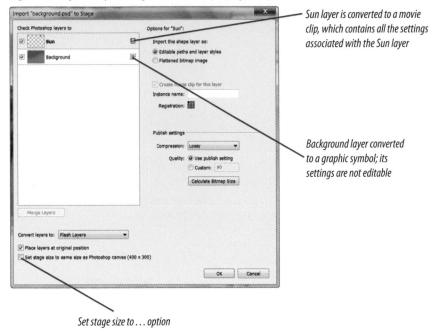

Sun layer is converted to a movie clip, which contains all the settings associated with the Sun layer

Background layer converted to a graphic symbol; its settings are not editable

Set stage size to . . . option not selected

Figure 7 *The imported background graphic placed on the Stage*

Set position here

Set the width and height here

Figure 8 *Bitmap Properties dialog box*

Bitmap Properties

Options   ActionScript

Background

Update
Import...
Test

400 x 300 pixels at 32 bits per pixel

☑ Allow smoothing

Compression: Photo (JPEG) ▼

Quality: ○ Use publish setting: 80

⊙ Custom: 70

☐ Enable deblocking

JPEG: quality = 70: original = 480.0 kb, compressed = 1.4 kb, 0% of original

OK   Cancel

Item Preview window

Original size of graphic; changing the size of the object on the Stage does not affect the original bitmap symbol

Compressed size of the graphic

Change the compression settings of a bitmap

1. Display the Library panel, then double-click the **background.psd Assets** folder to display the Assets folder and the symbols for the two objects: the Background bitmap symbol and the Sun movie clip symbol.

   Note: When you specified in the Import dialog box that the Sun layer would be imported as "Editable paths and layer styles", the movie clip that contains the graphic information was created.

2. Right-click (Win) or [control]-click (Mac) the **Background bitmap symbol** in the Library panel, then click **Properties** to open the Bitmap Properties dialog box.

3. Click the **Allow smoothing check box** to select it.

4. Verify that Photo (JPEG) is selected for Compression, then click the **Custom option button** in the Quality area.

5. Type **100** in the Custom text box, then click **Test**.

   Study the quality of the graphic in the Preview window and notice the compressed size of the graphic is approximately 25 kb.

6. Change the Custom setting to **20**, then click **Test**.

   Notice the quality of the graphic has diminished as the compressed file size has dropped.

7. Change the Custom setting to **70**, then click **Test**.

   Your screen should resemble Figure 8. The compressed size of the graphic has been reduced to less than 2 kb, with no significant reduction in the appearance of the image.

8. Click **OK**.

9. Save your work.

You compared the quality and file sizes of different compressions and then compressed a bitmap file.

Break Apart Bitmaps
AND USE BITMAP FILLS

What You'll Do

In this lesson, you will break apart bitmap graphics and manipulate bitmap fill graphics to create new effects.

Breaking Apart Bitmaps

Bitmap graphics, unlike vector graphics, are made up of groups of pixels. You can break apart a bitmap graphic and edit individual pixels. Breaking apart a bitmap graphic allows increased flexibility in how you can use it within a movie. If you do break apart a bitmap graphic, you can select different areas of the graphic (with the Selection tool, as well as the Lasso Tool and its Magic Wand tool options) to manipulate them separately from the graphic as a whole, including deleting an area or changing its color. In addition, you can use the Eraser tool to delete parts of a bitmap graphic that has been broken apart.

QUICK **TIP**

There is no need to break apart a bitmap graphic that you do not plan to manipulate.

Using the Lasso Tool and the Magic Wand Tool

The Lasso tool lets you select an irregularly shaped part of a graphic, which you can then move, scale, rotate, reshape, or delete. You can use the Magic Wand tool, which is available in the Options area of the Tools panel when the Lasso tool is selected, to select areas of similar color in a bitmap graphic you have broken apart. For example, if you have a graphic of a girl with a blue background and you decide to delete the blue background, you can use the magic wand to select the blue background and then delete the selection. If there are other shades of blue adjacent to the background, you can use the magic wand settings to specify a color similarity threshold number between 0 and 200. A higher number means more similar colors will be selected.

QUICK **TIP**

Introducing bitmaps will always increase the file size of your movie, resulting in increased download times for the users.

Using Bitmap Fills

Until now, you have been applying solid colors and gradient fills to objects. Flash allows you to apply a bitmap fill to any drawn shape or text that has been broken apart. A **bitmap fill** is created by breaking apart a bitmap graphic and using it to fill another graphic. To do this, you break apart a bitmap graphic, use the Eyedropper tool to select the graphic, and then use the Paint Bucket tool to apply the bitmap fill to a different graphic.

QUICK TIP

The Paint Bucket tool has a lock modifier that can be used to apply a bitmap fill or gradient across multiple graphics. You can toggle the lock off and on using the Lock Fill option, which is available in the Options area at the bottom of the Tools panel when the Paint Bucket tool is selected. Usually, you toggle the lock off if you are filling only one object.

Figure 9 shows different bitmap fill effects. You can apply a bitmap fill to any drawn shape.

If necessary, Flash will tile (repeat) the bitmap to fill the shape. You can use the Gradient Transform tool to change the size, shape, rotation, and skew of your fill, which allows you to position the original graphic exactly as you want it in the new shape.

In addition to filling shapes with a bitmap, you can also apply your bitmaps as a fill by using the Brush tool. This process involves breaking apart the bitmap graphic, selecting it with the Eyedropper tool, and then choosing a Brush tool and brush size. When you begin painting, you will see your bitmap graphic as a fill.

Selecting a Bitmap Fill Using the Color Panel

If the bitmap graphic you want to use for a fill is not on the Stage, you can use the Color panel to select it. The process is to open the Color panel, choose Bitmap as the Type of fill, and then select the bitmap of your choice from the library area. If you select Bitmap fill using the Color panel and there are no bitmaps available in the library area, a dialog box opens so you can navigate to the file you want to use as the bitmap fill. In this situation, you do not have to break apart the bitmap. Figure 10 shows the Color panel with a bitmap fill selected.

Figure 9 *Different bitmap fill effects*

Bitmap fill applied with the Brush tool

Bitmap fill in a circle applied with the Paint Bucket tool

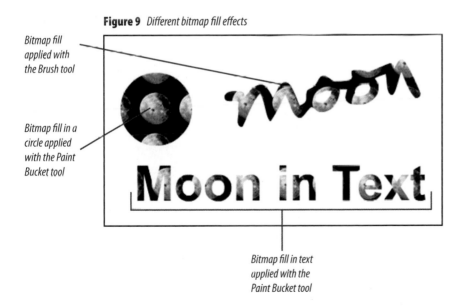

Bitmap fill in text applied with the Paint Bucket tool

Figure 10 *Bitmap fill selected in Color panel*

Use the list arrow to select Bitmap fill as the Type

Bitmap fill is selected

Bitmaps available in the Color library on the Color panel when Bitmap fill is selected

Break apart a bitmap

1. Verify the gsamples.fla document is open, click **File** on the menu bar, point to **Import**, then click **Import to Library**.

2. Click the **list arrow** for the file types, click **JPEG Image (*.jpg)**, click **moon.jpg**, then click **Open**.

3. Insert a **new layer**, move it to just above the background layer, then name it **moon**.

4. Click **frame 1** on the moon layer, then drag the **moon graphic symbol** to the Stage, as shown in Figure 11.

5. Verify the moon is selected, click **Modify** on the menu bar, then click **Break Apart**.

6. Click the **Selection tool** 🕭 , then click the **Pasteboard** to deselect the moon graphic.

7. Click the **Lasso tool** ✐ on the Tools panel, then click the **Magic Wand Settings tool** 🪄 in the Options area of the Tools panel.

   Note: Use the tool tip to be sure to select the Magic Wand Settings tool.

8. Click the **Smoothing list arrow** in the Magic Wand Settings dialog box, click **Pixels**, set the Threshold to **20**, then click **OK**.

9. Click the **Magic Wand tool** 🪄 in the Options area of the Tools panel, point to the **blue background** of the moon graphic as shown in Figure 12, then click to select the blue background.

10. Click **Edit** on the menu bar, then click **Cut**.

11. Click the **Selection tool** 🕭 , drag the **moon graphic** to the upper-right corner of the Stage, click the **Pasteboard**, then compare your Stage to Figure 13.

You broke apart and edited a bitmap graphic.

Figure 11 *Moon on Stage after importing*

Figure 12 *Using the Magic Wand to select the background color*

Figure 13 *Positioning the moon image*

Importing and Modifying Graphics

Figure 14 *Selecting a bitmap fill*

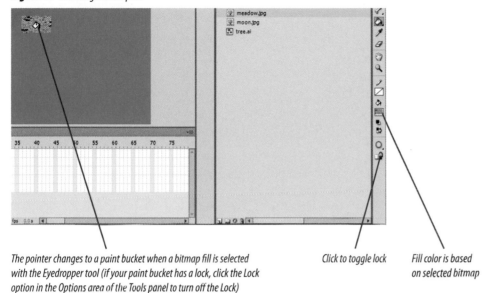

The pointer changes to a paint bucket when a bitmap fill is selected with the Eyedropper tool (if your paint bucket has a lock, click the Lock option in the Options area of the Tools panel to turn off the Lock)

Click to toggle lock　*Fill color is based on selected bitmap*

Figure 15 *Filling a shape with a bitmap*

Meadow bitmap tiles (repeats) to fill the rectangle

Use and edit a bitmap fill

1. Click **File** on the menu bar, point to **Import**, click **Import to Library**, then open **meadow.jpg**.

2. Insert a **new layer**, move it to just below the tree1 layer on the Timeline, then name it **meadow**.

3. Click **frame 1** of the meadow layer, then drag the **meadow graphic symbol** from the Library panel to an empty area of the Stage.

4. Click **Modify** on the menu bar, then click **Break Apart**.

5. Click the **Eyedropper tool** 🖊 on the Tools panel, click the **meadow graphic** on the Stage, then compare your screen to Figure 14.

   The Eyedropper tool lets you select a fill from an existing object so you can apply it to another object. Notice the color swatch for the Fill color tool in the Tools panel displays the meadow pattern and the pointer changes to a paint bucket.

6. Click the **Selection tool** ▶ on the Tools panel, then click the meadow graphic on the Stage to select it.

7. Click **Edit** on the menu bar, then click **Cut** to remove the graphic from the Stage.

8. Select the **Rectangle tool** ▢ on the Tools panel, then set the Stroke color to No Stroke ⊿.

9. Using Figure 15 as a guide, draw a **rectangle** across the bottom of the Stage that covers a small part of the tree trunk.

   The rectangle fills with a tiling bitmap of the meadow.

10. Save your work.

You used the Eyedropper tool to select a fill from an object, then applied the fill to another object.

Trace Bitmap
GRAPHICS

What You'll Do

In this lesson, you will trace a bitmap graphic to create vectors and special effects.

Understanding Tracing

Tracing is an outstanding feature if you are illustration-challenged or if you need to convert a bitmap graphic into a vector graphic for animation purposes. When you apply the trace function, you change a bitmap graphic into vector paths and fills with varying degrees of detail. If you keep all the detail in a graphic, you end up with very detailed, intricate vector paths, which tend to increase file size. If you remove some of the detail, you can turn a photograph into a more abstract-looking drawing, which usually results in a smaller file size.

Once traced, you can remove the original graphic from the library and work with only the traced paths and shapes, thereby reducing the movie's file size. The traced shapes act just like shapes you have drawn, with fills, lines, and strokes that you can manipulate and change. Tracing allows a graphic to act as a graphic drawn directly in Flash, which is why you are able to select vector fills based on color and change the color. You can also select vector paths (lines) and manipulate the paths to alter the shape of a graphic.

Figure 16 shows the before and after effects of tracing a graphic. In this example, you can see how tracing makes the original photograph appear more abstract.

Using the Trace Settings

It is possible to trace a graphic using very detailed or less detailed settings. Your traced graphic will look more like the original graphic if you retain more detail. If you want the traced graphic to look more abstract, use less detail. Remember, the greater the detail, the greater the file size. In Figure 17, three different trace effects are created by adjusting the trace values.

There are four options that affect how detailed the trace will appear: Color threshold, Minimum area, Corner threshold, and Curve fit. Color threshold compares two side-by-side pixels; if the difference is less than the color threshold, the two are considered the same color. Color threshold options include integers between 1 and 500. Minimum area sets the number of surrounding pixels to consider, with options between 1 and 1000. Corner threshold works with sharp edges to retain them or smooth them out. Curve fit determines how smoothly outlines are drawn. Figure 18 shows the Trace Bitmap dialog box. You can use the Preview button to display how various settings will affect the graphic.

One of the challenges with using the trace feature comes when you try to animate a traced graphic. Tracing creates paths and shapes, but every piece of the original graphic remains on one layer. To animate or tween between pieces of the shape, you often have to isolate parts of the object onto their own layers. Figure 19 shows the sections of the moon that have been isolated. The sections are selected by color according to

the settings in the Trace Bitmap dialog box. The Selection tool is used to click a color and drag the color section. Once isolated, a selection can be converted to a graphic symbol and animated.

QUICK TIP

You can no longer trace a bitmap graphic once you break it apart. The magic wand tool does not work on traced bitmaps, instead use the Selection tool or the Eraser tool.

Figure 16 *Before and after tracing a bitmap*

Figure 17 *Three different effects with different trace settings*

Figure 18 *Trace Bitmap dialog box*

Figure 19 *Dividing a traced graphic by color*

Sections of the moon selected by color and moved

Trace a bitmap graphic

1. Click the **Selection tool** ▶ on the Tools panel, click the **moon graphic** on the Stage to select it, then press **[Delete]**.

2. Click **frame 1** on the moon layer to select the frame, then drag the **moon.jpg graphic** from the Library panel to the upper-right corner of the Stage.

3. Verify the moon is selected, click **Modify** on the menu bar, point to **Bitmap**, then click **Trace Bitmap**.

4. Type **60** in the Color threshold text box.

5. Double-click the **value** in the Minimum area text box, then type **10**.

6. Click the **Corner threshold list arrow** to view the options, then click **Normal**.

7. Click the **Curve fit list arrow** to view the options, then click **Normal**,

8. Click **OK**, click the **Pasteboard** to deselect the moon, then compare your graphic to Figure 20.

9. Click the **Zoom tool** 🔍 on the Tools panel, then click the **moon** to enlarge it, as shown in Figure 21.

You traced a bitmap graphic and zoomed in on it.

Figure 20 *The traced bitmap image*

Bitmap graphic traced

Figure 21 *Zooming in on the moon*

Importing and Modifying Graphics

Figure 22 *Specifying a fill color*

New fill color

Figure 23 *Changing the fill color*

Figure 24 *The completed screen*

Your moon may
appear different

Edit a traced bitmap graphic

1. Click the **Selection tool** ▶ on the Tools panel.

2. Click the **Paint Bucket tool** � on the Tools panel, then verify the Lock Fill option 🔒 in the Options area of the Tools panel is not selected.

3. Set the Fill color to **#B7DEFF**, as shown in Figure 22, then press **[Enter]**.

4. Click various parts of the moon graphic with the Paint Bucket tool � to change the color to resemble Figure 23.

   Note: Click Edit on the menu bar, then click Undo to use the undo command, as needed.

5. Click the **Selection tool** ▶ on the Tools panel.

6. Set the view to **Fit in Window**.

   Your screen should resemble Figure 24.

7. Save your work, then close the document.

You edited a traced bitmap graphic by changing the color of parts of the bitmap.

Import graphics.

1. Create a new Flash document with a size of **550 × 400** pixels and a white background color, the view set to Fit in Window, and the frame rate set to **9** fps, then save it as **skillsDemo7.fla**.
2. Click the Library tab to display the Library panel.
3. Import the logo.png file from the drive and folder where your Data Files are stored to the library.
4. Import fullMoon.jpg to the library.
5. Import mountain.jpg to the library.
6. Import nightsky.jpg to the library.
   (*Note*: You can import more than one graphic at a time by selecting multiple graphics. Click a graphic, then press and hold [Ctrl] (Win) or [command] (Mac) and click another graphic.)
7. Save your work.

Break apart bitmaps and use bitmap fills.

1. Rename Layer 1 **nightsky**.
2. Click frame 1 on the nightsky layer, then drag the nightsky graphic to the Stage and break it apart.
3. Click the nightsky graphic with the Eyedropper tool, then delete the nightsky graphic from the Stage.
4. Use the Rectangle tool to create a rectangle (with nightsky for the fill and no stroke color) that spans the width of the Stage and covers the top half of the Stage.
5. Insert a new layer, name it **logo**, click frame 1 on the logo layer, and drag the logo graphic symbol to the upper-left corner of the Stage.
6. Insert a new layer named **mountain**, click frame 1 on the mountain layer, and drag the mountain symbol to the bottom-center of the Stage.
7. Use the Properties panel to change the width of the mountain so that it is as wide as the Stage, 550 pixels, then move the mountain graphic so it is flush with the bottom and sides of the Stage.
8. Lock the nightsky and logo layers.
9. Save your work.

Trace bitmap graphics.

1. Trace the mountain graphic, using settings of **100** for Color threshold, **10** for Minimum area, and Normal for Corner threshold and Curve fit.
2. Deselect the graphic.
3. Verify the Fill color on the Tools panel displays the nightsky and the Stroke color is set to No Stroke.
4. Use the Paint Bucket tool to change the blue sky, in the background of the mountain, to stars.
5. Lock the mountain layer.
6. Save your work.

Create an animation.

1. Add a keyframe to frame 30 of each layer.
2. Insert a new layer at the top of the Timeline and name it **moon**. Do not add a keyframe to frame 30 on this layer.
3. Click frame 1 of the moon layer.
4. Drag the fullMoon graphic to the Stage and break it apart.
5. Click a blank area of the Pasteboard to deselect the graphic.

6. Click the Lasso tool on the Tools panel, click the Magic Wand Settings button in the Options area of the Tools panel, then set the Threshold to **10** and the Smoothing to Pixels.

7. Use the Magic Wand to select the blue background, then delete the background.

8. Use the Selection tool to select the moon and convert it to a movie clip symbol with the name mc_Moon.

9. Change the view to 50%.

10. Move the moon off the left side of the Stage and above the mountains.

11. Insert a motion tween that moves the moon across the Stage and off the right side of the Stage.

12. Verify the motion span on the Timeline extends to frame 30.

13. Using the Selection tool, point to just below the motion path on the Stage, then click and drag the path to create an arc shaped path.

14. Click frame 1 on the moon layer, then use the Properties panel to set the rotation to **2** times.

15. Test the movie, then close the Flash Player window.

16. Click frame 23 on the moon layer, then compare your movie to Figure 25.

17. Lock all layers.

18. Save your work, then exit Flash.

Figure 25 *Completed Skills Review*

Importing and Modifying Graphics

Ultimate Tours is rolling out a new "summer in December" promotion in the coming months and wants a Flash website to showcase a series of tours to Florida, Bermuda, and the Caribbean. The website should use bright, "tropical" colors and have a family appeal. Though you will eventually animate this site, Ultimate Tours would first like to see still pictures of what you are planning to do.

1. Open a new Flash document, then save it as **ultimateTours7.fla**.
2. Set the movie properties, including the size and background color as desired.
3. Create the following text objects using Classic Text on separate layers, then lock the layers:
   - A primary headline **Ultimate Tours Presents...** with an appropriate font and color.
   - A subheading **Our new "Summer in December" Tour Packages!** in a smaller font size.
4. Import the following JPG files from the drive and folder where your Data Files are stored to the Library panel (alternately, you can create your own graphics, obtain graphics from your computer or the Internet, or create graphics from scanned media):

   gtravel1.jpg   gtravel4.jpg
   gtravel2.jpg   gtravel5.jpg
   gtravel3.jpg   gtravel6.jpg
5. Using the Library panel, rename the graphics **sand**, **umbrella**, **boat**, **castle**, **starfish**, and **boy**.
6. Drag the sand graphic to the Stage, break it apart, create a bitmap fill, then delete the sand graphic from the Stage.
7. Add a layer and create a rectangle using the sand bitmap fill that appears as a background for the other graphics.
8. Add the castle, boat, boy, umbrella, and starfish to the Stage to create an appealing vacation collage, as follows:
   - Use separate layers.
   - Trace each graphic to give it an artistic look. (*Hint*: Some of the sample files have a white background. To delete the background or any part of the graphic after tracing the graphic, use the Selection tool to select the desired part(s) and delete them or use the Eraser tool. *Note*: The magic wand will only work on bitmap graphics that have been broken apart. It will not work on traced bitmaps.)
   - Resize and arrange the graphics as desired.
   - Lock each layer when not in use.
9. Add a layer and create the two buttons, Home and Buy Now. Use the Paint Brush tool with the sand bitmap fill (or another bitmap fill associated with this file).
10. Lock all the layers.
11. Save your work, then compare your image to the example shown in Figure 26.

Figure 26   *Sample completed Project Builder 1*

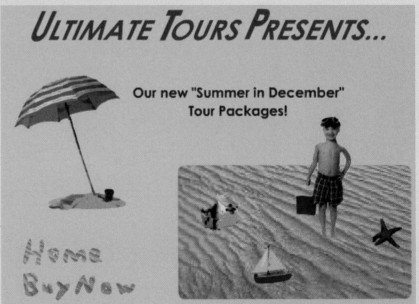

You have been asked to create several sample designs for the main screen of a new student art, poetry, and fiction anthology application called AnthoArt. This application will showcase artwork that includes painting, woodcuts, and photography, as well as writing (including poetry and fiction). Design the application so that it will be suitable for a smartphone.

1. Open a new Flash document and save it as **anthoArt7.fla**.
2. Set the movie properties, including the size (width: 480, height: 800) and background color, as desired.
3. Import the following JPG files from the drive and folder where your Data Files are stored to the Library panel (alternately, you can create your own graphics, obtain graphics from your computer or the Internet, or create graphics from scanned media):
   gantho1.jpg
   gantho2.jpg
   gantho3.jpg
   gantho4.jpg
4. Using the Library panel, rename the graphics as **shells**, **rainbow**, **leaves**, and **squash**.
5. Create a collage on the Stage using the four graphics and include subtitles as part of your design. Be sure to break apart some graphics and use the Trace Bitmap feature for some of the graphics. (*Note*: You do not need to use all four graphics in your collage.)

6. Create the title **AnthoArt**, using a bitmap fill for some or all of the letters. (*Hint*: Break apart the text until the text has a dot pattern.)
7. Create an Enter button, using one of the graphics as a bitmap fill.
8. Lock all the layers.
9. Save your work, then compare your movie image to the example shown in Figure 27.

Figure 27 *Sample completed Project Builder 2*

Figure 28 shows the home page of the Smithsonian website. Study the figure and complete the following. For each question, indicate how you determined your answer.

1. Connect to the Internet, type the URL *www.si.edu*.
2. Open a document in a word processor or open a new Flash document, save the file as **dpc7**, then answer the following questions. (*Hint*: Use the Text tool in Flash.)
   - Are photographs used well in this website? Why or why not?
   - Could the goals and intent of the website be accomplished without the use of photographs?
   - Do the graphics contribute to the design of the site? If so, how?
   - Which file format do you think was used for the images?
   - Can you guess what file format the logo was before it was brought into Flash? Or, do you think it was recreated in the application?
   - Do you think the graphics in this site should be changed in any way? How?
   - Who do you think is the target audience for this website?

Figure 28 *Design Project*
Courtesy of the Smithsonian Institution. www.si.edu

Importing and Modifying Graphics

To showcase your broad range of skills, you want to add some screen design work to your portfolio. This will allow you to improve upon and continue to use artwork you created previously. Try to create at least four samples of your work.

1. Open portfolio6.fla (the project you created in Portfolio Project, Chapter 6), then save it as **portfolio7.fla**.
2. Lock all layers.
3. Add a new layer and name it **screen designs**.
4. Insert a keyframe on the screen designs layer, one frame past the last frame in the movie.
5. Create a heading with the text **Sample Screen Designs**.
6. Import the graphics that will be used on this page to the Library panel. (*Note*: You can use the Publish Settings option in Flash to create PNG and JPG images of the websites you have created for this course. Alternately, you can use other images for the graphics that you place on this page.)
7. Place the graphics on the Stage so that their placement is visually pleasing.
8. Copy the Home button from another part of the movie to this frame.
9. Lock the screen designs layer.
10. Insert a new layer and name it **portfolioCase**.
11. Import the portfolioCase.jpg file to the Library panel. (*Note*: You can use another image, such as a photo of yourself, for the graphic that appears in the center of the home page.)

12. Select frame 1 of the portfolioCase layer, place the graphic on the Stage, break it apart, and delete the blue background.
13. Import the ganthro2.jpg file to the Library panel, then rename it **rainbow**.
14. Use the rainbow graphic to create a bitmap fill, then apply the fill to the portfolio case. (*Hints*: Turn off the Lock option for the Paint Bucket tool in the Options area of the Tools panel. Drag the rainbow graphic to the Stage, click the Bucket tool, open the Color panel, change to Bitmap fill, click the rainbow bitmap fill, then click in the middle of the portfolio case. Delete the rainbow graphic from the Stage.)

15. Insert a layer, name it **myName**, then create a text block that uses the settings of your choice to place your name on the portfolio case.
16. Insert a blank keyframe in frame 2 on the portfolioCase and myName layers.
17. Add ActionScript code to the Web Sites button on the home page that jumps the playhead to the frame that displays the Screen Designs page. Be sure to add a stop action so that the movie stops at the screen designs page, too.
18. Lock all layers, save your work, then compare your screens to the example shown in Figure 29.

Figure 29 *Sample completed Portfolio Project*

CHAPTER 8 BUILDING COMPLEX ANIMATIONS

1. Plan for complex applications and animations

2. Create an animated graphic symbol

3. Create a movie clip symbol

4. Animate buttons using movie clip symbols

5. Edit an animation using the Motion Editor

CHAPTER 8 BUILDING COMPLEX ANIMATIONS

Introduction

As your applications become more complex and you begin utilizing more advanced features of Flash, planning your work is critical. Part of the planning process is determining how to develop a clean Timeline, that is, with objects that are easy to recognize and manipulate, and how to optimize file size by reusing symbols as much as possible.

Creating animated graphic symbols and movie clip symbols can help meet both goals. A well-built application consists of many small pieces put together in animations that can be used in the application. These pieces often include movies nested within movies. For example, in an earlier chapter, you created a movie within a movie by using movie clip symbols of rotating wheels on a moving car. While the concept of movies within movies might sound confusing, it is actually very logical from a file management, media management, and animation perspective. Building movies with 40 layers and lengthy tween spans can be unwieldy. The alternative is to split the many animations on the Stage into smaller, reusable pieces, and then insert these smaller pieces as needed. Creating Flash movies using reusable pieces such as movie clip symbols allows you to have fewer motion tweens and layers in the movie. Creating animated graphic symbols and movie clip symbols also allows you greater flexibility in adding ActionScript to elements, as well as in placing elements on and off the Stage.

Plan for Complex Applications
AND ANIMATIONS

What You'll Do

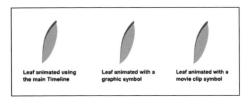

Leaf animated using | Leaf animated with a | Leaf animated with a
the main Timeline | graphic symbol | movie clip symbol

In this lesson, you will work with and compare animated graphic and movie clip symbols.

Making Effective Use of Symbols and the Library Panel

It is important to plan out in advance what you are trying to accomplish in an application. In addition to making development work easier, planning ahead also allows you to organize your Library panel with more accuracy. Consider the following questions as you plan your project:

■ Are there any repeated elements on the Stage? If yes, you should make them into graphic symbols. Graphic symbols should include any still element that is used on the Stage more than once. Graphic symbols might also be elements that you want to be able to tween. Keep in mind one graphic symbol can contain other graphic symbols. For example, you could have a sailboat in which the sails are graphic symbols within the boat symbol.

■ Are there any repeating or complex animations, or elements on the Stage that animate while the rest of the application is still? If so, make these animated graphic symbols or movie clip symbols.

■ What kind of interactivity will your Flash application have? You can assign

ActionScript to button symbols and to movie clip symbols, but not to graphic symbols. You should use button symbols for elements used for navigation or elements that you want to be clickable. Button symbols can contain both graphic and movie clip symbols inside them.

Remember, your Library panel should house all of the building blocks for your applications. To build a logical Library panel, you should have a solid plan in place for the different elements you expect to use.

Understanding Animated Graphic Symbols

Just as you can create a graphic symbol from multiple objects on the Stage, you can convert an entire multiple-frame, multiple-layer animation into a single **animated graphic symbol** that you can store in the Library panel. Creating a single animated graphic symbol removes all of the associated keyframes, layers, and tweening of the animation from your Timeline, which results in a much cleaner Timeline. Animated graphic symbols can also reduce file size if you expect to use the animation in more than one place in a movie.

Compare the two Timelines in Figure 1. On the left is a tree animated through the main Timeline; each individual leaf on the tree has its own layer. On the right is a Timeline for a movie with the same animation but with the leaves grouped into an animated graphic symbol and appearing on a single layer.

An animated graphic symbol is tied to the Timeline of the movie in which you place the symbol. This means that there must be enough frames on the Timeline for the animation to run, and that if the movie stops, the animation stops too.

Understanding Movie Clip Symbols

A **movie clip symbol**, which is essentially a movie within a movie, is a more robust way to store complex animations in the Library panel. The biggest difference between a movie clip symbol and an animated graphic symbol is that the movie clip symbol retains its own independent Timeline when you insert an instance of the symbol into a movie. This creates a nested effect, which means the movie clip instance Timeline plays within the main Timeline. Because the movie clip instance Timeline is independent of the main Timeline, it will repeat if its Timeline is shorter than the main Timeline. For example, if the main Timeline is 40 frames in length and the movie clip instance's Timeline is 10 frames in length, when the movie clip instance is inserted in frame 1 of the main Timeline it will repeat 4 times. This would be useful if you have an animation, such as a flashing logo, that you want to repeat as the main Timeline is playing. One technique for stopping an animated movie clip is to insert a blank keyframe at the end of the layer on the main Timeline that displays the movie clip.

Figure 1 *Comparing Timelines*

Multiple layers on the main Timeline are used to animate the leaves of a tree

Animated graphic symbol, placed on one layer on the main Timeline, contains the animation for all the leaves

In addition, you can use ActionScript to control the playing of a movie clip. For instance, you could have buttons that start and stop a movie clip.

Consider Figure 2, which looks like a still drawing of a living room. However, if it were animated, the fire could be crackling and the candles flickering. To create the animation for these elements (the fire and the candle flame), each one of these animated elements might reside in its own movie clip symbol (one containing the fire animation and a different one containing the candle flame). That way, when placed on the Stage in a movie, each of the movie clip symbols would move according to its own independent Timeline, as well as only taking up one layer and, potentially, only one keyframe on the Timeline. Not only does this help to organize the different pieces of a movie, it also allows you to isolate animated elements and have animations repeat. For example, the animation of the candle flame could be done by using a few frames in which the flame is moved back and forth one time. The animation could be converted to a movie clip with its own Timeline. This allows the movie clip to be repeated (independent of the main Timeline) giving the flame a fluttering effect.

In this lesson, you will view the same animation (animated leaf) created in three different ways: using the main Timeline, a graphic symbol, and a movie clip.

Figure 2 *Using movie clip symbols*

You could create one movie clip symbol of a flickering flame, and use it to animate all three candles

You could create one movie clip symbol of the fire, which would continuously crackle and move as fires do

Figure 3 *Adding an animated graphic symbol to the Stage*

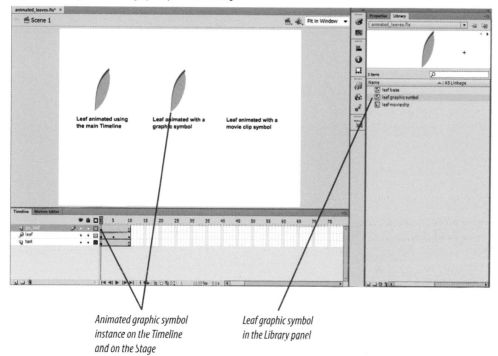

Animated graphic symbol
instance on the Timeline
and on the Stage

Leaf graphic symbol
in the Library panel

Work with an animated graphic symbol

1. Open fl8_1.fla, then save it as **animated_leaves.fla**.

2. Display the Library panel.

3. Press [**Enter**] (Win) or [**return**] (Mac) to play the animation.

   The motion tween in the leaf layer on the Timeline causes the leaf to move.

4. Double-click the **leaf graphic symbol** in the Library panel to display it in the edit window.

5. Press [**Enter**] (Win) or [**return**] (Mac) to play the animation.

   This is the same animation as the one on the main Timeline. It was developed by creating a new graphic symbol (named leaf graphic symbol) of the leaf, copying the motion tween on the main Timeline, and pasting it into the Timeline of this leaf graphic symbol.

6. Click **Scene 1** at the top left of the workspace to return to the main Timeline.

7. Insert a **new layer** above the leaf layer, then name it **gs_leaf**.

8. Click **frame 1** on the gs_leaf layer, then drag the **leaf graphic symbol** from the Library panel to the Stage above the text, as shown in Figure 3.

   The animated graphic symbol version of the leaf still takes up 10 frames on the Timeline, but the symbol's motion tween (blue shading and keyframe on the Timeline) does not display because it is saved as part of the graphic symbol.

9. Press [**Enter**] (Win) or [**return**] (Mac) to view the animations.

You opened a graphic symbol animation in the edit window and you moved an instance of an animated graphic symbol to the Stage.

Work with a movie clip symbol

1. Insert a **new layer** above the gs_leaf layer, then name it **mc_leaf**.

2. Drag the **leaf movie clip symbol** from the Library panel to the Stage above the text, as shown in Figure 4.

3. Click **frame 1** on the mc_leaf layer, then press **[Enter]** (Win) or **[return]** (Mac) to view the animations.

   The movie clip symbol version of the leaf does not move because movie clips on the Stage play only when you export, publish, or test the movie in the Flash Player. Although this movie clip has been provided for you to use in this lesson, you will learn how to create this movie clip symbol in a later lesson.

4. Click **Control** on the menu bar, point to **Test Movie**, then click **in Flash Professional** to test the movie.

   All three leaves animate in place continually.

5. Close the Flash Player window.

6. Save your work.

You placed an instance of a movie clip symbol on the Stage, then tested the movie.

Assign a stop action to the Timeline

1. Insert a **new layer** above the mc_leaf layer, then name it **stopAction**.

2. Insert a **keyframe** in frame 8 of the stopAction layer.

3. Open the Actions panel, then verify the Script Assist button is active.

(continued)

Figure 4 *Adding a movie clip symbol to the Stage*

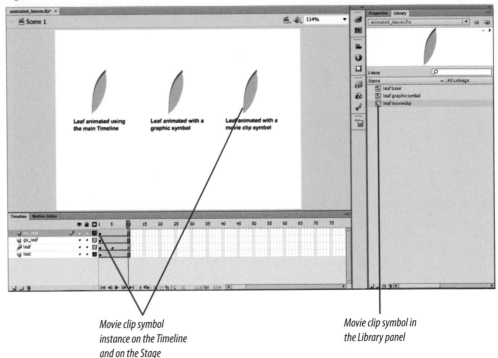

Movie clip symbol instance on the Timeline and on the Stage

Movie clip symbol in the Library panel

Figure 5 *Inserting a* `stop` *action using the Actions panel*

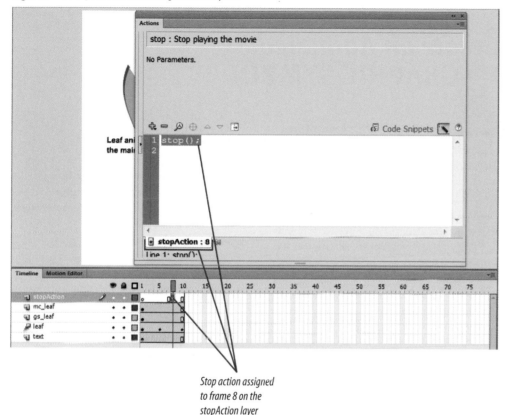

Stop action assigned
to frame 8 on the
stopAction layer

4. Verify that stopAction:8 is displayed in the lower-left corner of the Actions panel Script pane.

   This indicates that the ActionScript code will be assigned to frame 8 on the stopAction layer.

5. Click the **Add a new item to the script button** in the Script Assist window, point to **Global Functions**, point to **Timeline Control**, then click **stop**.

   Your screen should resemble Figure 5.

6. Test the movie.

   The first two instances move briefly and then stop because of the stop action in frame 8 on the main Timeline. The movement of the first two instances of the leaf are dependent on the main Timeline. Only the movie clip symbol continues to move because it has an independent Timeline.

7. Close the Flash Player window.

8. Click **frame 8** on the stopAction layer, click **Modify** on the menu bar, point to **Timeline**, then click **Clear Keyframe**.

9. Click **frame 1** on the stopAction layer.

10. Open the Actions panel, verify stopAction:1 is displayed in the lower-left corner of the Script pane, click the **Add a new item to the script button** in the Script Assist window, point to **Global Functions**, point to **Timeline Control**, then click **stop**.

11. Close the Actions panel.

12. Test the movie.

    The first two instances do not move at all because of the stop action in frame 1 on the main Timeline. Only the movie clip symbol moves because it has an independent Timeline.

13. Save your work, then close the movie.

You assigned a stop action to the Timeline and tested the movie.

Create an Animated
GRAPHIC SYMBOL

What You'll Do

In this lesson, you will convert an animation on the Timeline into an animated graphic symbol.

Using Graphic Symbols for Animations

Most of the time, you will want to use movie clip symbols instead of animated graphic symbols to store animations. However, there are some situations where creating an animated graphic symbol is useful, such as a sequential animation you want to play only one time, rather than repeat continuously like a movie clip. Or, you might want an animation to synchronize with other elements on the Stage, and because animated graphic symbols use the main Timeline, it can be easier to achieve this effect. Also, you can preview animated graphic symbols you place on the Stage right from the Flash editing environment by dragging the playhead back and forth across the Timeline (also called scrubbing). This makes animated graphic symbols easy to test within a Flash movie.

You create an animated graphic symbol in the same way you create a static graphic symbol, by choosing the Graphic option in the Create New Symbol dialog box. In the Library panel, an animated graphic symbol looks the same as a static graphic symbol. However, when you select the animated graphic symbol or a movie clip symbol, it is displayed with Stop and Play buttons in the Item Preview window in the Library panel. You can click these buttons, shown in Figure 6, for testing purposes.

NEW Copying Motion Tweens, Frames, and Layers from the Timeline

Despite good preliminary planning, you may end up drawing and animating objects in a movie, and decide later that the animation would be better placed inside an animated graphic or movie clip symbol. Fortunately, it is easy to copy motion tweens, frames, and layers from the main Timeline and paste them into a new symbol.

To copy multiple layers and frames from within a movie to a symbol, first select the layers and keyframes that you want to copy. To select multiple frames in one or more layers, click the first frame you want to select, and then drag to the last frame. Also, you can click the first frame, press and hold [Shift], and then click the last frame in order to select those frames and all the frames in between.

To select noncontiguous layers, click the name of the first layer you want to select, press and hold [Ctrl] (Win) or [command] (Mac), and then click each layer name. To select contiguous layers, click the first layer name, press and hold [Shift], and then click the last layer name in order to select those layers and all the layers in between. Figure 7 shows a selection across multiple frames and layers. Once you select the layers, click Edit on the menu bar, point to Timeline, and then click Cut or Copy Layers. Create or open the symbol, place the insertion

point in a keyframe, click Edit on the menu bar, point to Timeline, and then click Paste Layers. Flash pastes each individual layer from the original movie into the Timeline for the symbol, and even maintains the layer names.

Note that you cannot copy sound or interactivity in an animation from the main Timeline to an animated graphic symbol. If you want to include sound or interactivity in an animation, you should create a movie clip symbol instead of a graphic symbol.

Figure 6 *Stop and Play buttons in the Library panel Item Preview window*

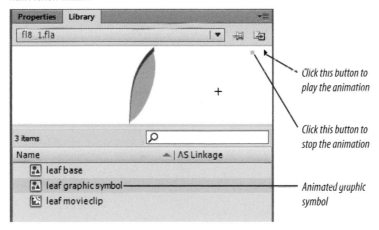

Click this button to play the animation

Click this button to stop the animation

Animated graphic symbol

Figure 7 *Multiple frames and layers selected*

Delete objects from the Timeline

1. Open fl8_2.fla, then save it as **animated_trees.fla**.

2. Verify the Library panel is open, drag the **border** at the top of the Timeline up to display the trunk layer and all 11 leaf layers, then set the view to **Fit in Window**.

3. Play the movie.

   The leaves animate on 11 separate layers.

4. Click the **trunk layer** to select it, press and hold **[Shift]**, click the **leaf eleven layer**, then release **[Shift]**.

   The trunk layer, all numbered leaf layers, and all frames in each layer on the Timeline are selected, as shown in Figure 8.

   TIP You can press and hold [Ctrl] (Win) or [command] (Mac), then click one or more layer names to select all frames in each layer you click.

5. Click **Edit** on the menu bar, point to **Timeline**, then click **Cut Layers**.

   The layers are removed from the Timeline and the tree is no longer visible on the Stage.

   You selected and then cut the layers on the Timeline that made up the tree.

Move frames to create an animated graphic symbol

1. Click **Insert** on the menu bar, then click **New Symbol**.

2. Type **animated tree** in the Name text box, select **Graphic** as the type, then click **OK**.

   You are now in the edit window for the animated tree graphic symbol.

3. Click **Edit** on the menu bar, point to **Timeline**, then click **Paste Layers**.

   (continued)

Figure 8 *Layers and frames selected on main Timeline*

Selecting the frames on the Timeline also selects the elements on the Stage

Figure 9 *Layers and frames pasted on graphic symbol Timeline*

Figure 10 *Moving an instance of the tree symbol to the Stage*

The tree symbol takes up only one layer on the Timeline

Figure 11 *Resizing the second instance of the tree symbol*

Lesson 2   Create an Animated Graphic Symbol

The tree trunk and leaves appear on the Stage, as shown in Figure 9. You may need to scroll the Stage to view the entire tree.

4. Click **Layer 1** on the Timeline, then click the **Delete icon** 🗑 on the Timeline status bar to delete the layer.

5. Play the movie, then click **Scene 1** at the top left of the workspace to return to the main Timeline.

6. Click **ESSENTIALS** on the title bar, then click **Reset 'Essentials'**.

You pasted layers from the main Timeline into a graphic symbol to create an animated graphic symbol. You then deleted a layer that had no objects on it.

Move an animated graphic symbol to the Stage

1. Insert a **new layer** above the background layer, then name it **trees**.

2. Click **frame 1** on the trees layer, then drag the **animated tree graphic symbol** from the Library panel to the left side of the Stage, as shown in Figure 10.

3. Play the movie.

4. Click **frame 1** on the trees layer, then drag the **animated tree graphic symbol** from the Library panel to the right side of the Stage to create another instance of the tree.

5. Click the **Properties panel**, then in the POSITION AND SIZE area, verify the Lock icon 🔗 is not broken, then set the width to **64**.

6. Position the tree as shown in Figure 11.

7. Play the movie and watch the leaves animate on the Stage.

8. Save your work, then close the movie.

You created two instances of an animated graphic symbol on the Stage.

Create a Movie
CLIP SYMBOL

What You'll Do

In this lesson, you will create a movie clip symbol and nest movie clip symbols within one another.

Using Movie Clip Symbols for Animations

Movie clip symbols are usually the most efficient choice for creating and storing complex animations. The main advantage of movie clip symbols is that they maintain their own independent Timeline, which is especially useful for animating continuous or looping actions. Movie clip symbols require only one frame in the main movie, regardless of the complexity of the animation, which can make it easier to work with the Timeline.

Movie clip symbols offer many other sophisticated features not available with animated graphic symbols. For instance, you can add sound and associate ActionScript statements to movie clip symbols, or you can create an animation for a movie clip in the main Timeline (such as a motion tween) while another movie clip continues to play its own animation on its independent Timeline. For example, you could have an animation of a plane flying across the screen developed as a motion tween on the main Timeline. At the same time, you could have an animation of a spinning windmill developed as another

movie clip that plays continuously. In addition, you can use movie clip symbols to animate a button.

To start building a movie clip symbol, create a new symbol and then choose Movie Clip in the Create New Symbol dialog box. You can create the movie clip animation from scratch, or cut and copy frames and layers from the main Timeline, as you did with the animated graphic symbol in the previous lesson. You can also copy a motion tween from another animated object and paste it to a movie clip symbol.

QUICK **TIP**

While you're working with the main Timeline, you see only a static image of the first frame of a movie clip symbol on the Stage. To view the full animation, you must export, publish, or test the movie.

Nesting Movie Clips

As you learned in Chapter 4, a movie clip symbol is often made up of many other movie clips, a process called **nesting**. You can nest as many movie clip symbols inside another movie clip as you like. You can also place a symbol, graphic, or button inside a movie clip symbol. Figure 12 shows a diagram of nesting.

Nested movie clips create a **parent-child relationship** that will become increasingly important as you enhance the interactivity of your movies and begin to deploy more sophisticated ActionScript statements. When you insert a movie clip inside another movie clip, the inserted clip is considered the child and the original clip the parent. These relationships are hierarchical, as indicated in Figure 12. Notice that both the movie clips and the graphic symbol are children of the parent clip. Also, keep in mind that if you place an instance of a parent clip into a movie

and then change it, you will also affect all its nested child clips. Any time you change the instance of a parent clip, the associated child clips update automatically. For example, if you have a car that is the parent clip and it has wheels that are child clips and you resize the car, the wheels resize proportionally.

Understanding the Movie Explorer Panel

The Movie Explorer panel, shown in Figure 13, allows you to inspect the nesting structure of your entire Flash movie. This is a useful reference to print so, as you work on a movie,

you can easily view the movie's structure and see which elements are nested inside each other. You can also apply a filter to view just the elements you want. To access the Movie Explorer, click Window on the menu bar, then click Movie Explorer.

The Panel options button opens the Options menu, which you can use to select a variety of actions to perform on the elements listed in the Movie Explorer. For example, you can go to the element on the Stage and Timeline, find the element in the Library panel, or open all panels relevant to the element so you can edit the object using the panels.

Figure 12 *Diagram of a nested movie clip animation*

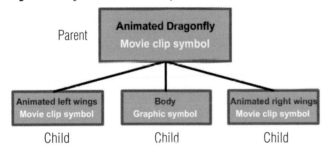

Figure 13 *Movie Explorer panel*

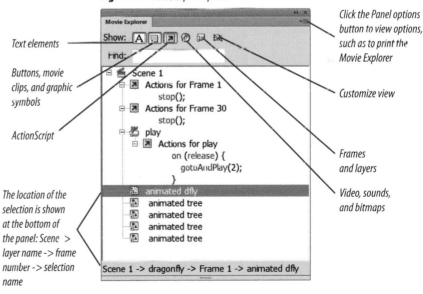

Create a movie clip symbol

1. Open fl8_3.fla, save it as **dragonfly.fla**, then change the frame rate to **10** fps.

2. Display the Library panel, then notice the symbols.

   The Library panel contains the dfly body, left wings, and right wings graphic symbols, as well as the animated left wings movie clip symbol. These symbols will form the basis of your movie clip.

3. Click the **animated left wings movie clip symbol** in the Library panel, then click the **Play button ▶** in the Item Preview window.

   Note: Be sure you click the movie clip symbol and not the name next to the movie clip symbol.

   The wings appear to flutter. Next, you will create another movie clip symbol to animate a set of right wings for the dragonfly.

4. Click **Insert** on the menu bar, then click **New Symbol**.

5. Type **animated right wings** in the Name text box, select **Movie Clip** for the type, then click **OK** to display the edit window.

6. Click **frame 1** on Layer 1 on the Timeline, then drag the **right wings graphic symbol** from the Library panel to the center of the Stage so that the circle is over the centering cross-hair, as shown in Figure 14.

7. Display the Properties panel, click **1** on the Timeline, then click the **wings**.

8. Change the X and Y coordinates to X: **0**, Y: **0**.

   Setting the coordinates to 0,0 provides an anchor point that will remain the same as you resize the wings, which provides the appearance of fluttering.

   (continued)

Figure 14 *Positioning the wings in the edit window*

Place circle on the wings over the centering cross-hair; use the arrow keys as needed to align the cross-hairs

right wings graphic symbol

Building Complex Animations

Figure 15 *Setting values for frame 5 of the motion tween*

Frame 5 selected

Be sure this appears as a broken link

Set these values

Figure 16 *Assembled animated dragonfly*

Animated left wings movie clip symbol

Animated right wings movie clip symbol

9. Click **Insert** on the menu bar, then click **Motion Tween**.

10. Click **frame 5** on the Timeline, click the **wings**, then use the Properties panel to set the following values: W: **47**, H: **57**, as shown in Figure 15.

    Note: Make sure the Link icon for the width and height is broken.

11. Click **frame 10** on the Timeline, click the **wings**, then use the Properties panel to set the following values: W: **84**, H: **57**.

12. Play the animation.

13. Click **Scene 1** at the top left of the workspace to return to the main Timeline.

You created a movie clip symbol containing a motion tween animation.

Nest movie clip symbols

1. Click **Insert** on the menu bar, then click **New Symbol**.

2. Type **animated dfly** in the Name text box, verify Movie Clip is selected for the type, then click **OK**.

3. Drag the **dfly body graphic symbol** from the Library panel to the center of the Stage.

4. Drag the **animated left wings movie clip symbol** from the Library panel to the Stage, then attach it to the upper-left side of the dragonfly's body.

5. Drag the **animated right wings movie clip symbol** to the upper-right side of the body.

    Compare your image to Figure 16, and use the arrow keys to make adjustments as needed.

6. Click **Scene 1** at the top left of the workspace to return to the main Timeline.

You nested two movie clips inside a new movie clip symbol.

Move the movie clip symbol to the Stage, rotate, and resize it

1. Insert a **new layer** above the trees layer, then name it **dragonfly**.

2. Click **frame 1** on the dragonfly layer, then drag the **animated dfly movie clip symbol** from the Library panel so it is on top of the left tree on the Stage, as shown in Figure 17.

3. Play the movie.

   Because the dragonfly is an animated movie clip, the animation does not play on the Stage.

4. Test the movie to view the animation, then close the Flash Player window.

5. Verify the dragonfly graphic on the Stage is selected.

6. Click **Modify** on the menu bar, point to **Transform**, then click **Scale and Rotate**.

7. Type **180** for the Rotate value, then click **OK**.

8. Display the Properties panel, click **frame 1** on the dragonfly layer, then click the **dragonfly**.

9. Verify the Lock icon is unbroken, change the width to **49** in the Properties panel, use the Selection pointer ▸⊕ to place the dragonfly so it is centered on the branches, then save your work.

You added an instance of a movie clip symbol to the Stage, rotated it 180 degrees, and resized it.

Animate an instance of a movie clip and resize an object

1. Click **frame 1** on the dragonfly layer, click **Insert** on the menu bar, then click **Motion Tween**.

(continued)

Figure 17 *Animated dragonfly instance placed on the Stage*

Dragonfly on the Stage

The movie clip takes up only one layer on the Timeline

Building Complex Animations

Figure 18 *Reshaping the path with the Selection tool*

Drag the motion
path down

Figure 19 *Dragging the Bezier handle up to complete the curve*

Drag the
handle up

Figure 20 *Completed path*

Your path may vary

2. Click **frame 10** on the dragonfly layer, then drag the **dragonfly** to the leaves on the small tree.

3. Using the **Selection pointer** ↖₊, point to the middle of the motion path, then, when the pointer changes to ↖, drag the **path** down, as shown in Figure 18.

4. Click the **Subselection tool** ▷ , point to the left end of the motion path, then, when the pointer changes to an arrow with an unfilled square ↖□, click to display the Bezier handles.

5. Point to the right-side handle, then, when the pointer changes to a delta symbol ▶, drag the **handle** up to the position shown in Figure 19.

6. Drag the **solid path** down slightly using the Subselection pointer with a filled square ↖■.

   Notice the dots from the original path are now on the reshaped path, as shown in Figure 20.

7. Click **frame 1** on the dragonfly layer, then click **Orient to path** in the Properties panel.

8. Click the **Free Transform tool** 🔲, then rotate a corner handle to align the front of the dragonfly to the path.

9. Click **frame 10** on the dragonfly layer, click the **dragonfly**, then resize the dragonfly to width **22**.

10. Drag the **tween span** on the dragonfly layer to **frame 30**, then insert **keyframes** in frame 30 on the other layers.

11. Test the movie, close the Flash Player window, then save your work.

You animated and resized an instance of a movie clip.

Animate Buttons Using
MOVIE CLIP SYMBOLS

What You'll Do

In this lesson, you will create an animated button and put together a short interactive movie using ActionScript.

Understanding Animated Buttons

As you learned in a previous chapter, a button symbol does not have the standard Timeline but instead has four states associated with it. You can animate a button by nesting a movie clip symbol inside any one of the three visible states of the button: Up, Over, or Down— although Up and Over are the most common placements for nesting movie clips.

Depending on the state in which you nest the symbol, you will have different results. If you nest the animation inside the Up state, the movie/button will continue to animate as long as the button is visible on the Stage in the main Timeline. If you nest the movie inside the Over state, the animation will be visible only when users mouse over the button. If the animation is nested inside the Down state, users will see only a brief flicker of animation when they click the mouse. The first two are the most common placements for nesting a movie clip and both have obvious interface benefits as well—if your users see something animated, they are more inclined to interact with it and discover it is actually a button.

Building an Animated Button Symbol

To build an animated button symbol, you need at least two symbols in the Library panel. First, you need to create a movie clip symbol with the animation. In building this animation, place the movie clip symbol in the Up state if you want the animation to run repeatedly even if the movie is not running. Otherwise, place the movie clip symbol in the Over state if you want the animation to run only when the mouse pointer is over the button.

Once you have built the movie clip symbol, you need to create a button symbol in which to nest the animation. Remember, because movie clips have independent Timelines, the clip will run continually while the button symbol is on the Stage if the movie clip is placed in the Up state, even if the main movie pauses or stops. Figure 21 shows the Information bar for the edit window of a movie clip symbol nested inside a button.

As with a movie clip, you must publish the movie or test it using the Flash Player to see the animation of a button. The Enable Simple Buttons option will not play the movie clip—you will see only a static view of the first frame of the movie clip.

Creating an Interactive Movie

Adding interactivity to a movie simply means you are asking your user to be involved in the movie in some way other than watching it. It can be as simple as adding a button for a user to click or giving the user a choice to make. Interactivity can also be complex, for example, the game shown in Figure 22 in which a user must assemble a puzzle. Because adding interactivity means you are forcing users to become involved in your movie, you are more likely to hold your users' interest.

You can also create complex interactions by using ActionScript in combination with movie clip symbols. With ActionScript, you can set up movie clips to play, pause, or perform other actions based on user input such as clicking the mouse or pressing a key on the keyboard, similar to the interactions you can create with a button. You can also use ActionScript to instruct movie clips to perform actions without waiting for user input and to jump to specific frames on the Timeline of a movie clip symbol.

Figure 21 *Movie clip symbol nested inside a button*

⇦ 🎬 Scene 1 👆 play 🎞 animated left wings

Button symbol   *Animated movie clip*

Figure 22 *Interactive game created with symbols, buttons, and ActionScript*

Drag and drop the states to the correct place

Borders
Quit

You have 0 correct

Buttons control game variables

Counter keeps track of score as you play the game

Users drag pieces to the correct place in the puzzle

Create an animated button by nesting an animation in the button's Up state

1. Verify that the dragonfly document is open, click **Insert** on the menu bar, then click **New Symbol**.

2. Type **play** in the Name text box, change the Type to **Button**, then click **OK**.

3. Click the **Up frame** on Layer 1, click the **Text tool** T on the Tools panel, then click the **Text tool pointer** ⊢ᴛ in the center of the Stage.

4. Use the Properties panel to change the Character family to **Verdana**, the style to **bold**, the size to **24**, and the color to **black**.

    Note: If you see TFL Text at the top of the Properties panel, click the list arrow and then select Classic Text. If you see Dynamic Text or Input Text below Classic Text, click the list arrow and then select Static Text.

5. Type **PLAY**.

6. Click the **Selection tool** ⬉ on the Tools panel, drag the **animated left wings movie clip symbol** from the Library panel to the left of the word "PLAY," then drag the **animated right wings movie clip symbol** from the Library panel to the right side of the word "PLAY", as shown in Figure 23.

7. Click the **Selection tool** ⬉ on the Tools panel, click the word **PLAY** on the Stage, click the **Text (fill) color box** on the Properties panel, position the Eyedropper pointer 🖋 over a wing, then click.

    (continued)

Figure 23 *Adding the animated wings to the text*

The wings are nested movie clip symbols

Building Complex Animations

Figure 24 *Setting the Hit area*

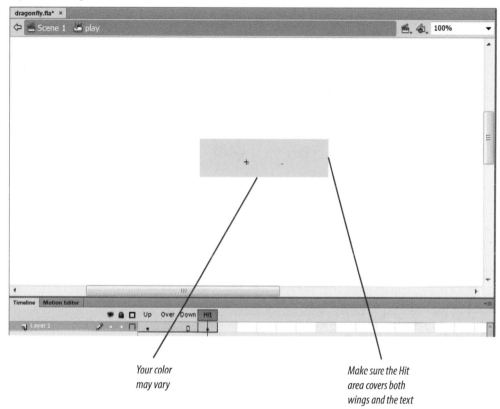

Your color
may vary

Make sure the Hit
area covers both
wings and the text

TIP When you move the Eyedropper pointer to the Stage,
do not pass over any other clickable element in the
Properties panel. If, as you move the Eyedropper
pointer, the pointer changes to a shape other than
the Eyedropper, go back and click the Text (fill) color
box and try again.

The text and the wings are now the same color.

8. Insert a **keyframe** in the Hit frame of the
   button Timeline, select the **Rectangle tool**
   on the Tools panel, then draw a **box**
   around both sets of wings and the text, as
   shown in Figure 24.

TIP Remember that the Hit state is invisible on the
Stage, but it defines the clickable area of a button.

9. Click the **Selection tool** on the
   Tools panel.
10. Click **Scene 1** at the top left of the workspace
    to return to the main Timeline.

*You created a button symbol and placed an animation inside the
Up state of the button symbol.*

Place the animated button on the Stage

1. Insert a **new layer** above the dragonfly layer, name it **button**, then click **frame 1** on the button layer.

2. Drag the **play button symbol** from the Library panel to the lower-right corner on the Stage, as shown in Figure 25.

3. Insert a **new layer** above the button layer, then name it **actions**.

4. Open the Actions panel, then click **frame 1** on the actions layer.

5. Verify that the Script Assist button is selected and that actions:1 is displayed in the lower-left corner of the Actions panel Script pane.

6. Click **Add a new item to the script button** in the Script Assist window, point to **Global Functions**, point to **Timeline Control**, click **stop**, then collapse the Actions panel.

7. Click **Control** on the menu bar, point to **Test Movie**, then click **in Flash Professional**.

   The wings flutter on the animated button and on the dragonfly in the tree. Notice that the dragonfly in the tree does not fly on the motion path and the leaves on the trees do not animate. This is because both the dragonfly's motion and the leaves are dependent on the main Timeline, which is stopped on frame 1.

8. Close the Flash Player window.

You placed an animated button on the Stage and added a stop action.

Figure 25 *Placing the button on the Stage*

The animated button is made up of text and two movie clip symbols

Figure 26 *Adding the button action in the Actions panel*

Event	Action
on (release)	gotoAndPlay()

Clicking the PLAY button will play frame 2

Add a button action

1. Click the **Selection tool** , then click the **PLAY button** on the Stage to select it.

2. Display the Actions panel, then verify that the play button symbol is displayed in the lower-left corner of the Actions panel Script pane.

3. Click **Add a new item to the script button** , point to **Global Functions**, point to **Movie Clip Control**, then click **on**.

4. Click **Add a new item to the script button** , point to **Global Functions**, point to **Timeline Control**, then click **goto**.

5. Change the Frame number to **2**, as shown in Figure 26.

6. Click **frame 30** on the actions layer, click **Insert** on the menu bar, point to **Timeline**, then click **Blank Keyframe**.

7. Click **Add a new item to the script button** , point to **Global Functions**, point to **Timeline Control**, click **stop**, then close the Actions panel.

8. Click **Control** on the menu bar, point to **Test Movie**, then click **in Flash Professional**.

   The dragonfly in the tree and the PLAY button are animated because they use their movie clip Timelines, which are independent of the main Timeline.

9. Click the **PLAY button**.

   The leaves on the trees animate and the dragonfly flies on the motion path, which are actions associated with the main Timeline.

10. Close the Flash Player window, save your work, then close the movie.

You added actions to the movie, creating interactivity.

Edit an Animation Using
THE MOTION EDITOR

What You'll Do

In this lesson, you will use the Motion Editor to make changes in the properties of an animation.

Understanding the Motion Editor

Flash provides a feature called Motion Editor that allows you to edit motion tween animations by changing the property values such as the position, rotation, color effects, and ease value. The advantages of using the Motion Editor are that you can quickly make changes to an animation without having to use the Properties panel and you can view the effect of a change while it is being made. In addition, you can more precisely control the changes that are to be made. Figure 27 shows the Motion Editor panel displayed below the Stage. The Essentials workspace groups the Timeline and Motion Editor panels. When Motion Editor is clicked the Motion Editor panel opens in place of the Timeline panel at the bottom of the Flash workspace. In Figure 27, the Stage view has been set to 25% so that the entire Motion Editor panel can be seen. The PLAY button, which has been given a motion tween, is selected and all changes made in the Motion Editor will affect this button symbol.

The Motion Editor includes several columns with the headings across the top of the panel: Property, Value, Ease, Keyframe, and Graph. The Property, Value, and Ease columns are used together. They represent the properties of the selected object (in this case the button symbol) and are grouped into three categories: Basic motion, Transformation, and Eases.

- Basic motion includes the position of the button symbol (X and Y values) on the Stage, the Rotation Z value, and the type of ease, if any, for each property. Currently, the button symbol has X and Y coordinates of 400 px and 370 px, respectively. No rotation and no ease values have been specified.
- Transformation includes skew and scale (used to resize the symbol) values; color effects such as transparency and brightness; and filters such as drop shadow, blur, and glow. None of these properties have been changed.

Building Complex Animations

- Eases has several types including slow, medium, and fast, as well as values from −100 to 100. Setting the type of ease and ease value for a specific property is a two-step process. If you want to specify an ease (for example, when moving an object), first you select the type of ease and the value within this category. Then, you click the list arrow for a property, such as the X coordinate, and select the ease type.

The Keyframe column is used to add and remove keyframes. When you need to change a property you must select a keyframe or insert one. You insert a keyframe by right-clicking (Win) or [control]-clicking (Mac) the frame and choosing Add Keyframe. Keyframes are displayed on the graph as black rectangles. Currently there are keyframes in frames 1 and 30 because the motion tween begins and ends on these frames.

The Graph column provides a frame-by-frame visual representation of the values specified for the associated properties. You can change these values. For example, if you want to change the position of the object on the Stage, you can enter a value for the X or Y coordinates or you can drag the keyframe in frame 1 for the X or Y coordinates up or down.

Figure 27 *The Motion Editor panel*

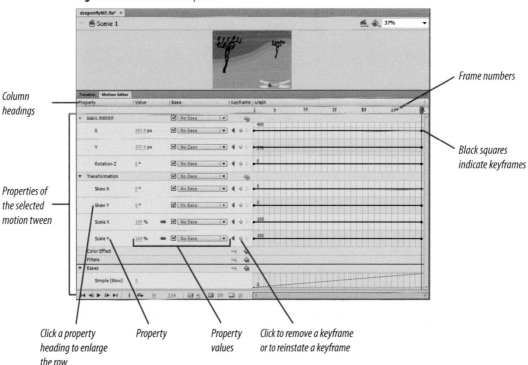

Frame numbers

Column headings

Black squares indicate keyframes

Properties of the selected motion tween

Click a property heading to enlarge the row

Property

Property values

Click to remove a keyframe or to reinstate a keyframe

Use the Motion Editor to change properties of a motion tween animation

1. Open dragonfly.fla, then save it as **dragonflyME.fla**.

2. Click **frame 1** on the button layer, insert a **motion tween**, click **frame 30**, then insert a **keyframe**.

3. Change the View to Fit in Window, then collapse the Properties panel.

4. Click **Motion Editor** on the Timeline.

5. Drag the **top** of the Motion Editor panel up to display the Motion Editor panel.

6. Click the **Viewable Frames value** at the bottom of the Motion Editor and change the value to **30**, as shown in Figure 28.

7. Click **30** on the Motion Editor Graph Timeline.

8. In the Basic motion area, click the **Y value**, type **80**, then press **[Enter]** (Win) or **[return]** (Mac).

   Notice the button symbol on the Stage moves and the graph line on the Motion Editor changes.

9. Change the rotation Z value to **320**.

(continued)

Figure 28 *Displaying the entire Motion Editor panel*

Drag top line of the Motion Editor panel up to display the entire panel

Viewable Frames value

Select No Ease list arrow in the Basic motion area

Frame 30 selected on the Motion Editor Graph Timeline

Figure 29 *Selecting a keyframe to drag*

Point to the
black square

Figure 30 *The completed Motion Editor panel*

10. In the Transformation area, verify the links for the X and Y scales are not broken, then change the Scale X to **10%**.

    Notice the Scale Y is set to 10% automatically because the lock is not broken.

11. In the Eases area, change the Simple (Slow) value to **100**.

12. On the Basic motion bar, click the **No Ease list arrow**, then click **Simple (Slow)**.

    All the ease settings in the Basic Motion area change to Simple (Slow).

13. Click **Control** on the menu bar, point to **Test Movie**, then click **in Flash Professional**.

14. Click the **PLAY button**.

15. Close the Flash Player window.

16. Point to the **keyframe** in frame 30 on the X coordinate graph line, as shown in Figure 29.

17. Drag the **line** up to change the value to approximately **420** and notice how the top of the motion path on the Stage moves toward the tree.

    Your screen should resemble Figure 30.

18. Test the movie, click the **PLAY button**, then close the Flash Player window.

19. Save your work, close the document, then exit Flash.

You used the Motion Editor to change the properties of a motion tween animation.

Plan for complex applications and animations, and create an animated graphic symbol.

1. Start Flash, open fl8_4.fla from the drive and folder where your Data Files are stored, then save it as **skillsDemo8.fla**.
2. Set the view to Fit in Window.

   In this Flash document, you will create a movie that will display a clock (a movie clip) with a minute hand (a movie clip) and an hour hand (a movie clip) that are rapidly spinning. The clock will be a button so that when the user clicks the clock it displays wings (two movie clips) and flies around the screen. All of the necessary graphic objects are available in the Library panel. The movie currently has a background graphic (water and clouds) and a text title (Time Flies).

Create a movie clip symbol.

1. Create a new movie clip symbol named **mc_minuteHand**.
2. Verify you are in the edit window for the mc_minuteHand movie clip, then drag the g_minute hand graphic symbol to the Stage.
3. Use the Properties panel to set the X and Y position values to 0 and 0.
4. Click the Free Transform tool and verify the object is selected.
5. Change the view to 800%, then drag the transformation point (the white circle) of the minute hand object to the middle of the colored circle at the bottom of the object. This will set the pivot point for the object as it spins around.
6. Click frame 1, then create a motion tween.

7. Drag the end of the tween span on the Timeline back to frame 5.
8. Verify frame 5 is selected, then use the Properties panel to set the rotate value to 1 and the direction to clockwise.
9. Play the movie clip, then return to the main Timeline.
10. Change the view to Fit in window, then create a new movie clip symbol named **mc_hourHand**.
11. Verify you are in the edit window for the mc_hourHand movie clip, then drag the g_hour hand graphic symbol to the Stage.
12. Use the Properties panel to set the X and Y position values to 0 and 0.
13. Change the view to 800%, then drag the transformation point (white circle) to the middle of the bottom of the object (the blue circle), which is actually to the left.
14. Click frame 5, then insert a keyframe.
15. Click Modify on the menu bar, click Transform, click Scale and Rotate, set the rotate value to 30 degrees, then click OK.
16. Click frame 10, insert a keyframe, then repeat Step 15 to set the rotate value to 30 degrees.
17. Repeat Step 15 for frames 15, 20, 25, 30, 35, 40, 45, 50, 55, and 60. (*Hint*: Do not just copy and paste frames because the action of rotating the hand will not be copied and pasted to the new frames. You can use shortcut keys. The [F6] key will insert a keyframe. The [Ctrl]+[Alt]+S keys (Win) or [option]+[command]+S (Mac) display the Scale and Rotate dialog box. Then pressing [Enter] Win or [return] [Mac] will accept the values in the dialog box.)
18. Play the movie clip, then return to the main Timeline.

19. Create a new movie clip symbol named **mc_clock**.
20. Verify you are in the edit window for the mc_clock movie clip, rename Layer 1 **clockFace**, then drag the g_clock face graphic symbol to the Stage.
21. Use the Properties panel to set the X and Y position values to 0 and 0.
22. Add a new layer, name it **hourHand**, zoom to 400, scroll to see the clock, drag the mc_hourHand movie clip so the colored circle at the bottom of the hand aligns with the clock's registration symbol.
23. Add a new layer, name it **minuteHand**, drag the mc_minuteHand movie clip to the middle of the clock so that the bottoms of the objects overlap, use the arrow keys to align the two hands, then change to Fit in Window.
24. Add a new layer named **wings**, move it below the clockFace layer, then click frame 1 on the wings layer.
25. Drag the mc_left wings symbol to the upper-left side of the clock, then drag the mc_right wings symbol to the upper-right side of the clock.
26. Use the Free Transform tool and the arrow keys to rotate the wings as needed to place the wings so they appear to be connected to the clock.
27. Insert keyframes in frame 60 on all the layers, then return to the main Timeline.
28. Add a layer, name it **clock**, insert a keyframe in frame 2 on the layer.
29. Drag the mc_clock movie clip symbol to the lower middle of the Stage.

Animate the movie clip symbol.

1. Verify frame 2 on the clock layer is selected, then create a motion tween.

2. Select frame 60 on the clock layer, then drag the clock to the upper-left corner of the Stage.
3. Use the Properties panel to resize the clock to approximately one-fourth of its original size, then adjust the position of the clock so it is in the upper-left corner of the Stage, as shown in Figure 31.
4. Use the Selection tool to reshape the motion path to an arc.
5. Use the Subselection tool to display the Bezier handles and reshape the motion path to an S curve, then compare your screen to Figure 31.

Animate buttons using movie clip symbols.

1. Display the mc_clock symbol in the edit window.
2. Select the clockface and both hands layers (not the wings layer).
3. Click Edit on the menu bar, point to Timeline, click Copy Layers, then return to the main Timeline.
4. Create a new movie clip symbol with the name **mc_clockButton**.
5. Verify you are in the edit window for the mc_clockButton symbol, click frame 1, click Edit on the menu bar, point to Timeline, click Paste Layers, then return to the main Timeline. (*Hint:* If your clock has wings, delete the object in the edit window, return to the main Timeline, open mc_clock and move the wings to the wings layer, then repeat Step 5.)
6. Create a new button symbol with the name **b_clockButton**, then insert the mc_clockButton symbol into the Up state of the button.

7. Insert a keyframe in the Hit state of the button, return to the main Timeline, insert a new layer above the clock layer, then name it **button**.
8. Click frame 1 on the button layer, then click the Edit Multiple Frames icon at the bottom of the Timeline.
9. Drag the b_clockButton symbol to the Stage and place it directly on top of the clock. (*Hint:* Use the arrow keys to align the two clocks.)
10. Turn off the Edit Multiple Frames feature, then remove frames 2–60 on the button layer.
11. Insert a new layer above the button layer, name it **stopAction**, then insert stop actions in frame 1 and 60. (*Hint:* Be sure to add a keyframe to frame 60.)
12. Add a goto action to the button on the Stage, and specify 2 as the frame to go to. (*Hint:* Be sure the button symbol is displayed in the lower-left corner of the Actions panel Script pane.)
13. Test your movie, be sure to click the clock button, then save your work.

Figure 31 *Motion path for clock movie clip symbol*

Edit an animation using the Motion Editor.

1. Save the document as **skillsDemo8-ME.fla**.
2. Click frame 1 on the gtext layer. The text block has been converted to a graphic symbol, a motion tween has been inserted and a keyframe placed in frame 60.
3. Change the view to Fit in Window, display the Motion Editor panel and adjust the panel height to view the entire panel.
4. Change the viewable frames to 60.
5. Verify the text symbol is selected, click 60 on the Graph Timeline and make the following changes:
   - X value: 450
   - Y value: 350
   - Z value: 360
   - Scale X value: 50
   - Color Effect: Tint, black, 50% (*Hint:* Click the Add Color, Filter, or Ease button on the Color Effect bar, then change the settings.)
6. Test the movie, then compare your screen with Figure 32.
7. Save your work, then exit Flash.

Figure 32 *Completed Skills Review*

Ultimate Tours has decided it wants to add animation to the opening page of its "Summer in December" website, which is promoting a series of tours to Florida, Bermuda, and the Caribbean. The management would like the animation to draw attention to the company name and to the navigation button (which in this example is the sun graphic) so visitors will click to find out more information about specific tours. Though the site is still at an early stage, they would like to see some prototypes of potential animations. The company would like a new look that differs from the prototype developed in Chapter 7 (ultimateTours7.fla).

1. Start a new Flash document and save it as **ultimateTours8.fla**.
2. On paper, plan how you might add animations to this page that will fulfill the criteria Ultimate Tours has established.
3. Build the animation you have planned for emphasizing the company name or the promotion subtitle text. For example, you might convert the text of the promotion ("Our new Summer …") to a graphic symbol, then create a movie clip symbol in which the text dissolves and reappears, changes color, rotates, or moves across the screen.
4. Build the animation you have planned that will encourage visitors to click the continue button. For example, you might create an animation of a yellow ball representing the sun rolling out from the heading. Then, you could create a direction line telling visitors to click the sun to continue. (*Note:* For this project, the button does not have to be active.)
5. Save your work, then compare your image to the example shown in Figure 33.

Figure 33 *Sample completed Project Builder 1*

Photo courtesy of J. Shuman.

Building Complex Animations

You have been asked to create a short interactive application on ocean life for the local elementary school, which is planning a visit to an oceanographic institute. This project should be colorful, interactive, and full of images that appeal to 7- to 12-year-old students. The application should be designed to be delivered on a smartphone.

The opening screen should show some images of sea creatures which, when clicked, lead to more information. You must include at least three clickable objects on this opening screen.

1. Obtain some images of fish, coral, and other ocean creatures from resources on your computer or the Internet, or from scanned media. (*Note*: Be sure to use only images you have permission to use.)
2. Create a new Flash document, then save it as **ocean_life8.fla**.
3. Set the document properties, including the size and background color, if desired. (*Hint:* For a mobile app, set the size to 480 × 800.)
4. Create animated movie clips for at least three ocean creatures. Use different types of animation for these movie clips. For example, you might use motion tweening to move, resize, or rotate objects, or fade them in or out.
5. Use the Motion Editor to make adjustments to one of the tweens.
6. Create buttons for the ocean creature images using your animated movies in the Up state and also

designating a Hit state. (*Hint*: Be creative about the appearance of the buttons—use different shapes and sizes, or try cropping and making the images themselves clickable.)

7. Place the three buttons on the Stage.
8. Add some explanatory text.
9. Save your work and compare your image to the example shown in Figure 34.

Figure 34 *Sample completed Project Builder 2*

 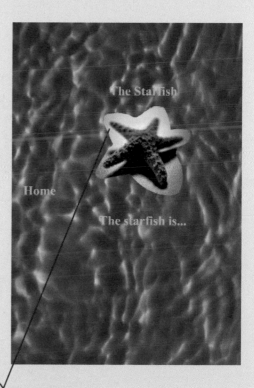

The starfish movie clip contains the graphic image of the starfish and a motion tween that causes the starfish to rotate and get larger as it rotates when the application opens; clicking the starfish opens a new screen

Figure 35 shows a birthday card created in Flash. Study the figure and complete the following. For each question, indicate how you determined your answer.

1. Connect to the Internet, then go to *http://www.rubberchickencards.com/site/search .htm?id=197*.

2. Open a document in a word processor or create a new Flash document, save the file as **dpc8**, then answer the following questions. (*Hint*: Use the Text tool in Flash.)

   - Without seeing the source file for this movie, make a list of objects you believe to be in the Library panel and why you think they should be stored there.
   - Do you think all the images in this work were drawn in Flash? Explain.
   - What in this movie could be animated?
   - Would you use animated graphic symbols or movie clip symbols to create the animations? Explain.
   - Are there any animated graphic symbols or movie clip symbols you could create once and use in multiple places?
   - What other buttons would you add and why?
   - Suppose you want to create an animation in which one jester strums his lute, some text appears and then dissolves, the other jester bangs his

tambourine, more text appears and dissolves, then both jesters play simultaneously while the words "Happy Birthday" float across the screen. Plan a strategy for creating this animation that will streamline the Timeline, reuse symbols to conserve file size, and allow you to easily set up the timing of the sequence so the text appears at the appropriate time.

Figure 35 *Design Project*

© 2006–2010 rubberchickencards.com™, rubberchicken.com™. http://www.rubberchickencards.com/site/search.htm?id = 197

You have decided to create a mobile application that will provide potential clients with current samples of your work. To add some pizzazz, you want to have visitors see a navigation button animate when they mouse over it. The animation should be fairly subtle and elegant, and showcase your animation skills.

1. Start a new Flash document and save it as **portfolio8.fla**.
2. Set the Stage dimensions to width: 640 and height: 960, the dimensions for the iOS mobile screen.
3. Create a movie clip symbol named **animated button**.
4. Inside the movie clip symbol create an animation that would be appropriate for the mouse-over of your primary navigation buttons in the portfolio.
5. Open each of your button symbols and place the animation in the Over state. (*Hint*: Insert a keyframe in the Over state, then drag the animated button movie clip to the Stage. It will be a nested movie clip within the button symbol.)
6. Save your work, then compare your movie to the example shown in Figure 36. (*Note*: Each of the balls rotate and flip when the pointer rolls over it.)

Figure 36 *Sample completed Portfolio Project*

CHAPTER 9 INTRODUCTION TO ACTIONSCRIPT 3.0

1. Understand ActionScript 3.0
2. Work with instances of movie clip symbols
3. Use code snippets
4. Work with variables

CHAPTER **9** INTRODUCTION
TO ACTIONSCRIPT 3.0

Introduction

Until now, you have generally used ActionScript 2.0 (AS2) to code various actions, such as stop events within frames and goto events within buttons. Using AS2 allows you to use Script Assist to enter code that controls the Timeline and creates user interactivity. ActionScript 3.0 (AS3) allows you to do everything you did using AS2 and more. In addition, using AS3 significantly improves the performance of Flash movies by delivering large and complex applications, such as games and websites, more rapidly. Increased performance greatly enhances the user experience by not having to wait for movies to download, as well as making complex animations work more smoothly.

AS2 and AS3 are scripting languages with intuitive code (instructions) such as *gotoAndPlay*. However, AS3 is based on Object Oriented Programming (OOP) standards. OOP is a way to organize code (a set of instructions). You use AS3 code to define objects and send messages between objects. Conceptually, you have been working in an object oriented environment in the previous chapters. That is, you have been working with items (objects) on the Stage and assigning them actions or having them react to actions.

You can build on this conceptual knowledge formed while using AS2 to learn AS3 and to apply the basic concepts of Object Oriented Programming, including understanding its terminology and understanding the rules (the syntax) regarding how AS3 code is written. Having a basic understanding of AS2 gives you a frame of reference as you begin learning AS3.

The goal of this chapter is for you to understand how you can use AS3 to create applications. The examples used in this chapter are simple but give you a basic understanding of AS3 and how AS3 can be used to create complex applications that would be more difficult, time consuming, less flexible or even impossible to create using AS2. Indeed, many new features of recent editions of Flash (especially CS5 and CS6) require that the movie be created with AS3. These features include inverse kinematics (using the Bone tool), 3D effects, and mobile events. Adobe requires a basic knowledge of ActionScript 3.0 for its Associate's certification. Thus, having fundamental skills in AS3 makes a person more employable.

Understand ACTIONSCRIPT 3.0

What You'll Do

In this lesson, you will use ActionScript to create an object, animate the object, and create interactivity.

Understanding How ActionScript 3.0 Works

In the previous chapters, the process for creating movies has focused on the Timeline and on using Flash tools (such as the Tools panel, the Properties panel, and the Library panel). You selected a frame on a layer, used tools to create and place objects on the Stage, and used menu items to animate the objects. For example, in previous chapters, you used Flash tools to draw an oval on the Stage with a specific color and size. Then you used the menu options to change the drawing into a symbol, such as a button, and the edit window to change the colors of the button states and to specify the hit area. Finally, you selected the button instance on the Stage and used the Actions panel and AS2 code to specify an *on release* mouse event and *goto* action that jumps the playhead to another frame that has a motion tween.

Depending on the complexity and length of an application, the Timeline for a movie created in this manner could get very long and have many layers. With AS3, the emphasis shifts from the Timeline to objects, both on and off the Stage. So, for example, with AS3, all of the AS2 examples cited above

can be done without using the drawing tools, menu system, or edit window. That is, you can write the code directly in the Actions panel that defines the button and specifies the event (*mouse click*) that triggers the action (*goto*) or simply plays the motion tween without moving the playhead. This provides a great deal more flexibility because the code can be reused or executed from other places in the movie.

When you start a new Flash Movie, you choose AS2 or AS3. Specifying AS3 means that when writing code in the Actions panel you must adhere to the AS3 rules. Specifying AS3 code does not prevent you from using the features (drawing tools to create and place objects on the Stage, to create Timeline animations, and so on) that you have already learned. In fact, most Flash movies are a combination of these activities and ActionScript code. However, you can only develop using one ActionScript version. You can switch versions (using the Publish Settings option), but, if you do, then all of the code that you have developed already will need to be rewritten.

In order to understand AS3, you must understand the concept of objects. In AS3, an object is an instance similar to the instances you created from movie clip, graphic, and button symbols. In previous chapters, the instances you placed on the Stage were defined (form, color, size, and so on) by the symbols used to create the instances. With AS3, instances are defined by **classes** instead of by symbols. This is useful because a class has certain attributes (properties) and functionality (methods) that are passed on to its objects. The **properties** of an object describe the object, such as the size and color; the **methods** explain what the object can do, such as rotate or accept a mouse click, or what can be done to an object, such as fill it with color. (*Note*: The properties of a class are similar to those of an instance of a symbol, which are also passed on.) Figure 1 summarizes the concepts and terminology related to Classes, Objects, Properties, and Methods.

The Flash program has many predefined classes, such as the Shape class, which are available for use as soon as you start an AS3 document. If a class is not predefined in Flash, you can import a class, such as Tween, or you can create your own class. For example, you could create a cell phone class. After creating the cell phone class, when you place an instance of the cell phone class on the Stage, it has all of the properties of the class and can perform all of the methods associated with the class. The class contains the AS3 code that defines the object. Based on the AS3 code, Flash knows what the object is and what it can do. As you work with AS3, you will be working with objects that are defined by their class. For example, you will use the Shape class to create instances of objects, such as circles and rectangles.

Understanding Display Lists and the addChild() Method

Flash files have a **display list**. The display list is transparent to the user but Flash uses it to manage every object on the screen when the movie is published. In order for an object to be on the display list, it must be part of the **DisplayObjects** class. Objects that can be part of the display list include movie clips, buttons, text, shapes, bitmaps, and video. Objects created with AS3 are not automatically visible on the screen when a movie is published. They must be added to the display list with the **addChild()** method. The syntax for using the addChild method is addChild(my_Object), where my_Object is the name of the object to be added to the display list. Each time you create an object that you want to be visible on the screen in the Flash Player when the movie is published, you must use the addChild() method. Likewise, if you want to remove an object from the display list, then you must use the removeChild() method.

Figure 1 *Summary of specific AS3 concepts and terms*

Term	Definition	Example	Notes
Class	AS3 code that defines the attributes (properties) and functionality (methods) of an object	CellPhone	A class can have a subclass such as smartphones
Object	One instance of a class that inherits the attributes (properties) and functionality (methods) of that class	myCellPhone	
Property	Each attribute of an object, such as its size or color (i.e. "What does it look like")	Height, width, color, weight, screen, buttons, and so on.	
Method	The functionality of an object (i.e. "What can it do" or "What can be done to it")	makeCall, receiveCall, textMessage, recordVideo, takePicture, and so on.	

Understanding Variables and Data Types

A **variable** is a container that holds data. You assign each variable a **data type**, which indicates the class used to populate the variable. There are scores of data types including Number, String (text), MovieClip, and Shape. The syntax for creating a variable is *var variableName:DataType*, where you specify the variable name and the data type. So, using this syntax, you could create a variable to hold a user's age by typing **var age:Number**. In this example, the variable name is age and data type is Number. It is useful to create a variable name that says something about the information that is held in the variable. And, it is imperative to use the correct data type, which can be found in the Help section of Flash CS6. An important use of variables is to hold instances of objects that can be referred to throughout the AS3 code. For example, you could create a variable named myAnimatedLogo_mc with MovieClip as the data type and assign it an animated movie clip. Then anytime you wanted to display the movie clip you would use that variable in your code.

Getting Started with AS3

The process for working with AS3 is to plan your application including how you will be developing objects (such as by importing them to the Library, drawing them on the Stage, or creating them using AS3), and how you will be using the Timeline (such as by developing motion tweens using the Timeline or by developing the motion tweens using AS3). The planning also involves how to construct the user interactivity (such as using buttons, goto actions, and so on). Figure 2 shows a simple movie that has a border and a circle. Figure 2 also shows the Actions panel with the code used to develop the circle. The movie uses two layers and only one frame on the Timeline. The Flash drawing tools were used to create the border, which was placed on its own layer. AS3 was used to create the circle. The process for creating a circle using AS3 is to add a layer with an appropriate name, such as actions, then open the Actions panel and type in the code. The Shape class is used to create a vector object (lines, arcs, circle, and rectangles) and the Graphics subclass is used to create the circle named my_circle. The Graphics subclass has several methods (such as drawCircle) that make it easy to create various shapes. An explanation of the code follows.

`var my_circle:Shape = new Shape();`

This line of code does three things. First, it creates a variable called my_circle. (Remember, you must determine the variable name.) Next, it specifies Shape as the data type for the variable. Then, it creates an instance of the class by specifying new Shape (), which means it will create an instance of the circle. (*Note*: Many data types, such as Shape and MovieClip, describe the class used to fill the variable. So, they are both data types and classes.)

`my_circle.graphics.beginFill(0x00FF00);`

This line of code uses the beginFill method for the graphics subclass to specify the fill color property for the object. The first two characters (0x) indicate that a hexadecimal value will follow. You have used hexadecimal numbers with the Fill Color tool on the Tools panel. 00FF00 is a shade of green. Notice you do not type the # sign before the numbers when you are specifying a color code in AS3.

`my_circle.graphics.drawCircle (250, 100, 20);`

This line of code uses the drawCircle method for the graphics subclass to set the location and size of the object. The first two values are the X and Y Stage coordinates and the last value is the radius of the circle. So, this circle will be located in the top middle of the Stage and have a diameter of 40 px (that is, the radius 20 times 2).

Figure 2 *A movie with a circle and the AS3 code used to create the circle*

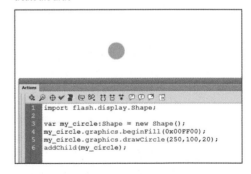

```
addChild(my_circle);
```

This line of code adds the object (my_circle) to the display list so that the object will be visible on the screen based on the Timeline when the movie is played in the Flash Player.

With just four lines of code you can create a circle and specify a fill color, size, and Stage location. Other properties that are easy to add would be a stroke (line size and color) and a transparency (alpha) value. You might also add a line of code to indicate the fill process is complete (my_circle.graphics.endFill();). This line was omitted in order to simplify the example.

When this movie is published, frame 1 plays displaying the area with the blue border and the green circle. Now the question is "Why not just draw the circle on the Stage, convert it to a symbol, and give it an instance name?" The answer is once you have created this object and placed it in a variable container it becomes easily accessible for inclusion in other AS3 code. In addition, using display objects rather than drawn objects reduces the Flash file size significantly because code generated that creates an object by drawing on the Stage is less efficient than code written in the Actions panel to create an object.

Importing Classes

Many, but not all, classes are built into a Flash document. By including only commonly used classes, such as Shape, the Flash file size can be kept smaller. Depending on the configuration of the Flash program on the computer you are using, these built-in classes may be added automatically to the Actions panel as you type AS3 code that references the class. For example, the code import flash.display.Shape; may appear in the Actions panel when you type: var my_circle:Shape = new Shape(); which references the Shape class. If the import code does not appear, the code you typed will still work. However, for some classes, you need to import them as shown in the following section on adding Tweens.

Adding Tweens Using ActionScript 3

To make the example we have been discussing more interesting, we can use AS3 to add a motion tween to the circle in order to have it move down the Stage by changing the location of its y coordinate. AS3 provides a Tween class that can be used to create motion tweens. Before you can use the Tween class, you must import it. Tweens involve a change in an object's size, transparency, or position, and these changes could also involve easing. Therefore, in addition to importing the Tween class, you need to import the Easing class too. The code for these two imports is:

```
import fl.transitions.Tween;
```

```
import fl.transitions.casing.*;
```

After importing these two classes, the following code can be added to create a tween that causes the circle to move down the screen.

```
var moveCircle:Tween = new Tween(my_
    circle,"y",None.easeOut,0,220, 5, true)
```

This line of code does several things:

```
var moveCircle:Tween
```

Creates a variable named moveCircle and specifies Tween as the data type.

```
new Tween
```

Creates an instance of the object (the circle created using AS3).

```
(my_circle
```

Identifies the object to be animated.

```
y
```

Identifies the property of the object that is to be controlled, i.e., the y location on the Stage.

```
None.easeOut
```

Specifies the type of ease (in, out) for the tween. In this case there is no ease.

```
0
```

Specifies the object's starting y position.

```
220
```

Specifies the object's ending y position.

```
5, true)
```

These two values work together. The first value indicates the duration of the tween in either the number of seconds or the number of frames. The second value indicates if the duration is to be specified in seconds or frames. A true value specifies seconds. A false value specifies frames.

The entire line of code causes the circle to move from its current location 220 pixels down the Stage in 5 seconds.

Adding Interactivity Using AS3

Now that an object and a motion tween have been developed using AS3, a button could be used to provide interactivity, such as playing an animation when the user clicks the button.

A common type of interactivity is to have the user click a button, which causes some action (such as the playhead jumping to a frame on the Timeline that plays a motion tween). With AS2, you used Script Assist to assign a button action, such as *on release*, and then you specified the results, such as *gotoAndPlay*. With AS3, you do not assign code to a button or any other objects on the Stage; instead, you reference the object within the code. Figure 3 shows a button added to the Stage in frame 1 of a layer named button. This button was created using the Flash drawing tools. The drawing was converted to a button symbol named b_play, and the Properties panel was used to give the button an instance name of playBtn. The instance name can be used in AS3 code to reference the button. There are three steps involved in a basic button interaction.

1. An event, such as a mouse click, occurs.
2. Flash recognizes that the event has occurred by using an **Event Listener**. Flash is constantly "listening" to "hear" when an event occurs.
3. Flash executes a block of code in response to the event. The block of code is called a **function**. The important thing about functions is that they are reusable blocks of code. They can be written one time and executed as often as desired, which helps keep the file size of a Flash movie small.

An example of the AS3 code that carries out these three steps follows.

playBtn.addEventListener(MouseEvent. CLICK, animateCircle);

This line of code does three things:

playBtn.addEventListener

Adds an event listener method to the instance (playBtn) of the button on the Stage.

MouseEvent.CLICK

Identifies the event as a mouse click (there are several other mouse events such as MOUSE_OVER, MOUSE_UP, and MOUSE_DOWN).

animateCircle

Creates a function named animateCircle. In the same way that you must give a variable a name, you also must create the name for the function. It is helpful to give functions meaningful names.

The function has been named and now it needs to be defined. This involves using the function (animateCircle), specifying the event type (MouseEvent), and typing the lines of code that are to be executed inside curly braces {}. The following code defines the animateCircle function in response to a mouse event.

function animateCircle(event:MouseEvent)

{

var moveCircle:Tween = new Tween(my_circle,"y",None.easeOut,0,220, 5, true);

}

Figure 3 *A button added to the Stage in frame 1*

Instance name for object on the Stage

Notice that the code for the moveCircle tween is within the curly braces. As a result, the code for the moveCircle tween will be executed when the user clicks the Play button on the Stage because, when the Event Listener for the playBtn "hears" the click event, it "calls" the animateCircle function.

A variation of this function would be to include the code that creates the circle within the curly braces, followed by the code shown above to animate the circle. Then, when the user clicks the Play button, the circle appears and is animated.

Understanding ActionScript 3.0 Syntax and Format

AS3 is a strict code environment. This means when you write AS3 code, you must adhere to specific syntax rules including spelling, punctuation, capitalization, and use of special characters. For example, you must use exact case for action names, such as when typing the gotoAndPlay action, you must be sure to capitalize the "A" and "P." Also, remember the structure, that is the how the lines of code are organized and formatted, is critical. For example, a semicolon(;) terminates an ActionScript statement. Text strings appear between quotation marks. Actions are enclosed in curly braces—{}—as shown in Figure 4. In addition, there are certain conventions that, while not required,

are considered good coding practices. These will be pointed out as you work through the chapter. A seemingly minor mistake, such as typing a colon instead of a semicolon, will cause an error when the ActionScript code is executed. If you need help, you can display code hints. Code hints give the syntax or possible parameters for an action in a pop-up window as you are entering the action. To see a code hint, type the action statement, and then type an opening parenthesis. To dismiss the code hint, type a closing parenthesis or press [Esc]. To disable the code hints, click Edit on the menu bar, click Preferences, and then click to deselect the Code Hints check box in the ActionScript category.

Flash provides two features that are useful when working with the Actions panel, **Check syntax** and **Auto format**. Clicking the Check syntax button checks for any errors in the syntax of the coding and, if found, displays a message in the Compiler Errors panel. The Compiler Errors panel appears grouped with the Timeline/Output/Motion Editor panel set. You can use the information in the Compiler Errors panel to help determine what changes need to be made. In many cases the mistakes are in spelling or use of special characters.

The Auto format button formats the code in accordance with ActionScript formatting conventions. Clicking the Auto format button may add spaces, lines, and indents to make the code more readable.

Figure 4 *Syntax for AS3 code*

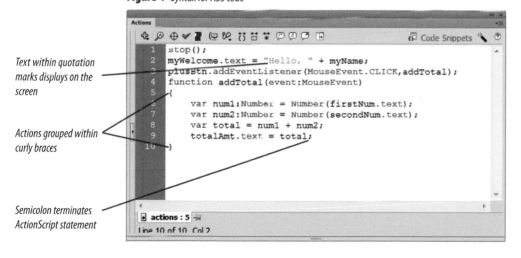

Text within quotation marks displays on the screen

Actions grouped within curly braces

Semicolon terminates ActionScript statement

```
1   stop();
2   myWelcome.text = "Hello, " + myName;
3   plusBtn.addEventListener(MouseEvent.CLICK,addTotal);
4   function addTotal(event:MouseEvent)
5   {
6       var num1:Number = Number(firstNum.text);
7       var num2:Number = Number(secondNum.text);
8       var total = num1 + num2;
9       totalAmt.text = total;
10  }
```

actions : 5

Line 10 of 10 Col 2

Using the Actions Panel

The specific steps used when working with AS3 vary depending on what you would like done within your movie. The process can be as simple as starting a new AS3 Flash document, opening the Actions panel and typing the desired code. Or, the process can be as complex as utilizing the Timeline, adding content and functionality spread throughout multiple layers (in the same way you added content in an AS2 document), and then using AS3 code to enhance the movie. Either approach involves the Actions panel. (*Note*: When you work with ActionScript you are creating a text file. It is possible to create the file outside of Flash using programs designed for writing and debugging AS3 code, such as Adobe Flash Builder.)

The Actions panel has two windows (left one and right one) and three panes, as shown in Figure 5:

- **Actions toolbox pane**—provides the categories of actions that can be selected to build ActionScript code. This provides an alternative to typing code in the Script pane.
- **Script navigator pane**—provides a list of frames that contain scripts used in the movie. This pane can be used to quickly locate a frame and display its code in the Script pane.
- **Script pane**—used to type in the code and a toolbar for editing the code.

Configuring the Actions Panel

In previous chapters, you have used the Actions Panel mainly to insert code using Script Assist.

As just discussed, there are two windows, left and right, in the Actions panel. The left window displays the Actions toolbox pane and the Script navigator pane. The right window displays the Script pane where the ActionScript code is displayed and edited. You will need to display the right window at all times. Before writing any code, be sure to check the layer name and frame number/name displayed in the lower-left corner of the Script pane to verify it is the frame you want to apply the code to. You can collapse and expand the left window by clicking the Expand/Collapse arrow between the windows. You can resize the windows by dragging the border between the two windows left or right. You can resize the panes in the left window by dragging the border between the two panes up or down. You can press [F9] to open and close the Actions panel.

Figure 5 *Actions panel ready to enter AS3 code*

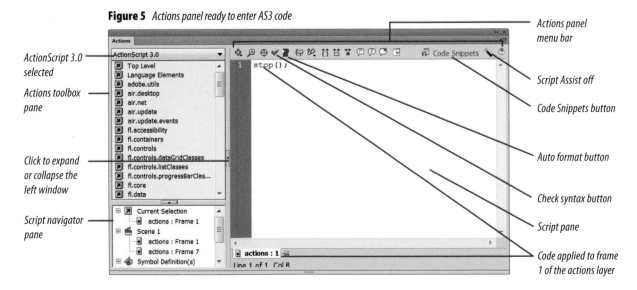

ActionScript 3.0 selected

Actions toolbox pane

Click to expand or collapse the left window

Script navigator pane

Actions panel menu bar

Script Assist off

Code Snippets button

Auto format button

Check syntax button

Script pane

Code applied to frame 1 of the actions layer

Figure 6 *The code to create a circle applied to the actions:1 frame*

```
Actions
import flash.display.Shape;

var my_circle:Shape = new Shape();
my_circle.graphics.beginFill(0x00FF00);
my_circle.graphics.drawCircle(250,100,20);
addChild(my_circle);
```

This statement may be added automatically as you type the code to create a shape.
Note: Ignore code hints throughout this chapter if they appear as you type.

Using the Check syntax and Auto format buttons

It is good practice to always check syntax after typing code. Click the Check syntax button throughout this chapter after typing code even if you are not directed to do so in the steps. The Compiler Errors panel opens and is grouped with the Timeline/Output/Motion Editor panel set. The status bar indicates the number of errors and warnings. If there is an error, a message appears in the Compiler Errors panel. Use the message to help fix the error. Some errors may not be recognized until the movie is tested in the Flash Player.

It is also good practice to use the Auto format button to ensure your code is formatted according to AS3 structure. This will make your code easier to read and easier to find errors, if any.

Use ActionScript to create an object

1. Open fl9_1.fla, then save it as **CircleObject.fla**.
2. Change the view to Fit in Window.

   This movie has one layer named border with a blue border in frame 1.
3. Insert a **new layer**, name it **actions**, then click **frame 1** on the actions layer.
4. Open the Actions panel, then collapse the Actions panel left window if it is open.
5. Verify actions:1 is displayed in the lower-left corner of the Script pane, then turn off Script Assist if it is active.
6. Click at the top of the Script pane, then type the following as shown in Figure 6.

   var my_circle:Shape = new Shape();

   my_circle.graphics.beginFill(0x00FF00);

   my_circle.graphics.drawCircle(250, 100, 20);

   addChild(my_circle);
7. Click the **Check syntax button** ✔ on the Actions panel menu bar and correct any errors.
8. Collapse the Actions panel, then press **[Enter]** (Win) or **[return]** (Mac) to play the movie.

   Nothing appears on the Stage. The object only appears when the movie is published.
9. Click **Control** on the menu bar, point to **Test Movie**, then click **in Flash Professional**.

   The green circle appears in the Flash Player window.
10. Close the Flash Player window, then save your work.

You used ActionScript 3.0 to create and display an object.

Use ActionScript to change the properties of an object

1. Save the document as **CircleObject2.fla**.

2. Open the Actions panel, then change the fill color of the object to **0xFF0000**.

3. Test the movie and notice the color of the circle is now red.

4. Close the Flash Player window.

5. Change the position of the object to **50**, **50** and the radius to **40**.

6. Test the movie, notice the red circle is larger and in the upper-left corner of the Flash Player window, then close the Flash Player window.

7. Drag the **mouse pointer** to highlight the four lines of code starting with var.

8. **Right-click** (Win) or **[control]-click** (Mac) the code, then click **Copy**.

9. Click the end of the addChild line, then press **[Enter]** (Win) or **[return]** (Mac) to move down a line.

10. **Right-click** (Win) or **[control]-click** (Mac) the new blank line, then click **Paste**.

11. For the newly copied lines change the four occurrences of my_circle to **my_circle2**, then change the position to **250**, **250**, as shown in Figure 7.

12. Test the movie.

    Notice another object (my_circle2) is displayed.

13. Close the Flash Player window, save your work, close the Actions panel, then close the movie.

You used ActionScript 3.0 to change the properties of an object and create a second object.

Figure 7 *The code to create a second circle applied to the actions:1 frame*

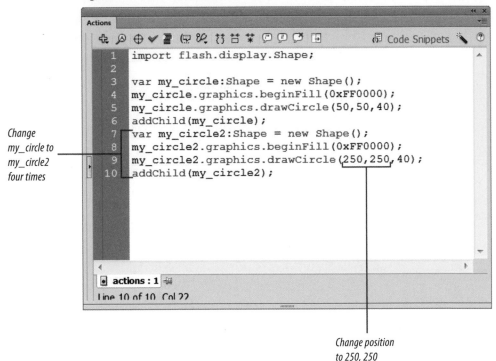

Change my_circle to my_circle2 four times

Change position to 250, 250

Figure 8 *The code to allow the Tween class to be used and applied to the actions:1 frame*

Type these
2 lines

Insertion
point initially
placed before
var

Figure 9 *The code to create the motion tween*

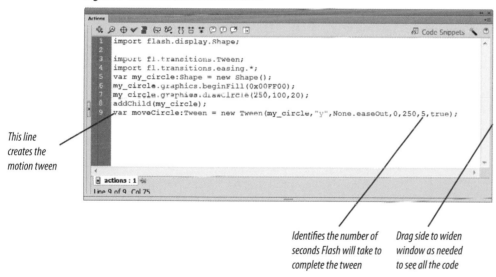

This line
creates the
motion tween

Identifies the number of
seconds Flash will take to
complete the tween

Drag side to widen
window as needed
to see all the code

Use ActionScript 3.0 to create a motion tween

1. Open CircleObject.fla, then save it as **CircleTween.fla**.
2. Change the view to Fit in Window.
3. Click **frame 1** on the actions layer, then display the Actions panel.
   Note: Pressing F9 (Win) or [option]+F9 (Mac) opens and closes the Actions panel.
4. Click before **var** on line 3 to position the insertion line at the beginning of that line.
   Note: If code was not automatically added to your Actions panel, then your line numbers will differ from those referenced In the text and shown in the figure. Your code needs to match the figure exactly but your line numbers do not.
5. Press **[Enter]** (Win) or **[return]** (Mac) to create a blank line.
6. Click the blank **line 3**, then type the following two lines as shown in Figure 8.
   import fl.transitions.Tween;
   import fl.transitions.easing.*;
   This code allows the Tween class to be used.
7. Click the end of the last line of code, then press **[Enter]** (Win) or **[return]** (Mac) to move to a blank line.
8. Type the following code on one line.
   var moveCircle:Tween = new Tween (my_circle,"y",None.easeOut,0,250, 5, true);
   Your Actions panel should match Figure 9.
9. Test the movie, then close the Flash Player window.
10. Change the seconds (5) in the code to **2**.

(continued)

11. Test the movie, then close the Flash Player window.

12. Save your work, close the Actions panel, then close the document.

You used ActionScript to create a motion tween and changed the speed of the tween.

Use ActionScript to create user interactivity

1. Open fl9_2.fla, then save it as **CircleInteractive.fla**.

2. Change the view to Fit in Window.

   This movie has three layers: border, button, and actions. The border and the button were created with the Flash tools. The actions layer has code that animates a circle.

3. Test the movie, let the animation play, then click the **Play button**.

   Notice there is no effect when the Play button is clicked.

4. Close the Flash Player window.

5. Click the **Play button** on the Stage, display the Properties panel, then notice the instance name is playBtn.

   This instance name will be used in the code you develop.

6. Click **frame 1** on the actions layer, then display the Actions panel.

7. Click **line 5** in the Script pane, press **[Enter]** (Win) or **[return]** (Mac) to move to line 6, which is blank.

8. Type the code on line 6, as shown in Figure 10.

(continued)

Figure 10 *The code to create an event listener for a mouse click on the playBtn instance*

```
import flash.display.Shape;

import fl.transitions.Tween;
import fl.transitions.easing.*;

playBtn.addEventListener(MouseEvent.CLICK, animateCircle);
var my_circleNew:Shape = new Shape();
my_circleNew.graphics.beginFill(0xFF0000);
my_circleNew.graphics.drawCircle(50, 50, 40);
addChild(my_circleNew);
var moveCircle:Tween = new Tween(my_circleNew,"y",None.easeOut,0,300,2,true);
```

This line creates the event listener

Introduction to ActionScript 3.0

Figure 11 *The completed code for the animateCircle function*

```
Actions
Code Snippets
1   import flash.display.Shape;
2
3   import fl.transitions.Tween;
4   import fl.transitions.easing.*;
5   import flash.events.MouseEvent;
6
7   playBtn.addEventListener(MouseEvent.CLICK, animateCircle);
8   function animateCircle(event:MouseEvent)
9   {
10  var my_circleNew:Shape = new Shape();
11  my_circleNew.graphics.beginFill(0xFF0000);
12  my_circleNew.graphics.drawCircle(50, 50, 40);
13  addChild(my_circleNew);
14  var moveCircle:Tween = new Tween(my_circleNew,"y",None.easeOut,0,300,2,true);
15  }

actions : 1
Line 15 of 15  Col 2
```

This statement may be added automatically as you type the code for a MouseEvent

Enclosing code in curly braces

Some code, such as the code used to define a function, is enclosed in curly braces. Usually, once you type the opening brace and press [Enter] (Win) or [return] (Mac), the closing brace is added automatically; you type the code between the two braces. Sometimes, however, if you are enclosing code previously created, then you need to type the closing brace at the end of the code as seen in this set of steps.

This creates an event listener for a mouse click on the playBtn instance and names a function (in this case animateCircle) to be executed.

9. Press **[Enter]** (Win) or **[return]** (Mac), then type the following.

   function animateCircle(event:MouseEvent)

   {

   These two lines of code begin the process of identifying the block of code included in the function, named animateCircle.

10. Click the blank line at the bottom of the code, then type **}**.

    This curly brace indicates the end of the function's block of code. Your screen should match Figure 11.

11. Test the movie, click the **Play button**, then notice the object appears and animates.

12. Click the **Play button** again, then notice another instance of the object appears and is animated.

    Each time the Play button is clicked, the function is called and the code is executed. If you wanted to show only one instance, you would add code at the beginning of the function to check for an existing instance and to clear it if one is found before running the animation.

13. Close the Flash Player window, save your work, close the Actions panel, then close the document.

You used ActionScript to add user interactivity to a button.

Work with Instances
OF MOVIE CLIP SYMBOLS

What You'll Do

In this lesson, you will use ActionScript to control instances of movie clip symbols.

Working with Movie Clips

Most large Flash applications include many movie clips. Using movie clips helps you manage your document by breaking complex tasks into smaller components, and using movie clips also lets you reuse content and reduce file size. Another advantage to movie clips is you can use actions with them, allowing you greater control over the objects on the Stage.

You can set the actions you associate with movie clips to run when a user performs an action, to run automatically when the movie plays, or to run when a condition is met, such as if the movie clip has been dropped on top of another movie clip. Some common uses of AS3 with movie clips include creating actions that run a specific frame within the movie clip's Timeline and making a movie clip draggable, so users can move it in games, to shopping carts, or in simulations.

> **QUICK TIP**
>
> AS3 used with movie clips will run only when you test, export, or publish your movie.

Exporting a Movie Clip for Use in ActionScript

When a movie clip has been created and added to the Library panel it is not yet ready to be used with ActionScript. To keep the file size down, objects in the Library are not by default included in the swf file when the movie is published. Objects placed on the Stage are automatically included in a swf file. However, objects that are added at runtime, such as those created using ActionScript, need to be identified. This is done by turning on the Export for ActionScript feature found in the Symbol Properties dialog box. Figure 12 shows the process for exporting a movie clip, named PurpleShirt, for use in ActionScript. First, you open the Symbol Properties dialog box and check the Export for ActionScript check box in the ActionScript Linkage area of the dialog box. A class is created that references the movie clip. You can specify a class name, such as PurpleShirtMC as shown in Figure 12, or accept the default name. This name appears in the AS Linkage column of the Library panel. The AS linkage name can be used to reference the movie clip in

ActionScript code. For example, as shown below and in Figure 13, a variable can be used to create an instance of a movie clip, then the addChild method can be used to have the instance appear on the screen when the movie is published.

var PurpleShirtInstance:PurpleShirtMC=
    new PurpleShirtMC();

There are two parts to this line of code.

var PurpleShirt:PurpleShirtMC

This creates a variable with the name PurpleShirtInstance and uses PurpleShirtMC as the data type, which in this case is the movie clip data type. (*Note*: Flash knows that PurpleShirtMC is a Movie Clip data type because PurpleShirtMC is linked with PurpleShirt in the Library. PurpleShirt is a movie clip so that makes PurpleShirtMC a Movie Clip data type. You could have typed MovieClip for the data type but instead you used the more meaningful name PurpleShirtMC, which you specified in the Symbol Properties dialog box.)

= new PurpleShirtMC();

This creates a new instance of the PurpleShirt movie clip using the PurpleShirtMC AS linkage name which is used to reference the movie clip.

QUICKTIP

To ensure that your ActionScript will run correctly, do not include spaces in movie clip symbol instance names.

Figure 12 *The process for exporting a movie clip for use in AS3*

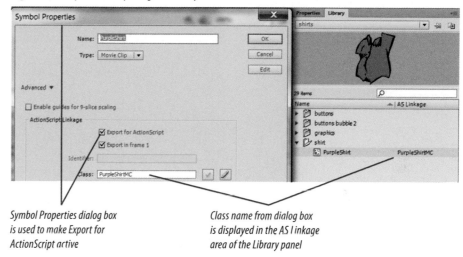

Symbol Properties dialog box is used to make Export for ActionScript active

Class name from dialog box is displayed in the AS Iinkage area of the Library panel

Figure 13 *Using a variable to create an instance of a movie clip on the Stage*

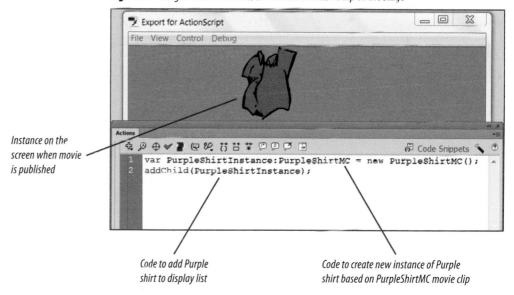

Instance on the screen when movie is published

Code to add Purple shirt to display list

Code to create new instance of Purple shirt based on PurpleShirtMC movie clip

Make movie clip instances so they can be referenced in ActionScript

1. Open fl9_3.fla, then save it as **shirts.fla**.

   This movie has five layers and one frame.

   Note: If you receive a message that a font is missing, you can replace the font with the default font or any other appropriate font.

2. Test the movie, then click each of the buttons.

   None of the buttons are functional.

3. Close the Flash Player window.

4. Display the Library panel, then open the **shirt folder**.

5. Click each of the movie clips and view it in the Item Preview window.

   In the completed movie, when the user clicks a button, the appropriate movie clip (displaying a color or pattern) will appear on the shirt.

6. **Right-click** (Win) or **[control]-click** (Mac) **PurpleShirt** in the Library panel, then click **Properties**.

7. Click **Advanced** in the Symbol Properties dialog box to expand the box if it is not already expanded.

8. Click the **Export for ActionScript check box** if it is not already checked.

   Flash automatically inserts PurpleShirt for the Class name.

9. Change PurpleShirt to **PurpleShirtMC**, as shown in Figure 14, then click **OK**.

   A message appears indicating that Flash will create a definition for this class.

   (*Note:* If Flash does not recognize a class you specify, it automatically defines the class using the information provided in the Symbol Properties dialog box.)

   (continued)

Figure 14 *Changing the class name*

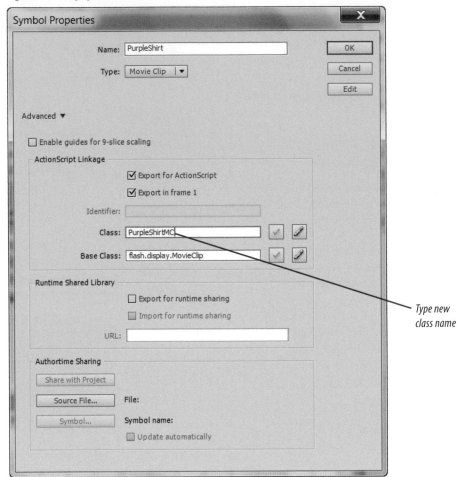

Type new class name

Figure 15 *Viewing the AS linkage name in the Library panel*

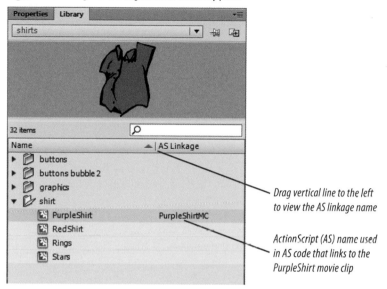

Drag vertical line to the left to view the AS linkage name

ActionScript (AS) name used in AS code that links to the PurpleShirt movie clip

Figure 16 *The code for creating the four variables*

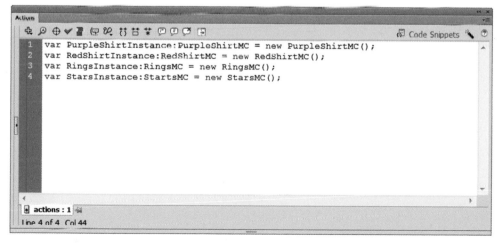

10. Click **OK**.

11. Drag the **vertical line** next to AS Linkage in the Library panel to the left to view the AS Linkage name, as shown in Figure 15.

12. Repeat Steps 6-10 for the remaining three movie clips giving them class names of **RedShirtMC**, **RingsMC**, and **StarsMC**.

    The class names and the AS linkage names are the same.

13. Insert a **new layer** at the top of the Timeline, then name it **actions**.

14. Click **frame 1** on the actions layer.

15. Open the **Actions panel**, then type the following code on one line.

    var PurpleShirtInstance:PurpleShirtMC = new PurpleShirtMC();

    This creates a variable named PurpleShirtInstance, sets the data type to PurpleShirtMC, and creates an instance of the object.

16. Type the code for the other three objects as shown in Figure 16.

17. Close the Actions panel.

18. Save your work.

You specified Export for ActionScript for movie clip symbols in the Symbol Properties dialog box, gave a class name to each one, then created a variable and instance for each movie clip so the movie clips can be referenced in AS3 code.

Add an event listener and function to a button instance

1. Click the **purple button** on the Stage to select it.

2. Display the Properties panel, then note the instance name of the button.

3. Click **frame 1** on the actions layer, open the Actions panel, verify the insertion point is at the end of the last line of code, press **[Enter]** (Win) or **[return]** (Mac) one time, then type the following on one line.

   purpleBtn.addEventListener(MouseEvent. CLICK, displayPurple);

   This adds an event listener to the button instance named purpleBtn. It also specifies the event as a mouse click event and defines a function, displayPurple, that will execute when the event occurs.

4. Press **[Enter]** (Win) or **[return]** (Mac) to move the insertion point to the next blank line, then type the following on two lines.

   function displayPurple(event:MouseEvent)
   {

   These two lines of code begin the block of code for the function, displayPurple. Any code placed after the brace { will be part of the block of code that is executed when the purple button is clicked.

5. Press **[Enter]** (Win) or **[return]** (Mac) to move the insertion point to the next blank line, then type the following on one line, as shown in Figure 17.

   addChild(PurpleShirtInstance).x=125, (PurpleShirtInstance).y=93;

   (continued)

Figure 17 *The code for creating an event listener and function for a button*

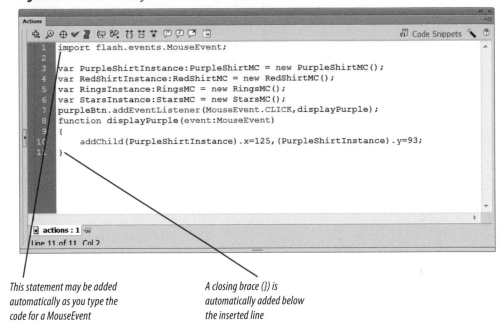

```
import flash.events.MouseEvent;

var PurpleShirtInstance:PurpleShirtMC = new PurpleShirtMC();
var RedShirtInstance:RedShirtMC = new RedShirtMC();
var RingsInstance:RingsMC = new RingsMC();
var StarsInstance:StarsMC = new StarsMC();
purpleBtn.addEventListener(MouseEvent.CLICK,displayPurple);
function displayPurple(event:MouseEvent)
{
    addChild(PurpleShirtInstance).x=125,(PurpleShirtInstance).y=93;
}
```

This statement may be added automatically as you type the code for a MouseEvent

A closing brace (}) is automatically added below the inserted line

Figure 18 *The completed code for all the buttons*

```
Actions
import flash.events.MouseEvent;

var PurpleShirtInstance:PurpleShirtMC = new PurpleShirtMC();
var RedShirtInstance:RedShirtMC = new RedShirtMC();
var RingsInstance:RingsMC = new RingsMC();
var StarsInstance:StarsMC = new StarsMC();
purpleBtn.addEventListener(MouseEvent.CLICK,displayPurple);
function displayPurple(event:MouseEvent)
{
    addChild(PurpleShirtInstance).x=125,(PurpleShirtInstance).y=93;
}
redBtn.addEventListener(MouseEvent.CLICK,displayRed);
function displayRed(event:MouseEvent)
{
    addChild(RedShirtInstance).x=125,(RedShirtInstance).y=93;
}
ringsBtn.addEventListener(MouseEvent.CLICK,displayRings);
function displayRings(event:MouseEvent)
{
    addChild(RingsInstance).x=125,(RingsInstance).y=93;
}
starsBtn.addEventListener(MouseEvent.CLICK,displayStars);
function displayStars(event:MouseEvent)
{
    addChild(StarsInstance).x=125,(StarsInstance).y=93;
}
```

`actions : 1`
Line 26 of 26, Col 2

You can copy the AS3 code for the purpleBtn, paste it in the Script pane, and then replace information specific to the purpleBtn object with information specific to another object, such as redBtn

This code adds the PurpleShirtInstance to the display list and places an instance of the purple shirt at x and y coordinates 125 and 93, respectively.

6. Click the **Check syntax button** ✓ in the Script pane, then correct any errors.

7. Click the **Auto format button** 🖹, then compare your Script pane to Figure 17 on the previous page.

8. Test the movie, click the **purple button**, then close the Flash Player window.

9. Complete the code for the other buttons as shown in Figure 18.

   Note: You can copy and paste the purpleBtn code and then change all instances of purple (or PurpleShirt) to red (or RedShirt), rings, or stars respectively, and making sure to match capitalization of the word or phrase you are replacing.

10. Save your work.

You added event listeners and functions that display objects on the Stage.

Change the visibility of objects

1. Test the movie, click the **Purple button**, then click the **Red button**.

   The red shirt covers the purple shirt.

2. Click the **Stars button**, then click the **Rings button**.

   The rings are placed on top of the stars. To have only one pattern appear at a time, you can change the visibility values for the instances.

3. Close the Flash Player window, then add the following below the addChild(RingsInstance) line and before the closing }, as shown in Figure 19.

   RingsInstance.visible = true;

   This code sets the visible property of the RingsInstance (rings pattern on the Stage) to true when the Rings button is clicked.

4. Add the following below the RingsInstance.visible=true; line and before the closing }.

   StarsInstance.visible = false;

   This code sets the visible property of the StarsInstance (star pattern on the Stage) to false when the Rings button is clicked. So, these two lines of code cause the rings to display and the stars to disappear when the Rings button is clicked.

   (continued)

Figure 19 *Setting the visibility for the RingsInstance to true*

```
17   ringsBtn.addEventListener(MouseEvent.CLICK,displayRings);
18   function displayRings(event:MouseEvent)
19   {
20       addChild(RingsInstance).x=125,(RingsInstance).y=93;
21       RingsInstance.visible = true;
22   }
23   starsBtn.addEventListener(MouseEvent.CLICK,displayStars);
24   function displayStars(event:MouseEvent)
25   {
26       addChild(StarsInstance).x=125,(StarsInstance).y=93;
27   }
```

Note: your line numbers may vary

Type this line to set the visibility for the object to true

Introduction to ActionScript 3.0

Figure 20 *The completed code to set all the visibility values*

```
Actions
                                                          Code Snippets
1   import flash.events.MouseEvent;
2
3   var PurpleShirtInstance:PurpleShirtMC = new PurpleShirtMC();
4   var RedShirtInstance:RedShirtMC = new RedShirtMC();
5   var RingsInstance:RingsMC = new RingsMC();
6   var StarsInstance:StarsMC = new StarsMC();
7   purpleBtn.addEventListener(MouseEvent.CLICK,displayPurple);
8   function displayPurple(event:MouseEvent)
9   {
10      addChild(PurpleShirtInstance).x=125,(PurpleShirtInstance).y=93;
11  }
12  redBtn.addEventListener(MouseEvent.CLICK,displayRed);
13  function displayRed(event:MouseEvent)
14  {
15      addChild(RedShirtInstance).x=125,(RedShirtInstance).y=93;
16  }
17  ringsBtn.addEventListener(MouseEvent.CLICK,displayRings);
18  function displayRings(event:MouseEvent)
19  {
20      addChild(RingsInstance).x=125,(RingsInstance).y=93;
21      RingsInstance.visible = true;
22      StarsInstance.visible = false;
23  }
24  starsBtn.addEventListener(MouseEvent.CLICK,displayStars);
25  function displayStars(event:MouseEvent)
26  {
27      addChild(StarsInstance).x=125,(StarsInstance).y=93;
28      StarsInstance.visible = true;
29      RingsInstance.visible = false;
30  }

actions : 1
Line 29 of 30  Col 32
```

Code to set
visibility values

5. Add the following below the addChild(StarsInstance) line.

   StarsInstance.visible = true;

   RingsInstance.visible = false;

   This code causes the stars to display and the rings to disappear when the Stars button is clicked.

6. Click the **Check syntax button** ✔ in the Script pane, then correct any errors.

7. Click the **Auto format button** ☰ , then compare your Script pane to Figure 20.

8. Test the movie, then click each button several times.

9. Close the Flash Player window, then close the Actions panel.

10. Save your work, then close the document.

You used ActionScript to set the visibility values of objects.

Use
CODE SNIPPETS

What You'll Do

In this lesson, you will use code snippets to make a movie clip draggable.

Working with Code Snippets

In Chapter 6, you were introduced to code snippets, which are predefined blocks of AS3 code that provide a quick way to insert AS3 code into the Script pane. You used code snippets to add events and gestures to mobile applications in earlier lessons. Code snippets are provided for a number of features that can be added to an application including navigation, animation, audio, and video. Figure 21 shows the Code Snippets panel with the list of categories and the Timeline Navigation category expanded

Figure 21 *The Code Snippets panel*

to show the code snippets available in that category. Figure 22 shows the "Click to Go to Frame and Play" code snippet after it has been inserted in the Script pane. The code begins with several comment lines that are grayed out. These are instructions that guide you through the use of the code. The code starts in line 11 with an add mouse click event listener for a button instance named startBtn followed by a function named fl_ClickToGoToAndPlayFromFrame. This is a generic function name that you can change to be more descriptive of what is happening in the function. Line 13 identifies the start of the function and line 15 has the code that is executed when the user clicks the startBtn. The instructions indicate that you replace the number 5 with the frame number you would like the playhead to move to when the symbol instance (startBtn) is clicked. The process for using this code snippet follows.

- Create a button symbol and give it an instance name.
- Select the button instance on the Stage. (*Note*: Even though you select the button on the Stage, the AS3 code will be placed in a frame on a layer named actions (or Actions), not in a frame containing the button. If there is no layer named actions or Actions, Flash will create one and name it Actions.)
- Open the Code Snippets panel and click the desired snippet to enter that code in the Script pane.
- Edit the code as needed, such as changing the function name and editing the actions you want executed. For instance, you can change the frame number that the function should go to and play when the code is executed.

Think of code snippets as templates that allow you to make changes to customize the code. These could be changes in function names, frame numbers, or properties such as ease values.

Figure 22 *The Script pane after adding a code snippet*

Name of code snippet

Comment lines explaining the code and giving instructions; /* marks the beginning and */ marks the end of comments

Button with event listener

A function with gotoAndPlay code

A number that increments is appended to the function name each time the code snippet is used (your number may differ)

Void is an optional keyword that indicates the function does not return a value

Frame movie will go to and play

Adding Comments to Your AS3 Code

As you write more and more code, it becomes useful to provide comments, like those shown in Figure 22, to help clarify what is happening in a particular section of code. Comments can be inserted easily using the Apply block comment button or Apply line comment button on the Actions menu bar. You can also add a comment to your ActionScript code by typing a slash and an asterisk (/*) at the beginning and an asterisk and a slash (*/) at the end of one or more lines of text. Any code between this set of symbols is treated as a comment and it is ignored when the ActionScript code runs. Alternately, if your comment is only a single line, you can place two slashes (//) at the beginning of the line, and that line will be ignored when the ActionScript runs. Comments appear in the Script pane as gray text, and they are not part of the executable code.

Understanding Interactive Movie Clips

Using AS3 with movie clip symbols offers many opportunities for creating a richer user experience. With the startDrag and stopDrag actions, you can make a movie clip draggable while a movie is playing; that is, you can allow a user to click the movie clip and then move it to another location on the screen. You have probably seen draggable movie clips in games created with Flash, as shown in Figure 23, or in user interface features such as scroll bars and sliders in web applications created with Flash.

AS3 code can also change the properties of movie clip symbols as a movie is playing. You can control such properties as position, rotation, color, size, and whether the movie clip is visible or hidden. Actions that change movie clip properties are often used in combination with actions that test for user input or interactions. For example, you can create ActionScript that makes a movie clip disappear when it is dragged onto another movie clip.

QUICK TIP

As you work through this lesson, you will be opening the Actions and Code Snippets panels and viewing objects on the Stage. If your workspace gets cluttered, you can move, collapse, and resize panels as needed to work more efficiently. If the workspace becomes confusing you can click the ESSENTIALS button above the menu bar and choose Reset 'Essentials'.

Figure 23 *Draggable movie clips in a Flash game*

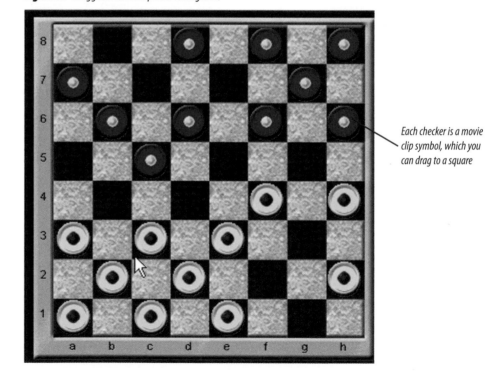

Each checker is a movie clip symbol, which you can drag to a square

Figure 24 *The startBtn instance name displayed in the code snippet*

startBtn instance name

Use code snippets to make a button interactive

1. Open fl9_4.fla, then save it as **shapes.fla**.
2. Drag the **playhead** through the Timeline.

   This movie contains two screens. The first screen has a button that will be used to jump the playhead to the second screen.
3. Click the **Start button** to select it.

   Note: You select the Start button so that Flash knows which object instance to apply the code snippet code to.
4. Display the Properties panel, then type **startBtn** for the instance name.
5. Click **Window** on the menu bar, then click **Code Snippets**.
6. Click the **Timeline Navigation expand icon** ▶ to display the options.
7. Verify the Start button is selected on the Stage, then click **Click to Go to Frame and Play** in the Code Snippets panel.
8. Click the **Show description icon** ⓘ, then read the description of the code.
9. Click the **Show code icon** {}, **scroll** to the bottom of the code, then verify startBtn (the Start button's instance name) is displayed, as shown in Figure 24.

   (continued)

10. Click **5** in the code, type **7**, click the **Insert button**, then watch as the code is inserted into frame 1 of the actions layer.

11. Click **frame 1** on the actions layer, then display the Actions panel.

12. Read the code and verify your code resembles Figure 25.

13. Test the movie, click the **Start button**, close the Flash Player window, then save your work.

You used code snippets to add interactivity to a button.

Use code snippets to enter code into the Script pane

1. Collapse the Code Snippets panel and the Actions panel.

2. Click **7** on the Timeline to display the next screen, then click the **black square** in the Start Bin.

3. Display the Properties panel, then type **square** for the instance name.

4. Display the Code Snippets panel, then click the **Actions expand icon** ▶.

5. Verify the black square is selected on the Stage.

6. Click **Drag and Drop** in the Code Snippets panel.

7. Click the **Show description icon** ⓘ, then **read** the description of the code.

8. Click the **Show code icon** { }, **scroll** to the bottom of the code, then verify square (the black square's instance name) is displayed, as shown in Figure 26.

9. Click the **Insert button**, then watch as the code is inserted into frame 7 of the actions layer.

(continued)

Figure 25 *The completed code for the ClickToGoToAndPlayFromFrame function*

The default value (5) for the frame to go to is changed to 7

Figure 26 *The Drag and Drop code snippet with the instance name (square) displayed*

instance name of the black square movie clip

Figure 27 *The code snippet displayed in the Actions panel*

```
Actions
1   stop();
2   /* Drag and Drop
3   Makes the specified symbol instance moveable with drag and drop.
4   */
5
6   square.addEventListener(MouseEvent.MOUSE_DOWN, fl_ClickToDrag_5);
7
8   function fl_ClickToDrag_5(event:MouseEvent):void
9   {
10      square.startDrag();
11  }
12
13  stage.addEventListener(MouseEvent.MOUSE_UP, fl_ReleaseToDrop_5);
14
15  function fl_ReleaseToDrop_5(event:MouseEvent):void
16  {
17      square.stopDrag();
18  }
```

```
actions : 7
Line 18 of 18, Col 2
```

10. Click **frame 7** of the actions layer, then display the Actions panel.

11. Read the comments and code, as shown in Figure 27.

    Line 6 of the code adds a mouse down event listener for the square instance and a function named fl_ClickToDrag_5 (*Note*: The 5 may vary).

    Lines 8–11 of the code defines the function so that when the mouse pointer is over the square and the mouse button is pressed, the square will be draggable.

    Line 13 of the code adds a mouse up event listener to the Stage and a function named fl_ReleaseToDrop_5. That is, when the mouse pointer is on the Stage and the mouse button is released, Flash will recognize it as a mouse up event.

    Lines 15–18 of the code defines the function so that when the mouse button is released, the square will not be moveable.

12. Test the movie, then click the **Start button**.

13. Drag the **black square** in the Start Bin to on top of the yellow square in the Drop Bin, then release the mouse button.

14. Close the Flash Player Window, then close the Actions and Code Snippets panels.

15. Save your work, then close the document.

You used code snippets to add interactivity to a movie and to enable an object to be draggable.

Work
WITH VARIABLES

What You'll Do

In this lesson, you will use ActionScript to create interactive Text and Number variables.

Understanding Variables

As you have already learned, a **variable** is a container that holds information. Variables are dynamic; that is, the information they contain changes depending on an action a user takes or another aspect of how the movie plays. For example, a variable would be used in a Flash game that keeps track of scores or in a form in which a user enters credit card information while making an online purchase. As already seen in previous lessons, you create variables in ActionScript with the **var** keyword. You have to specify a name and a data type for the variable when you create it.

To create a **String variable**, which is a sequence of characters including letters, numbers, and punctuation, place quotation marks around the string. For example, the ActionScript statement var myExam:String = "Pop Quiz"; creates a variable named myExam with a String data type and the string "Pop Quiz" assigned to the myExam variable.

To create a **Number variable**, you can just write the number (you do not need quotation marks around the number). For example, var myScore:Number = 93; creates a variable named myScore with a Number data type, and the number 93 assigned to the myScore

variable. No quotation marks are needed around a value assigned to a Number variable.

Flash includes the following data types for variables: String, Number, Boolean, Object, and MovieClip, which you worked with in an earlier lesson. See the Flash Help system for a full explanation of each type.

QUICK **TIP**

To ensure your ActionScript will run correctly, do not include spaces in variable names.

Using Text Fields to Collect User Information

One of the most powerful uses of variables is to collect and work with information from users. To do this, you create input text fields to collect the data and dynamic text fields to display the data. Once a variable is created, you can manipulate variables using ActionScript. For example, if you want to display a person's name in a dynamic text field, you can create a variable that collects the person's name in an input box and then, using the same variable, displays the person's name in a dynamic text field. You can even write AS code to include a greeting, such as Hello, before the person's name when it is displayed.

An **input text field** takes information entered by a user and stores it as a variable. To create an input box, you select the Text tool, open the Properties panel, and change the text type to Input, as shown in Figure 28. You can also set properties, such as font family and style, whether the input text box appears with a border, and the maximum number of characters allotted for user input. Then, you use the Text tool to draw the box on the Stage and assign an instance name to it.

A **dynamic text field** displays information derived from variables. A dynamic text field can be used together with an input text box. For example, you could have a user enter his/her name into an input text field in one part of a movie and have the name displayed in a dynamic text box in another part of the movie. You create a dynamic text box the same way you create an input text box by using the Text tool and Properties panel, but you select Dynamic Text as the text type.

Text input fields work with string data. If you want the user to input numbers so calculations can be performed, you must convert the String data type to a Number data type. For example, you could have an input text box with an instance name of inputAge where the user types in her age. The following code could be used to change the data that the user types from text to a number.

```
var age:Number = Number(inputAge.text);
```

In the code, a variable named age is created with the Number data type. Then, the data

from the inputAge text box is converted to a number and assigned to the variable age. This process of changing one data type to another is called **casting**.

Embedding Fonts

When you include input text fields in your Flash movie you need to embed the font so that it is available to the users no matter what fonts they have on their computer. Embedding the font ensures the text maintains the appearance

you desire. The process for embedding fonts is to click the Embed button in the Character area of the Properties panel. This displays the Font Embedding dialog box that you use to specify which font(s) and characters to embed. A font file is created that accompanies the swf file when the Flash document is published. If a font has not been embedded in a Flash movie and it is not present on your computer, you may receive a Font not found message. You can choose to have Flash display a substitute font.

Figure 28 *Using the Properties panel to create an input text field*

- Text type list arrow
- Input Text selected as the text type
- Embed button
- Change Character settings
- Show border around text button (active)
- Behavior set to Single Line

Understanding Expressions

Expressions are formulas for manipulating or evaluating the information in variables. This can range from string expressions that concatenate (join together) user and system-derived text (as in a paragraph that inserts a user's name right in the text) to numeric expressions that perform mathematical calculations like addition, subtraction, or incrementing a value. Flash also lets you enter logical expressions that perform true/false comparisons on numbers and strings, with which you can create conditional statements and branching.

Note that some expressions have different results depending on whether they are performed on String or Number variables. For example, the comparison operators >, >=, <, and <= determine alphabetical order when used with String variables, and the mathematical operator + concatenates strings. In addition, the equal sign is used to test whether or not two values are identical.

Figure 29 shows an expression in which the value of one variable (num1) is added to the value of another variable (num2) and the result is assigned to a third variable (total). The code defines the addTotal function that is executed when the plusBtn object is clicked.

Figure 29 *Example of an expression used for a calculation*

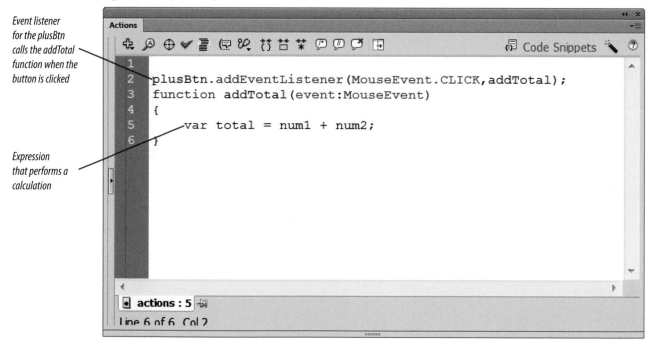

Event listener for the plusBtn calls the addTotal function when the button is clicked

Expression that performs a calculation

```
plusBtn.addEventListener(MouseEvent.CLICK,addTotal);
function addTotal(event:MouseEvent)
{
    var total = num1 + num2;
}
```

Figure 30 *Drawing the text box for the input text field*

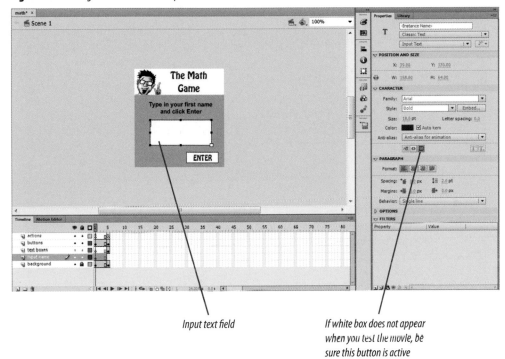

Input text field

If white box does not appear
when you test the movie, be
sure this button is active

Create an input text box

1. Open fl9_5.fla, then save it as **math.fla**.

2. Drag the **playhead** through the Timeline.

   This movie has two screens, an introduction that allows you to type in a name, and a calculations screen to enter numbers and perform calculations.

3. Click **frame 1** on the input name layer, then click the **Text tool** T on the Tools panel.

4. Verify the Properties panel is displayed, verify Classic Text is displayed, click the **Text type list arrow**, then click **Input Text**.

5. Make the following changes: Family: **Arial**; Style: **Bold**; Size: **18**; Color: **#990000**, click the **Show border around text button** 🔲 to turn it on, set the alignment to Align Left ≣ , then verify the Behavior is set to Single line.

   Note: If the Properties panel does not display the CHARACTER area, click the pasteboard, make the changes above, then delete the text box on the pasteboard.

6. Draw a **text box** as shown in Figure 30.

TIP Use the Selection tool pointer to move the box and the handles to resize the box.

7. Verify the text box is selected on the Stage, then use the Properties panel to enter **inputNameBox** as the instance name.

8. Test the movie.

   A white input text box appears on the screen. In addition, a message appears in the Output panel indicating that fonts should be embedded.

9. Try to type **Jesse** into the input name box.

(continued)

The letters do not appear because the font is not available at runtime.

10. Close the Flash Player window.

You created an input text box in which users can type their name. You also specified the formatting for the input text.

Embed fonts for use with input text fields

1. Click the **Selection tool** ![selection tool icon] on the Tools panel, then click the **input text box** on the Stage to select it.

   Note: If you cannot select the input text box, click the Pasteboard, and then click the input text box.

2. Verify the Properties panel is displayed, then note the font that appears in the Character area.

3. Click the **Embed button** in the Character area.

   The Font Embedding dialog box appears with the name of font, Arial, that was specified for the input text box. The font style, Bold, is displayed along with the embedded font name (Font 1).

4. Click **Uppercase**, **Lowercase**, **Numerals**, and **Punctuation** in the Character ranges area to select them.

   These character ranges are added to the Font 1 embedded font, as shown in Figure 31.

5. Click **OK** to close the dialog box.

6. Test the movie, type **Jesse** in the input box, then click the **Enter button**.

7. Close the Flash Player window.

8. Save your work.

You embedded a font for an input text box.

Figure 31 *Selecting the font character ranges in the Font Embedding dialog box*

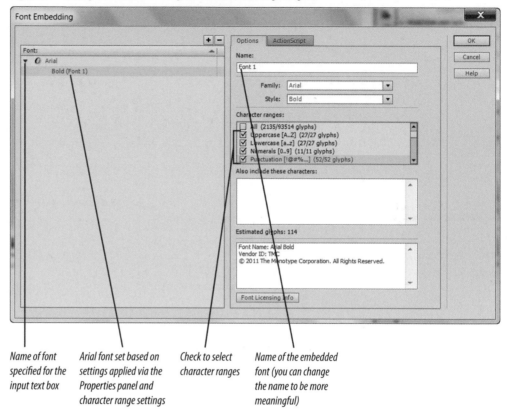

Name of font specified for the input text box

Arial font set based on settings applied via the Properties panel and character range settings

Check to select character ranges

Name of the embedded font (you can change the name to be more meaningful)

Font Embedding dialog box

When you embed a font, the Font Embedding dialog box displays the current font. The dialog box also displays the font style (in this case Bold) and Font 1. The number 1 indicates this is the first font to be embedded. If you were to embed another font it would be designated Font 2. You can specify the Character ranges for Font 1 by selecting it and clicking on the desired check boxes.

Figure 32 *Drawing the text box for the dynamic text field*

Text box is a dynamic
text field

Dynamic Text selected
as the text type

Create a dynamic text box

1. Click the **Selection tool** on the Tools panel, then click the **Timeline tab** to display the Timeline.

2. Insert a **new layer** above the input name layer, then name it **hello**.

3. Insert a **keyframe** in frame 5 of the hello layer.

4. Click the **Text tool** T on the Tools panel, then use the Properties panel to change the text type to **Dynamic Text**.

5. Click the white area next to the character's head, and then use the Selection tool to move or resize the box as necessary so it matches Figure 32.

6. Verify the text box is selected.

7. Use the Properties panel to enter **myWelcome** as the instance name.

8. Save your work.

You created a dynamic text box to hold the name the user enters.

Use ActionScript to collect and modify String variables

1. Click **frame 1** on the actions layer, then display the Actions panel.

2. Click after the **;** in stop();, press **[Enter]** (Win) or **[return]** (Mac) to insert a blank line, then type:

   var myName:String = "";

   This defines a variable named myName with a String (text) data type. This variable will be used to hold the name typed into the input text box. The "" gives the variable an initial value of null (that is, an empty container).

3. Click before the **g** in the goto line within the function, press **[Enter]** (Win) or **[return]** (Mac) to insert a blank line, press **[↑]**, then type:

   myName = inputNameBox.text;

   This takes the text that is typed in the input text box and assigns it to the myName variable. The .text indicates a text property.

4. Verify your Script pane matches Figure 33.

5. Click **frame 5** on the actions layer.

6. Expand the Actions panel, type the following below the stop(); line.

   myWelcome.text = "Hello, " + myName;

   This statement takes the value in the myName variable and concatenates it with Hello, . So, when the user clicks the Enter button, this ActionScript takes the name the user has entered in the myName input field, prefaces it with the word "Hello, " then displays the text string in the myWelcome dynamic text box.

7. Click the **Check syntax button** ✔ .

   (continued)

Figure 33 *The script pane showing the code that collects the data from the input field*

```
1  stop();
2  var myName:String = "";
3
4  enterBtn.addEventListener(MouseEvent.CLICK, CaptureInputandGoTo);
5
6  function CaptureInputandGoTo(event:MouseEvent):void
7  {
8      myName = inputNameBox.text;
9      gotoAndPlay(5);
10 }
11
```

Data typed into the inputNameBox (which is the instance name assigned to the input text box created earlier) is assigned to the myName variable (which is a String variable)

Figure 34 *The completed code to have the input text appear in the dynamic text box*

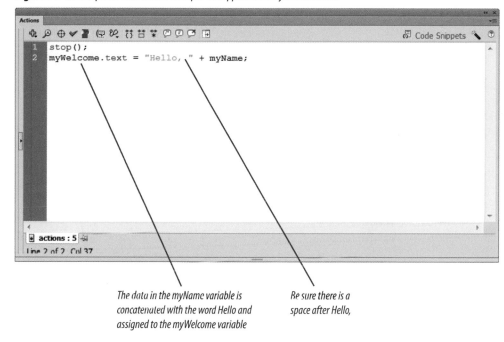

```
1  stop();
2  myWelcome.text = "Hello, " + myName;
```

The data in the myName variable is concatenated with the word Hello and assigned to the myWelcome variable

Be sure there is a space after Hello,

If there are errors in the code, check your code and be sure it matches the code in Figure 34.

8. Click the **Auto format button** ▤ in the Script pane.

9. Test the movie, click the **name input field**, type **Jesse**, then click the **Enter button**.

   The name "Jesse" appears in the dynamic text field, prefaced by "Hello, ".

10. Close the Flash Player window, close the Actions panel, then save your work.

You used ActionScript to modify a text variable and place it in a dynamic text box.

Use ActionScript to perform a mathematical operation on a numeric variable

1. Verify the calculation screen is displayed.

   This screen already contains two input text boxes (below First Number and Second Number) and a dynamic text box (next to Total).

2. Click the **Selection tool** ▶ , click the **Input text box** below First Number, then give it an instance name of **firstNum**.

3. Click the **Input text box** below Second Number, then give it an instance name of **secondNum**.

4. Click the **Dynamic text box** next to Total, then give it an instance name of **totalAmt**.

5. Click the **plus button**, then give it an instance name of **plusBtn**.

6. Click **frame 5** of the actions layer, open the Actions panel, then type the code that follows on the line below the myWelcome line. Type the code all on one line.

   (continued)

plusBtn.addEventListener(MouseEvent.CLICK, addTotal);

This adds a mouse click event listener to the plusBtn instance and creates a function named addTotal.

7. Type the remaining lines of code shown in Figure 35 below the plusBtn line.

   This code defines the block of code for the addTotal function that is called when the user clicks the plusBtn button. The first two lines of code inside the curly braces take the input typed by the user in the First Number and Second Number input text boxes and assigns them to number variables. The third line adds the two numeric variables and assigns the result to a variable named total. The last line assigns the value in the total variable to the totalAmt text field (the instance name for the dynamic text field) and displays it in the Total text box.

8. Test the movie, type a **name**, then click the **Enter button**.

9. Type a **number** into the First Number box, type a **number** into the Second Number box, then click the **plus button**.

10. Close the Flash Player window, then save your work.

You used ActionScript to create a mathematical operation that works with variables.

Copy ActionScript code

1. Click the **Selection tool** ▶ on the Tools panel, click the **minus button** on the Stage to select it, verify the Properties panel is displayed, then type **minusBtn** for the instance name.

(continued)

Figure 35 *The completed code to perform a calculation on input data*

You may see an import statement in line 1

Event listener that calls the addTotal function when the plusBtn is clicked

Takes the text from the input text fields and assigns it to numeric variables

Adds the numeric variables and assigns the result to another variable named total

Assigns the value in the total variable to totalAmt, which is the instance name of the dynamic text field

Type this code on one line

```
stop();
myWelcome.text = "Hello, " + myName;
plusBtn.addEventListener(MouseEvent.CLICK,addTotal);
function addTotal(event:MouseEvent)
{
    var num1:Number = Number(firstNum.text);
    var num2:Number = Number(secondNum.text);
    var total = num1 + num2;
    totalAmt.text = total;
}
```

actions : 5
Line 10 of 10, Col 2

Figure 36 *Highlighting the code*

Drag the mouse
pointer to highlight
the lines of code

```
1  stop();
2  myWelcome.text = "Hello, " + myName;
3  plusBtn.addEventListener(MouseEvent.CLICK,addTotal);
4  function addTotal(event:MouseEvent)
5  {
6      var num1:Number = Number(firstNum.text);
7      var num2:Number = Number(secondNum.text);
8      var total = num1 + num2;
9      totalAmt.text = total;
10 }
```

actions : 5
Line 3 of 10 Col 1

Figure 37 *The completed ActionScript to perform the mathematical calculations*

```
19  multBtn.addEventListener(MouseEvent.CLICK, multTotal);
20  function multTotal(event:MouseEvent)
21  {
22      var num1:Number = Number(firstNum.text);
23      var num2:Number = Number(secondNum.text);
24      var total = num1 * num2;
25      totalAmt.text = total;
26  }
27  divBtn.addEventListener(MouseEvent.CLICK,divTotal);
28  function divTotal(event:MouseEvent)
29  {
30      var num1:Number = Number(firstNum.text);
31      var num2:Number = Number(secondNum.text);
32      var total = num1 / num2;
33      totalAmt.text = total;
34  }
```

actions : 5
Line 34 of 34 Col 2

2. Click **frame 5** on the actions layer, then display the Actions panel.

3. Drag the **mouse pointer** to highlight the plusBtn line and the function lines as shown in Figure 36.

4. **Right-click** (Win) or **[control]-click** (Mac) the highlighted text, then click **Copy**.

5. Click at the end of the code, press **[Enter]** (Win) or **[return]** (Mac) to insert a blank line below the code, then **right-click** (Win) or **[control]-click** (Mac) and click **Paste**.

6. Change **plusBtn** to **minusBtn**, change **addTotal** to **subtTotal** for both instances of addTotal, then change **+** to **−**.

   This creates a new mouse click event listener for the minus button and changes the function to subtract the numbers typed into the input boxes.

7. Test the movie, enter **two numbers**, then click the **minus button**.

8. Close the Flash Player window.

9. Repeat Steps 1 – 6 for the multiplication and division buttons using **multBtn** and **divBtn** for the instance names; **multTotal** and **divTotal** for the function names; an asterisk (*****) for the multiplication operator; and a slash (**/**) for the division operator.

10. Compare your screen to Figure 37.

11. Test the movie, type in various numbers and test all of the buttons, then close the Flash Player window.

12. Close the Actions panel, save your work, then close the document.

Your copied ActionScript code from one object to another and made changes to the code.

Use ActionScript to create an object and change its properties.

(*Hint*: Use the Check syntax and Auto format features to verify ActionScript code you type.)

1. Start Flash, open a new ActionScript 3.0 document, then save it as **skillsDemo9-object.fla**.
2. Rename Layer1 **actions**.
3. Display the Actions panel.
4. Type the code to create a rectangle using the variable name **myRectangle** with a **Shape** data type, a **000099** fill, positioned at **100** pixels for the x and y coordinates, and with a width of **50** pixels and a height of **80** pixels (*Note*: The code for drawing a rectangle is drawRect (x-coordinate, y-coordinate, width, height). Then type the code to add the object to the display list.
5. Check the syntax and format the code.
6. Test the movie, then close the Flash Player window.
7. Change the rectangle color to **660000** and the x position to **50**.
8. Test the movie, close the Flash Player window, then change the x position to **100**.
9. Test the movie to verify your change, close the Flash Player window, then save your work.

Use ActionScript to create a motion tween and user interactivity.

1. Add the code to import the tween and easing classes.
2. Add the code to create a variable named **animateRectangle** with a **Tween** data type, create an instance of the myRectangle object, then specify an x movement, with no ease, with a starting point of **0** and ending point of **300** in **3** seconds.
3. Test the movie, then close the Flash Player.

4. Click frame 1 of the actions layer, then type a stop action at the top of the Actions panel.
5. Insert a new layer, then name it **button**.
6. Click frame 1 of the button layer, then create a button on the Stage and give it an instance name of **playBtn**.
7. Click frame 1 of the actions layer, display the Actions panel, then type the code above the existing line of code that begins var myRectangle ... and that will add a mouse click event listener to the button and define a function.
8. Type the code to create the function that will animate the object. (*Hint*: Move the code that defines the variable and the tween code to within the curly braces of the function.)
9. Check the syntax and format the code.
10. Close the Actions panel.
11. Test the movie, then click the button.
12. Close the Flash Player window, save your work then close the document.

Add an event listener and function to a button instance.

1. Open fl9_6.fla, then save it as **skillsDemo9-seasons.fla**.
2. Scrub the playhead to look at all the frames in the movie. This movie has two screens, which are displayed in frames 1 and 6. There are stop actions in frames 1 and 6.
3. Click the Start button on the Stage and give it an instance name of **startBtn**.
4. Click frame 1 on the actions layer, then open the Actions panel.
5. Type the code for an event listener to the startBtn object that will execute a function (you specify

the function name, such as playSeason) when the startBtn object is clicked.
6. Type the code for the function that will cause the playhead to go to and play frame 6.
7. Check the syntax and format the code.
8. Test the movie and click the Start button.
9. Close the Flash Player window, then save your work.

Add Code to make a button interactive.

1. Click the tick mark for 6 on the Timeline.
2. Click the Restart button on the Stage and give it an instance name of **restartBtn**.
3. Click frame 6 on the actions layer.
4. Add code for an event listener to the restartBtn object that will execute a function (you specify the function name) when the restartBtn object is clicked.
5. Add code for the function that will cause the playhead to go to and play frame 1.
6. Check the syntax and format the code.
7. Test the movie, click the Start button, then click the Restart button.
8. Close the Flash Player window, then save your work.

Use code snippets to enter code into the script pane.

1. Click the scarf on the Stage to select it, then give it an instance name of **scarfDrag**.
2. Open the Code Snippets panel, then expand the Actions folder.
3. Verify the scarf is selected on the Stage, then double-click the Drag and Drop code snippet in the Actions folder to insert the code snippet.
4. Close the Code Snippets panel.
5. View the code in the Actions panel.

6. Change stage to **scarfDrag** for the mouse up event listener. (*Hint*: This will prevent a click anywhere on the Stage from executing the function.)
7. Test the movie, click the Start button, then drag and drop the scarf under one of the pictures. (*Note*: For this test of the movie, you are simply testing the drag and drop functionality of the scarf.)
8. Close the Flash Player window, then close the Actions panel.
9. Save your work.

Make movie clip instances able to be referenced with ActionScript.

1. Display the Library panel, then expand the movieclips folder.
2. Right-click (Win) or [control]-click (Mac) winterScene, then click Properties.
3. Display the Advanced area of the Symbol Properties dialog box, check Export for ActionScript, change the class name to **winterSceneMC**, then click OK twice.
4. Click frame 6 on the actions layer, then open the Actions panel.
5. Add code on a blank line after the closing brace for the gotoAndPlay function to create a variable named **winterSceneInstance**, set the data type to **winterSceneMC**, and create an instance of the object.
6. Add code to add the Instance to the display list so that it appears on the screen when the movie is viewed in the Flash Player. (*Hint*: Use the addChild method and set the x value to **310** and the y value to **2**.)
7. Check the syntax and format the code.
8. Test the movie, then click the Start button to view the winter scene that has been added.

9. Close the Flash Player window.
10. Add code within the fl_ReleaseToDrop function for the mouse up event to set the visible property of the winterSceneInstance to false.
11. Add the same code (setting the visible property to false for the winterSceneInstance) above the gotoAndPlay(1); line in the function for restartBtn. This will prevent the winterInstance object from appearing on the first screen when the Restart button is clicked.
12. Test the movie, click the Start button, then drag and drop the scarf below the winter scene, which causes the winter image to disappear.
13. Close the Flash Player window.
14. Close the Actions panel, then save your work.

Create an input text field box.

1. Insert a new layer above the background layer, then name it **input text**.
2. Click frame 6 on the input text layer, then insert a blank keyframe.
3. Click frame 1 of the input text layer.
4. Click the Text tool, display the Properties panel, then make the following changes: Family: Arial; Style: Bold; Size: **14**; Color: **#000099**; Paragraph Format: Align left.
5. Click the Text type list arrow in the Properties panel, click Input Text, verify Show border around text button is active, then verify the Behavior is set to Single line.
6. Draw a text box below "What is your favorite season?".
7. Verify the text box is selected on the Stage, then type **inputSeason** for the instance name.
8. Save your work.

Embedding fonts for use with input text fields.

1. Click the Selection tool, then click the input text box on the Stage to select it.
2. Display the Properties panel, then note the font that appears in the CHARACTER area.
3. Click the Embed button in the CHARACTER area.
4. Click Uppercase, Lowercase, Numerals, and Punctuation in the Character ranges area to select them.
5. Click the Add new font button. (*Note*: If Font 1 already appears in your dialog box, the new font will be named Font 2.)
6. Click OK to close the dialog box.
7. Test the movie, type **Winter** in the input box, then click the Start button. (*Note*: If you cannot type in the box, close the Flash Player window, use the Selection tool to click the input text box, then set the text type to Input Text. Also, check the Font Embedding dialog box to ensure the font has been embedded.)
8. Close the Flash Player window.
9. Save your work.

Create a dynamic text box.

1. Insert a new layer above the input text layer, then name it **display text**.
2. Insert a keyframe in frame 6 of the display text layer.
3. Click the Text tool, use the Properties panel to change the text type to Dynamic Text with the same font settings as the Input text, except change the font color to white.

4. Click the Show border around text button to deselect the button, then select the Multiline option as the Behavior in the PARAGRAPH area on the Properties panel.
5. Draw a text box above the scarf approximately the same height as the images.
6. Type **myFavorite** as the instance name for the dynamic text box.
7. Save your work.

Use ActionScript to collect and modify String variables.

1. Click frame 1 on the actions layer, then display the Actions panel.
2. Insert a blank line below the stop(); line, then type the code to create a variable named **mySeason** with the **String** data type and an initial null value.
3. Insert a blank line above the goto line within the function, then type the code to assign the text entered into the inputSeason text box to the mySeason variable.
4. Click frame 6 on the actions layer, open the Actions panel, insert a line below the stop(); line, then type the code to assign the data in the mySeason variable to the myFavorite dynamic text box after the words "I like ". (*Note*: Be sure there is a space after the word "like" and before the period.)
5. Check the syntax, then auto format the code.
6. Test the movie, type **Winter** in the input text box, then click the Start button and view the text displayed above the scarf.

7. Drag and drop the scarf below the winter scene.
8. Close the Flash Player window, close the Actions panel, then save your work.

Use ActionScript to perform a math calculation.

1. Insert a new layer above the scarf game layer, then name it **temperature**.
2. Insert a keyframe in frame 6 of the temperature layer.
3. Select the Text tool, change the font size to 10, the color to black, and the text type to Static Text. (*Hint*: If the Properties panel does not display the CHARACTER area, click the pasteboard, make the changes above, then delete the text box on the pasteboard. Also, change the Anti-alias setting to Anti-alias for Readability to make the text more readable.)
4. Use the Text tool to type **Enter Fahrenheit Click for Celsius**, as shown in Figure 38.
5. Add an input text field box below "Click" with Arial, bold, 12 pt, black with a border, and single line Behavior.
6. Add an instance name of **tempIn** for the input text box.
7. Create a dynamic text box to the right of the input text box, then give it an instance name of **celTemp**.
8. Create a button with a **Convert** label, place it below the text boxes, then give it an instance name of **convertBtn**.

9. Click frame 6 on the actions layer, then open the Actions panel.
10. Type the code to add a click event listener to the convertBtn object that creates a function named **convert**.
11. Type the code to associate the function with a mouse event, then type the three lines of code that are executed when the convertBtn object is clicked causing the convert function to execute.
    - A variable named **fahrenheit** with a Number data type that is assigned tempIn text as a number
    - A variable named **celsius** that is assigned a formula for converting the value in the fahrenheit variable to a Celsius value: ((fahrenheit-32)/9*5)
    - The celsius variable assigned to the celTemp dynamic text box.
12. Test the movie, enter a season, click the Start button, drag the scarf to beneath the winter scene, type **70** for the Fahrenheit value, then click the Convert button.
13. Continue adding Fahrenheit values, then click the Restart button and repeat the process.
14. Close the Flash Player window.
15. Save your work, then close the document.
16. Exit Flash.

Figure 38 *Completed Skills Review*

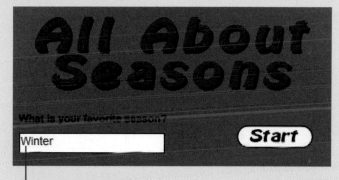

Dynamic text box

Input text box

Static text box

Dynamic text box displaying calculation

Input text box

Introduction to ActionScript 3.0

Ultimate Tours wants to add screens to their website that will provide information for the Package Tour of the month. The information will include the destination, features for various types of accommodations, and cost per week. Ultimate Tours would like the screens to be interactive and allow the visitor to enter a name (which is displayed later), enter the number of adults (used to calculate the cost) going on the trip, and select the type of accommodations (used to calculate the cost). It would also like the screens to have some visual interest beyond just a series of text and numbers so that it engages the visitor.

1. Open ultimateTours8.fla (the file you created in Chapter 8 Project Builder 1) and save it as **ultimateTours8-reference.fla.** This movie was done using ActionScript 2.0.
2. Start a new ActionScript 3.0 document, name it **ultimateTours9.fla**, then move the assets from the ultimateTours8-reference.fla file to the new AS 3.0 document. (*Hint*: You can move the assets from one document to another using the Library panel. Open both documents. With the new document active, open the Library panel and click the Display movies list arrow to display the list of all open documents. Click the ultimateTours8-reference.fla document to display its Library panel. Drag the desired items (including folders) to the Stage. Then delete them from the Stage.)
3. Use the assets from the ultimateTours8-reference.fla file to recreate page 1 in the AS 3.0 document.
4. Create a second screen that is displayed when the visitor clicks the sun navigation button on the home screen. The second screen is a movie clip that contains the destination information. (*Hint*: To create a movie clip screen, create a new movie clip symbol and use the edit window to design the screen. Then return to the main Timeline, insert a keyframe where the new screen will appear, drag the movie clip from the Library panel and align it on the Stage.)
5. Refer to Figure 39 as you include the following on the second screen. Be sure to include all elements and to check spelling and punctuation.
   - A background that is the same as the home screen but that has been dimmed (e.g. set the brightness to 55)
   - A heading with the destination **Cozumel**
   - A static text box with the text: **Enter your name:**; followed by an input text box that allows the visitor to enter a name
   - Two buttons: one that, when clicked, displays the features associated with Deluxe accommodations in a box, and another button, that when clicked, displays the features associated with Standard accommodations in a box (*Hint*: Use a movie clip with the Export for ActionScript feature turned on.)
   - Two additional buttons: one that, when clicked, displays a third screen with the price package for Deluxe accommodations; a different button that, when clicked, displays a fourth screen with the price package for the Standard accommodations
6. Buttons on screen 2 and their functions include:
   - A Deluxe button
     - Displays the features associated with Deluxe accommodations; create as a movie clip within the destination movie clip
   - A Standard button
     - Displays the features associated with Standard accommodations; create as a movie clip with the destination movie clip
   - Two "Click to see your Package Price" buttons— one for Deluxe accommodations (screen 3) and one for Standard accommodations (screen 4)
     - Displays Welcome text and the name that was entered into the input field on screen 2
     - Displays an input box for entering the number of adults
     - Calculates the package cost by multiplying the accommodation amount times the number of adults from the input text box
     - Displays the package cost in a dynamic text field
   - The sun graphic included as part of each of the buttons
7. Include the following on the third and fourth screens:
   - Same background and heading as on the second screen
   - A dynamic text box that displays a message (such as Welcome,) followed by the name from the input text box on screen 2
   - A static text box with the text: **Enter number of adults:**; followed by an input text box that allows the visitor to enter a number (the number of adults going on the trip)
   - A button that, when clicked, calculates the cost
   - A static text block that displays the words **Total cost: $**

- A dynamic text field that follows the words Total cost: $ and displays a number that is calculated based on the number of adults times the rate for the type of accommodation selected (2000 for Deluxe and 1000 for Standard) (*Hint*: Put these numbers in the ActionScript code when calculating the total cost.)
- The selected accommodation type and its list of features

- A back button that when clicked displays screen 2 (Cozumel)

8. Save your work, compare your image to the example shown in Figure 39, then close the document and exit Flash.

Figure 39 *Sample completed Project Builder 1*

Screen 1

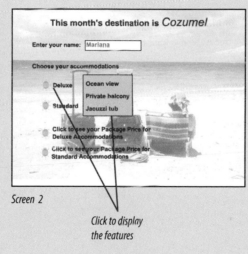

Screen 2

Click to display the features

Screen 3

Calculation based on the number of adults and the type of accommodation

Introduction to ActionScript 3.0

You work in the multimedia department of a school. An instructor asks you to build an interactive study guide in Flash that includes a series of practice test questions and that can be displayed on a smartphone. The instructor would like to see a prototype of a matching style test question. The prototype should include feedback showing students the correct answer.

1. Create a new Flash ActionScript 3.0 document, then save it as **dragToMatch.fla**.
2. Set the movie properties, including the size (height: 480 × width: 800), background color, graphics, and text headings as desired.
3. Use the Text tool to create a drag and drop matching-style exercise of your own, or use the example shown in this Project Builder. The exercise should have at least four choices.
4. Create an input text box in which students can type their names.
5. Create a dynamic text box to display the student's name and a message.
6. Create a feedback screen to indicate the correct answers. The feedback screen shows where the answers should have been dropped.
7. Create navigation buttons to jump to the various screens in the application.
8. Save your work, then compare your application to the example shown in Figure 40.

Figure 40 *Sample completed Project Builder 2*

Opening screen

Matching screen

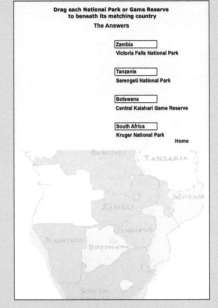

Answers screen

Figure 41 shows a page from a website created using Flash. Study the figure and complete the following. For each question, indicate how you determined your answer.

1. Connect to the Internet, type the following URL *www.nyphilkids.org/games/main.phtml?*, click instrument Frenzy, then read and follow the directions on the screen to play the game.

2. Open a document in a word processor or create a new Flash document, save the file as **dpc9**, then answer the following questions. (*Hint*: Use the Text tool in Flash.)

   In this game, the visitor uses the arrow keys on the keyboard to move the maestro back and forth. The maestro has to catch the instrument as it drops. The visitor then moves the maestro to the correct bin for the captured instrument and presses the down arrow to drop it in the bin by category (woodwind, brass, percussion, strings). If the instrument is dropped into the correct bin, the visitor is awarded points. Missed catches are also tabulated.

   - What are some actions that could be used to enable the user to drag and drop an instrument in the correct bin rather than using the arrow keys?

- Which elements of the movie must be movie clip symbols? Would all the movie clips need instance names?
- What actions would allow the visitor to enter a name at the beginning of the game and have the name displayed at the end of the game?

- When the question mark (?) button near the lower right of the screen is clicked, instructions for playing the game appear. How would you create this navigation?
- Suppose you wanted the Maestro's eyes to animate when the mouse pointer moved over them. How would you do this?

Figure 41 *Design Project*
Courtesy of New York Philharmonic Kidzone. www.nyphilkids.org/games/main.phtml?

In a previous chapter, you created a screen for your digital portfolio that contained thumbnail pictures of work samples. Another way to highlight your work might be to create a slide show that runs continuously, to display different samples. Such a strategy could motivate the visitor to look at more samples.

1. Open portfolio8.fla, then save it as **portfolio8-reference.fla**.
   This movie was done using ActionScript 2.0.
2. Start a new ActionScript 3.0 document, name it **portfolio9.fla**, then move the assets from the portfolio8-reference.fla file to the new AS 3.0 document. (*Hint*: You can move the assets from one document to another using the Library panel. Open both documents. With the new document active, open the Library panel and click the Display movies list arrow to display the list of all open documents. Click the portfolio8-reference.fla document to display its Library

panel. Drag the desired items (including folders) to the Stage. Then delete them from the Stage.)

3. Use the assets from portfolio8-reference.fla to recreate screen 1 in the AS 3.0 document.
4. Create a series of screen shots with at least four samples of your work, or use the screen shots you created for the Portfolio Project at the end of Chapter 7.
5. Create a new screen with the title **My Samples**.
6. Create a movie clip symbol that includes a series of screens, each screen should show one sample of your work and some explanatory text about that sample. Each sample and associated text should appear in a separate frame. The samples should be spaced out on the movie clip Timeline to allow a few seconds between when one screen appears and the next one appears.
7. Return to the main Timeline and the first frame for the My Portfolio screen. Use the Samples button to jump to frame 2, which is the My Samples screen.

8. Add a button with the text **Slide Show** on the My Samples screen, then program the Over and Down states for the button in any way you'd like.
9. Turn on the Export for ActionScript feature for the movie clip and use the AS linkage name in the code when creating a variable that will become an instance of the object.
10. Type the code that displays the movie clip when the user clicks the Slide Show button. Use the addChild method, and the x and y values to position the movie clip on the Stage.
11. Use a home button to create navigation from the samples screen to the main portfolio screen. Add a line of code in the function to turn off the visibility of the movie clip when the home button is clicked. This will prevent the movie clip from appearing on the home screen.
12. Save your work, then compare your movie to the example shown in Figure 42.

Figure 42 *Sample completed Portfolio Project*

CHAPTER 10
USING ACTIONSCRIPT TO ENHANCE USER EXPERIENCE

1. Create complex interactivity

2. Load movies at runtime

3. Work with conditional actions

4. Use ActionScript to create external links

CHAPTER 10

USING ACTIONSCRIPT TO ENHANCE USER EXPERIENCE

Introduction

In this chapter, you will continue to build on your knowledge of ActionScript, with an emphasis on adding actions that encourage user interaction and enhance the user experience. Some examples of how you can use ActionScript to accomplish these goals follow. You can replace the mouse cursor with a custom cursor. You can track user interactions and offer feedback based on the data you gather. You can break your applications into multiple, smaller movies and then use ActionScript to load these movies when appropriate, which will help you organize a large application or website and provide users relief from lengthy downloads.

You can create conditional actions to implement complex branching in your movies. You can create looping actions to help streamline your ActionScript and to provide a way to repeat a set of actions based on a value provided by the user or on a task you want the user to perform.

With all the new actions and cool techniques you will see in this chapter, remember that you're still just scratching the surface of ActionScript. The more you research and experiment, the more surprised you will be by all you can accomplish with ActionScript, and the more your users will appreciate your efforts.

```
1   import flash.events.MouseEvent;
2   stop();
3   Mouse.hide();
4   stage.addEventListener(MouseEvent.MOUSE_MOVE,follow);
5   function follow(Event:MouseEvent)
6   {
7       myCursor.x = mouseX;
8       myCursor.y = mouseY;
9   }
10  startBtn.addEventListener(MouseEvent.CLICK, goto2);
11  function goto2(Event:MouseEvent)
12  {
13      gotoAndPlay(2);
14  }
```

```
6
7   {
8       if (myName == "B")
9       {
10          gotoAndStop(2);
11      }
12      else
13      {
14          if (myName == "B")
15          {
16              gotoAndStop(3);
17          }
18          else
19          {
20              if (myName == "C")
21              {
22                  gotoAndStop(4);
23              }
24          }
25      }
26  }
27
```

```
10
11
12  fishBtn.addEventListener(MouseEvent.CLICK,loadMovie1);
13  function loadMovie1(event:MouseEvent)
14  {
15      myLoader.load(new URLRequest("fish.swf"));
16      addChild(myLoader);
17  }
18
19
20
21
22
23
```

```
3
4   websiteBtn.addEventListener(MouseEvent.CLICK,goWeb);
5   function goWeb(Event:MouseEvent)
6   {
7       var targetURL:URLRequest = new URLRequest("http://www.adobe.com/");
8       navigateToURL(targetURL,"_blank");
9   }
10
11
12
13
14
15
16
```

Create Complex
INTERACTIVITY

What You'll Do

 In this lesson, you will use ActionScript to create a custom cursor, create conditional actions, and count user interactions.

Creating a Custom Cursor

Creating a custom cursor is a fun way to make a Flash site distinctive. You might create a cursor with your face on it for a personal site, or you can tie the cursor into the theme of the site, such as using a picture of a yo-yo for an e-business site selling toys. You can also integrate a custom cursor with the purpose of the site; for example, in a game site, the custom cursor might be a cartoon figure the user leads through a maze with the mouse. The custom cursor can be a graphic, photograph, or even an animation. The only requirement is that it be a movie clip symbol.

The first step toward implementing a custom cursor is to hide the regular cursor. You do this with the *Mouse.hide* method. There is a corresponding *Mouse.show* method you can use to redisplay the cursor at any point. After hiding the regular cursor you display the custom cursor. This means you will have two cursors on the Stage, but only the custom cursor is visible.

The next step is to set up an event listener that "listens" for when the mouse moves. When the mouse moves, a function is called which causes the custom cursor to follow the hidden cursor. Flash tracks the x and y Stage position of the hidden cursor. By setting the custom cursor to the same x and y coordinates, it follows the hidden cursor.

Mouse movement is tracked by mouseX and mouseY properties, which return the coordinates of the mouse pointer. As the user moves the mouse, the mouseX and mouseY values are updated constantly to reflect the current position of the mouse pointer. Because the custom cursor is following the hidden cursor, these values are assigned to the coordinates of the custom cursor (which is an instance of a movie clip). Figure 1 shows the ActionScript for a custom cursor implemented using this method.

Using Multiple Objects to Call a Function

One of the values of ActionScript 3.0 is the ability to reuse lines of code. This is especially applicable to functions (which are made up of blocks of code). For example, you could have one event listener (such as MOUSE_DOWN) that **calls** (executes) the same function (such as *startToDrag*) for more than one object (such as for a circle, square, and triangle). Figure 2 shows three objects (with instance names of mySquare, myTriangle, and myCircle) that, when they receive a MOUSE_DOWN event, will call the

clickToDrag function. The function has one line of code that makes the object receiving the MOUSE_DOWN event draggable. Notice that the instance names of the objects are not used in the function. Rather, *event.target* is specified as the draggable object. *Event.target* refers to the instance that is assigned to the event listener. So, if the mySquare object receives the MOUSE_DOWN event it becomes the event.target, which means the mySquare object becomes draggable. Without *event.target*, you would need to type the same function three times, once for each object.

Creating Conditional Actions

If-then statements are familiar to anyone who has had minimal programming exposure.

ActionScript includes an *if* action that can test whether certain conditions have been met and, if so, can perform other actions. (You used an *if* statement when you created the preloader in a previous chapter.) Conditional statements offer many possibilities for building more interactive movies. You should enclose all the actions you want Flash to carry out in braces following the *if* action. If the conditions are not met, the actions in the braces are ignored, and Flash jumps to the next action.

When creating conditions in ActionScript, you must use two equal signs (= =). A single equal sign (=) assigns a specific value to a variable. For example, n=9 in ActionScript assigns the value 9 to a variable named n,

Figure 1 *ActionScript to create a custom cursor by setting X and Y coordinates*

myCursor is the instance name of the custom cursor movie clip symbol

The mouseX and mouseY coordinates are passed to the custom cursor

Figure 2 *Three objects that call the same function*

These three objects call the same function, clickToDrag

event.target refers to whichever object (mySquare, myTriangle, myCircle) calls the function

Name of function

but n == 9 is a conditional statement that checks if the variable n has a value of 9, and if so, performs another action. Figure 3 shows an example of a conditional statement.

Working with Parent Movie Clips

In Chapter 9, you learned about the display list, which is a list of all of the items that will be visible on the screen in a Flash document.

In Chapter 9, you used the *addChild* method when you wanted to add an object to the display list. The display list includes movie clips, drawn shapes, text fields, videos, and bitmaps. Items on the display list are display objects. Some of these display objects can have children. For example, a movie clip could be made up of one drawn shape, such as a square. The square would be a child of the movie clip and the movie clip would be a parent of the square. This is important because when you want to refer to the square in your ActionScript code you would really need to refer to its parent movie clip. You do this using this format:

parent == (*movie clip instance name of the parent*)

In this example, a parent is identified by its movie clip instance name. Any object that is part of the movie clip is a child of the movie clip. Thus, this code structure can be used to refer to a child of a movie clip. For example, let's say you have written the code to make a black square (a movie clip with an instance name of mySquare) a draggable object. You want the black square to be dragged to and dropped on the yellow square (an object which is the child of a movie clip with an instance name of targetSquare). In order to determine if the black square was dropped on the yellow square, you would use the dropTarget

Figure 3 *Example of a conditional statement*

Double equal signs used because this is part of a conditional if statement; the double equal signs tell the program to check to see if the value of n is 9

This action is only carried out when n is equal to 9

Using ActionScript to Enhance User Experience

property. This concept is illustrated in Figure 4 and discussed next:

`if(mySquare.dropTarget.parent==targetSquare)`

if makes this a conditional statement; it lets you know that something will happen if the condition (the dropTarget) is correct.

mySquare is the instance name of the movie clip that is being dragged, in this example the black square.

dropTarget is the property that specifies the condition that must be met in order for the *if* statement to be fulfilled; in this case, dropTarget means the object (the black square) must be dropped on a target, as identified in the next part of the code.

parent==targetSquare specifies the targetSquare movie clip as a parent, and therefore its child (the yellow square object) would be the drop target.

The entire line of code checks to see if the drop target of the object being dragged (mySquare) is a child (yellow square) of the targetSquare movie clip.

Tracking User Interactions

One aspect of interactivity involves responding to user actions, such as jumping to a different point in a movie when a user clicks a button. Another aspect involves providing users with individual feedback based on the actions they take or information they supply. This can be as simple as creating a dynamic text box to display the user's name in a greeting, as you did in Chapter 9. Or, this can be as complex as using ActionScript to gather and display more complex information, such as the number of times a user clicks the mouse or a user's progress in a game or quiz. Collecting such information presents many opportunities to offer users custom feedback. Tracking interactions can also provide you with insight on the way people work with your site or application.

The increment and decrement actions are useful when tracking user interactions. The **increment action**, ++ (two plus signs), adds 1 unit to a variable or expression; the **decrement action**, – – (two minus signs), subtracts 1 unit. For example, the ActionScript statement x++ is the equivalent of the expression $x = x+1$. Both add 1 to the variable. You might use the increment operator to keep track of and display the number of correct answers a user has given during an online test.

QUICK TIP

The increment and decrement operators are also useful when setting up the number of times to run a conditional loop. For example, you might want to allow a user to attempt to answer a question a specified number of times before providing the correct answer to the user.

Figure 4 *Using parent to target a shape within a movie clip instance*

```
Actions
                                                          Code Snippets
 15
 16   mySquare.addEventListener(MouseEvent.MOUSE_UP,clickToDrop1);
 17   function clickToDrop1(Event:MouseEvent)
 18   {
 19        reply.text = "";
 20        if (mySquare.dropTarget.parent == targetSquare)
 21        {
```

This is checking to see if the mySquare object (the black square) has been dropped on top of the child (yellow square object) of the parent movie clip with the instance name of targetSquare

Hide the cursor

1. Open fl10_1.fla from the drive and folder where your Data Files are stored, then save it as **interactive.fla**.

2. Drag the **playhead** to view the contents of the frames.

   This movie has two screens, a welcome screen in frame 1 and a drag and drop screen in frame 2.

3. Click **frame 1** on the actions layer, then open the Actions panel.

   Frame 1 of the actions layer has an import flash.events.MouseEvent statement; a stop action, and a goto action for the Start button.

4. Click **frame 2** on the actions layer.

   Frame 2 of the actions layer has an import flash.events.MouseEvent statement and a stop action.

5. Click **frame 1** on the actions layer, then type the following line of code below the stop(); line in the Script pane, as shown in Figure 5: **Mouse.hide();**

6. Test the movie.

   The mouse cursor is not visible.

TIP The cursor reverts to the shape for your operating system when you position the mouse pointer on the title bar or menu bar of the Flash Player window.

7. Close the Flash Player window.

8. Collapse the Actions panel.

9. Save your work.

You used ActionScript to hide the mouse cursor.

Figure 5 *ActionScript to hide the mouse cursor*

Code to type ⟶

```
import flash.events.MouseEvent;
stop();
Mouse.hide();
startBtn.addEventListener(MouseEvent.CLICK, goto2);
function goto2(Event:MouseEvent)
{
    gotoAndPlay(2);
}
```

Using ActionScript to Enhance User Experience

Figure 6 *Instance of the custom cursor movie clip symbol on the Stage*

Create a custom cursor using X and Y coordinates

1. Insert a **new layer** above the shapes layer, name it **cursor**, then click **frame 1**.

2. Display the Library panel, open the movieClips folder, then drag the **cursor movie clip symbol** to the center of the Stage, as shown in Figure 6.

3. Verify the cursor movie clip symbol is selected on the Stage, display the Properties panel, type **myCursor** for the instance name, then press **[Enter]** (Win) or **[return]** (Mac).

4. Click **frame 1** of the actions layer, display the Actions panel, then type the following as a single line of code below the Mouse.hide(); line:

   stage.addEventListener(MouseEvent. MOUSE_MOVE, follow);

   This creates an event listener that "listens" for the mouse to move. Also, it names a function (*follow*) that is called when the mouse moves.

   (continued)

5. Press **[Enter]** (Win) or **[return]** (Mac), then type the following lines of code, as shown in Figure 7:

function follow(Event:MouseEvent)
{
myCursor.x = mouseX;
myCursor.y = mouseY;

This defines the function (named *follow*) to set the x and y positions of the custom cursor (myCursor) to the x and y positions of the regular cursor, which is hidden.

Note: A closing right brace (}) is added automatically when you press [Enter (Win) or [return] (Mac) after typing the opening left brace ({).

6. Test the movie, use the custom cursor to click the **Start button** on the first screen, then try to drag and drop the shapes on the second screen.

7. Close the Flash Player window.

8. Save your work.

You used ActionScript to designate an instance of a movie clip symbol to act as the mouse cursor using X and Y coordinates.

Use multiple objects to call a function

1. Click **frame 2** on the actions layer, then display the Actions panel.

2. Type the following line of code below the stop(); line:

mySquare.addEventListener(MouseEvent.
MOUSE_DOWN, clickToDrag);

This creates an event listener and names a function, *clickToDrag*, that is called when there is a MOUSE_DOWN event on the mySquare object.

(continued)

Figure 7 *ActionScript that sets the position of the custom cursor to the position of the regular cursor*

```
1  import flash.events.MouseEvent;
2  stop();
3  Mouse.hide();
4  stage.addEventListener(MouseEvent.MOUSE_MOVE,follow);
5  function follow(Event:MouseEvent)
6  {
7      myCursor.x = mouseX;
8      myCursor.y = mouseY;
9  }
10 startBtn.addEventListener(MouseEvent.CLICK, goto2);
11 function goto2(Event:MouseEvent)
12 {
13     gotoAndPlay(2);
14 }
```

actions : 1

Line 8 of 14 Col 22

Closing right brace is added automatically; do not type

Code to type

Use of Capitalization in Coding

In general, it is important to match capitalization when typing AS3 code. However, in some instances when typing AS3 code, you can use either uppercase or lowercase for initial capitalization. An example is Event:MouseEvent that can be written event:MouseEvent.

Using ActionScript to Enhance User Experience

Figure 8 *ActionScript to define the clickToDrag function using event.target*

Closing right brace is
added automatically;
do not type

Code to type

3. Press **[Enter]** (Win) or **[return]** (Mac), then type the following two lines of code:

   myTriangle.addEventListener(MouseEvent. MOUSE_DOWN, clickToDrag);

   myCircle.addEventListener(MouseEvent. MOUSE_DOWN, clickToDrag);

   This code creates MOUSE_DOWN event listeners for the myTriangle and myCircle objects and calls the same function, *clickToDrag*.

4. Press **[Enter]** (Win) or **[return]** (Mac), then type the following lines of code, as shown in Figure 8:

   function clickToDrag(event:MouseEvent)

   {

   event.target.startDrag();

   This defines the *clickToDrag* function as a mouse event and allows the event.target object to be draggable. Recall that event.target refers to the object that calls the function, so in this example, the object that hears the event "MOUSE_DOWN" will be the object that can be dragged (startDrag). When the black square (mySquare) is clicked, it will be draggable. When the black triangle (myTriangle) is clicked, it will be draggable. When the black circle (myCircle) is clicked, it will be draggable.

5. Test the movie, click the **Start button**, drag the **black square** around the screen, then release the mouse button.

   Notice the object is draggable. However, you are not able to drop the object at this time.

6. Close the Flash Player window, close the Action panel, then save your work.

You used event.target to allow multiple objects to call the same function.

Create dynamic text boxes

1. Insert a **new layer** above the shapes layer, then name it **text boxes**.

2. Click **frame 2** on the text boxes layer, then insert a **keyframe**.

3. Click the **Text tool** T on the Tools panel, display the Properties panel, click the **Text type list arrow**, click **Dynamic Text**, click the **Show border around text button** 🔲 to select it, click the **Align center** button 🔳 in the PARAGRAPH area.

4. Use the Properties panel to set the text properties to: Family: **Arial**; Style: **Bold**; Size: **12**; Text fill color: **#990000**.

5. Using Figure 9 as a guide, draw a **text box** below the words Mouse clicks.

6. With the text box selected, type **mouseClicks** for the instance name.

7. Using Figure 10 as a guide, create **two more dynamic text boxes**.

8. Give the middle text box an instance name of **reply** and the right side text box an instance name of **piecesLeft**.

9. Click the **Embed button** in the CHARACTER area of the Properties panel, then click the check boxes for **Uppercase**, **Lowercase**, **Numerals,** and **Punctuation** to select them.

10. Click **OK**.

11. Save your work.

You created three dynamic text boxes, gave them instance names, and embedded a font set.

Figure 9 *Drawing the dynamic text box*

Dynamic text box (if your box is not white, be sure the "Show border around text button" option is active)

Figure 10 *Drawing the other dynamic text boxes*

If one of the text boxes overlaps other elements on the screen, click the Selection tool on the Tools panel after drawing the text box, then use the mouse or arrow keys to move the box

Using ActionScript to Enhance User Experience

Figure 11 *Creating a conditional statement*

```
Actions
1   import flash.events.MouseEvent;
2   stop();
3   mySquare.addEventListener(MouseEvent.MOUSE_DOWN,clickToDrag);
4   myTriangle.addEventListener(MouseEvent.MOUSE_DOWN,clickToDrag);
5   myCircle.addEventListener(MouseEvent.MOUSE_DOWN,clickToDrag);
6   function clickToDrag(event:MouseEvent)
7   {
8       event.target.startDrag();
9   }
10  mySquare.addEventListener(MouseEvent.MOUSE_UP,clickToDrop1);
11  function clickToDrop1(Event:MouseEvent)
12  {
13      if(mySquare.dropTarget.parent == targetSquare)
14  }

actions : 2
Line 13 of 14  Col 48
```

Closing brace added
automatically;
do not type

Code to type

Be sure to type two
equal signs (==) with
no space between

Create a conditional statement

1. Click **frame 2** on the actions layer, then open the Actions panel.

2. Insert a **blank line** below the last line of code, then type the following as a single line of code:

   mySquare.addEventListener(MouseEvent. MOUSE_UP, clickToDrop1);

   This adds a mouse up event listener to the mySquare object on the Stage and names a function *clickToDrop1*.

3. Press **[Enter]** Win or **[return]** (Mac) to add a new line, then type the following lines of code:

   function clickToDrop1(Event:MouseEvent)

   {

   This begins the process of defining the *clickToDrop1* function.

4. Press **[Enter]** Win or **[return]** (Mac) to add a new line, then type the following as a single line of code, as shown in Figure 11:

   if (mySquare.dropTarget.parent == targetSquare)

   This creates a conditional statement that says if mySquare is dropped on targetSquare then complete the following lines of code. (*Note*: targetSquare is the instance name of the parent movie clip named square T, and the yellow square is the child of the parent movie clip.)

   (continued)

5. Press **[Enter]** Win or **[return]** (Mac) to add a new line before the closing brace (}), then type the following lines of code:

    {

    reply.text = "Good Job!";

    targetSquare.visible = false;

    The two lines within the curly braces identify the code to be executed if the conditional statement is true. The first line assigns *Good Job!* to reply.text, which is the middle text box on the screen. The second line causes the targetSquare object to disappear from view.

6. Insert a **blank line** between the last two curly braces (}) at the end of the code, then type **mySquare.stopDrag();** as shown in Figure 12.

    Notice the stopDrag line is placed outside the conditional statement so that it is executed whether or not the statement is true. The closing brace (}) completes the block of code for the *clickToDrop1* function.

7. Test the movie, click the **Start button**, then drag the **black square** to the yellow square.

    Notice *Good Job!* is displayed in the reply text box and the yellow square (targetSquare instance) disappears from the screen.

    Note: If errors occur, compare your code to Figure 12, check your layers for the correct object placement, verify the text boxes are dynamic and have the correct instance names, and make sure you have embedded the font.

8. Close the Flash Player window.

9. Save your work.

You created a conditional statement within a function.

Figure 12 *Placing the stopDrag line outside the conditional statement*

Code for clickToDrop1 function

Code to type

Nested code requires its own set of braces

```
import flash.events.MouseEvent;
stop();
mySquare.addEventListener(MouseEvent.MOUSE_DOWN,clickToDrag);
myTriangle.addEventListener(MouseEvent.MOUSE_DOWN,clickToDrag);
myCircle.addEventListener(MouseEvent.MOUSE_DOWN,clickToDrag);
function clickToDrag(event:MouseEvent)
{
    event.target.startDrag();
}
mySquare.addEventListener(MouseEvent.MOUSE_UP,clickToDrop1);
function clickToDrop1(Event:MouseEvent)
{
    if (mySquare.dropTarget.parent == targetSquare)
    {
        reply.text = "Good Job!";
        targetSquare.visible = false;
    }
    mySquare.stopDrag();
}
```

Figure 13 *ActionScript to increment the variable value and assign it to a text box*

Code to type ──────

```
1   import flash.events.MouseEvent;
2   stop();
3   var myClicks:Number = 0;
4   var objectsLeft:Number = 3;
5   mouseClicks.text = String(myClicks);
6   piecesLeft.text = String(objectsLeft);
7   mySquare.addEventListener(MouseEvent.MOUSE_DOWN,clickToDrag);
8   myTriangle.addEventListener(MouseEvent.MOUSE_DOWN,clickToDrag);
9   myCircle.addEventListener(MouseEvent.MOUSE_DOWN,clickToDrag);
10  function clickToDrag(event:MouseEvent)
11  {
12      event.target.startDrag();
13  }
14  mySquare.addEventListener(MouseEvent.MOUSE_UP,clickToDrop1);
15  function clickToDrop1(Event:MouseEvent)
16  {
17      if (mySquare.dropTarget.parent == targetSquare)
18      {
19          reply.text = "Good Job!";
20          targetSquare.visible = false;
21      }
22      mySquare.stopDrag();
23      myClicks++;
24      mouseClicks.text = String(myClicks);
25  }
```

actions : 2
Line 24 of 25 Col 38

Changing the Data Type to Display Data in Dynamic Text Boxes

Dynamic text boxes display characters (including numbers) as string data. Therefore, if you have a number that is to be displayed in a dynamic text box it must be changed to a string data type. The process is to append *.text* to the instance name of the dynamic text box using the format: *instanceName.text*. Then, take the numeric variable and preface it with String using the format: *String(variable Name)*. Finally, the text box (using the instance name) is assigned the value in the variable using the following format: *instanceName.text = String(variableName)*. If the variable name is **myClicks** and the dynamic text box instance name is **mouseClicks** the code would be **mouseClicks.text = String(myClicks)**.

Track user interactions

1. Be sure actions:2 is the active layer (as noted in the lower left corner of the Actions panel), then insert a **blank line** after the stop(); line in the Actions panel.

2. Type the following lines of code:

   var myClicks:Number = 0;

   var objectsLeft:Number = 3;

   The first line creates a numeric variable named myClicks and assigns it an initial value of 0. This variable will keep track of the number of times the mouse button is clicked. The second line creates a numeric variable named objectsLeft and assigns it an initial value of 3. The number for this variable will be reduced each time an objected is dragged.

3. Press **[Enter]** Win or **[return]** (Mac) to add a new line, then type the following lines:

   mouseClicks.text = String(myClicks);

   piecesLeft.text = String(objectsLeft);

   The first line takes the numeric value in the myClicks variable, changes it into a string value and assigns it to the mouseClicks text box. The second line takes the numeric value in the objectsLeft variable, changes it into a string value, and assigns it to the piecesLeft text box. This allows the numeric values to be displayed in the dynamic text field boxes.

4. Type the following lines of code after the mySquare.stopDrag line and before the closing brace (}), as shown in Figure 13:

   myClicks++;

   mouseClicks.text = String(myClicks);

   (continued)

The first line increments the value for myClicks by 1. The second line updates the value in the mouseClicks text box.

5. Press **[Enter]** Win or **[return]** (Mac) to add a new line, then type the following lines of code, as shown in Figure 14:

objectsLeft--;

piecesLeft.text = String(objectsLeft);

The first line decrements the value for objectsLeft by 1. The second line updates the value in the piecesLeft text box.

Note: Be sure to type two minus signs (--) after objectsLeft.

6. Test the movie, then click the **Start button**.

Notice the Mouse clicks and Pieces left text boxes display the initial values.

Note: If errors occur, compare your code to Figure 14.

7. Drag the **black square** on top of the yellow square.

Notice the Mouse clicks and Pieces left text boxes display the updated values.

8. Close the Flash Player window.

9. Save your work.

You tracked user interactions with the increment and decrement operators.

Figure 14 *ActionScript to decrement the variable value and assign it to a text box*

```
Actions
Code Snippets
1   import flash.events.MouseEvent;
2   stop();
3   var myClicks:Number = 0;
4   var objectsLeft:Number = 3;
5   mouseClicks.text = String(myClicks);
6   piecesLeft.text = String(objectsLeft);
7   mySquare.addEventListener(MouseEvent.MOUSE_DOWN,clickToDrag);
8   myTriangle.addEventListener(MouseEvent.MOUSE_DOWN,clickToDrag);
9   myCircle.addEventListener(MouseEvent.MOUSE_DOWN,clickToDrag);
10  function clickToDrag(event:MouseEvent)
11  {
12      event.target.startDrag();
13  }
14  mySquare.addEventListener(MouseEvent.MOUSE_UP,clickToDrop1);
15  function clickToDrop1(Event:MouseEvent)
16  {
17      if (mySquare.dropTarget.parent == targetSquare)
18      {
19          reply.text = "Good Job!";
20          targetSquare.visible = false;
21      }
22      mySquare.stopDrag();
23      myClicks++;
24      mouseClicks.text = String(myClicks);
25      objectsLeft--;
26      piecesLeft.text = String(objectsLeft);
27  }
```

actions : 2

Line 26 of 27 Col 40

Code to type

Be sure to type two minus signs (--) with no space between

Figure 15 *Highlighting the lines of code*

```
10  function clickToDrag(event:MouseEvent)
11  {
12      event.target.startDrag();
13  }
14  mySquare.addEventListener(MouseEvent.MOUSE_UP,clickToDrop1);
15  function clickToDrop1(Event:MouseEvent)
16  {
17      if (mySquare.dropTarget.parent == targetSquare)
18      {
19          reply.text = "Good Job!";
20          targetSquare.visible = false;
21      }
22      mySquare.stopDrag();
23      myClicks++;
24      mouseClicks.text = String(myClicks);
25      objectsLeft--;
26      piecesLeft.text = String(objectsLeft);
27  }
```

actions : 2
Line 14 of 27, Col 1

Figure 16 *The copied and edited lines of code*

```
27      piecesLeft.text = String(objectsLeft);
28  }
29  myTriangle.addEventListener(MouseEvent.MOUSE_UP,clickToDrop2);
30  function clickToDrop2(Event:MouseEvent)
31  {
32      reply.text = "";
33      if (myTriangle.dropTarget.parent == targetTriangle)
34      {
35          reply.text = "Good Job!";
36          targetTriangle.visible = false;
37      }
38      myTriangle.stopDrag();
39      myClicks++;
40      mouseClicks.text = String(myClicks);
41      objectsLeft--;
42      piecesLeft.text = String(objectsLeft);
43  }
44  myCircle.addEventListener(MouseEvent.MOUSE_UP,clickToDrop3);
45  function clickToDrop3(Event:MouseEvent)
46  {
47      reply.text = "";
48      if (myCircle.dropTarget.parent == targetCircle)
49      {
50          reply.text = "Good Job!";
51          targetCircle.visible = false;
52      }
53      myCircle.stopDrag();
54      myClicks++;
55      mouseClicks.text = String(myClicks);
56      objectsLeft--;
57      piecesLeft.text = String(objectsLeft);
58  }
```

Code copied and edited for myTriangle

Code copied and edited for myCircle

actions : 2
Line 58 of 58, Col 2

Copy ActionScript code

1. **Drag the pointer** to highlight the lines shown in Figure 15.
2. **Right-click** (Win) or **[control]-click** (Mac) the highlighted area, then click **Copy**.
3. Insert a **blank line** at the bottom of the ActionScript code, **right-click** (Win) or **[control]-click** (Mac), then click **Paste**.
4. Change **mySquare** to **myTriangle** (3 occurrences) in the code you just pasted.
5. Change **clickToDrop1** to **clickToDrop2** (2 occurrences).
6. Change **targetSquare** to **targetTriangle** (2 occurrences).
7. Repeat Steps 3 through 6 using **myCircle**, **clickToDrop3**, and **targetCircle**.
8. Insert a **blank line** above the first *if* statement, then type:

   reply.text = "";

   This code will clear the text in the reply.text text box of the words "Good Job!".
9. Repeat Step 8 for the other two *if* statements.
10. Click the **Check syntax button** on the Actions panel menu bar, click the **Auto format button**, then compare your screen to Figure 16.
11. Test the movie, click the **Start button**, then drag **each of the objects** in the Start Bin to the corresponding objects in the Drop Bin.
12. Close the Flash Player window, then close the Actions panel.
13. Save your work, then close the document.

You copied ActionScript code and changed object names.

Load Movies
AT RUNTIME

What You'll Do

In this lesson, you will load and unload movies into the Flash Player so that they play along with the content of the original movie.

Understanding Multiple Movies

In previous chapters, you have seen how you can use scenes and movie clip symbols to break large applications into smaller, more manageable components. Another strategy is to split a single movie into a number of different movies, and then use ActionScript to load the movies as needed. For example, you might have an application with a number of discrete areas, not all of which are of interest to every user. By splitting each area into its own movie, you can save download time for the user because, instead of having to download a large application, the movie for each area will be downloaded only when it is needed or the user specifically requests it, such as by clicking a link. Multiple movies can create smoother transitions between screens because the new movies load into the current application screen. Using multiple movies can also help you keep organized during development of a movie, especially if different people are working on different parts of the application. Figure 17 shows an example of one way to use multiple movies.

Loading Movies

The *Loader* class along with the *addChild* method can be used to load an external movie (or other object such as a graphic, text block, or sound). You must know the name of the Flash Player movie file you want to load (Flash Player files have a .swf extension) and also its location. The location can be on your computer or on a network. The location is specified using the *URLRequest* class. When you are creating a link to a file, you can include an **absolute path**, which specifies the exact location of the file, or a **relative path**, which indicates the location based on the current location of your movie file. For example, if the SWF file you are referencing is in a folder named myMovie and your Flash document is in the same folder, you can include just the filename, without any path, in your code. Figure 18 shows the ActionScript for loading an SWF file located in the same folder as the Flash document.

You can load a new movie with the original document or into a movie clip symbol. If you load a new movie with the original document, the new movie inherits the frame rate, dimensions, and background color of the original document. When the new movie appears, it is placed in the upper-left corner of the original document, which may cause design issues if your movies are not the same size; make sure to test how the additional movies will load before publishing a site. You can specify the x and y Stage coordinates for the SWF file when loading it. Loading a new movie into a movie clip gives you more control over the size and placement of the movie. One useful technique is to create a blank movie clip symbol that you name, position on Stage where you want the new movie to appear, and then load the new movie into the blank movie clip symbol.

Unloading Movies

The *removeChild* method can be used to unload movies. Including this action when you no longer need a movie loaded can create smoother transitions between movies, ensure there's no visual residue between movies of different sizes, and reduce the memory required by the Flash Player. When a movie is unloaded, it is removed from the player but it is still available to be replayed without having to download it again.

Figure 17 *A Flash site that takes advantage of using multiple movies*

NASA/courtesy of nasaimages.org

Each tab could open a different SWF file, saving the user download time

Figure 18 *ActionScript for loading an SWF file in the same location as the Flash document*

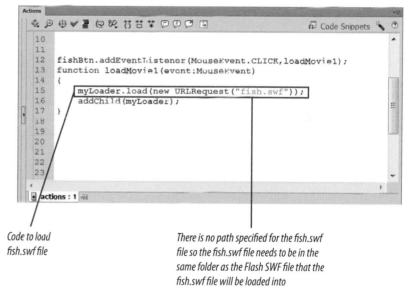

Code to load fish.swf file

There is no path specified for the fish.swf file so the fish.swf file needs to be in the same folder as the Flash SWF file that the fish.swf file will be loaded into

Load a movie

1. Open fl10_2.fla, then save it as **letterF.fla**.

   This movie has three buttons and the letter F displayed on the Stage. The instance names for the buttons are fishBtn, unloadBtn, and frogBtn.

   TIP The steps use relative paths to load new movies. Be sure to copy the two movies you will load, fish.swf and frog.swf, to the same drive and folder where you save the letterF.fla file.

2. Click **frame 1** on the actions layer, then open the Actions panel.

3. Type the following line of code below the stop(); line:

   var myLoader:Loader = new Loader();

   This creates a variable named myLoader with a Loader data type and creates an instance of the Loader.

4. Press **[Enter]** Win or **[return]** (Mac), then type the following as a single line of code:

   fishBtn.addEventListener(MouseEvent. CLICK, loadMovie1);

   This creates an event listener for a mouse event for the fishBtn and names a function, loadMovie1.

5. Press **[Enter]** Win or **[return]** (Mac) to add a new line, then type the following lines of code, as shown in Figure 19:

   function loadMovie1(event:MouseEvent)

   {

   myLoader.load(new URLRequest("fish. swf"));

   addChild(myLoader);

   (continued)

Figure 19 *ActionScript to define the* loadMovie1 *function*

```
1  import flash.display.Loader;
2  import flash.events.MouseEvent;
3  import flash.net.URLRequest;
4
5  stop();
6  var myLoader:Loader = new Loader();
7  fishBtn.addEventListener(MouseEvent.CLICK,loadMovie1);
8  function loadMovie1(event:MouseEvent)
9  {
10     myLoader.load(new URLRequest("fish.swf"));
11     addChild(myLoader);
12 }
```

actions : 1

Line 11 of 12, Col 21

Closing brace added automatically; do not type

Code to type

These lines may appear as you enter the code

Figure 20 *ActionScript to add event listener for the frogBtn object*

```
Actions
1   import flash.display.Loader;
2   import flash.events.MouseEvent;
3   import flash.net.URLRequest;
4
5   stop();
6   var myLoader:Loader = new Loader();
7   fishBtn.addEventListener(MouseEvent.CLICK,loadMovie1);
8   function loadMovie1(event:MouseEvent)
9   {
10      myLoader.load(new URLRequest("fish.swf"));
11      addChild(myLoader);
12  }
13  frogBtn.addEventListener(MouseEvent.CLICK,loadMovie2);
14  function loadMovie2(event:MouseEvent)
15  {
16      myLoader.load(new URLRequest("frog.swf"));
17      addChild(myLoader);
18  }
```

actions : 1

Line 17 of 18   Col 21

fishBtn code copied, pasted, and adjusted to call movie for frogBtn

This defines the function loadMovie1. The myLoader line uses the URLRequest class to specify the SWF file to load into the myLoader variable. The addChild line places the variable myLoader on the display list so that it is visible on the screen.

6. Test the movie, then click the **fish button**.

   The fish animation appears on top of the F.

7. Close the Flash Player window.

8. Copy and paste the code used for the fish button to add the event listener and function for the **frogBtn object**, then adjust the wording in the code, as shown in Figure 20, to correspond to the frogBtn. Change fishBtn to frogBtn, fish.swf to frog.swf and loadMovie1 to loadMovie2 (2 occurrences).

9. Click the **Check syntax button** ✔, then click the **Auto format button** ≣.

10. Test the movie, click the **frog button**, then click the **fish button**.

11. Close the Flash Player window.

12. Save your work.

You created the ActionScript to load external SWF files at runtime.

Unload movies

1. Add a new **blank line** below the last line of code, which is a closing brace, then type the following as a single line of code:

   unloadBtn.addEventListener(MouseEvent.CLICK, removeMovie);

   This creates an event listener for a mouse event that calls a function named removeMovie when the unloadBtn object on the Stage is clicked. This code is needed if you want to remove the fish or the frog and display just the letter F and the buttons.

2. Press **[Enter]** Win or **[return]** (Mac) to add a new line, then type the following lines of code, as shown in Figure 21:

   function removeMovie(event:MouseEvent)

   {

   removeChild(myLoader);

   This defines the *removeMovie* function and uses the *removeChild* method to remove the *myLoader* variable from the display list so it is no longer visible on the screen.

3. Click the **Check syntax button** ✔, then click the **Auto format button** ≡.

4. Play the movie, click the **fish button**, then click the **unload button**.

5. Close the Flash Player window.

6. Save your work.

You used the removeChild *method to remove a movie from the screen.*

Figure 21 *ActionScript to define the removeMovie function*

```
import flash.display.Loader;
import flash.events.MouseEvent;
import flash.net.URLRequest;

stop();
var myLoader:Loader = new Loader();
fishBtn.addEventListener(MouseEvent.CLICK,loadMovie1);
function loadMovie1(event:MouseEvent)
{
    myLoader.load(new URLRequest("fish.swf"));
    addChild(myLoader);
}
frogBtn.addEventListener(MouseEvent.CLICK,loadMovie2);
function loadMovie2(event:MouseEvent)
{
    myLoader.load(new URLRequest("frog.swf"));
    addChild(myLoader);
}
unloadBtn.addEventListener(MouseEvent.CLICK,removeMovie);
function removeMovie(event:MouseEvent)
{
    removeChild(myLoader);
}
```

Line 22 of 23 Col 24

Closing brace added automatically; do not type

Code to type

Figure 22 *Changing the y coordinate value*

```
Actions

1   import flash.display.Loader;
2   import flash.events.MouseEvent;
3   import flash.net.URLRequest;
4
5   stop();
6   var myLoader:Loader = new Loader();
7   myLoader.x = 0;
8   myLoader.y = 50;
9   fishBtn.addEventListener(MouseEvent.CLICK,loadMovie1);
10  function loadMovie1(event:MouseEvent)
11  {
12      myLoader.load(new URLRequest("fish.swf"));
13      addChild(myLoader);
14  }
15  frogBtn.addEventListener(MouseEvent.CLICK,loadMovie2);
16  function loadMovie2(event:MouseEvent)
17  {
18      myLoader.load(new URLRequest("frog.swf"));
19      addChild(myLoader);
20  }
21  unloadBtn.addEventListener(MouseEvent.CLICK,removeMovie);
22  function removeMovie(event:MouseEvent)
23  {
24      removeChild(myLoader);
25  }

                                           Code Snippets

actions : 1
Line 8 of 25  Col 16
```

Code to set the placement of the SWF file

Set the Stage position when loading a movie

1. Insert a **new line** below the var myLoader:Loader=new Loader(); line, then type the following lines of code:

   myLoader.x = 0;

   myLoader.y = 0;

   This code sets the x and y coordinates for the myLoader variable, which determines where the movie will appear on the screen.

2. Test the movie, then click the **fish button**.

   The fish appears in the center of the screen.

3. Close the Flash Player window.

4. Change the myLoader.y value from 0 to **50**, as shown in Figure 22.

5. Test the movie, then click the **fish button**.

   The fish appears lower on the screen.

6. Close the Flash Player window.

7. Close the Actions panel.

8. Save your work, then close the document.

You set and then changed the Stage position when loading a movie.

Work With CONDITIONAL ACTIONS

What You'll Do

In this lesson, you will work with conditional actions and use ActionScript to duplicate movie clip symbols.

Using the Else and Else If Statements

In Chapter 9, you used the *if* statement to test for a condition. If the condition was true, the *if* statement ran a series of actions enclosed in curly braces. Otherwise, it skipped the actions in braces and ran the next set of actions in the Script pane.

ActionScript also includes an *else* statement you can use to create more sophisticated branching. An *else* statement lets you specify one set of actions to run if a condition is true, and an alternate set to run if the condition is false. If a condition has more than two possible states, you can use *else if* to set up a series of possible branches. For example, if you are creating an online test, there might be several possible answers a student could provide, and you might want to create a different branch for each answer. Figure 23 shows ActionScript that uses *else if* to create multiple branches.

Creating Conditional Loops

A **loop** is an action or set of actions that repeat as long as a condition exists. Creating a loop can be as simple as taking a variable, assigning a value to it, executing a statement, and if the statement is false, adding one to the variable and trying again. You can often just use an *if* action to create a loop, which is what you did when you created the preloader in an earlier chapter.

ActionScript includes other actions you can use to create more sophisticated conditional loops. The *for*, *while*, and *do while* loops all let you set up conditions for a loop and actions to run repeatedly. The *for* loop uses a series of arguments to set up a condition, a series of actions to take if the condition is true, and a counter that keeps track of the number of loops. This counter is often used in conjunction with the condition, for instance, to run the loop a user-specified number of times. The *while* and *do while* loops let you enter a series of actions to run while a condition is true. The difference is that *do while* runs the actions at least one time, then evaluates if the condition is true, whereas *while* evaluates the condition and then runs the actions if the conditions are met. Figure 24 shows an example of using the *while* statement to create a loop.

Using the Password Line Type in an Input Field

You may not want passwords to be visible onscreen as users enter them. For security, you can set an input text field to display asterisks rather than the actual keystrokes being typed by a user. To do this, click the Text tool, be sure the text type is set to Input Text, display the Properties panel for the Input Text field, click the Line type list arrow for the Behavior option in the PARAGRAPH area, and then click Password.

Using the Math.random Function

There are times in a Flash application that you may need to generate numbers at random. For example, you may be developing a game and want a character to appear on the screen in a different position each time the user clicks a button. The x and y Stage coordinate values for the character could be generated using the *Math.random* function. This function returns a random number that is equal to or greater than 0 and less than 1 (that is 0 to .999…). This random number can be used to obtain a value that is in a desired range. For instance, if you want to calculate a number that is equal to or above 100 and less than 200, you use the number generated by the *Math.random* function and multiply it by 100, then you would add 100. If the random number that is generated is 0, the calculated number would be 100 ((0*100) + 100). If the random number that is generated is .999, the calculated number would be 199.9 ((.999*100)+100).

Figure 23 *ActionScript using* else if *statements to create multiple branches*

```
 6
 7  {
 8      if (myName == "A")
 9      {
10          gotoAndStop(2);
11      }
12      else
13      {
14          if (myName == "B")
15          {
16              gotoAndStop(3);
17          }
18          else
19          {
20              if (myName == "C")
21              {
22                  gotoAndStop(4);
23              }
24          }
25      }
26  }
27
```

Figure 24 *ActionScript to create a loop using the* while *statement*

```
 8
 9  function loadFish(event:MouseEvent)
10  {
11      var amount:Number = Number(numberIn.text);
12      var n:Number = 0;
13      while (n < amount)
14      {
15          myLoader.load(new URLRequest("fish.swf"));
16          addChild(myLoader);
17          n++;
18      }
19  }
20
21
```

This code creates a loop that continues to load the fish.swf file while the variable n is less than the value in the variable named amount

Create conditional branching using if and else statements

1. Open fl10_3.fla, then save it as **branching.fla**.

2. Drag the **playhead** to view the three screens.

   This application has three screens. The first screen requires a user to type a password and click a login button, the second screen displays Access Granted, and the third screen displays Access Denied.

3. Use the Selection tool ▶ to click the **white input text box** in frame 1 on the Stage, display the Properties panel, then type **pwEntered** for the instance name.

4. Click the **login button** on the Stage to select it, then give it an instance name of **loginBtn**.

5. Click **frame 1** on the actions layer, open the Actions panel, then click below the stop(); line.

6. Press **[Enter]** (Win) or **[return]** (Mac), then type the following as a single line of code:

   loginBtn.addEventListener(MouseEvent. CLICK, checkPW);

   This creates an event listener for the loginBtn object and names the function, *checkPW*, that will be called when the loginBtn object is clicked.

7. Press **[Enter]** (Win) or **[return]** (Mac), then type the following lines of code, as shown in Figure 25:

   function checkPW(Event:MouseEvent)

   {

   if (pwEntered.text == "letmein")

   The first line identifies the function (*checkPW*). The if line checks to see if the text typed by the user in the password input text box is letmein.

   (continued)

Figure 25 *The function that includes an* if *statement*

Closing brace added automatically; do not type

Code to type

This line may appear as you enter the code

Use of Semicolon in Code

Remember that a semicolon is used in code to indicate the end of a statement. A semicolon appears at the end of most lines of code. However, a semicolon is not used at the end of a line of code that is followed by a set of braces, such as a line of code that starts a function or a line of code that starts a conditional statement (*if, else, else while*).

Using ActionScript to Enhance User Experience

Figure 26 *The completed code to test user input*

Opening and closing curly braces for the checkPW *function*

```
1  import flash.ui.Mouse;
2
3  stop();
4
5  loginBtn.addEventListener(MouseEvent.CLICK,checkPW);
6  function checkPW(Event:MouseEvent)
7  {
8      if (pwEntered.text == "letmein")
9      {
10         gotoAndStop(2);
11     }
12 }
```

Opening and closing curly braces for nested gotoAndStop *code*

8. Press **[Enter]** (Win) or **[return]** Mac to add a new blank line, then type the following lines of code as shown in Figure 26:

   {

   gotoAndStop(2);

   This code tells the program what to do if the *if* statement is true, that is, if the user typed letmein in the password input text box.

   Notice the two sets of curly braces. The gotoAndPlay code is nested inside the *checkPW* function code. Each set of codes (the *checkPW* function code and the gotoAndStop code) must have its own set of curly braces.

9. Click the **Check Syntax button** .

10. Click the **Auto format button** .

11. Test the movie, type **notsure**, then click the **login button**.

    Nothing happens using the text string notsure.

12. Change **notsure** to **letmein**, then click the **login button**.

    The second screen appears.

13. Close the Flash Player window.

14. Close the Actions panel.

15. Save your work.

You used an if *statement to create a conditional branch based on user behavior (input of password).*

Provide user feedback

1. Insert a **new layer** above the password input box layer, then name it **tries output box**.

2. Click the **Text tool** on the Tools panel, change the Text type to **Dynamic text**, then be sure Show border around text button 🔳 is not selected.

3. Draw the **text box** shown in Figure 27, then give it an instance name of **tries**.

4. Click **frame 1** on the actions layer, display the Actions panel, then click below the stop(); line.

5. Type **var n:Number = 0;** to create a numeric variable named n.

6. Click after the **right brace (})** below the gotoAndStop line to set the insertion line as shown in Figure 28.

7. Press **[Enter]** (Win) or **[return]** (Mac) to add a blank line, then type the following lines of code:

   else

   {

   This starts the else statement. The else statement will be executed if the user does not type the correct password, letmein.

8. Press **[Enter]** (Win) or **[return]** (Mac), then type the following lines of code:

   n++;

   tries.text = "Sorry, "+(3-n)+" tries left";

   pwEntered.text = "";

   The first line increments the variable n by 1. The second line subtracts the value of n from 3, concatenates it with Sorry . . . tries left, and places the text string in the tries dynamic text box. The third line clears the password that the user typed in the pwEntered input text box.

   (continued)

Figure 27 *Drawing the dynamic text box*

Create this dynamic text box

Figure 28 *Setting the insertion line*

Insertion line

```
1   import flash.ui.Mouse;
2
3   stop();
4   var n:Number = 0;
5   loginBtn.addEventListener(MouseEvent.CLICK,checkPW);
6   function checkPW(Event:MouseEvent)
7   {
8       if (pwEntered.text == "letmein")
9       {
10          gotoAndStop(2);
11      }
12  }
```

actions : 1

Line 11 of 12, Col 3

Using ActionScript to Enhance User Experience

Figure 29 *Completed code to create a conditional branch based on user input*

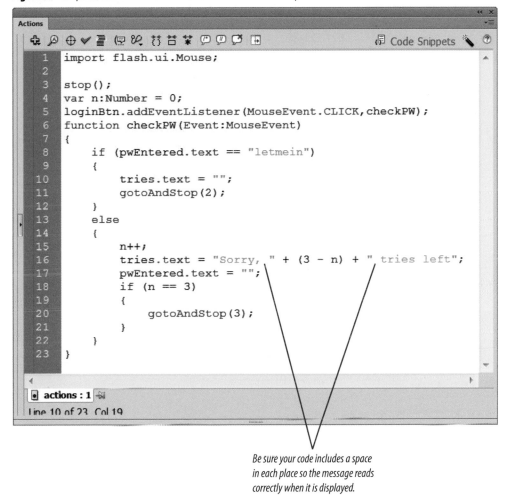

```
Actions
⊕ ⌕ ⊕ ✔ ≣ ⌕⚙ ⟨⟩ ⟨⟩ ✱ ⟨⟩ ⟨⟩ ⟨⟩ ⊞                    ⟨⟩ Code Snippets ✎ ⟨?⟩
 1    import flash.ui.Mouse;
 2
 3    stop();
 4    var n:Number = 0;
 5    loginBtn.addEventListener(MouseEvent.CLICK,checkPW);
 6    function checkPW(Event:MouseEvent)
 7    {
 8        if (pwEntered.text == "letmein")
 9        {
10            tries.text = "";
11            gotoAndStop(2);
12        }
13        else
14        {
15            n++;
16            tries.text = "Sorry, " + (3 - n) + " tries left";
17            pwEntered.text = "";
18            if (n == 3)
19            {
20                gotoAndStop(3);
21            }
22        }
23    }
```

`actions : 1`

Line 10 of 23 Col 19

Be sure your code includes a space in each place so the message reads correctly when it is displayed.

9. Press **[Enter]** (Win) or **[return]** (Mac), then type the following lines of code:

   if (n == 3)

   {

   gotoAndStop(3);

   The first line checks to see if n is equal to 3. If so, the code within the braces is executed which jumps the playhead to screen 3. Screen 3 displays the words Access Denied.

10. Insert a blank line above the gotoAnd Stop(2); line and type the following:

    tries.text = "";

    This clears the entry in the tries text box so the entry will not appear on screen 2.

11. Click the **Check Syntax button** ✔ , click the **Auto format button** ≣ , then compare your screen to Figure 29.

12. Test the movie, type **notsure** for the password, then click the **login button**.

13. Type **notsure** and click the login button two more times.

    The Access Denied screen appears and the number of tries left is displayed.

14. Close the Flash Player window.

15. Test the movie, type **letmein** for the password, then click the **login button**.

    The Access Granted screen appears.

16. Close the Flash Player window, then close the Actions panel.

17. Click the **password input box** on the Stage to select it, click the **Behavior list arrow** in the PARAGRAPH area of the Properties panel, then click **Password**.

   (continued)

18. Test the movie, type **letmein**.

    Notice asterisks are displayed in place of the letters as you type.

19. Click the **login button**.

    The Access Granted screen appears.

20. Close the Flash Player window, save your work, then close the movie.

You used if *and* else *statements to provide feedback to the user.*

Create a while loop to duplicate movie clip symbols

1. Open fl10_4.fla, then save it as **duplicator.fla**.

    This movie has one screen that allows the user to determine how many times to duplicate the head on the screen. The user enters a number and clicks the duplicator button, which causes that number of heads to appear in random locations on the screen.

2. Insert a **new layer** above the duplicate button layer, then name it **number input box**.

3. Click the **Text tool** T on the Tools panel, change the text type to **Input**, click the Show border around text button 圖 to make it active, change the Behavior to **Single line**, then draw the **text box** shown in Figure 30.

4. Enter **numberIn** for the instance name.

5. Click **frame 1** on the actions layer, open the Actions panel, then type the following as a single line of code below the stop(); line:

    duplicateBtn.
    addEventListener(MouseEvent.CLICK,
    runDuplicate);

    (continued)

Figure 30 *Drawing the input text box*

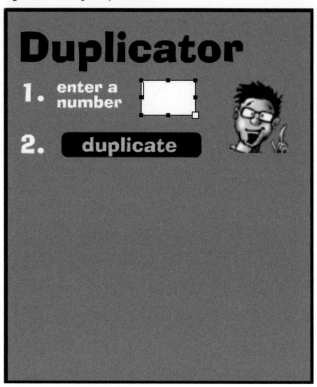

Figure 31 *Setting the condition for the* while *loop*

```
import flash.events.MouseEvent;

stop();
duplicateBtn.addEventListener(MouseEvent.CLICK,runDuplicate);
function runDuplicate(event:MouseEvent)
{
    var amount:Number = Number(numberIn.text);
    var n:Number = 0;
    while (n<amount)
    {
}
```

This line may appear as you enter the code

This closing brace was added automatically as part of the runDuplicate function

This creates an event listener for duplicateBtn (the instance name of the button) and names a function, runDuplicate, that is called when the duplicateBtn object is clicked.

6. Press **[Enter]** (Win) or **[return]** (Mac) to add a blank line, then type the following lines of code:

function runDuplicate(event:MouseEvent)

{

The first line identifies the function (runDuplicate). The left brace ({) signifies the start of the code that defines the function.

7. Press **[Enter]** (Win) or **[return]** (Mac) to add a blank line, then refer to Figure 31 as you type the following lines of code:

var amount:Number = Number (numberIn.text);

var n:Number = 0;

The first line creates a numeric variable named amount and assigns it the number entered by the user in the numberIn input box. The second line creates a numeric variable named n and gives it a value of 0.

8. Press **[Enter]** (Win) or **[return]** (Mac) to add a blank line, then type the following lines of code, as shown in Figure 31:

while (n < amount)

{

The first line sets the condition for the while loop. That is, the loop will continue as long as the value in the amount variable is less than the value in the n variable. The { brace signifies the start of the code contained in the loop.

(continued)

9. Press **[Enter]** (Win) or **[return]** (Mac) to add a blank line, then type the following:

   var faceInstance:faceMC = new faceMC();

   This line creates a variable named faceInstance and creates an instance of the faceMC movie clip.

10. Press **[Enter]** (Win) or **[return]** (Mac) to add a blank line, then type the **addChild** code, as shown in Figure 32, and that follows:

    addChild(faceInstance).x = (Math.random()*150)+50, (faceInstance).y = (Math.random()*200)+50;

    This line adds the faceInstance object at a random location on the screen and keeps the object within the boundaries of the Stage.

    (continued)

Figure 32 *The* addChild *line*

```
Actions
import flash.events.MouseEvent;

stop();
duplicateBtn.addEventListener(MouseEvent.CLICK,runDuplicate);
function runDuplicate(event:MouseEvent)
{
    var amount:Number = Number(numberIn.text);
    var n:Number = 0;
    while (n<amount)
    {
        var faceInstance:faceMC = new faceMC();
        addChild(faceInstance).x = (Math.random()*150)+50,(faceInstance).y = (Math.random()*200)+50;
    }
}
```

actions : 1
Line 12 of 14 Col 95

Code to type

Using ActionScript to Enhance User Experience

Figure 33 *Completed code to create a loop based on user input*

```
Actions
   import flash.events.MouseEvent;

   stop();
   duplicateBtn.addEventListener(MouseEvent.CLICK,runDuplicate);
   function runDuplicate(event:MouseEvent)
   {
       var amount:Number = Number(numberIn.text);
       var n:Number = 0;
       while (n<amount)
       {
           var faceInstance:faceMC = new faceMC();
           addChild(faceInstance).x = (Math.random()*150)+50,(faceInstance).y = (Math.random()*200)+50;
           n++;
       }
   }

 actions : 1
Line 13 of 15  Col 7
```

11. Press **[Enter]** (Win) or **[return]** (Mac) to add a blank line, then type the following:

    n++;

    This line increments n by 1.

12. Click the **Check Syntax button** ✔ , click the **Auto format button** ≣ , then compare your Script pane with Figure 33.

13. Test the movie, type **5** in the enter number box, then click the **duplicate button**.

TIP Compare your Actions panel to Figure 33. If you encounter any errors, be sure the Text type is set to Input text and, if you see asterisks when you type, change the Behavior setting to Single line.

14. Close the Flash Player window, save your work, then close the document.

You used a while *statement to create a loop that duplicates a movie clip symbol the number of times specified by the user.*

Use ActionScript
TO CREATE EXTERNAL LINKS

What You'll Do

 In this lesson, you will create email and web page links.

Creating a Link to a Website

Many websites contain links to other sites. You might create links to lead the user to a related site or just to another site you want to share. The *URLRequest* class along with the *navigateToURL* function, shown in Figure 34, let you open another file or jump from a button or movie clip symbol to another website. The new site or file can appear in the same browser window as your site or in a new browser window. Table 1 displays the target options for a website and external file links.

QUICK TIP

You can also enter the HTML filename of a specific window or frame as a target. This might be appropriate if you have multiple links on a page and want a separate window to open for one of the links that the user follows but not for the other links.

When you use *URLRequest* to jump to another website, you must supply the URL for the file. Make sure to include the entire URL, including the protocol prefix, for example, *http://www.adobe.com*, which is known as an absolute path.

Figure 34 *ActionScript to display a website*

The variable name targetURL is given a URLRequest data type and then assigned the URL

Using ActionScript to Enhance User Experience

Creating a Mailto: Link

You can also use *URLRequest* to create an email link from a button or movie clip symbol. When a user clicks an email link, a new email message window opens, with the TO: address field already filled in with an address you have specified, as shown in Figure 35. To create an email link, include mailto: and then the email address in the URL field of the *URLRequest* statement. If you want to create an email link from text, not a button or movie clip symbol, you can use the Properties panel.

TABLE 1: TARGET OPTIONS FOR WEBSITE LINKS	
Option	**Opens site or link in:**
_self	The current window
_blank	A new window
_parent	The parent of the current frame (a frame is a part of a web page)
_top	The top-level frame in the current window

© Cengage Learning 2013

Figure 35 *New message window for a maito:link*

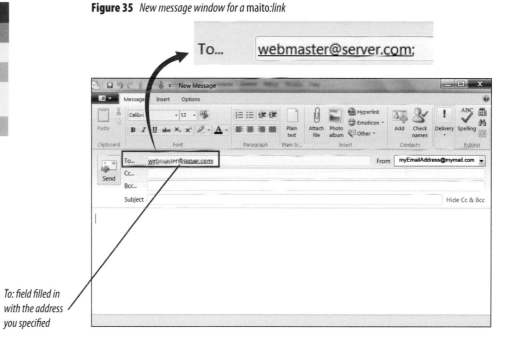

To: field filled in with the address you specified

Create a website link

1. Open fl10_5.fla, then save it as **links.fla**.
2. Click **frame 1** on the actions layer, open the Actions panel, then type the following as a single line of code:

   websiteBtn.addEventListener(MouseEvent.CLICK, goWeb);

   This creates an event listener for a mouse event and names a function (goWeb) that is called when the websiteBtn object is clicked.

3. Press **[Enter]** (Win) or **[return]** (Mac) to add a blank line, then type:

   function goWeb(Event:MouseEvent)

   This starts the definition of the function goWeb.

4. Press **[Enter]** (Win) or **[return]** (Mac) to add a blank line, then type these three lines of code, as shown in Figure 36:

   {
   var targetURL:URLRequest = new URLRequest("http://www.adobe.com/");
   navigateToURL(targetURL,"_blank");

5. Compare your screen to Figure 36, test the movie, then click the Visit our Website button.

   The Adobe website opens in a browser window. If the browser does not open in a window, click the flashing browser button on the taskbar to display the browser window.

   Note: If you are not connected to the Internet, you will not be able to view the site.

6. Close the browser, close the Flash Player window, then save your work.

You linked a button to a website.

Figure 36 *ActionScript code to create a website link*

These lines may appear as you enter the code

Code to create a website link

Creates a variable named targetURL with the data type URLRequest

navigateToURL function displays the website in a new browser window

Specifies the URL for the website to be displayed

Using ActionScript to Enhance User Experience

Figure 37 *ActionScript code to create an email link*

```
Actions
import flash.events.MouseEvent;
import flash.net.URLRequest;

websiteBtn.addEventListener(MouseEvent.CLICK,goWeb);
function goWeb(Event:MouseEvent)
{
    var targetURL:URLRequest = new URLRequest("http://www.adobe.com/");
    navigateToURL(targetURL,"_blank");
}

emailBtn.addEventListener(MouseEvent.CLICK,goEmail);
function goEmail(Event:MouseEvent)
{
    var emailTo:URLRequest = new URLRequest("mailTo:webmaster@server.com");
    navigateToURL(emailTo,"_blank");
}
```

Code to create an email link

Creates a variable named emailTo with the data type URLRequest

navigateToURL *function displays an email form in a new window*

Specifies the URL for the email address to be displayed

Create a link to an email address

1. Display the Actions panel, click after the **last curly brace** (}), Press **[Enter]** (Win) or **[return]** (Mac) twice to add two blank lines, then type:

    emailBtn.addEventListener(MouseEvent. CLICK, goEmail);

    This creates an event listener and names a function (goEmail) that is called when the emailBtn object is clicked.

2. Press **[Enter]** (Win) or **[return]** (Mac) to add a blank line, then type:

    function goEmail(Event:MouseEvent)

    This starts the definition of the function goEmail.

3. Press **[Enter]** (Win) or **[return]** (Mac) to add a blank line, then type the three lines of code, as shown in Figure 37:

    {

    var emailTo:URLRequest = new URLRequest ("mailTo:webmaster@server.com");

    navigateToURL(emailTo, "_blank");

4. Compare your screen to Figure 37, test the movie, then click the email button.

    A new email message window opens in your default email program, with the To: field already filled in.

    TIP If an email message window does not appear, your computer may not have access to an email program. If a security warning appears, click Allow.

5. Close the email form window without saving changes, then close the Flash Player window.

6. Save your work, close the document, then exit Flash.

You linked a button to an email address.

Create complex interactivity.

(*Note*: It is good practice to use the Check syntax button and the Auto format button each time you complete the code for an action. This allows you to troubleshoot the code as you go.)

1. Start Flash, open fl10_6.fla, then save it as **skillsDemo10.fla**.
2. Scrub the playhead to view the contents of the frames.

   This is a game in which the user tries to click a moving target, and then, when the user clicks the End button, he or she receives feedback that is based on the number of hits. (*Note*: All of the buttons have been given intuitive instance names. For example, the button on the Stage with the text, Go, has an instance name of goBtn.)

3. Click 1 on the Timeline, click the white dynamic text box at the top of the Stage, then type **hitsBox** for the instance name.
4. Click frame 1 on the actions layer, open the Actions panel, then add a blank line below the stop(): line.

   You will hide the mouse cursor and enable a custom cursor named arrow. However, first you will create a variable named arrow with a data type of arrow_cursorMC, which is a movie clip in the Library that contains the custom cursor. Because you are assigning the movie clip to a variable and using

the variable in the code, you do not need to specify an instance name for the movie clip custom cursor as you did in Lesson 1. (*Note*: The arrow_cursorMC movie clip has been given a linkage name, arrow_cursorMC, which means the Export for ActionScript is enabled.) Creating the variable will allow you to use the *addChild* method so that the cursor can be added to the display list, which means it can appear on the Stage.

5. Type the following:
   var arrow:arrow_cursorMC = new arrow_cursorMC;
6. Move to the next line and type the *mouse hide* method, then move to the next line.
7. Add a stage mouse move event listener and specify **followMouse** for the function name, then move to the next line and type the code to associate the function with a mouse event.
8. Move to the next line and define the block of code for the followMouse function that will set arrow.x and arrow.y to follow the mouseX and mouseY, then move to the next line.
9. Type **addChild(arrow);** to add the arrow to the display list. (*Note*: Be sure the lines that define what will be executed when the function is called are enclosed within left and right braces ({}).)
10. Click after the right brace (}) that completes the function (*Note*: this right brace should have been added automatically while you were typing the function definition), then move to the next line.

Load movies at runtime.

1. Create a variable named **myLoader** with a data type of Loader and create a new instance of the Loader, then move to the next line. (*Note*: myLoader will be used to load an SWF file with animated text that will display on the first screen as the flash application opens.)
2. Type the two lines that set the myLoader x and y properties to 0, then move to the next line.
3. Type the URLRequest statement so that myLoader loads "textAnimation.swf", then on the next line use the *addChild* method to add myLoader to the display list. (*Hint*: This is similar to the exercise you completed in Lesson 2; however, loading this SWF file is not associated with clicking a button.)

   This completes the code to load the SWF file into the movie. (*Note*: Be sure that the textAnimation.swf file is in the same folder as your skillsDemo10.fla file.)

4. Add a line to the bottom of the ActionScript code, then create a variable named **hits** with a Number data type and a value of 0.
5. Move to the next line and type an event listener that will call a function named **runIT** when the user clicks the goBtn object on the Stage.
6. Move to the next line and type the code to associate the function with a mouse event.

7. Move to the next line and define the block of code for the runIT function as follows. (*Note*: Be sure to enclose the lines of code that define what will be executed when the function is called within left and right braces ({}). After completing this Skills Review, you will have blocks of code that are nested within other blocks of code. It is important to be sure you always have an opening left brace and a closing right brace for each block of code.)

    - Create a variable named **heartInstance** with a targetMC data type and new targetMC instance. (*Note*: The movie clip named targetMC is in the Library and contains an animation of a heart moving around the screen.)
    - Use the *addChild* method to add an instance of the heartInstance object using an x coordinate of 260 and y coordinate of 220. *Hint*: This will keep the animation of the moving heart within the boundaries of the Stage. This one line of code is. addChild(heartInstance). x = **260**, (heartInstance). y = **220**;
    - Type an event listener that will call a function named **hitIT** when the user clicks the heartInstance object on the Stage.
    - Move to the next line and define the block of code for the hitIT function as follows: (*Note*: Be sure to enclose the lines of code that define what will be executed when the function is called within left and right braces ({}).)
    - A line of code that increments the variable hits by 1. (*Note*: You created the hits variable with a Number data type earlier.)
    - A line of code that takes the value in the hits variable and changes it to a String data type, then assigns it to the hitsBox text box. (*Note*: This will display the number of hits that are recorded as the user clicks on the heartInstance object.)
    - Move to the line after the closing brace for the function and create an event listener that will call a function named **goto2** when the endBtn object is clicked.
    - Move to the next line and type the code to associate the function with a mouse event.
    - Move to the next line and define the block of code for the goto2 function as follows: (*Note*: Be sure to enclose the lines of code that define what will be executed when the function is called within left and right braces ({}).)
    - A line of code that uses the *removeChild* method to remove myLoader from the display list so the animated text will not be visible on the next screen.
    - A line of code that uses the *removeChild* method to remove heartInstance from the display list so the heart will not be visible on the next screen.
    - A line of code that causes the playhead to go to and play frame 2.

8. Verify a right brace (}) ends the function.
9. Check the syntax and auto format the code.
10. Collapse the Actions panel, then click frame 2 on the Timeline.
11. Click the dynamic text box just below score, then give it an instance name of **scoreBox**.
12. Click the dynamic text box just above the Start Over button, then give it an instance name of **messageBox**.
13. Click frame 2 on the actions layer, open the Actions panel, then add a blank line below the stop(); line.
14. Type the statement that takes the value in the hits variable and changes it to a string data type and then assigns it to the scoreBox text box. (*Note*: This will display the number of hits the user had when trying to click on the heartInstance object.)

Using ActionScript to Enhance User Experience

Work with conditional actions.

1. On the next line, type the *if-else* code that will check the number of hits. If the number is greater than 4 have **Super!** appear in the messageBox text box. If not, have the message **Nice Try!** appear in the text box.

2. On the line after the closing brace, create an event listener that calls a function named **goHome** when the user clicks the startoverBtn object.

3. Move to the next line and type the code to associate the function with a mouse event.

4. On the next line, define the block of code for the goHome function to include:
   - A *removeChild* method that removes the arrow. (*Note*: This will remove the custom cursor because it will be added at frame 1.)
   - A gotoAndPlay action that jumps the playhead to frame 1.

Use ActionScript to create an external link.

1. After the closing right brace for the *goHome* function, create an event listener that calls a function named **goEmail** when the user clicks the commentsBtn object.

2. Move to the next line and type the code to associate the function with a mouse event.

3. On the next line, define the block of code for the *goEmail* function to include a URLRequest and *navigateToURL* method that will display an email form with the To line filled in with your email address.

4. Check the syntax and auto format the code.

5. Test the movie, compare your image to Figure 38, then save your work. (*Hint:* To increase the difficulty of the game, increase the frame rate. This causes the targetMC movie clip (the hearts) to change position more quickly.)

Figure 38 *Completed Skills Review*

Ultimate Tours would like you to build a banner for its website which, when a button on the banner is clicked, will load a new movie containing its latest travel specials. By creating the banner in one SWF file and the specials in another, Ultimate Tours can update the specials at any time, just by replacing one file. As a way to encourage users to look at and interact with the banner, they would also like you to create a button that links to the *www.weather.com* website.

1. Open fl10_7.fla, then rename the file **ultimateTours10**.

   This movie contains a heading, two buttons, and a red backdrop. The blank area on the left is where the new movie, named specials.swf, will be loaded.

2. Click the "see specials" button on the Stage, then give it an instance name of **specialsBtn**.
3. Click the "get weather" button on the Stage, then give it an instance name of **weatherBtn**.
4. Click frame 1 of the actions layer, then open the Actions panel.
5. Add a blank line beneath the stop(); line.
6. Type the code that creates a variable named **myLoader**, with a Loader data type, and creates an instance of the new Loader.
7. Type two lines of code to set the myLoader.x value to **20** and the myLoader.y value to **10**.

8. Type the code to create an event listener that calls a function (with a name of your choosing) when the user clicks on the specialsBtn object.
9. Type the block of code to define the function to use the URLRequest class to load specials.swf.

   Note: You will need to have the specials.swf file in the same folder as the ultimateTours10.fla file.

10. Use the *addChild* method to add the myLoader instance to the display list so that it becomes visible on the screen.
11. Add a blank line below the last line of code, then type the code to create an event listener that calls a function

(with a name of your choosing) when the user clicks on the weatherBtn object.
12. Type the block of code to associate the function with a mouse event and to define the function to use the URLRequest class and the *navigateToURL* function to link to the http://www.weather.com website using a new window.
13. Check the syntax and auto format the code.
14. Test the movie, click the see specials button, compare your image to Figure 39, then click the get weather button.
15. Close your browser, save your work, then close the document.

Figure 39 *Completed Project Builder 1*

You have volunteered to use Flash to create an interactive, educational counting game that will get first-graders comfortable with computers. The game will display a random number of cookies spilled from a cookie jar, ask students to count the cookies, type the number, and then give feedback on whether or not the answer is correct. The application will be designed for smartphones.

1. Open fl10_8.fla, then save it as **counting_game10.fla**.
2. Click frame 1 on the Timeline, click the input box above the go button, then give it an instance name of **checkBox**.
3. Click frame 1 on the actions layer, then open the Actions panel.
   Notice that some code has already been included in the file. The code in Line 2 creates a numeric variable named numberOfCookies, which has been given the value of 0. This variable will be assigned a random number between 1 and 10 inclusive. The code in Line 3 is an event listener that calls a function named getCookies when the startBtn object is clicked. The code in Lines 4-8 defines the getCookies function. The code in Line 6 assigns a number between 1 and 10 inclusive to the numberOfCookies variable. This is done using the *Math.random* and the *Math.floor* methods. The *Math.random* method returns a value between 0 and .999 that is multiplied by 10 and adds 1. So, the range for *Math.random* is 1 to 10.999.

The *Math.floor* method takes the number that was calculated using the *Math.random* method and changes it into a whole number that does not exceed the specified range (in this case 1 through 10). The code in Line 7 creates a numeric variable named n, which will be used in a counter.

4. Complete the *getCookies* function by typing code for the following before the closing right brace:
   ■ Add a line below the last line of code and before the closing right brace to create a while loop that loops while n is less than numberOfCookies.
   ■ Define the while loop as follows and place the code inside a new set of left and right braces.
      ● Type a line that creates a variable named **cookieInstance** that has a **cookieMC** data type and then create a new instance of the cookieMC. (*Note*: cookieMC is the movie clip that contains an image of the cookie.)
      ● Add another line of code that uses the *addChild* method to add cookieInstance to the display list and positions it in a random location. (*Hint*: See Figure 32 for the format. The x values should be 166 and 36, and the y values should be 150 and 220. This will ensure the cookies will overlap with the cookie jar.)
      ● Add another line of code that increments n by 1.
   ■ Verify both the while loop block of code and the *getCookies* function block of code end with right braces (}).

5. After the closing right brace for the *getCookies* function, type an event listener that calls a function when the goBtn object is clicked. Name the function **checkNumberTyped**.
6. Define the function as an *if-else* statement. If the number entered by the user into the input box (checkBox.text) is equal to the number of cookies (numberOfCookies) generated by the *Math.random* function, then have the playhead got to and play frame 2; else have the playhead go to and play frame 3.
7. Check the syntax and auto format the code.
8. Click frame 2 on the Timeline, click the dynamic text box just below the heading on the Stage and give it an instance name of **right**.
9. Click frame 2 on the actions layer, then display the Actions panel.

   The code in Line 2 adds an event listener that "listens" for an ENTER_FRAME event and names a function (**correct**). The enter frame event causes the function named correct to be executed when the playhead moves to frame 2.

10. Type the line of code between the left and right braces ({}) that takes the value in the numberOfCookies variable and changes it to a String data type, then assigns it to the dynamic text box named **right**. (*Hint*: The format to change a numeric var to a string is: Textboxname.text = String(var);)

11. Check the syntax and auto format the code.
12. Click frame 3 on the Timeline, click the dynamic text box on the Stage and give it an instance name of **wrong**.
13. Click frame 2 on the actions layer and copy the code for the event listener and the function called correct, then click frame 3 on the actions layer and paste the code on a new line following stop();.
14. Edit the code pasted into frame 3 on the actions layer so the function name is **incorrect** and the text box name is **wrong**.
15. Check the syntax and auto format the code.
16. Test the movie several times by entering both correct and incorrect numbers for the number of cookies displayed.
17. Lock all layers.
18. Compare your image to Figure 40, save your work, then close the document.

Figure 40 *Completed Project Builder 2*

Using ActionScript to Enhance User Experience

Figure 41 shows a page from a website created using Flash. Study the figure and complete the following. For each question, indicate how you determined your answer.

1. Connect to the Internet, go to this URL: *http://v4.2a-archive.com,* and then click ENTER.

2. Open a document in a word processor or open a new Flash document, save the file as **dpc10**, then answer the following questions. (*Hint*: Use the Text tool in Flash.)

   ■ What is the purpose of this site? Does the design of the site contribute to its purpose?

   ■ Move the mouse pointer around the screen and note the different effects as you pass over links and buttons. How could these effects be achieved with ActionScript?

   ■ Click the links in the main navigation bar. What changes occur on the screen? Do you think the links are jumping to a different frame in this movie or loading a new movie? What specific actions could be used to achieve this effect?

   ■ List some of the advantages of loading a new movie for links, in the context of this site.

   ■ Click the Portfolio link, then click the VIEW button for the featured website. (*Note*: The VIEW button is under the slide show that is running for the featured website.) What happens? What specific actions might be associated with the View button to achieve this effect?

Figure 41 *Design Project*
Copyright © 2003 2Advanced Studios, LLC. http://v4.2a-archive.com

Using ActionScript to Enhance User Experience

You have decided to create a new portfolio with five screens, each in a separate frame and on a separate layer. One screen contains examples of the Flash work you have done throughout this book, and one creates a password-protected, clients-only area. You will create the links to your Flash movies by loading new SWF files. You can use your favorites from the files you have developed throughout this book, or any other SWF files you have created on your own.

1. Open a new Flash document, then save it as **portfolio10.fla**.
2. Create a screen with a heading of **home** in frame 1 on a layer called Home Page. Add another layer named **Navigation-buttons** and create three buttons named **home**, **flash samples**, and **clients only**.
3. Create a screen in frame 2 on a layer called **Flash Samples**, using a format that fits in visually with the rest of your site. On this screen include a title and at least three buttons, each of which, when clicked, loads a new Flash movie. (*Hint*: New movies appear starting in the middle of the current movie. You may need to reduce the size of your SWF files or change the x and y coordinates of the loader to position the movies as desired. Be sure the SWF files are in the same folder as your movie.)
4. Create a screen in frame 3 on a layer called **Clients Only**. On this screen, create the text "Enter password" and an input text box with the instance name **enterPW**.
5. Create another screen that says: **Welcome to the client's area**.

6. Create another screen that says: **Sorry, that is not correct. Please contact me to receive or verify your password**. Then, add a button to the page which, when clicked, opens the user's default email program to a new mail message with your email address filled in.
7. On the Clients Only screen that prompts for a password, create a button with the text **Submit**. Set up a conditional action which, if the user types the word "password" in the input text box, jumps to the "Welcome" screen, or, if the user types anything else, jumps to the "Sorry" screen.
8. Add events to the buttons on the home screen which, when clicked, jump to the appropriate screen: the home button goes to screen 1, the flash samples button goes to the flash samples screen, and the clients only button goes to the clients only screen.
9. Create a variable named myLoader with a Loader data type and add an instance of the loader. Specify the X and Y Stage location for the loader. (*Hint*: Place these three lines in frame 1 of your actions layer just below a stop(); statement.)
10. Add myLoader.unload(); event (assuming your loader variable is named myLoader) to the function called by the home, samples and clients only navigation buttons on the home screen. (*Note*: If you don't add this action, the movies you load on the Flash Samples screen will remain loaded, even when you navigate away from the samples screen. Add these statements above the goto statements in each function.)
11. Check the syntax and auto format the code.

12. Test the movie, then compare your movie to Figure 42.
13. Save your work.

Figure 42 *Sample completed Portfolio Project*

CHAPTER 11

ADDING SOUND
AND VIDEO

1. Work with sound

2. Specify synchronization options

3. Modify sounds

4. Use ActionScript with sound

5. Work with video

CHAPTER 11

ADDING SOUND AND VIDEO

Introduction

Like animation and interactivity, sound and video are important tools you can use to express a message, engage users, and make your site or application appealing to visitors. In an earlier chapter, you added sound to the Timeline and to a button and you added video to a Flash application. In this chapter, you will see that there is much more you can do with sound and video in Flash. For example, you can set a short sound clip to play continuously, creating a musical backdrop for your application. Or, you can synchronize sound with an animation or movie clip, perhaps providing a voice-over that explains what's happening on the screen. You can use new video features, such as adding cue points, which allow users to navigate to different parts of a video clip. You can add cue points to a video directly in Flash using the Properties panel.

Sound and video can add significantly to the size of published applications, so you should plan ahead and try to use them strategically. Apply sound and video only where it will have the most impact. Flash includes a number of compression options that can help you achieve a balance between quality and file size when using these elements in your applications. Effective and judicious use of sound and video are key ingredients in making a Flash site or application a truly multimedia experience.

TOOLS YOU'LL USE

Work with
SOUND

What You'll Do

In this lesson, you will add background music to a movie and work with layering and repeating sounds.

Importing Sound Files

One way to add sound to an object (such as a button) or the Timeline in Flash, is to import sound files to the Library panel. Table 1 shows the types of sound files you can import. In addition to imported sound files, Flash provides dozens of sound effects such as sirens wailing, dogs barking, and lightning cracking. These are found in the Common Libraries panel on the Windows menu. You can add a sound using the Timeline, or you can use ActionScript to add a sound during runtime.

Adding a Sound to the Timeline

When you want a sound to play in the background, rather than tie it to a specific object on the Stage, you can add an instance of the sound to a frame on the Timeline. You can select a keyframe on a layer on the Timeline and then drag a sound from the Library panel to the Stage to add the sound to the selected keyframe, or you can select a keyframe on a layer on the Timeline and then add a sound to the selected keyframe through the Properties panel. Using the Properties panel is the recommended method because you can select the sound file you want to use, set the number of times you want the sound file to repeat,

and set effects related to the sound file, such as fade in and fade out.

Sounds are represented on the Timeline by either a straight or waveform line, as shown in Figure 1. The approximate duration of the sound is indicated by the number of frames the line occupies. Although the line extends no further than the last frame of the movie, if the sound is longer in duration than the length of the movie in seconds, the sound may continue playing after the playhead has reached the last frame of the movie.

You can play multiple sounds at once by placing the sounds on different layers. For example, you might have background music that plays continuously, but then play accent sounds at various points to act as a supplement or counterpoint to the background. Or you might have a background sound on one layer and a voice-over or narration on another layer. You can stagger where each sound begins by creating a keyframe at a later point on the Timeline, and then adding the sound to this keyframe.

Understanding Event Sounds

By default, sounds you add in Flash are considered **event sounds**. Like movie clip symbols, event sounds play independently of the Timeline. The sound starts in the keyframe to which you add it, but it can continue playing even after the last frame in the main Timeline is played. In addition, event sounds may play at a faster or slower rate than indicated by the frames on the Timeline, depending on the speed of the computer on which the movie is played.

Event sounds have an advantage in that you can use them as many times as you like in a movie, with no increase in the file size of your published movie. However, when a movie is played over the web, event sounds do not begin until the entire sound file is downloaded; this may cause a disconnect between sound and images for some users.

There is another type of sound in Flash, called **stream sound**. Stream sounds are similar to animated graphic symbols because they are closely tied to the main Timeline. Thus, even if a stream sound is longer than a movie, a stream sound stops at the end of the movie.

When loading sound files externally, instead of from the Library panel, stream sounds can start playing as your computer begins to download them, which means users do not have to wait for the entire sound file to download before the movie starts. You will work with stream sounds in the next lesson. The same sound file can be designated as either an event sound or a stream sound, depending on the setting you choose.

Figure 1 *A sound on the Timeline*

This layer contains the sound

Sound file on Timeline

Repeating Sounds

The Repeat feature lets you replay a sound a specified number of times. This is useful in certain situations, such as creating background music for a movie. If you want your audio to loop continuously, you can select the Loop option by clicking the Repeat list arrow in the SOUND area on the Properties panel, and then selecting Loop.

TABLE 1: SOUND FILES THAT FLASH IMPORTS		
Sound type	**Windows**	**Mac**
Adobe Soundbooth (.asnd)	Yes	Yes
Waveform Audio File (.wav)	Yes	Yes, requires QuickTime
Audio Interchange File (.aiff), (.aif)	Yes, requires QuickTime	Yes
MPEG-1 Audio level 3 (.mp3)	Yes	Yes
Sound only QuickTime movies (.mov), (.qt)	Yes, requires QuickTime	Yes, requires QuickTime
System 7 sounds (.snd)	No	Yes, requires QuickTime
Sound Designer II (.sd2)	No	Yes, requires QuickTime
SunAU (.au)	Yes, requires QuickTime	Yes, requires QuickTime

© Cengage Learning 2013

Add sound to a Timeline

1. Open fl11_1.fla from the drive and folder where your Data Files are stored, then save it as **nightclub.fla**.

2. Display the Library panel, expand the Audio folder to display the list of audio files, click **accent1**, then click the **Play button** ▶ in the Item Preview area at the top of the Library panel to preview the sound.

3. Preview the **accent2** and **background** sounds.

4. Insert a **new layer** above the sign layer, then name it **audioBackground**.

5. Click **frame 1** on the audioBackground layer, display the Properties panel, click the **Name list arrow** in the SOUND area, click **background**, then verify that Event appears in the Sync sound list box, as shown in Figure 2.

   Flash adds the sound file to the layer, as indicated by the blue horizontal line through the frames on the audioBackground layer.

TIP The Library panel already contains several sounds, so when you click the Name list arrow in the SOUND area, a list appears of all sound files that have been imported into the Library panel.

6. Test the movie.

   The background music sound clip plays, ending after about 12 seconds, which is how long it takes to play the sound file one time.

7. Close the Flash Player window.

You added a sound to the Timeline and verified it was an event sound.

Figure 2 *Selecting a sound file in the Properties panel*

Click the list arrow to see a list of sounds in the Library panel

If necessary, click the list arrow, then select Event

Adding Sound and Video

Figure 3 *A Timeline with layered sounds*

Sounds end at
these frames

Layer sounds

1. Insert a **new layer** above the audioBackground layer, then name it **accent1**.

2. Click **frame 1** on the accent1 layer, click the **Name list arrow** in the SOUND area on the Properties panel, click **accent1**, then verify that Event appears in the Sync list box.

3. Insert a **new layer** above the accent1 layer, then name it **accent2**.

4. Insert a **keyframe** in frame 30 on the accent2 layer.

5. Click the **Frame view button** at the top right side of the Timeline, then click **Tiny** to display more frames.

6. Click the **Name list arrow** in the SOUND area on the Properties panel, click **accent2**, verify that Event appears in the Sync list box, then compare your screen to Figure 3.

7. Test the movie.

   All three sound files play simultaneously for a short time. However, since the sound clips are of different durations, they do not all play to the end of the movie.

   TIP When you look at the Timeline, sound lines are blue and layer border lines are black.

8. Close the Flash Player window.

You layered sounds of different durations.

Create a repeating sound

1. Click **frame 1** on the audioBackground layer, verify that Repeat is displayed in the SOUND area on the Properties panel, change the Number of times to repeat to **3**, then compare your screen to Figure 4.

   The sound line on the audioBackground layer now stretches to the end of the movie, frame 200.

2. Click **frame 1** on the accent1 layer, then use the Properties panel to change the Number of times to repeat to **5**.

3. Click **frame 30** on the accent2 layer, then use the Properties panel to change the Number of times to repeat to **4**.

   Since the accent2 sound starts in a later keyframe than the accent1 sound, you do not have to repeat it as many times to have it play until the end of the movie.

TIP You select Loop when you want a sound to play continuously. You select Repeat and select a number when you want a sound file to play a set number of times. The default setting is Repeat 1, which indicates the sound will play one time.

4. Lock the three audio layers.

(continued)

Figure 4 *Specifying the number of times a sound repeats*

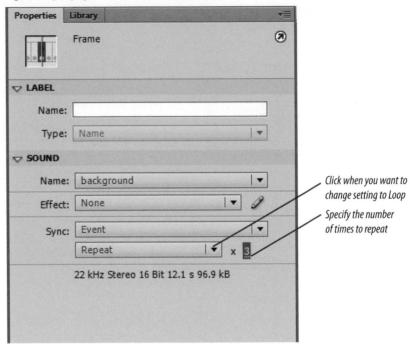

Click when you want to change setting to Loop

Specify the number of times to repeat

Adding Sound and Video

Figure 5 *Sounds in Timeline extend to end of movie*

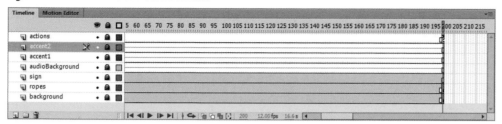

5. Drag the **playhead** to frame 200 on the Timeline, as shown in Figure 5.

   All the sounds now extend to the same ending frame, frame 200, which is the frame where the animation of the sign ends.

6. Test the movie and let it play until all the sounds stop.

   The sound files play simultaneously during the animation of the sign. You can tell the animation has ended when the words "Vectors Nightclub" stop flashing. The blue lines on the Timeline representing the sound waves end at frame 200, the last frame of the movie. However, because the sounds are event sounds, they continue to play even after the playhead reaches frame 200, each stopping only when it reaches the end of the number of repetitions you specified.

7. Close the Flash Player window.

8. Click the **Frame view button** 🔻📼 at the top right of the Timeline, then click **Normal** to display fewer frames.

9. Drag the **scroll bar** at the bottom of the Timeline to the left to display frame 1.

10. Save your work.

You set three sounds to repeat, which causes them to play simultaneously to the same ending frame, frame 200. However, because the sounds have a repeat number associated with them they continue to play past frame 200 until the repeat number has been executed.

Specify
SYNCHRONIZATION OPTIONS

What You'll Do

In this lesson, you will synchronize a stream sound with an animation, and you will set a button to play a sound in the Over state and stop playing the sound in the Up state.

Understanding Synchronization Options

As you've seen, Event is the default synchronization sound option in the Properties panel. You can also choose from one of three other synchronization options: Start, Stop, and Stream, as shown in Figure 6.

Understanding Stream Sounds

Unlike event sounds, stream sounds are tied to the Timeline and the number of frames on the Timeline. When you add a sound and set it to stream, Flash breaks the sound into individual sound clips and then associates each clip with a specific frame on the Timeline. The frame rate of your movie determines the number of clips that Flash creates. If the sound is longer than the number of frames on the Timeline, the sound still stops at the end of the movie.

One important use of stream sounds is to synchronize animation and audio, since the sounds can be better coordinated with the Timeline during both development and playback. If the computer playing a movie is slow, Flash will skip frames of an animation

to maintain synchronization with a stream sound. To avoid a jumbled or jerky playback, you should try to keep your animation simple when using a stream sound.

> **QUICK TIP**
>
> Once you set a sound to stream, you can preview the sound by pressing [Enter] (Win) or [return] (Mac) to play the movie on the Stage.

Understanding the Start and Stop Synchronization Options

A Start sound is similar to an event sound, but it will not play again if an instance of that sound is already playing. The Start option is often used with sounds associated with buttons or with movies that loop back to the beginning, in order to avoid overlapping sounds.

The Stop option lets you end an event sound at a specific keyframe. For example, you can start an event sound in frame 1 and then stop it playing in frame 40, even if the sound file is of a much longer duration. You insert a keyframe in the frame where you want to apply a Stop option, then you specify the name of the sound you want to stop in the Properties panel. If you want to stop multiple event sounds, you must insert a separate Stop option in a keyframe on each sound layer. Flash indicates a Stop option with a small square in the keyframe, as shown in Figure 7.

Figure 6 *The Sync sound options in the Properties panel*

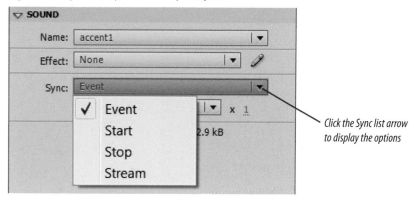

Click the Sync list arrow to display the options

Figure 7 *A Stop option on the Timeline and in the Properties panel*

Properties panel with Stop action

Timeline with stop action

The black rectangle indicates the end of the span of frames with the same content

The filled-in blue square above the keyframe indicates a Stop action

Sync set to Stop

Sound file Stop action will be applied to

Set synchronization to the Stream option

1. Verify that the nightclub.fla movie is open, click **Insert** on the menu bar, then click **New Symbol**.

2. Type **wordAnimation** in the Name text box, select Movie Clip for the Type, then click **OK**.

   The edit window for the wordAnimation movie clip symbol opens.

3. Rename Layer 1 as **audio**.

4. Insert a **keyframe** in frame 50.

5. Display the Actions panel, then type **stop();** as shown in Figure 8.

   Inserting a keyframe creates a movie clip of sufficient length (frames 1–50) for the sound to play, and adding a stop action to the keyframe stops the movie clip Timeline from repeating.

6. Close the Actions panel, click **frame 1** on the audio layer, click the **Name list arrow** in the SOUND area on the Properties panel, then click **bitmaps_free_vo**.

7. Click the **Sync list arrow**, click **Stream**, then compare your screen to Figure 9.

8. Press **[Enter]** (Win) or **[return]** (Mac), then listen to the audio.

   The sound file plays, "Tonight all bitmaps get in for free."

You created a movie clip, specified a stop action, added a sound, and set the synchronization of a sound to stream.

Figure 8 *Adding a stop action*

Be sure Script Assist is not active; you cannot type in the Script pane if Script Assist is active

Figure 9 *The streaming sound in the Timeline and Properties panel*

Audio layer

Sync option is set to Stream

Sound that will stream

Figure 10 *The Swap Symbol dialog box*

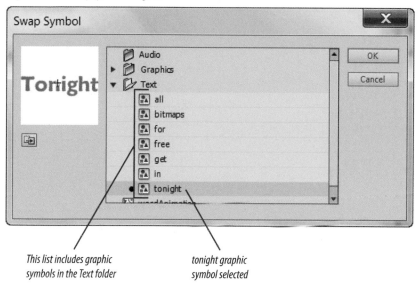

This list includes graphic
symbols in the Text folder

tonight graphic
symbol selected

Figure 11 *Selecting a symbol to swap*

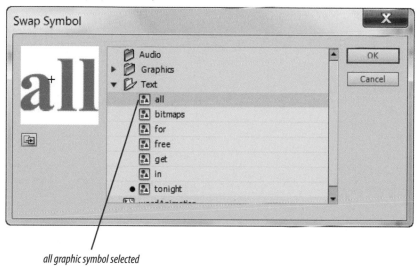

all graphic symbol selected

Synchronize a stream sound with an animation

1. Insert a **new layer** above the audio layer in the wordAnimation movie clip, then name it **text**.

   You will add text that synchronizes with a voice-over.

2. Insert a **keyframe** in frame 13 on the text layer, display the Library panel, expand the Text folder to view the text graphic symbols, then drag the **tonight graphic symbol** approximately to the middle of the Stage.

3. Change the view to **Fit in window**.

4. Display the Properties panel, change the X value to **–48.9**, change the Y value to **–8.5**, then press **[Enter]** (Win) or **[return]** (Mac).

   The word Tonight appears centered on the Stage.

5. Click the **Selection tool** ▶ on the Tools panel, insert a **keyframe** in frame 19 on the text layer, click the word **Tonight** on the Stage to select it, click the **Swap button** in the Properties panel to open the Swap Symbol dialog box as shown in Figure 10.

TIP The Swap Symbol dialog box lets you replace an object on the Stage with a different object, keeping all other properties the same, including any actions you have assigned to the original object.

6. Click the **all graphic symbol** in the Swap Symbol dialog box as shown in Figure 11, then click **OK**.

   Flash replaces the instance of the tonight graphic symbol with an instance of the all graphic symbol.

(continued)

7. Insert a **keyframe** in frame 23 on the text layer, click the word **all** on the Stage to select it, click the **Swap button**, click the **bitmaps graphic symbol** in the Swap Symbol dialog box, then click **OK**.

8. Insert a **keyframe** in frame 31 on the text layer, click the word **Bitmaps** on the Stage to select it, click the **Swap button**, click the **get graphic symbol** in the Swap Symbol dialog box, then click **OK**.

9. Insert a **keyframe** in frame 32 on the text layer, click the word **Get** on the Stage to select it, click the **Swap button**, click the **in graphic symbol** in the Swap Symbol dialog box, then click **OK**.

10. Insert a **keyframe** in frame 35 on the text layer, click the word **in** on the Stage to select it, click the **Swap button**, click the **for graphic symbol** in the Swap Symbol dialog box, then click **OK**.

11. Insert a **keyframe** in frame 37 on the text layer, click the word **for** on the Stage to select it, click the **Swap button**, click the **free graphic symbol** in the Swap Symbol dialog box, click **OK**, then compare your Timeline to Figure 12.

12. Click **1** on the Timeline, then press **[Enter]** (Win) or **[return]** (Mac), to view the words as they synchronize with sound.

13. Click **Scene 1** at the top left of the workspace to return to the main Timeline.

You created a text animation, then synchronized the appearance of each word in the animation with a voice-over saying the word.

Figure 12 *The wordAnimation movie clip symbol Timeline*

The keyframes containing graphic symbols on the text layer synchronize with the spoken words on the audio layer

Adding Sound and Video

Figure 13 *Movie clip symbol on the Stage*

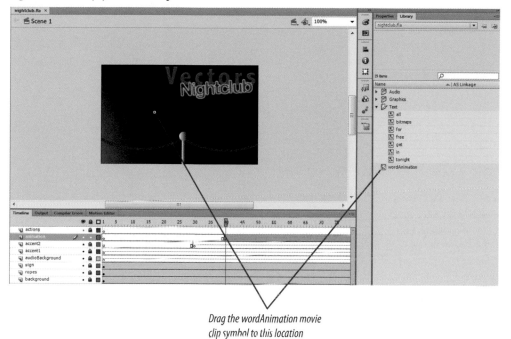

Drag the wordAnimation movie
clip symbol to this location

Add the synchronized animation to the Stage

1. Insert a **new layer** above the accent2 layer, then name it **animation**.

2. Insert a **keyframe** in frame 40 on the animation layer.

3. Display the Library panel, then drag the **wordAnimation movie clip symbol** from the Library panel to the left side of the Stage, as shown in Figure 13.

4. Test the movie.

   The words and stream sounds appear synchronized.

5. Close the Flash Player window.

6. Save your work.

7. Close the movie.

You added an animation synchronized with sound to the Stage.

Set synchronization to the Start option

1. Open fl11_2.fla, then save it as **superTips.fla**.

2. Display the Library panel, open the buttons folder, then double-click the **gel Right button** to display the edit window.

3. Drag the **playhead** through the Timeline.

    The gel Right button symbol currently has four layers, which create the visual effects of the button, such as the arrow changing color when the pointer rolls over it.

4. Insert a **new layer** above the button-arrow layer, name it **audio**, then insert a **keyframe** in the Over frame on the audio layer.

5. Display the Properties panel, click the **Name list arrow** in the SOUND area, then click **accent2**.

    Flash adds the sound file, as indicated by the straight line on the audio layer, which will start to play once you move the mouse pointer over the button, and it will continue to play even after you move off the button.

6. Click the **Sync list arrow**, click **Start**, then compare your screen to Figure 14.

7. Click **Scene 1** at the top left of the workspace to return to the main Timeline.

8. Test the movie, position the mouse pointer over a button, then move the mouse pointer off the button.

    The music starts playing when you hover over a button, and it continues even if you move the mouse pointer away from the button.

9. Close the Flash Player window.

You added sound to the Over state of a button.

Figure 14 *Inserting a Start option in the Over state of a button*

Sound added to
the Over frame

Sync sound option
set to Start

Adding Sound and Video

Figure 15 *Inserting a Stop option in the Up state of a button*

Blue shading indicates
Stop option in Up frame

Sync option set to Stop

Set synchronization to the Stop option

1. Display the Library panel, then double-click the **gel Right button** in the Library panel to open it in the edit window.

2. Click the **Up frame** on the audio layer.

3. Display the Properties panel, click the **Name list arrow** in the SOUND area, then click **accent2**.

4. Click the **Sync list arrow**, click **Stop**, then compare your screen to Figure 15.

5. Click **Scene 1** at the top left of the workspace to return to the main Timeline.

6. Test the movie.

7. Position the mouse pointer over a button, then move the mouse pointer off the button.

   Note: If you click a button, close the Flash Player window and repeat Steps 6 and 7.

   The music stops playing when you move the mouse pointer away from the button.

8. Close the Flash Player window.

9. Save your work, then close the file.

You directed a sound to stop when a button is in the Up state.

Modify SOUNDS

What You'll Do

 In this lesson, you will edit when one sound begins and create a custom sound effect for another sound.

Editing Sounds for Length

In most cases, you will want to edit and enhance sounds in a sound-editing program before you import them into Flash. However, Flash does include some basic editing features you can use on sounds you have already imported.

You can trim the length of a sound file using the Edit Envelope dialog box, shown in Figure 16. By moving the Time In and Time Out controls, you can set where the sound will start and stop playing. Adjusting the controls lets you delete unwanted sounds and remove silent sections at the start and end of sounds, which reduces the file size of the published application. You can preview the edits you make to a sound by clicking the Play button at the bottom-left corner of the Edit Envelope dialog box. Other buttons in this dialog box let you zoom the display of the sound in or out and set the units in the center of the dialog box to seconds or frames, which can help you determine the length of event sounds and make frame-by-frame adjustments to stream sounds.

Changing Sound Effects

Flash includes the following effects you can apply to sounds:

- Left Channel plays the sound only in the left channel or speaker.
- Right Channel plays the sound only in the right channel or speaker.
- Fade Left to Right gradually shifts the sound from the left channel to the right channel over the duration of the sound.
- Fade Right to Left gradually shifts the sound from the right channel to the left channel over the duration of the sound.
- Fade In increases the volume of the sound as it begins to play.
- Fade Out decreases the volume of the sound as it ends.

You can set these options either in the Properties panel of the frame to which you have added the sound, or in the Edit Envelope dialog box for the sound.

An additional option—Custom—lets you create your own volume variations over the duration of a sound. By clicking the channel sound line and then moving the envelope handle toward the top (to make the sound louder) or bottom (to make the sound quieter), you can specify up to eight locations where you want the sound to fade in, fade out, or play at less than 100% volume. For stereo sounds, you can set different custom envelopes for the two channels. Figure 17 shows a custom volume envelope.

Figure 16 *The Edit Envelope dialog box*

Envelope handle for left channel

Sound line for left channel

Envelope handle for right channel

Sound line for right channel

Play sound   Stop sound

Time In control

Time Out control

Units in frames

Zoom in   Zoom out   Display units in seconds

Display units in frames

Figure 17 *A custom volume envelope*

Sound decreases in volume here

Sound increases in volume here

Edit a sound using the Time In control

1. Open nightclub.fla, then save it as **vectors.fla**.

2. Insert a **new layer** above the animation layer, then name it **voice_intro**.

3. Click **frame 1** on the voice_intro layer, click the **Name list arrow** in the SOUND area on the Properties panel, click **hello_vo**, click the **Sync list arrow**, then click **Stream**.

4. Test the movie, then close the Flash Player window.

5. Click the **Edit sound envelope button** in the Properties panel, click the **Effect list arrow**, then click **Custom**.

   You will edit the sound file so it plays only the words "Vectors Nightclub."

6. Click the **Frames button** in the Edit Envelope dialog box to select it, if it is not already selected.

7. Click the **Zoom out button** repeatedly until you can see the entire sound with the frames, as shown in Figure 18.

8. Click the **Play sound button** in the Edit Envelope dialog box.

9. Click and drag the **Time In control** to frame 30, then compare your image to Figure 19.

10. Click the **Play sound button** in the Edit Envelope dialog box.

    Only the last two words of the sound, "Vectors Nightclub," should play. If necessary, adjust the Time In control.

11. Click **OK** to close the Edit Envelope window, then test the movie.

12. Close the Flash Player window.

You changed the point at which a sound begins playing.

Figure 18 *Zooming the hello_vo sound in the Edit Envelope dialog box*

Left channel envelope

Frame 50

Timeline In control

Each mark is 10 frames

Right channel envelope

Click Zoom out button until sound is visible

Figure 19 *Trimming the length of a sound*

The part of the sound with the white background will play

Drag the Time In control to frame 30, which is when only 4 tick marks are visible in the white area

Each mark is now 5 frames

Figure 20 *Decreasing the volume of both channels*

Drag the envelope handles one at a time to the lowest part of each envelope

Figure 21 *Increasing the volume of the left channel*

Drag the new handle to the highest point in the envelope

Right channel handle

Edit envelopes to create custom volume effects

1. Unlock the audioBackground layer, then click **frame 1** on the layer.

2. Click the **Effect list arrow** in the Properties panel, then click **Custom**.

   Note: You can also select Custom using the Effect list arrow in the Edit Envelope dialog box.

3. Click the **Zoom out button** 🔍 until the frames display 5, 10, 15, and 20, drag the **envelope handle** for the left channel and the **envelope handle** for the right channel down to the lowest point to decrease the sound in both channels, then compare your dialog box to Figure 20.

4. Click the **left channel sound line** on frame 20.

   New envelope handles appear on frame 20 for both the left and right channel envelope sound lines.

5. Drag the **new handle** on the left channel up to the highest point, as shown in Figure 21.

6. Drag the **new handle** on the right channel up to its highest point.

7. Click the **Play sound button** ▶ in the Edit Envelope dialog box.

   The music fades in gradually in both channels.

8. Click the **Stop sound button** ■, then click **OK** in the Edit Envelope dialog box.

9. Lock all the layers, save your work, then close the movie.

You established a fade in effect for a sound file by dragging envelope handles to create a custom envelope.

Use ActionScript
WITH SOUND

What You'll Do

In this lesson, you will use ActionScript to play and stop sounds.

Understanding ActionScript and Sound

ActionScript and sound are a powerful combination. You can use actions to set how and when sounds play in an application, and to start or stop sounds in response to user interactions. You can also use events to trigger an action such as navigating to a frame or scene based on when a sound ends.

To reference a sound from the Library panel in ActionScript, you must enable the Export for ActionScript option in the Linkage area of the Sound Properties dialog box, as shown in Figure 22. In the dialog box, you make sure a sound in the Library panel that is referenced in ActionScript will be exported for use by the ActionScript, and you also assign a class name which is the name you will use to identify the sound in ActionScript. You can make the class name the same name as the sound name, or you can assign a new class name. By default, Flash assigns the sound name as the class name.

A **sound object** is a way for ActionScript to recognize and control a sound. Creating a sound object is similar to creating an instance of a sound on the Stage, except it happens entirely in ActionScript. First, you create a variable and then you give it a Sound data type using the class name specified as the Linkage name in the Library panel. (*Note:* Flash knows that the class name represents the Sound class because it was specified in the Sound Properties dialog box.) Then you assign an instance of the sound class to the variable, as shown in Figure 23. This links the sound file to the sound object.

Starting and Stopping Sounds with ActionScript

Once you have created a sound object and attached a sound to it, you can begin controlling the sound using ActionScript.

The *Sound.play* method is used to start playing a sound. When using this action, you substitute the variable name of a sound object for "Sound." For example, if you have a sound object named "BackgroundMusic," you would include the action *BackgroundMusic.play* to play the sound. *Sound.play* includes optional parameters that let you specify a sound offset (for example, if you want to start playing a sound that is 15 seconds long at the 10-second mark) and also the number of times to repeat the sound.

The *stopAll* method of the *SoundMixer* class stops all sounds currently playing, regardless of whether the sound is an event or stream sound. It's a good idea to include a *stopAll* statement at the end of a movie, especially if the movie uses event sounds.

To stop a single sound you can use the *stop()*; method of the *SoundChannel* class. The ActionScript to assign a sound to a sound channel and to use the sound channel to control the playing of the sound follows.

var channel1:SoundChannel;

channel1 = safariSnd.play()

channel1.stop();

The first line of code creates a variable named channel1 with a SoundChannel data type. The second line of code plays a sound named safariSnd using the SoundChannel variable. The last line of code stops any sound assigned to the channel1 variable.

Figure 22 *The Sound Properties dialog box*

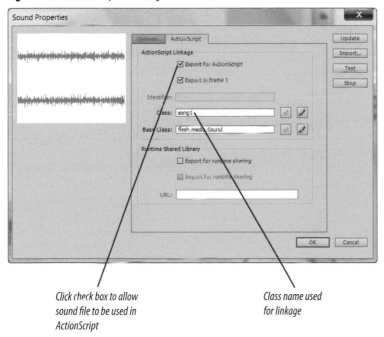

Click check box to allow sound file to be used in ActionScript

Class name used for linkage

Figure 23 *Example of ActionScript to create a sound object*

A variable (named snd) with a Sound data type; the Sound data type is identified by using the class name (song1) that was specified in the Linkage area of the Sound Properties dialog box

Assigning an instance of the Sound class to the variable

Link a sound file with a movie

1. Open fl11_3.fla, save it as **levels.fla**, then test the movie.

2. Click the **start button**, then click the **mute button**.

   The animation plays and stops, but there is no sound.

3. Close the Flash Player window.

4. Display the Library panel, right-click (Win) or [control]-click (Mac) the **song1 audio file**, then click **Properties** to open the Sound Properties dialog box.

5. Click the **ActionScript tab** to display the Linkage area if it is not already displayed, click the **Export for ActionScript check box** to select it as shown in Figure 24, then verify Export for runtime sharing is not checked.

6. Click **OK**.

   A message appears indicating that Flash will automatically generate a definition for the class.

7. Click **OK**.

8. Display the Library panel, then notice that song1 is displayed in the Linkage column.

You used the Sound Properties dialog box to create a linkage class and to ensure a sound will be exported for ActionScript.

Start a sound using ActionScript

1. Click **frame 1** on the actions layer, then open the Actions panel.

   The current ActionScript code causes the playhead to go to and play the frame labeled startBars when the start button is clicked. The startBars frame is the first frame in the colorBars movie clip, and it is the frame where the animation starts. Remember a movie clip has its own Timeline.

   (continued)

Figure 24 *Using the Sound Properties dialog box to enable the Export for ActionScript option*

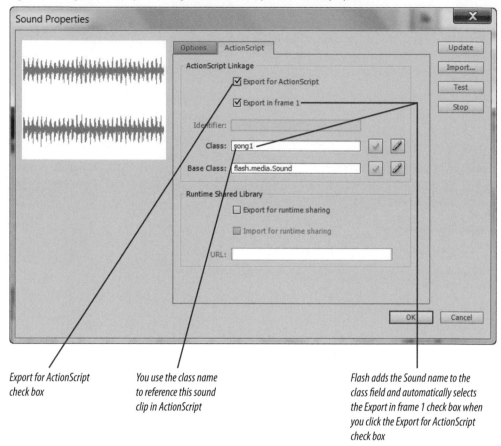

Export for ActionScript check box

You use the class name to reference this sound clip in ActionScript

Flash adds the Sound name to the class field and automatically selects the Export in frame 1 check box when you click the Export for ActionScript check box

Figure 25 *ActionScript to create a new sound object*

```
1  stop();
2  startBtn.addEventListener(MouseEvent.CLICK, playAn
3  function playAn(Event:MouseEvent)
4  {
5      colorBars.gotoAndPlay("startBars");
6      var snd:song1 = new song1();
7  }
8
9  muteBtn.addEventListener(MouseEvent.CLICK, stopAn)
10 function stopAn(Event:MouseEvent)
11 {
12     colorBars.gotoAndPlay("stopBars");
13 }
```

Creates a variable named snd and gives it a song1 data type (song1 is the new class you created), and creates an instance of the class

actions : 1

Line 6 of 13 Col 30

Figure 26 *ActionScript to stop all sounds when mute button is clicked*

Code to make SoundMixer class available

ActionScript code to play the song1 sound file

New code to type; stops all sound when mute button clicked

```
1  import flash.media.SoundMixer;
2  stop();
3  startBtn.addEventListener(MouseEvent.CLICK, playAn
4  function playAn(Event:MouseEvent)
5  {
6      colorBars.gotoAndPlay("startBars");
7      var snd:song1 = new song1();
8      snd.play();
9  }
10
11 muteBtn.addEventListener(MouseEvent.CLICK, stopAn)
12 function stopAn(Event:MouseEvent)
13 {
14     colorBars.gotoAndPlay("stopBars");
15     SoundMixer.stopAll();
16 }
```

actions : 1

Line 15 of 16 Col 23

2. Type the following line below the colorBars line in the playAn function, as shown in Figure 25:
   var snd:song1 = new song1();
3. Press **[Enter]** (Win) or **[return]** (Mac), then type the following line.
   snd.play();
   This line causes the snd variable containing the song1 instance to play.
4. Test the movie, click the **start button**, then click the **mute button**.
   The sound file plays when you click start; when you click mute, the color bars stop playing, but the sound file does not.
5. Close the Flash Player window.

You wrote the ActionScript for a button that creates a sound object, attaches a sound to the object, and plays the sound.

Stop sounds using ActionScript

1. Display the Actions panel.
2. Type the following above the stop(); line:
   import flash.media.SoundMixer;
   This line makes the SoundMixer class available.
3. Type the following line below the colorBars line in the stopAn function, as shown in Figure 26:
   SoundMixer.stopAll();
   This line stops all sounds currently playing.
4. Close the Actions panel, then test the movie.
5. Click the **start button**, click the **mute button**, then click the **start button** again.
   The music plays when you click start, then stops when you click mute.
6. Close the Flash Player window.
7. Save your work, then close the document.

You added actions to stop sounds from playing.

Work with VIDEO

What You'll Do

In this lesson, you will import an external video, set cue points, and use ActionScript to allow users to navigate through the video.

Understanding Loading an External Video

In a previous chapter, you learned how to convert a video clip to the FLV file format. Then you embedded the video into a Flash application. Embedded video becomes part of the SWF file similar to other objects, such as sound and graphics. Embedding video is best used with small video clips in order to keep the SWF file size small. Flash provides another process, progressive downloading, for including video in a Flash application. Progressive downloading uses a video Component and ActionScript to load an external FLV file into an SWF file, allowing the video to play when the SWF file is played. The FLV file resides outside the SWF file and can begin playing soon after the first part of the file has been downloaded. This keeps the SWF file smaller than when the video is embedded. The video Component is a built-in object, with playback controls, that displays the video on the Stage.

The process for loading an external video follows:

- Start a Flash ActionScript 3.0 document and select the layer and frame where the video will be displayed.

- Import the video using the Import Video option from the Import command on the File menu.
- Use the Browse button in the Import Video dialog box to navigate to the folder where the video is located and choose the video. This will tell Flash where the video file is located. (*Note*: If the video file is not an .flv file you will need to use the Adobe Media Encoder to convert it.)
- Check the Load external video with playback component option, and click the Next button.
- The Skinning screen appears, as shown in Figure 27. The video's skin determines the appearance and position of the video controls. You use this screen to choose how the FLVPlayback Component will appear and what controls (play, pause, rewind, and so on) will be available. You can choose from a variety of predefined skins or you can choose not to have any skin or controls at all. You can obtain skins from third party developers and even create your own custom skins. When you are finished making your choices on this screen, you click the Next button.
- The Finish Video Import screen appears, indicating the file and its location as well as

Adding Sound and Video

information on the video Component and its skin. When you are finished reviewing the screen, you click the Finish button.

The FLVPlayback Component is displayed on the Stage. You can use the controls to play the video without having to publish the movie. This allows you to preview the video and to add features to the video, such as cue points.

Introducing Cue Points

A relatively new and extremely useful feature of Flash video is the ability to add cue points directly in Flash using the Properties panel. Cue points are indicators on the video timeline that you specify. For example, you may have a video that runs for 20 seconds and 12 seconds into the video there is a scene that you want the user to be able to jump to. You can specify a

cue point at the 12 second mark, give it a name, and use the name in ActionScript. This process is similar to creating frame labels on the Flash Timeline that are used in ActionScript to have the playhead jump to the frame when a button is clicked. To create a cue point, you scrub the seek bar to locate the desired position for the cue point, then use the CUE POINTS area of the Properties panel to add a cue point and give it a name, as shown in Figure 28.

Using Cue Points in ActionScript

The FLVPlayback class allows you to load FLV video files. The findCuePoint method finds a cue point and the seek method seeks the time (in milliseconds) associated with the cue point. The code within a function called by a button click that displays the video at a cue point follows.

```
function goLion(Event:MouseEvent)
{
var myvid:Object = MyVideo.
    findCuePoint("lion");

MyVideo.seek(myvid.time);

}
```

The first highlighted line of code creates a variable named "myvid" with an Object data type. MyVideo is the instance name of the video FLVPlayback Component and "lion" is the name of the cue point. Thus, the "lion" cue point is assigned to the myvid object.

The second highlighted line of code takes the time in the myvid object (that is the cue point time) and seeks (jumps to) it in the MyVideo instance (the video on the Stage).

Figure 27 *The Skinning screen in the Import Video dialog box*

Preview of the selected skin   *Click to view Skin options*   *Click to view color palette of available control bar colors*

Figure 28 *Setting a cue point*

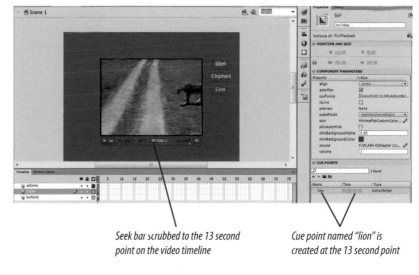

Seek bar scrubbed to the 13 second point on the video timeline   *Cue point named "lion" is created at the 13 second point*

Load an external video

1. Open fl11_4.fla, then save it as **safari.fla**.

2. Insert a **new layer**, name it **video**, then click **frame 1** of the video layer.

3. Click **File** on the menu bar, point to **Import**, then click **Import Video**.

    The Import Video dialog box opens with the Select Video screen active.

4. Click the **Browse** button, navigate to the folder where your data files are stored, click **safari.flv**, then click **Open**.

5. Verify Load external video with playback component is selected, as shown in Figure 29, then click the **Next button**.

6. Read the information on the Skinning screen, then click the **Next button**.

7. Read the information on the Finishing screen, then click the **Finish button**.

    The FLVPlayback Component appears, see Figure 30, centered on the Stage with the video loaded.

8. Click the center of the FLVPlayback Component on the Stage to select it, click the **play button** ▶ on the playback Component.

    The video plays in the FLVPlayback Component. Notice the video has three parts: the title, the elephant, and the lion.

9. Click the center of the FLVPlayback Component on the Stage to select it.

10. Display the Properties panel, then type **myVideo** for the instance name.

11. Save your work.

You imported a video that is loaded into an FLVPlayback Component, then you played the video on the Stage and in the Flash Player window.

Figure 29 *Completed Select Video screen*

Your file path may differ

Load external video option selected

Figure 30 *FLVPlayback Component on the Stage with video loaded*

Play button   Go to first frame button   Seek bar   Time Indicator   Volume indicator

Figure 31 *COMPONENT PARAMETERS area of the Properties panel*

Instance name of the FLVPlayback Component on the Stage

Properties of the FLVPlayback Component

Area to create and list cue points

Figure 32 *Adding a cue point named start*

Add ActionScript Cue Point button

Type name here

Time associated with cue point

Set cue points

1. Click the **Go to first frame button** ▐◀ on the FLVPlayback component to set the time indicator to 0.

2. Display the Library panel and notice the FLVPlayback Component is listed.

3. Display the Properties panel, expand the COMPONENT PARAMETERS, then view the properties for the FLVPlayback Component as shown in Figure 31.

   This area has information about the FLVPlayback Component, including the alignment on the Stage, the skin, and the source video file. The CUE POINTS area is used to add and display cue points. Currently, there are no cue points.

4. Click the **Add ActionScript Cue Point button** ➕

5. Click **Cue Point 1** in the Name column, then type **start**, as shown in Figure 32.

   This creates a cue point named start at the beginning of the video (00:00:00:00).

6. Drag the **seek bar** on the FLVPlayback Component until the elephant appears (approximately 1 second as indicated by the time listed on the FLVPlayback Component control bar.

7. Click the **Add ActionScript Cue Point button** ➕, click **Cue Point 2** in the Name column, then type **elephant**.

8. Drag the **seek bar** on the FLVPlayback Component until the road appears that the lion crosses (approximately 11 seconds).

9. Click the **Add ActionScript Cue Point button** ➕, click **Cue Point 3** in the Name column, type **lion**, then press **[Enter]** (Win) or **[return]** (Mac).

10. Save your work.

You created three cue points for the video.

Use ActionScript with cue points

1. Insert a **new layer**, name it **actions**, click **frame 1** on the actions layer, open the Actions panel, then type the following as a single line of code:

   lionBtn.addEventListener(MouseEvent. CLICK, goLion);

2. Press **[Enter]** (Win) or **[return]** (Mac) to move down a line, then type the following:

   function goLion(Event:MouseEvent)

3. Press **[Enter]** (Win) or **[return]** (Mac) to move down a line, type **{**, then press **[Enter]** (Win) or **[return]** (Mac).

4. Type the following between the curly braces as a single line of code:

   var myvidLion:Object = myVideo. findCuePoint("lion");

5. Press **[Enter]** (Win) or **[return]** (Mac) to move down a line, then type the following:

   myVideo.seek(myvidLion.time);

   This line takes the time in the myvidLion variable (that is the cue point time) and seeks (jumps to) it in the myVideo instance on the Stage.

6. Test the movie, click the **Lion button**, then close the Flash Player window.

7. Display the Actions panel, then use Figure 33 to complete the ActionScript code for the other two buttons.

8. Test the movie, click all the buttons, then close the Flash Player window.

9. Save your work.

You created a navigation process for the user by using cue points in ActionScript.

Figure 33 *The completed ActionScript for the cue points*

```
import flash.events.MouseEvent;

lionBtn.addEventListener(MouseEvent.CLICK, goLion);
function goLion(Event:MouseEvent)
{
    var myvidLion:Object = myVideo.findCuePoint("lion");
    myVideo.seek(myvidLion.time);
}
elephantBtn.addEventListener(MouseEvent.CLICK, goElephant);
function goElephant(Event:MouseEvent)
{
    var myvidElephant:Object = myVideo.findCuePoint("elephant");
    myVideo.seek(myvidElephant.time);
}
startBtn.addEventListener(MouseEvent.CLICK, goStart);
function goStart(Event:MouseEvent)
{
    var myvidStart:Object = myVideo.findCuePoint("start");
    myVideo.seek(myvidStart.time);
}
```

Creates an event listener that calls the goLion function when the lionBtn object is clicked

Creates a variable named myvidLion that has an Object data type and assigns the cue point named "lion" to the variable

Figure 34 *The completed ActionScript to play and stop a sound*

Creates a variable named safariSnd with a Sound data type; the Sound data type is identified by using the class name (safari) that was specified in the Linkage area of the Sound Properties dialog box

Creates a variable named channel1 with a SoundChannel data type

Plays the sound (safariSnd) using the SoundChannel channel1 variable

Code to stop a sound

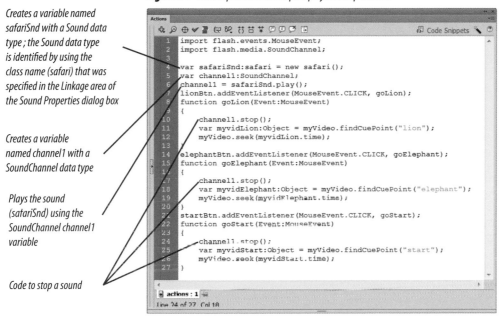

```
import flash.events.MouseEvent;
import flash.media.SoundChannel;

var safariSnd:safari = new safari();
var channel1:SoundChannel;
channel1 = safariSnd.play();
lionBtn.addEventListener(MouseEvent.CLICK, goLion);
function goLion(Event:MouseEvent)
{
    channel1.stop();
    var myvidLion:Object = myVideo.findCuePoint("lion");
    myVideo.seek(myvidLion.time);
}
elephantBtn.addEventListener(MouseEvent.CLICK, goElephant);
function goElephant(Event:MouseEvent)
{
    channel1.stop();
    var myvidElephant:Object = myVideo.findCuePoint("elephant");
    myVideo.seek(myvidElephant.time);
}
startBtn.addEventListener(MouseEvent.CLICK, goStart);
function goStart(Event:MouseEvent)
{
    channel1.stop();
    var myvidStart:Object = myVideo.findCuePoint("start");
    myVideo.seek(myvidStart.time);
}
```

How to Create a Sound Object

A **sound object** is a way for ActionScript to recognize and control a sound. Creating a sound object is similar to creating an instance of a sound on the Stage, except it happens entirely in ActionScript. Line 4 of Figure 34 shows the process. First, you create a variable (safariSnd) and then you give it a Sound data type using the class name specified as the Linkage name in the Library panel (safari). (*Note:* Flash knows that the class name represents the sound class because it was specified in the Sound Properties dialog box.) Then you assign an instance of the sound class to the variable (= new safari). This links the sound file (which is safari.wav as displayed in the Library panel) to the sound object.

Combine sound and video

1. Double-click the **Elephant button** on the Stage to open it in the edit window.

2. Click the **Down frame**, display the Properties panel, click the **Name list arrow** in the SOUND area, then click **elephant.wav**.

3. Verify Sync is set to Event, then click **Scene 1** to return to the main Timeline.

4. Repeat Steps 1-3 for the **Lion button** using the **lion.mp3** sound file.

5. Click **Scene 1** to return to the main Timeline, display the Library panel, then play the **safari.wav** sound.

6. Click **frame 1** on the actions layer, then open the Actions panel.

7. Type the following 3 lines of code above the lionBtn event listener line:

   var safariSnd:safari = new safari();

   var channel1:SoundChannel;

   channel1 = safariSnd.play();

8. Type the following within the function for each of the buttons as shown in Figure 34:

   channel1.stop();

   This stops the playing of the safariSnd sound file.

9. Test the movie, click each button, then close the Flash Player window.

10. Save your work, then close the document.

You added event sounds to buttons and used ActionScript to play and stop a sound.

Work with sound.

1. Start Flash, open fl11_5.fla, then save it as **skillsDemo11.fla**.
2. Move the playhead through the Timeline of the movie. Notice there are two screens that are partially completed. The callouts in Figure 35 indicate the types of changes you will make to the movie.
3. Insert a new layer above the buttons layer, then name it **ambient1**.
4. Click frame 1 on the ambient1 layer, then select the background_loop1 sound from the Name list in the SOUND area on the Properties panel, which adds it to frame 1 on the ambient1 layer.
5. Set the synchronization for the sound on the ambient1 layer to Event, then set the number of times to repeat to 10.
6. Insert a new layer above the ambient1 layer, then name it **ambient2**.
7. Click frame 1 on the ambient2 layer, then select the background_loop2 sound from the Name list in the SOUND area on the Properties panel, which adds it to frame 1 on the ambient2 layer.
8. Verify the synchronization for the sound on the ambient2 layer is set to Event, then set the number of times to repeat to 10.
9. Insert a new layer above the ambient2 layer, name it **song**, then add an instance of the song1 sound to frame 15 on the song layer. (*Hint*: Insert a keyframe in frame 15 before you add the sound.)
10. Verify the synchronization for the sound on the song layer is set to Event, then set the number of times to repeat to 10.
11. Save your work.

Specify synchronization options.

1. Create a new movie clip symbol named **animated_text**.
2. Name Layer 1 of the animated_text movie clip symbol **audio**, click frame 1 on the audio layer, select the music_selector_audio sound from the Name list in the SOUND area on the Properties panel, which adds it to frame 1 on the new layer, then set the synchronization to Stream. (*Note*: You will not see the audio file on the Stage or in the Timeline yet.)
3. Insert a keyframe in frame 75 on the audio layer, then add a stop action to the keyframe. (*Hint*: Adding a keyframe lets you see the full stream sound. Adding the stop action keeps the movie clip from repeating.)
4. Insert a new layer above the audio layer, name it **text**, insert a keyframe in frame 13 on the layer, then drag the Welcome graphic symbol from the Text folder in the Library panel to the Stage.

Figure 35 *Completed Skills Review*

Voice-over and background music begin when screen is displayed; voice-over is synchronized with words

5. Display the Properties panel, change the value in the X text box to −58.5 and the value in the Y text box to −16.7, then press [Enter] (Win) or [return] (Mac).
6. Insert a keyframe in frame 17 on the text layer, select the word "Welcome" on the Stage, click the Swap button on the Properties panel, click the "to" graphic symbol, then click OK.
7. Insert a keyframe in frame 20 on the text layer, select the word "to" on the Stage, click the Swap button on the Properties panel, click the "the" graphic symbol, then click OK.
8. Insert a keyframe in frame 23 on the text layer, select the word "the" on the Stage, click the Swap button on the Properties panel, click the "music" graphic symbol, then click OK.
9. Insert a keyframe in frame 27 on the text layer, select the word "Music" on the Stage, click the Swap button on the Properties panel, click the "selector" graphic symbol, then click OK.

Click the mute button to stop all sounds

Click the start over button to stop currently playing sounds and restart song from the beginning

Adding Sound and Video

10. Insert a blank keyframe in frame 45 on the text layer.
11. Click frame 1, then press [Enter] (Win) or [return] (Mac) to play the movie clip. (*Note*: The audio includes the word *online*, but no text appears on the Stage. It is difficult to hear the voice over the music. You will make adjustments to correct this later in this Skills Review.)
12. Return to the main Timeline.
13. Create a new layer above the song layer, name it **animation**, click frame 1 on the layer, then add an instance of the animated_text movie clip symbol from the Library panel to anywhere on the Stage.
14. Display the Properties panel for the movie clip symbol instance, change the value in the X text box to 120 and the value in the Y text box to 40, then press [Enter] (Win) or [return] (Mac).
15. Click frame 1 on the buttons layer, double-click the right arrow button on the Stage to open it in the edit window, add a layer, then name it **sound**.
16. Insert a keyframe in the Down frame on the sound layer, then use the Properties panel to add an instance of the Plastic Click sound to the frame and set the synchronization to Start.
17. Click the Up frame on the sound layer, add an instance of the Plastic Click sound to the frame, then set the Sync sound to Stop.
18. Return to the main Timeline, test the movie, then save your work.

Modify sounds.

1. Open the animated_text movie clip in the edit window, then click frame 1 on the audio layer.

2. Display the Properties panel, then click the Edit sound envelope button on the Properties panel.
3. Show units in Frames, then zoom out the view in the Edit Envelope dialog box until you can see the waveform for the entire sound, as shown in Figure 36.
4. Play the sound.
5. Drag the Time Out control (located on the Timeline at the end of the waveform, about frame 70) left to approximately frame 31, then play the sound in the Edit Envelope dialog box to verify that the word "online" does not play.
6. Click OK, then return to the main Timeline.

7. Click frame 1 on the ambient1 layer, then click the Edit sound envelope button on the Properties panel.
8. Play the sound, then stop the sound.
9. Reduce the volume by dragging the envelope handles in both channels so the sound line is just above the bottom of the envelope, as shown in Figure 37 on the next page.
10. Play the sound. (*Hint*: If you do not hear the sound, drag the envelope handles up slightly. Adjust the sound lines as needed until you hear the sound playing softly.)
11. Click OK to accept changes and close the Edit Envelope dialog box.

Figure 36 *The Edit Envelope dialog box*

Each hash mark indicates increments of 10 frames

Time Out control

12. Click frame 1 on the ambient2 layer, then click the Edit sound envelope button on the Properties panel.
13. Play the sound, then stop the sound.
14. Drag the envelope handles in both channels to just above the bottom of the envelope, then play the sound. (*Note*: Continue to adjust the handles and play the sound until you are satisfied that the sound plays softly in the background.)
15. Click OK to accept changes and close the Edit Envelope dialog box.
16. Save your work.

Use ActionScript with sound.

1. Select the song1 sound in the Sounds folder in the Library panel, then display the Sound Properties dialog box for the song1 sound symbol. (*Hint*: Click the Panel options list arrow in the Library panel title bar, then click Properties.)
2. Click the ActionScript tab, select the Export for ActionScript check box in the ActionScript Linkage area of the Sound Properties dialog box, then click OK twice.
3. Unlock the actions layer, click frame 14 on the actions layer, then open the Actions panel.
4. Add a SoundMixer.stopAll(); statement below the gotoAndPlay statement within the function that is called when the startBtn object is clicked.
5. Move down a line and create a variable with the name **snd** and a data type of song1 (the class name specified when you completed the Linkage area of the Sound Properties dialog box) and create an new instance of the sound object.
6. Move down a line and add a snd.play(); statement to play the sound object.
7. Use the Check syntax and Auto format buttons to check your code.

8. Click frame 30 on the actions layer, then display the Actions panel. (*Note*: There are two event listeners, one for the mute button and one for the start over button. Each function for the event listeners has a gotoAndPlay action that plays a section of the waveform (a movie clip) Timeline.)
9. Add a SoundMixer.stopAll(); statement below the gotoAndPlay ("mute"); statement and within the function braces.

10. Add the following two lines of code below the gotoAndPlay ("start"); statement:

    var snd:song1 = new song1();
    snd.play();

11. Use the Check syntax and Auto format buttons to check your code, then lock the actions layer.
12. Test the movie, then save your work.
13. Close the file, then exit Flash.

Figure 37 *Volume adjusted by changing the placement of the sound line in each channel*

Envelope handles

Work with video.

1. Create a new ActionScript 3.0 file, then save it as **skillsDemo11-video.fla**.
2. Rename Layer 1 as **buttons**.
3. Refer to Figure 38 as you set the Stage background color and create two buttons at the bottom right side of the Stage with labels Lake and Waterfall, then give them instance names of **lakeBtn** and **waterfallBtn**. (*Note*: You do not need to match the Figure exactly, use colors and shapes that appeal to you.)
4. Add a layer, name it **video**, then select frame 1.
5. Import wilderness.flv as an external video.
6. Give the FLVPlayback Component an instance name of **myVideo**.
7. Use the Properties panel to add cue points named **lake** and **waterfall** at the points they appear in the video.
8. Add a layer and name it **actions**.
9. Open the Actions panel, then complete the ActionScript to add an event listener for each button that calls a function (**goLake** and **goWaterfall**, respectively) to seek the location on the video corresponding to the respective cue points.
10. Test the movie, click the Waterfall button first, then click the Lake button.
11. Compare your screen to Figure 38, close the Flash Player window, then save your work.

Combine sound and video.

1. Import the waterfall.wav file from the drive and folder where your Data Files are stored to the Library, change the properties to Export for ActionScript, then specify **waterfall** for the class name.

2. Click frame 1 on the actions layer, then open the Actions panel.
3. Position the insertion point above the waterfallBtn event listener statement, then create a variable named **waterfallSnd** with a waterfall data type (waterfall is the Sound class you created in Step 1), and create a new instance of the sound.
4. Move down a line and create a variable named **channel1** with a SoundChannel data type.

Figure 38 *Completed Skills Review - Video*

5. Add a statement within the goWaterfall function that uses the channel1 variable to play waterfallSnd.
6. Add a statement as the first line of code within the goLake function that stops the sound being played in the channel1 variable.
7. Test the movie, click the Waterfall button first, then click the Lake button.
8. Close the Flash Player window, save your work , then close the Flash document.
9. Exit Flash.

Ultimate Tours would like you to create a banner promoting its "Japan on a Budget" tours. The graphics for the banner are complete; now you need to add music and a voice-over. Ultimate Tours would like a musical background to play continuously while the banner is displayed, and they have also provided a voice-over they would like to be synchronized with text on the screen, as shown in Figure 39. Finally, Ultimate Tours would like an accent sound to play when a visitor clicks the navigation button on the banner.

1. Open fl11_6.fla, then save the file as **ultimateTours11.fla**.
2. Test the movie and notice the text banner that appears across the screen against different background images.
3. Insert a new layer above the text animation layer, name it **audio**, use the Properties panel to add the sound named ultimate_background to frame 1 on the layer, then set synchronization to Event.
4. Set repetition for the sound to **2** to ensure the music plays the entire time the banner is displayed.
5. Display the Library panel, open the movie clips folder, then open the words movie clip symbol in the edit window.
6. Insert a new layer above the text layer, name it **audio**, use the Properties panel to add the ultimate_voiceover sound to the layer, then set synchronization to Stream.

7. Move the keyframes that control when each word of text appears on the Stage to synchronize with when the word is spoken in the voice-over. (*Hint*: Use the playhead to hear the stream sound and use the wave pattern as a clue to when a sound is played. Drag the keyframes on the text layer to create the synchronization effect. *Note*: To move a keyframe, click the keyframe you want to move to select it. Press and hold the mouse pointer on the keyframe until the pointer changes to 🖑. Use the 🖑 pointer to drag the keyframe to the new location, then release the mouse button.)

8. Return to the main Timeline, open the Library panel, open the buttons folder, then double-click the Circle with arrow button to open it in the edit window.
9. Edit the arrow button to play the Switch Small Plastic sound when a visitor clicks the button. (*Hint*: Be sure to specify the Sync setting as Event.)
10. Return to the main Timeline, test the movie, then close the Flash Player window.
11. Select frame 1 on the audio layer, then use the Edit Envelope dialog box to reduce the volume of the ultimate_background sound.
12. Test the movie, then close the Flash Player window.
13. Save your work.

Figure 39 *Sample completed Project Builder 1*

Voice-over is synchronized with appearance of words

Sound plays when visitor clicks button

You work for a software game company. Your newest game, "Match the Shapes," will be developed in Flash and marketed to preschoolers. You are working on a prototype of the game to show upper management. You have already completed the visual aspects of the prototype; now you must add sound.

1. Open interactive.fla, then save it as **game_prototype11.fla**. (*Note*: You created the interactive.fla file in Chapter 10.)
2. Test the movie to see how the matching game works, then close the Flash Player window.
3. Change the frame rate to 12 frames per second.
4. Import the following sound files to the Library. (*Hint*: Click File on the menu bar, point to Import, then click Import to Library).
   ambient_audio.wav
   welcome_voiceover.wav
   crowd_yes.wav

5. Create a new folder in the Library panel named **sounds**, then drag the files to the sounds folder in the Library panel.
6. Add a new layer above the cursor layer and name it **ambient**.
7. Using the Properties panel, add the ambient_audio sound as an event sound to frame 1 only. Repeat the sound **2** times to ensure it plays the entire time the visitor is viewing the screen. Set the Effect in the Properties panel to Fade in. Remove frame 2 on the ambient layer.
8. Test the movie, then close the Flash Player window.
9. Create a movie clip named **welcome** with three layers, each extending 50 frames. The first layer should have the welcome_voiceover audio clip as a stream sound. The second layer should have text blocks with the words **"Welcome to Match the Shapes"** that are synchronized with the welcome_voiceover audio clip. Each word in the phrase appears one at a time and stays on the Stage as new words are added to the phrase. You will need to add a keyframe in each frame where you want a new word to appear. After adding the keyframe, be sure to click the edit window to deselect any words that are selected in the window before adding the next word. Use two lines for the text and keep the total width below 200 pixels. (*Hint*: You can display the Rulers to check the width.) The third layer should have a stop action at the end of the movie clip.

10. Display the first screen and delete the "Welcome to Match the Shapes" heading and the Instructions text block from the backdrop layer, but be sure the rest of the elements, such as the orange background, stay. (*Hint*: You will need to unlock the layer before you can delete the text.)

11. Add a new layer above the backdrop layer and name it **welcome**. Then add the welcome movie clip to frame 1 of the layer. Remove frame 2 from the layer.

12. Add a statement to the Start button function that stops all sounds before the playhead jumps to frame 2.

13. Have a sound play each time the user correctly drags an object from the start bin to the drop bin. (*Note*: Be sure you set the audio file to Export to ActionScript and give the file a linkage name, such as goodSnd. Insert two lines of ActionScript in frame 2 on the actions layer that create a sound variable, then play an instance of the sound variable. Be sure to add these two lines of code above the reply.text = "Good Job!"; line for each shape.)

14. Test the movie, then close the Flash Player window.

15. Save your work and compare your screens to Figure 40, then close the document.

Figure 40 *Sample completed Project Builder 2*

Voice-over and text are synchronized

Sound plays when visitor successfully drops a shape into the correct position in the drop bin

Figure 41 shows a page from a website that might have been created using Flash. Study the figure and complete the following. For each question, indicate how you determined your answer.

1. Connect to the Internet, then go to *http://www.americaslibrary.gov/jp/bball/ jp_bball_early_2.html*.

2. Open a document in a word processor or open a new Flash document, save the file as **dpc11**, then answer the following questions. (*Hint*: Use the Text tool in Flash.)
   - Currently, this site does not have any sounds. How might sound be used to enhance this site?
   - If this site were created in Flash, how might you incorporate sounds?
   - What user controls might be appropriate when including sound In a Flash application and why?

Figure 41 *Design Project*

"First Nine of the Cincinnati (Red Stockings) Base Ball Club." Tuchfarber, Walkley & Moelmann, 1869. Prints and Photographs Division, featured in American Treasures of the Library of Congress. www.americaslibrary.gov/jp/bball/jp_bball_early_4.html

Union prisoners at Salisbury, North Carolina play baseball in 1863

How Baseball Began
When a group in New York City got together in 1845 to regulate the rules of baseball, they decided that to get a base runner out, an opposing player need only tag him with the ball instead of hitting him with it. From then on, baseball was played using a hard ball, and soon the game began to be played on a much larger scale. Baseball became an organized sport in the 1840s and 1850s. People even played it during the Civil War. In this print you can see Union soldiers playing a baseball game in a Confederate prisoner-of-war camp in North Carolina. Do you know where the first baseball teams were established?

 Click for enlargement and credits

 page 2 of 4

Library Of Congress | Legal Notices | Privacy | Site Map | Contact Us

In the previous chapter, you created a portfolio for your work samples and a password-protected, clients-only area. Now you will add sound to the Flash application. If you have access to sound-recording software, you can record your own voice-overs that describe the samples being shown. You can import sound clips or use the sounds found in the Sounds area of the Common Libraries panel. Alternatively, you can use the sample files provided in this chapter as musical background sounds. Finally, you will add a video to your portfolio.

Work with sound.

1. Open portfolio10.fla, then save it as **portfolio11.fla**.
2. Use sound files from the Common Libraries panel, or import to the Library panel sound files you have acquired or created, such as voice-overs describing your work, or import the following sound files from the drive and folder where your Data Files are stored:
   accent1.mp3
   accent2.mp3
   background.mp3
   portfolio_voiceover.wav
3. Add a new layer named **music**, then add a background sound that plays when the movie starts. Have the background sound stop when a user clicks any of the buttons.
4. Add a sound to each button on the home page that is heard when the button is clicked.
5. Use ActionScript to add a sound from the Library panel to the Games button on the flash samples page.

6. Add a sound when the user successfully enters the correct password and gains access to the clients area.
7. If you are using the musical backgrounds, experiment with adding effects to the sounds, such as fades or shifts between channels.
8. Test the movie.
9. Save your work, then compare your movie to Figure 42.

Work with video.

1. Save portfolio11.fla as **portfolio11-video.fla**.
2. Add a new layer to the Timeline, name it **video**, then insert a keyframe in frame 6 of the layer.

3. Add keyframes to frame 6 of the Navigation-buttons, Border, and actions layers.
4. Add a keyframe to frame 4 of the video layer, then add a button with a label **Video** to the Stage to the right of My Portfolio.
5. Name the instance of the button, **videoBtn**.
6. Click frame 4 on the actions layer and open the Actions panel.
7. Type the code to add an event listener to the videoBtn object so that a function named **goVideo** is called when the button is clicked.

Figure 42 *Sample completed Portfolio Project*

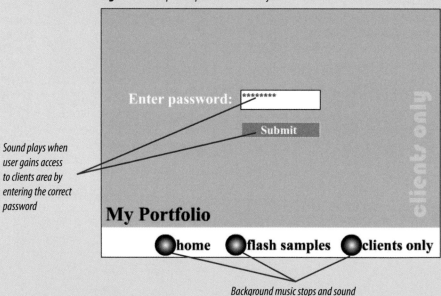

Sound plays when user gains access to clients area by entering the correct password

Background music stops and sound plays when buttons are clicked

Adding Sound and Video

8. Type the code to create the goVideo function that jumps the playhead to frame 6.

9. Click frame 6 on the video layer, then import the flv file named catFun.flv.

10. Play the video on the Stage, then create two cue points: one named **bag** that starts near the beginning of the video and the other named **string** that is near the middle of the video. Also create two buttons to the right of the FLVPlayer Component: one labeled **bag** and the other labeled **string**. Give the buttons instance names of **bagBtn** and **stringBtn** respectively.

11. Click frame 6 on the actions layer and open the Actions panel.

12. Type the code to add event listeners to the bagBtn and stringBtn objects that call functions when they are clicked.

13. Type the code for the function for each event listener that creates a variable as an object type and assigns an instance of the video with the findCuePoint method and cue point name. Then type the code to seek the time for each cue point of the video.

14. Test the movie, navigate to the clients area screen, enter the correct password (*Hint*: password), click submit, click the Video button, click the bag button, compare your screen to Figure 43, then click the string button.

15. Close the Flash Player window, then save your work.

16. Open the Library panel.

17. Open Sounds from the Common Libraries option of the Window menu.

18. Select Animal Mammal Carnivore Cat Domestic Cat Meow 02.mp3, then drag it to the Library panel.

19. Change the properties to Export for ActionScript with a class name of **cat**.

20. Display the Actions panel, then type the code at the top of the panel that creates a variable with a sound (cat) data type.

21. On the next line add a variable with a **SoundChannel** data type.

22. On the next line add the code to have the cat sound play.

23. Test the movie, navigate to the clients area screen, then click the Video button.

24. Close the Flash Player window, save your work, then close the document.

25. Exit Flash.

Figure 43 *Completed Portfolio - Video*

CHAPTER 12

DEVELOPING MOBILE APPLICATIONS

1. Use the Mobile Content Simulator
2. Repurpose mobile applications
3. Use the Accelerometer
4. Use touch and gesture events

CHAPTER 12 DEVELOPING MOBILE APPLICATIONS

Introduction

The enormous popularity of mobile devices (smartphones and tablets) has driven a need for the development of applications that run on these devices. These applications include games (such as the popular Angry Birds); educational applications (such as Curious George); informational applications (such as the National Park Service); and business applications (such as Photoshop Touch). Adobe has responded to this need by incorporating new features in its latest version of Flash that allow easy development and deployment of mobile applications. These features include Code Snippets for Touch and Gesture events, such as tap, zoom, and rotate; Apple iOS and Android publish settings; and templates for Android applications. In addition, Flash provides a feature that allows you to test a mobile application using the on-screen **Mobile Content Simulator**. The Simulator displays the application as it would appear on a mobile phone, and allows you to

use events and gestures such as touch, zoom, and swipe to see how the application reacts.

The actual development process for mobile applications is not significantly different from stand-alone and web applications. Both require identifying the purpose, target audience, treatment and specification, as covered in Chapter 1. However, there are considerations that need to be addressed when developing for mobile devices as opposed to desktop displays. These include screen size (smaller), processor speed (slower), and user interactivity (touch, swipe, pinch, and so on).

In Chapter 6 you learned about Adobe AIR and had a brief introduction to using Flash to develop mobile applications. You may want to review Chapter 6 Lessons 4 and 5, which covers the process for publishing Android applications and testing them on a smartphone connected to your computer. If you have access to an Android device you should use it to test the applications you develop in this chapter.

```
3
4    Multitouch.inputMode = MultitouchInputMode.GESTURE;
5
6    stage.addEventListener(TransformGestureEvent.GESTURE_SWIPE, fl_Swipe);
7
8    function fl_Swipe(event:TransformGestureEvent)
9    {
10       if (event.offsetX == 1)
11       {
12           prevFrame();
13       }
14       else if (event.offsetX == -1)
15       {
16           nextFrame();
17       }
18   }
19
```

Actions : 1

Document Settings

Dimensions: 230 px (width) x 250 px (height)

☑ Adjust 3D Perspective Angle to preserve current stage projection
☐ Scale content with stage

Ruler units: Pixels   Match: ○ Default ○ Contents ○ Printer

Background color:

Frame rate: 12.00

Auto-Save: ☐ 10 minutes

Make Default

New from Template

Category: Advertising, AIR for Android, Animation, Banners, Media Playback, Presentations, Sample Files

Templates: 800 x 480 Blank, Accelerometer, Fling, Options Menu, Swipe Gallery

Description: Android document with ball object reacting to accelerometer.

Use the Mobile Content SIMULATOR

What You'll Do

In this lesson, you will use the Mobile Content Simulator to test a mobile application

Understanding the Simulator

Throughout the development process it is important to test the application to determine if it is performing as planned. Ideally, developers would like to test their mobile application on all of the targeted devices. Given the number of mobile devices available today this is not feasible. Flash provides a new feature in CS6 called the Mobile Content Simulator. As the name implies, this feature allows you to simulate the use of an application on a mobile device, specifically a smartphone. The process is to begin developing an application and, when you are ready to test out a feature such as a pinch and zoom event, you select the Test movie option from the Control menu. Then you select in AIR Debug Launcher (Mobile). All mobile applications developed in Flash are AIR files, which means they do not need the Flash Player to run. So, the AIR Debug Launcher (Mobile) is used to test a mobile application.

After selecting in AIR Debug Launcher (Mobile), two windows appear as shown in Figure 1. The Simulator window is used to simulate the movement of the phone and the actions of the user. The figure shows the Simulator window with the Accelerometer area open. The AIR preview window, which is labeled "Device", displays the application as it will be seen on a user's phone as the Simulator is manipulated in the Simulator window. The Accelerometer area is used to simulate the user's movement of the phone. For example, if you have a ball on the screen and you tilt the phone graphic in the Simulator window, the ball in the AIR preview window will respond by moving around the screen.

Figure 2 shows the Simulator window with two other areas that can be displayed in the Simulator window: the Touch and Gesture area and the Geolocation area. The Touch and Gesture screen is used to simulate user actions such as drag, zoom, and swipe. The Geolocation

Developing Mobile Applications

screen is used to test an application that utilizes location data.

In addition to these features, other features available via the Simulator window are listed below:

- Menu, Back, Search buttons—used to simulate the operation of buttons found on Android phones; you must use ActionScript to simulate the operation of these buttons.

- Accelerometer Settings button—used to change the view of the phone
- Accelerometer X, Y, and Z settings—used to tilt and rotate the phone
- Touch and Gesture Touch layer check box—used to make the application respond to touch and gesture events
- Touch and Gesture Alpha setting—used to simulate various lighting conditions, such as the glare from the sun

- Touch and Gesture radio buttons—used to select the desired event to simulate
- Geolocation options—used to enter location data for the application

QUICK TIP

You use the "in Air Debug Launcher (Mobile)" specifically to test apps for smartphones. You use the 'in Air Debug Launcher (Desktop)" to test apps for other mobile devices, such as tablets.

Figure 1 *The Mobile Content Simulator window and the AIR preview window*

Simulator window with Accelerometer feature expanded

AIR preview window

Figure 2 *The Touch and Gesture and the Geolocation screens*

Simulator window with Touch and Gesture feature expanded

Simulator window with Geolocation feature expanded

The Output Panel

When you test an application using the Mobile Content Simulator, information about the file will be displayed in the Output panel. At a minimum, the size of the SWF file after it has been decompressed is displayed, as shown in Figure 3. Initially, when a Flash FLA file is published, it is compressed to reduce the file size. In order to be viewed it needs to be decompressed, a process that is transparent to the user. A common use for the Output panel is when a developer is debugging an application, that is, the programmer uses information in the Output panel to determine where in the ActionScript code a problem occurs and fixes it. One technique is to use a trace statement to display information as the application is running, such as:

```
trace("Seconds elapsed: " +
    fl_SecondsElapsed);
```

This line of code sends the number of seconds that have elapsed since the start of the application to the Output panel as shown in Figure 3.

The Output panel is grouped with the Timeline and Motion Editor panels.

Figure 3 *The Output panel*

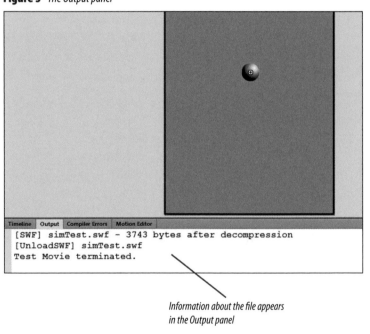

Information about the file appears in the Output panel

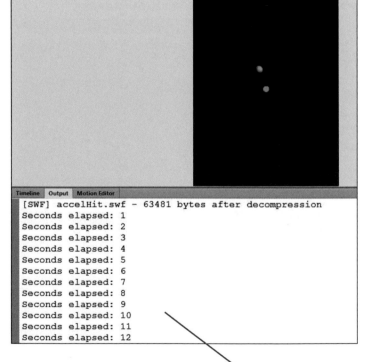

Trace statement in the ActionScript code causes information to be displayed in the Output panel as the application is running

Figure 4 *Inserting code using a Code Snippet*

Show code icon

Use the Simulator

1. Open fl12_01.fla, save it as **simTest.fla**, then change the view to **Fit in Window**.

   This is an Android application that has a background and a movie symbol object named grayBall_mc.

2. Click the **ball** on the Stage, then give the ball an instance name of **grayBall**.

3. Click **Window** on the menu bar, then click **Code Snippets**.

4. Click the **Mobile Touch Events expand icon** ▶, then click **Touch and Drag Event**.

5. Click the **Show code icon** {} as shown in Figure 4, then click the **Insert button**.

   Notice an Actions layer has been added. Frame 1 on the Actions layer contains the code for the Touch and Drag event.

6. Click the **ball** on the Stage, click **Window** on the menu bar, then click **Code Snippets**.

7. Click the **Mobile Actions expand icon** ▶, then click **Move with Accelerometer**.

8. Click the **Show code icon** {} , then click the **Insert button**.

   The code for the Move with Accelerometer event has been added to frame 1 on the Actions layer.

   (continued)

9. Click **Control** on the menu bar, point to **Test Movie**, then click **in AIR Debug Launcher (Mobile)**.

   The Mobile Content Simulator window appears along with the AIR preview window, which is labeled Device.

10. Click the **Settings button** ⚙ in the Simulator window, then click **Flat**.

    Notice you only see the end of the device in the Simulator window, as if the user is looking at the top of the device.

11. Change the **X** setting to -90 as shown in Figure 5, then press **[Enter]** (Win) or **[return]** (Mac).

    This changes the orientation of the simulated device to show it as though the user is holding it face up.

12. Point to the center of the device as shown in Figure 6, hold down the mouse button, then rotate the mouse in a small circular motion to simulate moving the device.

    Notice how the ball in the AIR preview window moves as the device in the Simulator window moves. Notice also how the x, y, and z axes in the Simulator window also move as the device is rotated.

    Note: If the ball moves off the screen, close the AIR preview window and repeat, Steps 9–12. The ActionScript for the Move with Accelerometer does not have code to prevent the ball from leaving the screen.

    (continued)

Figure 5 *Changing the Simulator settings for the Accelerometer*

Settings button

Type -90 here, type the minus symbol before the value

Figure 6 *Positioning the pointer on the device*

Point here

These lines represent the x, y, and z axes orientation for the device

Figure 7 *Setting the width and height of the symbol*

Touch and
Gesture
area active

Alpha slider

Symbol
width and
height
settings

Symbol
resized

13. Click **TOUCH AND GESTURE** in the Simulator window, then click the **Touch layer check box** to select it.

14. Change the alpha setting to **10%**, then change it to **60%** and notice how the AIR preview window changes.

15. Verify the Click and drag radio button is selected, then click and drag the **ball** in the AIR preview window.

    Note: The touch symbol simulates the user touching the screen.

16. Change the touch symbol width and height to **40**, point to the **ball** as shown in Figure 7, then click and drag the **ball** in the AIR preview window.

17. Close the AIR preview window to return to the Flash workspace.

18. Save your work, then close the application.

You used the Code Snippets panel to add mobile events to an application and tested the application using the Mobile Content Simulator.

Repurpose Mobile
APPLICATIONS

What You'll Do

In this lesson, you will repurpose an application for a
mobile phone and a tablet

Repurposing Mobile Applications

A goal of mobile developers is to be able to
create one application and use it for a variety of
phones and tablets. This reduces development
time and allows assets, such as photos,
graphics and text to be reused. Ultimately,
this lowers overall development costs.
Mobile devices have significant variation in
screen sizes, as shown in Table 1. Therefore,
repurposing an application often requires
resizing the objects on the Stage. A new feature
of Flash allows objects to be resized as the
dimensions of the Stage are changed. Figure 8
shows the Document Settings dialog box that
can be used to change the Stage dimensions.
Notice the Scale content with stage option. By
selecting this option, the size of the objects
on the Stage will be changed automatically
to correspond with the change in the Stage
dimensions. Figure 9 shows an application in
which the Stage size has been reduced. Notice
how the objects have been resized.

Changing the size of the objects may not be
enough to optimize the application for playback

TABLE 1: SCREEN SIZES OF VARIOUS PHONE AND TABLET MOBILE DEVICES		
Phone	**Screen H × W (pixels)**	**Operating System**
Apple iPhone	960 × 640	iOS
Motorola Atrix	960 × 540	Android
HTC Thunderbolt	480 × 800	Android
T-Mobile G2x	400 × 800	Android
Tablet		
Samsung Galaxy	1280 × 800	Android
Apple iPad	2048 × 1536	iOS
Amazon Kindle Fire	1024 × 600	Android
Motorola XOOM	1280 × 800	Android

© Cengage Learning 2013

on a specific device. Selected objects may need additional resizing as well as repositioning. For example, an application that is designed to be displayed in portrait orientation on a smartphone may not appear as intended on a tablet device without rearranging the objects for display in landscape orientation. In addition, buttons that are a part of a phone application may need to have their hit area enlarged to make it easier for users to tap them.

While applications can be made scalable, developers need to set an initial target including the device type and operating system. The most popular smartphones run the Android operating system or the Apple iOS operating system used on the iPhone. Fortunately, the development and deployment process for these two types of devices are similar.

Figure 8 *The Scale content with stage option*

Select this option to have objects on the Stage resize as the Stage dimensions are changed

Figure 9 *Stage objects scaled as the Stage size is changed*

Resize an application for a smartphone

1. Open fl12_02, then save it as **phoneF.fla**.

   The Stage dimensions are width: 230 px and height: 250 px.

2. Test the movie, then close the Flash Player window.

3. Click **Modify** on the menu bar, then click **Document**.

4. Change the dimensions to width: **480** and height: **800**, a common size for smartphones.

5. Click the **Scale content with stage check box** to select the option, then click **OK**.

6. Change the view to **Fit in Window**, then test the movie.

7. Click each button to view the resized objects, then close the Flash Player window.

8. Click **File** on the menu bar, then click **Publish Settings** to display the Publish Settings dialog box.

9. Click the **Publish Target list arrow** ▼ as shown in Figure 10, click **AIR 3.2 for Android**, then click **OK**.

10. Click **Control** on the menu bar, point to **Test Movie**, click **in AIR Debug Launcher (Mobile)**, then click the buttons to play the application.

    Notice the blank space that appears at the bottom of the smartphone screen. This area is reserved for the phone's menu buttons

11. Close the AIR preview window, then save your work.

You resized an application specifying that the content be scaled.

Figure 10 *The Publish Target options*

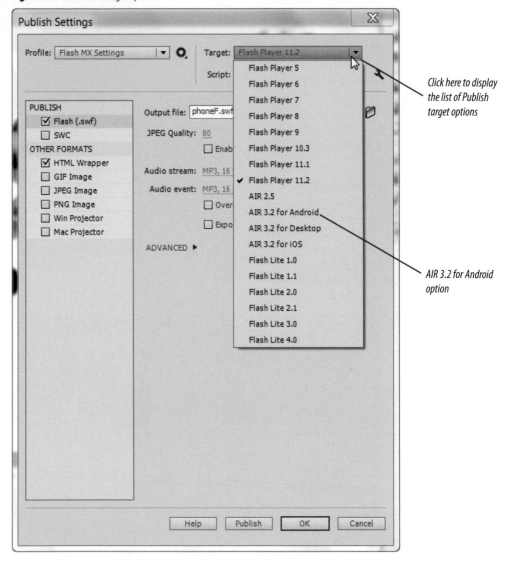

Click here to display the list of Publish target options

AIR 3.2 for Android option

Figure 11 *Repositioning the buttons*

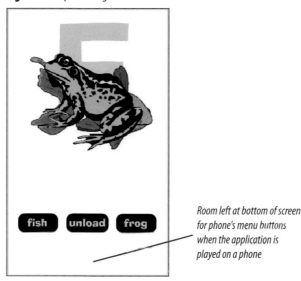

Room left at bottom of screen
for phone's menu buttons
when the application is
played on a phone

Figure 12 *Changing the hit area*

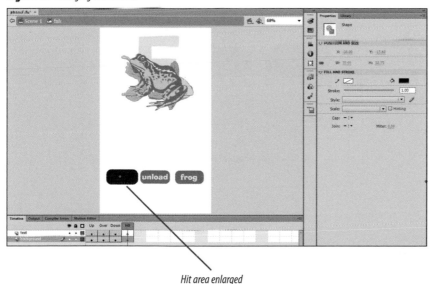

Hit area enlarged
and repositioned

Alter objects and reposition them

1. **Unlock** all layers.
2. Click a blank area of the Stage to deselect all the objects.
3. Click the **Selection tool** ➤ on the tool panel, click the **fish button**, press **[Shift]**, then click the **unload** and **frog buttons** to select all three buttons.
4. Reposition the buttons near the bottom of the Stage (while still leaving space for the phone's menu buttons), as shown in Figure 11.
5. Double-click the **fish button** to display it in the edit window.
6. Click the **Hit frame** of the background layer, then click the **black oval** that covers the button.
7. Display the Properties panel, verify the lock icon ☜ is locked, resize the oval to a width of **70**, then use the arrow keys to position the black oval over the button, as shown in Figure 12.
8. Click **Scene 1** to return to the main Timeline.
9. Repeat Steps 5 through 8 to enlarge the hit area for the unload and frog buttons.

(continued)

10. Click the **F** on the Stage.

11. Display the Properties panel, then verify the lock icon 🔗 in the POSITION AND SIZE area is locked.

12. Change the width to **400**.

13. Verify F is selected, click the **Style list arrow** ▼ in the COLOR EFFECT area of the Properties panel, then click **Alpha**.

14. Change the Alpha setting to **50%**.

15. Reposition the letter F, the fish, and the frog to resemble Figure 13.

16. Click **Control** on the menu bar, point to **Test Movie**, then click **in AIR Debug Launcher (Mobile)**.

17. Click each button to play the application.

18. Close the AIR preview window.

19. Save your work.

You resized and repositioned selected objects to make the application more appropriate for a smartphone.

Figure 13 *Repositioning the objects on the Stage*

Developing Mobile Applications

Figure 14 *Repositioning the objects*

Resize an application for a tablet device

1. Save the application as **tabletF.fla**.
2. Click **Modify** on the menu bar, then click **Document**.
3. Change the width to **1280**, click the **Scale content with stage check box** to select it, then click **OK**.
4. Change the view to **Fit in Window**.
5. Change the Stage background color to **#009900**.
6. Click the letter **F**, then display the Properties panel.

   Notice the width of the letter F has increased from 400.
7. Reposition the three buttons, the fish, and frog to the approximate location shown in Figure 14.
8. Click **Control** on the menu bar, point to **Test Movie**, then click **in AIR Debug Launcher (Desktop)**.

   Note: Because you are testing for a tablet and not a phone, you use the Desktop setting and not the Simulator window.
9. Click the buttons, then close the AIR preview window.
10. Save your work.
11. Close the application.

You changed the dimensions of an application to accommodate a tablet device and resized and repositioned selected objects.

Use the
ACCELEROMETER

What You'll Do

In this lesson, you will use the accelerometer feature of a mobile device

Understanding the Accelerometer

When playing games on a mobile device one of the most often used features is having objects move in response to the movement of the device. That is, the user tilts or rotates the device and an object(s) moves. This could be as simple as a ball rolling around the screen or as complex as an avatar moving through a virtual environment. The device's built-in accelerometer controls this movement and ActionScript code in Flash controls the accelerometer. That is, ActionScript code is used to access the device's accelerometer and determine such things as the sensitivity of the object to the movement of the device and whether or not the object remains on the screen. Figure 15 shows the code to access the accelerometer which is explained in the following.

```
var fl_Accel:Accelerometer = new
    Accelerometer();
```

This line of code creates a variable named fl_Accel with a data type of Accelerometer.

```
fl_Accel.addEventListener(Accelerometer
    Event.UPDATE, moveBall);
```

This line of code creates an Accelerometer event listener that listens for movement in the device (denoted by the word UPDATE) and calls the moveBall function.

```
function moveBall(event:Accelerometer
    Event)
```

This line of code identifies the moveBall function.

```
ball.x −= event.accelerationX;
```

```
ball.y += event.accelerationY;
```

The first line of the code above adjusts the x position of the object with the instance name ball according to the movement of the device along its x axis. The second line of code adjusts the y position of the object with the instance name ball according to the movement of the device along its y axis.

You can increase the sensitivity of the object by increasing the amount of movement of the object in relation to the movement of the device. This is done by multiplying the event.accelerationX and event.accelerationY by some number. For example, the lines of code listed next increase the x and y movement of the ball by a factor of 30 in relation to the movement of the device.

ball.y −= event.accelerationX*30;

ball.y += event.accelerationY*30;

Keeping the Object on the Screen

In most cases you want the object to remain on the Stage. If an object moves off the screen it may be difficult to have it reappear. The code that keeps the ball from moving off the Stage is shown in Figure 16 and discussed next. The screen size for this sample discussion is 480 wide and 800 high, a standard size for Android smartphones.

if (ball.x > (480 - ball.width / 2))

This line of code checks to see if the x position of the ball is greater than the width of the screen (480) minus the width of the ball divided by 2. This assumes the registration point (the point that is used to align the x and y coordinates) is in the middle of the ball. Thus, if the ball reaches the right edge of the screen the following code is executed:

{

ball.x = 480 - ball.width / 2;

}

This line of code sets the x position of the ball to 480 minus the width of the ball divided by 2. That is, it sets the right edge of the ball to the right edge of the screen.

Figure 15 *Code to access the device's accelerometer*

```
4
5
6    var fl_Accel:Accelerometer = new Accelerometer();
7    fl_Accel.addEventListener(AccelerometerEvent.UPDATE, moveBall);
8
9    function moveBall(event:AccelerometerEvent)
10   {
11       ball.x -= event.accelerationX;
12       ball.y += event.accelerationY;
13   }
14
15
16
17
```

Actions : 1

Line 17 of 19 Col 1

Figure 16 *Code to keep the object on the screen*

```
21
22       if (ball.x > (480 - ball.width / 2))
23       {
24           ball.x = 480 - ball.width / 2;
25       }
26       if (ball.x < (0 + ball.width / 2))
27       {
28           ball.x = 0 + ball.width / 2;
29       }
30       if (ball.y > (800 - ball.width / 2))
31       {
32           ball.y = 800 - ball.width / 2;
33       }
34       if (ball.y < (0 + ball.width / 2))
35       {
36           ball.y = 0 + ball.width / 2;
37       }
38
```

Actions : 1

Line 37 of 82 Col 3

```
if (ball.x < (0 + ball.width / 2))

{

ball.x = 0 + ball.width / 2;

}

if (ball.y > (800 - ball.width / 2))

{

    ball.y = 800 - ball.width / 2;

}

if (ball.y < (0 + ball.width / 2))

{

    ball.y = 0 + ball.width / 2;

}
```

These last twelve lines of the code keep the ball within the boundary of each side of the screen. Each of the *if* statements checks the location of the ball based on its x or y coordinate and adjusts the location of the ball if necessary.

Using Templates

Flash provides several templates for developing mobile applications for Android devices. Figure 17 shows the New from Template dialog box with AIR for Android on the Templates tab selected. Selecting a template displays a preview screen and a description. In this case the Accelerometer template is selected displaying a green ball on a black grid background and the description: "Android document with ball object reacting to accelerometer." Templates are useful for a number of reasons. First, they help in learning what a specific feature does, e.g., "What does the Accelerometer do?" Second, they help in learning how to incorporate a specific feature into an application by using the ActionScript code that is provided. Third, they can be used in prototyping to quickly explore an idea without costly in-depth development time. Fourth, they can be used as a starting place in creating an application by swapping and rearranging objects and enhancing the ActionScript code.

Figure 17 *The New from Template dialog box*

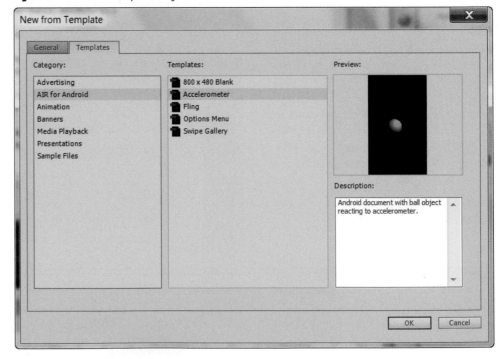

Using a Timer

A timer is a useful feature that is often used in games as the user competes to get the fastest time while completing an activity. Flash provides a code snippet that can be used to keep track of elapsed time. Because the elapsed time is tracked in a variable, the time is available to be used in other code such as displaying it in a text box on the screen. The code for creating a timer is shown in Figure 18 and explained next.

var fl_TimerInstance:Timer = new Timer(1000, 30);

This line of code creates a variable named fl_TimerInstance and gives it a Timer data type. The 1000 specifies 1000 milliseconds (1 second) as the time interval at which the timer is triggered. The 30 specifies the number of times the timer is triggered. Thus, the timer is triggered every second for 30 seconds. Both of these numbers can be changed.

fl_TimerInstance.addEventListener (TimerEvent.TIMER, fl_TimerHandler);

This line of code creates an instance of the timer, adds an event listener that listens for the start of the timer and a function (fl_TimerHandler) to call when the timer starts.

fl_TimerInstance.start();

This line of code starts the instance of the timer.

var fl_SecondsElapsed:Number = 1;

This line of code creates a variable named fl_SecondsElaspsed, gives it a Number data type, and assigns an initial value of 1 to the variable.

function fl_TimerHandler (event:TimerEvent):void

{

   trace("Seconds elapsed: " + fl_SecondsElapsed);

   fl_SecondsElapsed++;

}

These last five lines of code identify the fl_TimerHandler function. When the function is called, which is continuously, a trace statement displays the elapsed seconds in the Output panel of the Timeline/ Output/Motion Editor panel set. This can be used for debugging the application. Also, the variable holding the elapsed seconds, fl_SecondsElapsed, is increased by one.

Figure 18 *Code to create a timer*

```
var fl_TimerInstance:Timer = new Timer(1000, 30);
fl_TimerInstance.addEventListener(TimerEvent.TIMER, fl_TimerHandler);
fl_TimerInstance.start();

var fl_SecondsElapsed:Number = 1;

function fl_TimerHandler(event:TimerEvent):void
{
    trace("Seconds elapsed: " + fl_SecondsElapsed);
    fl_SecondsElapsed++;
}
```

Use the Accelerometer

1. Click **File** on the menu bar, click **New**, then click the **Templates** tab.

2. Click **Air for Android** in the left pane of the New from Template dialog box, click **Accelerometer** in the right pane, then view the Preview window and read the description.

3. Click **OK**.

4. Change the view to **Fit in Window**.

5. Save the movie as **accel.fla**.

6. Click **Control** on the menu bar, point to **Test Movie**, then click in **AIR Debug Launcher (Mobile)**.

7. Click the **Settings button** 🔧 in the Simulator window, then click **Flat**.

8. Change the **X** setting to **-90** as shown in Figure 19, then press **[Enter]** (Win) or **[return]** (Mac).

9. Point to the center of the device in the Simulator window, hold down the mouse button, then rotate the **mouse** in a small circular motion to simulate moving the device.

    Notice how the ball in the AIR preview window moves as the device in the Simulator window moves and how it never leaves the screen.

TIP You can also place the pointers on other areas of the device in the Simulator window to manipulate it.

10. Close the AIR preview window.

    This closes the Simulator window and displays the Flash workspace.

You used the Mobile Content Simulator to test a Flash Accelerator template.

Figure 19 *Changing the X setting*

X value changed to -90

Figure 20 *Displaying the open files*

Click here to view the open FLA files

List of files open in Flash

Tabs show files open in Flash

Swap objects

1. Save the file as **accelDragonfly.fla**.

2. Change the frame rate to **30**.

3. Open **dragonfly-bkgrnd.fla** from the location where you store your data files.

4. Display **accelDragonFly.fla**, click frame **1** on the Ball layer.

5. Display the Library panel, then click the **Open files list arrow** ▼ below the Library panel tab to display the files currently open in Flash, as shown in Figure 20.

6. Click **dragonfly-bkgrnd.fla** to display the Library contents for this file.

7. Drag the **animated dfly** movie clip to the Stage.

   This places the animated dfly movie clip and its associated graphics and symbols into the AccelDragonfly.fla library.

8. Click the **Open files list arrow** ▼ below the Library panel tab, then click **accelDragonfly.fla** to display the contents of its library.

9. Click the **Selection tool** ▶ on the Tools panel, click the **dfly movie clip** on the Stage to select it, then press **[Delete]** to remove it from the Stage.

10. Click the **green ball** to select it, click **Modify** on the menu bar, point to **Symbol**, then click **Swap Symbol**.

    The Swap Symbol dialog box appears.

11. Click **animated dfly**, then click **OK**.

    The dfly movie clip symbol replaces the green ball movie clip symbol.

(continued)

12. Click **Control** on the menu bar, point to **Test Movie**, then click **in AIR Debug Launcher (Mobile)**.

13. Click the **Settings button** ⚙ in the Simulator window, then click **Flat**.

14. Change the **X** setting **-90**.

15. Point to the lower left of the device, hold down the mouse button, then **rotate** the mouse in a small circular motion to simulate moving the device.

16. Close the AIR preview window.

17. Display the **Timeline panel**, unlock the **Background layer**, click **frame 1** on the Background layer, then press **[Delete]** to delete the background object.

    The Stage is black.

18. Display the Library panel, click the **Open files list arrow** ▼ below the Library panel tab to display the open files, then click **dragonfly-bkgrnd.fla** to display the Library contents for this file.

19. Verify frame 1 on the Background layer is selected, then drag the **trees movie clip** to the Stage and center it, as shown in Figure 21.

20. Test the movie using the in AIR Debug Launcher (Mobile) option, change the settings to flat and -90, then move the device to have the wings circle the bottom tree and return to the top tree.

21. Close the AIR preview window.

22. Save your work, then close both applications.

You swapped symbols, changed the background of a movie, and tested it using the Mobile Content Simulator.

Figure 21 *Centering the trees movie clip on the Stage*

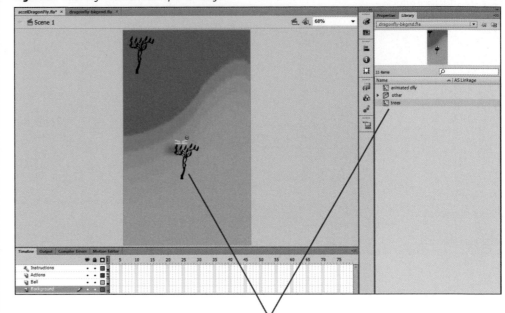

trees movie clip dragged from the Library panel and centered on the Stage

Figure 22 *Positioning the circle*

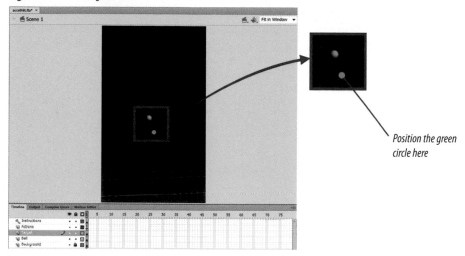

Position the green
circle here

Figure 23 *The completed text box*

The outline of the text
box will not appear
when the text box is
not selected.

Add a target to an application

1. Open a new Air for Android Accelerometer template file, save is as **accelHit.fla.**

2. Change the view to **Fit in Window**.

3. Click the **ball** on the Stage to select it, then use the Properties panel to change the ball size to **27x27**.

4. Insert a new layer above the Ball layer, then name it **Target**.

5. Click **frame 1** on the Target layer, then draw a circle on the Stage with size: **20 × 20**, fill color: **00AA00**, and stroke set to **No Stroke**.

6. Position the circle as shown in Figure 22, then change the object to a movie clip symbol with the name **target_mc**.

7. Verify the circle is selected, then use the Properties panel to give it an instance name of **theTarget**.

8. Insert a layer above the Target layer, then name it **Text box**.

9. Click **frame 1** of the **Text box layer**, select the Text tool, then use the Properties panel to change the Text type to **Dynamic Text** with the following: Character Family: **Planet Benson 2** (or a font of your choice); Size: **40**; Color: **CCCCCC**; Paragraph Format: **Align center**; Behavior: **Multiline**.

10. Draw the text box near the top of the Stage, change the dimensions to Width: **440** and Height: **66**, center the text box across the Stage, then give it an instance name of **textb**. Your screen should resemble Figure 23.

TIP Be sure to break the lock in the POSITION AND SIZE area before setting the width and height.

11. Lock all layers, then save your work.

You created an object to be used as a target and added a dynamic text box.

Detect a collision and provide feedback

1. Change the frame rate to **20**.

2. Click **frame 1** on the Actions layer, then open the Actions panel.

3. Click the **Auto format icon** ☰ at the top of the Actions panel.

4. Type the following between the last two braces, as shown in Figure 24.

   if (ball.hitTestObject (theTarget))

   {

         textb.text = "a Hit";

   }

   This code checks to see if the ball collides with the green dot (instance name of theTarget) and, if so, the words "a Hit" are displayed in the dynamic text box named textb.

5. Click the **Auto format icon** ☰ .

6. Test the application using the Mobile Content Simulator and change the settings to flat and -90.

TIP Change the settings to flat and -90 each time you are asked to test the application in the Mobile Content Simulator in this chapter.

7. Manipulate the Simulator in the Simulator window so that the ball in the AIR preview window collides with the green dot and notice the words "a Hit" are displayed in the dynamic text box.

8. Close the AIR preview window, then save your work.

You added ActionScript code to cause text to output when one object collides with another.

Figure 24 *The code to detect a collision and provide feedback*

Actions

```
21          }
22          if (ball.x < (0 + ball.width / 2))
23          {
24              ball.x = 0 + ball.width / 2;
25          }
26          if (ball.y > (800 - ball.width / 2))
27          {
28              ball.y = 800 - ball.width / 2;
29          }
30          if (ball.y < (0 + ball.width / 2))
31          {
32              ball.y = 0 + ball.width / 2;
33          }
34          if (ball.hitTestObject(theTarget))
35          {
36              textb.text = "a Hit";
37          }
38      }
```

Type these 4 lines of code → (lines 34-37)

Actions : 1

Line 37 of 38 Col 3

Figure 25 *Adding the code to cause the number of seconds to display in the text box*

```
35        {
36            textb.text = "a Hit";
37        }
38  }/* Simple Timer
39  Displays a countdown timer in the Output panel until 30 seconds elapse.
40  This code is a good place to start for creating timers for your own purposes.
41
42  Instructions:
43  1. To change the number of seconds in the timer, change the value 30 in the
44  first line below to the number of seconds you want.
45  */
46
47  var fl_TimerInstance:Timer = new Timer(1000,30);
48  fl_TimerInstance.addEventListener(TimerEvent.TIMER, fl_TimerHandler);
49  fl_TimerInstance.start();
50
51  var fl_SecondsElapsed:Number = 1;
52
53  function fl_TimerHandler(event:TimerEvent):void
54  {
55        trace("Seconds elapsed: " + fl_SecondsElapsed);
56        fl_SecondsElapsed++;
57        textb.text = String(fl_SecondsElapsed);
58  }
```

Actions : 1

Line 57 of 58 Col 41

Type this line
of code

Add a timer to an application

1. Click **frame 1** on the Actions layer.

2. Click **Window** on the menu bar, then click **Code Snippets**.

3. Click the **Actions expand icon** ▶, click **Simple Timer**, click the **Show description icon** ⓘ, then read the description.

4. Click the **Show code icon** {}, read the code, then click the **Insert** button.

5. Display the Actions panel, then scroll to the bottom of the panel to view the timer code.

   Notice the variable that keeps track of the elapsed seconds is named fl_SecondsElapsed. You will use this variable to display the seconds in the dynamic text box you named textb.

6. Insert a line below fl_SecondsElapsed++; then type the following as shown in Figure 25:

   textb.text = String(fl_SecondsElapsed);

   This line of code causes the number of seconds to display in the text box. Because the code is within the function and the function is running continuously, the number of seconds is displayed continuously.

7. Test the application using the Mobile Content Simulator and notice the timer running in the text box.

8. Manipulate the Simulator in the Simulator window so that the ball in the AIR preview window collides with the green dot and notice the words "a Hit" are again displayed in the dynamic text box.

9. Close the AIR preview window, then save your work.

You added a Code Snippet to cause the number of seconds on the timer to display in the text box.

Change the output in a dynamic text box

1. Display the Actions panel.

2. Change the textb.text = "a Hit"; line of code to:

   textb.text = ("a Hit at " + fl_SecondsElapsed + " seconds");

   This line of code causes the words "a Hit at " followed by the number of elapsed seconds followed by the word "seconds" to be displayed when the ball collides with the green dot.

3. Test the application using the Mobile Content Simulator and notice the timer running in the text box.

4. Manipulate the Simulator in the Simulator window so that the ball in the AIR preview window collides with the green dot and notice the words "a Hit at (a number) seconds" are displayed in the dynamic text box as shown in Figure 26.

   Notice the words disappear and the timer continues to run. You can stop the timer and also have the ball disappear.

5. Close the AIR preview window.

   (continued)

Figure 26 *The text box displaying the text and the elapsed seconds*

Developing Mobile Applications

Figure 27 *The code to stop the timer and remove the ball from the screen*

```
35          {
36              textb.text = ("a Hit at " + fl_SecondsElapsed + " seconds");
37              fl_TimerInstance.stop();
38              ball.visible = false;
39          }
40     }/* Simple Timer
41     Displays a countdown timer in the Output panel until 30 seconds elapse.
42     This code is a good place to start for creating timers for your own purposes.
43
44     Instructions:
45     1. To change the number of seconds in the timer, change the value 30 in the
46     first line below to the number of seconds you want.
47     */
48     var fl_TimerInstance:Timer = new Timer(1000,30);
49     fl_TimerInstance.addEventListener(TimerEvent.TIMER, fl_TimerHandler);
50     fl_TimerInstance.start();
51     var fl_SecondsElapsed:Number = 1;
52     function fl_TimerHandler(event:TimerEvent):void
53     {
54         trace("Seconds elapsed: " + fl_SecondsElapsed);
55         fl_SecondsElapsed++;
56         textb.text = String(fl_SecondsElapsed);
57     }
```

Type these
2 lines of
code

6. Add the following two lines of code below the textb line as shown in Figure 27:

    fl_TimerInstance.stop();

    ball.visible = false;

    These two lines of code are placed within the *if* statement that checks to see if the ball collides with the dot, so they are executed when the collision occurs. The first line stops the timer so that the number of seconds that has elapsed from the start of the application to the collision is displayed. The second line sets the visibility property of the ball to false which causes the ball to disappear.

7. Test the application using the Mobile Content Simulator and notice the timer running in the text box.

8. Manipulate the Simulator in the Simulator window so that the ball in the AIR preview window collides with the green dot.

    Notice that when the ball collides with the dot, the timer stops (that is, the seconds do not change) and the ball disappears.

9. Close the AIR preview window.

10. Save your work.

11. Close the application.

You added code to cause the output to specify an exact number, stop a timer, and cause an object to disappear from the screen.

Use Touch and GESTURE EVENTS

What You'll Do

Paintings courtesy of B. VanDyke Shuman

 In this lesson, you will use the Mobile Content Simulator to test touch and gesture events on a mobile device

Using Touch and Gesture Events

In addition to the Accelerometer, you can use the Mobile Content Simulator to test an application that includes Touch and Gesture events, such as drag, swipe, and zoom. In Chapter 6, you used Code Snippets to add the mobile gesture Pinch to Zoom. Figure 28 shows the Code Snippet for the *Swipe to Go to Next/ Previous Frame and Stop* mobile action. This mobile action can be used instead of a button that is clicked to move the playhead to the next or previous frame. This code is discussed next.

Multitouch.inputMode = MultitouchInput Mode.GESTURE;

This line of code configures the Multitouch class so that the multitouch gesture event can be detected.

stage.addEventListener (TransformGesture Event.GESTURE_SWIPE, fl_Swipe);

This line of code creates an event listener that listens for a swipe gesture event on the Stage and then calls a function named fl_Swipe.

function fl_Swipe (event:TransformGestureEvent)

This line of code identifies the fl_Swipe function.

Figure 28 *Code snippet for the Swipe to Go to Next/Previous Frame and Stop mobile action*

```
{
    if (event.offsetX == 1)
    {
        prevFrame();
    }
    else if (event.offsetX == −1)
    {
        nextFrame();
    }
}
```

These ten lines of code are contained within the function. The first *if* statement checks to see if the offsetX is positive, indicating a left to right swipe. If so, the playhead moves to the previous frame. Otherwise, if the offset is negative, which indicates a right to left swipe, the playhead moves to the next frame. Additional *if* statements can be added to check if the offsetY is positive or negative (indicating a swipe from top to bottom or bottom to top).

The Swipe Event code snippet is useful if you want to develop an application that allows the user to move back and forth through a series of frames. You can add this code snippet to an existing application or you can use the Swipe Gallery template, which already includes the Swipe Event code. Figure 29 shows the New from Template dialog box with the Swipe Gallery template selected. This template is useful if you want to develop an application that allows the user to move back and forth

through a series of screens, such as a gallery of paintings. Unlike the previous example, all of the screens are contained in a single frame. The Preview screen in Figure 29 shows the number 1 on a red background. This template contains four screens numbered 1–4, but only screen 1 is displayed. The other three screens, numbered 2–4, are off the right side of the Stage. The description says: "Android document with code for swipe gesture to slide a movie clip of items." Essentially, all four screens are contained in a movie clip, which in this template is called imageHolder, that can be swiped left to right or right to left to display one screen at a time. The swipe gesture event is similar to the code above except that the swipe gesture causes the movie clip to display the next or previous screen rather than the playhead moving to the next or previous frame. Because it is a movie clip you can add more screens as desired.

There is a fine distinction between the use of swiping to a frame and swiping to a screen. You use the swipe to frame when the content you have created is contained in frames. You use the swipe to screen when the content you have created is contained in a movie clip, where each frame in the movie clip is considered a screen. Each screen contains a movie clip or other content. The content contained in the swipe movie clip (imageHolder) is stored as movie clip symbols (NobleEye_mc, WildBlue_mc, and WildGold_mc in the lesson example that follows). Generally, swiping to a screen is used when related content is displayed linearly, such as a series of photos. Whereas, swiping to a frame might be used to display distinct sections of an application, such as moving from a welcome screen to a main menu screen.

Figure 29 *New from Template dialog box with the Swipe Gallery template selected*

Use the swipe gesture

1. Click **File** on the menu bar, click **New**, click the **Templates tab**, click **AIR for Android**, click **Swipe Gallery**, then click **OK**.

2. Save the file as **WildHorses.fla**.

3. Change the view to **25%**.

   Notice the four objects. Each is about 425 × 575. The Stage is set to 480 × 800. The red object with the number 1 is currently on the Stage. The others are to the right of the Stage.

4. Click **Control** on the menu bar, point to **Test Movie**, then click **in AIR Debug Launcher (Mobile)**.

5. Click the **TOUCH AND GESTURE expand icon** ▶, then click the **Touch layer check box** to select it.

6. Click the **Swipe option button** to select it.

   The instructions on how to simulate the swipe action in the Mobile Content Simulator are listed in the Instructions area at the bottom of the Simulator window.

7. Point to the right side of the number 1, then notice the circle object that appears with the arrow cursor, as shown in Figure 30.

   This circle represents the user's touch point on their smartphone.

8. Press and slowly swipe to the **left**, then release the mouse.

9. Continue to swipe until the 4 is displayed, then swipe in the other direction until the **1** is displayed.

10. Close the AIR preview window to return to the Flash workspace.

   (continued)

Figure 30 *Pointing to the AIR preview window displays the circle object*

TOUCH AND GESTURE pane expanded

Touch layer check box

Swipe option button selected

Instruction area provides information about the selected Gesture option

The circle object

Developing Mobile Applications

Figure 31 *Deleting the number 2*
Painting courtesy of B. VanDyke Shuman.

*If you delete the orange box instead of
the number 2, click Edit on the menu bar,
click Undo Delete, then repeat step 20.*

11. Change the view to **Fit in Window**.

12. Click **File** on the menu bar, click **Import**, then click **Import to Library**.

13. Navigate to your Data files, then import **NobleEye.jpg**, **WildBlue.jpg** and **WildGold.jpg**.

14. Display the Library panel, then drag **NobleEye.jpg** to the Stage.

15. Verify the NobleEye.jpg object is selected, click **Modify** on the menu bar, click **Convert to Symbol**, change the symbol name to **NobleEye_mc**, select **Movie Clip** as the type, verify the registration point is set to center, then click **OK**.

    You can convert the jpg image into any symbol (movie clip, graphic or button). Converting it into a movie clip rather than a graphic symbol provides more flexibility if you decide to target the symbol in your ActionScript code.

16. Verify **NobleEye_mc** is selected on the Stage, then press **[Delete]** to remove it from the Stage.

17. Repeat Steps 14–16 for the other JPG files naming them **WildBlue_mc** and **WildGold_mc**.

18. Double-click **1** on the Stage to open the **imageHolder movie clip** in the edit window.

    The imageHolder movie clip is the default movie clip for the Swipe template. The movie clips you created using the jpg images will be nested in the swipe imageHolder movie clip.

19. Change the view to **25%**.

20. Click **2** in the orange box to select the number 2 only, then press **[Delete]** to remove it.

    Your screen should resemble Figure 31.

    (continued)

21. Click the **orange placeholder**, click **Modify** on the menu bar, point to **Symbol**, then click **Swap Symbol**.

22. Click **NobleEye_mc** in the Swap Symbol dialog box, then click **OK**.

Notice the horse graphic displays a tint. This is part of the Swipe Gallery template.

23. Display the Properties panel, then click the **Style list arrow** ▼ in the COLOR EFFECT area to display the list, as shown in Figure 32.

24. Click **None**.

25. Repeat Steps 21–25 for the **WildBlue.jpg** and **WildGold.jpg** graphics swapping them for the purple and green placeholders, respectively.

26. Change the view to **Fit in Window**.

27. Click **1** on the Stage to select it, then press **[Delete]**.

(continued)

Figure 32 *The list of style options*
Painting courtesy of B. VanDyke Shuman.

Tint applied as part of Swipe template

Style options

Style list arrow

Developing Mobile Applications

Figure 33 *A title for screen 1*

Painting courtesy of B. VanDyke Shuman.

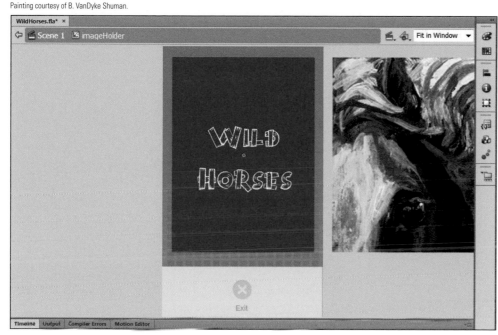

28. Select the **Text tool** T on the Tools panel, then verify the Text type is set to Static Text on the Properties panel.

29. Using a font of your choice add a title to screen 1 similar to Figure 33.

30. Click **Scene 1** to return to the main timeline.

31. Click **Control** on the menu bar, point to **Test Movie**, then click **in AIR Debug Launcher (Mobile)**.

32. Click the **TOUCH AND GESTURE expand icon** ▶ , then click the **Touch layer check box** to select it.

33. Click the **Swipe radio button** to select it.

34. Point to the right side of the text heading, then press and swipe until each of the 3 horses is displayed, then swipe in the other direction.

35. Close the AIR preview window.

36. Save your work.

You started a new AIR for Android Swipe template, swapped graphics, and tested the application in the Mobile Content Simulator.

Use the zoom gesture

1. Save the application as **WildHorsesZoom.fla**.

2. Double-click the screen with the Wild Horses heading to display it in the edit window.

3. Click the **Wild Horses text** to select it.

4. Click **Modify** on the menu bar, then click **Convert to Symbol**.

5. Change the name to **WHtext_mc** and the type to **Movie Clip**, then click **OK**.

6. Verify the text is selected, then use the Properties panel to enter an instance name of **WHtext** as shown in Figure 34.

7. Click **Window** on the menu bar, then click **Code Snippets**.

8. Click the **Mobile Gesture Events expand icon** ▶ , then click **Pinch to Zoom Event**.

9. Click the **Show description icon** ⓘ , then read the description.

10. Click the **Show code icon** {} , read the code, then click the **Insert button**.

    Notice a new layer is inserted with the name Actions and the code is placed in frame 1 of the Actions layer.

11. Click **Scene 1** to return to the main Timeline.

    (continued)

Figure 34 *Entering an instance name*
Painting courtesy of B. VanDyke Shuman.

Instance name

Developing Mobile Applications

Figure 35 *Setting the 1ˢᵗ touch point*

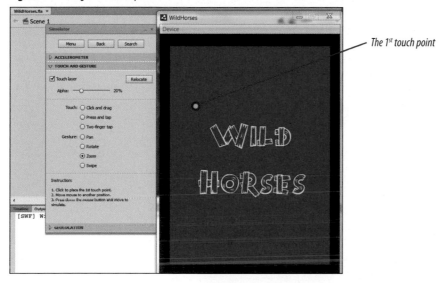

The 1ˢᵗ touch point

Figure 36 *Pointing to the position for the 2ⁿᵈ touch point*

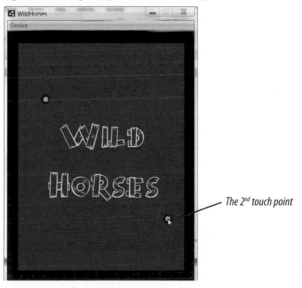

The 2ⁿᵈ touch point

12. Click **Control** on the menu bar, point to **Test Movie**, then click **in AIR Debug Launcher (Mobile)**.

13. Click the **TOUCH AND GESTURE expand icon ▶**, then click the **Touch layer check box** to select it.

14. Click the **Zoom option button** to select it.

15. Read the instructions at the bottom of the panel.

16. Click to set **touch point 1**, as shown in Figure 35.

17. Point to the position shown in Figure 36, hold down but do not release the mouse button to identify touch point 2, slowly drag **touch point 2** toward touch point 1 until they touch, then drag **touch point 2** away from touch point 1.

    The text zooms in and out.

18. Click to set **touch point 1** above the text, point below the text, hold down but do not release the mouse button to identify touch point 2, slowly drag **touch point 2** toward touch point 1 until they pass each other, then drag **touch point 2** away from touch point 1.

    Notice the position of the touch points determines how the text will be shaped as the zoom occurs.

19. Close the AIR preview window.

20. Save then close the application.

You added a Code Snippet to allow for a zoom gesture and tested the feature in the mobile AIR debug launcher.

Repurpose an application and use the Mobile Content Simulator.

1. Open fl12_3.fla, then save it as **skillsDemo12-rep.fla**.
   This game is similar to the one you created in Chapter 10. The stage size is 500 × 400.
2. Click Control on the menu bar, point to Test Movie, then click in Flash Professional.
3. Play the game, then close the Flash Player window.
4. Click Modify on the menu bar, then click Document.
5. Change the width to **480** and the height to **800**, a standard size for a smartphone.
6. Click the Scale content with stage check box to select it, then click OK.
7. Change the view to Fit in Window.
8. Change the backdrop fill color and border to fit the new Stage size.
9. Change the Publish Setting target to AIR 3.2 for Android.
10. Test the movie in the Mobile Content Simulator.
11. Close the AIR preview window.

Add a mobile gesture event.

1. Click the Hit the Target Game heading on the Stage to select it.
2. Display the Code Snippets panel.
3. Select the Pinch to Zoom Event in the Mobile Gesture Events folder, then insert the code.
4. Test the application in the Mobile Content Simulator.
5. Display the Touch and Gesture screen.
6. Click the Touch layer check box to select it, then click the Zoom radio button.
7. Use the pointer to zoom the heading out.

8. Click the Touch layer check box to deselect it, then continue to play the game and compare your work to Figure 37. (*Note*: No touch gestures have been applied to the Go and End buttons and the heart, so you need to turn off the Touch layer to continue playing the game.)
9. Close the AIR preview window.
10. Save and close the application.

Use a template to create an accelerometer application.

1. Open a new AIR for Android Accelerometer template application, then save it as **skillsDemo12-collide.fla**.
2. Select the green ball on the Stage and change the width and height to **30** pixels.
3. Draw a red ball with a height and width of **15** pixels and center the ball on the Stage. (*Hint*: Be sure the lock icon is locked.)
4. Change the ball to a movie clip symbol with the name **rball_mc**.
5. Give the red ball an instance name of **rball**.
6. Verify the red ball is selected, then display the Code Snippets panel.
7. Expand the Mobile Actions folder, then insert the Move with Accelerator action.
8. Click frame 1 of the Actions layer, then display the Actions panel.
9. Scroll down the panel and review the code.
   Both balls will move in response to the movement of the device. However, notice the difference between the accelerometer code for the green ball (instance name ball) and the red ball (instance name rball). The green ball, which is part of the template, contains code that keeps the ball on the Stage. The red ball, which is controlled by the code snippet does not have code to keep it on the Stage. This will be part of the application, that is, the user will try to have the green ball collide with the red ball before the red ball moves off the Stage.
10. Close the Actions panel, then display the Mobile Content Simulator.
11. Change the Accelerometer settings to Camera view: **Flat** and X: **-90**.
12. Slowly rotate the center of the simulator phone. Notice that both objects move.
13. Continue to move the phone until the red ball disappears.
14. Close the AIR preview window to return to the Flash workspace.

Add a timer.

1. Display the Code Snippet panel.
2. Open the Actions folder, then insert the Simple Timer code.
3. Display the Actions panel, then scroll to display the timer code. (Notice the trace statement that is used to display the number of seconds that have elapsed proceeded by the words: "Seconds elapsed: ".)
4. Use the Mobile Content Simulator to test the application and notice how the Output panel displays the elapsed seconds but the seconds are not displayed in the AIR preview window. (*Note*: You may need to move the Mobile Content Simulator windows to view the Output panel.)
5. Close the AIR preview window.

Display elapsed time and add collision.

1. Add a layer and name it **text box**.
2. Select frame 1 of the text box layer.
3. Create a dynamic text box using the following settings: **Arial**, **bold**, **20** pt, **white** color, **no border**, **center aligned**.
4. Draw the text box near the top of the Stage and center it across the Stage.
5. Give the text box an instance name of **textb**.
6. Click frame 1 on the actions layer, then display the Actions panel.
7. Type the following as one line of code beneath the ball.y += accelY * 30; line of code.
   textb.text = ("Elapsed time" + fl_SecondsElapsed + "seconds");
   This line of code displays the phrase: Elapsed time (number of seconds) seconds. The phrase is displayed in the text box (instance name textb). (*Note*: fl_SecondsElapsed may have an underscore (__) followed by a number appended to it. For example, it may display as fl_SecondsElapsed_2. This is caused by inserting more than one instance of the code.)
8. Use the Mobile Content Simulator to test the application, then notice the text and seconds that are displayed and compare your work to Figure 37.
9. Close the AIR preview window.
10. Click frame 1 on the Actions layer, display the Actions panel, then type the following code as the last *if* statement code within the moveBall function.
    (*Note*: Be sure the code comes after the last curly brace (}) of the *if* statement for the ball.y = 0 + ball.width / 2; line and before the curly brace (}) that follows the line.)

```
if (ball.hitTestObject(rball))
{
        fl_TimerInstance.stop();
        rball.visible = false;
}
```
(*Note*: The closing brace should be added automatically so you should not have to type it.)

This code checks to see if the green ball (instance name ball) hits the red ball (instance name rball). If so, it stops the timer and has the red ball disappear. (*Note*: fl_TimerInstance may have an underscore (__) followed by a number appended to it. For example, it may display as fl_TimerInstance_2.

Figure 37 *Completed Skills Review*

This is caused by inserting more than one instance of the code.)
11. Use the Mobile Content Simulator to test the application.
12. Move the simulator phone until the balls collide and notice that the time stops and the red ball disappears.
13. Close the AIR preview window.
14. Save your work, then close the application.
    (*Note*: You may want to change the application's frame rate and/or the size of the balls in order to change the difficulty of the application. Also, you could change the seconds for the timer so that it displays longer than 30 seconds.)

Ultimate Tours would like you to create a prototype of a smartphone app that has the user play a matching game involving currency symbols. To play the game, users drag and drop a currency symbol onto its name, as shown in Figure 38. If they get it correct, a message displays and if not, a different message appears. The prototype should be created as simply as possible using code snippets where appropriate.

Create the application.

1. Open a new AIR for Android application, save it as **ultimateTours12.fla**, then use Figure 38 as a guide to complete the steps that follow.
2. Change the Stage color.
3. Add a layer, name it, then create a heading.
4. Add a layer, name it, then create the four terms (Dollar, Euro, Yen, Pound).
5. Change each of the terms to a movie clip symbol with an appropriate name.
6. Give the Dollar, Euro and Yen movie clip terms appropriate instance names.
7. Give the Pound movie clip term the instance name: **pound**.

8. Add a layer, name it, then use the drawing tools to create a currency symbol.
9. Change the currency symbol to a movie clip with an appropriate name.
10. Give the currency movie clip the instance name: **pdcurrency**.
11. Add a layer, name it, then create a dynamic text box.
12. Give the text box the instance name: **textb**.
13. Select the currency symbol on the Stage, then display the Code Snippet panel.
14. Insert a Touch and Drag mobile touch event.
15. Click frame 1 of the Actions layer, open the Actions panel, then scroll to the bottom of the panel.
16. Add the following 2 lines just below the stopTouchDrag line but before the closing brace.

```
if (pdcurrency.hitTestObject(pound))
{
        textb.text = ("That's it!");
}
else
{
        textb.text = ("Sorry, try again.");
}
```

(*Note*: Watch carefully as you type the code. Remember that some closing braces are added automatically so do not type a duplicate brace. Your finished typed code should match the code in the book exactly.)

These lines test if the currency symbol (instance name pdcurrency) has hit the correct term (instance name pound). If so, the text *That's it!* displays in the text box (instance name textb). If not the text *Sorry, try again.* displays in the text box.

17. Use the Auto format and Check syntax buttons at the top of the Actions panel and correct any code errors.
18. Save your work.

Test the application.

1. Open the Mobile Content Simulator, then expand the Touch and Gesture area.
2. Select the Touch layer check box, then drag and release the currency symbol several times to view the text that appears in the text box.
3. Close the AIR preview window.
4. Save your work, then close the application.

Figure 38 *Sample completed Project Builder 1*

You have been asked to develop a prototype application that demonstrates the use of the swipe event on a phone application. You will start with a template and repurpose it.

Use a template to create a swipe application.

1. Open a new AIR for Android Swipe Gallery template application, then save it as **swipePrototype.fla**.
2. Change the view to 50%.
3. Open the imageHolder movie clip in the edit window.
4. Click on a numbered screen and note the size of the graphic, which is smaller than the size of the Stage.
5. Return to the main Timeline.
6. Obtain three graphics, such as JPG photos, and resize them to fit the dimension of the swipe template screen (that is, the colored area with the number).

7. Import the three graphics to the Library.
8. Drag each file to the stage, change it to a movie clip, and delete it from the Stage.
9. Open the imageHolder movie clip in the edit window and change the view to 50%.
10. Delete the number 1 on the first screen, then add a title, change it to a movie clip, and give it an instance name.
11. Delete the other numbers, swap symbols with the three new movie clips, and remove the tint from each image.
12. Return to the main Timeline.
13. Display the Mobile Content Simulator.
14. Use the Touch and Gesture Swipe gesture to display the screens.
15. Close the AIR preview window.

Add a zoom gesture.

1. Open the imageHolder in the edit window.
2. Select the movie clip on the second screen on the Stage and give it an instance name.
3. Insert a Pinch to Zoom Event for the movie clip from the Mobile Gestures Events options.
4. Return to the main Timeline.
5. Display the Mobile Content Simulator.
6. Use the Touch and Gesture Swipe gesture to swipe and display the second screen.
7. Change to the Zoom gesture and zoom in and out on the screen.
8. Close the AIR preview window.
9. Save and close the application.

Figure 39 *Sample completed Project Builder 2*
Photos courtesy of J. Shuman.

Figure 40 shows a USA.gov mobile application that provides information on Southern California deserts. Those interested in recreation activities such as camping, hiking and boating as well as touring these areas will benefit from this application. The map is the opening screen for the application. The second screen is displayed when Recreation is clicked on the menu bar.

1. Connect to the Internet, then go to http://apps.usa.gov/ca_desert.shtml.

2. Open a document in a word processor or open a new Flash document, save the file as **dpc12**, then answer the following questions. (*Hint*: Use the Text tool in Flash.)

   - Could this application have been repurposed from a web site?
   - What mobile touch and gestures events might be used to enhance this application?
   - What suggestions would you make to improve the design, and why?

Figure 40 *Design Project*

Courtesy of USA.gov. http://apps.usa.gov/ca-desert.shtml

In the previous chapter, you created a portfolio for your work samples that included sound and a password-protected, clients-only area. Now you will repurpose the application for a smartphone and test it using the Mobile Content Simulator.

Resize the Stage.

1. Open portfolio11.fla, then save it as **portfolio12.fla**. (*Note*: You will need to have math.swf, shirt.swf, and shirt2.swf in the same folder as the portfolio12.fla because these files are loaded into the application when the user clicks specific buttons.)
2. Test the application in the Flash player window, then close the Flash Player window.
3. Use the Document Settings dialog box to change the Stage dimensions to 480 width and 800 height, then choose to scale the content to the Stage.
4. Change the view to Fit in Window. Notice the border does not fit the Stage.
5. Test the movie in the Flash player window and notice the graphics are displayed on the top half of the Stage.

Resize the Stage objects.

Note: You may want to lock and unlock layers as you work with the objects on the Stage so that you are only working with the desired objects.

1. Change the border to have it fit around the entire Stage.
2. Change the navigation buttons' white background to have it fit the width of the Stage.

3. Move the top of the white background for the navigation buttons to the mid-point of the Stage, move the text My Portfolio above the white bar, then move the navigation buttons so they are evenly spaced within the white bar.
4. Display frame 2 and notice the small size of the Games, Shirt Selector and Pattern Select buttons.
5. Resize (including the hit area) and reposition the buttons as shown in Figure 41. (*Hint*: Depending on how these three buttons were created in your file named portfolio11.fla, you may want to recreate them here. You can display a button in the edit window, select and delete the text, and then use the text tool to type a larger button label. Once you are satisfied with the button label, you can enlarge the hit area.)
6. Test the movie in the Flash player window, then close the window.
7. Save your work.

Change the publish settings for a mobile device.

1. Use the Publish Settings dialog box to change the Target to AIR 3.2 for Android.
2. Display the Mobile Content Simulator.
3. Display the Touch and Gesture events screen in the Simulator window.
4. Select the Touch layer check box, then select the Two-finger tap touch option.
5. Click on the flash samples button. There is no response because the ActionScript for this application does not contain any mobile event code.
6. Close the AIR preview window.

Add mobile events.

You can add mobile event code snippets and then replace the default action in the code snippet with the action(s) in the current ActionScript code. For example, when the user clicks on the flash samples button three lines of code are used to stop all sounds, unload any SWF files, and jump the playhead to frame 2. When you insert the Two Finger Tap event code snippet, the code causes the object being tapped to double in size. So, you merely replace the code that doubles the size of the object with the three lines of code already in the Actions panel.

1. Click frame 1 on the actions layer.
2. Click the flash samples button on the Stage to select it and notice the instance name displayed on the Properties panel.
3. Display the Code Snippets panel and insert the Two Finger Tap Event which is located in the Mobile Gesture Events folder.
4. Click frame 1 on the actions layer, then display the Action panel.
5. Copy the three lines of code (SoundMixer, myLoader, gotoAndStop) within the function called when the samplesBtn (or the instance name of your flash samples button) is clicked.
6. Replace the two lines of code (samplesBtn.scaleX *= 2; samplesBtn.scaleY *= 2) in the Code Snippet with the three lines of copied code.

7. Scroll to display the original samplesBtn addEventListener code (including the three lines you copied) that creates the function that is called when the user clicks on the button, then delete the block (seven lines) of code associated with the samplesBtn.
8. Test the application and use the Two-finger tap touch option to tap the flash samples button.
9. Close the AIR preview window.
10. Save and close the application.

Figure 41 *Sample completed Portfolio Project*

ADOBE RICH MEDIA COMMUNICATIONS USING FLASH PROFESSIONAL CS6		
Objective (Note that some objectives have additional coverage online on Cengage Brain.)	**Chapter**	**Page(s)**
Domain 1.0 Setting Project Requirements		
1.1 Identify the purpose, audience, and audience needs for rich media content.		
1.1a Identify information that determines purpose, audience, and audience needs for rich media content.	1	1-42-43, online
1.2 Identify rich media content that is relevant to the purpose of the media in which it will be used (websites, mobile devices, and so on).		
1.2a Identify criteria for determining whether content is relevant to the purpose.	1	1-42-43
1.3 Understand options for producing accessible rich media content.		
1.3a Explain why including accessible content in rich media elements *matters* to clients and the target audience.	1	1-45
1.3b Identify elements of a SWF movie that can be read by screen readers.	1	1-45, online
1.3c List examples of project requirements that result in accessible rich media content.	1	1-45, online
1.4 Demonstrate knowledge of standard copyright rules (related terms, obtaining permission, and citing copyrighted material).		
1.4a Use copyright terms correctly, such as "copyrighted," "fair use doctrine," "intellectual property," and "derivative works."	7	7-7, online
1.4b Identify when permission must be obtained to use copyrighted material.	7	7-7
1.4c Identify methods used to indicate content as copyrighted.		online
1.4d Recognize proper methods for citing websites, images, sounds, video, and text from the Internet.		
1.5 Understand project management tasks and responsibilities.		
1.5a Identify items that might appear on a project plan.	1	1-46
1.5b Identify phases that might appear on a project plan.	1	1-46
1.5c Identify deliverables that might be produced during the project.	1	1-42-45, online
1.5d Identify common problems and issues in project management.	1	1-42, online

ADOBE RICH MEDIA COMMUNICATIONS USING FLASH PROFESSIONAL CS6		
Objective (Note that some objectives have additional coverage online on Cengage Brain.)	**Chapter**	**Page(s)**
1.6 Communicate with others (such as peers and clients) about design and content plans.		
1.6a Demonstrate knowledge of techniques for gathering feedback on design and content plans from others (such as peers and clients).	1	1-45
Domain 2.0 Identifying Rich Media Design Elements		
2.1 Identify general and Flash-specific best practices for designing rich media content for a website.		
2.1a Identify attributes of a website, game, mobile app, or rich Internet application that demonstrate consistency.	1	1-42-46
2.1b Identify techniques in Flash used to produce consistent elements.	1	1-19; 3-2, 3-4, 3-5
2.1c Identify the benefits of consistency.	1	1-44-45
2.1d Demonstrate knowledge of web-safe colors.		online
2.1e Identify criteria for deciding if content should be implemented by using rich media.	1	1-42-46, online
2.1f Demonstrate knowledge of the benefits of using motion presets.	1	1-21
2.1g Identify the benefits of authoring FLV files for Adobe AIR.		online
2.1h Identify the benefits of including metadata in SWFs.		online
2.2 Demonstrate knowledge of design elements and principles.		
2.2a Demonstrate knowledge of graphic design elements and principles.	1	1-42-46, online
2.2b Identify examples of horizontal symmetry, vertical symmetry, diagonal symmetry, radial symmetry, and asymmetric layout.	1	1-43, online
2.2c Recognize examples of page designs that violate design principles or best practices.	1	1-43-44
2.3 Identify general and Flash-specific techniques to create rich media elements that are accessible and readable.	1	1-41
2.3a Demonstrate knowledge of text formatting guidelines that improve readability.	2	2-32-41
2.3b Identify specific techniques used to make rich media content accessible to viewers with visual, auditory, and motor impairments.	1	1-45, online

	ADOBE RICH MEDIA COMMUNICATIONS USING FLASH PROFESSIONAL CS6		
	Objective (Note that some objectives have additional coverage online on Cengage Brain.)	**Chapter**	**Page(s)**
2.4	Use a storyboard to produce rich media elements.		
	2.4a Demonstrate knowledge of storyboards.	1	1-44-45
	2.4b List kinds of information that need to be communicated through a storyboard.	1	1-44-45
2.5	Organize a Flash document		
	2.5a Demonstrate knowledge of structural elements used to organize a Flash document.	2,3	2-42, 3-10-15
Domain 3.0 Understanding Adobe Flash CS6 Interface			
3.1	Identify elements of the Flash interface.		
	3.1a Identify and label elements of the Flash interface.	1	1-4-8, 8-28 – 8-29, 12-6, online
	3.1b Demonstrate knowledge of how to show and hide panels, including the Property inspector.	1	1-5-8
	3.1c Demonstrate knowledge of preset and custom workspaces.	1	1-8-10
3.2	Use the Property Inspector.		
	3.2a Demonstrate knowledge of the various functions of the Property inspector.	1	1-5, 1-17, 1-27-29, 37, 41, 1-5, 1-25 – 1-28
3.3	Use the Timeline.		
	3.3a Identify and label elements of the Timeline and their functions.	1, 4	1-5, 1-11, 1-30-35, 2-43, 4-5
	3.3b Demonstrate an understanding of frame rate and how it affects the playback, timing, and size of the finished published movie.	1	1-33-34
	3.3c Demonstrate knowledge of using layers to arrange content on the Stage.	1	1-32-33
	3.3d Demonstrate knowledge of how to add, name, arrange, delete, and organize layers into folders.	1,2	1-32-37, 2-42-43
	3.3e Demonstrate knowledge of how to preview a document (movie) by using the Timeline.	1	1-12-13

ADOBE RICH MEDIA COMMUNICATIONS USING FLASH PROFESSIONAL CS6		
Objective (Note that some objectives have additional coverage online on Cengage Brain.)	Chapter	Page(s)
3.3f Demonstrate knowledge of how to add, delete, and rename layers.	2	2-42-54
3.3g Demonstrate knowledge of how to change the frame rate of a document.	1	1-37
3.3h Demonstrate knowledge of how to adjust layer properties.	2	2-42-54
3.4 Adjust document properties.		
3.4a List global document settings that can be adjusted by using the Document Settings dialog box.	1	1-17, online
3.4b Demonstrate knowledge of how to adjust document properties.	1	1-17
3.5 Use Flash guides and rulers.		
3.5a Demonstrate knowledge of how to show and hide rulers.	2	2-6-7, 2-14-15
3.5b Demonstrate knowledge of how to add and remove guides.	2	2-6-8
3.5c Demonstrate knowledge of guide properties.	2	2-4, 2-9, online
3.5d Demonstrate knowledge of how to set or change guide properties.	2	2-6-7, 2-14-15
3.6 Use the Motion Editor.		
3.6a Demonstrate knowledge of object-based animation.	1	1-19-20, 1-23-26
3.6b Demonstrate knowledge of motion paths and how to modify them with Bezier controls.	2	2-6-9
3.6c Demonstrate knowledge of how to adjust the timing of an animation.	1	1-37
3.7 Understand Flash file types.		
3.7a Demonstrate knowledge of the differences between a Flash document (FLA), a published file (SWF), and a Flash video file (FLV).	1,5	1-12, 1-38-39, 5-12-13
3.7b Demonstrate knowledge of the difference between a video file and a Flash video in which the video has been embedded or linked.	5,11	5-12-13, 11-26-27
3.7c Demonstrate knowledge of XMP and XFL file types.		online
3.8 Identify best practices for managing the file size of a published Flash document.		
3.8a Identify best practices for managing the file size of published Flash document.	6	6-10

ADOBE RICH MEDIA COMMUNICATIONS USING FLASH PROFESSIONAL CS6		
Objective (Note that some objectives have additional coverage online on Cengage Brain.)	**Chapter**	**Page(s)**
Domain 4.0 Building Rich Media Elements by Using Flash CS6		
4.1 Make rich media content development decisions based on your analysis and interpretation of design specifications.		
4.1a Demonstrate knowledge of the relationship between end-user requirements and design and development decisions.	1	1-42-46
4.1b Identify rich content that is affected by end-user technical factors.	1	1-42-43
4.2 Use tools on the Tools panel to select, create, and manipulate graphics and text.		
4.2a Identify or label the tools on the Tools panel.	2	2-4-7
4.2b Demonstrate knowledge of the difference between the Selection and Subselection tools.	2	2-4-5, 2-15, 2-29
4.2c Demonstrate knowledge of the terms "bitmap" and "vector" as used in drawing graphics in Flash.	2	2-2
4.2d Demonstrate knowledge of selection techniques used for working with and modifying shapes.	2	2-5, 2-18-31
4.2e Given a set of tools, identify which tools are used for selection.	2	2-4-6
4.2f Given a set of tools, identify which tools are used for drawing or creating shapes.	2	2-4-6, 4-42 – 4-45
4.2g Given a set of tools, identify which tools are used for modifying shapes.	2	2-4-6, 2-19, 2-22, 7-13
4.3 Import and modify graphics.		
4.3a Demonstrate knowledge of how to import graphics.	3	3-30-32
4.3b Identify which graphic file types can be imported to a Flash document.	7	7-4-10
4.3c Demonstrate knowledge of the difference between importing to the Stage and to the Library panel.	7	7-4
4.3d Demonstrate knowledge of techniques to modify graphics such as break apart, trace bitmap, and swap bitmap.	3,7,11	3-5, 3-9, 7-16-19, 11-13-14
4.3e Demonstrate knowledge of how to break apart a graphic.	3	3-5, 3-9
4.3f Demonstrate knowledge of how to trace a bitmap graphic.	7	7-16-19

ADOBE RICH MEDIA COMMUNICATIONS USING FLASH PROFESSIONAL CS6		
Objective (Note that some objectives have additional coverage online on Cengage Brain.)	Chapter	Page(s)
4.3g Demonstrate knowledge of how to swap a graphic or symbol on the Stage with another graphic or symbol stored in the document library.	11	11-13-14
4.3h Demonstrate knowledge of recommended graphic file types to use when importing images to a Flash document.	7	7-4-6
4.4 Create text.		
4.4a Demonstrate knowledge of text types.	2,9	2-32-33, 9-30-31
4.4b Demonstrate knowledge of how to create static text fields.	2	2-34
4.4c Demonstrate knowledge of the terms "expanding-width text block" and "fixed-width text block."	2	2-32, 2-34
4.4d Demonstrate knowledge of how to create and convert expanding-width and fixed-width text blocks.	2	2-32, 2-34
4.4e Demonstrate knowledge of Text Layout Framework (TLF).	2	2-32-33, 2-38-41; online
4.4f Demonstrate knowledge of how to create text by using the TLF tool.	2	2-38-41
4.5 Adjust text properties.	2	2-28-33
4.5a Identify which text properties can be adjusted by using the Property inspector.	2	2-32-41
4.5b Demonstrate knowledge of how to change font and font size by using the Property inspector.	2	2-34
4.5c Demonstrate knowledge of how to adjust text color.	2	2-34
4.5d Demonstrate knowledge of how to size a block of static text.	2	2-34
4.5e Demonstrate knowledge of how to change the alignment of static text.	2	2-34
4.5f Demonstrate knowledge of the anti-aliasing option for text.	9	9-42
4.5g Add graphic filters to text.	2	2-35
4.6 Create objects and convert them to symbols, including graphics, movie clips, and buttons.		
4.6a Demonstrate knowledge of the characteristics of graphic, movie clip, and button symbols.	3	3-4-5
4.6b Demonstrate knowledge of how to convert an existing object (shape, text, graphic) into a symbol.	3	3-6

ADOBE RICH MEDIA COMMUNICATIONS USING FLASH PROFESSIONAL CS6		
Objective (Note that some objectives have additional coverage online on Cengage Brain.)	**Chapter**	**Page(s)**
4.6c Demonstrate knowledge of how to create a new symbol.	3	3-18
4.6d Demonstrate knowledge of the states (up, down, over, hit) of a button symbol.	3	3-16-17
4.6e Demonstrate knowledge of how to add over, down, and hit states to a button symbol.	3	3-18-19
4.6f Identify uses of transparent or invisible button symbols.	5	5-2-3, 5-26
4.7 Understand symbols and the library.		
4.7a Demonstrate knowledge of symbols.	3	3-4-5
4.7b Demonstrate knowledge of the library, including types of objects stored in the library.	1,3	1-5, 3-2
4.7c Identify the benefits of using symbols in a movie.	3	3-2
4.7d Demonstrate knowledge of the difference between a symbol and an instance of a symbol.	3	3-2, 3-4-9
4.7e Demonstrate knowledge of how to create patterns from symbols.	2	2-14-15, 5-43
4.8 Edit symbols and instances.		
4.8a Demonstrate knowledge of how to edit symbols from the Stage and from the library.	3	3-7-9
4.8b Demonstrate knowledge of how to edit an instance of a symbol.	3	3-9
4.8c Demonstrate knowledge of the difference between editing a symbol and editing an instance of a symbol.	3	3-7-9
4.9 Create masks.		
4.9a Demonstrate knowledge of masks.	5	5-4-5
4.9b Demonstrate knowledge of how to create a mask layer and apply a mask.	5	5-6-7
4.10 Create animations (changes in shape, position, size, color, and transparency).		
4.10a Demonstrate knowledge of the terms "tween," "motion tween," "shape tween," and "keyframe animation."	1,4	1-19-20, 4-2-35
4.10b Demonstrate knowledge of the differences between a motion tween, shape tween, and classic tween.	4	4-2-35

ACA CERTIFICATION GRID

(CONTINUED)

ADOBE RICH MEDIA COMMUNICATIONS USING FLASH PROFESSIONAL CS6

Objective (Note that some objectives have additional coverage online on Cengage Brain.)	Chapter	Page(s)
4.10c Identify the conditions and constraints for creating motion and shape tweens.	4	4-30-31
4.10d Demonstrate knowledge of the object-based tweening model and the Motion Editor.	1,4,8	1-19-20, 23-26, 4-4-5, 8-28-29
4.10e Demonstrate knowledge of the terms "frame," "keyframe," and "blank keyframe."	1,4	1-33-34, 4-22
4.10f Demonstrate knowledge of how to insert, remove, manipulate and clear keyframes and frames.	4	4-22
4.10g Identify advantages of using frame labels.	3	3-25
4.10h Demonstrate knowledge of how to create frame labels.	3	3-25
4.10i Demonstrate knowledge of how to create a shape tween.	4	4-32
4.10j Demonstrate knowledge of how to create a motion tween.	4	4-7-9
4.10k Demonstrate knowledge of the differences between animating text and animating symbols.	4	4-42
4.10l Demonstrate knowledge of ways to animate text.	4	4-42-49
4.10m Demonstrate knowledge of how to create effects such as fade in or fade out animation, change in color over time, and change in size.	1,4	1-21, 1-28, 4-47
4.10n Demonstrate knowledge of animating one or a series of symbols, shapes, or objects by using inverse kinematics with the Bone tool and adjusting Spring properties.	5	5-28-35
4.10o Demonstrate knowledge of best practices for shape tweening.	4	4-30-31
4.10p Demonstrate knowledge of how to identify and resolve tweening errors.		
4.10q Demonstrate knowledge of how to create and use a motion guide to animate shapes, text, and symbols along a path.	4	4-20-23
4.10r Demonstrate knowledge of how to create motion presets.	1	1-21, 1-30-31

ADOBE RICH MEDIA COMMUNICATIONS USING FLASH PROFESSIONAL CS6			
Objective (Note that some objectives have additional coverage online on Cengage Brain.)		**Chapter**	**Page(s)**
4.11	Add simple controls through ActionScript 3.0.		
	4.11a Demonstrate knowledge of simple actions (stop, gotoAndPlay, navigateToURL, SoundMixer. stopAll).	9	9-2, 9-4-9, 10-34, 10-36, 11-23, 11-25
	4.11b Demonstrate knowledge of basic concepts in object-oriented programming: function, variable, class, object, method, property.	9	9-5-9, 9-20-21
	4.11c Demonstrate knowledge of event-handling concepts in ActionScript 3.0: event source, event listener, listener function.	9	9-8-9, 9-14-15, online
	4.11d Demonstrate knowledge of how to add simple actions to a movie using ScriptAssist mode.	9	9-2, 9-10-11
	4.11e Demonstrate knowledge of code snippets.	9	9-24-29, online
4.12	Import and use sound.	5,10	5-8-11, 10-4-31
	4.12a Identify audio file types that can be imported for use in a Flash document.	5,11	5-8-9, 11-5
	4.12b Demonstrate knowledge of the terms "stream" and "event."	11	11-5, 11-10-11
	4.12c Demonstrate knowledge of how to import a sound file.	11	11-4
	4.12d Demonstrate knowledge of how to add sound to the Timeline.	5,11	5-10-11, 11-4-6
	4.12e Demonstrate knowledge of how to edit audio, including fading audio in and out.	11	11-18-21
4.13	Add and export video.		
	4.13a Identify video file formats that can be included in a Flash document.	5	5-12-13
	4.13b Demonstrate knowledge of rules and best practices for incorporating video in a Flash document.	5,11	5-12-13, 11-26-28
	4.13c Demonstrate knowledge of how to create Flash video files (FLV).	5,11	5-12-17, 11-26-28
	4.13d Demonstrate knowledge of how to use the Adobe Media Encoder.	5	5-13-15

ADOBE RICH MEDIA COMMUNICATIONS USING FLASH PROFESSIONAL CS6		
Objective (Note that some objectives have additional coverage online on Cengage Brain.)	Chapter	Page(s)
4.14 Publish and export Flash documents.		
4.14a Identify ways to optimizing a Flash document for the target audience.	6	6-10
4.14b Demonstrate knowledge of publish settings.	1	1-12, 1-38-39
4.14c Demonstrate knowledge of file types that can be generated when publishing a document.	1,6	1-38-39, 6-4-5
4.14d Demonstrate knowledge of how to generate a SWF file.	1	1-12-16
4.14e Demonstrate knowledge of how to publish to AIR for desktop, AIR for Android, and AIR for iOS.	6	6-22-37
4.14f Demonstrate knowledge of how to export images and movies.		
4.15 Make a document accessible.		
4.15a Demonstrate knowledge of how to set accessibility options for the entire document.	1	1-45, online
4.15b Demonstrate knowledge of how to set accessibility options for an individual object or movie clip symbol.	1	1-45, online
4.15c Demonstrate knowledge of why to hide objects from screen readers.		online
4.15d Demonstrate knowledge of how to hide objects from screen readers.		online
Domain 5.0 Evaluating Rich Media Elements by Using Flash CS6		
5.1 Conduct basic technical tests.		
5.1a Identify what to look for when conducting a technical test of a document.	6	6-10-15
5.1b Demonstrate knowledge of the differences between testing and previewing a movie.	1	1-12-16
5.1c Demonstrate knowledge of how to check spelling in a Flash document.		online
5.1d Demonstrate knowledge of how to test a Flash document against a storyboard.	1	1-43-45
5.2 Identify techniques for basic usability tests.	6	6-10, 6-15
5.2a Demonstrate knowledge of elements involved in conducting a usability test, such as observation and interviews.	1	1-45

Read the following information carefully!

Find out from your instructor the location where you will store your files.

■ To complete many of the chapters in this book, you need to use the Data Files provided on Cengage Brain.

■ Your instructor will tell you where to post the files. Your instructor will also tell you where you will store the files you create and modify.

Copy and organize your Data Files.

■ Use the Data Files List to organize your files to a USB storage device, network folder, hard drive, or other storage device.

■ Create a subfolder for each chapter in the location where you are storing your files, and name it according to the chapter title (e.g., chapter_1).

■ For each chapter you are assigned, copy the files listed in the **Data File Supplied** column into that chapter's folder. Note that you can also copy each folder and its contents to the storage location rather than creating the folders yourself.

Find and keep track of your Data Files and completed files.

■ Use the **Data File Supplied** column to make sure you have the files you need before starting the chapter or exercise indicated in the **Chapter** column.

■ Use the **Student Creates File** column to find out the filename you use when saving your new file for the exercise.

■ The **Used in** column tells you the lesson or end of chapter exercise where you will use the file.

Files Used in this Book

ADOBE FLASH CS6			
Chapter	**Data File Supplied**	**Student Creates New File**	**Used In**
1		workspace.fla	Lesson 1
	fl1_1.fla		Lesson 2
		tween.fla	Lesson 3
	*tween.fla	layers.fla	Lesson 4
	*layers.fla		Lesson 5
			Lesson 6
	fl1_2.fla		Skills Review
		demonstration.fla	Project Builder 1
	fl1_3.fla		Project Builder 2
		dpc1.doc	Design Project
			Portfolio Project

*Created in a previous Lesson or Skills Review in current chapter

ADOBE FLASH CS6			
Chapter	Data File Supplied	Student Creates New File	Used In
2	fl2_1.fla		Lesson 1
	fl2_2.fla		
	fl2_3.fla		
	fl2_4.fla		Lesson 4
	fl2_5.fla		Lesson 5
	fl2_6.fla		Skills Review
		ultimateTours2.fla	Project Builder 1
		theJazzClub2.fla	Project Builder 2
		dpc2.doc	Design Project
		portfolio2.fla	Portfolio Project

ADOBE FLASH CS6			
Chapter	**Data File Supplied**	**Student Creates New File**	**Used In**
3	fl3_1.fla		Lesson 1
	fl3_2.fla		Lessons 2-4
	islandview.jpg	sailing.fla	Lesson 5
	sailboat.ai		
	fl3_3.fla		Skills Review
	BeachScene.jpg		
	**ultimatetours2.fla		Project Builder 1
	UTLogo.png		
		isa3.fla	Project Builder 2
		dpc3.doc	Design Project
	**portfolio2.fla		Portfolio Project

**Created in a previous chapter

ADOBE FLASH CS6			
Chapter	Data File Supplied	Student Creates New File	Used In
4	fl4_1.fla		Lesson 1
	fl4_2.fla		
	fl4_3.fla		Lesson 2
	fl4_4.fla		Lesson 3
	fl4_5.fla		
	fl4_6.fla		Lesson 4
	fl4_7.fla		
	fl4_8.fla		
	fl4_9.fla		Lesson 5
	fl4_10.fla		Lesson 6
	fl4_11.fla		Skills Review
	fl4_12.fla		Project Builder 1
	ship.gif		
	fl4_13.fla		Project Builder 2
		dpc4.doc	Design Project
	**portfolio3.fla		Portfolio Project
5	fl5_1.fla		Lesson 1
	fl5_2.fla		Lesson 2
	CarSnd.wav		
	beep.wav		

**Created in a previous chapter

ADOBE FLASH CS6			
Chapter	**Data File Supplied**	**Student Creates New File**	**Used In**
5, continued	fl5_3.fla		Lesson 3
	fireworks.mov		
	fl5_4.fla		Lesson 4
	fl5_5.fla		Lesson 5
	fl5_6.fla		
	fl5_7.fla		Lesson 6
	fl5_8.fla		Lesson 7
	fl5_9.fla		Skills Review
	fl5_10.fla		
	fl5_11.fla		
	*decoLand.fla		
	tour-video.mov		
	fl5_12.fla		Project Builder 1
	**ultimatetours4.fla		
	fl5_13.fla		Project Builder 2
		dpc5.doc	Design Project
	**portfolio4.fla		Portfolio Project

*Created in a previous Lesson or Skills Review in current chapter
**Created in a previous chapter

ADOBE FLASH CS6			
Chapter	Data File Supplied	Student Creates New File	Used In
6	fl6_1.fla		Lesson 1
	fl6_2.fla		Lesson 2
	fl6_3.fla		Lesson 3
	fl6_4.fla		Lesson 4
	Match16.png		
	Match32.png		
	Match48.png		
	Match128.png		
	fl6_5.fla	SanteFe.fla	Lesson 5
	Game36.png		
	Game48.png		
	Game72.png		
	SFimage.jpg		
	SF36.png		
	SF48.png		
	SF72.png		
	fl6_6.fla		Skills Review
	fl6_7.fla		
	sedona16.png		
	sedona32.png		

ADOBE FLASH CS6			
Chapter	**Data File Supplied**	**Student Creates New File**	**Used In**
6, continued	sedona48.png		
	sedona128.png		
	sedonaImage.png		
	sedona36.png		
	sedona72.png		
	fl6_8.fla		Project Builder 1
	**ultimatetours5.fla		
	uTours16.png		
	uTours32.png		
	uTours48.png		
	uTours128.png		
	publish16.png		Project Builder 2
	publish32.png		
	publish36.png		
	publish48.png		
	publish72.png		
	publish128.png		
		dpc6.doc	Design Project
	**portfolio5.fla		Portfolio Project

**Created in a previous chapter

ADOBE FLASH CS6			
Chapter	Data File Supplied	Student Creates New File	Used In
7	background.psd	gsamples.fla	Lesson 1
	dragonfly.png		
	tree.ai		
	meadow.jpg		Lesson 2
	moon.jpg		
	*gsamples.fla		Lesson 3
	fullMoon.jpg	skillsDemo7.fla	Skills Review
	logo.png		
	nightsky.jpg		
	mountain.jpg		
	gtravel1.jpg	ultimateTours7.fla	Project Builder 1
	gtravel2.jpg		
	gtravel3.jpg		
	gtravel4.jpg		
	gtravel5.jpg		
	gtravel6.jpg		

*Created in a previous Lesson or Skills Review in current chapter

ADOBE FLASH CS6			
Chapter	**Data File Supplied**	**Student Creates New File**	**Used In**
7, continued	gantho1.jpg	anthoArt7.fla	Project Builder 2
	gantho2.jpg		
	gantho3.jpg		
	gantho4.jpg		
		dpc7.doc	Design Project
	portfolioCase.jpg	portfolio7.fla	Portfolio Project
8	fl8_1.fla		Lesson 1
	fl8_2.fla		Lesson 2
	fl8_3.fla		Lessons 3-4
	**dragonfly.fla		Lesson 5
	fl8_4.fla		Skills Review
		ultimatetours8.fla	Project Builder 1
		ocean_life8.fla	Project Builder 2
		dpc8.doc	Design Project
		portfolio8.fla	Portfolio Project

**Created in a previous chapter

ADOBE FLASH CS6			
Chapter	Data File Supplied	Student Creates New File	Used In
9	fl9_1.fla		Lesson 1
	fl9_2.fla		
	fl9_3.fla		Lesson 2
	fl9_4.fla		Lesson 3
	fl9_5.fla		Lesson 4
	fl9_6.fla	skillsDemo9-object.fla	Skills Review
	**ultimatetours8.fla		Project Builder 1
		dragToMatch.fla	Project Builder 2
		dpc9.doc	Design Project
	**portfolio8.fla		Portfolio Project
10	fl10_1.fla		Lesson 1
	fl10_2.fla		Lesson 2
	fish.swf		
	frog.swf		
	fl10_3.fla		Lesson 3
	fl10_4.fla		
	fl10_5.fla		Lesson 4
	fl10_6.fla		Skills Review
	textAnimation.swf		

**Created in a previous chapter

ADOBE FLASH CS6			
Chapter	**Data File Supplied**	**Student Creates New File**	**Used In**
10, continued	fl10_7.fla		Project Builder 1
	specials.swf		
	fl10_8.fla		Project Builder 2
		dpc10.doc	Design Project
	math.swf	portfolio10.fla	Portfolio Project
	shirt.swf		
	shirt2.swf		
11	fl11_1.fla		Lesson 1
	fl11_2.fla		Lesson 2
	*nightclub.fla		Lesson 3
	fl11_3.fla		Lesson 4
	fl11_4.fla		Lesson 5
	safari.flv		
	fl11_5.fla		Skills Review

*Created in a previous Lesson or Skills Review in current chapter

ADOBE FLASH CS6			
Chapter	**Data File Supplied**	**Student Creates New File**	**Used In**
11, continued	waterfall.wav		
	wilderness.flv		
	fl11_6.fla		Project Builder 1
	**interactive.fla		Project Builder 2
	ambient_audio.wav		
	crowd_yes.wav		
	welcome_voiceover.wav		
		dpc11.doc	Design Project
	**portfolio10.fla		Portfolio Project
	accent1.mp3		
	accent2.mp3		
	background.mp3		
	catFun.flv		
	portfolio_voiceover.wav		

**Created in a previous chapter

ADOBE FLASH CS6			
Chapter	**Data File Supplied**	**Student Creates New File**	**Used In**
12	fl12_1.fla		Lesson 1
	fl12_2.fla		Lesson 2
	dragonfly-bkgrnd.fla	accel.fla	Lesson 3
		accelDragonfly.fla	
		accelHit.fla	
	NobleEye.jpg	WildHorses.fla	Lesson 4
	WildBlue.jpg	WildHorsesZoom.fla	
	WildGold.jpg		
	fl12_3.fla	skillsDemo12-collide.fla	Skills Review
		ultimateTours12.fla	Project Builder 1
		swipePrototype.fla	Project Builder 2
		dpc12.doc	Design Project
	**portfolio11.fla		Portfolio Project
	math.swf		
	shirt.swf		
	shirt2.swf		
13	fl13_1.fla		Lesson 1
	rosario.jpg		Lesson 2
	rosario.txt		

**Created in a previous chapter

ADOBE FLASH CS6			
Chapter	Data File Supplied	Student Creates New File	Used In
13, continued	animation.swf		
	sunset.jpg		
	fl13_2.fla		Skills Review
	*mySamples.fla		
	kayaking.jpg		
	kayaking.txt		
	kayaker.swf		
	fl13_3.fla		Project Builder 1
	destination.swf		
	kapalua.jpg		
	kapalua.txt		
		isa_survey1.fla	Project Builder 2
		dpc13.doc	Design Project
	fl13_4.fla		Portfolio Project
	AutumnVineyrds.jpg		
	DistantVineyards.jpg		
	Mustangs.jpg		
	Novlight.jpg		
	Rendezvous.jpg		
	ValleyRespite.jpg		

*Created in a previous Lesson or Skills Review in current chapter

3D Effects
A process in Flash that animates 2D objects through 3D space with 3D Transformation tools.

A

Absolute path
A path containing an external link that references a link on a web page outside of the current website, and includes the protocol "http" and the URL, or address, of the web page.

Accelerometer
A built-in feature of mobile devices that causes objects on the screen to move in response to the movement of the device.

Actions panel
The panel where you create and edit ActionScript code for an object or a frame.

Actions Toolbox pane
The section of the Actions panel displaying the categories of actions that can be selected to build ActionsScript code.

ActionScript
The Adobe Flash scripting language used by developers to add interactivity to movies, control objects, exchange data, and create complex animations.

ActionScript 3.0 (AS3)
The version of Flash ActionScript that is based on Object Oriented Programming (OOP) standards that provides a way to organize code (a set of instructions).

addChild() method
The method used to add objects to the display list.

Adobe Flash CS6
A development tool that allows you to create compelling interactive experiences, often by using animation.

AIR (Adobe Integrated Runtime)
A Flash technology used to create applications that can be played without a browser. An AIR app can be displayed on mobile devices, on stand-alone computers, on the Internet, and even on television sets.

AIR for Android
A feature of Flash that allows you to publish Flash FLA files so that they run on Android devices (smartphones and tablets).

AIR for iOS
A feature of Flash that allows you to publish Flash FLA files so that they run on iOS devices (iPhones and iPads).

Animated graphic symbol
An animation stored as a single, reusable symbol in the Library panel.

Animation
The perception of motion caused by the rapid display of a series of still images.

Anti-aliasing
The process of smoothing the edges of a graphic so they appear less jagged.

Applications (also called apps)
Products such as interactive games, tutorials, demonstrations, business and informational programs that can be incorporated in a website,

deployed on a desktop computer or delivered on a mobile device.

Auto format
A button in the Actions panel that, when clicked, formats the code in accordance with ActionScript formatting conventions.

B

Balance
In screen design, the distribution of optical weight in the layout. Optical weight is the ability of an object to attract the viewer's eye, as determined by the object's size, shape, color, and other factors.

Bandwidth Profiler
A feature used when testing a Flash movie that allows you to view a graphical representation of the size of each frame and the frame-by-frame download process.

Bitmap fill
A fill that is created by breaking apart a bitmap graphic and using it to fill another graphic.

Bitmap image
An image based on pixels, rather than mathematical formulas. Also referred to as a raster image.

Break apart
The process of breaking apart text to place each character in a separate text block. Also, the process of separating groups, instances, and bitmaps into ungrouped, editable elements.

Broadband
A type of data transmission, such as DSL and cable, in which a wide band of frequencies is available to transmit more information at the same time.

Button symbol
Object on the Stage that is used to provide interactivity, such as jumping to another frame on the Timeline.

——————— **C** ———————

Calls
The term used to describe what happens when code executes (or calls) a function.

Casting
The process of changing one data type to another.

Check syntax
The Check syntax button checks for any errors in the syntax of the coding and, if found, displays a message in the Compiler Errors panel.

Class
ActionScript 3.0 code that defines the attributes and functionality of an object.

Code hints
Hints appearing in a pop-up window that give the syntax or possible parameters for an action.

Code Snippets
Predefined blocks of ActionScript 3.0 code that provide a quick way to insert AS3 code into the Script pane.

Components
Predeveloped movie clips that can quickly add functionality to a movie by dragging and dropping them from the Components panel to the Stage. Commonly used for creating forms

with boxes for entering user data (name, address, and so on), check boxes, drop-down menus and video playback objects.

Conditional action
ActionScript that tests whether or not certain conditions have been met and, if so, can perform other actions.

Controller
A window that provides the playback controls for a movie.

Coordinate
The position on the Stage of a pixel as measured across (X coordinate) and down (Y coordinate) the Stage.

Copyright
A legal protection for the particular and tangible expression of an idea.

Cue Points
Indicators on the video timeline that can be used in ActionScript. For example, you could specify a cue point at a location in a video that you want the user to be able to jump to by clicking a button.

——————— **D** ———————

Data type
Indicates the class used to populate the variable.

Deco Tool
Tool used to create drawing effects that can be used to quickly create environments, such as city landscapes, and to create various animations

Decrement action
An ActionScript operator, indicated by—(two minus signs), that subtracts 1 unit from a variable or expression.

Device Central
A program used to test Flash movies on various models of mobile devices.

Display list
A list used by Flash to make objects visible to the user when a movie is published. Objects are added to the display list using the addChild() method of ActionScript 3.0.

DisplayObject
The class that contains objects that can be part of the display list.

Dock
A collection of panels or buttons surrounded by a dark gray bar. The arrows in the dock are used to maximize and minimize the panels.

Document
A Flash file which, by default, is given the .fla file extension.

Drop Zone
A blue outline area that indicates where a panel can be moved.

DSL
A broadband Internet connection speed that is available through phone lines.

Dynamic text field
A text box created on the Stage with the Text tool that displays information derived from variables.

——————— **E** ———————

Embedded fonts
Fonts that are available to the users no matter what fonts they have on their computer and ensures the text maintains the desired appearance. A font file is created that accompanies the swf file when the Flash document is published.

Embedded video
A video file that has been imported into a Flash document and becomes part of the SWF file.

Event Listener
ActionScript 3.0 code that "listens" to "hear" when an event occurs. For example, a button object might listen for a mouse click.

Event sound
A sound that plays independently of the Timeline. The sound starts in the keyframe to which it is added, but it can continue playing even after a movie ends. An event sound must download completely before it begins playing.

Expressions
Formulas for manipulating or evaluating the information in variables.

External links
Links from a Flash file or movie to another website, another file, or an e-mail program.

——————— **F** ———————

File Transfer Protocol (FTP)
A standard method for transferring files from a development site to a web server.

Filters
Special effects, such as drop shadows, that can be applied to text using options on the Filters area in the Properties panel.

Flash
See Adobe Flash CS6

Flash Player
A free program from Adobe that allows Flash movies (.swf and .exe formats) to be viewed on a computer.

Flowchart
A visual representation of how the contents in an application or a website are organized and how various screens are linked.

Frame-by-frame animation
An animation created by specifying the object that is to appear in each frame of a sequence of frames (also called a frame animation).

Frame label
A text name for a keyframe, which can be referenced within ActionScript code.

Frames
Individual cells that make up the Timeline in Flash.

Function
An ActionScript 3.0 statement that executes a block of code in response to the event. For example, a function might include a gotoAndPlay action in response to a mouse click on a button.

——————— **G** ———————

Gradient
A color fill that makes a gradual transition from one color to another causing the colors to blend into one another.

Graphic Symbols
Objects, such as drawings, that are converted to symbols and stored in the Library panel. A graphic symbol is the original object. An instance (copy) of a symbol can be made by dragging the symbol from the Library to the Stage.

Graphics Interchange Format (GIF)
A graphics file format that creates compressed bitmap images. GIF graphics are viewable on the web.

Guide layers
Layers used to align objects on the Stage.

——————— **H** ———————

Increment action
An ActionScript operator, indicated by ++ (two plus signs), that adds 1 unit to a variable or expression.

Input text field
A text field created on the Stage with the Text tool that takes information entered by a user and stores it as a variable.

Instances
Editable copies of symbols that are placed on the Stage.

Inverse Kinematics
A process using a bone structure that allows objects to be animated in natural ways, such as a character running, jumping, or kicking.

Inter-screen unity
Refers to the design that viewers encounter as they navigate from one screen to another, and it provides consistency throughout the application.

Intra-screen unity
Refers to how the various screen objects relate and how they all fit in.

——————— **J** ———————

Joint Photographic Experts Group (JPEG)
A graphics file format that is especially useful for photographic images. JPEG graphics are viewable on the web.

——————— **K** ———————

Keyframe
A frame that signifies a change in a movie, such as the end of an animation.

L

Layers
Rows on the Timeline that are used to organize objects and that allow the stacking of objects on the Stage.

Level
A hierarchical designation used when loading new movies into the current movie; similar to layers on the Timeline.

Library panel
The panel that contains the objects (graphics, buttons, sounds, movie clips, etc.) that are used in a Flash movie.

Linkage class name
The name used to identify a sound from the Library panel in an ActionScript statement. You specify a linkage identifier in the Sound Properties dialog box.

Loader Component
A Component that can load external jpg graphic files and swf movie files.

Loop
An action or a set of actions that repeat as long as the condition exists.

M

Main Timeline
The primary Timeline for a Flash movie that is displayed when you start a new Flash document.

Marquee
Created when you drag the Selection tool pointer around the entire object to select it.

Mask layer
A layer used to cover up the objects on another layer(s) and, at the same time, create a window through which you can view various objects on the other layer.

Menu bar
A bar across the top of the program window that is located under the program title bar and lists the names of the menus that contain commands.

Merge Drawing Model
A drawing mode that causes overlapping drawings (objects) to merge so that a change in the top object, such as moving it, may affect the object beneath it.

Method
In ActionScript 3.0, the functionality of an object, that is, what it can do. For example, a button can listen for a mouse click.

Mobile Content Simulator
A feature in Flash that allows you to test mobile applications. The simulator displays the application as it would appear on a mobile phone and allows you to use events and gestures, such as swipe and zoom, to see how the application reacts.

Morphing
The animation process of changing one object into another, sometimes unrelated, object. For example, animating a car to change into a bus.

Motion Editor
Used to edit motion tween animations by changing the property values such as the position, rotation, color effects, and ease value.

Motion guide
Feature that allows you to draw a path and attach motion-tweened animations to the path. A motion guide has its own layer.

Motion path
A dotted line on the Stage that represents the path the object takes from the beginning frame to the ending frame of a motion tween.

Motion span
See tween span.

Motion Tween Presets
Pre-built animations that can be applied to objects in Flash. For example, applying a bouncing effect to a ball.

Motion tweening
The process used in Flash to automatically fill in the frames between keyframes in an animation that changes the properties of an object such as the position, size, or color. Motion tweening works on symbols and groups.

Movement
In screen design, the way the viewer's eye moves through the objects on the screen.

Movie clip symbol
An animation stored as a single, reusable symbol in the Library panel. It has its own Timeline, independent of the main Timeline.

MP3 (MPEG-1 Audio Layer 3)
A sound compression option primarily used for music and longer streaming sounds, but which can also be applied to speech.

N

Nesting
Including another symbol within a symbol, such as nesting a graphic symbol, button, or another movie clip symbol within a movie clip symbol.

Number variable
In ActionScript, a variable type that contains a number with which you can use arithmetic operators, such as addition and subtraction. To create a number variable use the Number data type.

O

Object Drawing Model
A drawing mode that allows you to overlap objects, which are then kept separate, so that changes in one object do not affect another object. You must break apart these objects before being able to select their stroke and fills.

Objects
Items, such as drawings and text, that are placed on the Stage and can be edited and manipulated. In ActionScript 3.0, an instance of a class that inherits the attributes (properties) and functionality (methods) of a class.

Onion Skin
Feature that displays the outlines of an animated object so that the positions of the object in a series of frames can be viewed all at once.

P

Panel sets
In Flash, groups of the most commonly used panels, such as the Properties and Library panels.

Panels
Individual windows in Flash used to view, organize, and modify objects and features in a movie.

Parameters
Properties of Components, such as autoload, that can be changed using the Properties panel or the Component Inspector.

Parent-child relationship
A description of the hierarchical relationship that develops between nested symbols, especially nested movie clip symbols. When you insert a movie clip inside another movie clip, the inserted clip is considered the child and the original clip is the parent.

Pasteboard
The gray area surrounding the Flash Stage where objects can be placed and manipulated. Neither the Pasteboard nor objects placed on it appear in the movie unless the objects move onto the Stage during the playing of the movie.

Persistence of vision
The phenomenon of the eye capturing and holding an image for one-tenth of a second before Processing another image. This enables the rapid display of a series of still images to give the impression of motion and creates an animation.

Pixel
Each dot in a bitmap graphic. Pixels have an exact position on the screen and a precise color.

Playhead
An indicator specifying which frame is playing in the Timeline of a Flash movie.

Portable Network Graphics (PNG)
A graphics file format developed specifically for images that are to be used on the web.

Pose layer
Refers to the Armature layer, which is added to the Timeline when create a bone structure.

Preloader
An animation and ActionScript code (which could be a movie clip) that is played at the beginning of a movie to provide feedback to the viewer on the progress of downloading the movie frames.

Progressive download
The process of delivering an external Flash FLV video file at runtime.

Projector
A standalone executable movie, such as a Windows .exe file.

Properties panel (also called Property inspector)
In Flash, the panel that displays the properties of the selected object, such as size and color, on the Stage or the selected frame. The Properties panel can be used to edit selected properties.

Property
An attribute of an object such as its size or color.

Property inspector
A panel that allows you to display and edit the properties of a selected object or frame. See Properties panel.

Publish
The process used to generate the files necessary for delivering Flash movies on the web, such as SWF and HTML files.

Q

QuickTime
A file format used for movies and animations that requires a QuickTime Player.

R

Raster image
An image based on pixels, rather than mathematical formulas. Also referred to as a bitmap image.

Raw
A sound compression option that exports a sound with no compression. You can set stereo to mono conversion and a sampling rate.

Registration point
The point on an object that is used to position the object on the Stage using ActionScript code.

Relative path
A path to a file based on the current location of the Flash .swf file referencing the file.

Rulers
On screen markers that help you precisely measure and position an object. Rulers can be displayed using the View menu.

───────── **S** ─────────

Scene
A Timeline designated for a specific part of the movie. Scenes are a way to organize long movies by dividing the movie into sections.

Script Assist
A feature found in the Actions panel which can be used to generate ActionScript without having to write programming code.

Script Navigator pane
The section of the Actions panel that provides a list of elements (objects, movie clips, frames) that contain scripts. It can be used to quickly locate an object, such as a button, or a frame and display the ActionScript code.

Script pane
The section of the Actions panel that displays the code and a toolbar for editing the code. Also, displays the Script Assist dialog box.

Shape hints
Indicators used to control the shape of a complex object as it changes appearance during an animation.

Shape tweening
The process of animating an object so that its shape changes. Shape tweening requires editable graphics.

Sound object
A built-in object that allows ActionScript to recognize and control a sound. To associate a specific sound with a sound object, use a variable with a sound class type.

Specifications
A list of what will be included in each screen including the arrangement of each element and the functionality of each object (for example, what happens when you click the button labeled Skip Intro).

Speech compression
A sound compression option best used for voice-overs and other speech. You can set a sampling rate when you choose this option.

Stage
The area of the Flash workspace that contains the objects that are part of the movie and that will be seen by the viewers.

Start synchronization option
A synchronization option that can be applied to sounds and that acts just like event sounds, but that will not begin again if an instance of the sound is already playing.

Stop synchronization option
A synchronization option that can be applied to sounds and lets you end an event sound at a specific keyframe.

Storyboard
A series of sketches that illustrate the sequence of events in an animation.

Streaming sound
A sound that is tied to the Timeline. No matter its length, a streaming sound stops at the end of the movie. Streaming sounds can start playing as they download.

Streaming video
The process of delivering video content using a constant connection established with a Flash Communication Server.

String variable
In ActionScript, a sequence of characters including letters, numbers, and punctuation. To create a string variable, use the Sting data type and enclose the string in double quotation marks.

Symbols
The basic building blocks of a Flash application. There are three types: graphic, button, and movie clip.

───────── **T** ─────────

T1
An extremely fast Internet connection that is widely used by businesses.

Target
A reference in an action to a movie clip symbol or other object that includes a path and name.

Text Layout Format (TLF)
A text tool option that provides advanced text features such as flowing text, character coloring and column creation.

Time In control, Time Out control
Controls in the Edit Envelope dialog box that let you trim the length of a sound file.

Timeline
The component of Flash used to organize and control the movie's contents over time by specifying when each object appears on the Stage.

Tools panel
The component of Flash that contains a set of tools used to draw, select, and edit graphics and text. It is divided into four sections.

Touch and Gesture Events
Features of mobile device applications such as drag, swipe, and zoom.

Trace
The process of turning a bitmap image into vector paths for animation and other purposes.

Transformation point
The point used to orient an object as it is being animated. For example, a rotating object will rotate around the transformation point. Also, the point of an object that snaps to a motion guide.

Tween span
The number of frames in a motion tween.

Tweening
The process of filling the in-between frames in an animation.

Unity
Intra-screen unity refers to how the various screen objects relate in screen design. Inter-screen unity refers to the design that viewers encounter as they navigate from one screen to another.

V

var age:Number
A variable used to hold a user's age.

Variable
A container that holds information and is used in ActionScript code.

Vector graphic
An image calculated and stored according to mathematical formulas rather than pixels, resulting in a smaller file size and the ability to resize the image without a loss in quality.

Web server
A computer dedicated to hosting websites that is connected to the Internet and configured with software to handle requests from browsers.

Workspace
The area in the Flash program window where you work with documents, movies, tools, and panels. The Flash workspace can be customized.

Oval Primitive tool, 2–35
Oval tool, 1–18, 2–5, 2–9
Over state
    animated buttons, 8–20
    buttons, 3–16, 3–20
overlapping objects, stacking order, 2–46

Paint Bucket tool, 2–5, 7–13
panel(s), 1–5—8, 1–9—10. *See also specific panels*
    closing, 1–7
    floating, 1–7
    rearranging, 1–6—7
Panel options button, 8–15
Panel options menu, Library panel, 3–10
panel sets, 1–6
paragraphs, 2–37
parent movie clips, ActionScript, 10–6—7
parent-child relationship, 8–15
Particle System tool, 5–43
password line type In input field, 10–25
paths
    absolute, 10–18
    motion. *See* motion paths
    orienting objects to, motion tween animations, 4–13
    relative, 10–18
Pen tool, 2–4, 2–10—11
Pencil tool, 2–5, 2–12
Permissions tab settings, AIR for Android Settings dialog
        box, 6–30
persistence of vision, 4–2
personal uses of Flash, 1–1
Perspective Angle property, 5–36
Photoshop files (PSD file format), importing graphics, 7–6,
        7–10
pixels, 2–2, 3–30
planning
    animations, 8–4
    applications, 1–42—47

play actions, assigning to buttons, 3–27
Play command, 1–13
playback system, planning applications, 1–43
playing multiple sounds at once, 11–4—5
plus sign (+), increment operator, 10–7
PNG file format, 6–4
    importing graphics, 7–5, 7–8
PolyStar tool, 2–5
pose layer, IK objects, 5–29
positioning. *See also* moving
    drop-down buttons, 5–20—21
    movies on Stage while loading, 10–23
    objects, applications for mobile devices, 12–14
    objects on Stage, 2–6—7, 2–16—17, 7–8
    Stage, 1–8
predefined classes, AS3, 9–5
preloaders, 6–16—21
    adding actions to, 6–19
    adding layers for, 6–18
    creating animations, 6–20
    preloading movies, 6–16—17
    testing, 6–21
previewing
    animated graphic symbols, 8–10
    buttons, 3–20—21
    movies, 1–12
Primitive Oval tool, 2–5
Primitive Rectangle tool, 2–5
progressive downloading, 5–12
project management, 1–46
projector files, 1–39, 6–2
properties, objects, 9–5
    changing using AS3, 9–12
Properties icon, Library panel, 3–11
Properties panel, 1–5
    adding sounds to Timeline, 11–4
    CHARACTER area, 2–38
    creating input text fields, 9–31

Filters option, 2–39
    linking static text to websites or external files, 10–35
    selecting sound files, 5–8, 5–9, 11–6
    shape tween animations, 4–31
    synchronizing sound to video, 5–17
    text objects, 2–37
Property inspector. *See* Properties panel
Property keyframe, 1–33, 4–6
PSD file format, importing graphics, 7–6, 7–10
Publish command, 1–12
Publish feature, settings, 6–4—5
Publish Preview command, 6–5
Publish Settings dialog box, 6–4, 6–5, 6–22, 6–23
Publish Target list, 6–25
publishing applications, 6–1—37
    AIR applications, 6–22—24
    applications for mobile devices, 6–36—37
    default settings, 6–6
    file formats, 6–4—9
    preloaders. *See* preloaders
    projector files, 6–2
    reducing file size. *See* reducing file size
    Simulator, 6–2

QT file format, 5–9, 11–5

raster graphics, 7–4
rate of change, adjusting, shape tween animations, 4–34
rearranging panels, 1–6—7
Rectangle Primitive tool, 2–34—35
Rectangle tool, 1–18, 1–22, 2–5, 2–9
reducing file size, 6–10—15
    Bandwidth Profiler, 6–10—11, 6–14
    guidelines, 6–10
    Simulate Download feature, 6–11, 6–12—13
registration points, classic tween animations, 4–21
relative paths, 10–18
release mouse event, 3–24

positioning movies on, while loading, 10–23
positioning objects on, 2–6—7, 2–16—17, 7–8
specifying color, 1–38, 1–41
view, 1–11
Standard Guide layer type, 2–46
Start option, synchronizing sounds, 11–10, 11–11, 11–16
starting Flash, 1–9
stop actions
  assigning to frames, 3–26—27
  assigning to Timeline, 8–8—9
stop(); method, *SoundChannel* class, 11–23
Stop option, synchronizing sounds, 11–10—11, 11–17
stopAll method, *SoundMixer* class, 11–23
storyboards, 1–44—45
Stream option, synchronizing sounds, 11–11, 11–12
stream sounds, 11–5
  stopping, 11–11
  synchronizing, 11–10, 11–11, 11–13—14
  Timeline, 11–10
streaming video, 5–12
string data, converting to Number data type, 9–31
String data type, text input fields, 9–31
String variables, 9–30, 9–36—37
  collecting and modifying, 9–36—37
stroke(s), colors, 2–21, 2–24
Stroke Color tool, 2–5
Subselection tool, 2–4, 2–29, 2–33
Swap Color tool, 2–6
Swap Symbol dialog box, 11–13
swapping objects, accelerometer, 12–21—22
SWF file format, 6–4
  loading external FLV files, 5–12, 11–26
  tracking changes in file size, 6–11
swipe gesture, 12–30—33
symbol(s)
  button, 3–4
  creating, 3–6
  editing in edit window, 3–8

graphic. *See* animated graphic symbols; graphic symbols
  importing AI files as, 7–9
  Library panel. *See* Library panel
  movie clip. *See* movie clip symbols
  types, 3–4
Symbol Properties dialog box, 9–16
Symmetry Brush, 5–43
synchronizing sounds, 11–10—17
  adding synchronized animation to Stage, 11–15
  with animation, 11–10, 11–13—14
  with a button, 5–8, 11
  Event option, 11–10, 11–11
  event sounds, 11–11
  Start option, 11–10, 11–11, 11–16
  Stop option, 11–10—11, 11–17
  Stream option, 11–11, 11–12
  stream sounds, 11–10, 11–11, 11–13—14
  to video, 5–17
syntax, AS3, 9–6, 9–9

Tab title, Library panel, 3–10
tablet devices, resizing applications for, 12–15
targets, adding to applications, 12–23
templates, accelerometer, 12–18
Test Movie command, 1–13—14
testing
  apps on mobile devices, 6–32
  buttons, 3–20—21
  movies, 1–13—14, 1–16, 6–10—13
  preloaders, 6–21
text, 2–36—45
  applying gradients, 2–41
  changing attributes, 2–36—37, 2–38
  entering, 2–36, 2–38
  filters, 2–39
  paragraphs, 2–37
  skewing, 2–40
  transforming, 2–37

text blocks, 2–37
  changing for Classic text, 2–36
  making into a button, 4–48
  resizing, 2–38
text boxes. *See* dynamic text boxes; embedding fonts
text fields, collecting user information using, 9–30—31, 9–33—34
Text Layout Framework (TLF), 2–36, 2–37, 2–42—45
Text Layout Framework mode, 2–36
text objects, aligning, 2–40
Text tool, 2–4, 2–38, 2–39, 2–40
Time In control, editing sounds, 11–18, 11–20
Time Out control, editing sounds, 11–18
Timeline, 1–4, 1–5, 1–32—37
  adding sound, 11–4—5, 11–6
  assigning stop actions, 8–8—9
  copying motion tweens, frames, and layers from, 8–10—11
  deleting objects, 8–12
  display, 1–11
  frames, 1–33, 1–37
  interpreting, 1–33—34
  keyframes, 1–33
  layers, 1–32—33, 1–35, 1–36, 1–37
  Layers area, 2–47
  resizing, 1–8, 1–11
  returning to, 3–17
  stream sounds, 11–10
  viewing features, 1–36
Timeline Control, 3–28
timers, accelerometer, 12–19, 12–25
TLF (Text Layout Framework), 2–36, 2–37, 2–42—45
Toggle Sorting Order icon, Library panel, 3–11
tool(s). *See also specific tools*
  for creating vector graphics, 2–6
  grouped, 2–6
  options, 2–6, 2–12
Toolbox pane, Actions panel, 3–25, 3–26